The R[...]

D1099611

Pro
& the Côte d'Azur

written and researched by

Kate Baillie, Chris Pitts
and Neville Walker

with additional contributions by

Ross Velton and Nick Woodford

ROUGH
GUIDES

NEW YORK • LONDON • DELHI

www.roughguides.com

Contents

A taste of Provence
colour section following
p.168

La Provence sportive
colour section following
p.328

3

◄◄ Lavender field near Comps-sur-Artuby ◄ Cassis

Introduction to

Provence
& the Côte d'Azur

**The ancient Provençal version of Genesis maintains that
prior to introducing Adam, the Creator realized he had
several materials left over; large expanses of celestial
blue, all kinds of rocks, arable soil filled with seeds for a
sumptuous flora, and a variety of as yet unused tastes and
smells from the most subtle to the most powerful. "Well,"
He thinks, "why don't I make a beautiful résumé of my
world, my own special paradise?" And so Provence came
into being.**

This paradise encompasses the snow-peaked lower Alps
and their foothills, which in the east descend to the
sea's edge, and to the west extend almost to the Rhône.
In central Provence, the wild, high plateaux are cut by
the deepest cleft in the surface of Europe – the Grand
Canyon du Verdon. The coastal hinterland is made up
of range after range of steep, forested hills in which the
warm scent of pines, eucalyptus and wild herbs intoxicates the senses. The
shore is an ever-changing series of geometric bays giving way to chaotic
outcrops of glimmering rock and deep, narrow inlets, like miniature Norwegian fjords – the *calanques*. In the Camargue, the shoreline itself becomes
an abstraction as land and sea merge in infinite horizons. Away from the
Rhône delta there is nowhere that does not have its frame of hills, or
mountains, or strange sudden eruptions of rock.

But all these elements would be nothing without the Mediterranean
light, which is at its best in spring and autumn. It is both soft and brightly
theatrical, as if each landscape had lighting rigged up by an expert for
maximum colour and definition with minimum glare. It is no surprise

4

that of all the arts, painting should be the one that owes so much of its European history over the last hundred years to the beauty and escapism of this world. Most of the great artists of the Modern period came to the region to paint or sculpt – among them Matisse, Renoir, Signac, Léger, Dufy, Bonnard, Chagall, Cocteau and Picasso – and many of their works are exhibited in museums throughout the region.

Food and wine are the other great pleasures of Provence, with the produce that grows here – olives and garlic, asparagus and courgettes, grapes, melons and strawberries, *cêpe* and *morille* mushrooms, almonds and sweet chestnuts, basil and wild thyme, to name but a few – forming an essential part of the hot, sensual

▶ Fish market in Aix-en-Provence

Fact file

• The Provence-Alpes-Côte d'Azur (PACA) *région* is one of 22 in France, divided into six *départements*, each governed by a local *préfecture*. Once notorious as a stronghold of the extreme-right *Front National*, Provence has edged to the left politically in recent years and is currently controlled by a coalition of socialists, greens and communists.

• Bordered by the Rhône River to the west, the Alps to the north and the east, and the Mediterranean to the south, PACA covers 31,400 square kilometres. The region contains some of the most geographically diverse terrain in France, ranging from scrub and pine forests, through canyons and beaches, to arid hills, limestone outcrops and alpine peaks. It is also home to several unique ecosystems, including the wetlands of the Camargue, the fjord-like *calanques* and the Grand Canyon du Verdon, Europe's deepest canyon.

• Provence is the third largest *région* in France in terms of population, with some 4,800,000 residents. Some ninety percent live in urban areas, while the rural Haute-Provence has one of the lowest population densities in France. Catholicism is the dominant religion, although in Marseille around a quarter of the population is Muslim. Small Jewish and Protestant communities also exist.

• The region is France's third most important economically and attracts more visitors than any other; a staggering 35 million annually. Despite economic regeneration in the Marseille area, however, unemployment in PACA remains high.

5

environment. The wines, too, from the dry, light rosés of the Côtes de Provence to the deep and delicate reds of the Côtes du Rhône and Châteauneuf-du-Pape, both complement and owe their brilliance to the intensity of sunshine.

Such earthly pleasures, however, have been both a blessing and a curse. Successive waves of invaders and visitors have found the paradise they sought in Provence, and at the height of summer on the Riviera an unoccupied strip of beach can seem a far-fetched idea.

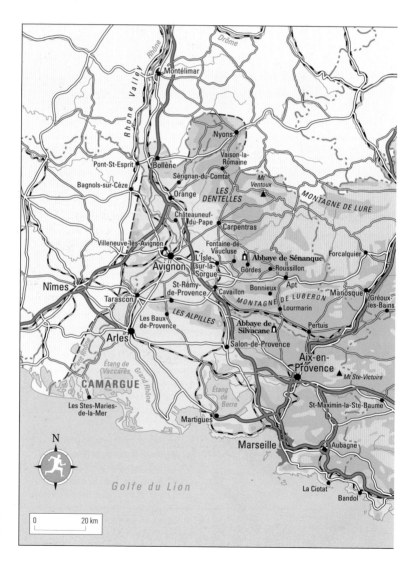

Where to go

This is a large region, and a diverse one, whose contrasting land-scapes encompass the rural fields and villages of inland Provence, the remote mountainous regions of the Alpes-Maritime in the east and north, and the high-rise developments and autoroutes of the Riviera in the south. The Riviera's capital is **Nice**, an intriguing and

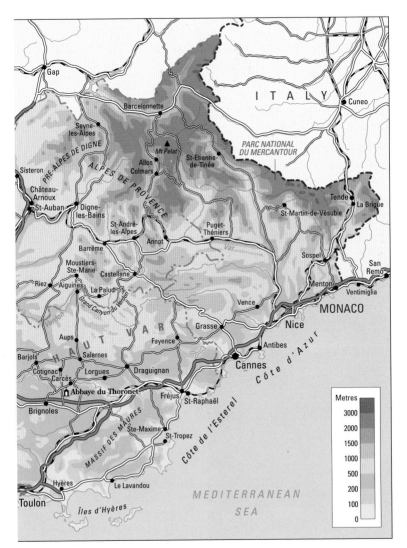

vibrant blend of Italianate influence, faded Belle Époque splendour and first-class art. The town makes a perfect base from which to explore the region, with wonderful food, affordable accommodation and lively night-life. To the north of the city, densely wooded alpine foothills are home to a series of exquisite and unspoilt **perched villages**, while to the east, the lower Corniche links the picturesque coastal towns of **Villefranche**, **St-Jean-Cap-Ferrat** and **Beaulieu**: the higher roads offer some of Europe's most spectacular coastal driving en route to the perched village of **Èze** and the tiny principality of **Monaco**. Beyond here lie the resort and castle of **Roquebrune Cap Martin**, and the charming town of **Menton**, on the Italian border, with its lemon groves and atmospheric old quarter. The Riviera's western half claims its best beaches – at jazzy **Juan-les-Pins** and at **Cannes**, a glitzy centre of designer shopping and film. The Riviera also boasts some heavyweight cultural attractions, with the Picasso museum in **Antibes**, Renoir's house at **Cagnes-sur-Mer** and the superb **Fondation Maeght** and **Fernand Léger** museums in the attractive perched villages of **St-Paul-de-Vence** and **Biot** respectively. The world's perfume capital, **Grasse**, and the ancient town of **Vence** both shelter in the hills behind the busy coastal resorts, while for a real escape from the bustle of the coast, the tranquil **Îles des Lérins** lie just a few kilometres offshore.

▲ Boats in Les Calanques

West of the ancient Massif of the **Esterel**, beyond the Roman towns of **Fréjus** and **St Raphaël**, lie the dark wooded hills of the **Massif des Maures**. Here, the coast is home to the infamous hot spots of **Ste-Maxime** and **St-Tropez**, still a byword for glamour and excess almost fifty years after Bardot put it firmly on the jetsetters' map. In dramatic contrast, the **Corniche des Maures** stretches to the west, its series of low-key resorts interspersed by blissfully unspoilt strips of Mediterranean coastline. Beyond lies the original Côte d'Azur resort of **Hyères** with its elegant villas, fascinating old town, and offshore **Îles d'Hyères**, a Mecca for nature lovers, naturists and divers.

Further west, past the great natural harbour of **Toulon** and

The cuisine of the south

The south of France is renowned for its simple, healthy **cuisine**, based on top-quality olive oil, herbs, garlic and vegetables, all grown or produced in the region. Fish is also essential to two of Provence's great dishes – *bourride* and *bouillabaisse*.

Not surprisingly, the region has been fertile territory for some great **chefs**. **Auguste Escoffier**, one of the best-known names of European cuisine, and creator of the peach Melba, was born in Villeneuve-Loubet in 1846 before going on to achieve international fame through his association with hotelier César Ritz. His style of cuisine, based very much on cream, butter and rich sauces, dominated the restaurant world for much of the twentieth century, though more recent Provençal chefs have turned to a healthier form of cooking. In the 1970s, Légion d'Honneur winner **Roger Vergé** brought culinary fame to the hilltop village of Mougins near Cannes thanks to his "cuisine of the sun" based on fresh herbs and local produce.

Current celebrity superchef **Alain Ducasse** is a Vergé protégé, and although not born in Provence, is very much associated with the region: his *Louis XV* restaurant at the *Hotel de Paris* in Monaco was the first hotel restaurant to win three Michelin stars. In addition to a culinary empire that stretches as far as Paris, London and New York, Ducasse still runs several restaurants in the south of France and three country hotels: *La Bastide de Moustiers* at Moustiers Ste-Marie (see p.000), *Le Domaine des Andéols* near Gordes, and *L'Hostellerie de l'Abbaye* de la Celle near Brignoles. **Joël Robuchon** is yet another celebrity chef to cook up a storm in the principality of Monaco, while in Mougins **Alain Llorca** has taken over the reins at the *Moulin de Mougins* as Roger Vergé's hand-picked successor.

the superb wine country of the **Bandol** AC, lies the buzzing metropolis of **Marseille**. The region's largest city, this tough port has recently overcome its former sleazy reputation to become a lively, cosmopolitan, and often very likeable spot in which to spend a few days. On its eastern edge lie the **calanques**, a series of beautiful rocky coves accessible to walkers and boaters, with the picture-postcard village of **Cassis** and the working port of **La Ciotat** beyond, linked by the spectacular **Corniche des Crêtes**. North of Marseille is the elegant city of **Aix**, with its handsome stone houses, café-lined boulevards and some of Provence's best markets. It was here that Cézanne lived and painted,

▶ Produce market near Mont Ventoux

9

taking his inspiration from the countryside around the nearby **Mont Ste-Victoire**.

Beyond Aix lies the Lower Rhône Valley, home to some of Provence's most ancient cities: **Arles** and **Orange** both still boast some spectacular Roman structures, while **Avignon**, city of the popes and for centuries one of the great artistic centres of France, has an immaculately preserved medieval core and, of course, its famous bridge. The Rhône runs by the vineyards of **Châteauneuf-du-Pape** and the impressive fortifications of

Villeneuve-lès-Avignon, before meeting the sea at the unique lagoon-studded marshlands of the **Camargue**, with its rich variety of wildlife including bulls, horses and flamingos.

Inland from Marseille is the **Luberon** region, a fertile rural hinterland whose attractive old villages are now dominated by second-home owners. Nearby lie two of Provence's great medieval monasteries, at **Silvacane** and **Sénanque**. Beyond the **plateau de Vaucluse** rise the imposing **Mont Ventoux** and the jagged pinnacles of the **Dentelles de Montmirail**, with its brace of celebrated wine-producing towns including **Beaumes de Venise**, known for its sweet dessert wines. East of the Luberon is the heartland of Provence, whose archetypal landscape of lavender fields dotted with old stone villages stretches northwards towards the dramatic **Grand Canyon du Verdon**. The countryside surrounding the canyon is rich in archeological evidence of man's long occupation of the region, with the area around the towns of **Riez**, **Valensole** and **Forcalquier** providing an exquisite taster of rural Provence.

Beyond the canyon but within easy reach of the Riviera, narrow **clues**, or gorges, open onto a secret landscape perfect for cycling and horse-riding, with the fortified towns of **Entrevaux** and **Colmars** defining the old frontier between France and Savoy. A third fortress town, **Sisteron**, on the Durance, marks the gateway to the mountains and the **Alps** proper, where the delightful town of **Barçelonette** provides skiing

The art of Provence

Describing the south of France in a letter to Pissarro, Cézanne once wrote, "the silhouettes you see here are not only black and white, but also blue, red, brown and violet." His words go some way towards explaining the region's attraction for **painters**, and indeed over the last hundred years or so, Provence and the Côte d'Azur have been home and inspiration to some of the greatest names of modern art – **Van Gogh**, **Renoir**, **Matisse** and **Picasso** among them. The brilliant **southern light** was one of the most influential factors in their work here, with Matisse remarking that, had he gone on painting in the north, "there would have been cloudiness, greys, colours shading off into the distance...". Instead, during his time in Nice he produced some of his most famous, colourful works, such as *Interior with Egyptian Curtains* (*Le Rideau égyptien*) and *Icarus* (*Icare*). Van Gogh, too, was profoundly influenced by the region, and it was in Provence that he fully developed his distinct style of bright, contrasting colours. His landscapes of olive trees, cypresses and harvest scenes, such as *La Sieste* and *Champ de Blé et Cyprès* (*Wheat Field With Cypresses*), all pay tribute to the intensity of the **Provençal sun**.

Whilst the landscape and light of the south influenced the painters so strongly, they in turn had a major impact on the region. Hand-in-hand with the various writers and socialites who flocked to the Côte d'Azur during the interwar years, their artistic, and touristic, legacy helped to shape the region that exists today.

Movie mania

The Côte d'Azur may not be as synonymous with **film making** as Hollywood, but its role in the evolution of cinema is just as important. It was in the seaside town of La Ciotat (see p.000) that the movie camera was invented by the Lumière brothers, who, in 1895, filmed the first ever moving picture – a less than glamorous shot of local workers leaving the family-owned car factory at closing time. As early as the 1920s, Nice was producing many of France's most innovative films in the Victorine Film Studios, and local writers Marcel Pagnol and Jean Cocteau were among the many who set their movies in the area. But it was **Brigitte Bardot**, and **French New Wave cinema** that really put the Riviera on the map, with Roger Vadim's *Et Dieu Créa la Femme* (1956) being the first in a long series of classic postwar films shot along the coast. Over the next few years, films such as Hitchcock's *To Catch a Thief* (1956), shot along the corniches, and *Masque de Fer* (1962) helped to confirm the south's reputation as a glamorous movie location. Today, although the production studios of Nice no longer make movies, the world's top stars are still drawn to the Riviera by the annual **Cannes Film Festival** (see p.000) whose Palme d'Or awards remain among the film industry's most prestigious prizes.

and snowboarding in winter and kayaking and hiking in the summer. Stretching south from here towards the **Roya valley** and the border with Italy is the **Parc National du Mercantour**, a genuine wilderness, whose only permanent inhabitants are its wildlife: ibex, chamois, wolves and golden eagles.

When to go

Beware **the coast** at the height of summer. The heat and humidity can be overpowering and the crowds, the exhaust fumes and the costs overwhelming. For **swimming,** the best months are from June to mid-October, with May a little on the cool side, but only by summer standards. As for sunbathing, that can be done from **February through to October**. February is one of the best months for the Côte d'Azur – museums, hotels and restaurants are mostly open, the mimosa is in blossom, and the contrast with northern Europe's climate at its most delicious. The worst month is **November** when almost everything is shut and the weather turns cold and wet.

The same applies to inland Provence. Remember that the lower Alps are usually under snow from late November to early April (though recent winters have had snow in Nice followed by no falls on the lower ski resorts). October can erupt in storms that quickly clear, and in May, too, weather can be erratic. In **summer**, vegetation is at its most barren save for high up in the mountains. Wild bilberries and raspberries, purple gentians and leaves turning red to gold are the rewards of **autumn** walks. **Springtime** brings such a profusion of wild flowers you hardly dare to walk. In March, a thousand almond orchards blossom.

13

▲ Olive grave

The only drawback with the off seasons is the **Mistral wind**. This is a violent, cold, northern airstream that is sucked down the valley of the Rhône whenever there's a depression over the sea. It can last for days, wrecking every fantasy of carefree Mediterranean climes. Winter is its worst season but it rarely blows east of Toulon, so be prepared to move that way.

Average daytime temperatures

	Jan	Feb	Mar	Apr	May	Jun	Jul	Aug	Sep	Oct	Nov	Dec
Central Provence												
	12.2	11.9	14.2	18.5	20.8	26.6	28.1	28.4	25.2	22.1	16.8	14.1
Rhône Valley												
	7.4	6.7	10.8	15.8	17.3	25.6	27.6	27.6	23.5	16.5	10.4	7.8
Riviera/Côte d'Azur												
	12.2	11.9	14.2	18.5	20.8	26.6	28.1	28.4	25.2	22.2	16.8	14.1

Average sea temperatures

	May	June	July	Aug	Sept	Oct
Montpellier to Toulon						
	15	19	19	20	20	17
Île du Levant to Menton						
	17	19	20	22	22	19

All temperatures are in **Centigrade**: to convert to **Fahrenheit** multiply by 9/5 and add 32. For a recorded **weather forecast** phone ☎32.50 (€0.34/min), or check ⓦwww.meteo.fr.

25

things not to miss

It's not possible to see everything that Provence has to offer in one trip – and we don't suggest you try. What follows is a selective taste of the region's highlights: outstanding beaches and ancient sites, natural wonders and colourful festivals. They're arranged in five colour-coded categories, which you can browse through to find the very best things to see and experience. All highlights have a page reference to take you straight into the guide, where you can find out more.

01 Les Calanques Page **91** • Take a boat trip to these hidden inlets east of Marseille, where the shimmering white rock shelters crystal-clear waters.

02 Les Baux Page **111** • The eleventh-century citadel and picture-perfect *village perché* of Les Baux offer incredible views south over La Grande Crau to the sea.

03 The gypsy pilgrimage, Ste-Maries-de-la-Mer
Page **129** • An annual spectacle of music, dancing and religious ritual dating from the sixteenth century.

04 Grand Canyon du Verdon Page **259** • Cycle, walk or bungee-jump in Europe's largest canyon.

05 Boulevard de la Croisette in Cannes Page **367** • Walk, jog or rollerblade along the Riviera's most glamorous seafront promenade. In summer, you'll share it with a jostling crowd and a few Hollywood starlets; in winter, you'll have the whole stretch to yourself.

07 Fondation Maeght

Page **402** ● Don't miss this highly original art museum, whose building and setting are as impressive as the modern works of art inside.

06 Dining al fresco in Vieux Nice

Page **424** ● Sit outside a Vieux Nice café watching the vibrant street life, and tuck into *salade niçoise*, *pissaladière* or a slice of *socca* straight from the pan.

08 Abbaye de Sénanque

Page **231** ● The twelfth-century Cistercian abbey of Sénanque is enhanced by its beautiful position, surrounded by lavender fields.

09 **Mont Ste-Victoire by Paul Cézanne** Page **204** • Walk up to the top of the mountain that inspired so much of Cézanne's work.

10 **Festival d'Avignon** Page **140** • July and early August is the time to visit Avignon, when its ancient monuments provide the backdrop to a riot of theatre, music and dance.

11 **The perched village of Peillon** Page **428** • Built for defence, the region's *villages perchés* are much admired for their maze of streets, mellow stone houses and spectacular settings.

13 **Relaxing on the Riviera** Page **422** • Waiters will serve chilled wine and lobster mayonnaise on the swanky hotel beaches of Nice – if your wallet can stand the strain.

12 **Parc National du Mercantour** Page **282** • Ride, hike, canoe or ski in this alpine wilderness that is home to the Vallée des Merveilles and its four-thousand-year-old rock carvings.

14 Avignon's Palais des Papes Pages **146** • The vast medieval building was home to a succession of popes during Avignon's fourteenth-century heyday.

15 Matisse Museum, Nice Page **422** • Set amid Roman ruins and olive groves, Nice's Matisse Museum includes work from almost every period of the artist's life.

16 Go topless in Saint Tropez Page **336** • Despite the hype and commercialism, St-Tropez's beaches are still among the best on the Riviera.

17 **The vineyards of Châteauneuf-du-Pape** Page **157** ● Sample a glass of Provence's world-famous wine at the *domaine* where it was made.

18 **Marseille** Pages **59** ● Don't let its former reputation put you off visiting this earthy, multi-ethnic Mediterranean metropolis with good food, great bars, excellent football and bags of culture.

19 **Bouillabaisse** Page **77** ● Marseille is the best place to sample this renowned fish stew.

20 **Roman Amphitheatre, Orange** Page **161** • Beautifully preserved, Orange's fifth-century theatre is still used for performances in the summer.

21 **The markets of Aix-en-Provence** Page **203** • The cathedral city of Aix is home to Provence's best markets, selling everything from live rabbits to hand-made clothes.

22 **Breaking the bank at Monte Carlo** Page **443** • If you're going to lose your shirt, there's no finer place to do so than amid the Belle Époque elegance of Monaco's opulent casino.

23 **Driving the Riviera's corniches** Page **431** • Check out the spectacular views on one of the world's most memorable drives.

24 **The Camargue** Page **124** ● Saddle up one of the white Camargue horses and explore this watery marshland on horseback.

25 **Cassis** Page **89** ● Cassis harbour is the place to sample spiky *oursins* (sea urchins), washed down with a bottle of crisp, white wine.

Basics

Basics

Getting there

With two of France's largest provincial airports at Nice and Marseille and a further international airport at Toulon-Hyères, getting to Provence by air is usually the quickest and cheapest option from the UK or Ireland, with the competition between the low-cost airlines and the established carriers helping to keep costs down. There are few direct intercontinental flights to the region, though, so long-haul travellers from the USA, Canada, Australia, New Zealand and South Africa are more likely to fly into a major European hub such as Paris or London, then transfer to a short flight, or complete the journey by train. Eurostar rail services through the Channel Tunnel link to the fast TGV system, making rail a viable alternative, although you'll need to change at Paris or Lille. It's possible to reach Marseille or Nice by bus and car from the UK, too, though the journey can take up to 24 hours.

Airfares for long-haul flights depend on the **season**, with the highest being around June to August, when the weather is best; fares drop during the "shoulder" seasons – September, April and May – and you'll get the best prices during the low season, October to March (excluding Christmas and New Year when prices are hiked up and seats are at a premium). Flights from the UK and Ireland don't vary seasonally as much but prices peak at weekends and if you book late.

Flights from the UK and Ireland

With the rapid increase in the number of **budget airlines** between the UK, Ireland and France, flying is a cheap and convenient option, particularly if you're leaving from or heading to one of the regional airports. Budget airlines bmibaby, easyJet, flybe and Ryanair serve a variety of destinations in Provence, including Avignon, Marseille, Nice and Toulon-Hyères. Bear in mind, though, that budget airline routes and destinations have a tendency to change regularly, so it's wise to keep an eye on the airlines' websites (see p.31). **Tickets** work on a quota system, and it's wise to book as early as possible for the really cheap seats, which if you're lucky can cost as little as a penny, with airport taxes and surcharges on top often coming to only £16–20 each way. To keep costs down, be as flexible as possible – flying midweek at an ungodly hour will probably secure the cheapest tickets.

It's still worth checking out the **traditional carriers**, such as Air France, British Airways and Aer Lingus, which have slashed their fares for short flights to compete with the upstart budget carriers. Low-season return **fares** to Marseille or Nice from London with British Airways can cost less than £70 including taxes; note that as flag carriers are more orientated towards business travellers, it's not always cheapest to fly midweek. A flight from Dublin to Marseille with Aer Lingus costs around €111 if booked in advance; the service operates from June to mid-September; fares from Dublin to Nice are similar and the service runs year-round.

British Airways flies daily from London Heathrow and Gatwick to **Nice** and from Gatwick to **Marseille**. bmibaby flies from Birmingham daily to Nice and twice a week to Marseille. flybe links Exeter and Southampton with Nice from May to October and March to October respectively and also has seasonal flights from these UK regional airports to **Avignon**. easyJet flies to Nice from Bristol, Liverpool, London Gatwick, Luton and Stansted. Ryanair links Dublin, Glasgow and London Stansted with Marseille.

Flights from the US and Canada

There are few direct flights from the US and Canada to Provence. Delta Airlines flies year-round from JFK airport in **New York** to Nice from around $560 in the winter low season, with prices rising to around $1200 at the summer peak. Additionally, Canadian charter carrier Air Transat links **Montreal** with Nice and Marseille during the summer months (approximately April/May–Oct), with frequency of flights highest during the July and August holiday period. **Prices** start at around CAN$749 return to Marseille, rising to CAN$1359 at the summer peak; fares to Nice are broadly comparable, though somewhat lower at the height of the season than the equivalent flights to Marseille.

These direct flights aside, most journeys to Provence from North America will involve a **transfer**, either using an internal North American flight to hook up with the Delta or Air Transat flights or else flying direct to Paris or some other major European hub, with onward connections by air or train.

Several major airlines have **scheduled flights to Paris** from the US and Canada. Air France operates frequent flights from around fifteen North American cities all year round and has a dense network of internal flights in France for forward connection, including frequent flights to Nice, Marseille, Toulon-Hyères and Avignon. Many internal Air France flights depart from Paris Orly airport, which requires a cross-town transfer from Charles de Gaulle, but there are also internal flights to Marseille and Nice from Charles de Gaulle, which is the main portal for intercontinental flights. Other airlines offering direct services to Paris from a variety of US cities include: American Airlines from **New York**, **Chicago**, **Dallas** and **Miami**, Continental from **Newark** and **Houston**, Delta from **Atlanta**, **Boston** and **Cincinnati**, Northwest from **Detroit**, United from **Chicago** and **Washington DC** and US Airways from **Philadelphia**. Flights typically leave early evening, with those from the East Coast arriving in Paris early the next day.

Typical midweek round-trip **fares** in low season are around $500 from Chicago, $600–700 from Houston, $600 from Los Angeles and $500–600 from New York, rising to double these prices or more in the high season. Air Canada offers non-stop flights to Paris from Montreal and Toronto, both from around CAN$725 in the low season, rising to around CAN$1350 in the summer. Air Transat offers good-value charter flights from several Canadian cities,

with prices from Montreal under CAN$500 midweek in the low season, rising to around CAN$950 in the summer.

Another option is to take one of the other **European carriers**, such as British Airways, Iberia, or Lufthansa, from the US or Canada to their home base and then continue on to Provence – each has onward connections to both Marseille and Nice.

Flights from Australia, New Zealand and South Africa

There are **no direct flights** to Provence from Australia, New Zealand or South Africa. Most visitors will therefore fly to Paris or London, where they can **transfer** to a flight to Nice or Marseille or – if flying into Paris – onto an ultra-fast TGV **train** for onward connection to the south. Flights via Asia or the Middle East, with a transfer or overnight stop at the airline's hub, are generally the cheapest option; those routed through the US tend to be slightly pricier.

Air France offers the most competitive ticket **prices** from **Australia**, with special web offers dramatically reducing the cost of travel, so that off-season flights from Brisbane to Marseille can cost as little as AUS$1404, though the journey involves two **changes of plane** to reach Provence. Alternatively, typical off-season fares from Sydney to Marseille with Air France are around AUS$1850. Qantas operates codeshare flights to Paris with Air France via Singapore from Melbourne and Sydney, with flights from Sydney for around AUS$2200 in November and AUS$2800 in July; prices from Melbourne are slightly lower but vary seasonally in the same way. Singapore Airlines is generally cheaper, with off-season flights from Sydney via Singapore around AUS$2000 and high-season prices under AUS$2400; again, Melbourne flights are cheaper. Singapore Airlines routes travellers from **Adelaide**, **Perth** and **Brisbane** via Singapore at similarly competitive rates. British Airways offers the most convenient option of all, flying from Sydney via London Heathrow to Nice with only one change of plane from AUS$2262 in the low season, and from Melbourne for slightly less. Its connections to Marseille are not quite as

Fly less – stay longer! Travel and climate change

Climate change is the single biggest issue facing our planet. It is caused by a build-up in the atmosphere of carbon dioxide and other greenhouse gases, which are emitted by many sources – including planes. Already, flights account for around 3–4% of human-induced global warming: that figure may sound small, but it is rising year on year and threatens to counteract the progress made by reducing greenhouse emissions in other areas.

Rough Guides regard travel, overall, as a global benefit, and feel strongly that the advantages to developing economies are important, as are the opportunities for greater contact and awareness among peoples. But we all have a responsibility to limit our personal "carbon footprint". That means giving thought to how often we fly and what we can do to redress the harm that our trips create.

Flying and climate change

Pretty much every form of motorized travel generates CO_2, but planes are particularly bad offenders, releasing large volumes of greenhouse gases at altitudes where their impact is far more harmful. Flying also allows us to travel much further than we would contemplate doing by road or rail, so the emissions attributable to each passenger become truly shocking. For example, one person taking a return flight between Europe and California produces the equivalent impact of 2.5 tonnes of CO_2 – similar to the yearly output of the average UK car.

Less harmful planes may evolve but it will be decades before they replace the current fleet – which could be too late for avoiding climate chaos. In the meantime, there are limited options for concerned travellers: to reduce the amount we travel by air (take fewer trips, stay longer!), to avoid night flights (when plane contrails trap heat from Earth but can't reflect sunlight back to space), and to make the trips we do take "climate neutral" via a carbon offset scheme.

Carbon offset schemes

Offset schemes run by Ⓦ www.climatecare.org, Ⓦ www.carbonneutral.com and others allow you to "neutralize" the greenhouse gases that you are responsible for releasing. Their websites have simple calculators that let you work out the impact of any flight. Once that's done, you can pay to fund projects that will reduce future carbon emissions by an equivalent amount (such as the distribution of low-energy light bulbs and cooking stoves in developing countries). Please take the time to visit our website and make your trip climate neutral.

Ⓦ www.roughguides.com/climatechange

---

convenient, involving a bus transfer between Heathrow and Gatwick airports. BA flights to Nice from Auckland involve two changes of plane, with fares around NZ$2770.

As well as flights from Brisbane, Melbourne, Perth and Sydney, Emirates operates services from **New Zealand**, with flights from **Auckland** and **Christchurch** via Dubai, and is also competitive on price, with off-season return fares from just over AUS$2000 or NZ$2000; Cathay Pacific flights from Adelaide, Auckland, Brisbane, Cairns, Melbourne, Perth and Sydney via Hong Kong are a little more expensive than Emirates or Singapore Airlines.

From **South Africa**, Air France again offers the most competitive prices, with off-season return fares from **Johannesburg** via Paris to Nice from around ZAR6650; South African Airways flights from Johannesburg route via Frankfurt and start at just under ZAR8000. British Airways flies from **Cape Town** via London Heathrow to Nice off-season for ZAR9176; fares from Johannesburg are lower.

By train

Eurostar operates frequent high-speed passenger **trains** daily from Waterloo International to France via the **Channel Tunnel**;

most but not all services stop at Ashford in Kent (40min from London). Travellers to **Marseille** bypass Paris, changing trains at Lille; the journey takes around seven hours, with cheapest non-flexible fares from around £109 return and early morning trains most likely to be cheaper. **Nice**-bound travellers have to change at Paris, transferring from the Gare du Nord to the Gare du Lyon; the journey time is around ten hours and fares start at around £119. Fares to **Avignon** are comparable to those to Marseille; the journey time is around forty minutes less. On Saturdays from July to mid-September there is a **direct service** between London and Avignon in both directions, with a journey time of just over six hours.

For visitors arriving off long haul flights in **Paris**, fast, direct **TGV** trains link Charles de Gaulle airport with Marseille in a little under four hours, with one-way fares from around €58; direct trains from Charles de Gaulle to Nice take around six and a half hours, with one-way fares from around €67.

Rail passes

The **Eurail Pass**, which offers unlimited first-class rail travel in eighteen European countries including France, is only available to **non-European residents** and can either be bought prior to arriving in Europe or at a higher price at a Eurail Aid Office, but it's an expensive option if you're only visiting Provence and don't intend to travel more widely in Europe. Less expensive and of more obvious use, given the geographical proximity of Provence to Italy, are the various Eurail **France-Italy** passes (from US$285), which offer unrestricted first- or second-class travel for anything between four and ten days in a two-month period. A **Saver** version of the pass (from US$255 per person) is available for two or more people travelling together, and there's also a **Youth** pass (from US$215) valid for second-class rail travel for those under the age of 26.

Inter Rail passes offer unlimited second-class rail travel but are only available to **European residents**; you will be asked to provide proof of residency before being allowed to purchase one. The passes come in adult, under-26 and under-12 versions, and can be bought to cover one or two of the Inter Rail **zones** or the entire network. Provence, as part of France, is included in Zone E with the Benelux countries. Single-zone passes (£215/€286 adult; £145/€195 under-26) are valid for sixteen days, two-zone passes (£295/€396 adult; £205/€275 under-26) for 22 days and Global (all zones) tickets (£405/€546 adult; £285/€385 under-26) for one calendar month. Inter Rail passes do not include travel within your country of residence, though pass holders are eligible for **discounts** on rail fares to and from the border of the relevant zone as well as reductions on Eurostar and cross-Channel ferries.

A three- to nine-day **France Railpass** (from £103/US$222 adult) is valid for one month and can be booked three months in advance, with the cheapest adult prices available for groups of two to five people travelling together. The pass does not include the price of seat reservations, which are compulsory on some services such as TGV.

By bus

Eurolines, a network of European **bus** companies, offers services from London Victoria to Lyon with onward connections to **Marseille**, **Hyères**, **Toulon**, **Cannes** and **Nice**; journey time to Marseille is 21hrs 45min and to Nice approximately 24 hours, and involves a change at Lyon. Buses are air-conditioned and fitted with toilets. **Fares** (London–Marseille on a Promo 15 return fare £79; Nice on a Eurolines Value Return fare £86) are cheaper than the equivalent train journeys but are likely to be undercut by budget airlines for much of the year, making the somewhat gruelling journey worth considering only if avoiding tight airline baggage restrictions is a consideration.

Also worth investigating is **Busabout**, a **hop-on, hop-off** bus network operating throughout Europe in summer (May–Oct). Buses depart every two to three days on three cross-continental loops – northern, southern and western; the western loop links Paris with Nice via Switzerland, with onward links to northern Spain and back to Paris; the southern loop links Nice with northern Italy, Switzerland, Austria and southern Germany. A single loop costs £289.

By car

Getting to Provence by car from the **UK** is relatively straightforward, with the **Channel Tunnel** or one of the short **ferry** crossings from Kent the quickest ways to access the French autoroute network. From Calais, the best route follows the E17 to the east of Paris via Troyes and Dijon – avoiding the capital's congestion – linking with the E15, which continues via Lyon south to Provence. For much of the journey, **traffic** is light; usually, it's only south of Lyon that congestion is a problem.

From **Ireland**, Brittany Ferries links Cork with Roscoff in Brittany, while Irish Ferries links Rosslare with Roscoff and with Cherbourg – routes which eliminate the need to drive across the UK, but with the downside that they are not as direct as from Calais and involve some stretches of off-autoroute driving.

Return **fares** to take your car through the Channel Tunnel start from just under £100. **Ferry** prices are seasonal and depend on the size of your vehicle and the time you choose to cross; midweek sailings are cheaper, as are some night crossings or crossings in the middle of the day. An easy way to compare prices is via Ferry Savers (℡0870 066 9612, ⓦwww.ferrysavers.com) and EuroDrive (℡0870 423 5540, ⓦwww.eurodrive.co.uk), both of which offer cut-price fares; the latter caters only for people taking their cars across the Channel. Return fares from the UK are now available for less than £40 if booked in advance on the Norfolk Line Dover–Dunkerque service, or from around £70 on the shorter Dover–Calais route. Off-season return prices from Ireland start from around €340 for a car, two adults and two children.

Airlines, agents and operators

Online booking

ⓦwww.expedia.co.uk (in UK),
ⓦwww.expedia.com (in US)
ⓦwww.expedia.ca (in Canada)
ⓦwww.lastminute.com (in UK)
ⓦwww.opodo.co.uk (in UK)
ⓦwww.orbitz.com (in US)

ⓦwww.travelocity.co.uk (in UK), ⓦwww.travelocity.com (in US), ⓦwww.travelocity.ca (in Canada), ⓦwww.zuji.com.au (in Australia), ⓦwww.zuji.co.nz (in New Zealand).

Airlines

Aer Lingus UK ℡0870/876 5000, Ireland ℡0818/365 000, US and Canada ℡1-800/IRISH-AIR, ⓦwww.aerlingus.com.

Air Canada UK ℡0871/220 1111, Ireland ℡01/679 3958, US and Canada ℡1-888/247-2262, Australia ℡1300/655 767, New Zealand ℡0508/747 767, ⓦwww.aircanada.com.

Air France UK ℡0870/142 4343, US ℡1-800/237-2747, Canada ℡1-800/667-2747, Australia ℡1300/390 190, South Africa ℡0861/340 340, ⓦwww.airfrance.com.

Air Transat Canada ℡1-866/847-1112, ⓦwww.airtransat.com.

American Airlines UK ℡0845/778 9789, Ireland ℡01/602 0550, US and Canada ℡1-800/433-7300, Australia ℡1800/673 486, New Zealand ℡0800/445 442, ⓦwww.aa.com.

bmi UK ℡0870/607 0555 or 0222, Ireland ℡01/407 3036, US ℡1-800/788-0555, ⓦwww.flybmi.com.

bmibaby UK ℡0871/224 0224, Ireland ℡1890/340 122, ⓦwww.bmibaby.com.

British Airways UK ℡0870/850 9850, Ireland ℡1890/626 747, US and Canada ℡1-800/AIRWAYS, Australia ℡1300/767 177, New Zealand ℡09/966 9777, South Africa ℡114/418 600, ⓦwww.ba.com.

Cathay Pacific UK ℡020/8834 8888, US ℡1-800/233-2742, Canada ℡1-800/268-6868, Australia ℡13 17 47, New Zealand ℡09/379 0861, South Africa ℡11/700 8900, ⓦwww.cathaypacific.com.

Continental Airlines UK ℡0845/607 6760, Ireland ℡1890/925 252, US and Canada ℡1-800/523-3273, Australia ℡02/9244 2242, New Zealand ℡09/308 3350, ⓦwww.continental.com.

Delta UK ℡0845/600 0950, Ireland ℡1850/882 031 or 01/407 3165, US and Canada ℡1-800/221-1212, Australia ℡1300/302 849, New Zealand ℡09/977 2232, ⓦwww.delta.com.

easyJet UK ℡0905/821 0905, ⓦwww.easyjet.com.

Emirates UK ℡0870/243 2222, US and Canada ℡1-800/777-3999, Australia ℡03/9940 7807, New Zealand ℡05/0836 4728, South Africa ℡0861/363 728, ⓦwww.emirates.com.

flybe UK ℡0871/700 0535, Ireland/International ℡0044/13922 68500, ⓦwww.flybe.com.

Iberia UK ☏ 0870/609 0500, Ireland ☏ 0818/462 000, US ☏ 1-800/772-4642, South Africa ☏ 011/884 5909, ⊛ www.iberia.com.

Lufthansa UK ☏ 0870/837 7747, Ireland ☏ 01/844 5544, US ☏ 1-800/399-5838, Canada ☏ 1-800/563-5954, Australia ☏ 1300/655 727, New Zealand ☏ 0800/945 220, South Africa ☏ 0861/842 538, ⊛ www.lufthansa.com.

Northwest/KLM UK ☏ 0870/507 4074, US ☏ 1-800/225-2525, Australia ☏ 1-300/767 310, ⊛ www.nwa.com.

Qantas Airways UK ☏ 0845/774 7767, Ireland ☏ 01/407 3278, US and Canada ☏ 1-800/227-4500, Australia ☏ 13 13 13, New Zealand ☏ 0800/808 767 or 09/357 8900, South Africa ☏ 11/441 8550, ⊛ www.qantas.com.

Ryanair UK ☏ 0871/246 0000, Ireland ☏ 0818/303 030, ⊛ www.ryanair.com.

Singapore Airlines UK ☏ 0844/800 2380, Ireland ☏ 01/671 0722, US ☏ 1-800/742-3333, Canada ☏ 1-800/663-3046, Australia ☏ 13 10 11, New Zealand ☏ 0800/808 909, South Africa ☏ 11/880 8560 or 8566, ⊛ www.singaporeair.com.

South African Airways UK ☏ 0870/747 1111, US and Canada ☏ 1-800/722-9675, Australia ☏ 1800/221 699, New Zealand ☏ 09/977 2237, South Africa ☏ 11/978 1111, ⊛ www.flysaa.com.

United Airlines UK ☏ 0845/844 4777, US ☏ 1-800/UNITED-1, Australia ☏ 13 17 77, ⊛ www.united.com.

US Airways UK ☏ 0845/600 3300, Ireland ☏ 1890/925 065, US and Canada ☏ 1-800/428-4322, ⊛ www.usair.com.

Agents and operators

Abercrombie & Kent US ☏ 1-800/554 7016, ⊛ www.abercrombiekent.com. Deluxe canal and river cruises and trekking packages.

Adventure Center US ☏ 1-800/227 8747, ⊛ www.adventurecenter.com. Small group hiking or cycling tours. Eight-day 'Hiking in Provence' $960.

The Alternative Travel Group UK ☏ 01865/315 678, ⊛ www.atg-oxford.co.uk. Five- and eight-day walking tours in the Luberon from £370.

Back Door Travel US ☏ 425/771-8303, ⊛ www.ricksteves.com. Small group travel. Twelve-day Paris & Provence trip $2595 plus flight.

Backroads US ☏ 1-800-GO-ACTIVE, ⊛ www.backroads.com. Trendy bike tour company offering a six-day Provence Biking trip for $2798.

Belle France UK ☏ 0870/405 4056, ⊛ www.bellefrance.co.uk. Cycling, walking, painting and motoring holidays in and around St Rémy and the Camargue.

Butterfield & Robinson US & Canada ☏ 1-866/551-9090, ⊛ www.butterfield.com. Seven-day Provençal biking tours CAN$5695.

Canvas Holidays UK ☏ 0870/192 1154, ⊛ www.canvasholidays.co.uk. Camping holidays on the Côte d'Azur.

CIT Holidays ☏ 1300/361 500, ⊛ www.cittravel .com.au. Australian operator offering mid-priced hotels in major resorts on the Riviera, in Aix, Avignon and Marseille.

Club Cantabrica UK ☏ 01727/866 177, ⊛ www .cantabrica.co.uk. Specializing in the upper end of the mobile home, caravan and campsite market, with sites in Antibes and Port Grimaud.

Contiki Tours UK ☏ 020/8290 6422, ⊛ www .contiki.com. Holidays in Provence for those aged 18–35.

Dominique's Villas UK ☏ 020/7738 8772, ⊛ www.dominiquesvillas.co.uk. Up-market agency with a diverse range of tempting properties, mostly for larger groups.

ebookers UK ☏ 0871/223 5000, Ireland ☏ 01/488 3507, ⊛ www.ebookers.com, ⊛ www.ebookers .ie. Low fares on an extensive selection of scheduled flights and package deals.

Euro-Bike & Walking Tours US & Canada ☏ 1-800/321-6060, ⊛ www.eurobike.com. Biking and hiking tours; seven-day 'A taste of Provence' cycle trip costs $3200.

Eurocamp UK ☏ 0870/901 9410, ⊛ www .eurocamp.co.uk. Camping at or near the coast and at Castellane.

Explore Holidays ☏ 02/9423 8080, ⊛ www .exploreholidays.com.au. Australian operator offering two- to five-star hotel packages, predominantly in Nice.

The French Experience US & Canada ☏ 212/986-3800, ⊛ www.frenchexperience.com. Twenty-two-day apartment packages on the Riviera from around $800.

French Travel Connection ⊛ www.frenchtravel .com.au. Cultural and wine tours, hotels and cycling tours.

Holiday in France ☏ 01225/310 822, ⊛ www .holidayinfrance.co.uk. Up-market villas and houses to rent, including some very large properties.

Gîtes de France ☏ +33 1/1.42.81.28.53 ⊛ www .gites-de-france.com. National federation that rents out houses, cottages and chalets, often in scenic rural locations.

Individual Travellers Company UK ☏ 0870/078 0189, ⊛ www.indiv-travellers.com. Villas and houses for rent in Provence, including numerous smaller properties.

Inntravel UK ☏ 01653/617 945, ⊛ www.inntravel .co.uk. Award-winning operator offering exclusive walking, riding and cycling holidays. Six-night 'Scented Hills of the South' walking tour from £525.

Keycamp ☎ 0870/700 0740, Ⓦ www.keycamp .co.uk. Camping and mobile home holidays on the Côte d'Azur.

Lagrange Holidays ☎ 020/7371 6111, Ⓦ www .lagrange-vacances.com. Self-catering and hotel-based holidays both on the Côte d'Azur and in inland Provence.

Martin Randall Travel ☎ 020/8742 3355, Ⓦ www.martinrandall.com. Cultural tours on specialist themes including art, archaeology and gastronomy. Seven-day 'Roman and Medieval Provence' tour £1650.

Mountain Travel Sobek US & Canada ☎ 1-888/ MTSOBEK, Ⓦ www.mtsobek.com. Hiking trips in Provence; eight-day 'Colors of Provence' tour $3450.

Peregrine Adventures UK ☎ 0844/736 0170, Australia ☎ 1300/854 444, Ⓦ www.peregrine.net .au. Small group adventure and cultural tours. Eight-day 'Secrets of Provence' cycling tour £990.

Trailfinders UK ☎ 0845/050 5940, Ireland ☎ 01/677 7888, Australia ☎ 1300/780 212, Ⓦ www.trailfinders.com. One of the best-informed and most efficient agents for independent travellers.

STA Travel UK ☎ 0871/230 0040, US ☎ 1-800/781-4040, Australia ☎ 1300/733 035, New Zealand ☎ 0800/474 400, South Africa ☎ 0861/781 781, Ⓦ www.statravel.com. Worldwide specialists in independent travel; also student IDs, travel insurance, car rental, rail passes, and more. Good discounts for students and under-26s.

Susie Madron's Cycling for Softies ☎ 0161/248 8282, Ⓦ www.cycling-for-softies .co.uk. Up-market cycling holidays starting from and finishing at St Rémy.

Walkabout Gourmet Adventures ☎ 02/9980 2928, Ⓦ www.walkaboutgourmet.com. Walking tours with an emphasis on good food. 'A Week in Provence' in Haute Provence costs AUS$2965.

Wilderness Travel US & Canada ☎ 1-800/368-2794, Ⓦ www.wildernesstravel.com. Nine-day 'Hiking Haute Provence' trips from $3895.

Rail contacts

CIT World Travel Australia ☎ 1300/361 500, Ⓦ www.cittravel.com.au.
Eurail Ⓦ www.eurail.com.
European Rail UK ☎ 020/7387 0444, Ⓦ www.europeanrail.com.

Europrail International Canada ☎ 1-888/667-9734, Ⓦ www.europrail.net.
Eurostar UK ☎ 0870/518 6186, outside UK ☎ 0044/1233 617 575, Ⓦ www.eurostar.com.
Inter Rail Ⓦ www.interrailnet.com.
Rail Europe UK ☎ 0870/837 1371, US ☎ 1-877/257-2887, Canada ☎ 1-800/361-RAIL, Ⓦ www.raileurope.com/us, Ⓦ www.raileurope.co.uk.
Rail Plus Australia ☎ 613/9642 8644, New Zealand ☎ 649/377 5415, Ⓦ www.railplus.co.nz.
STA Travel UK ☎ 0871/230 0040, US ☎ 1-800/781-4040, Australia ☎ 1300/733 035, New Zealand ☎ 0800/474 400, South Africa ☎ 0861/781 781, Ⓦ www.statravel.com.
Trailfinders UK ☎ 0845/050 5940, Ireland ☎ 01/677 7888, Australia ☎ 1300/780 212, Ⓦ www.trailfinders.com.

Bus contacts

Busabout UK ☎ 020/7950 1661, Ⓦ www.busabout.com.
Eurolines UK ☎ 0870/580 8080, Ⓦ www.nationalexpress.com/eurolines.
STA Travel UK ☎ 0871/230 0040, US ☎ 1-800/781-4040, Australia ☎ 1300/733 035, New Zealand ☎ 0800/474 400, South Africa ☎ 0861/781 781, Ⓦ www.statravel.com.
Trailfinders UK ☎ 0845/050 5940, Ireland ☎ 01/677 7888, Australia ☎ 1300/780 212, Ⓦ www.trailfinders.com.

Ferry contacts

Brittany Ferries UK ☎ 0870/907 6103, Ireland ☎ 021/427 7801, Ⓦ www.brittany-ferries.com.
Irish Ferries Ireland ☎ 0818/300 400, Ⓦ www.irishferries.com.
Norfolkline UK ☎ 0870/870 1020, Ⓦ www.norfolkline.com.
P&O Ferries UK ☎ 0870/598 0333, Ⓦ www.poferries.com.
Sea France UK ☎ 0870/443 1653, Ⓦ www.seafrance.com.
Speedferries UK ☎ 0870/220 0570.
Transmanche UK ☎ 0800/917 1201, Ⓦ www.transmancheferries.com.

Channel Tunnel

Eurotunnel UK ☎ 0870/535 3535, Ⓦ www.eurotunnel.com.

Getting around

Travelling by train is the most reliable and economical means of visiting Provence's main cities. Once you reach your destination you can use the local bus networks to get around, both in the town and out into the surrounding areas. Away from the major towns, however, the rail network is sparse, and bus services are infrequent and often extremely slow, so having independent transport is an important factor if you want to be free to explore out of town.

By train

SNCF (☏ 36.35, ⊛ www.voyages-sncf.com) is the French national rail network, responsible for the vast majority of rail services in Provence. Pride of the network is the high-speed **TGV** (*train à grande vitesse*), which is capable of speeds of over 300kph and which links the region with Paris and the rest of France, with stations at Orange, Avignon, Aix and Marseille, before continuing via Toulon, Hyères and Les Arcs-Draguignan to serve most of the major Riviera resorts, including St Raphaël, Cannes, Nice and Monaco.

Though the TGV is the fastest way to arrive in Provence by rail, the requirement to reserve seats reduces the convenience of the service for **inter-town** hop-on, hop-off travel, and once in Provence you'll find the **TER** (Transport Express Régional) services more useful. These trains are slower but often still impressively modern and comfortable, and stop at more intermediate stations than the TGV. You can also carry a **bicycle** free of charge on these trains, stowing it either in the baggage car or in the bicycle spaces provided. In addition to the principle lines along the Rhône valley and the coast, a second major line heads north from Marseille through Aix and along the Durance to Manosque, Sisteron and beyond, towards Gap and Grenoble; another line heads north from Nice towards the Italian border at Tende, linking many of the communities of the *pays-arrière niçois* with the coast.

Tickets can be bought through the website ⊛ www.voyages-sncf.com, which has an English language option, by phone on ☏ 36.35 or at SNCF stations, and must be validated in the bright yellow *compostage de billets* machines prior to boarding the train. **Timetables** are divided into blue and white periods (*périodes bleues* and *périodes blanches*), with the cheapest travel during the blue off-peak periods.

Variable **reductions** on ticket prices are available if you buy from three months to two weeks in advance, and last-minute offers on the Voyages SNCF website the week before you travel often include reductions of 50 percent. In addition, **Découverte à Deux** tariffs produce 25 percent reductions for two or more people travelling together, provided they stay a minimum of one night away; **Découverte Séjour** fares offer the same discount for single travellers, provided they travel a minimum of 200km and that their stay includes a Saturday night. There are also **Découverte 12–25** fares for children and young adults and **Découverte Senior** fares for the over-60s, each offering a 25 percent saving and without the minimum stay restrictions of the other Découverte fares. A **Découverte Enfant+** tariff for accompanied children under the age of 12 is also available. Larger reductions of 30 to 50 percent are possible within Provence on the TER network using the **discount passes** €15 Carte Jeune or €30 Carte Tout Public, both valid for a year. You'll need ID and a photo to buy either, and you'll have to use the train a lot to justify the cost of purchase.

Provence's 'other' rail network is the narrow-gauge **Chemin de Fer de Provence** (⊛ www.trainprovence.com), a wonderfully scenic (if slow), meandering ride from Nice to Digne.

By bus

Along the coast and between the major towns, Provence is well served by **buses**, with the best and most frequent routes being the fast Aix–Marseille shuttle via the autoroute, and the services that link Nice with the other principal resorts along the Riviera. In more remote rural areas bus services meet the needs of schools and shoppers visiting local markets, and are in any case infrequent and often slow.

SNCF buses are useful for getting to places on the rail network no longer served by passenger trains, such as intermediate stops on the Manosque–Sisteron line and the entire Château Arnoux–Digne line. **Inter-urban buses** are otherwise coordinated on a departmental basis, with **timetables** and other information often available online: ⓦwww.lepilote.com in Bouches du Rhône for Marseille and surroundings; ⓦwww.transports.var.fr for the Var, ⓦwww.vaucluse.fr for Avignon, the Vaucluse and around; ⓦwww.rca.tam.fr for Nice and the Riviera. The Alpes de Haute-Provence produces a timetable in book form, available at bus stations and tourist offices on request. Most towns have a central **gare routière** (bus station), frequently – though not invariably – close to the gare SNCF.

By car

Away from the big cities Provence is superb driving country – whether on the **coastal roads** that feature in so many new car commercials, or on the zig-zagging **mountain routes**. Driving allows you to explore the more remote villages and the most dramatic landscapes, which are otherwise inaccessible; roads such as the Route Napoléon, the Grande Corniche and the roads around the Grand Canyon du Verdon were built expressly to give breathtaking views. In the **cities**, driving is a much less attractive option – the old historic parts of many towns are all but inaccessible by car, car crime remains a problem and traffic and parking conditions can be nightmarish, particularly in Nice and Marseille.

Unleaded (95 and 98 octane), diesel (*gazole*) and LPG **fuel** are all readily available. In common with other European countries, fuel **costs** are somewhat higher than North American drivers will be used to – around €.35 per litre for unleaded. Most places accept credit cards, though note that in the Marseille region some large filling stations insist on prepayment before you fill up, and that in rural areas, filling stations are scarce, pumps are often automated out of hours and foreign credit cards are generally not accepted. It's therefore a good idea to keep your tank topped up, especially if you will be touring in remote parts of Provence. Outside the travel-to-work area of Marseille, **tolls** apply on the autoroutes: you pick up a ticket at the entrance to a toll section and pay in cash or by credit card when you leave the toll area. In contrast to the rest of France, autoroutes in Provence tend to be congested.

Car rental agencies cluster around the airports at Nice and Marseille and at major rail stations, with most well-known international agencies represented; addresses are listed throughout the guide. Prepaying via a website usually produces a much better rate, and there is sometimes a difference in price between booking from home on the web and using the local French website. **Rates** for the smallest cars (Citroën C1 or similar) start at around €175 for a week – prices do vary considerably between agents, so it's worth shopping around. When comparing prices, however, be sure to check what the quoted price does and does not include.

Standard **speed limits** are 50kph in built-up areas, 90kph outside built-up areas and 110kph on dual carriageways, with a limit of 130kph on autoroutes in fine weather, reduced to 110kph in the rain. Speed limits are also lower on autoroutes that pass through urban areas. Radar detectors are illegal and EU drivers exceeding the speed limit by more than 40kph can have their licence seized immediately; on-the-spot **fines** for motoring offences are severe – though along the Riviera in particular you wouldn't know it, as people drive fast and erratically, with lack of attention often a problem at junctions and lights.

Car rental agencies

Alamo UK ☏0870/400 4562, US ☏1-800/462-5266, ⓦwww.alamo.com.
Auto Europe US and Canada ☏1-888/223-5555, ⓦwww.autoeurope.com.

Avis UK ☎ 0870/606 0100, Ireland ☎ 021/428 1111, US and Canada ☎ 1-800/331-1212, Australia ☎ 02/9353 9000, New Zealand ☎ 09/526 2847, ⓦ www.avis.com.

Budget UK ☎ 0870/156 5656, US ☎ 1-800/527-0700, Canada ☎ 1-800/268-8900, Australia ☎ 1300/362 848, New Zealand ☎ 0800/283 438, ⓦ www.budget.com.

Dollar UK ☎ 0808/234 7524, Ireland ☎ 1800/575 800, US ☎ 1-800/800-3665, Canada 1-800/229-0984, ⓦ www.dollar.com.

Europcar UK ☎ 0870/607 5000, Ireland ☎ 01/614 2800, US & Canada ☎ 1-877/940-6900, Australia ☎ 393/306 160, ⓦ www.europcar.com.

Europe by Car US ☎ 1-800/223-1516, ⓦ www.europebycar.com.

Hertz UK ☎ 020/7026 0077, Ireland ☎ 01/870 5777, US & Canada ☎ 1-800/654-3131, Australia ☎ 13 30 39, New Zealand ☎ 0800/654 321, ⓦ www.hertz.com.

Holiday Autos UK ☎ 0870/400 4461, Ireland ☎ 01/872 9366, US ☎ 866/392-9288, Australia ☎ 299/394 433, South Africa ☎ 11/2340 597, ⓦ www.holidayautos.co.uk.

National UK ☎ 0870/400 4581, US ☎ 1-800/CAR-RENT, New Zealand ☎ 0800/800 115, ⓦ www.nationalcar.com.

SIXT UK ☎ 0870/156 7567, Ireland ☎ 061/206 088, US ☎ 1-888/SIXT CAR, ⓦ www.e-sixt.com.

Suncars UK ☎ 0870/902 8021, Ireland ☎ 1850/201 416, ⓦ www.suncars.com.

Thrifty UK ☎ 01494/751 500, Ireland ☎ 01/800 515 800, US and Canada ☎ 1-800/847-4389, Australia ☎ 1300/367 227, New Zealand ☎ 0800/737 070, ⓦ www.thrifty.com.

By bike

As the proliferation of specialist cycling tours demonstrates, **cycling** on backstreets in rural Provence can be a delightful experience, if a strenuous one at times due to the often rugged terrain. Cycles can easily be **hired**, particularly down on the coast where most towns have a branch of the Holiday Bikes chain (ⓦ www.holiday-bikes.com), which also rents out motorcycles and scooters. You can even take your bike free of charge on the regional TER **trains** – there's a €10 charge if you want to take them on the TGV, however.

Information on cycling **tours** can be found on p.32–33.

Accommodation

Finding accommodation on the spot in the larger towns and cities in Provence is generally not a problem for much of the year, outside of the July and August high season. On the Riviera things get more difficult earlier in the year, however: in May, the Cannes Film Festival makes it extremely difficult to find reasonably priced accommodation in the western Riviera, while the Monaco Grand Prix creates the same problem on the stretch of coast to the east of Nice. Booking a couple of nights in advance is reassuring at any time of year, and spares you the effort of trudging around looking for somewhere.

Hotels

Hotels in Provence, as in the rest of France, are **graded** according to the standard of accommodation on a zero- to five-star scale, with zero representing the most basic hotels and five stars the most luxurious, though the system is a little haphazard, often having more to do with ratio of bathrooms to guests than with quality; ungraded and single-star hotels are often very good. **Single rooms** – if the hotel has any – are only marginally cheaper than doubles, so sharing always slashes costs, especially since many hotels willingly provide rooms with extra beds for three or more people at good discounts.

Accommodation price codes

Throughout this guide, hotels and guesthouses have been priced on a scale of
❶–❾, indicating the lowest price you could expect to pay for a double room in high
season. What you get for your money varies enormously between establishments,
and in lower-priced hotels you should expect to pay considerably more for en-suite
facilities. Equally, how much comfort you get for your money depends on where in
the region you stay – your money will go further outside the most popular resorts,
in cities such as Toulon or Marseille and in certain smaller towns.

❶ Under €30   ❹ €55–69   ❼ €100–124
❷ €30–39   ❺ €70–84   ❽ €125–150
❸ €40–54   ❻ €85–99   ❾ Over €150

There used to be an entire class of one-
and zero-star, small, **family-run hotels** in
most Provençal towns and cities, reliably
cheap but often very variable in the standard
of accommodation they offered. Stiff competition from the budget chains has led to the
weaker among these hotels closing down in
large numbers, with those that survive
increasingly sharpening up their act with
more en-suite rooms, brighter decor and
satellite TV – so that standards in the
cheapest hotels are higher than they were,
but too often, so are the prices.

Breakfast, which is not normally included,
can add upto €15 per person to the bill,
sometimes more – though there is no
obligation to take it. The cost of eating
dinner in a hotel's restaurant can be a more
important factor to bear in mind when
deciding where to stay. It's actually illegal for
hotels to insist on your taking **half board**
(*demi-pension*), though you'll come across
some that do, especially during the summer
peak. This can work to your advantage,
however, since the food may well be
excellent and considerably cheaper than a
meal in a restaurant.

Note that many **family-run hotels** close
for two or three weeks a year in low season.
In smaller towns and villages they may also
close for one or two nights a week, usually
Sunday or Monday. Details are given where
relevant in the Guide, but dates change from
year to year and some places may decide to
close for a few days in low season if they
have no bookings. The best precaution is to
phone ahead to check.

Prices in the swankier **resorts** such as
Cannes or St Tropez tend to be higher than

in the rest of the region – though Nice has a
good supply of cheap accommodation
throughout most of the year – and in high
season (July–Aug) prices soar in the Côte
d'Azur resorts.

There are a number of well-respected **hotel
federations** represented in Provence. The
biggest and most useful of these is Logis de
France (☎01.45.84.83.84, ⊛www.logis-de
-france.fr), an association of over 3500 hotels
nationwide. Two other, more up-market federations worth mentioning are Châteaux &
Hôtels de France (☎01.72.72.92.02, ⊛www
.chateauxhotels.com) and Relais & Châteaux
(UK & Ireland ☎44 800 2000 02, US &
Canada ☎1 800 735 2478, Australia ☎2
9299 2280, New Zealand ☎00 800 254
50066, ⊛www.relaischateaux.com), which
specializes in stylish, elegant hotels.

Aix-en-Provence and Toulon participate in
the "**Bon Weekend en Villes**" programme,
whereby you get two nights for the price of
one at participating hotels. In most cases the
offer is restricted to the winter period (Nov–
March). Further details are available from
tourist offices or online at ⊛www.bon-week
-end-en-villes.com.

Chambres d'hôtes and gîtes

Chambres d'hôtes (bed and breakfasts in
private houses) are fairly widespread, particularly in small villages. They vary in standard
and are rarely an especially cheap option –
usually costing the equivalent of a two-star
hotel, sometimes more if they're particularly
elegant. However, if you're lucky, they may
be good sources of traditional home
cooking. Details of a selection of these are

Budget chain hotels

A very useful option – especially if you're driving and looking for somewhere late at night – are the **chain hotels** located at motorway exits and on the outskirts of major towns. They may be soulless, but you can count on a decent and reliable standard. Among the biggest and cheapest (from around €26 for a three-person room with communal toilets and showers) is the one-star Formule 1 chain (☎08.92.68.56.85, ⊛www.hotelformule1.com). Other budget chains include B&B (☎08.92.78.29.29, ⊛www.hotel-bb.com), the slightly more comfortable Première Classe (☎08.25.00.30.03, ⊛www.premiereclasse.fr) and Etap Hôtel (☎08.92.68.89.00, ⊛www.etaphotel.com). More up market but still affordable chains are Ibis (☎08.92.68.66.86, ⊛www.ibishotel.com) and Campanile (☎01.64.62.46.00, ⊛www.campanile.fr), where en-suite rooms with satellite TV and direct-dial phones cost from around €40–50; some of these higher-quality budget hotels also have good city centre positions.

given in the Guide; full lists are available from tourist offices.

If you're planning to stay a week or more in any one place it might be worth considering renting **self-catering** accommodation. This will generally consist of self-contained country cottages known as **gîtes** or *gîtes ruraux*. Many *gîtes* are in converted barns or farm outbuildings, though some can be quite grand.

Lists of both *gîtes* and *chambres d'hôtes* are available from the government-funded agency Gîtes de France (☎01.49.70.75.75, ⊛www.gites-de-france.fr), where you can search for accommodation by type, as well as by area.

Hostels, gîtes d'étape and refuges

At between €10 and €16 per night for a dormitory bed, sometimes with breakfast thrown in, **youth hostels** – *auberges de jeunesse* – are invaluable for single travellers on a **budget**. Some now offer rooms, occasionally en suite, but they don't necessarily work out cheaper than hotels – particularly if you've had to pay a taxi fare to reach them. However, many allow you to cut costs by eating in their cheap canteens, while in a few you can prepare your own meals in the communal kitchens.

Slightly confusingly, there are two rival **French hostelling associations**: the Fédération Unie des Auberges de Jeunesse (FUAJ; ☎01.44.89.87.27, ⊛www.fuaj.org), or the much smaller Ligue Française pour

les Auberges de Jeunesse (LFAJ; ☎01.44.16.78.78, ⊛www.auberges-de-jeunesse.com). Normally, to stay at FUAJ or LFAJ hostels you must show a current **Hostelling International (HI) membership card**. It's usually cheaper and easier to join before you leave home, provided your national Youth Hostel association is a full member of HI; visit ⊛www.hihostels.com for details of membership prices, and for worldwide booking facilities. Alternatively, you can purchase a HI card in LFAJ hostels for €15.25 (€10.70 for those under 26 years of age); at FUAJ hostels you can buy individual "welcome stamps" at a rate of €2.90 per night; after six nights you are entitled to the HI card.

Alone among Provençal cities, **Nice** has a sizeable **independent** hostel sector, with most of the **backpacker** places clustered in the area south of the *gare SNCF*. Standards vary widely, but the best of these hostels are at least as good as the traditional youth hostels and they generally have a less institutional feel; prices tend to be a little higher, in the €15–22 range.

In the countryside, another hostel-style alternative exists in the form of **gîtes d'étape**. Aimed primarily at hikers and long-distance bikers, *gîtes d'étape* are often run by the local village or municipality and are less formal than hostels. They provide bunk beds and primitive kitchen and washing facilities from around €10 per person. In the mountains there are **refuge** huts on the main GR routes; these are extremely basic and not always very friendly places, and must be booked three weeks in advance in high summer. **Costs** per night are usually around €15 depending on facilities. The refuges in the Mercantour are run by the Club Alpin Français des Alpes-Maritimes (Ⓦwww. cafnice.org), whose website lists details of the refuges under its care and the contact details for making reservations, which are handled by each individual refuge.

Camping

Most villages and towns in Provence have at least one **campsite** (notable exceptions being Marseille, which has none, and Nice, which has only one, a long way out). Camping is extremely popular with the French and, especially for those from the north, Provence is a favourite destination. The cheapest sites – from around €11 – are often the *camping municipaux* run by the local authority in small communes in rural Provence. Another countryside option – usually with minimal facilities – is camping *à*

la ferme – on private **farmland**. Local tourist offices will usually have lists of such sites.

On the Côte d'Azur, **commercial sites** can be monstrously large, with hundreds of *emplacements* and elaborate facilities including swimming pools and restaurants; you should reckon on paying anything up to €20–28 per night for a car, tent and two people in high season on the coast. Contact information for campsites is given in the text of the Guide; check ahead for space availability. The price is also indicated, along with the French grading, from one to four stars, which indicates the sophistication of the facilities.

Camping rough (*camping sauvage*) is strongly discouraged in summer due to the high risk of forest fires; in any case, you should never camp rough without first asking the landowner's permission, as farmers have been known to shoot first and ask questions later. Camping on the **beach** is not permitted in major resorts and is not terribly desirable either, since promenades are generally too brightly lit to allow a decent night's sleep.

Food and drink

Food is as good a reason as any for going to Provence. The region boasts one of the greatest cuisines of France, as well as some very fine wines in the Vaucluse, on the coast and at Châteauneuf-du-Pape.

Provence boasts a considerable number of top gourmet **restaurants**, particularly in the cities and along the Côte d'Azur, where – if your budget can stretch to perhaps €100 or more – you can enjoy the creations of some of France's most celebrated kitchens in fine style. Unfortunately, the risk of a mediocre or even bad meal in the heavily touristed areas is ever greater, but if you take your time – treating the business of choosing a place as an appetizer in itself – you should be able to eat well without spending a fortune.

The **markets** of Provence are a sensual treat as well as a lively social event; the best ones are listed in the Guide. The region is

also the homeland of **pastis**, the aniseed-flavoured spirit traditionally served with a bowl of olives before meals.

For a **glossary** of food and drink terms, see p.491–499; for more on the region's food, see the Food colour section.

Breakfast

Depending on the class of hotel or hostel, **breakfast** may be a simple affair of coffee and freshly baked baguette with jam and butter, or a much more elaborate affair involving croissants or a hot and cold buffet – though the splendour of the breakfast buffet will be reflected in the **bill**: a breakfast buffet in even a mid-range hotel might set you back €12 per day, whereas a simpler bread-and-coffee affair in a cheaper hotel might be half that or less. If you're sure that you're going to be staying in town it can be cheaper and just as convenient to opt out and go instead to a local café for a croissant, *pain au chocolat* (a chocolate-filled croissant) or a sandwich, washed down with coffee or hot chocolate – though if you decide to do this, be sure your hotel understands you do not require breakfast so it is not added to your bill.

Lunch and dinner

At lunchtime, and sometimes in the evening, you'll find many restaurants and cafés offer good-value **plats du jour** (chef's specials) at prices below the **à la carte** menu prices. You'll also come across lunchtime **formules** – a menu of limited or no choice, including perhaps a main course and a drink. Most restaurants also have one or more elaborate **prix-fixe** (set-price) menus, which usually offer a limited selection of the dishes available on the full à la carte menu at a reduced price. The usual accompaniment to a full meal is wine; stick to the house wine – often served in 25 or 50cl *pichets* – if you want to keep the bill down.

If you want to experience the full glory of **Provençal cooking** you really need to eat in a **restaurant**. It's still perfectly possible to eat magnificently well for €25 or less in a small, family-run restaurant where you'll enjoy hearty, home-cooked dishes such as *daube de boeuf* or *pieds et paquets*, though the restaurant business is a highly competitive one, particularly in the resorts, and the real gems are not as easy to find as they were. The grander establishments make full use of the high quality of the local produce to create **haute cuisine** with a Provençal accent but at distinctly international prices, particularly in jet-set hotspots such as St Tropez, Monaco or Mougins.

One very appealing and affordable alternative to Provençal cuisine – particularly in Marseille – is **North African** food; other inexpensive ethnic options include the numerous **Asian** fast food buffets, though the quality of Chinese, Vietnamese and Thai cooking in Provence is very variable, even in the more up market restaurants, and some visitors may find the food rather bland, as spicing tends to be toned down to suit less adventurous French palates. **Indian** or **Mexican** food, should you find it, similarly tends to lack the customary fiery heat.

For vegetarians in particular the numerous **pizzerias** can be a godsend, usually advertising pizza cooked *au feu de bois* – in a wood-fired oven – and served with a drizzle of oil. Pizza tends to be one of the cheapest options, though quality and price vary enormously. Fresh **pasta**, a speciality of Nice, is affordable and often very good – and another safe option for veggies.

Brasseries and cafés vary widely in price and style, from those that are merely large bars serving a restricted food menu to very grand (and expensive) affairs resembling the celebrated Parisian eateries of the Left Bank; generally speaking, brasseries serve **quick meals** at any time of the day, including salads and lighter options. Whereas in a restaurant the attitude to the chef's creations can be highly reverential, a brasserie is as much a place to see and be seen, drink a beer or coffee or read the newspaper as to linger over food. **Crêperies and salons de thé** are also a good bet for light meals.

Snacks and street food

Provence – and especially the city of Nice – is a wonderful place to eat on the hoof. Colourful **markets** are an excellent source of fresh produce, meats and cheeses, while **patisseries** often sell the delicious savoury *pain fougasse*, a finger-shaped bread that may contain olives, anchovies, sausage, cheese or bacon. Along the Riviera the **sandwich** of choice is the hearty *pan bagnat*, a delicious mix of tuna, hard-boiled egg and bitter *mesclun* salad leaves drizzled with oil, usually available for less than €5; **Niçois street food** includes the simple onion tart *pissaladière*, *farcis* (vegetables stuffed with a meat mixture) and hot wedges of *socca* – a pancake made with chickpea flour. In **Marseille** in particular, other options include Tunisian snacks such as *brik à l'oeuf* (a delicious filo pastry snack stuffed with soft-set egg), spicy Merguez sausages and Middle Eastern falafel.

Drinks

As in the rest of France, **coffee** is the beverage of choice, served long and milky as a *café au lait* at breakfast time and drunk short and strong as an *express* (espresso) later in the day – ask for *une crème* or *une grande crème* if you want a coffee with milk in a café. Ordinary **tea** is usually Liptons, served in the cup with a tea bag; ask for *un peu de lait frais* if you want it with milk, English style. Herb or fruit teas – known as infusions or *tisanes* – are also widely available.

Draught **beer** – usually Kronenbourg – is one of the cheaper alcoholic drinks you can buy; you'll also see French and Belgian bottled beers and, in larger towns and cities, a big international selection in Dutch- or Irish-style pubs.

Provençal **wines** include the very grand vintages of Châteauneuf-du-Pape, the renowned wines of Vacqueyras, Gigondas and Bandol, and the famous dessert wines of Beaumes de Venise; prices for these nobler wines can be understandably high, but there's plenty of inexpensive Côtes du Luberon or Côtes de Provence wine to enjoy too. Red, white and rosé varieties are available in all price ranges, and in the summer heat in particular the allure of a crisp, pale Provençal rosé can be irresistible.

For those in search of something stronger, **pastis** is the ubiquitous *aperitif*, and there's also an abundance of cognac, armagnac and various flavoured *eaux de vie*, of which the most delicious is Poire Williams; *marc* is a spirit distilled from grape pulp. Cocktails are served at most late-night bars and discos.

The media

Getting hold of international editions of English-language newspapers and magazines in Provence is relatively easy. Newsstands at airports and railway stations and branches of Virgin in the major cities invariably stock the major publications, though such is the influx of English-speaking expatriates that these days you may just as easily find the latest edition of the Wall Street Journal or Financial Times on sale in some idyllic village in the Luberon.

Newspapers and magazines

Of the national **French dailies**, *Le Monde* (🌐 www.lemonde.fr) is the most respected, though it can be a bit tedious; *Libération* (🌐 www.liberation.com) is moderately left-wing, independent and more colloquial, *L'Humanité* (🌐 www.humanite.presse.fr) is communist and *Le Figaro* (🌐 www.lefigaro.fr) is the most respected of the right-leaning newspapers. That said, if you can read French, you're more likely as a visitor to find one of the major regional newspapers such as Marseille's *La Provence* or Nice's down-market *Nice Matin* useful, if not for their indifferent news coverage then for their listings.

Also worth seeking out is the English-language magazine *Riviera Reporter* (🌐 www.riviera-reporter.com), which you can pick up at English bookshops and occasionally at tourist offices, and which, though aimed more at expats than visitors, often contains articles of interest.

Radio

Broadcasting out of Monaco and faithfully reflecting its British expat audience with a down-home local radio mix of suburban chat and middle-of-the-road hits, **Riviera Radio**

(106.5FM in France, 106.3FM in Monaco, @www.rivieraradio.mc) is also very useful for visitors to the Côte d'Azur, thanks to its news and events coverage. If you're driving on the southern French autoroutes, **Radio Trafic** (107.7FM) broadcasts a mix of French and international hits interspersed with French and English-language traffic bulletins. **English-language** broadcasts can be heard on the BBC (@www.bbc.co.uk/worldservice), Radio Canada (@www.rcinet.ca), and Voice of America (@www.voa.gov). See their websites for local frequencies.

Television

French TV has six **channels**: three public (France 2, France 3 and Arte/France 5), one subscription (Canal Plus – with some unencrypted programmes), and two commercial open broadcasts (TF1 and M6). Of these, TF1 and France 2 are the most popular, showing a broad range of programmes. Hotels frequently offer a **satellite TV** package that includes additional cable channels, including usually at least one in English – generally either CNN or BBC World.

Festivals

Provence is home to some of France's most celebrated **festivals**. The real cultural heavyweights are the **Avignon** (@www.festival-avignon.com) and **Aix** (@www.festival-aix.com) festivals, which use the historic settings of the two cities to stunning effect as a backdrop for high culture in the early summer. Also internationally known are **Juan-les-Pins**' Jazz à Juan, the region's most prestigious **jazz festival**, and its equivalent in **Nice**, and the Chorégies d'Orange **opera festival** (@www.choregies.asso.fr) at the Roman theatre in **Orange** in July. Most famous of all Provence's festivals is the **Cannes Film Festival** (@www.festival-cannes.fr), held every year in May, but this is a trade-only event and, other than the occasional glimpse of a Hollywood star surrounded by paparazzi, you're unlikely to feel a part of it.

Much more accessible are Nice's pre-Lent **carnival** (@www.nicecarnaval.com) with its celebrated *Bataille de Fleurs*, Menton's annual *Fête du Citron* (lemon festival) in

February and the gathering of the gypsies in *Les Stes Maries de la Mer* in May.

Arles and Fréjus still have Spanish–style *férias* or **bullfights**, while Marseille's *Fiesta des Suds* world **music and arts festival** (@www.docks-des-suds.org) strikes a more contemporary and cosmopolitan note in the industrial setting of the city's docklands each October.

The principality of **Monaco** makes up for its modest size with a packed programme of events of its own, from the **Monte Carlo Rally** in January (@www.acm.mc) to the *Printemps des Arts* (@www.printemps-des-arts.mc) arts festival in March and April and the **Grand Prix** (@www.acm.mc) in May.

On a less spectacular scale, many small towns and villages in Provence have more traditional and authentic, small-scale **fêtes** of their own, a contrast to the hype and glitz of the coast and well worth checking out if you happen to be in the region at the right time. Details of the most popular festivals, as well as many smaller-scale events, are listed throughout the Guide.

Sports and outdoor activities

Spectator sports

Football is the most popular **spectator sport** in Provence, especially in Marseille, home of Olympique de Marseille, one of the top French teams. Motor racing takes precedence in Monaco, while enthusiasm for **cycle racing** is as great as anywhere in France, and the annual **Tour de France** generally has a stage in Provence, most notoriously on Mont Ventoux. In and around the Camargue, the number one spectator sport is **bullfighting**; though not to everyone's taste, it is, at least, less gruesome than the variety practised in Spain. The world-famous **Formula One Grand Prix** takes place in Monaco in May, while some of Provence's remote inland routes make perfect terrain for **rallying**. Monaco and Nice host international **Tennis Open** championships.

The characteristic Provençal sporting pastime is **pétanque**, the region's version of *boules*, which you'll see played in practically every town or village square, in parks and sometimes in purpose-built arenas. The principle is the same as in bowls, but the terrain is rough, never grass, and the area of play much smaller.

Sailing and watersports

There can scarcely be a coast anywhere in the world with as many **yachting facilities** as the Côte d'Azur, and most coastal resorts have at least one marina and often more. The characteristic Riviera boat is a flashy motor cruiser rather than an elegant yacht, and a disproportionate number of craft seem to spend most of their time in port being used as a venue for showing off. The chief problem for **watersports** enthusiasts on the Côte d'Azur is simple congestion, with the thousands of yachts dodging jetskis, motorboats and windsurfers and adding up to a traffic headache – not least because the offshore powerboat racers seem to drive with no more care than the sports car speed fiends show on land. Nonetheless, the sea is warm and placid and there are plenty of opportunities to hire equipment.

Elsewhere, there are opportunities for **diving** in the clear waters around Cassis, along the Corniche des Maures and at Fréjus. **Swimming** is most enjoyable in the *calanques* of Marseille or around the quieter and more remote beaches away from the big cities; purpose-built **water parks** on the coast offer extensive facilities in exchange for their rather steep entry prices.

Sailing and watersports operators

Absolute Boat ☎06.11.73.30.56, ⓦwww.absoluteboat.com. *The* place in Cannes to charter that drop-dead speedboat or motor yacht for film festival posing, if money is no object.

AM Catamaran ☎04.92.93.16.39, ⓦwww.am-catamaran.com. Half-day cruises along the Côte d'Azur on a giant catamaran. Various itineraries from Antibes, St Raphaël and St Tropez; from €40 for half a day.

Aqualand ⓦwww.aqualand.fr. Operator of family water parks, with parks at St-Cyr Sur Mer, Fréjus and Ste-Maxime.

Bateau École Var ☎04.94.83.11.21, ⓦwww.bateau-ecole-var.com. Sailing school based at Port Santa Lucia in St Raphaël.

Bormes Plongée ☎04.94.64.91.28, ⓦwww.bormesplongee.com. Diving tuition for adults and children, off Port Cros and Porquerolles.

Centre Cassidain de Plongée ☎04.42.01.89.16, ⓦwww.centrecassidaindeplongee.fr. Diving in the bay of Cassis and the *calanques*.

École de Croisière Sillages ☎06.10.27.13.83, ⓦwww.sillages.fr. Sailing school based at the old harbour in St Raphaël; all levels, including beginners, accepted.

Mio Palmo Plongée ☎04.94.15.43.10, ⓦwww.mio.palmo.free.fr. Diving on the exquisite Cap Lardier.

Water Glisse Passion ☎06.61.85.59.27. Waterskiing school on La Nartelle beach, Ste-Maxime.

Yachtazur ☎04.94.53.69.34, ⓦwww.yachtazur .com. Yacht charters from the port at Fréjus, from around €990 per week off-season, with skippers available at extra cost.

Outdoor and adventure activities

With its benign climate and superb natural spaces, Provence makes a superb venue for **outdoor sports and adventure pursuits**. The beautiful alpine scenery makes superb **walking** country, particularly around the Grand Canyon du Verdon and in the Parc National du Mercantour (🕸www.mercantour.eu). The Grand Canyon du Verdon (see p.259) is popular for **hiking**, **rafting**, **canyoning**, **kayaking**, **rock climbing**, **hang-gliding**, **mountain biking** and **horse-riding**: Castellane and La Palud Sur Verdon are the two main centres for active sports in the gorge; nearby St-André-les-Alpes is popular for **paragliding** and hang-gliding, and Fayence is a centre for **gliding**. Gentler airborne pursuits include **hot-air ballooning** in the Pays de Forcalquier. Closer to the coast, the Gorge du Loup is another centre for canyoning.

The Camargue is Provence's most famous centre for **horse-riding**; information on holidays on horseback is included in "Agents and operators" p.32.

Cycling is popular almost everywhere, with bicycle rental available in most major towns, and there are numerous organised cycling **tours** available (see "Agents and operators" p.32). **Bike rental** information is given throughout the Guide. The Estérel is an increasingly popular centre for mountain biking.

Outdoor and adventure operators

Aboard Rafting ☎04.92.83.76.11, 🕸www.aboard-rafting.com. Castellane-based outfit organising rafting in the Grand Canyon du Verdon. Also offers air boating, canyoning, water rambling, mountain biking and many other activities.

Aerozarbre ☎06.20.23.47.55, 🕸www.aerozarbre.asso.fr. Treetop assault courses at Buoux in the southern Luberon.

Club Alpin Français des Alpes-Maritimes ☎04.93.62.59.99, 🕸www.cafnice.org. Nice-based branch of the national mountaineering union, which manages refuges in the Parc National du Mercantour.

Envol de Provence ☎04.94.90.86.13, 🕸www.envolprovence.com. Paragliding school at Signes, near St-Maximin de la Sainte-Baume.

Holiday Bikes 🕸www.holiday-bikes.com. Leading rental agency for bikes and scooters in the region, with outlets in most coastal resorts.

Luclimb Adventure ☎04.90.65.07.53, 🕸www.luclimb.com. Rock-climbing in the Dentelles, plus canyoning, Via Ferrata, hiking.

Montgolfière Vol-Terre ☎04.90.05.61.46, 🕸www.vol-terre.com. Balloon flights over the Luberon.

La Palud Sur Verdon 🕸www.lapaludsurverdon .com. Website of the Maison des Gorges du Verdon, with masses of links for climbing guides, canyoning, walking, horse-riding and mountain biking in and around the Grand Canyon du Verdon.

Parc National du Mercantour 🕸www .mercantour.eu. Web portal in English for the national park that straddles the French-Italian border.

Les Poneys de Sophie ☎06.70.75.28.91. Riding instruction at all levels, plus trekking from stables at St Aygulf, near Fréjus.

Relais Équestre de la Mène ☎06.11.81.11.32, 🕸www.rem83.fr. Horse-riding in the Massif des Maures.

Rustr'aille Colorado ☎04.90.04.96.53, 🕸www.parapente.biz. Tandem paragliding jumps above the Colorado Provençal.

Velo Loisir en Luberon ☎04.92.79.05.82, 🕸www.veloloisirluberon.com. Network of mapped cycle routes in the Luberon, with affiliated accommodation, cycle hire and repair, etc.

Verdon Passion ☎04.92.74.69.77, 🕸www .verdon-passion. Moustiers-Ste-Marie-based activity outfit organising canyoning, climbing, paragliding, etc.

Skiing and snowboarding

Thanks to the unique topography of the region, it's possible to **ski** remarkably close to the coast – the closest resort to the Côte d'Azur being Gréolières-les-Neiges, a short distance from Grasse. More reliable snow and more extensive facilities are, however, found inland: at Valberg, Isola 2000, La Foux d'Allos, Auron and in the resorts around Barçelonette.

Ski resorts

Auron 🕸www.auron.com. Resort with ski school, snowboarding club and 135km of pistes.

La Foux d'Allos ☎04.92.83.02.81, 🕸www.valdallos.com. Purpose-built, high-altitude ski resort in the Val d'Allos, which has 230km of pistes – the most extensive network in the southern Alps.

Isola 2000 ☎08.05.81.15.15, 🕸www.isola2000.com. Ski resort at an altitude of 2000m on the fringe of the Parc National du Mercantour, with 120km of pistes.

Valberg ☎ 04.93.23.24.25, ⓦ www.valberg.com. Resort claiming the best snow record in the region, with a separate area for snowboarders, a ski school and black runs.

La Vallée de l'Ubaye ⓦ www.ubaye.com. The region around Barçelonnette harbours several skiing resorts, including Le Sauze Super Sauze, Sainte Anne la Condamine and Pra Loup, whose pistes link up with those of La Foux d'Allos.

Shopping

Provence offers a rich variety of local **crafts and produce** to buy as souvenirs, with everything from *santons* in Aubagne or Marseille to high quality glassware in Biot and fine (and sometimes not so fine) art and handicrafts in every chic village along the Côte d'Azur.

Food can be a particular joy to buy, from soft nougat and farmhouse honey to olive oil and fine wine, *marrons glacés* from Collobrières and *calissons* from Aix. One of the joys of shopping in Provence is the opportunity to taste oils and wines as you go;

Clothing and shoe sizes

Women's dresses and skirts

American	4	6	8	10	12	14	16	18
British	8	10	12	14	16	18	20	22
Continental	38	40	42	44	46	48	50	52

Women's blouses and sweaters

American	6	8	10	12	14	16	18
British	30	32	34	36	38	40	42
Continental	40	42	44	46	48	50	52

Women's shoes

American	5	6	7	8	9	10	11
British	3	4	5	6	7	8	9
Continental	36	37	38	39	40	41	42

Men's suits

American	34	36	38	40	42	44	46	48
British	34	36	38	40	42	44	46	48
Continental	44	46	48	50	52	54	56	58

Men's shirts

American	14	15	15.5	16	16.5	17	17.5	18
British	14	15	15.5	16	16.5	17	17.5	18
Continental	36	38	39	41	42	43	44	45

Men's shoes

American	7	7.5	8	8.5	9.5	10	10.5	11	11.5
British	6	7	7.5	8	9	9.5	10	11	12
Continental	39	40	41	42	43	44	45	46	47

another is the sheer colour and choice in the region's many excellent markets.

Most larger towns have considerable shopping facilities in the centre, including perhaps a **department store** as well as the usual range of **fashion** and **footwear** chain stores; most Provençal towns of any size also have sizeable edge-of-town **retail** **parks** which include not only mammoth supermarkets but also discount shoe and clothing retailers. Some of the Côte d'Azur resorts – in particular St Tropez, Cannes, Nice and Monte Carlo – also have a considerable selection of luxury stores, with all the usual international **designer** names present.

Travelling with children

Travelling with **children and babies** presents no particular problems in Provence. They're generally welcome everywhere, including most bars and restaurants. Hotels charge by the room, with a small supplement for a cot or additional bed. Some restaurants – especially in resorts – have specific children's menus. You'll have no difficulty finding disposable nappies, but watch out for baby foods with added sugar and salt and for rich milk powders. **Price reductions** for children are commonplace in museums and attractions and on public transport, with the under-3s or -4s often going free – for instance, children under four travel free on SNCF **trains**.

Tourist offices can help with information on activities specifically aimed at children; along the coast in particular there is no shortage of **attractions** to keep children amused, from funfairs to water parks to zoos. Navigating the steep and cobbled streets of the typical Provençal *village perché*, however, is unlikely to amuse most parents. Most **medicines** are available over the counter at pharmacies. Finally, it is rare to see women breastfeed in public, and you may encourage disapproving stares if you try it.

Travel essentials

Costs

Though France is not a particularly expensive country to visit compared with its European neighbours, Provence is one of the more expensive regions of the country: prices in some of the chic hotspots on the Côte d'Azur can rival those in the more prestigious *arrondissements* of Paris, and costs for accommodation on the coast soar during the July and August peak season when foreign visitors have to compete with the French for scarce hotel rooms.

For a reasonably comfortable stay, including a hotel room for two, a light restaurant lunch and a proper restaurant dinner, plus moving around, café stops and museum visits, you need to allow a **budget** of around £67/$130/€100 a day per person. By counting the pennies, staying at youth hostels (around £10–13.50/$15–26/€15–20 bed and breakfast) or camping (from around £7.50/$14.50/€11 for two people), and being strong-willed about extra cups of coffee and doses of culture, you could manage on £40/$78/€60 a day – or even less if you're surviving on street snacks and market food.

As in other European Union countries, you'll routinely find that Value Added Tax (*TVA*) makes up part of your hotel, restaurant or shopping bill – but prices are usually quoted inclusive of the **tax**. At restaurants you only need to leave an additional cash **tip** if you feel you have received service out of the ordinary, since restaurant prices almost always include a service charge. It's customary to tip porters, tour guides, taxi drivers and hairdressers between one and two euros.

Crime and personal safety

Though certain sections of **Marseille**, **Toulon** and **Nice** have a distinctly dodgy feel, violent crime against tourists is pretty rare. **Petty theft**, however, is endemic along the Côte d'Azur and also a problem in the more crowded part of the big cities, and occasional, serious crimes – as in 2006 when the footballer Patrick Vieira and his family were gassed unconscious in their sleep at their Cannes home by burglars – contribute to the region's somewhat lurid reputation for crime.

Visitors to the region should take the normal **precautions**: don't wave money or travellers' cheques around, never let cameras and other valuables out of your sight and carry wallets and bags securely, particularly in crowded places. The best

security of all is to have a good **insurance** policy and to keep a record of the numbers you'll need if you have to cancel credit cards, as well as the relevant details of your valuables.

Drivers face perhaps the greatest problems, particularly with regard to break-ins: never leave valuables in an unattended car. Drivers on the Riviera in particular are susceptible to robbery by thieves on motorbikes while stuck in heavy traffic.

There are two main types of **police** in France – the Police Nationale and the Gendarmerie Nationale. The former deals with all crime, parking and traffic affairs within large and mid-sized towns, where you'll find them in the Commissariat de Police. The Gendarmerie Nationale covers the rural areas.

Pedestrians should take great care when crossing roads – inattentiveness is still a great problem among French drivers and many pay little heed to pedestrian crossings or lights. Do not step onto a crossing assuming traffic will stop for you.

Drug use is just as prevalent in Provence as anywhere else in Europe – and just as risky. People caught smuggling or possessing drugs, even just a few grams of marijuana, are liable to find themselves in jail. Should you be arrested on any charge, you have the right to contact your consulate (addresses given in the relevant sections in the Guide), though don't expect much sympathy.

As a long-standing stronghold of the extreme right, Provence has acquired a regrettable reputation for **racism**. The majority of racist incidents are focused against the Arab community and occur largely, but by no means exclusively, within the cities. As a result, particularly Arab, but also black and Asian visitors, may encounter an unwelcome degree of curiosity or

Emergency numbers and helpline contacts

Police ☏17.
Medical emergencies/ambulance ☏15.
Fire brigade/paramedics (*pompiers*) ☏18.
Rape crisis (*SOS Viol*) ☏08.00.05.95.95.
Homophobia (SOS Homophobie; 8–10pm) ☏08.10.10.81.35.

suspicion from shopkeepers, hoteliers and the like. If you suffer a **racial assault**, contact the police, your consulate or one of the local anti-racism organizations (though they may not have English-speakers): SOS Racism (Ⓦwww.sos-racisme.org) and Ligue Internationale Contre le Racisme et l'Antisémitisme (LICRA; Ⓦwww.licra.org) – the latter has contacts in most major towns in the region. One other useful resource for travellers is the Paris-based, **English-speaking helpline** SOS Help (Ⓣ01.46.21.46.46, daily 3–11pm; Ⓦwww.soshelpline.org). The service is manned by trained volunteers who not only provide a confidential listening service, but also offer practical information for foreigners facing problems in France.

Travellers with disabilities

For travellers with **disabilities**, and particularly those using wheelchairs, haphazard parking habits, stepped village streets and cobbled paving are among the challenges of a visit to Provence – with the proliferation of dog mess on many pavements an additional and unwelcome hazard. Many **hotels** have lifts, but it's worth checking that your wheelchair will fit before booking – some smaller hotels still have the diminutive older-style lift shaft with the staircase wrapped around it. Museums, stations and other sites are gradually being adapted with **ramps** or other forms of access, though provision varies and is rarely comprehensive.

The national association APF (Association des Paralysées de France) is a useful source of information and has representatives in each *département*. SNCF produces a very useful guide for **travellers** with disabilities, *Le Mémento du Voyageur Handicapé*. It's in French only, but if you read the language it does contain useful information on the accessibility of major stations, plus contact numbers for accessible or adapted **transport** in major towns and cities. The public transport situation is improving as transport networks are modernized: Nice's new Tramway, for instance, has been designed to be fully accessible.

APF – Association des Paralysées de France
Ⓦwww.apf.asso.fr (in French).
Avignon Ⓣ 04.90.16.47.40

La Garde (Var) Ⓣ 04.98.01.30.50
Manosque Ⓣ 04.92.71.74.50
Marseille Ⓣ 04.91.79.99.99
Nice Ⓣ 04.92.07.98.00

Electricity

The French electricity supply runs at 220V, using plugs with two round pins. If you need a transformer, it's best to buy one before leaving home, though you can find them in large department stores in France.

Entry requirements

EU citizens can travel freely in Provence and can stay for an unlimited amount of time, while those from **Australia, Canada, New Zealand and the United States**, among other countries, do not need a visa for a stay of up to ninety days. **South African** citizens require a short-stay visa for up to ninety days, and a long-stay visa for anything after that. You'll need to have a return ticket, and provide evidence that you have accommodation in France, and to provide information on any family or private connections in the country. Be aware, however, that the situation can change and it's advisable to check with your nearest French embassy or consulate before departure.

All **non-EU citizens** who wish to remain longer than ninety days must apply to the local *mairie* or town hall for a **residence permit** (a *titre de séjour*, also known as a *carte de séjour*), for which you will have to show proof of – among other things – a regular income or sufficient funds to support yourself, evidence of medical insurance and the appropriate visa (if required).

For further information about visa regulations consult the Ministry of Foreign Affairs website: Ⓦwww.diplomatie.gouv.fr.

Visa requirements for **Monaco** (an independent principality) are identical to those of France; there are no border controls between the two.

Gay and lesbian travellers

The prevalence of conservative, right-wing attitudes has traditionally meant **lesbian and gay** life in Provence is rather discreet, but in the cities at least that is now changing: both

Nice and Marseille have annual gay pride celebrations and if the bar scene is still fairly low-key compared with Paris or Lyon, it is at least growing – **Nice** in particular has quite a respectable range of lesbian and gay-friendly accommodation, cafés, bars and clubs, and the atmosphere in the city has improved noticeably in recent years.

Perhaps the most relaxed attitudes can be found in the smaller, chic resorts such as **Cannes** and **St Tropez**, where the gay presence is both long-established and relatively integrated into the mainstream. Away from the coast, both **Aix** and **Avignon** have small-scale but lively bar scenes.

The national gay magazine *Têtu* is widely available but more useful listings are found in the free bar **magazines** such as *Guide, Nous* and *Link Xtra*.

Health

There are no compulsory vaccinations for visiting Provence, tap water is safe to drink and most travellers to Provence will encounter little in the way of **health problems**: sunburn, heat exhaustion and insect bites are the most usual complaints. If you do need to access healthcare, standards of treatment in France are among the best in the world.

Under the French **health system**, all services, including doctor's consultations, prescribed medicines, hospital stays and ambulance call-outs, incur a charge which you have to pay upfront. **EU citizens** are entitled to a refund (usually between 70 and 100 percent) of medical and dental expenses, providing the doctor is govern-ment-registered (*un médecin conventionné*) and provided you have the correct documen-tation (the **European Health Insurance Card** – EHIC; application forms available from main post offices in the UK). This can still leave a hefty shortfall, however, especially after a stay in hospital, so you might want to take out some additional insurance. All **non-EU visitors** should ensure they have adequate medical insurance cover.

For **minor complaints** go to a *pharmacie*, signalled by an illuminated green cross. You'll find at least one in every small town and even some villages. They keep normal shop hours (roughly 9am–noon & 3–6pm), though

some stay open late and in larger towns at least one (known as the *pharmacie de garde*) is open 24 hours according to a rota; details are displayed in all pharmacy windows.

For anything more serious you can get the name of a **doctor** from a pharmacy, local police station, tourist office or your hotel. Alternatively, look under "Médecins" in the *Yellow Pages*.

In **emergencies**, you will always be admitted to the nearest general hospital (*centre hospitalier*). Phone numbers and addresses of hospitals in all the main cities are given in the Guide. The national number for the **ambulance** service is ☎ 15.

Medical resources for travellers

CDC ☎ 1-877/394-8747, ⊛ www.cdc.gov/travel.
Official US government travel health site.
Department of Health ⊛ www.dh.gov.uk/travellers.
Official UK government travel health site, with details of how to get the EHIC card plus information on healthcare in France.

Insurance

Even though **EU citizens** are entitled to healthcare privileges in France, you'd do well to take out an **insurance policy** before travelling to cover against theft, loss, illness or injury. A typical travel insurance policy usually provides cover for the loss of baggage, tickets and – up to a certain limit – cash or cheques, as well as cancellation or curtailment of your journey. Most of them exclude so-called dangerous sports, unless an extra premium is paid.; in France this can mean skiing, whitewater rafting, rock-climbing and potholing, and the policy should cover mountain rescue services, helicopter ambulances and the like. Many policies can be chopped and changed to exclude coverage you don't need – for example, sickness and accident benefits can often be excluded or included at will.

If you do take medical coverage, ascertain whether benefits will be paid as treatment proceeds or only after you return home, and if there is a 24-hour medical emergency number. When securing **baggage cover**, make sure that the per-article limit – typically under £500/$750 and sometimes as little as £250/$400 – will cover your most valuable possession. If you need to make a claim, you should keep **receipts** for medicines and medical treatment, and in the event you have anything stolen, you must obtain an official statement from the police (called a *constat de vol*).

Rough Guides has teamed up with Columbus Direct to offer you **travel insurance** that can be tailored to suit your needs. Products include a low-cost **backpacker** option for long stays; a **short break** option for city getaways; a typical **package holiday** option; and others. There are also annual **multi-trip** policies for those who travel regularly. Different sports and activities (trekking, skiing, etc) can usually be covered if required.

See our website (ⓦwww.roughguides insurance.com) for eligibility and purchasing options. Alternatively, UK residents should call ☏0870/033 9988; Australians should call ☏1300/669 999 and New Zealanders ☏0800/55 9911. All other nationalities should call ☏+44 870/890 2843.

Internet

Many tourist hotels in Provence provide **Internet** access to guests as a free service; in larger hotels and the big budget chains it's often possible to connect to the net using WiFi, though there's usually a charge involved. **Internet cafés** are relatively easy to find, particularly in Nice where they cluster in the streets south and east of the *Gare SNCF* and are often associated with businesses offering cheap international phone calls.

Note that some Internet cafés advertise English-language format **keyboards**; if not, expect terminals to have French format (non-QWERTY) keyboards which may take some getting used to. Expect to pay around €4 per hour, with some cafés charging relatively higher rates for shorter time periods.

Laundry

Inexpensive self-service laundries or *laveries automatiques* are commonplace in Provençal towns, and are listed in the guide for larger destinations such as Nice. They are often unattended, so come armed with small change. Machines are graded in different wash sizes, costing in the region of €5 for 7kg. The alternative *blanchisserie* or pressing services are more expensive, as are hotel laundry services: Most hotels forbid doing laundry in your room, though you should get away with just one or two items.

Living in Provence

EU citizens are free to work in France on the same basis as a French citizen. This means you no longer have to apply for a residence or work permit except in very rare cases – contact your nearest French consulate for further information. **Non-EU citizens**, however, will need both a work permit (*autorisation de travail*) and a residence permit; again, contact your nearest French consulate or, if already in France, your local *mairie* or *préfecture* to check what rules apply in your particular situation.

Most **non-EU citizens** who manage to survive for long periods of time in France do it on luck, brazenness and willingness to live in pretty basic conditions. In the towns, bar work, club work, teaching English, translating or working as an au pair are some of the ways people scrape by; in the countryside, the options come down to seasonal fruit- or grape-picking, teaching English, busking or DIY odd-jobbing; there may also be seasonal work in ski resorts. Remember that unemployment is high: the current rate stands at almost ten percent and is on the rise.

When **looking for a job**, a good starting point is to get hold of one of the books on working abroad published by Vacation Work (ⓦwww.vacationwork.co.uk). In France, check out the "*Offres d'Emploi*" (Job Offers) in *Le Monde*, *Le Figaro* and the local newspapers such as *La Provence* in Marseille or *Nice Matin*; it may also be worth checking the business section of the *Riviera Times* (ⓦwww.rivieratimes.com) or the classified sections of *Anglo Info* (ⓦriviera.angloinfo .com; ⓦprovence.angloinfo.com). You can also try visiting local job agencies – tourist information offices should be able to tell you where they are.

Study and work programmes

AFS Intercultural Programs UK ☏0113/242 6136, US ☏1-800/AFS-INFO, Canada ☏1-800/361-7248 or 514/288-3282, Australia ☏1300/131 736 or ☏02/9215 0077, New Zealand ☏0800/600 300 or 04/494 6020, South Africa ☏11/447 2673, international enquiries

☏1-212/807-8686, ⓦwww.afs.org. Intercultural exchange organization with programmes in over 50 countries.

American Institute for Foreign Study US ☏1-866/906-2437, ⓦwww.aifs.com. Language study and cultural immersion, as well as au pair and Camp America programmes.

Mail

Post offices, known as "La Poste" (ⓦwww.laposte.fr) and identified by bright yellow-and-blue signs, are generally open from around 8.30am to 6pm or 7pm Monday to Friday, and from 8.30am to noon on Saturday. However, these hours aren't set in stone: smaller branches tend to keep shorter hours and may close for an hour or so at lunch.

For **sending letters**, remember that you can buy stamps (*timbres*) with less queuing from *tabacs* and newsagents. Standard letters (20g or less) and postcards within France and to other European Union countries cost €0.80, or €0.95 to North America, Australia and New Zealand. Inside larger post offices you'll find rows of yellow-coloured *guichets automatiques* – automatic stamp machines with instructions available in English where you can weigh letters and packages and buy the appropriate **stamps**; sticky labels and tape are also dispensed. To post your letter on the street, look for the bright yellow postboxes.

To send **bulkier items** overseas you can buy a 2kg Boite Postexport – the price is €16.15 for European Union countries and Switzerland and €17.70 for the rest of the world.

Maps

In addition to the maps in this guide and the various free town plans and regional **maps** you'll be offered along the way, the one extra map you might want is a good, up-to-date **road map** of the region. The 1:100,000 maps produced by Michelin (ⓦwww.viamichelin.fr) or the Institut Géographique National (IGN; ⓦwww.ign.fr) are excellent. Both companies also issue good regional maps either as individual sheets or in one large spiral-bound "*atlas routier*"; Michelin's version is available in English as the *France Tourist & Motoring Atlas* (£12.99).

If **walking**, it's worth investing in the more detailed (1:25,000) IGN maps (see above).

Free town maps handed out by tourist offices are often surprisingly good, particularly those sponsored by the Galeries Lafayette department store group; the quality of free maps covering rural areas is more variable and they tend to be geared more towards inspiring you than providing practical information. **Rough Guides** also produces a map of France.

Money

The **currency** in both Provence and the principality of Monaco is the **Euro**, divided into 100 cents (though the French still often refer to these as *centimes*). At the time of writing the exchange rate was €1=£0.67/US $1.31.

ATMs are widespread and accept credit or debit cards carrying Visa or Cirrus symbols; most such machines operate in a selection of languages including English. Note that as your bank will charge you a fee, it's more economical to draw larger sums less frequently than to withdraw small amounts.

Credit and debit cards are also widely accepted in shops, hotels and restaurants, although some smaller establishments don't accept cards, or only for sums above a certain amount. Visa – called Carte Bleue in France – is almost universally recognized, followed by MasterCard (also known as EuroCard). American Express ranks a bit lower. Note that French cards operate on the **chip and pin** system, as in the UK.

Another option is a **pre-paid debit card**; you load up the account with funds before you leave, and then just throw the card away when you've finished with it. They are available through Travelex (ⓦwww.cashpassportcard.com) and in the UK through American Express (ⓦwww.americanexpress.com/uk).

Banks are typically open Monday to Friday from around 8.30am until 5.30pm; in larger branches those hours may be longer, but smaller branches may close for an hour or even two in the middle of the day. Note that stand-alone **bureaux de change** are not as commonplace since the introduction of the Euro eliminated much of their business; generally, it's just as easy to go to a bank or post office if you need to change money or travellers' cheques.

Public holidays

January 1 New Year's Day
Easter Sunday
Easter Monday
Ascension Day (forty days after Easter)
Pentecost or Whitsun (seventh Sunday after Easter)
May 1 Labour Day
May 8 Victory in Europe (VE) Day 1945
July 14 Bastille Day
August 15 Assumption of the Virgin Mary
November 1 All Saints' Day
November 11 Armistice Day 1918
December 25 Christmas Day

Opening hours and public holidays

Outside the big towns and cities, almost everything in Provence closes for a couple of hours at midday, including shops, museums, tourist offices and most banks. Basic **working hours** are roughly 8am–noon and 2–6pm, with shops usually staying open until 7pm or sometimes later. In major cities, many businesses and museums open continuously with no break for lunch; if in doubt, it's worth checking ahead before making a special journey. Small **food shops** may not reopen till halfway through the afternoon, closing around 7.30pm or 8pm, just before the evening meal. The standard **closing day** is Sunday, though some food shops and newsagents are open in the morning.

Museums typically open around 9am and take a long lunch break, reopening at 2 or 3pm then staying open until 5.30 or 6pm; hours are almost invariably longer in summer. If in doubt, check before setting out. **Churches and cathedrals** rarely post opening hours, but are generally open during the working day, though smaller churches, particularly in remote villages, are often locked except when mass is on.

Phones

If you want to use your **mobile/cellphone**, contact your phone provider to check whether it will work in France and what the **call charges** are – they tend to be pretty exorbitant, and remember you're likely to be charged extra for receiving calls. French mobile phones operate on the European

International dialling codes

Calling France from home
France international access code + 33 + city code.

Calling home from abroad
Note that the initial zero is omitted from the area code when dialling the UK, Ireland, Australia and New Zealand from abroad.

UK international access code + 44 + city code.
Ireland international access code + 353 + city code.
US and Canada international access code + 1 + area code.
Australia international access code + 61 + city code.
New Zealand international access code + 64 + city code.
South Africa international access code + 27 + city code.

GSM standard, so US cellphones won't work in France unless you have a tri-band phone.

If you are going to be in France for any length of time and will be making and receiving a lot of local calls, it may be worth your while buying a **French SIM card** (which will give you a local phone number) and prepaid recharge cards (*mobicartes*). You can buy a SIM card from any of the big mobile providers (France Télécom's Orange, SFR and Boygues Telecom), all of which have high-street outlets. They cost from around €30, and you'll need to have an address in France to register – that of your hotel or a friend will usually suffice.

Time

France is in the Central European Time Zone (GMT+1). This means it is one hour ahead of the UK, six hours ahead of Eastern Standard Time and nine hours ahead of Pacific Standard Time. Daylight Saving Time (GMT+2) in France lasts from the last Sunday of March to the last Sunday of October.

Tourist information

Most communities of any size in Provence, from major cities to even the smallest village, have a **tourist information office**, and generally the standard of information they produce is excellent. Major tourist centres in particular produce glossy information brochures with very comprehensive listings of accommodation, restaurants and cultural or leisure activities.

Local tourist **websites** are listed throughout the Guide; in addition, good regional sites include: **Alpes de Haute Provence** (Ⓦwww.alpes-haute-provence.com), with information on the alpine regions of Provence; **Guide Riviera** (Ⓦwww.guideriviera.com), the official

site for tourism on the Côte d'Azur; **Provence Guide** (Ⓦwww.provenceguide.com), site for tourism in the Vaucluse, including Avignon, Orange, the Dentelles and the Luberon; **Visit Provence** (Ⓦwww.visitprovence.com), a tourist web portal for the Bouches du Rhône *département* which includes Marseille and Aix-en-Provence.

Tourist offices and government sites

Australian Department of Foreign Affairs
Ⓦwww.dfat.gov.au, Ⓦwww.smartraveller.gov.au.
British Foreign & Commonwealth Office
Ⓦwww.fco.gov.uk.
Canadian Department of Foreign Affairs
Ⓦwww.dfait-maeci.gc.ca.
Irish Department of Foreign Affairs
Ⓦwww.foreignaffairs.gov.ie.
New Zealand Ministry of Foreign Affairs
Ⓦwww.mft.govt.nz.
US State Department Ⓦwww.travel.state.gov.

French tourist offices in your home country

In the UK Maison de la France, 178 Piccadilly, London W1J 9AL ☏09068/244 123, Ⓦuk.franceguide.com.
In Ireland ☏15 60 235 235, Ⓦie.franceguide.com.
In the US 444 Madison Ave, NY 10022, New York ☏514/288-1904; 9454 Wilshire Boulevard, Suite 210, Beverly Hills 90212, CA ☏514/288-1904 Ⓦus.franceguide.com; Consulate General of France 205 N. Michigan Ave, Suite 3770, Chicago 60601, Illinois ☏514/288-1904
In Canada Maison de la France, 1800 Ave McGill College, Suite 1010, Montreal, Quebec H3A 3J6 ☏514/288-2026, Ⓦca-en.franceguide.com.
In Australia Maison de la France, Level 13, 25 Bligh St, Sydney 2000, NSW ☏02/9231 5244, Ⓦau.franceguide.com.
In South Africa Maison de la France, PO Box 41022, Craighall 2024 ☏11/523 82 92, Ⓦza.franceguide.com.

Guide

Guide

Marseille and around

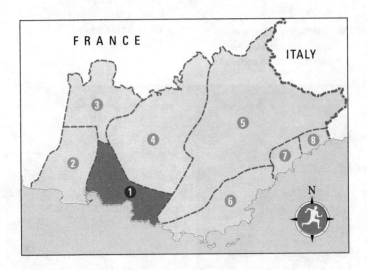

CHAPTER 1   # Highlights

* **The Vieux Port, Marseille** An intoxicating blend of food, history, water and sunlight at the very heart of France's great Mediterranean metropolis. See p.66

* **L'Unité d'Habitation, Marseille** Le Corbusier's masterpiece is a truly ground-breaking piece of modernist architecture. See p.74

* **Château d'If** The most compelling of Marseille's islands was the setting for Dumas' The Count of Monte Cristo. See p.76

* **Calanques** Whether you walk, swim or simply take a boat trip, don't miss the clear waters and deep fjord-like inlets of the coastline between Marseille and Cassis. See p.81

* **Corniche des Crêtes** Don't get blown away by the coast's most spectacular drive, from Cassis to La Ciotat. See p.92

△ Notre Dame de la Gorde, Marseille

Marseille and around

The **Marseille** conurbation is by far the most populated and industrial-ized part of Provence, and indeed of southern France. After Lyon and Paris it is France's third-largest urban region. It's an area where tourism takes a back seat to other, not always so aesthetically pleasing industries: to shipping in Marseille; and heavy petrochemicals around the Étang de Berre. Yet the area also has vast tracts of deserted mountainous countryside and a shoreline of high cliffs, deep jagged inlets and sand beaches with stretches still untouched by the holiday industry.

For visitors, the great attraction is the city of Marseille itself, a vital commer-cial port for more than two millennia. France's second city is, for all its notorious reputation, a wonderful place with a distinctive, unconventional character that never ceases to surprise.

The first foreigners to settle in Provence, the ancient **Greeks** from Phocaea and their less amiable successors from **Rome**, left evidence of their sophistica-tion around the **Étang de Berre**, at **Les Lecques**, and most of all at Marseille. Museums in Marseille guard reminders of the indigenous peoples of Provence whose civilization the Romans destroyed.

Military connections are strong in this region. **Salon-de-Provence** trains French air-force pilots but also preserves reminders of Nostrodamus; **Aubagne** is home to the French Foreign Legion but also to the characters of **Pagnol**.

But the barracks of Aubagne and the petrochemical industries and tanker terminals around the Étang de Berre aside, there are still great **seaside attrac-tions**: the pine-covered rocks of the **Estaque**; the *calanques* (rocky inlets) between Marseille and **Cassis**; the sand beaches of La Ciotat bay; and the heights from which to view the coast, most notably on the **route des Crêtes**. The area also has great **wines** at Cassis, and great **seafood**, particularly in Marseille, home of the famous sea-fish dish, *bouillabaisse*.

Marseille

The most renowned French city after Paris, **MARSEILLE** has, like the French capital, both prospered and been ransacked over the centuries. It has lost its

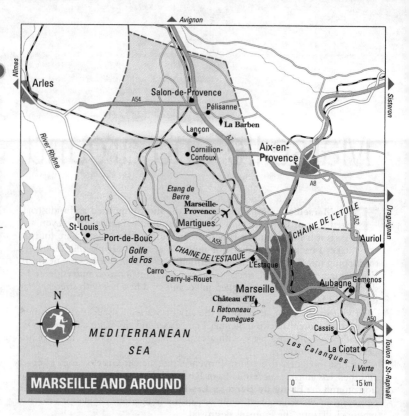

Avignon

Nîmes

Arles

Salon-de-Provence

Pélisanne

La Barben

Lançon

Cornillion-Confoux

Aix-en-Provence

Etang de Berre

Marseille-Provence ✈

Port-St-Louis

Martigues

Port-de-Bouc

Golfe de Fos

Carro

Carry-le-Rouet

CHAINE DE L'ESTAQUE

L'Estaque

CHAINE DE L'ETOILE

Auriol

Aubagne

Gemenos

Sisteron

Draguignan

Marseille

Château d'If

I. Ratonneau

I. Pomègues

N

MEDITERRANEAN SEA

Cassis

Les Calanques

La Ciotat

I. Verte

Toulon & St-Raphaël

MARSEILLE AND AROUND

0   15 km

privileges to sundry French kings and foreign armies, refound its fortunes, suffered plagues, religious bigotry, republican and royalist terror and had its own Commune and Bastille-storming. It was the presence of so many Revolutionaries from Marseille marching their way from the Rhine to Paris in 1792 which gave the name to the Hymn of the Army of the Rhine that became the national anthem, *La Marseillaise*.

Marseille has been a trading city for over two and a half thousand years, ever since ancient Greeks from Ionia discovered shelter in the Lacydon inlet, today the Vieux Port, and came to an agreement with the local Ligurian tribe. The story goes that the locals, noticing the exotic cargo of the strangers' boats, sent them off to the king's castle where the princess's wedding preparations were in full swing. The Ligurian royal custom at the time was that the king's daughter could choose her husband from among her father's guests. As the leader of the Greek party walked through the castle gate, he was handed a drink by a woman and discovered that she was the princess and that he was the bridegroom. The king gave the couple the hill on the north side of the Lacydon and Massalia came into being. And there ends, more or less, Marseille's association with romance.

Which is not to say Marseille cannot be romantic. It has a powerful magnetism as a true Mediterranean city, surrounded by mountains and graced with hidden corners that have the unexpected air of fishing villages. Built (for the most part

Race, politics and football

Marseille has all the social, economic and **political tensions** of France writ large. To some extent it is a divided city, with the ethnic French living on one side of La Canebière, and the large, vibrant North African community on the other: needless to say, racism is rife, as are poverty, bad housing and rising unemployment, particularly amongst the young. On top of this socially explosive mixture, Marseille has also had to contend with a reputation for protection rackets and shoot-outs, violent crime and prostitution, and corruption and drug-laundering – thanks in part to *The French Connection*. It's a reputation that is not without foundation: a gun attack on a brasserie, *Les Marronniers*, left three dead (including an alleged drug dealer) in April 2006, and though the incident happened far off the tourist trail in the thirteenth arrondissement, it was an unwelcome reminder of the bar massacres of the 1970s and attracted headlines worldwide. Nevertheless, though parts of the city do feel palpably dodgy, Marseille's reputation for danger is if anything overplayed, its social problems no different to those in many other French cities, as the 2005 riots – which began in the *banlieue* of Paris, not Marseille – proved.

One sphere of city life that has been as tumultuous and murky as its reputation would have it, however, is that of **politics**. There is plenty of grassroots support for the *Front National* and for Le Pen, who shocked Europe with his strong showing in the first round of the 2002 French presidential elections before being convincingly seen off by Jacques Chirac. Marseille's most notorious politician during recent decades, however, was **Bernard Tapie**, a millionaire businessman with the common touch who entered politics in the 1980s with the express intention of seeing off Le Pen's *Front National*, and who won the hearts of the Marseillais by making their football team, **Olympique de Marseille** (OM), great again – in 1993 they became the first French team to win the European Cup. Charges of fraud and tax evasion failed to dent Tapie's popularity, and in the 1994 European elections he gained around seventy percent of the vote. However, under his ownership, OM's finances went haywire and both owner and team were embroiled in a notorious scandal when it was discovered that Marseille had been guilty of chicanery and match-fixing in the 1992 season, enabling them to clinch the national Championship and qualify for their "glorious" European run of 1993. OM was relegated to the second division as punishment, and was taken over by a consortium of private business interests in conjunction with the town hall. Tapie was declared bankrupt and jailed for eight months for bribery and match-rigging. However, he wasn't a man to be kept down and, despite having defrauded OM of $15 million, the club welcomed him back as sporting director in 2001. Tapie hit the headlines twice in 2005; in September he won a €135 million lawsuit against the Crédit Lyonnais bank over the sale of his stake in the Adidas sportswear company; and in December 2005 he was convicted of tax fraud and sentenced to three years by a Paris court (a sentence he did not serve, as the judge took into account time Tapie had spent in prison previously).

A more universally admired – and multicultural – symbol of Marseille's footballing prowess is French national idol **Zinedine Zidane**, the Marseille-born son of Algerian parents and one of the leading members of the so-called "rainbow team" that won the 1998 World Cup. Zidane made use of his hero status during the 2002 election to speak out against Le Pen and in favour of Chirac. And though Zidane shocked France and the sporting world with his headbutt to Italian defender Marco Materazzi in the 2006 World Cup final, he was swiftly forgiven when he revealed the cause of his anger to be Materazzi's insulting comments about his mother and sister. Nevertheless, his sending off in what was anyway his last game for Les Bleus, was an ignominious end to a remarkable international career.

handsomely) of warm stone, it has its triumphal architecture; it has, too, the cosmopolitan atmosphere of a major port. Perhaps the most appealing quality is the down-to-earth nature of its inhabitants, who are gregarious, generous and endlessly talkative.

In recent years the city has undergone something of a renaissance, shaking off much of its old reputation for sleaze and danger to attract a wider range of visitors. The TGV has made it accessible to northerners, who can be seen picking up their hire cars at the Gare St-Charles on Friday nights. Slowly, the splendid facades along La Canebière are getting scrubbed up; the shops in the streets to the south of it are increasingly trendy or elegant, and the fruits of new investment are transforming the city's hitherto run-down face. The forward march of progress is not, however, relentless. All too often last year's prestige civic project becomes this year's broken and bottle-strewn fountain, and Marseille's easy tolerance of graffiti means it undoubtedly *looks* like the most violent city in France, with even the road signs on the city's autoroutes obscured. In short, it's a rough diamond. If you don't like your cities gritty, Marseille may not be for you. See past its occasional squalor, though, and chances are you'll warm to this down-to-earth, vital metropolis.

Arrival and information

Arriving by **car**, you'll descend into Marseille from the surrounding heights of one of three mountain ranges. From any direction the views encompass the barricade of high-rise concrete on the lower slopes, the vast roadstead with docks stretching miles north from the central **Vieux Port** and Marseille's classic landmark, the **Basilique de Notre-Dame-de-la-Garde**, perched on a high rock south of the Vieux Port. Follow signs for the Vieux Port to reach the city centre.

The city's **airport**, the Aéroport de Marseille-Provence, is 20km northwest of the city centre at Marignane; a shuttle bus runs to the **gare SNCF St-Charles** (6am–10.50pm; every 20min; later buses meet flights; €8.50), on the northern edge of 1er arrondissement on esplanade St-Charles. The new **gare routière** stands to the right of the station entrance, part of a project to transform the old station into a modern transport interchange, though for the time being buses to Aix depart from the Porte d'Aix. From esplanade St-Charles, a monumental staircase leads down to boulevard d'Athènes, which becomes boulevard Dugommier before reaching **La Canebière**, Marseille's main street. La Canebière runs to the head of the **Vieux Port**, a fifteen-minute walk to the right of the intersection. Marseille's main **tourist office** is at 4 La Canebière (June–Aug Mon–Sat 9am–7pm, Sun & public hols 10am–5pm; ☏04.91.13.89.00, ⓦwww.marseille-tourisme.com).

City transport

Marseille has an efficient **bus**, **métro** network, scheduled to be supplemented by two **tram** lines in 2007, running from Blancarde to Euroméditerranée and from Noailles to Les Caillols. You can get a plan of the **transport system** from RTM at 6 rue des Fabres (Mon–Fri 8.30am–6pm, Sat 9am–12.30pm & 2–5.30pm; ⓦwww.rtm.fr), one street north of La Canebière near the Bourse, the city's stock exchange. **Tickets** are flat rate for buses, trams and the métro and can be used for journeys combining all three as long as they take less than one hour. You can buy individual **tickets** (€1.70) from bus and tram drivers, and from métro ticket offices, or **multi-journey** *Cartes Libertés* (in increments of €2 and €6), which are valid for five and ten journeys respectively; these can be bought from métro stations, RTM kiosks and shops displaying the RTM sign. If you're likely to be hopping on and off public transport frequently, you might consider the good value one day *Carte Journée* (€4.50) or three-day *Carte 3* Jours (€6). Tickets need to be punched in the machines on the bus, on tramway platforms or at métro gates. The métro runs Monday to Thursday 5am to 9pm, and until 12.30am at weekends or when the football team is playing. **Night buses** run out from the centre from 9.30pm to 12.45am, from rue des Fabres: pick up a timetable from the RTM office or métro sales points or check them online.

Accommodation

Demand for accommodation in Marseille isn't as tied to the tourist season as in the coastal resorts, and finding a room in August is no more difficult than in November. **Hotels** are plentiful with lots of reasonable two and three star options around the Vieux Port and on the streets running south from it; real budget bargains are rarer and grander establishments virtually unknown. If you get stuck for a room, the main tourist office offers a free accommodation service. The cheapest options are the city's **youth hostels**, both quite a way from the centre.

Hotels

Alizé 35 quai des Belges, 1er ☎04.91.33.66.97, ⓦwww.alize-hotel.com. Comfortable, bright, soundproofed rooms; the more expensive ones look out onto the Vieux Port. Public areas are a little gloomy, however. ❺

Athènes 37 bd d'Athènes, 1er ☎04.91.90.03.83, ⓦwww.hotel-beaulieu-marseille.com. Right next to the train and bus stations; thin on charm but with rock-bottom prices, and a few rooms have balconies. ❶

Le Béarn 63 rue Sylvabelle, 6e ☎04.91.37.75.83, ⓦwww.hotel-bearn.com. Comfortable, friendly and inexpensive if a bit shabby, and close to the centre. ❷

Bellevue 34 quai du Port, 2e ☎04.96.17.05.40, ⒻÏ04.96.17.05.41. Boutique-style hotel on the port with chic modern decor and good prices, but no lift. ❻

Le Corbusier Unité d'Habitation, 280 bd Michelet, 8e ☎04.91.16.78.00, ⓦwww .hotellecorbusier.com. Stylish hotel on the third floor of the renowned architect's iconic high-rise (see p.75; book in advance. ❹

Edmond-Rostand 31 rue Dragon, 6e ☎04.91.37.74.95, ⓦwww.hoteledmondrostand .com. Helpful management, great charm and atmosphere, and well known, so you should book in advance. ❹

Esterel 124–125 rue Paradis, 6e ☎04.91.37.13.90, Ⓔhotel.esterel1@libertysurf.fr. Pleasant two-star

place in a good, animated location with all mod cons. ❸

Etap Hôtel Vieux Port 46 rue Sainte, 1er ☎08.92.68.05.82, ⓦwww.etaphotel.com. Big branch of the comfortable budget chain in a superb location close to the Vieux Port. ❸

Lutétia 38 allée Léon-Gambetta, 1er ☎04.91.50.81.78, ⓦwww.hotelmarseille.com. Right in the thick of things with pleasant, sound-proofed and a/c rooms. ❹

Manon 36 bd Louis-Salvator, 6e ☎04.91.48.67.01, ⒻÏ04.91.47.23.04. Comfortable, simple rooms and very central, though the location is a little noisy, between the Préfecture and cours Julien. ❷

New Hôtel Select 4 allée Léon-Gambetta, 1er ☎04.91.95.09.09, ⓦwww.new-hotel.com. Clean, modern, well-located, and popular with Japanese visitors. ❺

Hôtel du Palais 26 rue Breteuil, 6e ☎04.91.37.78.86, ⓦwww.hotelmarseille.com. Very smart three-star sister to La Residence du Vieux Port, in a great location a short walk from the Vieux Port. ❺

La Residence du Vieux Port 18 quai du Vieux Port ☎04.91.91.91.22, ⓦwww.hotelmarseille.com. Smart hotel with tasteful, conservative decor. All rooms have a view of the port and most have balconies. ❻

Le Richelieu 52 corniche Kennedy, 7e ☎04.91.31.01.92, ⓦwww.lerichelieu-marseille.com.

Friendly place, and one of the more affordable of the corniche hotels, overlooking the plage des Catalans. ③

Hôtel St Ferréol 19 rue Pisançon, corner rue St-Ferréol, 1er ☎04.91.33.12.21, ⓦwww .hotel-stferreol.com. Pretty decor, marble baths

with Jacuzzis, in a central pedestrianized area. Popular with gay visitors. ⑥

Tonic Hôtel 43 quai des Belges, 1er ☎04.91.55.67.46, ⓦwww.tonichotel.com. Smart and modern with a great port-side location close to the restaurants. ⑦

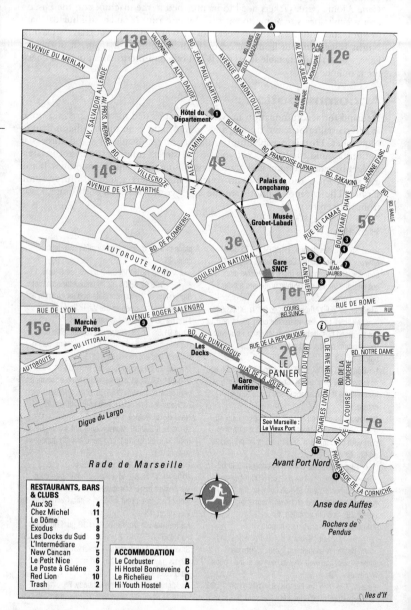

RESTAURANTS, BARS & CLUBS	
Aux 3G	4
Chez Michel	11
Le Dôme	1
Exodus	8
Les Docks du Sud	9
L'Intermédiare	7
New Cancan	5
Le Petit Nice	6
Le Poste à Galéne	3
Red Lion	10
Trash	2

ACCOMMODATION	
Le Corbuster	B
Hi Hostel Bonneveine	C
Le Richelieu	D
Hi Youth Hostel	A

Youth hostels and chambres d'hôtes

HI youth hostel 76 allée des Primevères, 12ᵉ
☎04.91.49.06.18, ⓦwww.fuaj.org. Bus #8 from
Centre Bourse (direction "St-Julien", stop "Bois
Luzy:). Cheap, clean youth hostel in a former

château a long way out from the centre. Curfew
11pm. Reception 7.30am–noon & 5–10.30pm.
Dormitory bed €9.50.
HI youth hostel Bonneveine impasse Bonfils,

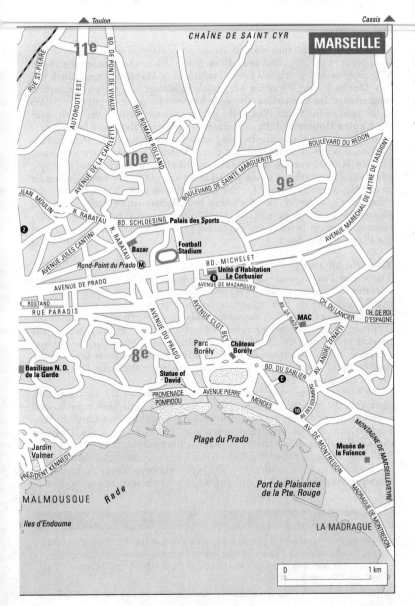

av J-Vidal, 8ᵉ ☎04.91.17.63.30, Ⓦwww.fuaj
.org. Mº rond-point du Prado, then bus
#44 (direction "Roy d'Espagne", stop "Place
Bonnefon") or night bus #583 from Vieux Port.
Recently renovated hostel just 200m from the
beach, with Internet access. Reception 7am–
1am, curfew at 1am. Closed mid-Dec to mid-Jan.

M & Mme Schaufelberger 2 rue St-Laurent, 2ᵉ
☎04.91.90.29.02. Ⓦwww.fleursdesoleil.fr
/crans-maisons/13-schaufel.html. Mº Vieux Port.
Chambre d'hôte on the fourteenth floor of a high-
rise in Le Panier with great views from the
balcony. Separate entrance and bathroom.
English is spoken by friendly owner. ❹

The City

Marseille is divided into sixteen arrondissements that spiral out from the
focal point of the city, the **Vieux Port**. Due north lies **Le Panier**, the Vieille
Ville and site of the original Greek settlement of Massalia; further north still
Les Docks are the focus for Marseille's ambitious inner city regeneration
programmes. **La Canebière**, the wide boulevard starting at quai des Belges
at the head of the Vieux Port, is the central east-west axis of the town, with
the **Centre Bourse** and the little streets of **quartier Belsunce** bordering it
to the north and the main shopping streets to the south. The main north-
south axis is **rue d'Aix**, becoming **cours Belsunce** then **cours St-Louis**,
rue de Rome, **avenue du Prado** and **boulevard Michelet**. The lively,
youngish quarter around **place Jean-Jaurès** and the trendy **cours Julien** lie
to the east of rue de Rome. On the headland west of the Vieux Port are the
village-like *quartiers* of **Les Catalans** and **Malmousque** from where the
Corniche heads south past the city's most favoured residential districts
towards the main beaches and expensive promenade bars and restaurants of
the **Plage du Prado**.

The Vieux Port

The **Vieux Port** is, more or less, the ancient harbour basin, and the original
inlet that the ancient Greeks sailed into. Historic resonances, however, are not
exactly deafening on first encounter, drowned as they are by the stalling or
speeding lanes of traffic. But the sunny **cafés** on the north and east side of the
port indulge the sedentary pleasures of observing street life; the morning **fish
market** on the quai des Belges provides some natural Marseillais theatre; and
the mass of seafood restaurants on the **pedestrianized streets** between the
southern quay and cours Estienne d'Orves ensure that the Vieux Port remains
the life centre of the city.

Two fortresses guard the harbour entrance. St-Jean, on the northern side,
dates from the Middle Ages when Marseille was an independent republic, and
is now only open when hosting exhibitions; its imposing Tour Carré du Roy
René is currently undergoing conversion to create a new national **Musée
des Civilisations d'Europe et de la Méditerranée**, scheduled to open in
2010. The enlargement of the Fort St-Jean in 1660, and the construction of
St-Nicolas fort, on the south side of the port, represented the city's final defeat
as a separate entity. Louis XIV ordered the new fort to keep an eye on the city

after he had sent in an army, suppressed the city's council, fined it, arrested all opposition and, in an early example of rate-capping, set ludicrously low limits on Marseille's subsequent expenditure and borrowing. The Fort St-Nicolas is still a military installation today.

The best view of the Vieux Port is from the **Palais du Pharo**, built on the headland beyond Fort St-Nicolas by Emperor Napoléon III for his wife and now used as a conference centre. Its surrounding park (8am–9pm) hides an underground *mediathèque* and exhibition space. For a wider-angle view, head up to the city's highest point, **Notre-Dame-de-la-Garde**, on boulevard André-Aune (daily: summer 7am–7pm; winter 7.30am–5.30pm; bus #60), which tops the hill south of the harbour. Crowned by a monumental gold Madonna and Child, the Second Empire landmark is a monstrous riot of neo-Byzantine design, the most distinctive of Marseille's landmarks and immaculate after recent restoration. Inside, model ships hang from the rafters while the paintings and drawings displayed are by turns kitsch, unintentionally comic and deeply moving, as they depict the shipwrecks, house fires and car crashes from which the virgin has supposedly rescued grateful believers. A World War I soldier's helmet pierced by a bullet hole is a prominent exhibit.

There are two small museums on the south side of the port which are worth checking out. The **Musée du Santon**, 47 rue Neuve Ste-Catherine (guided visits only: Tues & Thurs 2.30pm; free), is part of the Carbonel workshop, one of the most renowned producers of the crib figures for which Provence is famous. The **Maison de l'Artisanat et des Métiers d'Art**, 21 cours Estienne d'Orves (Tues–Sat 1–6pm; free), hosts excellent temporary exhibitions on Marseillais themes. Two doors away is the intellectual haunt of *Les Arcenaulx*: a restaurant, *salon de thé* and bookshop.

A short way inland from the Fort St-Nicolas, above the Bassin de Carénage and the slip road for the Vieux Port's tunnel, is Marseille's oldest church, the **Abbaye St-Victor** (daily 9am–7pm; €2 entry to crypt). Originally part of a monastery founded in the fifth century on the burial site of various martyrs, the church was built, enlarged and fortified – a vital requirement given its position outside the city walls – over a period of two hundred years from the middle of the tenth century. It certainly looks and feels more like a fortress with the walls of the choir almost three metres thick, and it's no conventional ecclesiastical beauty. Nevertheless the crypt, in particular, is fascinating: a crumbling warren of rounded and propped-up arches, small side chapels and secretive passageways, its proportions are more impressive than the church above and it contains a number of sarcophagi, including one with the remains of St Maurice.

Present Christian worship in the city has as its headquarters a less gloomy edifice. The **Cathédrale de la Major** (Tues–Sat 10am–noon & 2–5.30pm; Sun 9am–12.30pm & 2–6pm), on the north side of the Vieux Port overlooking the modern docks, is a striped neo-Byzantine solid block that completely overshadows its forlorn predecessor, the Romanesque **Vieille Major**, which stands alongside, closed, shuttered and structurally undermined by the road tunnel beneath it.

Opposite the two cathedrals, on esplanade de la Touret, a mural illustrates the ancient Greeks arriving at Marseille, and at the end of the esplanade, opposite Fort St-Jean, is the small Romanesque **Church of St-Laurent**, built on the site of a Greek Temple of Apollo (Mon–Fri 2–6pm).

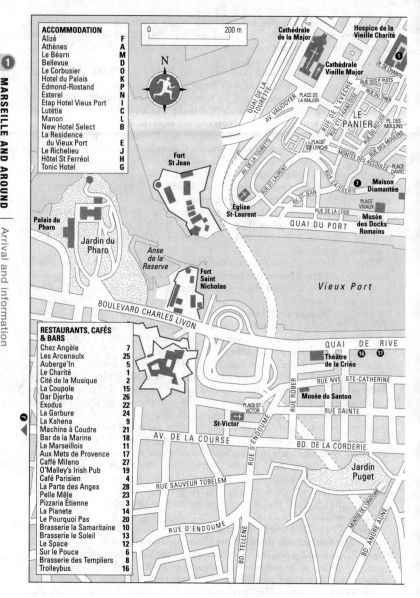

ACCOMMODATION

Alizé	F
Athènes	A
Le Béarn	M
Bellevue	D
Le Corbusier	O
Hotel du Palais	K
Edmond-Rostand	P
Esterel	N
Etap Hotel Vieux Port	I
Lutétia	C
Manon	L
New Hotel Select	B
La Residence du Vieux Port	E
Le Richelieu	J
Hôtel St Ferréol	H
Tonic Hotel	G

RESTAURANTS, CAFÉS & BARS

Chez Angèle	7
Les Arcenaulx	25
Auberge'In	5
Le Charité	1
Cité de la Musique	2
La Coupole	15
Dar Djerba	26
Exodus	22
La Garbure	24
La Kahena	9
Machine à Coudre	21
Bar de la Marine	18
Le Marseillois	11
Aux Mets de Provence	17
Caffé Milano	27
O'Malley's Irish Pub	19
Café Parisien	4
La Parte des Anges	28
Pelle Mêle	23
Pizzaria Étienne	3
La Planete	14
Le Pourquoi Pas	20
Brasserie la Samaritaine	10
Brasserie le Soleil	13
Le Space	12
Sur le Pouce	6
Brasserie des Templiers	8
Trolleybus	16

Le Panier

Le Panier, the oldest part of Marseille, lies to the east of the cathedrals and stretches down to the Vieux Port. This is where the ancient Greeks built their Massalia, and where, up until World War II, tiny streets, steep steps and a jumble of houses irregularly connected, formed a Vieille Ville typical of this coast. In 1943, however, Marseille was under **German occupation** and the quarter

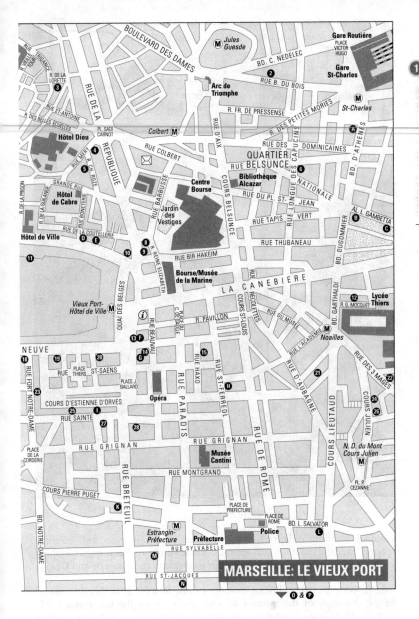

MARSEILLE: LE VIEUX PORT

represented everything the Nazis feared and hated, an uncontrollable warren providing shelter for *Untermenschen* of every sort, including Resistance leaders, Communists and Jews. They gave the twenty thousand inhabitants one day's notice to leave. While the curé of St-Laurent pealed the bells in protest, squads of SS moved in; they cleared the area and packed the people, including the curé, off to Fréjus, where concentration camp victims were selected. Out of seven

△ Le Panier

hundred children, only sixty-eight returned. Dynamite was laid, carefully sparing three old buildings that appealed to the Fascist aesthetic, and everything in the lower part of the quarter, from the waterside to rue Caisserie and Grande rue, was blown sky high.

After World War II, archeologists reaped some benefits from this destruction in the discovery of the remains of a warehouse from the first-century AD Roman docks. You can see vast food-storage jars for oil, grain and spices in their original positions, and part of the original jetty, along with models, mock-ups and a video to complete the picture, can be viewed at the **Musée des Docks Romains** on place de Vivaux (Tues–Sun: June–Sept 11am–6pm; Oct–May 10am–5pm; €2).

Though the quarter preserves some of its old identity at the top of the slope, the quayside buildings are solidly built but austere 1950s modern, with a hint of Art Deco in places. Amongst all this are the landmark buildings that the Nazis spared: the seventeenth-century **Hôtel de Ville** on the quay; the half-Gothic, half-Renaissance **Hôtel de Cabre** on the corner of rue Bonneterie and Grande rue; and the **Maison Diamantée** of 1620, so called for the pointed shape of its facade stonework, on rue de la Prison. This exceptionally beautiful building houses the **Musée de Vieux Marseille** (Tues–Sun 10am–5pm, €3), whose collections cover the lifestyles and maritime history of Marseille from the seventeenth century to the present day and include traditional costumes, crèches and *santons*, paintings, Provençal furniture and playing cards.

Overlooking the small **place Daviel** nearby is an impressive eighteenth-century bell tower, all that remains of the Église des Accoules, destroyed in 1794 as it had served as a meeting place for counter-revolutionaries after the French Revolution. To the north of here, above the place Daviel, is the vast nineteenth-century **Hôtel Dieu**, now a nursing college. At the junction of rue de la Prison and rue Caisserie, the steps of montée des Accoules lead up and across to **place de Lenche**, site of the Greek agora, a few blocks south of the cathedrals and a good café stop.

What's left of old Le Panier is above here, though the fifteen windmills of place des Moulins disappeared in the nineteenth century. If you climb rue du Réfuge you'll find yourself in a modern piazza, with new buildings in traditional styles, and an uninterrupted view of the refined **Hospice de la Vieille Charité** at the far end. This seventeenth-century workhouse, with a gorgeous Baroque chapel surrounded by handsome columned arcades in pink stone, is now a cultural centre, hosting some excellent temporary exhibitions and a very comfortable art house cinema, the **Miroir** (℡04.91.14.58.88) that often shows films in their original version. It is also home to two museums, a café and a bookshop. The **Musée d'Archéologie Méditerranéenne** (Tues–Sun: June–Sept 11am–6pm; Oct–May 10am–5pm; €2; combined ticket for entire complex €4.50) contains some very beautiful fourth- and fifth-century BC pottery and glass, an Egyptian collection with mummies and their accompanying boxes for internal organs plus a mummified crocodile. It also displays fascinating finds from a Celto-Légurian settlement at Roquepertuse, between Marseille and Aix, including a double-headed statue. The other permanent collection is the **Musée des Arts Africains, Océaniens et Amérindiens** (same hours and prices as Musée d'Archéologie), which in addition to its sculptures and masks has a collection of dried heads.

Euroméditerranée and Les Docks

From the Vieille Charité it's a short walk along rue Lorette and down a steep flight of steps to rue de la République, the formerly run-down nineteenth century boulevard that leads north from the Vieux Port. The walk is a graphic illustration of the ambitious nature of the regeneration scheme known as **Euroméditerranée**, for the stone buildings along the entire length of the rue de la République have had their facades cleaned and the commercial premises on their lower floors refurbished and frequently re-let to new occupants. The avenue ends at place de la Joliette, from which the magnificently restored buildings of **Les Docks** stretch alongside the autoroute viaduct, itself slated for removal and replacement by a new boulevard du Littoral. The sheer scale of the dock buildings makes their conversion into an office complex impressive, with one long central corridor lined with restaurants and a few shops linking the various atria between the original buildings. Most animated at its southern end close to place de la Joliette, the complex is – unusually for Marseille – a little sterile in its further reaches; nevertheless, it's worth continuing as far as the

Centre d'Informations (Mon–Thurs 10am–1pm & 2–6pm; Fri 10am–1pm & 2–5pm) just to see what else is planned for this part of the city. Already large new office buildings alongside the original warehouses are bringing in white collar, financial sector jobs and some of France's biggest corporate names, including BMP Paribas. One block to the south on boulevard des Dames, the delightful 1928 Art Deco building that once belonged to the **Compagnie Générale Transatlantique** – the celebrated French Line – is a reminder of the glamour that was once attached to sea travel, with murals depicting the old company's routes to North Africa, North and South America in the vestibule. The building is still occupied by shipping lines today.

La Canebière and around

La Canebière, the grandiose, if dilapidated, boulevard that runs for about a kilometre east from Marseille's port, is the undisputed hub of the town. Named after the hemp (*canabé*) that once grew here and provided the raw materials for the town's thriving rope-making trade, it was originally modelled on the Champs Elysées, though today it's too busy and scruffy for pavement-café idling and its shops are fairly lacklustre and almost outnumbered by the various banks and airline offices. It is also home, at the port end, to two museums. The **Musée de la Marine et de l'Economie** (daily 10am–6pm; €2) is housed on the ground floor of the Neoclassical stock exchange and contains a superb collection of model ships, including the legendary 1930s transatlantic liner *Normandie* and Marseille's very own prewar queen of the seas, the *Providence*. A bit further up at no. 11, the **Musée de la Mode** (Tues–Sun: June–Sept 11am–6pm, Oct–May 10am–5pm; €3) displays fashion and swimwear from 1945 to the present day, as well as hosting regular exhibitions; it also has a chi-chi restaurant.

Behind the stock exchange is the ugly **Centre Bourse** shopping centre and the **Jardin des Vestiges**, where the ancient port extended, curving northwards from the present quai des Belges. Excavations have revealed a stretch of the Greek port and bits of the city wall with the base of three square towers and a gateway, dated to the second or third century BC. The beautifully lit and spaced **Musée d'Histoire de Marseille**, inside the Centre Bourse (Mon–Sat noon–7pm; €2), shows the main finds of Marseillaise excavations, of which the most dramatic is a third-century AD wreck of a Roman trading vessel. There are models of the city, reconstructed boats, everyday items such as shoes and baskets, and a beautiful Roman mosaic of a dolphin, plus a great deal of information on text panels and a video about the Roman, Greek and pre-Greek settlements. Laws that were posted up in Greek Massalia are cited, forbidding

---

Marseille's Commune

Within the space of four years from its completion in 1867, the Marseille **Préfecture** had flown the imperial flag, the red flag and the tricolour. The red flag was flying in 1871, during Marseille's Commune. The counter-revolutionary forces advanced from Aubagne, encountering little resistance, and took the heights of Notre-Dame-de-la-Garde from where they directed their cannons down onto the Préfecture. The defeat was swifter but no less bloody than the fate of the Parisian Communards. One of the Marseillaise leaders, Gaston Crémieux, a young idealistic bourgeois with great charisma, escaped the initial carnage but was subsequently caught. Despite clemency pleas from all quarters of the city, Thiers, president of the newly formed Third Republic and a native of Marseille, would not relent and Crémieux was shot by a firing squad near the Pharo Palace in November 1871.

women to drink wine and allowing would-be suicides to take hemlock if the 600-strong parliament agreed.

The vast new **central library** on cours Belsunce is another of the regeneration projects gradually supplanting the dilapidated tenements north of La Canebière, its slick modernity softened by a Beaux-Arts portal that recalls the old Alcazar music hall where the likes of Tino Rossi and Yves Montand once performed. The continuation of cours Belsunce, rue d'Aix, stretches to **Porte d'Aix**, Marseille's Arc de Triomphe, modelled on the ancient Roman arch at Orange. This was part of the city's grandiose mid-nineteenth-century expansion which included the Cathédrale de la Major and the Joliette docks, paid for with the profits of military enterprise, most significantly the conquest of Algeria in 1830. Today it's a popular meeting place for the North African male community, as is the **quartier Belsunce** to the east. Bordered by cours Belsunce/rue d'Aix, boulevard d'Athènes and St-Charles, this dynamic district is home to hundreds of tiny shops selling North African food, music, household goods and cheap sportswear.

At the top end of boulevard d'Athènes, a monumental stairway leads up to **Gare St-Charles**. It was laid out in the 1920s with Art Deco railings, lamps and mammoth statues and has steps wide enough for people to sit and chat, play cards or, for some, simply to lie drunk without constituting an obstruction.

More Arab trading, on a smaller scale, takes place just south of La Canebière around the lively **Marché des Capucins** (Mon–Sat 8am–7pm) by the former Gare de l'Est. The streets around here are pretty seedy, with plenty of insalubrious hotels and, come nightfall, prostitutes on every corner, particularly along the handsome rue Sénac de Meilhan.

The prime shopping quarter of Marseille centres around three streets running south from La Canebière: rue de Rome, rue Paradis and rue St-Ferréol, which terminates at the pseudo-Renaissance **Préfecture**, where demonstrations in the city traditionally converge. The streets are full of chic, designer boutiques, whose shop fronts have been renovated to their original architectural condition. Tempting cafés and patisseries are dotted throughout the *quartier*, making it a good place to stop for a midday meal.

Between rue St-Ferréol and rue Paradis, on rue Grignan, is the city's most important art museum, the **Musée Cantini** (Tues–Sun: June–Sept 11am–6pm; Oct–May 10am–5pm; €3), housing paintings and sculptures dating from the end of the nineteenth century up to the 1950s. The Fauvists and Surrealists are well represented along with works by Matisse, Léger, Picasso, Ernst, Le Corbusier, Miró and Giacometti. Only a proportion of the permanent collection is displayed at any one time, and even less during the many excellent temporary exhibitions.

A few blocks east of rue de Rome, the streets around **cours Julien** are full of bars and music shops, and the *cours* itself, with its pools, fountains, restaurant tables and enticing boutiques, is populated by Marseille's arty and bohemian crowd and its diverse immigrant community. By day this is one of the most pleasant places to idle in the city, though almost every surface is buried under thick layers of graffiti and the atmosphere at night can be a little threatening, particularly at the top end around the métro station. Madame Zaza of Marseille, an original and affordable Marseillaise couturier, has her shop at no. 73; there are bookshops and art galleries to browse in, plus a stamp and secondhand book market, with antiques and junk every second Sunday in summer months. The **daily market**, known as **La Plaine**, on place Jean-Jaurès, supplements its food stalls with flowers on Saturdays and Wednesdays and with a flea market on Tuesdays and Thursdays.

Palais de Longchamp and around

The **Palais de Longchamp**, 2km inland from the port (buses #8, #80, #81 or #41 from La Canebière, or métro Longchamp-Cinq-Avenues), was completed in 1869, the year the Suez Canal opened, bringing a new boom for Marseillaise trade. It was built as the grandiose conclusion of an aqueduct at Roquefavour (no longer in use) bringing water from the Durance to the city. Water is still pumped into the centre of the colonnade connecting the two palatial wings of the building. Below, an enormous statue looks as if it's honouring some great feminist victory: three well-muscled women stand above four bulls wallowing passively in a pool from which a cascade drops the four or five storeys to ground level.

The palace's north wing houses the **Musée des Beaux-Arts** (closed for renovation; enquire at tourist office for more information) a slightly stuffy place but with its fair share of delights. Italian, French and Flemish old masters, including works by Rubens and Jordaens, occupy the lower level, while upstairs is dedicated to nineteenth-century French art, with works by Corot and Signac. Most unusual are the three paintings by Françoise Duparc (1726–76), while the nineteenth-century Marseille satirist Honoré Daumier, imprisoned for his vicious caricatures of Louis Philippe's government, has an entire room dedicated to his cartoons. The other wing of the palace is taken up with the **Musée d'Histoire Naturelle** (Tues–Sun 10am–5pm, €4), and its collection of mouldy stuffed animals and lots of fossils. Opposite the palace, at 140 bd Longchamp, is the **Musée Grobet-Labadi** (Tues–Sun: June–Sept 11am–6pm, Oct–May 10am–5pm, €2) a typically elegant late-nineteenth-century bourgeois town house filled with exquisite tapestries, paintings and objets d'art.

About 1km northeast of the palace, at the end of boulevard Mal-Juin, stands the futuristic **Hôtel du Département** (métro St-Just; guided visits by appointment, Mon–Fri 9.30am & 2.30pm; ☎04.91.21.29.77). Deliberately sited in the run-down St-Just-Chartreux *quartier*, the new seat of government for the Bouches-du-Rhône *département* was the biggest public building to be built in the French provinces, designed by English architect Will Alsop in characteristically expressive style. In front of the Hôtel stands the **Dôme**, a venue for shows and exhibitions.

South of the centre: Parc Chanot, Unité d'Habitation, MAC and Parc Borély

Avenue du Prado, the continuation of rue de Rome, is an eight-lane highway, with impressive fountains and one of the city's biggest **daily markets** between métros Castellane and Périer. At the rond-point du Prado, the avenue turns west to meet the corniche road.

The north-south axis continues as boulevard Michelet past **Parc Chanot**, home to Olympique de Marseille's ground. OM's reputation for occasional brilliance means that home matches are almost always sold out, but tickets may be available from the *OM Café* on the quai des Belges on the Vieux Port, with prices starting around €40. At the far side of the stadium on rue Raymond-Teisseire, the vast modern **Palais des Sports** hosts boxing matches, tennis, showjumping and other spectacles.

Beyond Parc Chanot, set back from the west side of the boulevard, is a mould-breaking piece of architecture, **Le Corbusier's Unité d'Habitation**, designed in 1946 and completed in 1952. A seventeen-storey housing complex on stilts, the Unité was the prototype for thousands of apartment buildings the world over, though the difference in quality between this – the *couture* original – and the industrially produced imitations becomes immediately apparent after a visit to the Unité. Confounding expectations, this concrete modernist structure is extremely complex, with 23 different apartment layouts, to suit single people and varying sized families: the larger appartments are split across two floors with balconies on both sides of the building, giving unhindered views of mountains and sea. It's a remarkably happy place; many of the original tenants are still in residence, and people chat and smile in the lobby. At ground level the building is decorated with Corbusier's famous human figure, the Modulor, while on the third floor is a small café-bar with its terrace and superlative Mediterranean views, and a hotel (see p.63). The iconic, sculptural rooftop recreational area is probably the highlight, and it's here that Le Corbusier's infatuation with ocean liners seems most obvious. Some parts of the roof are not open to visitors, but a stroll around the rooftop running track is essential. To reach the Unité take the métro to rond-point du Prado, then bus #21 (direction "Luminy").

Further south, at 69 av d'Haïfa (bus #23 or #45 from métro rond-point du Prado; stop "Haïfa" or "Marie-Louise"), is the contemporary art museum, **MAC** (Tues–Sun: June–Sept 11am–6pm; Oct–May 10am–5pm; €3). The permanent collection, displayed in perfect, pure-white surroundings, is the continuation of the Cantini collection, with works from the 1960s to the present. The artists include the Marseillais César and Ben, along with Buren, Christo, Klein, Niki de St-Phalle, Tinguely and Warhol. Between avenue d'Haïfa and the sea, just off avenue Prado, is **Parc Borély**, with ponds, palm trees, a rose garden, botanical gardens (daily 6am–9pm; free) and no restrictions about walking or picnicking on the grass. It was originally the grounds of the **Château Borély,** an eighteenth-century mansion that once hosted temporary art exhibitions and is currently undergoing restoration to turn it into a museum of decorative arts. Next to the park is the race course and beyond that the Plage du Prado.

The corniche and south to Les Goudes

The most popular stretch of sand close to the city centre is the small Plage des Catalans, a few blocks south of the Palais du Pharo. This marks the beginning of Marseille's **corniche Président-Kennedy**, initiated and partly built after the 1848 revolution, and currently being doubled in width by extending it out over the sea. Despite its inland bypass of the Malmousque peninsula, it's a corniche as good as any on the Riviera, with Belle Époque villas on the slopes above, the Îles d'Endoume and the Château d'If in the distance, cliffs below and high bridge piers for the road to cross the inlets of La Fausse-Monnaie and Les Auffes. Here, the Monument aux Morts de l'Armée d'Orient frames its statue against the setting sun, while further along the corniche, a modernist memorial commemorates the *pieds noirs* who returned from North Africa.

Prior to 1948, Malmousque and the **Vallon des Auffes** were inaccessible from the town unless you followed the "customs men's path" over the rocks or took a boat. There was nothing on Malmousque, but the Vallon des Auffes had a freshwater source and a small community of fishermen and rope-makers. Amazingly, it is not much different today, with fishing boats pulled up around the rocks, tiny jumbled houses and restaurants serving the catch. Only one road, rue du Vallon-des-Auffes, leads out; otherwise it's the long flights of steps up to the corniche.

Malmousque is now a very desirable residential district, favoured by the champagne-socialist set, and home to Marseille's most expensive hotel-restaurant, *Le Petit Nice*. Behind La Fausse-Monnaie inlet, a path leads to the Théâtre Silvain, an open-air theatre set in a wilderness of trees and flowers. There's more greenery, of a formal nature, a short way further along the corniche in the **Jardin Valmer** (bus #83; stop "Corniche J-Martin"), and you can explore the tiny streets that lead up into this prime district of mansions with high-walled gardens.

The corniche J-F-Kennedy ends at the Plage du Prado, the city's main sand beach backed by a wide strip of lawns and the ugly Espace Borély complex of shops and restaurants. The promenade continues, however, all the way to Montredon, with a glittering array of restaurants, clubs and cafés, best seen at night. Set in a huge park that extends to the foot of the Montagne de Marseille-leveyre is the **Musée de la Faïence** (157 av de Montredon, Tues–Sun: June–Sept 11am–6pm; Oct–May 10am–5pm; €2), in the elegant nineteenth-century Château Pastré (bus #19 from métro rond-point du Prado; stop "Montredon-Chancel"). The eighteenth- and nineteenth-century ceramics, many of them produced in Marseille, are of an exceptionally high standard, such as the vibrant productions of Théodore Deck, but there is also a small collection of novel modern pieces.

From Montredon to Les Goudes, where the gleaming white, beautifully desolate hills finally meet the sea and the coast road ends, there are easily accessible *calanques* (rocky inlets) that face the setting sun, ideal for evening swims and supper picnics. If you prefer to walk, the GR98 to Cassis starts from the top of avenue de la Grotte-Roland, off avenue de Montredon a short way beyond the Pastré park. It splits into the 98a which follows the ridge inland and 98b which descends to the sea at Callelongue, the last outpost of Les Goudes. Here, amid the rocky wilderness, is the improbable site of *La Grotte* (1 rue des Pébrons, ☎04.91.73.17.99), nowadays a rather fancy restaurant.

The islands

Blacker than the sea, blacker than the sky, rose like a phantom the giant of granite, whose projecting crags seemed like arms extended to seize their prey.

So the **Château d'If** (Jan–March Tues–Sun 9am–5pm, April & May daily 9am–5pm, June–Sept daily 9.30am–6.30pm, Sept–Dec Tues–Sun 9.30am–5pm; €5) appears to Edmond Dantès, hero of Alexandre Dumas' *The Count of Monte Cristo*, having made his watery escape after five years of incarceration as the innocent victim of treachery. In reality, most prisoners of this island fortress died before they reached the end of their sentences – unless they were nobles living in the less fetid upper-storey cells, such as one de Niozelles who was given six years for failing to take his hat off in the presence of Louis XIV, and Mirabeau, who had run up massive debts with shops in Aix. More often, the crimes were political. After the revocation of the Edict of Nantes in 1685, thousands of Marseillais Protestants, who refused to accept the new law, were sent to the galleys and their leaders entombed in the Château d'If. Revolutionaries of 1848 drew their last breath here.

Apart from the castle, there's not much else to the Île d'If; it's little more than a rock that you can swim off, with a small café-restaurant. Dumas fans will love it, others may raise an eyebrow at the cell marked "Dantès" in the same fashion as non-fictional inmates' names. However you find it, it's a horribly well-preserved sixteenth-century edifice and the views back towards Marseille are wonderful.

Boats leave from the quai des Belges from 9am onwards (hourly in summer; five daily in winter; €10), with the last boat back timed to coincide with the château's closing time; the journey takes twenty minutes. Alternatively, you can do a round trip taking in the other two islands of the Frioul archipelago, **Pomègues** and **Ratonneau** (€15), which are joined by a causeway enclosing a yachting harbour. In days gone by these islands were used as a quarantine station, most ineffectually in the early 1720s when a ship carrying the plague was given the go-ahead to dock in the city, resulting in the decimation of half the population.

Eating and drinking

Fish and seafood are the main ingredients of the Marseillais diet, and the superstar of dishes is the city's own invention, **bouillabaisse**, a saffron- and garlic-flavoured fish soup with croûtons and *rouille* to throw in. There are conflicting theories about which fish should be included and where and how they must be caught, though it's generally agreed that *rascasse* is essential. The other city speciality is *pieds et paquets*, mutton or lamb belly and trotters.

The best, and most expensive, **restaurants** are close to the corniche, though for international choice the trendy cours Julien is the best place to head and rue Sainte is a good bet for smart and fashionable dining close to the opera and Vieux Port. The pedestrian precinct behind the south quay of the Vieux Port is more tourist-oriented and fishy. Le Panier has a few tiny, inexpensive **bistros**, while cheap **snacks** can be found from the stands along cours Belsunce where you can buy *frites* and sandwiches stuffed with meat for under €3.

As Marseille is a Mediterranean city, people tend to stay up late in summer. Around the Vieux Port, from place Jean-Jaurès to cours Julien, and the Plage du Prado are the areas where there are always lots of people around and the **cafés** and **restaurants** open late, though even around the port you're unlikely to find anywhere to eat much after 11.30pm, even at weekends. Be warned that many restaurants take very long summer breaks.

Restaurants and cafés

L'Abri Côtier bd des Baigneurs, plage du Fortin, 8ᵉ ☎04.91.72.27.29. Smart beachside restaurant in Montredon, serving fish, meat and pizzas. It's a block or so down from the boulevard and a little tricky to find, despite the many signs. Menus from €28. Closed Oct–March.

Chez Angèle 50 rue Caisserie, 2ᵉ ☎04.91.90.63.35. Packed Le Panier local, dishing up fresh pasta and pizza. Closed lunchtimes Sat & Sun.

Les Arcenaulx 25 cours d'Estienne-d'Orves, 1ᵉʳ ☎04.91.59.80.40. Lovely, atmospheric intellectual haunt that is also a bookshop and *salon de thé*; the €22.50 lunch menu is good value, otherwise there's a €29.50 menu and a *ménu découverte* at €52. Last orders 11pm. Closed Sun.

Auberge'In 25 rue du Chevalier-Roze, 2ᵉ ☎04.91.90.51.59. Tucked into a health-food shop on the edge of Le Panier, with a vegetarian *menu fixe* for €13.50. Open for lunch Mon–Sat, dinner Fri & Sat only.

Le Charité Centre de la Vieille Charité, 2ᵉ. The cultural centre's tearoom; it's a little gloomy inside, but one of few decent lunchtime options in this part of town. Closed Mon.

La Coupole 5 rue Haxo, 1ᵉʳ ☎04.91.54.88.57. Elegant brasserie serving a midday *plat du jour* for €12. The seafood salads are a temptation. Open Mon–Sat 8am–8pm; closed Sun.

Dar Djerba 15 cours Julien, 6ᵉ ☎04.91.48.55.36. Excellent Tunisian restaurant with beautiful tiling, friendly service and a €22.90 menu. Closed Mon.

L'Épuisette Anse du Vallon des Auffes, 7ᵉ ☎04.91.52.17.82. This is the place to eat the Auffes catch at the water's edge. Menus at €54, €65 and €95. Closed Sun, Mon & August.

La Garbure 9 cours Julien, 6ᵉ ☎04.91.47.18.01. Rich specialities from southwest France, including Bresse chicken. Menus around €24. Closed Sat midday & Sun.

La Kahena 2 rue de la République, 2ᵉ ☎04.91.90.61.93. Popular Tunisian restaurant near the Vieux Port, with grills and couscous from €8.50. Open daily.

Le Marseillois quai du Port, 2ᵉ ☎04.91.90.72.52. Restaurant on the deck of an old sailing vessel in the Vieux Port. *Prix-fixe* menu €2. Closed Sun and Mon.

Aux Mets de Provence 18 quai Rive-Neuve, 7ᵉ ☎04.91.33.35.38. A Marseille institution with authentic Provençal cooking at the top of a steep staircase. Lunch menu at €40, otherwise €60 including wine. Closed Sat midday, Sun & Mon lunch.

Chez Michel 6 rue des Catalans, 7ᵉ ☎04.91.52.30.63. There's no debate about the *bouillabaisse* ingredients here. A basket of five fishes, including the elusive and most expensive one, the *rascasse*, is presented to the customer before the soup is made – and this is quite simply the place to eat this dish. Expect to pay €58 per person for the *bouillabaisse* alone. Closed second two weeks of Feb.

Caffé Milano 43 rue Sainte, 1er ☎04.91.33.14.33. Sleek, rather *BCBG* and hugely popular Italian. Meat-based *plats* around €14; pasta dishes around €10. Closed Sat lunch & Sun.

Café Parisien 1 place Sadi-Carnot, 2e. Very stylish mix of old elegance and modern chic, with pasta dishes from around €11 and meat mains from €14 up. Closed Sun.

La Part des Anges 33 rue Sainte, 1er ☎04.91.33.55.70. Wonderful *cave de vins* serving hearty food to mop up the classy alcohol; *plats* around €12. Open daily.

Pizzaria Étienne 43 rue Lorette, 2e; no phone. An old-fashioned Le Panier pizzeria; hectic, cramped and crowded.

La Planete 45 quai des Belges, 1er ☎04.91.33.14.82. About the cheapest *bouillabaisse* with *rascasse* you'll find, at around €19, and they show you the fish first. Open daily.

Brasserie la Samaritaine 2 quai du Port, 2e. The sunniest port-side bar with comfy terrace chairs. *Plats du jour* around €11, salads from €7.60. Open daily.

Brasserie le Soleil 27 quai des Belges, 1er. The main daytime gathering place for the city's gay community. Slick and modern, with omelettes around €7.50; pasta around €9. Open daily.

Sur le Pouce 2 rue des Convalescents, 1er. Very cheap Tunisian restaurant in the *quartier* Belsunce. Couscous €5.

Bars

Brasserie des Templiers 21 rue Reine-Elizabeth, 1er. Next to the Centre Bourse, with good beers, including Belgian varieties and Guinness, and quick *croques*.

O'Malley's Irish Pub 9 quai du Rive Neuve, 1er. A wildly popular Vieux Port boozer with the usual "Irish" trimmings plus, of course, Beamish and Guinness, and live music on Thurs.

Bar de la Marine 15 quai Rive-Neuve, 1er. A favourite bar for Vieux Port lounging, and inspiration for Pagnol's celebrated Marseille trilogy. Open daily.

Bar Le Petit Nice 26 place Jean-Jaurès, 1er. The place to head for on Saturday morning during the market, with an interesting selection of beers. Open Mon–Sat from 6.30am.

Le Red Lion 231 av Pierre-Mendès-France, 8e. Large, raucous British-style pub close to Plage Borély, with 11 types of beer on draught. Open until 4am Fri & Sat.

Lesbian and gay bars

Aux 3G 3 rue St-Pierre, 5e. Marseille's most popular lesbian bar, regularly packed to the rafters at weekends. Open Thurs & Sun 7pm–midnight, Fri & Sat 7pm–2am.

Le Space 9 rue Guy Moquet, 1er. Large, stylish, a/c DJ bar that attracts a young, trendy gay and lesbian, pre-club crowd. Open Sat 10pm–2am.

Trash 28 rue du Berceau, 5e. Slick, cruisy gay men's bar with DJ, live entertainment and plenty of dark corners. Open weekdays 9pm–2am, later at weekends.

Markets and food shops

The city's copious **street markets** provide a feast of fruit and veg, olives, cheeses, sausages and spit–roast chickens – everything you'd need for a picnic except for wine, which is most economically bought at supermarkets. The markets are also good for cheap clothes. La Plaine and avenue du Prado are the biggest; the Capucins the oldest.

Marseille's Sunday flea market, **Marché aux Puces**, is a brilliant spectacle and good for serious haggling. There's a relaxed atmosphere, plenty of cafés, and everything and anything for sale, including very cheap fruit and veg.

The markets

Quai des Belges Vieux Port, 1er; M° Vieux Port. Fish sold straight off the boats. Daily 8am–1pm.

Capucins place des Capucins, 1er; M° Noailles. Fish, fruit and veg. Mon–Sat 8am–7pm.

Place Carli 1er; M° Noailles. Antiquarian books and records. Mon–Sat all day.

Cours Julien 6e; M° N.-D.-du-Mont-Cours Julien. Food Mon–Sat 8am–1pm; stamps Sun 8am–1pm; antiquarian books second Sat of month 8am–1pm; bric-a-brac Tues & Thurs 8am–1pm; organic produce Wed 8am–1pm; flowers Wed & Sat 8am–1pm, secondhand goods second Sun of the month 8am–7pm.

Allées de Meilhan La Canebière, 1e; M° Réformés. Flowers Tues & Sat 8am–1pm; *santons* daily in Dec 10am–7pm.

Cours Pierre Puget 1er, M° Préfecture Estrangin. Fruit, veg and fish, Mon & Fri 8am–1pm; flowers Mon 8am–1pm, bric-a-brac Wed 8am–1pm.

La Plaine place Jean-Jaurès, 5e; M° N.-D.-du-Mont-Cours-Julien. Food Mon-Sat 8am–1pm; bric-a-brac Tues, Thurs & Sat 9am–1pm; flowers Wed 8am–1pm.

Prado av du Prado, 6e; M° Castellane and Périer. Fruit, veg, fish and general food produce daily 8am–1pm; flowers Fri 8am–1pm.

Marché aux Puces av du Cap-Pinède, 15e; bus #35 from the Vieux Port (stop "Cap-Pinède") or bus #36 or #70 from M° Bougainville (stop "Lyon"). Food Wed–Sun 8am–1pm; antiques Fri–Sun 9am–7pm; bric-a-brac Sat; flea market Sun 9am–7pm.

Joseph Thierry 1er, M° Réformés. Fruit, greens and fish Mon–Sat 8am–1pm.

Shops

Le Carthage 8 rue d'Aubagne, 1er. The best Tunisian patisseries and Turkish delight in town.

Plauchut 168 La Canebière, 1er. Excellent *patissier-chocolatier-glacier* and *salon de thé*, established in 1820.

Nightlife and entertainment

Marseille's **nightlife** has something for everyone, with plenty of live rock and jazz, nightclubs and discos, as well as theatre, opera and classical concerts. Theatre is particularly innovative and lively in Marseille. The Virgin Megastore at 75 rue St-Ferréol, the book and record shop FNAC on the top floor of the Centre Bourse and the tourist office's ticket bureau are the best places to go for **tickets and information** on gigs, concerts, theatre, free films and cultural events. Virgin also stocks a wide selection of English books and runs a café on the top floor, open, like the rest of the store, Monday to Saturday until 9pm and on Sundays until 8pm. There is a free weekly **listings** mag *Ventilo*, and a couple of monthlies, *César* and *Marseille In Situ,* both of which you can pick up from FNAC, Virgin, tourist offices, museums and cultural centres.

Live music and nightclubs

L'Affranchi 212 bd de St Marcel, 11e ℡04.91.35.09.19. Venue in the eastern suburbs with a varied programme of clubs and live gigs, including rai, hip-hop and reggae. Open from 8.30pm when concerts are on (mostly Sat).

Le Bazar 90 bd Rabatau, 8e ℡04.91.79.08.00. Big, mainstream disco playing house and occasionally hosting big-name international DJs. Open Thurs–Sun.

Cité de la Musique 4 rue Bernard-du-Bois, 1er ℡04.91.39.28.28. Jazz cellar and auditorium.

Les Docks des Suds – le Hangar à Sucres 12 rue Urbain V, 3e. ℡04.91.99.00.00. Vast warehouse that serves as the venue for Marseille's annual Fiesta des Suds world music festival. Les Docks des Suds is open daytimes Tues–Fri and Sun 9am–1pm & 2–6pm

Le Dôme 48 av de St-Just, 4e ℡04.91.12.21.21. Marseille's large-capacity live venue, hosting big-name and tame middle-of-the-road acts.

Exodus 9 rue des Trois Mages, 1e ℡04.91.42.02.39. Small performance space between cours Julien and place Jean-Jaurès, presenting world music and theatre with a strong focus on Africa and Asia. Live music events generally start at 8.30pm.

L'Intermédiare 63 place Jean-Jaurès, 6e ℡04.91.47.01.25. Loud, hip, smoky bar with a variety of live bands, from rock to jazz and world music, plus Old Skool DJ nights. Open Mon–Sat 6.30pm–2am.

Machine à Coudre 6 rue Jean-Roque, 1e ℡04.91.55.62.65. Music café hosting alternative rock and reggae acts. €4–7 entry charge

depending on act. Open Thurs–Sat.
Le Moulin 47 bd Perrin, 13ᵉ; Mᵒ St-Just;
℡04.91.06.33.94. An obscure venue in the
northwest of the city, specializing in weird and
wonderful European bands. Concerts start at
8.30pm; open daily 8–11pm.
New Cancan 3 rue Sénac, 1ᵉʳ ℡04.91.48.59.76.
Cheesy, dated and expensive, but the *New
Cancan* is nevertheless Marseille's best known
and longest running gay disco. Open Thurs–Sun
11pm–dawn

Pelle Mêle 8 place aux Huiles, 1ᵉʳ
℡04.91.54.85.26. Intimate, smart and lively jazz
bistro and piano bar. Open 6pm–2am daily.
Le Poste à Galène 103 rue Ferrari, 5ᵉ
℡04.91.47.57.99. Live pop, rock & electro plus
80s nights and a bar. Opens 8.30 or 9.30pm,
depending on the event.
Trolleybus 24 quai de Rive-Neuve, 7ᵉ
℡04.91.54.30.45. Disco in a series of vaulted
rooms; house, pop, electro, hip-hop and techno.
Closed Sun–Wed.

Film, opera, theatre and concerts

Alhambra 2 rue du Cinéma, 16ᵉ
℡04.91.03.84.66. Art house cinema occasionally
showing undubbed English-language films (*v.o*).
Ballet National de Marseille 20 bd Gabès, 8ᵉ
℡04.91.32.72.72. The home venue of the
famous dance company, founded in 1972 by
Roland Petit.
Creuset des Arts 21 rue Pagliano, 4ᵉ
℡04.91.06.57.02. Drama, comedy and live music
venue.
Espace Julien 39 cours Julien, 6ᵉ
℡04.91.24.34.10. A mixed-bag arts centre, with a
programme that embraces comedy, hip-hop,
chanson, variety and world music.
La Friche la Belle de Mai 41 rue Jobin, 3ᵉ
℡04.95.04.95.04. Interdisciplinary arts complex
occupying a former industrial site in the north of
the city, hosting theatre, dance, live music and arts
exhibitions.

Le Miroir 2 rue de la Charité, 2ᵉ ℡04.91.14.58.88.
Art house films in comfortable surroundings at the
Vieille Charité, often undubbed in *v.o*.
Opéra 2 rue Molière, 1ᵉʳ ℡04.91.55.11.10.
Symphony concerts and operas in a magnificent
setting, part Neoclassical, part Art Deco.
Théâtre de Lenche 4 place de Lenche, 2ᵉ
℡04.91.91.52.22. Everything from Cervantes to
Beckett is showcased at this Le Panier theatre.
Théâtre Massalia La Friche la Belle de Mai, 3ᵉ
℡04.95.04.95.70. Lively puppet theatre with
changing programme of adult (evening) and
children's (matinee) shows.
Théâtre National la Criée 30 quai de Rive-Neuve,
7ᵉ ℡04.96.17.80.00. Home of the Théâtre National
de Marseille and Marseille's best theatre.
Variétés 37 rue Vincent-Scotto, 1ᵉ
℡04.96.11.61.61. Cinema showing the odd
undubbed English-language film (*v.o*).

Listings

Airlines Air France 14 La Canebière, 1ᵉʳ
℡0820.820.820; Cathay Pacific 41 La Canebière,
1ᵉʳ ℡04.91.91.14.69.
Airport information ℡04.42.14.14.14, ⊛www
.marseille.aeroport.fr.
Bike hire Cycles Ulysse, 3 av du Parc Borély;
℡04.91.77.14.51; Tandem, 16 av du Parc Borély
℡04.91.22.64.80.
Bookshops Virgin, 75 rue St-Ferréol, 1ᵉʳ, has an
English books section; Maupetit, 140 La Canebière,
1er, is a good general French bookshop.
Bus information ℡04.91.91.92.10.
Car parks cours Estienne-d'Orves, 1ᵉʳ; cours
Julien, 6e; allées Léon-Gambetta, 1ᵉʳ; rue Breteuil,
6ᵉ; Centre Bourse, 1ᵉʳ; place Félix-Baret, 6ᵉ; and
place Géneal-de-Gaulle, 1ᵉʳ.
Car rental Avis, Gare St-Charles ℡08.20.61.16.36;
Budget, 40 bd de Plombières ℡04.91.64.40.03;
National Citer, 20 Bd Schloessing, 8ᵉ

℡04.91.83.05.05; Europcar, 59 Allées Léon-
Gambetta, 1ᵉʳ ℡08.25.82.56.80; Hertz, 21 bd
Maurice-Bourdet, 1ᵉʳ ℡04.91.14.04.24. All also
have head offices at the airport.
Consulates Britain, 24 av du Prado, 6ᵉ
℡04.91.15.72.10; USA, place Varian-Fry/12 bd
Paul-Peytral, 6ᵉ ℡04.91.54.92.00.
Emergencies Ambulance ℡15; SOS Médecins
℡04.91.52.91.52; 24hr casualty departments at
La Conception, 144 rue St-Pierre, 5ᵉ
℡04.91.38.36.52; and SOS Voyageurs, Gare St-
Charles, 3ᵉ ℡04.91.62.12.80.
Ferries SNCM, 61 bd des Dames ℡03260,
⊛www.sncm.fr. Runs ferries to Corsica, Tunisia
and Algeria.
Internet *Info-Café* 1 quai du Rive Neuve, 1ᵉʳ
℡04.91.33.74.98.
Lost property 18 rue de la Cathédrale, 2ᵉ
℡04.91.90.99.37.

Pharmacy Syndicat des Pharmaciens
☎ 04.91.15.72.61.
Police Commissariat Centrale, 2 rue Antoine-Becker, 2ᵉ (24 hr; ☎ 04.91.39.80.00).
Post office 1 place de l'Hôtel-des-Postes, 1ᵉʳ.

Taxis Marseille Taxi ☎ 04.91.02.20.20; Taxi Blanc Bleu ☎ 04.91.51.50.00, Eurotaxi (multilingual drivers) ☎ 04.91.05.31.98; disabled facilities ☎ 06.11.54.99.99.
Train information ☎ 3635.

L'Estaque and westwards

Marseille's docks and its northern coastal sprawl finally end at **L'ESTAQUE**, an erstwhile fishing village much loved by painters in the nineteenth century, and easy to get to by train (10min on Miramas train). It was no rural paradise even in 1867, as a gouache by Cézanne of the factory chimneys of L'Estaque shows (originally given to Madame Zola and now exhibited in his studio in Aix). Yet it still has fishing boats moored alongside yachts, and the very pleasant artificial beaches to the west ensure that L'Estaque remains a popular escape from the city. The simple terrace restaurant *L'Hippocampe* on the coast road a little west of the village (☎ 04.91.03.83.78; closed Sun eve & Mon) is the place to go for a fish **dinner**, or if you simply want a **snack**, the local *chichis* (hot, doughnut-like confections) from the *Chichis Fruguis* kiosk on the promenade are delicious.

Between L'Estaque and Carry-le-Rouet, the hills of the **Chaîne de l'Estaque** come right down to the coast, a gorgeous wilderness of white rock, pines and brilliant yellow scented broom. The shore is studded with picturesque little *calanques* where the real estate is exceptionally desirable and the water exceptionally clean; you can look across the roadstead of Marseille to the islands and the entrance of the Vieux Port. At weekends in summer, road access to these *calanques* is strictly limited and you may have to park some distance from the sea. The train tunnels its way above the shore while the main road, the N568, then D5, takes an inland route through **La Rove** and **Ensues-la-Redonne**, with smaller roads looping down to the fishing villages and summer holiday homes of **Niolon**, **Méjean** and **La Redonne**. At Méjean simple meals of grilled fish and *petites fritures* are served overlooking the tiny port at *Le Mange Tout* (☎ 04.42.45.91.68; closed Dec–Feb).

The peace and intimate scale of this coast end at the small but bustling resort of **CARRY-LE-ROUET**, its harbour encircled by popular restaurants and overshadowed by a rather unfortunate 1960s tower block, though the town has a modest swank and even boasts a casino. Carry was the home of the jazz singer Nina Simone towards the end of her life, and it was here that she died in 2003. The **tourist office** in the Espace Fernandel (July & Aug Mon–Sat 9am–noon & 3–6pm; Sept–June Tues–Sat 10am–noon & 2–5pm; ☎ 04.42.13.20.36, ⓦ www.carry-lerouet.com) has a list of hotels and private rooms, but there's no real reason to stop other than to visit the wonderful **restaurant**, *L'Escale*, on a terrace above the right-hand side of Carry's port, where the *gâteau de poissons* is divine (☎ 04.42.45.00.47; menus from €35; closed Sun eve, Mon & Jan). If you're **camping**, head further west to the tiny, relatively peaceful village of Tamaris, where there are several campsites including *Lou Cigalon*, corniche des Tamaris (☎ 04.42.49.61.71; ⓦ www.loucigalon.com, €19 per tent; closed Oct–March), and the neighbouring *Les Tamaris*, calanque des Tamaris (☎ 04.42.80.72.11; ⓦ www.camping-lestamaris.com, €19.20 per tent; closed Oct–March). Both are located on a pleasant, sandy cove.

Carry merges into its western neighbour Sausset-les-Pins, where the beaches are stony and artificial, without any break in the seaside houses and apartment buildings. For **beaches** it's best to head beyond Tamaris where there are long, sandy beaches around the pleasantly downmarket family resorts of **CARRO** and **LA COURONNE**, though you may be put off by the proximity of the petrochemical plants at the mouth of the Étang de Berre.

The south shore of the Étang de Berre

The shores of the 22-kilometre-long and 15-kilometre-wide **Étang de Berre**, northwest of L'Estaque, are not the most obvious holiday destination. The lagoon is heavily polluted, especially around the southern edges near Marseille's airport, and the sources are only too visible: oil refineries, petrochemical plants and tankers heading in and out of the Caronte Canal linking the lagoon with the vast industrial complex and port on the Golfe de Fos.

There are, however, some unexpected pockets worth exploring: the ancient remains at **St-Blaise**, the perched villages of **Miramas-le-Vieux** and **Cornillon-Confoux**, and, despite its close proximity to Europe's largest oil refinery, the town of **Martigues**.

Martigues

MARTIGUES straddles both sides of the Caronte Canal and the island in the middle, at the southwest corner of the Étang de Berre. In the sixteenth century when the union of three separate villages, Jonquières to the south, Ferrières to the north and the island, known simply as l'Île, created Martigues, there were many more canals than the three that remain today. But Martigues has joined the long list of places with waterways to be dubbed the 'Venice' of the region, and it deserves the compliment, however fatuous the comparison.

In the centre of l'Île, in front of the sumptuous facade of the airy Église de la Madeleine, a low bridge spans the Canal St-Sébastien where fishing boats moor and houses in ochre, pink and blue look straight down onto the water. This appealing spot is known as the **Miroir aux Oiseaux** and was painted by Corot, Ziem and others at the turn of the twentieth century. Some of these artists' works, including Ziem's *Vieux Port de Marseille*, can be seen in the wonderful **Musée Ziem** on boulevard du Juillet in Ferrières (July–Aug Mon & Wed–Sun 10am–noon & 2.30–6.30pm; Sept–June Mon & Wed–Sun 2.30–6.30pm; free). The collection includes works by the likes of Dérain, Dufy and Signac, while François Picabia's 1905 *Étang de Berre* shows the lagoon to be every bit as choppy as it is today. Upstairs is a well-presented local history display, as well as some more contemporary art exhibits.

Behind the idle strolling quaysides of l'Île's canal, new housing has been designed on a pre-modern, acute-angled layout. From **quai Toulmond** the white and green geometric shapes of the ridiculously expensive municipal offices across the water and the towering highway bridge above the Caronte Canal contrast with the masts and bright hulls of the pleasure boats tied up along the quay.

A nineteenth-century swing bridge alongside a modern metal road bridge joins l'Île to **Ferrières**, whose tiny streets of shops and bars spread back from the relaxed focal point of place Jean-Jaurès. To the south, the tanker passage of the Canal Galiffet is spanned by a drawbridge taking you into **Jonquières**, the third and most lively of Martigues' centres, with the best concentration of bars and restaurants lining the main axis of cours du 4 Septembre and esplanade des Belges.

Buses from Marseille stop on the quayside opposite the *Brasserie du Port* in Ferrières, a little west of the bridge. From the **gare SNCF** take bus #3 (direction Ferrières), to the centre. The plush modern **tourist office** (June & Sept Mon–Sat 9am–6.30pm, July–Aug Mon–Sat 9am–7pm, Sun 10am–1pm & 3–7pm; Oct–Easter Mon–Fri 9am–6.30pm, Sat 9am–12.30pm, Sun 10am–12.30pm, Sept & Easter–June also Sun 9.30am–1pm, ℡04.42.42.31.10; ⓦwww.mairie-martigues.fr) is in Ferrières, on the Rond Point, close to the police station and the *mairie*.

The best of the **hotels** is the *St-Roch*, avenue Georges-Braque, Ferrières (℡04.42.42.36.36; ⓦwww.hotelsaintroch.com; ❼), while *Le Cigalon*, 37 bd du 14 Juillet, Ferrières (℡04.42.80.49.16; ❸), is in a noisy spot but a lot cheaper.

A good time to visit is between late June and the end of August to see the spectacle of the *Sardinades*, when thousands of plates of grilled sardines are sold cheaply each evening along the quays near the *mediathèque* in the Quartier de L'Île. Aside from these, the **food** to look out for is *poutargue*, a paste made from salted mullet, and *melets*, seasoned fish fry fermented in olive oil. Three **restaurants** to try, all on l'Île, are *Bouchon à la Mer*, 19 quai Toulmond (℡04.42.49.41.41; menus from €28); the scenically situated *Le Miroir*, 4 rue Marcel-Galdy (℡04.42.80.50.45; menus from €22.20); and *Chez Marraine*, 2 rue des Cordonniers (℡04.42.49.37.48, à la carte only), where the €11 fish soup is especially good.

St-Mître-les-Remparts, St-Blaise

About 6km beyond Martigues, on the road to Istres, lies the walled village of **ST-MÎTRE-LES-REMPARTS**, with two original gateways allowing entrance to its minuscule, cramped heart. From the unusual church at the culmination of the corkscrew nest of streets you can see westwards over the Étang du Pourra and Étang d'Engenier towards the Fos complex.

From the main road the D51 leads away from St-Mître village up to a hill between two more lagoons, the Étang de Citis and Étang de Lavalduc. On the hill stands the twelfth-century Chapelle St-Blaise beside a thirteenth-century wall and the **Oppidum St-Blaise** archeological site (Mon–Fri 9am–12.30pm & 2–5.30pm; free). The ancient inhabitants of this well-defended site left their mark throughout eight distinct periods, from 7 BC to the fourteenth century. If the site is closed you can still walk around it, see the extraordinary surviving Greek ramparts through the fence, and generally enjoy the woods and water, which can sometimes appear pink because of the algae encouraged by a high salt content.

Salon-de-Provence and around

The northern exit from the Autoroute du Soleil to **SALON-DE-PROVENCE** takes you past a memorial to **Jean Moulin**, the Resistance leader who was parachuted into the nearby Alpilles range in order to coordinate the different *maquis* groupings in Vichy France. He was caught on June 21, 1943, tortured, deported and murdered by the Nazis. The bronze sculpture, by Marcel Courbier, is of a lithe figure landing from the sky like some latter-day Greek god, very beautiful though somewhat perplexing if you're not aware of the invisible parachute.

Today, one of Salon's principal activities is teaching air force pilots to fly – indeed, legendary 1930s singer Charles Trenet was just one of thousands to

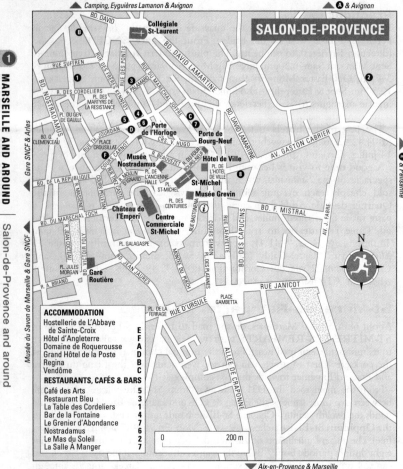

▲ Camping, Eyguières Lamanan & Avignon   ▲ ⒶＡ & Avignon

SALON-DE-PROVENCE

Collégiale St-Laurent

Porte de l'Horloge
Porte de Bourg-Neuf
Hôtel de Ville
Musée Nostradamus
St-Michel
Musée Grevin
Château de l'Emperi
Centre Commerciale St-Michel
Garé Routière

◄ Gare SNCF & Arles
◄ Musée du Savon de Marseille & Gare SNCF
Ⓔ & Pélisanne ►

N

ACCOMMODATION

Hostellerie de L'Abbaye de Sainte-Croix	E
Hôtel d'Angleterre	F
Domaine de Roquerousse	A
Grand Hôtel de la Poste	D
Regina	B
Vendôme	C

RESTAURANTS, CAFÉS & BARS

Café des Arts	5
Restaurant Bleu	3
La Table des Cordeliers	1
Bar de la Fontaine	4
Le Grenier d'Abondance	7
Nostradamus	6
Le Mas du Soleil	2
La Salle À Manger	7

0   200 m

▼ Aix-en-Provence & Marseille

undertake their military service here – and at times the planes scream overhead day and night. The clientele of the town's bars and restaurants usually includes blue-uniformed cadets from the École de l'Air at the **airforce base** to the south of the town. Salon is very proud of its role in the nation's strategic forces, not least because the base has given a welcome boost to the local economy for the last fifty years.

In medieval times, Salon's economy was dependent on its tanneries, a saffron crop and flocks of sheep reputed for the quality of their mutton. However, true prosperity arrived in the shape of the small black **olives** that produced an oil, *olivo selourenco*, of great gastronomic renown. By the end of the nineteenth century the Salonais were making soap from their oil, a highly profitable commodity manufactured in the most appalling conditions in subterranean mills. Those to whom the dividends accrued built opulent Belle Époque residences outside the old town walls, the grandest of which are to be found in the streets between the town centre and the *gare SNCF* to the west, and though

> ## Nostradamus and the Canal de Craponne
>
> Salon lies at the eastern edge of Provence's most arid region, La Crau, and suffered perennial droughts until the mid-sixteenth century, when the town's most famous resident, **Michel de Nostradamus**, financed the building of a canal. Engineered by **Adam de Craponne**, the waterway ran from the River Durance through a gap in the hills at Lamanon and across La Crau to the Étang de Berre, and today the area west of Salon is criss-crossed with similar canals. A contemporary account describes the people of Salon greeting the arrival of the waters with "applause, astonishment and joyful incredulity".

most have long since been given over to other uses or divided into apartments, they give the town a quiet, surprising grace.

The famous predictions of **Nostradamus** were composed in Salon, though the museum dedicated to him is less appealing than the mementoes of **Napoléon** in Salon's castle, the Château de l'Empéri. A good time to visit the town is mid-July when the **jazz festival** takes place, or in July and August for the annual **classical music festival** (Ⓦ www.festival-salon.fr) in the château.

Arrival, information and accommodation

From the **gare SNCF** on avenue Émile-Zola, the long straight boulevard Maréchal-Foch leads you on to cours Pelletan, at the edge of the Vieille Ville. Buses depart from the **gare routière** on place Jules-Morgan at the southern end of the *cours*. The **tourist office** (July–Aug Mon–Sat 9.30am–6.30pm, Sun 10am–12.30pm; Sept–June Mon–Sat 9.30am–12.30pm & 2–6pm; ℡ 04.90.56.27.60, Ⓦ www.visitsalondeprovence.com) is on the other side of the ring road around the Vieille Ville, at 56 cours Gimon.

Finding **accommodation** should not be too difficult, whatever time of year you visit. The *Grand Hôtel de la Poste*, 1 rue des Frères-Kennedy (℡ 04.90.56.01.94, Ⓦ grandhotel.provence.free.fr; ❷), and the renovated *Hôtel d'Angleterre*, 98 cours Carnot (℡ 04.90.56.01.10, Ⓦ www.hotel-dangleterre.biz; ❸), are comfortable and central; and the *Vendôme*, 34 rue Maréchal-Joffre (℡ 04.90.56.01.96, Ⓕ 04.90.56.48.78; ❸) has a pleasant courtyard setting. More luxury and a quieter location away from the town centre is on offer at *Le Mas du Soleil* 38 chemin Saint-Côme (℡ 04.90.56.06.53, Ⓦ www.lemasdusoleil.com; ❸), which also has an excellent restaurant. If you prefer to be in the country, the *Domaine de Roquerousse* (℡ 04.90.59.50.11, Ⓦ www.roquerousse.com; ❾), in the opposite direction to Salon from the northern autoroute exit, has sixteen rooms and ten self-contained units set in an extensive park. Otherwise, there's the seriously expensive *Hostellerie de L'Abbaye de Sainte-Croix*, 3km from Salon on the D16, route du Val-de-Cuech (℡ 04.90.56.24.55, Ⓦ www.relaischateaux.com/saintecroix; closed Jan–March; ❾), an ancient abbey in beautiful surroundings.

The canal-bank three-star **campsite**, *Camping Nostradamus* (℡ 04.90.56.08.36, Ⓦ www.camping-nostradamus.com; closed Nov–Feb, €16.10 per tent), on the D17 towards Eyguières and the Arles bus route (rte d'Eyguières), also has some **mobile homes**.

The Town

In the mid-1960s the town council initiated a programme of demolition and rebuilding in the **Vieille Ville**, which was completed in the late 1980s. Despite the swathes of redevelopment, however, Salon's commercial life has firmly established itself in the boulevards ringing the *Vielle Ville*, and the old town today has an artificial and rather lifeless feel to it.

Given the lack of life in this part of town, you might as well concentrate on the **Château de l'Empéri**, the centrepiece of the Vieille Ville. This massive structure is a proper medieval fortress, built to suit the worldliness of its former proprietors, the archbishops of Arles. It now houses the **National Military Art and History Museum** (Mon & Wed–Sun 10am–noon & 2–6pm; €3.05), covering the period from Louis XIV to World War I; the sections devoted to the Revolution and Napoleon are particularly fascinating.

Flights of gleaming steps run down the castle rock to place des Centuries, a wide-open space with little obvious purpose. It's overlooked by the Centre Commerciale St-Michel which houses the **Musée Grévin de la Provence** (Mon–Fri 9am–noon & 2–6pm; Sat & Sun 2–6pm; €3.05, or €5.35 including the Maison de Nostradamus), a series of waxwork scenes illustrating episodes from the legends and history of Provence, with taped commentaries available in several different languages. Opposite the Centre Commerciale, the thirteenth-century **Église St-Michel**, with two belfries, adds a touch of old-world charm to this rather dull windswept area, as does **rue Moulin-d'Isnard**, leading off the place de L'ancienne Halle, to the north of the square.

Just east of the place de L'ancienne Halle stands the **Maison de Nostradamus** (same hours as Musée Grévin; €3.05), on the street now named after the sooth-sayer. Nostradamus arrived in Salon in 1547, already famous for his aromatic plague cure, administered in Aix and Lyon, and married a rich widow. After some fairly long Italian travels, he returned to Salon and settled down to study the stars, the weather, cosmetics and the future of the world. Translations in numerous languages of his *Centuries*, the famous predictions, are displayed in the house along with pictures of events supposedly confirming them. There are waxwork tableaux and visuals meant to fill you with wonder, but nothing particularly earth shattering – the most interesting exhibit is the 1979 sculpture by François Bouché in the courtyard. Nostradamus died in Salon in 1566 and his tomb is in the Gothic Collégiale St-Laurent, at the top of rue du Maréchal-Joffre, north of the Vieille Ville.

To reach Collégiale St-Laurent from the museum, you'll pass through **Porte de l'Horloge**, the principal gateway to the Vieille Ville. This is a serious bit of seventeenth-century construction, with its Grecian columns, coats of arms, gargoyles and wrought-iron campanile. Through the arch is place Crousillat, which centres on a vast mushroom of moss concealing a three-statued fountain; a wonderful spot for a café break.

To the west of the *Vielle Ville* and located within a working *savonnerie*, the **Musée du Savon de Marseille**, 148 av Paul-Bourret (Mon–Thurs 9.30–11.30am & 1.45–5pm, Fri 9.30–11.30am & 1.45–4pm; €3, or €3.85 including factory tour), tells the story of soap-making in Provence from the Middle Ages onwards. Tours of the factory take place on Monday and Thursday at 10.30am and there is an on-site shop.

Eating and drinking

The best of central Salon's **restaurants** is *La Salle a Manger*, 6 rue Maréchal-Joffre (☎04.90.56.28.01; closed Sun & Mon), with wonderful Italianate decor and lovely Provençal food at very reasonable prices (weekday lunch menu at €15, otherwise €27; closed Sun & Mon) – it's very popular so book ahead. The *Hostellerie de L'Abbaye de Ste-Croix* (see p.85) and *Le Mas du Soleil*, 38 chemin de St-Côme (☎04.90.56.06.53), are both top-notch gourmet establishments, the latter being slightly more affordable, with two menus under €40. A more economical alternative is *La Table des Cordeliers*, 20 rue d'Hozier (☎04.90.56.53.42; closed Sun), in a former thirteenth-century chapel, which has menus at around €16.50 and €22.50, and for cheap, filling couscous there's the *Restaurant Bleu*, 32 rue Palamard (☎04.90.56.51.93; from €12).

The place for **café lounging** is around the fountain on place Crousillat, where you'll find *Bar de la Fontaine*, *Nostradamus* and the *Café des Arts*. On rue A-Moutin, opposite the Hôtel de Ville, there's a piano bar, *Le Grenier d'Abondance*.

Salon's famous olive oil and other produce can be bought at the busy Wednesday **market** on place Morgan or the Sunday market on place de-Gaulle.

Around Salon

Ten kilometres north of Salon, the main road and highway pass through a narrow gap in the hills by **LAMANON**, a village which was never much more than a stopover on the transhumance routes (used for the moving of flocks, and still followed by the Crau shepherds every June), though it does have a château. Above the village, hidden amongst rocks and trees, is a remarkable troglodyte village, the **GROTTES DE CALES**, which was inhabited from Neolithic times until the nineteenth century. Stairs lead down into grottoes, part natural, part constructed, with hooks and gutters carved into the rock; at the centre is a sacrificial temple. Access is free, though some parts of the complex are fenced off for safety reasons: follow the Montée de Cales which ascends from opposite the tourist office, where there's a small **museum** (Sun 2.30–5pm; free); the circuit of the *grottes* itself is on the GR6 footpath. The countryside west of Lamanon is typical of the dry Crau region: around **EYGUIÈRES** you may see llamas grazing along with goats and horses. Llamas are excellent at keeping trim forest firebreaks – so, too, are goats, but goats are forbidden from running loose in the forests, thanks to an unrevoked Napoleonic law.

Bears, elephants, big cats, hippos and a host of other non-native mammals and birds are kept for more conventional purposes at the **Château de la Barben** (château: April–Nov daily 10am-6pm; Dec–March Sat & Sun plus Mon–Fri during school hols 11am–noon & 2–5.30pm; €8; zoo: daily 10am-6pm; €12), 12km east of Salon, just beyond Pélissanne. This is very much a place to take young children, with plenty of entertainment such as miniature train rides, as well as the standard zoo delights. The château was lived in for a while by Napoléon's sister, Pauline Borghese, and her apartments are still decorated in imperial style, while the rest retains a feeling of seventeenth-century luxury.

The north shores of the Étang de Berre

The town of **Miramas**, to the north of the Étang de Berre, is a bland nineteenth-century creation, which exists solely because of its rail connections to the heavy industries of the coast. You may find yourself passing through here, but you're unlikely to want to linger.

In contrast, the honey-coloured, crumbly **MIRAMAS-LE-VIEUX**, perched on a hill 3km south of Miramas train station, is altogether more appealing, a typical Provençal medieval village – and refreshingly free of tourists. Narrow cobbled streets lead up past the pretty public gardens below place de la Mairie to the immaculately restored **St-Vincent church** and its tiny predecessor. Beyond is place du Château and its **castle** ruins. There are pottery shops and a couple of excellent ice-cream parlours, including *Le Quillé*, whose mouthwatering choice of flavours and fine terrace view attract a small evening crowd from the towns in the area.

Just to the south, on the Étang de Berre, is **ST-CHAMAS**, where port-side workers' houses are separated from the rest of the town by an aqueduct between two high rocks, one of which is colonized by a scenic grid of tightly terraced houses. Here, on the Monté des Pénitents, is a helpful little **tourist office** (Mon–Sat: mid-June to mid-Sept 9am–noon & 2–6pm; mid-Sept to mid-June 9am–noon & 1.30–5.30pm; ℡04.90.50.90.54, Ⓦwww.saintchamas.fr.st). A few metres further on up the hill is the path that accesses the top of the nineteenth-century **Pont de l'Horloge aqueduct**, an astonishing creation that affords the best (if slightly vertigo-inducing) views of the town from alongside its hallmark clock. This unpretentious town has several other interesting monuments, including a grandiose Hispanic-looking, seventeenth-century church, with a severely cracked, leaning bell tower, and **La Poudrerie gunpowder factory** that Louis XIV initiated in 1690, the economic mainstay of the town until its closure in 1974 and the site in 1936 of a terrible explosion that killed 53 workers. A twenty-minute walk south of the centre brings you to the elegant **Pont Flavien**, a first-century BC Roman triumphal bridge spanning the River Touloubre – an unexpected sight in the wasteland to the left of the main road to Aix.

Though not on the lagoon itself, the neighbouring rock-perched village of **CORNILLON-CONFOUX**, 4km east of St-Chamas, gives even better views of the Étang de Berre, taking in the Alpilles, the Luberon and sometimes even Mont Ventoux as well.

Aubagne

Marseille's suburbs extend relentlessly east along the highway and N8 corridor north of the Chine de St-Cyr. You reach **AUBAGNE** almost before you realize you've left Marseille, even though the landscape is now dominated by mountains on all sides. With a triangle of autoroutes around it and a series of dismal postwar developments which encroach on its historic core, the town is easy to pass by. Yet the town is not without cultural interest, as the headquarters of the French Foreign Legion and a major centre for the production of *santons*, the traditional Provençal Christmas figures. Its main claim to fame, however, is as the birthplace of writer and film-maker Marcel Pagnol (1895–1974) and the now much-altered setting for his tales. The international success in the 1980s of Claude Berri's films of Pagnol's *Jean de Florette* and *Manon des Sources*, starring Gérard Depardieu and Emmanuelle Béart, has widened Pagnol's appeal. In *Jean de Florette* an outsider inherits a property on the arid slopes of the Garlaban mountain, whose rocky crest rears like a stegasaurus's back, north of Aubagne. The local peasants who have blocked its spring watch him die from the struggle of fetching water, delighted that his new scientific methods won't upset their market share.

The soil around Aubagne is very fertile, and on Tuesday, Thursday, Saturday and Sunday mornings and Friday afternoons, you can take your pick of the flowers, fruit and vegetables from the excellent **market** stalls on cours Voltaire, cours Foch and the esplanade de-Gaulle. The soil also makes excellent pottery; hence the town's renown for *santons* and ceramics, and the only School of Ceramics in Provence, founded in 1989. From mid-July to the end of August and in December, a huge daily **market of ceramics** and **santons** takes place on the central street of cours Maréchal-Foch, and in December a giant crèche is set up with 120 figures. At any time of the year you can visit the potters' workshops in the Vieille Ville to the east of cours Maréchal-Foch: rue F-Mistral beyond the Hôtel de Ville is a good street to try. Other interesting displays of the art can be found at the top of the Vieille Ville in the **Ateliers Thérèse Neveu** (open daily during exhibitions only; free), in the cour de Clastre behind St-Saveur church.

The most impressive display of *santons* is to be found at **Le Petit Monde de Marcel Pagnol** (daily 9am–12.30pm & 2.30–6pm; free) in a diorama on esplanade de-Gaulle opposite the helpful **tourist office** on avenue Antide-Boyer (Mon–Sat 9am–noon & 2–6pm; ☎04.42.03.49.98, ⓦwww.aubagne.com). The finely detailed figures of Pagnol characters play out their parts on a model of the local district, complete with windmills, farms and villages. For real Pagnol fans, the tourist office supplies a map of all the places in his stories, and offers a range of guided tours in *Pays de Pagnol*.

Aubagne's other claim to fame is commemorated by the **Musée de la Légion Étrangère,** located within the barracks complex in the quartier Vienot on the other side of the A50 autoroute from the town centre (May–Sept Tues, Wed & Fri–Sun 10am–noon & 3–7pm; Oct–April Wed, Sat & Sun 10am–noon & 2–6pm; free). The tradition of foreigners serving in France's armies dates back to 1346, but the Legion as it exists today was created by King Louis Philippe in 1831. It received its baptism of fire in Algeria in 1832, and from then on was closely associated with North Africa for much of its history, founding the garrison at Sidi Bel Abbès in 1843. The town grew to be a modern city of 100,000 and remained the Legion's home until France withdrew from Algeria in 1962. How sudden that withdrawal was is demonstrated by the fact that just one year previously the Legion had opened a new Salle d'Honneur in Sidi Bel Abbès to commemorate its fallen. Today, the Salle d'Honneur is on the ground floor of the museum, and with its incessant soundtrack of martial music it's a suitably sombre place; just outside, present-day legionnaires can be seen drilling on the parade ground. The displays upstairs catalogue the Legion's campaigns and include the white *képis* familiar from cinematic depictions of Beau Geste.

Cassis

It's hard to imagine the little fishing port of **CASSIS**, on the main coast road south from Marseille, as a busy industrial harbour in the mid-nineteenth century, trading with Spain, Italy and Algeria. Its fortunes had declined by the time Dérain, Dufy and other Fauvist artists started visiting at the turn of the twentieth century. In the 1920s Virginia Woolf stayed while working on *To the Lighthouse*, and later Winston Churchill used to come to paint. These days it's scarcely an undiscovered secret, as one glance at the local property prices or the crowds in the port-side restaurants will tell you. The place bustles with activity: stalls

△ Moutes frites and Cassis rosé

sell artisans' handicrafts, guitarists busk round the port, and day-trippers endlessly circle the one-way system trying to find a parking space. But many people still rate Cassis the best resort this side of St-Tropez, its residents most of all.

Arrival, information and accommodation

Vehicle access to the central port area of Cassis is restricted, so **buses** drop their passengers at the *Gendarmerie* a little above the town, from where it's a short walk downhill to the port. The **gare SNCF** is 3km out of town, and connected to the town by a shuttle bus (Mon–Fri & Sat am) which takes around 15 minutes to reach Cassis. The modern **tourist office** is on the port at quai des Moulins (March–June & Sept–Oct Mon–Fri 9am–12.30pm & 2–6pm, Sat 9.30am–12.30pm & 2–5.30pm, Sun 10am–12.30pm; July–Aug Mon–Fri 9am–7pm, Sat & Sun 9.30am–12.30pm & 3–6pm; Nov–Feb Mon–Fri 9.30am–12.30pm & 2–5.30pm, Sat 10am–12.30pm & 2–5pm, Sun 10am–12.30pm; ☏08.92.25.98.92, Ⓦwww.cassis.fr).

Hotels

Le Clos de Arômes 10 rue Abbé Paul-Mouton ☏04.42.01.71.84, Ⓦwww.le-clos-des-aromes .com. Charming, quiet hotel a short way inland from the bustle of the port, with a lovely garden restaurant that is well regarded by locals. Closed Jan & Feb. ❹

Le Commerce 1 rue de Ste-Clair ☏04.42.01.09.10, Ⓕ04.42.01.14.17. Family-run hotel one block back from the port, with a restaurant. Closed mid-Nov to mid-Jan. ❸

Le Golfe 3 place du Grand Carnot ☏04.42.01.00.21, Ⓦwww.hotel-le-golfe-cassis.com. In the middle of all the action, overlooking the port, and with a lunchtime brasserie. Closed Nov–March. ❺

Le Grand Jardin 2 rue Pierre-Eydin ☏04.42.01.70.10, Ⓕ04.42.01.33.75. A pleasant hotel on a side street next to the Jardin Public and close to the centre of town. It has parking and is open all year. ❹

Joli Bois rte de la Gineste ☏04.42.01.02.68, Ⓕ04.42.01.18.24. Just off the main road to Marseille, 3km from Cassis. A bargain but it has only ten rooms, so best book ahead. It's in a pretty remote spot but there's plenty of parking space. ❷

Laurence 8 rue de l'Arène ☏04.42.01.88.78, Ⓦwww.cassis-hotel-laurence.com. A short way inland from the port and market, a/c and modernized. Some rooms have views of the harbour or château. Closed Nov & Dec. ❸

Le Provencal 7 av Victor-Hugo ☏04.42.01.72.13, Ⓕ04.42.01.39.58. A/c two-star hotel just steps from the harbour and one of the cheaper central options. ❸

Les Roches Blanches av des Calanques ☏04.42.01.09.30, Ⓦwww.roches-blanches-cassis .com. Handsome old hotel in a perfect position overlooking the bay, with smart rooms, terraces and a pine wood leading down to the water. ❻

Hostel and campsite

Les Cigales ☏04.42.01.07.34, Ⓕ04.42.01.34.18. Campsite on the corner of the rte de Marseille and av de la Marne, 1km from the port. €18.60 per tent. Closed mid-Nov to mid-March.

HI youth hostel *La Fontasse* ☏04.42.01.02.72. Ⓦwww.fuaj.org. In the hills above the *calanques* west of Cassis. By car from Cassis, take the D559 for 4km then turn left. The Cassis–Marseille bus stops on the D559 (bus stop "Les Calanques"). It's

2.5km walk from the centre of Cassis, towards the col de la Gardiole; take av des Calanques from the port. The hostel's facilities are basic (there are no showers, and power and water are rationed), but if you want to explore this wild, uninhabited stretch of limestone heights, the people running it will advise you enthusiastically. €9.50 per night. Reception 8–10.30am & 5–9pm. Closed Jan to mid-March

The Town

The white cliffs hemming it in and the value of its vineyards on the slopes above have prevented Cassis becoming a relentless sprawl, and the little modern development there is, is small scale. Port-side posing, eating *oursins* (sea urchins) and drinking aside, there's not much to do except sunbathe and look up at the ruins of the town's medieval **castle**. It was built in 1381 by the counts of Les Baux and refurbished last century by Monsieur Michelin, the authoritarian boss of the family tyres and guides firm, and it remains a private home.

Cassis has a small **museum** (summer Wed–Sat 10.30am–12.30pm & 3.30–6.30pm; winter Wed–Sat 10.30am–12.30pm & 2.30–5.30pm; free) in the seventeenth-century presbytery on rue Xavier-d'Authier just behind the tourist office. It has a bit of everything: nineteenth-century paintings and photographs of Cassis and Marseille, old furniture, costumes and Roman amphorae.

One of the most popular tourist activities is to take a **boat trip to the calanques** (from around €8), the long, narrow, deep, fjord-like inlets that cut into the limestone cliffs. Several companies operate from the port, but check if they let you off or just tour in and out, and be prepared for rough seas. If you're feeling energetic, you can **walk** along the GR98 footpath from the avenue des Calanques behind the western beach; it's about a ninety-minute walk to the furthest and best inlet, **En Vau**, where you can climb down rocks to the shore. Intrepid pine trees find root-holds, and sunbathers find ledges on the chaotic white cliffs. The water is deep blue and swimming between the vertical cliffs is an experience not to be missed. Note that from July until the second Saturday in September you have to stick to the coastal path or the sea from 11am to 4pm in order to lessen the fire risk.

Eating and drinking

Sea urchins accompanied by the delicious, crisp Cassis **white wine** are the speciality here. **Restaurant** tables are abundant along the port side on quai des Baux, quai Calandal and quai Barthélemy; prices vary but the best bet is to follow your nose, and seek out the most enticing fish smells. The authentic Provençal ratatouille and freshly caught fish at *Chez Gilbert*, 19 quai Baux (℡04.42.01.71.36; menu €27; closed Tues eve & Wed), are hard to beat; it also serves great *bouillabaisse*. *Nino*, at 1 quai Barthélemy (℡04.42.01.74.32; menus from €33; closed Sun eve & Mon), is an attractive blue-and-white restaurant, serving pasta, *bouillabaisse* and wonderful grilled fish, while *Romano*, 15 quai Barthélemy (℡04.42.01.08.16; lunch menu at €18, otherwise menus from €23.50), dishes up elaborate creations such as lobster ravioli or *gratinée* of mussels stuffed with garlic and parsley. The most beautiful gourmet restaurant in town is *La Presqu'Île*, on route des Calanques in the quartier

---

The Cosquer cave

In 1991, **Henri Cosquer**, a diver from Cassis, discovered paintings and engravings of animals, painted handprints and finger tracings in a cave between Marseille and Cassis, whose sole entrance is a long, sloping tunnel that starts 37m under the sea. The cave would have been accessible from dry land no later than the end of the last ice age and carbon dating has shown that the oldest work of art here was created around 27,000 years ago. Over a hundred animals have been identified, including seals, auks, horses, ibex, bisons, chamois, red deer and a giant deer known only from fossils. Fish are also featured along with sea creatures that might be jellyfish. Most of the finger tracings are done in charcoal and have fingertips missing, possibly to convey a sign language by bending fingers. For safety reasons it's not possible to visit the cave, though **diving schools** in Cassis organize dives in the bay and the *calanques*.

de Port-Miou, overlooking both the *calanques* and the bay of Cassis and offering exquisite fish dishes and traditional Provençal fare (☎04.42.01.03.77; menus €29 and €46; booking essential; closed Sun eve & Mon). For **drinking**, the *Bar Canaille*, on the corner of quai Calandal and quai des Baux, has the best *terrasse*, under the shade of a plane tree.

Cassis **wines**, from grapes grown on the slopes above the D559, are very special. Mistral described the white as "shining like a limpid diamond, tasting of the rosemary, heather and myrtle that covers our hills". If you arrive by train you can stop off at two **vineyards** on your way down the D1: the Domaine des Quatres Vents (☎04.42.01.01.12) and Clos d'Albizzi (☎ & ℱ04.42 .01.11.43). There are more along the D41 which loops east from the station, and along the D559 towards La Ciotat, and the tourist office's small English-language guide lists all the others. Alternatively, there's the **Maison des Vins** (☎04.42.01.15.61) on the D559 route de Marseille. For **picnic food** to go with the wine, head for the **market**, held around place Baragnon east of the port on Wednesday and Friday mornings, and for the numerous boulangeries in rue Victor-Hugo.

The Corniche des Crêtes

If you have a car or motorbike, the spectacular **Corniche des Crêtes** road south from Cassis to La Ciotat (the D141) is definitely a ride not to be missed. From Cassis the chemin St-Joseph turns off avenue de Provence, climbs at a maximum gradient to the Pas de la Colle, then follows the inland slopes of the Mont de la Canaille. Much of the landscape is often blackened by fire but every so often the road loops round a break in the chain to give you dramatic views over the sea. You can walk it as well in about three and a half hours: the path, beginning from Pas de la Colle, takes a precipitous straighter line passing the road at each outer loop. The Corniche is closed in high winds.

△ Corniche des Crêtes

La Ciotat and around

Cranes still loom incongruously over the old ship-building town of **LA CIOTAT**, where 300,000-tonne oil and gas tankers were built as recently as 1989. Today, the town's economy relies on property development, tourism, and mooring and repairing yachts, yet it remains a pleasantly unpretentious place, with a golden Vieille Ville above the bustling quayside, affordable hotels and restaurants, and an attractive beach stretching northeast from the port.

In 1895 **Auguste** and **Louis Lumière** filmed the first ever moving pictures in La Ciotat and in 1904 went on to develop the first colour photographs. The town celebrates its relatively unknown status as the cradle of cinema with an annual **film festival** in June.

Arrival, information and accommodation

The **gare SNCF** is 5km from the town centre but bus #21 is frequent at peak times and gets you to the Vieux Port in around twenty minutes. The Vieille Ville and port look out across the Baie de la Ciotat, whose inner curve provides the beaches and resort-style life of La Ciotat's beach-side extension, **La Ciotat Plage**. The **gare routière** is next to the **tourist office** (June–Sept Mon–Sat 9am–8pm, Sun 10am–1pm; Oct–May Mon–Sat 9am–noon & 2–6pm; ⊤04.42.08.61.32, ⓦwww.tourisme-laciotat.com), at the end of boulevard Anatole-France by the Vieux Port. **Bikes** can be hired from Cycle Lleba at 3b av F-Mistral (⊤04.42.83.60.30).

Hotels

Beaurivage 1 bd Beaurivage ⊤ & ⓕ04.42.98.04.34. Two-star hotel with parking, restaurant and a terrace. The more expensive rooms have sea views. Closed Oct–Feb. ❺

La Marine 1 av F-Gassion ⊤ & ⓕ04.42.08.35.11. ⓕ06.03.29.45.23. The best budget option in town, just above the Vieille Ville; a pleasant, very clean place with decent-sized rooms.

Popular with divers. Cheaper rooms lack bath or shower. ❷

Miramar 3 bd Beaurivage ⊤04.42.83.33.79, ⓦwww.miramarlaciotat.com. Possibly the best hotel in the town, set amid pines on the seafront. ❼

Hôtel la Rotonde 44 bd de la République ⊤04.42.08.67.50, ⓕ04.42.08.45.21. Modern hotel near La Marine and close to the old town. ❸

Campsite

St-Jean 30 av St-Jean ⊤04.42.83.13.01, ⓦwww .asther.com/stjean. Take bus #40 (direction "gare SNCF"; stop St-Jean Village). A three-star site by

the sea, this is the closest one to the centre and facilities include a tennis court. €23 per tent. Closed Oct–May.

The Town

The resplendently ornate nineteenth-century former *mairie* at the end of quai Ganteaume now houses the **Musée du Vieux Ciotat** (July–Aug Wed–Mon 4–7pm; Sept–June 3–6pm; €3.20), charting the history of the town back to its foundation by the ancient Greeks of Marseille when local shipbuilding began. Further down the quay is the seventeenth-century church, **Notre-Dame-du-Port**, with its Baroque facade and a striking early-seventeenth-century painting by André Gaudion of the *Descent of the Cross* alongside modern works of art. The streets of the Vieille Ville behind the church are uneventful and still a bit run-down, though the proliferation of estate agents in the town suggests that is set to change.

Film in La Ciotat

La Ciotat's train station has a commemorative plaque to the film *L'Arrivée d'un train en gare de La Ciotat*, which was one of a dozen or so films, including *Le déjeuner de bébé* and the comedy *L'Arroseur arrosé*, shown in the Château Lumière in September 1895. The audience jumped out of their seats as the image of the steam train hurtled towards them. Three months later the reels were taken to Paris for the capital's citizens to witness cinema for the first time.

La Ciotat marks its association with the artform with a couple of festivals. The **Cinestival** is an affordable event which takes place in late May or early June, usually revolving around a particular theme or genre and offering screenings at very low prices. The venues include the Lumière cinema and the Chapelle des Pénitents Bleus. A rather more glamorous event, the **Berceau du Cinema**, takes place around the same time at the Cinéma Lumière, screening a limited selection of films before an invited jury, which awards the *Lumières d'Honneur* prize. Tickets for these screenings can be obtained free in advance by writing to the Association Le Berceau du Cinéma, 20 rue Maréchal-Foch, 1300 La Ciotat (℡04.42.71.61.70, Ⓦwww.berceau-cinema.com).

To the east along the seafront, on the corner of boulevard A-France and boulevard Jean-Jaurès, is the crumbly **Eden Cinema**, the world's oldest movie house, currently closed to the public pending restoration. Further on, at plage Lumière, is a solid 1950s monument to Auguste and Louis Lumière who shot the world's first films in the garden of the family **château** at the top of allée Lumière. The house survives, but is private property and not open to the public. The brothers appear again in a mural on the covered market halls which house the modern **cinema** on place Evariste-Gras, visible as you walk up rue Régnier from boulevard Guérin north of the port. If you want to learn more about the brothers, the **Espace Simon Lumière** at 20 rue Maréchal-Foch (June–Sept Tues–Sat 4–7pm; Oct–May 3–6pm; free) has a small exhibition.

Boat trips depart from the Vieux Port for the ten-minute trip to the tiny offshore **Île Verte**, topped by a fort and with a small restaurant, *Chez Louisette*, which serves seafood. Both Vedette Voltigeur (℡04.42.83.11.44) and Vedette Monte Cristo (℡04.42.71.53.32) make the crossing to Île Verte daily, while Catameran Le Citharista (℡06.09.35.25.68) runs trips to the *calanques* of Cassis and Marseille (€17–23) from quai Ganteaume.

Alternatively, you could explore the remarkable contorted cliff beyond the shipyards that the city's founders named "the eagle's beak" and which is now protected as the **Parc du Mugel** (daily: April–Sept 8am–8pm; Oct–March 9am–6pm). A path leads up from the entrance through overgrown vegetation and past scooped vertical hollows to a narrow terrace overlooking the sea. The cliff face looks like the habitat of some gravity defying, burrowing beast rather than the result of erosion by wind and sea. To get there, take bus #30 (direction "La Garde"; stop "Mugel").

If you continue on bus #30 to Figuerolles you can reach the **Anse de Figuerolles** *calanque* down the avenue of the same name, and its neighbour, the **Gameau**. Both have pebbly beaches and a completely different dominant colour from the *calanques* of Cassis.

Eating, drinking and entertainment

La Ciotat's **restaurants** are not gastronomically renowned, though *Coquillages Franquin*, at 13 bd Anatole-France (℡04.42.83.59.50), serves perfectly respectable fish dishes on menus from €16.50, and *La Fresque*, just up from the quayside at 18 rue des Combattants (☎04.42.08.00.60), is a cut or two above the portside brasseries and glaciers, with the likes of duck stuffed with foie gras and cream of figs and menus from €18. Right on the port, pizzeria *La Mamma* (☎04.42.08.30.08) is one of the busiest spots in town, with decent pizzas from €8. There are plenty of **cafés** and **brasseries** on the quays: *Le Sirocco* does a lunchtime *formule* at €8; and there's a wide choice of places to drink, including *Best Of*, *Bar Continental* and *Pub Mexicain*, where the mojitos cost €5. The *Bar à Tine* overlooking the Cinema Lumière and the Tuesday market on place E-Gras is another pleasant place to drink. Also on place E-Gras, the *Atelier Convergences* is a lively piano bar and **jazz** venue. La Ciotat has a surprisingly animated cultural scene, including several gallery/exhibition spaces and the smart new *Théâtre du Golfe* on the seafront at boulevard Anatole-France (☎04.42.08.92.87).

There's a Sunday **market** on the quays, though the main shopping street is rue des Poilus, a little inland from the church of Notre Dame du Port. For a takeaway lunch, *Lou Pecadou*, a fishmonger's at no. 20, sells paella and other fish dishes from huge iron pans, and there are several boulangeries and an oriental patisserie nearby too.

Travel details

Trains

Aubagne to: Bandol (16–29 daily; 27 min); Cassis (16–28 daily; 8 min); La Ciotat (16–28 daily; 15 min); Marseille (19–26 daily; 15–20min); Toulon (16–29 daily; 42 min).

Marseille to: Aix (approx every 30min–1hr; 40min); Arles (16–22 daily; 50min); Aubagne (approx every 30min at peak times; 15–20min); Avignon (8–13 daily; 1hr 15min); Bandol (17–30 daily; 37–42min); Cannes (15–21 daily; 2hr 5min–2hr 20min); Carry-le-Rouet (8–14 daily; 25min); Cassis (16–29 daily; 22min); Cavaillon (2–4 daily; 55 min–1hr 15min); Hyères (1–4 daily; 1hr 15–1hr 30min); L'Estaque (10–20 daily; 10–20min); La Ciotat (18–31 daily; 30min); La Seyne-Six-Fours (16–27 daily; 52 min); Les Arcs-Draguignan (8–16 daily; 1hr 20min–2hr); Lyon (5–12 daily; 3hr 30min–3hr 40min); Martigues (8–14 daily; 40min); Menton (1–2 daily; 3hr 7min–3hr 20min); Miramas (approx every 15–30min at peak times; 30min–1hr 10min); Nice (14–20 daily; 2hr 20min–2hr 45min); Ollioules-Sanary (16–27 daily; 50min); Paris (TGV: 10–22 daily; 3hr 15min); St-Chamas (3–5 daily; 40min); St Cyr/Les Lecques (16–27 daily; 35min); St-Raphaël (14–21 daily; 1hr 30min–1hr 45min); Salon (2–3 daily; 45–55min); Tarascon (2 daily; 1hr); Toulon (every 20min at peak times; 40min–1hr 3min).

Miramas to: Arles (12–14 daily; 20min); Avignon (14–19 daily; 40min); Marseille (approx every 15min at peak times; 40min–1hr 20min).

Salon to: Avignon (4–6 daily; 45–55min); Marseille (3–4 daily; 55min); Miramas (9–13 daily; 10–30min).

Buses (Sundays and holidays reduced services)

Aubagne to: Aix (8 daily; 50min); Cassis (hourly; 30min); Gémenos (hourly Mon–Sat; 25min); La Ciotat (approx every 20 min–1hr; 25–40min); Marseille (every 5min at peak times; 25min).

Marseille to: Aix (every 5min at peak times; 30–50min); Apt (1–2 daily; 2hr 15min); Barçelonnette (1–3 daily; 3hr 50min–4hr 50min); Brignoles (2 daily; 1hr 15min); Carpentras (2–3 daily; 1hr 35min–2hr 20min); Cassis (7–14 daily; 40–50min); Digne (3–5 daily; 2hr 20min–2hr 50min); Forcalquier (1–4 daily; 2hr–2hr 15min); Grenoble (1 daily; 3hr 55min); La Ciotat (15 daily; 30–45min); Manosque (8–13 daily; 1hr 5min–1hr 30min); Martigues (every 15–45min; 45–50min) Pertuis (1–6 daily; lhr); St-Maximin (2 daily; 50–55min); Salon (6 daily; 1hr 10min); Sisteron (3–5 daily; 2hr 10min–2hr 25min).

Martigues to: Aix (6 daily; 1hr 20min); Carry le Rouet (1 daily; 42min); Marseille (every 15–40min; 45min); Salon (9 daily; 1hr).

Salon to: Aix TGV (6 daily, 55 mins); Aix (16 daily; 35–45min); Arles (7 daily; 50min–1hr 10min); Eyguières (7 daily; 15min); La Barben (1 daily; 30 min); Marignane Airport (6 daily; 35 min); Marseille (6 daily; 1hr 10min–1hr 20min); Martigues (9 daily; 55 min–1hr 10min); Miramas (9 daily; 25min).

Arles and the Camargue

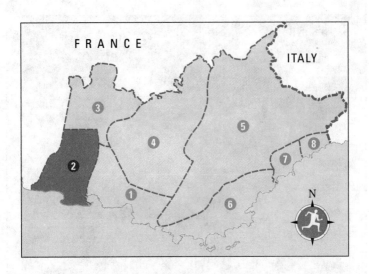

CHAPTER 2 # Highlights

* **Les Arènes** For its sheer size, Arles' ancient Roman amphitheatre is one of Provence's most impressive Roman remains. See p.104

* **Cathédrale des Images** This former quarry in the Valley of Hell has been the inspiration for many artists, including Dante and Cocteau. See p.112

* **St-Rémy-de-Provence** Enjoy the same views that inspired Van Gogh at this picturesque town at the base of the Alpilles. See p.112

* **The Camargue** The expansive marshland of the Rhône delta is home to pink flamingoes, white horses and unearthly, watery landscapes, as well as the colourful gypsy festival in Les Ste-Maries-de-la-Mer. See pp.124–132

△ White horses in the Camargue

Arles and the Camargue

Life in the Bouches du Rhône *département* west of the Étang de Berre revolves around the River Rhône, which flows south from Avignon to the sea. The river has always been a vital trading route, bringing wealth and fame to the towns that line its banks. The great castles at the riverside towns of **Tarascon** and **Beaucaire** are testament to the Rhône's strategic importance, while further south, at the point where the river divides into the Petit and Grand Rhône, **Arles** was once the centre of Roman Provincia – which stretched from the Pyrenees to the Alps – before becoming the capital of Gaul towards the end of the Roman era. Arles's great amphitheatre still seats thousands for summer entertainments, while further evidence of Roman occupation is apparent at **Glanum**, outside **St-Rémy-de-Provence**, where you can see the overlaid remains of Greek and Roman towns, and between Arles and St-Rémy, where the ancient **Barbegal mill** demonstrates the Romans' brilliant use of water power.

South of Arles, spreading across the Rhône delta, is the strange watery land of the **Camargue**, with a natural history and way of life quite distinct from surrounding regions. The wet expanses sustain flocks of flamingoes and a multitude of other birds, while black bulls and wild white horses graze on the edges of the marshes and lagoons. The Camargue also provides a sanctuary for unique social traditions – it is here, to the seaside resort of **Les Stes-Maries-de-la-Mer**, that **gypsies** come every May from all over the Mediterranean to celebrate their patron saint's day.

The modest plains to the north and east of Arles, enclosed by the River Durance and the Rhône and separated by the abrupt ridge of the **Alpilles**, are known as **La Petite Crau** and **La Grande Crau**. Here the villages and small towns have retained a nineteenth-century charm, living out the old customs and traditions revived by the great Provençal poet **Frédéric Mistral**, a native of La Petite Crau. This is the countryside that **Van Gogh** painted when he spent a year at Arles and then sought refuge in St-Rémy. Both towns celebrate his tragic brilliance.

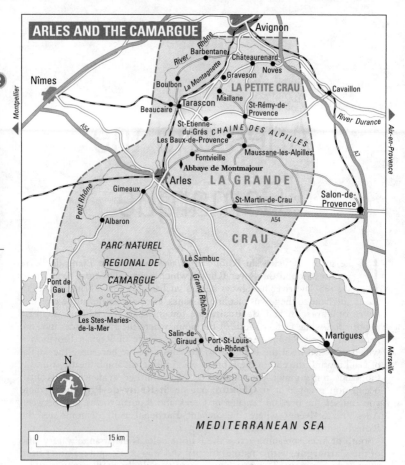

ARLES AND THE CAMARGUE

Avignon

Nîmes

Montpellier

Barbentane
Châteaurenard
River Rhône
Graveson
Noves
Boulbon
La Montagnette
LA PETITE CRAU
Cavaillon
Maillane
Tarascon
St-Rémy-de-
Provence
Beaucaire
A54
St-Etienne-
du-Grés
CHAÎNE DES ALPILLES
River Durance
Les Baux-de-Provence
Maussane-les-Alpilles
Fontvieille
Abbaye de Montmajour
Arles
LA GRANDE
Gimeaux
St-Martin-de-Crau
Salon-de-
Provence
Petit Rhône
A54
Albaron
CRAU
PARC NATUREL
REGIONAL DE
CAMARGUE
Le Sambuc
Grand Rhône
Pont de
Gau
Les Stes-Maries-
de-la-Mer
Salin-de-
Giraud
Port-St-Louis-
du-Rhône
Martigues

Aix-en-Provence

Marseille

N

MEDITERRANEAN SEA

0   15 km

Arles

ARLES, on the east bank of the Rhône, is a major town on the tourist circuit, its fame sealed by the extraordinarily well-preserved Roman amphitheatre, **Les Arènes**, at the city's heart, and backed by an impressive variety of other stones and monuments, both Roman and medieval. Roman Arles provided grain for most of the western empire and was one of the major ports for trade and shipbuilding; under Constantine, it became the capital of Gaul, Britain and Spain. After the Roman Empire crumbled, the city, along with Aix, regained its fortunes as a base for the counts of Provence before unification with France. For centuries it was Marseille's only rival, profiting from the inland trade route up the Rhône whenever France's enemies were blockading the port of Marseille. Arles began to decline when the arrival of train routes put an end to this advantage, and it was an inward-looking, depressed town that **Van Gogh**

came to in the late nineteenth century. It was a prolific, though lonely and unhappy period for the artist, ending with his self-mutilation and asylum in St-Rémy-de-Provence (see p.112). The **Fondation Vincent Van Gogh** pays tribute to him through the works of modern artists.

Today, despite the steady stream of tourists, Arles is a pleasantly laid-back place, springing to life for the **Saturday market** that brings everyone from the Camargue and La Crau into town. It also fills the year with a crowded calendar of festivals, of which the best known is the **Rencontres Internationales de**

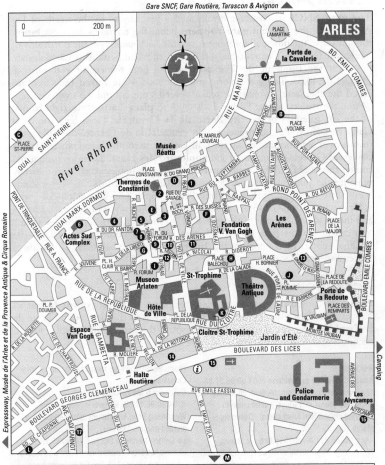

Gare SNCF, Gare Routière, Tarascon & Avignon ▲

ARLES

0   200 m

N

Expressway, Musée de l'Arles et de la Provence Antique & Cirque Romaine ◀

Camping ▶

ACCOMMODATION			
Acacias	A	Gauguin	B
Hôtel de l'Amphithéâtre	H	Grand Hôtel Nord Pinus	I
D'Arlatan	E	HI youth hostel	M
Calendal	J	La Muette	F
Le Cloître	K	Mireille	C
Constantin	L	Musée	D
Du Forum	G		

RESTAURANTS, CAFÉS & BARS			
Coco Bongo	14	Le Galoubet	5
L'Apostrophe	9	Le Grillon	13
Pâtisserie du Forum	8	La Gueule de Loup	11
Le Café La Nuit	12	Le Jardin du Manon	16
Cargo de Nuit	17	Le Vivier	2
La Charcuterie Arlésienne	10	L'Olivier	1
Chez Arianne	3	La Paillote	4
Lou Marquès	15	Soleileïs	7
L'Entrevue	6		

la **Photographie**, based around the National School of Photography, from July to mid-September; there's also the dance, music, folklore and theatre **Fêtes d'Arles** from early June to early July and the **Mosaïque Gitanes** with gypsy and flamenco dance and song in mid-July. For the locals – who say the photographic festival is only for Parisians – the key events are the annual opening of the bullfighting season with the **Fête des Gardians** on May 1, the crowning of the **Reine d'Arles**, once every three years – the last one took place in May 2005 – and the **rice harvest** festivities in mid-September.

Arrival and information

The **gare SNCF** is conveniently located a few blocks to the north of Les Arènes, with the adjacent **gare routière** being the terminus for most **buses**, though some, including all local buses, use the *halte routière* on the north side of boulevard Georges-Clemenceau, just east of rue Gambetta. Bus schedules are posted at the Boutique des Transports at the *halte routière*, or you can call ☎08.91.02.40.35. The *gare routière* and *halte routière* are linked by a free bus called the "Starlette", which also makes several stops around the town centre.

From the station, avenue Talabot leads south to **place Lamartine**, right by one of the old gateways of the city, **Porte de la Cavalerie**. From here rue de la Cavalerie takes you to Les Arènes and the centre. **Rue de l'Hôtel-de-Ville** is the main axis of old Arles, becoming rue Jean-Jaurès at its southern end where it meets boulevard Georges-Clemenceau and **boulevard des Lices**, the promenading and market thoroughfare. The main **tourist office** is on boulevard des Lices directly opposite the junction with rue Jean-Jaurès (Jan–March Mon–Sat 9am–4.45pm, Sun 10am–12.45pm; April–Sept daily 9am–6.45pm; Oct–Dec Mon–Sat 9am–4.45pm, Sun 10am–12.45pm; ☎04.90.18.41.20, ⓦwww.tourisme.ville-arles.fr), and there's also an annexe in the gare SNCF (Tues–Sat 9am–1pm & 2–4.45pm). You can hire **bikes** from Velo & Oxygen, 15 rue du Pont or Europbike, 1 rue Phillipe Lebon. To connect to the **Internet**, go to Cyber City, 41 rue du 4 Septembre, near place Voltaire.

Accommodation

Arles is well used to visitors and there are plenty of **hotel rooms** to suit all budgets. The best place to look for cheap rooms is in the area around Porte de la Cavalerie near the station. If you get stuck, the tourist office will find you accommodation for a €1 fee.

Hotels

Acacias 2 rue de la Cavalerie ☎04.90.96.37.88, ⓦwww.hotel-acacias.com. Modern, cheerfully decorated rooms in a friendly hotel close to the train station and town centre. Closed Nov–March. ④

Hôtel de l'Amphithéâtre 5 rue Diderot ☎04.90.96.10.30, ⓦwww.hotelamphitheatre .fr. Tasteful contemporary decor, spacious rooms and reasonable rates (especially for four-person rooms) make this hotel situated close to Les Arènes the best value in town. ③

D'Arlatan 26 rue du Sauvage ☎04.90.93.56.66, ⓦwww.hotel-arlatan.fr. Set in a beautiful old fifteenth-century mansion and decorated with antiques, this distinguished hotel has plenty of character, although the rooms can be rather small. Closed Jan. ⑥

Calendal 5 rue Porte de Laure ☎04.90.96.11.89, ⓦwww.lecalendal.com. Welcoming hotel with bright, a/c overlooking a shaded garden. ③

Le Cloître 16 rue du Cloître ☎04.90.96.29.50, ⓦwww.hotelcloitre.com. A cosy hotel where some rooms have views of St-Trophime. Closed Nov to late March. ③

Constantin 59 bd de Craponne, off bd Clemenceau ☎04.90.96.04.05, Pleasant, well maintained and comfortable, with prices kept down by its close proximity to the busy Nîmes highway (some traffic noise) and its location some distance from the centre. ③

Du Forum 10 place du Forum ☏04.90.93.48.95, ⓦwww.hotelduforum.com. Large rooms in an old house at the ancient heart of the city, with a swimming pool in the garden. A bit noisy and hot (a/c optional). Closed Nov–March. ❹

Gauguin 5 place Voltaire ☏04.90.96.14.35, ⓕ04.90.18.98.87. Simple, inexpensive rooms in a well run hotel. Booking advisable. ❷

Grand Hôtel Nord Pinus 14 place du Forum ☏04.90.93.44.44, ⓦwww.nord-pinus.com. Favoured by the *vedettes* of the bullring and decorated with their trophies, including a selection of stuffed bulls' heads. Despite all this, it's still one of the most luxurious and elegant options. ❾

Mireille 2 place St-Pierre ☏04.90.93.70.74, ⓦwww.hotel-mireille.com. On the other side of the river, with the more expensive and very luxurious rooms overlooking a swimming pool. Closed Nov to mid-March. ❺

La Muette 13–15 rue des Suisses ☏04.90.96.15.39, ⓦwww.hotel-muette.com. Renovated rooms with characterful old stone walls in a charming hotel close to Les Arènes. Closed Feb. ❸

Musée 11 rue du Grand-Prieuré ☏04.90.93.88.88, ⓦwww.hoteldumusee.com.fr. In a quiet location opposite the Musée Réattu, with small but welcoming rooms and a pretty communal patio. Closed Jan. ❸

Hostel and campsites

La Bienheureuse on the N453 at Raphèle-lès-Arles ☏04.90.98.48.06, ⓦwww.labienheureuse.com. Two-star site 7km out, but with regular buses from Arles (direction "Aix", stop "Raphèle"). This is the best of the local campsites. Its restaurant is furnished with pieces similar to those on display in the Museon Arlaten, and is full of pictures of popular Arles' traditions. €14.50 per tent.

City 67 rte de Crau ☏04.90.93.08.86, ⓦwww.camping-city.com. Two-star site with a pool 1.5km from town on the bus #2 route (direction "Pont de Crau", stop "Hermite"). €17 per tent. Closed Oct–March.

HI youth hostel 20 av Maréchal-Foch ☏04.90.96.18.25, ⓕ04.90.96.31.26. Reached with bus #4 (direction "Fourchon", stop "Foumier"), this rather dismal hostel has rock-hard beds (€14.55, including breakfast) in large dorms and spartan facilities. Reception 7–10am and 5–10pm; 11pm curfew. Closed late-Dec to early Feb.

The City

The centre of Arles fits into a neat triangle between bd Émile-Combes to the east, bds Clemenceau and des Lices to the south, and the Rhône to the west. The main square, with the cathedral and town hall, is **place de la République**, while the hub of popular life is **place du Forum**. Apart from the **Musée de l'Arles et de la Provence Antique**, south of the expressway,

---

Bullfighting in Arles and the Camargue

Bullfighting, or more properly *tauromachie* (roughly, "the art of the bull"), in Arles and the Camargue is generally not the Spanish-style *mise-à-mort*, and it's usually the bullfighters, or *razeteurs*, who get hurt, not the animal. The sport remains a passion with the locals, who treat the champion *razeteurs* like football stars, while the bulls are fêted and adored – before retirement they are given a final tour around the arena while people weep and throw flowers.

The **shows** involve various feats of daring and, being much closer to the scene, you will feel more involved than with other dangerous sports. The most common show is where the bull has a cockade at the base of its horns and ribbons tied between them. Using blunt razor-combs, the *razeteurs* have to cut the ribbons and get the cockades. For some shows, involving horsemen, arrows are shot at the bull, though these don't go in deep enough to make the animal bleed.

All this may leave you feeling cold, or sick, but it is your best way of experiencing **Les Arènes** in Arles. It may help to know that no betting goes on; people just add to the prize money as the game progresses. The tourist office, local papers and publicity around the arena will give you the details (around €5–15 per seat); be sure to check shows are not *mise-à-mort*.

the city's **Roman and medieval monuments** are all within easy walking distance of the centre.

Les Arènes and around

The amphitheatre, known as **Les Arènes**, in the centre of the city (see box below for opening hours; €5.50, combined ticket with the Thermes de Constantin), is the most impressive of the Roman monuments. It dates from the end of the first century AD and, to give an idea of its size, it used to shelter over two hundred dwellings and three churches, built into the two tiers of arches that form its oval surround. This medieval *quartier* was cleared in 1830 and Les Arènes was once more used for entertainment. Today, though not the largest Roman amphitheatre in existence and missing its third storey and most of the internal stairways and galleries, it is a very dramatic structure and a stunning venue seating 25,000 spectators for bullfights, theatre and music concerts.

Facing Les Arènes from the west, at 26 Rond-Point des Arènes, the Palais de Luppé houses the **Fondation Vincent Van Gogh** (April–June Tues–Sun 10am–6pm; July–Sept daily 10am–7pm; €7), which exhibits works by contemporary artists inspired by Van Gogh. Francis Bacon was the first to contribute with a painting based on Van Gogh's *The Painter on the Road to Tarascon,* which had been destroyed during World War II. Roy Lichtenstein repaints *The Sower*; Hockney, César and Jasper Johns also pay homage, as do musicians, poets, photographers and the fashion designer Christian Lacroix who grew up in Arles. The collection sometimes goes on tour, at which times it is replaced by an exhibition on one of the contributors.

The **Théâtre Antique**, just south of Les Arènes (see box on p.159 for opening hours; €3), comes to life in June and July during the dance and theatre festival and for the *Fête du Costume*, in which local folk groups parade in traditional dress. A resurrected Roman, however, would be appalled at the state of this entertainment venue, with only one pair of columns standing, all the statuary removed and the sides of the stage littered with broken bits of stone. It was built a hundred years earlier than Les Arènes and quarried for stones to build churches not long after the Roman Empire collapsed; it then became part of the city's fortifications, with one of the theatre wings being turned into the **Tour Roland**, whose height gives you an idea of where the top seats would have been. A convent and houses were later built over the area and it was only excavated at the turn of the twentieth century. Below the theatre the pleasant **Jardin d'Été** leads down to bd des Lices.

The quiet and attractive southeast corner of the city, between boulevard Émile-Combes, Les Arènes and the theatre, has vestiges of the ramparts built over the Roman walls down montée Vauban, and in the gardens running

Museums and monuments

If you're planning on visiting several of the city's sights, it's worth buying a **Pass Monument** (€13.50), which gives free admission to all Arles' museums and monuments except the Fondation Vincent Van Gogh. It's available from the tourist office and at the sights themselves. Opening hours for all Arles' monuments are the same – daily: March, April & Oct 9–11.30am & 2–5.30pm; May–Sept 9am–6pm; Nov–Feb 10–11.30am & 2–4.30pm. Note that in winter the amphitheatre and the cloisters do not close for lunch, while in summer the thermes is closed between noon and 2pm.

alongside the boulevard past the old Roman gateway, the **Porte de la Redoute**. Just by the gate you can see where the aqueduct from Barbegal (see p.110) brought water into the city.

Place de la République and around

West of Les Arènes stands **place de la République**, dominated by the **Cathédrale St-Trophime**, whose doorway boasts one of the most famous bits of twelfth-century Provençal stone carving in existence. It depicts the Last Judgement, trumpeted by angels playing with the enthusiasm of jazz musicians, while the damned are led naked and in chains down to hell; the blessed, all female and draped in long robes, processing upwards.

The cathedral itself was started in the Dark Ages on the spot where, in 597 AD, Saint Augustine was consecrated as the first bishop of the English. It was largely completed by the twelfth century. A font in the north aisle and an altar in the north transept, illustrating the parting of the Red Sea, were both originally Gallo-Roman sarcophagi. The high nave is decorated with d'Aubusson tapestries; you'll find more Romanesque and Gothic stone carving, this time with New Testament scenes enlivened with other myths such as Saint Martha leading away the tamed Tarasque (see p.122), in the extraordinarily beautiful **cloisters**, accessible from place de la République to the right of the cathedral (see box on p.104 for opening hours; €3.50).

An obelisk of Egyptian granite, that may once have stood in the middle of the Cirque Romaine (see p.107), stands in front of the cathedral, placed there by Louis XIV, who fancied himself as a latter-day Augustus. Across place de la République from the cathedral stands the palatial seventeenth-century **Hôtel de Ville**, inspired by the Palace of Versailles. You can walk through its vast entrance hall with its flattened vaulted roof, designed to avoid putting extra stress on the **Cryptoportiques** below: a huge, dark, dank horseshoe-shaped underground gallery, built by the Romans, possibly as a food store, possibly as a barracks for public slaves, but certainly to provide sturdy foundations for the forum above. The Cryptoportiques have been closed to visitors since July 2005 due to their own deteriorating state of firmness.

Immediately south of the place, on rue de la République, is the **Museon Arlaten** (daily: April–May & Sept 9.30am–12.30pm & 2–6pm; June–Aug 9.30am–1pm & 2–6.30pm; Oct–March 9.30am–12.30pm & 2–5pm; €4), set up in 1896 by Frédéric Mistral (see p.118) with his Nobel Prize money. In the room dedicated to the poet, a cringing notice piously instructs you to salute the great man's cradle. That apart, the collections of costumes, documents, tools, pictures and paraphernalia of Provençal life are extensive and intriguing. The evolution of Arlesian dress is charted in great detail for all social classes from the eighteenth century to World War I and includes a scene of a dressmaking shop. Two other life-size scenes portray a visit to a mother and newborn child, and a bourgeois Christmas dinner – not to be looked at if you're hungry. The room devoted to Provençal mythology, including a Tarasque from the Tarascon procession, is entertaining if not very enlightening.

Heading down rue du Président-Wilson from the Museon Arlaten and right into rue P.F-Rey brings you to the **Espace Van Gogh**, the former Hôtel-Dieu (hospital) where Van Gogh was treated. It now houses a *mediathèque* and university departments, with a bookshop and a *salon de thé* in the arcades. The flowerbeds in the courtyard are a recreation of the hospital garden based on Van Gogh's painting and the descriptions he wrote of the plants in letters to his sister.

Place du Forum to the river and Van Gogh

North of place de la République, **place du Forum** is still the centre of life in Arles today. In the square, you can see the pillars of an ancient archway and the first two steps of a monumental stairway that gave access to the Roman forum, now embedded in the corner of the *Nord-Pinus* hotel. The statue in the middle of the square is of Frédéric Mistral.

Heading north towards the river you reach the **Thermes de Constantin** (see box on p.104 for opening hours; €5.50, combined ticket with Les Arènes), the considerable ruins of what may well have been the biggest Roman baths in Provence. You can see the heating system below a thick Roman concrete floor and the divisions between the different areas, but there's nothing to help you imagine the original. The most striking feature, an apse in alternating brick and stonework, which sheltered one of the baths, is best viewed from outside on place Constantin.

To the right, along rue du Grand-Prieuré, is the entrance to the must-see **Musée Réattu** (daily: March–June & Oct 10am–12.30pm & 2–6.30pm; July–Sept 10am–7pm; Nov–Feb 1–6pm; €6.50) where, beside the rigid eighteenth-century classicism of works by the museum's founder and his contemporaries, there are some stunning twentieth-century pieces. Of the modern works, Picasso is the best represented with 57 ink and crayon sketches from between December 1970 and February 1971 which he donated to the museum. Amongst the split faces, clowns and hilarious Tarasque, is a beautifully simple portrait of Picasso's mother. Zadkine's bronze sculpture of a woman playing a violin, *Odalisque*, Mario Prassinos' black and white studies of the Alpilles, César's *Compression 1973* and works by contemporary artists are dotted about the landings, corridors and courtyard niches of this very beautiful fifteenth-century priory; there are also some very good temporary exhibitions.

If you walk to the back of the building, you'll see its gargoyles jutting over the river. There are lanterns along the river wall (and some wonderful sunsets), though much of the river front and its bars and bistros, where weary workers once drank and danced away their woes, was destroyed during World War II.

Another casualty of the bombing was the "Yellow House", on place Lamartine to the north of the centre, where **Van Gogh** lived before entering the hospital

△ Pont Van Gogh, Arles

at St-Rémy. However, the café painted in *Café de Nuit* is still open for business in place du Forum.

Van Gogh had arrived by train in February 1888 to be greeted by snow and a bitter Mistral wind. But he started painting straightaway, and in this period produced such celebrated canvases as *The Sunflowers*, *Van Gogh's Chair*, *The Red Vines* and *The Sower*. He used to wander along the riverbank wearing candles on his hat, watching the light of night-time; *The Starry Night* is the Rhône at Arles.

Van Gogh was desperate for Gauguin to join him, though at the same time worried about his friend's influence. From the daily letters he wrote to his brother Théo, it was clear that the artist found few kindred souls in Arles. Gauguin did eventually come and moved in with Van Gogh. The events of the night of December 23, when Vincent cut off his ear after chasing Gauguin with a razor blade, were recorded by the older artist fifteen years later. No one knows the exact provocation. Van Gogh was packed off to the Hôtel-Dieu hospital where he had the good fortune to be treated by a young and sympathetic doctor, Félix Rey. Van Gogh painted Rey's portrait while in the hospital as well as the hospital itself, in which the inmates are clearly suffering, not from violent frenzy, but from an unhappiness only Van Gogh could express.

Musée de l'Arles et de la Provence Antique and the Cirque Romaine

The **Musée de l'Arles et de la Provence Antique** stands on the spit of land between the Rhône and the Canal de l'Ecluse just west of the city centre (daily: April–Oct 9am–7pm; Nov–March 10am–5pm; €5.50). The triangular building, designed by Peruvian architect Henri Ciriani, is positioned on the axis of the **Cirque Romaine**, an enormous chariot racetrack that stretched for 450m from the museum to the town side of the expressway. Built in the middle of the second century AD, the track was 101m wide and allowed an audience of 20,000 to watch the chariot races. Although excavation of the track has been temporarily halted due to lack of funding, you can still look down into the existing digs crossed by av de la 1er Division Française Libre, the road in front of the museum. The models inside the museum, however, will give you a much better idea of Roman Arles' third major entertainment venue.

Inside, the museum is a treat: open-plan, flooded with natural light and immensely spacious. It covers the prehistory of the area and then takes you through the centuries of Roman rule from Julius Caesar's legionnaire base and the development during the reign of Augustus. It continues through the Christian era from the fourth century when Arles was Emperor Constantine's capital of Gaul, to the fifth century, the height of the city's importance as a trading centre. At that time, Emperor Honorius could say "the town's position, its communications and its crowd of visitors is such that there is no place in the world better suited to spreading, in every sense, the products of the earth". The exhibits are arranged chronologically as well as thematically, so, for example, there are sections on medicine, on the use of water power (with more details on the Barbegal mill; see p.110), on industry and agriculture. Fabulous mosaics are laid out with walkways above; and there are numerous sarcophagi with intricate sculpting depicting everything from music and lovers, to gladiators and Christian miracles.

Les Alyscamps

A couple of minutes' walk south from boulevard des Lices, down avenue des Alyscamps, lies the Roman's burial ground, **Les Alyscamps** (see box on p.104 for opening hours; €3.50), which was used by the wealthier Arlesians well into the Middle Ages. Now only one alleyway, foreshortened by a rail line, is preserved, although sarcophagi still line the shaded walk, whose tree trunks are azure blue in Van Gogh's rendering. Some of the tombs have an axe engraved on them, which is thought to have been the contemporary equivalent of a notice warning "Burglar alarm fitted". There are numerous tragedy masks, too, though any with special decoration have long since been removed to serve as municipal gifts, as happened often in the seventeenth century, or to reside in the museums. But there is still magic to this walk, which ends at the church of **St-Honorat** where more sarcophagi are stored.

Eating, drinking and entertainment

Arles has a good number of excellent-value **restaurants**. If you're looking for quick lunches, or just want to watch the world go by, there's a wide choice of **brasseries** on the main boulevards, of which the most appealing is *Coco Bongo*, 14 bd des Lices, which serves tapas and various cocktails. The most atmospheric place to eat, however, is place du Forum, where you can always get a decent *plat du jour* for around €10 at the cafés and bars lining the square.

Saturday is the big day of the week in Arles for the **market** that extends the length of boulevard Georges-Clemenceau, boulevard des Lices and boulevard Émile-Combes and many of the adjoining streets. A smaller food market takes place every Wednesday in place Lamartine, with bric-a-brac stalls spreading down boulevard Émile-Combes.

For all-round **entertainment**, the *Actes Sud* complex at 23 quai Marx-Dormoy (℡04.90.49.56.78), offers **classical concerts** and **films** (often in their original languages), along with meals, a bookshop and even a **hamam** (℡04.90.96.10.32).

Restaurants

La Charcuterie Arlésienne 51 rue des Arènes ℡04.90.96.56.96. A Lyonnaise-style deli; cramped, lively, with a variety of *assiettes de charcuterie* starting at €15. Closed Sun & Mon.

Chez Arianne 2 rue du Dr-Fanton ℡04.90.52.00.65. A small but appealing menu of home-made rabbit and chicken dishes for around €14, washed down with organic wines. Closed Mon.

L'Entrevue 23 quai Marx-Dormoy ℡04.90.93.37.28. Hip Moroccan café with an attached hamam. Tagines and couscous for €14–16. Closed Sun eve mid-Sept to mid-June.

Le Galoubet 18 rue du Dr-Fanton ℡04.90.93.18.11. Attractive, vine-covered terrace on which to sample modern Provençal cuisine; the €25 menu is particularly good value. Closed Sun, Mon & Wed lunch & Jan-Feb.

Le Grillon Corner of rond-point des Arènes & rue Girard-le-Bleu ℡04.90.96.70.97. Pleasant place overlooking Les Arènes with menus from €16, usually featuring a couple of seafood options along with the meat dishes. Closed Wed & Jan–Feb.

La Gueule de Loup 39 rue des Arènes ℡04.90.96.96.69. Cosy restaurant serving traditional dishes such as bull filet with anchovy sauce. Menus from €19; reservations recommended. Closed Sun & Mon lunch.

Le Jardin du Manon 14 av des Alyscamps ℡04.90.93.38.68. Hospitable Provençal restaurant offering elaborate regional dishes and delicious desserts, which you can enjoy in a small patio garden. Menus from €21. Closed Tues eve & Wed.

Lou Marquès *Hôtel Jules César*, 9 bd des Lices ℡04.90.52.52.52. A real gourmet delight where the specialities include langoustine risotto with Camargue rice and lobster cooked in Chateauneuf-du-Pape wine, all served with the utmost decorum; menus €40–80, main dishes around €25. Closed Sat & Sun Nov–March.

La Paillote 28 rue du Dr-Fanton ℡04.90.96.33.15. Very friendly place with a good €17 menu full of Provençal starters and main courses such as smoked ham braised in Porto. Closed Tues lunch & Wed eve.

Le Vivier 6 rue Dominique-Maïsto ℡04.90.49.60.64. The best place for fish and seafood, with the most expensive of the menus (€17–36) featuring a seafood platter including sea snails, clams, oysters and crab. Closed Sun & Mon lunch.

Cafés, bars and ice cream

L'Apostrophe 7 place du Forum ℡04.90.96.34.17. The youngest of the place du Forum bars, with modern decor and tables full of computer-users taking advantage of the free WiFi Internet access.

Le Café La Nuit place du Forum ☎04.90.96.44.56. If you sit on the terrace you'll find yourself in quite a few holiday snaps, as this is the setting of Van Gogh's *Café La Nuit*.

Cargo de Nuit 7 av Sadi-Carnot ☎04.90.49.55.99. A café-bar with an excellent line-up of live jazz, electronic and world music concerts, mainly on Fri & Sat evenings.

Pâtisserie du Forum 4 rue de la Liberté ☎04.90.96.03.72. A *salon de thé* with a whole pâtisserie full of goodies to go with the Earl Grey. Closed Sun.

Soleileïs 9 rue du Dr-Fanton ☎04.90.93.30.76. Delicious home-made ice cream with all-natural ingredients.

Listings

Car parks Parking des Lices, off bd des Lices; free parking in place Lamartine.

Car rental Avis at the gare SNCF (☎04.90.96.82.42); Europcar, 2 bis bd Victor-Hugo (☎04.90.93.23.24); Hertz, 2 bd Victor-Hugo (☎04.90.96.75.23); Rent-a-car, 1061 bd Émile-Combes (☎04.90.18.20.01).

Emergencies ☎15; Centre Hospitalier J-Imbert, quartier Fourchon (☎04.90.49.29.29).

Money exchange Rond-point des Arènes; several banks on rue de la République.

Pharmacy For a list of late-night pharmacies, call the gendarmerie on ☎04.90.52.50.60.

Police Bd des Lices, opposite the Jardin d'Été (☎04.90.52.50.60).

Post office 5 bd des Lices, 13200 Arles (Mon–Fri 8.45am–12.45pm & 1.45–6pm, Sat 8am–noon).

Swimming pool Stade Municipal off av Maréchal-Foch (July-Aug daily 10am–7pm).

Taxis ☎04.90.96.90.03, ☎04.90.49.69.59 or ☎04.90.93.31.16.

Trains Local ☎08.91.67.68.69; national ☎08.36.35.35.35.

La Grande Crau

La Grande Crau (or just plain La Crau) stretches east from Arles and the Rhône delta to Salon, and was once, a very long time ago, the bed of the Rhône and the Durance. The name Crau derives from a Greek word for "stony", certainly a dominant feature of this landscape. Legend has it that Hercules, having trouble taking on local Ligurians and the Mistral wind both at once, called on Zeus for aid, which arrived in the form of a pebblestone storm, water off a duck's back to the classical hero.

Much of the area is irrigated and planted with fruit trees protected by windbreaks of cypresses and poplars. But other parts are still a stony desert in summer when the grass between the pebbles shrivels up. As winter approaches, sections of the old Roman Via Aurelia are used as drove roads for sheep leaving their summer pastures in the mountains. In winter there are only the winds to contend with; in summer it is unbearably hot and shadeless.

There are some interesting stopoffs in the more amenable countryside between the western end of the Alpilles, the chain of hills that runs to the north of La Grande Crau, and Arles. The first is the extremely old **Chapelle St-Gabriel**, just 5km from Tarascon on the D33 to Les Baux, immediately after the junction with the main Avignon–Arles road. It's built on the site of a Gallo-Roman settlement, with a very appealing facade, possibly sculpted by the same artists responsible for St-Trophime's tympanum in Arles; Tarascon's tourist office has the keys, but there's not that much to see inside.

Between the chapel and a ruined medieval tower, the GR6 footpath heads up towards the Alpilles ridge and Les Baux (see p.110). For a ten-kilometre round walk you could follow the GR6 until you hit a small road, turn left down to **St-Étienne-du-Grés** and left again along the D32. There's a good **hotel** in St-Étienne, the *Mas Vidau*, impasse André Vidau (☎04.90.47.63.71, closed Jan–March ❸), with attractive rooms in an old farmhouse.

South of St-Gabriel is **FONTVIEILLE**, a popular pilgrimage for the French as the place where the writer Alphonse Daudet used to stay. The road past the small literary museum, **Moulin de Daudet** (daily: Feb & March 10am–noon & 2–6pm; April–Sept 9am–7pm; Oct–Dec 10am–noon & 2–6pm; €2.50), leads south to the crossroads with the D82 where the remains of two Roman aqueducts are visible. A little further south a left turning, signposted *Meunerie Romain*, brings you to the dramatic excavation of the **Barbegal mill**, a sixteen-wheel system powered by water from one of the aqueducts and constructed in 3 or 4 BC; it is estimated that the mill produced up to three tonnes of flour a day.

The road from Fontvieille to Arles takes you past the Romanesque ruins of the **Abbaye de Montmajour** (April–Sept daily 9.30am–6.30pm; Oct–March Tues–Sun 10am–5pm; €6.50), a five-minute ride from Arles itself on the Les Baux bus. Take heed when you climb the 124 steps of the fortified watch-tower, as your arrival will undoubtedly startle dozens of pigeons; the view from the top of La Grande Crau, the Rhône and the Alpilles is stunning. Below, in the **cloisters**, an excellent stone menagerie of beasts and devils enlivens the bases of the vaulting. Just 200m from the abbey, back in the direction of Fontvieille, the eleventh-century funerary chapel of **Ste-Croix**, with its perfect proportions and frieze of palm fronds, stands amid tombs cut out of the rock in a farmyard.

Les Baux-de-Provence

At the top of the Alpilles ridge, 15km northeast of Arles, lies the distinctly unreal fortified village of **LES BAUX-DE-PROVENCE**. Unreal partly because the ruins of the eleventh-century citadel are hard to distinguish from the edge of the plateau whose rock is both foundation and part of the structure. And unreal, too, because this Ville Morte (Dead City) and a vast area of the plateau around it are accessible only via a turnstile from the living village below, which remains a too-perfect collection of sixteenth- and seventeenth-century churches, chapels and mansions.

Les Baux once lived off the power and wealth of its medieval lords, who owed allegiance to none. When the dynasty died out at the end of the fourteenth century, the town, which had once numbered six thousand inhabitants, passed to the counts of Provence and then to the kings of France who, in 1632, razed the feudal citadel to the ground and fined the population into penury. From that date until the nineteenth century, both citadel and village were inhabited almost exclusively by bats and crows, until the discovery of bauxite (the aluminium ore takes its name from Les Baux) in the neighbouring hills, which gradually brought back some life to the village. Today tourism is the most important industry, with around 1.5 million visitors a year descending on the population of four hundred.

The village

The lived-in village has a great many beautiful buildings, among them those housing its half-a-dozen or so museums. One of the best museums is the **Musée Yves Brayer** in the Hôtel des Porcelets (mid-Feb to March & Oct–Dec daily except Tues 10am–12.30pm & 2–5.30pm; April–Sept daily 10am–12.30pm & 2–6.30pm; €4), showing the paintings of the twentieth-century figurative artist whose work also adorns the seventeenth-century

△ The ruins of Les Baux

Chapelle des Pénitents Blancs on place de l'Église. Changing exhibitions of the work of contemporary Provençal artists are displayed in the **Hôtel de Manville** (hours vary, so check with the tourist office; free). The museum of the **Fondation Louis Jou**, in the fifteenth-century Hôtel Jean de Brion (April–Oct Thurs–Sun 11am–1pm & 1.30–5pm; Nov–March by reservation only, ☏04.90.54.34.17; €3), contains the presses, wood lettering blocks and hand-printed books of the master typographer whose workshop opposite is still used for manual printing (products on sale in the boutique). The **Musée des Santons** in the old hôtel de ville (daily 9am–7pm; free) displays traditional Provençal nativity figures.

Follow the signs to the château for the entrance to the **Citadelle de la Ville Morte**, the main reason for coming to Les Baux (daily: Jan & Feb 9am–5pm; March–June, Sept & Oct 9am–6.30pm; July & Aug 9am–7.30pm; Nov & Dec 9.30am–5pm; €7.50), where there are several more museums amid the ruins. The **Musée d'Histoire des Baux** in the vaulted space of Tour de Brau has a collection of archeological remains and models to illustrate the village's history from medieval splendour to bauxite works. The most impressive ruins are those of the feudal castle demolished on Richelieu's orders; there's also the partially restored **Chapelle Castrale** and the **Tour Sarrasine**, the cemetery, ruined houses half carved out of the rocky escarpment, and some spectacular views, the best of which is out across La Grande Crau from beside the statue of the Provençal poet Charloun Riev at the southern edge of the plateau.

Practicalities

The **tourist office** is in the Maison du Roy on rue Porte Mage (daily: July–Sept 9.30am–1pm & 2–5.30pm; Oct–June 9.30am–12.30pm & 2–5.30pm; ☎04.90.54.34.39, ⓦ www.lesbauxdeprovence.com). You have to park – and pay – before entering the village and, as you'll soon discover, nothing in Les Baux comes cheap, least of all **accommodation**. There is just one moderately priced option, the *Hostellerie de la Reine Jeanne* (☎04.90.54.32.06, ⓦ www.la-reinejeanne.com; closed mid-Nov to mid-Feb; ❹), by the entrance to the village, which has very friendly staff, simple rooms with views of the citadelle and good **food** on menus starting at €22. If you feel like treating yourself, try the beautiful hotel-restaurant *Oustau de Baumanière* (☎04.90.54.33.07, ⓦ www.oustaudebaumaniere.com; ❾), just west of Les Baux on the road to the Val d'Enfer, which is spectacularly situated and elegantly luxurious. For less sumptuous fare, there are a couple of places selling crêpes, pizzas and other **snacks** along rue du Château.

The Val d'Enfer

Within walking distance of Les Baux, along the D27 leading north, is the valley of quarried and eroded rocks that has been named the **Val d'Enfer** (Valley of Hell). Dante, it is thought, came here while staying at Arles, and took his inspiration for the nine circles of the *Inferno*. Jean Cocteau used the old bauxite quarries and the contorted rocks for his film *Le Testament d'Orphée*, some of which was filmed in Les Baux itself.

More recently, the very same quarries have been turned into an audiovisual experience called the **Cathédrale des Images** (daily: March & Sept to early Jan 10am–6pm; April–Sept daily 10am–7pm; €7.30), signposted to the right downhill from Les Baux's car park. The projection is continuous, so you don't have to wait to go in. You are surrounded by images projected all over the floor, the ceilings and the walls of the vast rectangular caverns, and by music that resonates strangely in the captured space. The content of the thirty-minute shows, which changes yearly, doesn't really matter; it is just an extraordinary sensation, wandering on and through these changing shapes and colours. As an inventive use for a former worksite it can't be bettered.

St-Rémy-de-Provence and around

The scenery of La Grande Crau changes abruptly with the eruption of the **Chaîne des Alpilles**, whose peaks look like the surf of a wave about to engulf the plain. At the northern base of the Alpilles nestles **ST-RÉMY-DE-PROVENCE**, a dreamy place where Van Gogh sought psychiatric help and painted some of his most lyrical works. St-Rémy is a beautiful spot, as unspoilt as the villages around, and its old town (the Vieille Ville) is contained within a circle of boulevards no more than half a kilometre in diameter. Outside this ring, the modern town is sparingly laid out, so you don't have to plough your way through dense developments before you reach the heart of the city. Outside the old town, all the attractions lie within walking distance to the south: the **Roman arch**, the hospital of **St-Paul-de-Mausole**, the **Mas de la Pyramide** farmhouse in the old Roman quarries and the ruins of the ancient city of **Glanum**.

St-Rémy is ideally situated for exploration of the hills of the Alpilles, and is easy to get to by bus from either Arles or Avignon. The St-Rémy tourist office provides excellent free guides on **cycling** and **walking** routes in and around the Alpilles and has addresses for hiring **horses** and for **gliding** at a club that claims to hold the world record for the longest flight. Note, however, that due to the risk of fires the Alpilles is closed to walkers during the whole of the summer.

Arrival, information and accommodation

Arriving by **bus**, you'll be dropped at **place de la République**, the main square abutting the Vieille Ville to the west. The **tourist office** (June–Sept Mon–Sat 9am–12.30pm & 2–7pm, Sun 9am–noon; Oct–May Mon–Sat 9am–noon & 2–6pm; ☎04.90.92.05.22, ⓦwww.saintremy-de-provence.com) is just south of the centre on place Jean-Jaurès, between avenue Pasteur and avenue Durand-Maillane and reached by following boulevard Marceau until it becomes avenue Durand-Maillane. If you want to hire a **bike**, try Telecycles (☎04.90.92.83.15). The *Maison de la Presse* opposite *La Brasserie des Alpilles* stocks some **English-language newspapers** and paperbacks.

The town has a fairly wide choice of **accommodation**, though rates are on the high side. You may prefer to use one of the three campsites close by.

Hotels

Canto Cigalo chemin de Canto Cigalo ☎04.90.92.14.28, ⓦwww.cantocigalo.com. By the canal to the southeast of the old town, this quiet and comfortable hotel is in a secluded spot with a large garden. ❸

Le Castellet des Alpilles 6 place Mireille ☎04.90.92.07.21, ⓦwww.castelet-alpilles.com. South of the old town, past the tourist office; small and friendly, and some rooms with south-facing balconies and great views. Closed Nov–March. ❹

Cheval Blanc 6 av Fauconnet ☎04.90.92.09.28, ⓦwww.hotelcheval-blanc. One of the cheaper options (the four-person rooms are especially good value), very close to the old town. Closed Nov–Feb. ❸

Hostellerie le Chalet Fleuri 15 av Frédéric-Mistral ☎04.90.92.03.62, ⓕ04.90.92.60.28. An old-fashioned boarding house with renovated rooms: breakfast is served in the peaceful garden. Closed Jan. ❹

Gounod Ville Verte 18 place de la République ☎04.90.92.06.14, ⓦwww .hotel-gounod.com. Luxurious and centrally located hotel with ornately decorated rooms with mod cons such as flat-screen TVs. There's also a swimming pool and garden. Breakfast included. Closed late Feb to late March. ❼

Sous les Figuiers 3 av Taillandier ☎04.90.92.13.23, ⓦwww.hotel-charme-provence .com. Twelve well appointed rooms, some with their own private gardens. Swimming pool and an on-site artist's studio (art classes available). ❺

Villa Glanum 46 av Vincent-van-Gogh ☎04.90.92.03.59, ⓦwww.villaglanum.com. Next door to the archeological site; pleasant, not too expensive and has a pool. Most rooms with access for people with disabilities. ❹

Campsites

Le Mas de Nicolas av Plaisance du Touch ☎04.90.92.27.05, ⓦwww.camping-masdenicolas .com. A four-star municipal site, with its own pool, 2km along the rte de Mollèges to the northeast. Closed mid-Oct to mid-March. €17 per tent.

Monplaisir chemin Monplaisir ☎04.90.92.22.70, ⓦwww.camping-monplaisir.fr. Slightly closer, two-star campsite, 1km to the north along the rte de Maillane. Closed mid-Nov to Feb. €17.50 per tent.

Pegomas av Jean-Moulin ☎04.90.92.01.21, ⓦwww.campingpegomas.com. Three-star, with a pool, 1km east on the road to Cavaillon. Closed Nov–Feb. €15.40 per tent.

The Town

St-Rémy's compact centre makes it a pleasant place for strolling round the picturesque streets and their stylish shops, galleries and restaurants. Rue Carnot cuts through the old town from boulevard Mirabeau to boulevard Marceau to place Favier, where the **Musée des Alpilles** can be found.

The impressive archeological sites of **Glanum** and **Les Antiques** along with St-Rémy's other attractions, including **St-Paul-de-Mausole**, the psychiatric hospital whose most famous former patient is **Van Gogh**, lie south of the old town: about a ten-minute walk along av Pasteur, which becomes av Vincent-van-Gogh after the canal.

The Vieille Ville

The **Vieille Ville** is encircled by boulevards Marceau, Gambetta, Mirabeau and Victor-Hugo. To explore the old town take any of the streets leading off these boulevards and start wandering up alleyways and through immaculate leafy squares. From place de la République, on avenue de la Résistance, you'll pass the town's main church, the **Collégiale St-Martin**, a Neoclassical lump of a building of interest only for its renowned organ, painted in a surreal lime-green (recitals every Sat from July to mid-Sept at 5.30pm). The route from **rue du Parage** off boulevard Gambetta is particularly appealing with its central stream of clear water. Several ancient stately residences line its route as the street meanders up to **place Favier**, where you'll find St-Rémy's main museum.

The **Musée des Alpilles**, housed in the Hôtel Mistral de Mondragon on place Favier, a Renaissance mansion with a romantic interior courtyard (daily: July & Aug 10am–12.30pm & 2–7pm; March–June & Sept–Oct 10am–noon & 2–6pm; Nov–Feb 2–5pm; €3), gives a good introduction to the region. The collection features interesting displays on folklore, festivities and traditional crafts, plus intriguing local landscapes, some creepy portraits by Marshall Pétain's first wife and souvenirs of local boy Nostradamus.

To the south of place Favier, rue Millaud leads into **rue Hoche** where a fountain topped by a bust marks the house where **Nostradamus** was born. Only the facade of the house is contemporary with the futuristic savant, and it's not open to visitors. Heading east from here brings you to the eighteenth-century Hôtel d'Estrine, at 8 rue L'Estrine, now home of the **Centre d'Art Présence Van Gogh**. The centre hosts contemporary art exhibitions and has a permanent exhibition of Van Gogh reproductions and extracts from letters, plus an audiovisual presentation on the painter (April–Dec Tues–Sun 10am–1pm & 3–7pm; €3.20). A wide selection of Van Gogh books, prints and postcards is available from the shop.

There are many **art galleries** and boutiques scattered throughout St-Rémy, of which Le Grand Magasin, 24 rue de la Commune (June–Sept daily 10am–12.30pm & 2.30–7pm; Oct–May closed Mon), is one of the most interesting: it combines contemporary works of art with jewellery, accessories and household objects of a stylish and original nature.

South of the Vieille Ville

Outside the old town, a short way south of the tourist office on rue Jean-de-Nostredame, is the beautiful Romanesque **chapel of Notre-Dame-de-Pitié** (April–June, Sept & Oct Wed–Sun 2–6pm; July & Aug Wed–Sun 11am–1pm & 3–7pm; €2), which exhibits the art of the twentieth-century Greek painter, Mario Prassinos, who settled in the village of Eygalières, near St-Rémy. Tree forms, a favourite motif of his work, become a powerful graphic language in the series of oil paintings created for the chapel, *Les Peintures du Supplice* (*Paintings of the Suffering*), provoked by Prassinos' horror of torture.

If you keep heading south, following avenue Vincent-van-Gogh, you'll come to **Les Antiques**, a triumphal arch celebrating the Roman conquest of Marseille and a mausoleum thought to commemorate two grandsons of Augustus. Save for a certain amount of weather erosion, the mausoleum is perfectly intact. The arch is less so, but both display intricate patterning and a typically Roman sense of proportion. Les Antiques would have been a familiar sight to **Vincent van Gogh**, who, in 1889, requested that he be put away for several months. The hospital chosen by his friends was in the old monastery **St-Paul-de-Mausole**, a hundred metres or so east of Les Antiques, which remains a psychiatric clinic today. Although the regime was more prison than hospital, Van Gogh was allowed to wander out around the Alpilles and painted prolifically during his twelve-month stay. The church and cloisters can be visited (April–Oct Mon–Fri & Sun 9.30am–7pm, Sat 10am–7pm; €3.80); take avenue Edgar-Leroy or allée St-Paul from avenue Vincent-van-Gogh and continue straight ahead, following the "Zone Touris-tique" signs to the entrance. The actual hospital, which is closed to tourists, is just to the north of here. Inside, you'll be able to see a replica of Van Gogh's hospital room and several of the views that inspired the artist to produce the

150 canvases of this period, including paintings such as *Champs d'Oliviers, Le Faucher, Le Champ Clôturé* and *La Promenade du Soir*

Heading east along chemin des Carrières from the hospital, you'll see signs to the right for the **Mas de la Pyramide** (daily: June–Aug 9am–noon & 2–7pm; Sept–May 9am–noon & 2–5pm; worth waiting if there's no immediate answer to the bell at the gate; €4), an old troglodyte farm in the Roman quarries of Glanum with a field of lavender and a cherry orchard surrounded by cavernous openings into the rock, filled with ancient farm equipment and rusting bicycles. Standing in the centre of the lavender field is a twenty-metre slice of rock – the pyramid that gives the farm its name – revealing the depth of the ancient quarrying works. The farmhouse is part medieval, part Gallo-Roman and has some fascinating pictures of the owner's family who have lived here for generations.

Glanum

One of the most impressive ancient settlements in France, **GLANUM**, across the road from Les Antiques (April–Aug daily 10am–6.30pm; Sept–March Tues–Sat 10.30am–5pm; €6.50), was dug out from the alluvial deposits at the foot of the Alpilles. The site was originally a Neolithic homestead until the Gallo-Greeks, probably from Massalia (Marseille), built a city here between the second and first centuries BC. The Gallo-Romans constructed yet another town here from the end of the first century BC to the third century AD.

Glanum can be very difficult to get to grips with. Not only were the later buildings moulded on to the earlier ones, but also the fashion at the time of Christ was for a Hellenistic style. You can distinguish the Greek levels from the Roman most easily by the stones: the earlier civilization used massive hewn rocks while the Romans preferred smaller, more accurately shaped stones. The leaflet at the admission desk is helpful, as are the models and diagrams (with explanations in French) at the entrance.

Where the site narrows in the ravine at the southern end you'll find a Grecian edifice around a **spring**, the feature that made this location so desirable. Steps lead down to a pool, with a slab above for the libations of those too sick to descend. An inscription records that Agrippa was responsible for restoring it in 27 BC and for dedicating it to Valetudo, the Roman goddess of health. But **altars** to Hercules are still in evidence, while up the hill to the west are traces of a prehistoric settlement which also depended on this spring. The Gallo-Romans directed the water through canals to heat houses and of, course, to the **baths** that lie near the entrance to the site. There are superb sculptures on the Roman **Temples Geminées** (twin temples), as well as fragments of mosaics, fountains of both periods, and first-storey walls and columns.

Eating and entertainment

Throughout the year, you'll find plenty of **brasseries** and **restaurants** open in and around old St-Rémy. There are a few good options on rue Carnot: *Un Bouchon en Provence* at no. 51 (☎04.90.90.00.97; closed Thurs), has dinner menus for €16.50 and €22 focusing on Lyonnaise and Provençal cooking; and ⅍ *La Maison Jaune* at no. 15 (☎04.90.92.56.14; closed Mon & Sun eve in winter, Mon & Tues lunch in summer, plus Jan & Feb), has tempting à la carte offerings such as polenta and pigeon roasted in Baux wines, or menus for €34–62. Elsewhere, *La Gousse d'Ail* at 6 bd Marceau (☎04.90.92.16.87; closed Thurs & Fri lunch) has a €16 menu dedicated to vegetarians and hosts live jazz on Wednesday nights, while the trendy *XA*, 24 bd Mirabeau (℡04.90.92.41.23; closed Wed & Nov–March; €25 menu), serves excellent Asian-inspired food such as beef curry and shrimp with coriander and coconut milk. *Lou Planet*, at 7 place Favier (℡04.90.92.19.81; closed Oct–March), is a scenic and shaded spot to dine on crêpes (€5–7.50), and *Le Bistrot des Alpilles*, 15 bd Mirabeau (℡04.90.92.09.17; open till midnight), is a popular brasserie for *gigot d'agneau* and aïoli (dinner menu €25). Lastly, try *Le Jardin de Frédéric*, 8 bd Gambetta (℡04.90.92.27.76; closed Mon in low season), which specialises in Provençal dishes and has a €16 lunch menu.

If you're after **picnic fare**, do your shopping at the Wednesday morning **market** on the pedestrian streets of the old town or at the Saturday market in place de la Mairie. The *boulangerie* at 1 rue Carnot sells the special *épis*: a baguette made up of several rolls joined together in a zig-zag pattern. In season, you'll see and smell great bunches of basil and marjoram which are grown in abundance around St-Rémy. Aromatic oils are another speciality of the town; they are sold at *Chez Florame*, 34 bd Mirabeau (Easter–Sept daily 10am–12.30pm & 2.30–7pm; Oct–Easter closed Sun), where, from mid-July to mid-August, you can watch lavender being distilled.

The Ciné Palace on avenue Fauconnet sometimes screens undubbed English-language films (programme from the tourist office or at ℡04.90.92.37.41), but if you fancy something a little more lively, try the **disco**, *La Haute Galine*, quartier de la Galine (℡04.90.92.00.03), or the *Cocktail Club* **bar** on rue Roger-Salengro (running north from place de la République).

La Petite Crau and La Montagnette

Like La Grande Crau to the south, the plain, known as **La Petite Crau**, which stretches north from the Alpilles to the confluence of the Rhône and the Durance, is today a richly cultivated area with cherries and peaches as its main crops. Once, however, it was a swampy wasteland, the only extensive bit of solid ground being the rocky outcrop of **La Montagnette**, which runs parallel to the Rhône for 10km. Villages in the area are few and far between, built on the scattered bases of rock and often retaining their medieval elements of fortified walls and churches and tangled narrow streets. It is this Provence that inspired **Frédéric Mistral** and Vincent Van Gogh.

If you have your own **transport**, La Petite Crau and La Montagnette can easily be reached as day trips from St-Rémy, Tarascon or Avignon. By **bus**, it's more problematic, as services between the villages are sporadic. The Avignon–St-Rémy bus stops in Châteaurenard, while Boulbon, Barbentane and Tarascon are served by buses to Nîmes. There are no trains.

Markets

If you're in La Petite Crau on a Friday, the **Marché Paysan** in **Graveson**, place du Marché (early May to Oct 4–8pm) is not to be missed, with *paysans* from La Grande and La Petite Crau, the Camargue and from across the Durance selling their goats' cheeses, olives, flowers, and fruit and vegetables picked the same morning.

The ordinary morning markets here are on Friday in **Graveson**, Thursday in **Maillane** and **Noves**, Sunday in **Châteaurenard**, Wednesday in **Barbentane**, and Tuesday in **Rognonas**, the village just across the Durance from Avignon.

Châteaurenard and Noves

CHÂTEAURENARD, roughly halfway between St-Rémy and Avignon, is the main town in La Petite Crau and host to a massive wholesale fruit and vegetable market each Sunday; the produce is all locally grown and on market days the town is packed. Dominating the town's physical features are the two remaining towers of its Romanesque and Gothic medieval **castle** (May–Sept Tues-Sat 10am–noon & 2.30–6.30pm, Sun 2.30–6.30pm; Oct–April daily except Fri 3–5pm; €4), described by Frédéric Mistral as "twin horns on the forehead of a hill". Even if you're only passing through, it's worth taking the time to climb the castle's **Tour du Griffon** for the views across La Petite Crau to the Alpilles and La Montagnette. In a recess within the castle is engraved a 700-year-old troubadour poem, in Provençal, praising the beauty of the new building put up "by such a wise king".

Buses arrive on avenue Roger-Salengo, at the east end of which is the **tourist office** (July–Aug Mon–Sat 9am–noon & 3–7pm, Sun 10am–noon; Sept–June Mon–Sat 9am–noon & 2–5.45pm; ☎04.90.24.25.50, ⓦwww.chateaurenard.com). For cheap and basic **accommodation** try *Le Central*, 27 cours Carnot (☎04.90.94.10.90, ⓦwww.hotel-lecentral.com; ❸), or *Les Glycines*, 14 av Victor-Hugo (☎04.90.94.10.66, ⓦwww.resthotellesglycines.com; ❸), both with renovated rooms, the slightly better of which are at *Les Glycines*. Otherwise, there is a small and inexpensive **campsite**, *La Roquette*, at 746 av J-Mermoz (☎04.90.94.46.81, ⓦwww.camping-la-roquette.com; closed Nov–Feb; €9.70 per tent). For **food**, *La Buvette des Tours*, just below the castle, serves cheap salads, grills and pizzas on summer evenings (Wed–Sun). Alternatively, the lunch-only *Brasserie des Producteurs* at 4 rue R-Ginoux (☎04.90.94.04.61; closed Sun) offers menus from €12, while *Le Central* (see above; closed Jan) has a *plat du jour* for €7.50.

Five kilometres east of Châteaurenard, the little village of **NOVES** is typical of the area, with its fourteenth-century gateway. It is also where Laura, the subject of Petrarch's besotted sonnets, is reputed to have lived. If you fancy splashing out on a luxury stay, the *Auberge de Noves,* just outside Noves on the Châteaurenard road (☎04.90.24.28.28, ⓦwww.aubergedenoves.com; closed early Nov to mid-Dec; ❾), is a seriously expensive hotel-restaurant in a beautiful farmhouse with exquisite furnishings and impeccable service. Its restaurant (closed Sat lunch) serves such delicacies as foie gras, snails, truffles, lobster, along with plenty of fine wines (weekday lunch menu €40; dinner menu €85). For more basic comforts, Noves' **campsite** *Le Pilon d'Agel*, on the rte de Mollégès (☎04.90.95.16.23, ⓦwww.pilondagel.com; closed Oct–April; €15 per tent), offers a pool and access for people with disabilities.

Maillane and La Montagnette

The poet Frédéric Mistral was born in **MAILLANE** in 1830 and buried there in 1914. Primarily responsible for the early twentieth-century revival of all things Provençal, he won the Nobel Prize for Literature in 1904, a feat no other writer of a minority language has ever achieved. The house that he built and lived in from 1876 till the end of his life has been preserved intact as the **Museon Mistral**, 11 rue Lamartine (daily except Mon: April–Sept 9.30–11.30am & 2.30–6.30pm; Oct–March 10–11.30am & 2–4.30pm; €3.50).

La Petite Crau was Mistral's "sacred triangle", and its customs and legends were very often his primary source of inspiration. In his memoirs, Mistral describes the procession of St Anthime from **Graveson**, just north of Maillane, to La Montagnette, where on reaching the abbey church of **St-Michel-de-Frigolet**, the people spread out a feast on the perfumed grass and knocked back bottles of local wine for the rest of the day. If it hadn't rained by the time they reached home, they punished the saint by dipping him three times in a ditch.

The name of the abbey derives from *ferigoulo*, Provençal for thyme, which grows profusely in these hills, hence the perfumed grass of the feast. The thyme is also used to make a liqueur, *Le Frigolet*, which can be bought at the end of a guided tour of the **abbey church** and **cloisters** (Sun 4pm; €4). Mistral went to school in these buildings before they were returned to ecclesiastical use in the mid-nineteenth century. The highlight of the visit is the series of fourteen paintings on the *Mysteries of the Virgin Mary* by Mignard in the main church, though you may find the cloisters more spiritually inspiring.

The valleys that cut through the scrubbed white rock of **LA MONTAG-NETTE** are shaded by olive, almond and apricot trees, oaks and pines. The heights never extend above 200m, and the smell of thyme is omnipresent; easy and exhilarating **walking** country – although note that due to the risk of fires, walking is prohibited in La Montagnette from July to mid-September and horse riding restricted to between 6am and 11am.

Boulbon and Barbentane

One footpath from St-Michel-de-Frigolet takes you over the ridge and, after 5km or so, down to **BOULBON**. A strategic site overlooking the Rhône, Boulbon was heavily fortified in the Middle Ages, and today the ruins of its enormous fortress, built half within and half above a rocky escarpment, look like some picture-book crusader castle.

Eight kilometres from Boulbon, at the northern edge of La Montagnette in **BARBENTANE**, the fourteenth-century **Tour Anglica** keeps watch on the confluence of the Rhône and Durance. The town has two medieval gateways and a beautifully arcaded Renaissance building, the **Maison des Chevaliers**, plus a much more recent **Château** (guided tours April–June & Oct closed Wed; July–Sept daily 10am–noon & 2–6pm; Nov & Feb–March Sun only; €6.50), designed for grandeur rather than defence. This is a seventeenth-century ducal residence with gorgeous grey and white Tuscan marble floors, and all the vases, painted ceilings, chandeliers and delicate antique furniture that you would expect of a house still owned by generations of the same family of aristocrats. The Italianate gardens are the highlight.

For **hotel** accommodation in Barbentane, you can choose from the rudimentary comforts of *Hôtel St-Jean*, 1 le Cours (T & F 04.90.95.50.44; ❸), or the more comfortable *Castel Mouisson*, quartier Castel Mouisson (T 04.90.95.51.17, W www.hotel-castelmouisson.com; closed mid-Oct to mid-March; ❸), with good facilities and a pleasant garden and pool. There is a good **restaurant** in Maillane, *L'Oustalet Maianen* (T 04.90.95.76.17; closed Mon, Tues lunch, Sat lunch & Jan–Feb), with high quality Provençal dishes on menus at €25 and €39.

The Fête de Saint-Éloi

Boulbon celebrates the **Fête de Saint-Éloi** on the last Sunday of August. This involves chariots drawn by teams of horses in Saracen harness doing the rounds of the village, and much drinking by all the villagers. Elsewhere, notably in Graveson, Châteaurenard and Maillane, this saint, whose role is protector of beasts of burden, is celebrated on the penultimate Sunday of July.

Tarascon and Beaucaire

To the south of La Montagnette, the castles of **Beaucaire** and **Tarascon** face each other across the Rhône, the former in Languedoc on the west bank, the latter on the Provence side. Although both castles are regarded as classics, Tarascon's is the more interesting to visit; Beaucaire's tangled streets, however, make for more pleasant strolling. Tarascon has one of the most famous Provençal carnivals, based on an amphibious monster known as the *Tarasque*, and is home to the **Souleïado** textile company. Near Beaucaire, a reconstructed **Roman winery** has been put back to work.

Arrival, information and accommodation

Both towns are served by Tarascon's **train** station and have good **bus** links with Arles, Avignon and Nîmes. The **gare SNCF** is south of Tarascon's centre

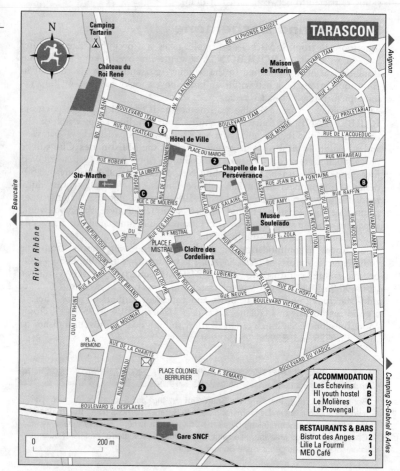

TARASCON

N

Camping Tartarin

Château du Roi René

Maison de Tartarin

BD. ALPHONSE DAUDET
BOULEVARD ITAM
RUE J. JAURÈS
RUE DU PROLETARIAT
BOULEVARD ITAM
AV. R. SALENGRO
BOULEVARD ITAM
RUE DU ROI RENÉ
RUE DU CHÂTEAU
RUE MONGE
RUE DE L'ACQUEDUC
Hôtel de Ville
PLACE DU MARCHÉ
RUE MIRABEAU
RUE ROBERT
Chapelle de la Persévérance
R. DE LA LIBERTÉ
RUE DE LA POISSONNERIE
RUE DU PROGRÈS
Ste-Marthe
RUE JEAN DE LA FONTAINE
RUE MILLAUD
RUE RASPAIL
RUE C. DE MOLIÈRES
RUE SALAIRE
RUE AMY
RUE RAFFIN
RUE PRUDHOM
RUE DE LA RÉVOLUTION
RUE DU JEU DE PAUME
BOULEVARD GAMBETTA
AV. DE LA RÉPUBLIQUE
Musée Souleïado
RUE DES HALLES
RUE DU PROGRÈS
R.F. MISTRAL
RUE E. ZOLA
RUE BLANQUI
RUE NICOLAS LAUGIER
PLACE F. MISTRAL
Cloître des Cordeliers
RUE LEDRU ROLLIN
RUE LUBIÈRES
R. PELLETAN
RUE DE L'HÔPITAL
COURS ARISTIDE BRIAND
RUE DU TOUR
RUE A. PERROT
RUE NEUVE
BOULEVARD VICTOR-HUGO
QUAI DU RHÔNE
RUE MOUNIAT
PL. A. BREMOND
RUE DE LA CHARITÉ
RUE GARIBALDI
PLACE COLONEL BERRURIER
AV. P. SEMARD
BOULEVARD DU VIADUC
BOULEVARD G. DESPLACES
Gare SNCF

River Rhône

Beaucaire

Avignon

Camping St-Gabriel & Arles

0   200 m

ACCOMMODATION
Les Échevins   A
HI youth hostel   B
Le Molières   C
Le Provençal   D

RESTAURANTS & BARS
Bistrot des Anges   2
Lilie La Fourmi   1
MEO Café   3

on boulevard Gustave-Desplaces (℡ 08.36.35.35.35). **Buses** arrive in front of the station, while opposite, on the other side of boulevard Gustave-Desplaces, is a **car park**, beyond which cours Aristide-Briand leads north to the road bridge across the Rhône. Tarascon's **tourist office** is at 16 bd Itam (July & Aug Mon–Sat 9am–7pm, Sun 9.30am–12.30pm; June & Sept Mon–Sat 9am–12.30pm & 2–6pm, Sun 9.30am–12.30pm; Oct–May Mon–Sat 9am–12.30pm & 2-5.30pm; ℡ 04.90.91.03.52, Ⓦ www.tarascon.org), a couple of hundred metres east of the château.

Beaucaire is bounded to the south by the Canal du Rhône which provides a pleasure port for the town before joining the river just below the bridge to Tarascon. Beaucaire's **tourist office** is at 24 cours Gambetta, overlooking the canal 300m from the bridge (April–June, Aug & Sept Mon–Fri 8.45am–12.15pm & 2–6pm, Sat 9.30am–12.30pm & 3–6pm: July Mon–Fri 8.45am–12.15pm & 2–6pm, Sat 9.30am–12.30pm & 3–6pm, Sun 9.30am–12.30pm; Oct–March Mon–Fri 8.45am–12.15pm & 2–6pm; ℡ 04.66.59.26.57, Ⓦ www .ot-beaucaire.fr). You can **hire boats** in Beaucaire at very reasonable prices from the Capitainerie du Port on cours Sadi-Carnot on the south side of the canal, opposite the tourist office.

Tarascon has more **accommodation** to offer than Beaucaire, including a youth hostel, but it should be easy to find a room in either town; and as the centre of Beaucaire is just a kilometre's walk away from that of Tarascon, across the bridge, it doesn't really matter which of the two you choose.

Hotels

Les Échevins 26 bd Itam, Tarascon
℡ 04.90.91.01.70, Ⓦ www.hotel-echevins.com. Reasonable rooms in a handsome town house. Closed Nov–April. ❹

Le Molieres 7 rue du Progres, Tarascon
℡ 04.90.43.52.52, Ⓦ www.chambres-tarascon .com. Three large, ornately decorated rooms in a grand seventeenth-century mansion right in the town centre. There's a garden and two small roof-top terraces. ❻

Napoléon 4 place Frédéric-Mistral, Beaucaire
℡ 04.66.59.05.17. A good budget choice by the river with very cheap singles. Only six rooms, so book ahead. ❷

Le Provençal 12 cours A-Briand, Tarascon
℡ 04.90.91.11.41, Ⓔ leprovencalmbc@orange.fr. Family-run hotel with paper-thin walls, but each room has en-suite facilities. Good location. ❷

Robinson rte de Remoulins, Beaucaire
℡ 04.66.59.21.32, Ⓦ www.hotel-robinson.fr. Two kilometres north of Beaucaire on the D986, with bright, pleasant rooms, a pool and tennis court. Closed early Feb to early March. ❹

Hostels and campsites

Youth hostel 31 bd Gambetta, Tarascon
℡ 04.90.91.04.08, Ⓔ tarascon@fuaj.org. About 850m northeast of the gare SNCF. Well-maintained town house with 65 dormitory beds; 11pm curfew. €11 per person (breakfast €3.40). Reception 8–9am & 6–10pm. Closed mid-Oct to mid-March.

Camping St-Gabriel Mas Ginoux, rte de Fontvieille, Tarascon ℡ & ℗ 04.90.91.19.83. A two-star site with a pool 5km southeast of town off the Arles road. €13.50 per tent. Closed mid-Dec to Jan.

Camping Tartarin rte de Vallabrègues, Tarascon
℡ 04.90.91.01.46, ℗ 04.90.47.64.54. A two-star site right beside the river, just north of the castle. €11.40 per tent. Closed Nov–March.

Tarascon

The **Château du Roi René**, to the north of the centre (April–Aug daily 10am–6.30pm; Sept–March Tues–Sun 10.30am–5pm; guided tours every hour; €6.50), is the obvious sight to head for, a vast impregnable mass of stone, beautifully restored to its defensive fifteenth-century pose. Its towers facing the enemy across the river are square and those at the back are round. Nowhere on the exterior is there any hint of softness. Inside, however, is another matter. The castle was a residence of King René of Provence, and of his father who planned

The Tarasque and Tartarin

On the last full weekend of June, the **Tarasque**, a mythical 6m-long creature with glaring eyes and shark-size teeth, storms the streets of Tarascon in the fashion of a Chinese dragon, its tail swishing back and forth to the screaming delight of all the children. It is said to have been tamed by Saint Martha after a long history of clambering out of the Rhône, gobbling people and destroying the ditches and dams of the Camargue with its long crocodile-like tail. The monster serves as a reminder of natural catastrophe, in particular floods, kept at bay in this region by the never totally reliable drainage ditches and walls. The weekend-long festivities involve public balls, bull and equestrian events and a firework and music finale.

Also celebrated at the same time is another local legend, that of **Tartarin**, a mid-nineteenth-century literary character, created by Alphonse Daudet who came from this part of Provence. Tartarin makes out he is a great adventurer, scaling Mont Blanc, hunting leopards in Algeria, bringing back exotic trees for his garden at 55 bis bd Itam. The address is real, and is dedicated to the fictional character: **Maison de Tartarin** (April–June & Sept Mon, Tues, Thurs & Fri 9.30am–noon & 2–7pm; July & Aug daily except Wed & Sun 9.30am–noon & 2–7pm; Oct Mon, Tues, Thurs & Fri 9am–noon & 1.30–6pm; €2), where a waxwork figure waits, gun in hand, in the hall. During the Tarasque procession, a local man, chosen for his fat-bellied figure, strolls through the town as Tartarin.

the building. It was designed with all the luxury that the period permitted. The mullioned windows and vaulted ceilings of the royal apartments and the spiral staircase that overlook the **cour d'honneur** all have graceful Gothic lines, and in the **Salle des Festins** (banqueting hall) on the ground floor and the **Salle d'Apparat** (stateroom) on the first floor, the wooden ceilings are painted with monsters and other medieval motifs. In several rooms graffiti dating from the fifteenth to the twentieth century testifies to the castle's long use as a prison. For example, in the **Salles des Gallères** are carvings of boats, some dating from the crusades, made by prisoners awaiting judgement. A visit ends with a climb up to the **roof**, from which revolutionaries and counter-revolutionaries were thrown in the 1790s. Aside from the sight of Tarascon's paper mill just downstream, the views are impressive and include, to the west, the far less substantial but still dramatic castle of Beaucaire.

The **Collégiale Royale Sainte-Marthe**, which stands across the street from the castle (daily: 8am–noon & 2–6pm; free), contains the tomb of Martha, the saint who saved the town from the Tarasque monster, in its crypt; St Martha also appears in the paintings by Nicolas Mignard and Vien that decorate the Gothic interior along with works by Pierre Parrocel and Van Loo.

In the centre of the town, on place Frédéric-Mistral off rue Ledru-Rollin, the sixteenth-century **Cloître des Cordeliers** (April–Sept Mon-Sat 10am–noon & 2.30–6.30pm; Oct-Nov Mon-Sat 10am–noon & 2–6pm; free) has had its three aisles of light cream stone beautifully restored. It's used for exhibitions, sometimes of contemporary paintings, often by young artists. Other exhibitions take place alongside a permanent collection of crib figures in the **Chapelle de la Persévérance** at 8 rue Proudhom (hours and price depend upon the exhibition; check at the tourist office), part of a former "refuge" for securing women and girls suspected of living "bad lives". Further down rue Proudhom, at no. 39, is the **Musée Souleïado** (May–Sept daily 10am–6pm; Oct–April Tues–Sat 10am–5pm; ☎04.90.91.50.51; €6.10), a tribute to the family business that revived the 200-year-old Tarascon tradition of making brightly coloured, patterned, printed fabrics, now sold in shops all over Provence. The museum houses the eighteenth-century wood blocks from which many of the patterns are still made, and tastefully displays products including a table setting dedicated to the bulls of the Camargue.

The rest of **the town**, with its streets of Renaissance town houses, the classical town hall and medieval arcades along rue des Halles, is relatively subdued, only really coming to life during the Tuesday morning **market**.

Beaucaire

A statue of a bull standing at the head of the Canal du Rhône greets you as you arrive in **BEAUCAIRE** from Tarascon. To the north, between the castle and the river, is a bullring and a theatre on the site of the old **champs de foire**. The fair, founded in 1217, was one of the largest in medieval Europe, attracting traders from both sides and both ends of the Mediterranean as well as merchants from the north along the Rhône. The fairs reached their heyday in the eighteenth century but died out in the nineteenth with the onset of rail freight.

The faded facades of the classical mansions and arcades around **place de la République**, **rue de la République** and **place Clemenceau**, many with plaques and historical descriptions (in French), give the town its character. The Mansart-designed **Hôtel de Ville** and the much more modern market halls on place Clemenceau are very attractive, as is the seventeenth-century house at 23 rue de la République. Between the two is the eighteenth-century church of **Notre-Dame-des-Pommiers**, with a frieze from its Romanesque predecessor embedded in the eastern wall, visible from rue Charlier.

To reach the **Château Royale de Beaucaire**, follow the ramparts north of the bridge and then cut into town on rue Victor-Hugo, cross place de la République and follow rue de la République until you reach place du Château. Every afternoon an hourly **falconry display** with medieval costumes and music is staged here (daily except Wed: April–June 2–4.30pm; July & Aug 3–6pm; March & Sept–Nov 2.30–4.30pm; €9). It's great for kids, and the birds perform very well, but it's a shame you can no longer ramble freely around the ruins or climb to the top of the tower to appreciate the great advantage it had over Tarascon, whose castle lies far below. The **gardens**, however, are open for independent exploration (daily except Tues: April–June 10am–noon & 2.15–6.15pm; July & Aug 10am–noon & 2–7.15pm; Sept & Oct 10am–noon & 2–6pm; Nov–March 10am–noon & 2–5.15pm; closed public hols; free), and contain the **Musée Auguste-Jacquet** (same hours; €4.40) with its small but interesting collection of Roman remains, mostly from a mausoleum, and documents relating to the medieval fair.

The castle was destroyed in 1632 on Richelieu's orders when the town gave support to one of the cardinal's rivals, the duc de Montmorency. However, one irregular-sided tower still stands intact with the battlements and machicolations typical of thirteenth-century military strategy. Despite Richelieu's efforts, most of the walls overlooking the river have survived, as has the monumental staircase linking the upper and lower sections of the castle and a Romanesque chapel.

Four kilometres along the road to Bellegarde lies the wine-producing domaine of **La Mas des Tourelles** (July & Aug daily 10am–noon & 2–7pm; April–June, Sept & Oct daily 2–6pm; Nov–March Sat only 2–6pm; €4.80, includes a tasting), where you'll find a reconstructed Roman winery with its oak trunk press and amphorae, or vases. The wine-maker and archeologist proprietor has put the Roman cellars to work again, using precise classical methods and recipes. Some of these are rather strange; apparently the Romans liked fortifying their wine with honey or seasoning it with fenugreek, dried iris bulbs, quince and pigs' blood.

Eating and drinking

Eating cheaply in Tarascon and Beaucaire is not a problem, but quality can be variable. In Tarascon, the best bet is the *Bistrot des Anges*, on place du Marché, which has alluring Provençal dishes such as *carpaccio de taureau* and seafood tart (℡04.90.91.05.11; €17 menu). Otherwise, *Lilie La Fourmi*, 14 bd Itam (℡06.62.25.55.93; closed Sun & evenings; €3.50–8), is a good spot for lunch, offering paninis or more filling hot meals. In Beaucaire, quai Générale-de-Gaulle, on the north side of the canal, is where you'll find the best concentration of restaurants and cafés, of which *Le Soleil*, at no. 30 (℡04.66.59.28.52), featuring *tellines* from the Camargue on its €16 menu, and *Nord au Sud*, at no. 27 ter, (℡04.66.59.02.55; €12), specializing in mussels, stand out. Beaucaire's most original food, however, is served at *Le Velo* on picturesque place de la République (℡06.10.48.17.32; €9–11), where the *plat du jour* could be melon soup or salmon cooked in tea. By far the best place for a **drink** is the trendy lounge-style *MEO Café*, on place Colonel Berrurier by the gare SNCF in Tarascon (℡04.90.91.47.74; weekdays until 9pm, weekend until 12.30pm).

Market day in Tarascon is on Tuesday and takes place along rue des Halles; in Beaucaire there's a market on Thursday and Sunday in the covered halls on place Clemenceau and cours Gambetta. On the first Friday of the month Beaucaire also has a **bric-a-brac** market on cours Gambetta.

The Camargue

The area below Arles, spreading across the Rhône delta and bounded to the west by the Petit Rhône, to the east by the Grand Rhône and to the south by the Mediterranean Sea, is known as the **Camargue**. This drained, ditched and now protected land is distinct from the rest of Provence in every sense, from its distinct wildlife and agriculture to the idiosyncratic people who have chosen to live here.

The region is home to the **bulls** and the **white horses** that the Camargue *gardians* or herdsmen ride. Neither animal is truly wild though both run in semi-liberty. In recent times new strains of bull have been introduced because numbers were getting perilously low. The Camargue horse remains a distinct breed, of unknown origin, is born dark brown or black, and turns white around its fourth year. It is never stabled, surviving the humid heat of summer and the wind-racked winter cold outdoors. The *gardians* likewise are a hardy community. Their traditional homes, or *cabanes*, are thatched and windowless one-storey structures, with bulls' horns over the doors to ward off evil spirits. They still conform, to some extent, to the popular cowboy myth, and play a major role in guarding Camarguais traditions. Throughout the summer, with spectacles involving bulls and horses in every village arena, they're kept busy and the work carries local glamour. Winter is a good deal harder, and fewer and fewer Camarguais property owners can afford the extravagant use of land that bull-rearing requires.

The two towns of the Camargue are as different as they could possibly be. **Les Stes-Maries–de–la–Mer** is the area's overcrowded resort, the place people living in and around Avignon come for a day at the beach and famous for its gypsy gathering in May. The much quieter **Salin-de-Giraud** is linked to the

Wildlife, agriculture and industry

The bulls and horses are just one element in the Camargue's exceptionally rich **wildlife**, which includes flamingoes, marsh- and seabirds, waterfowl and birds of prey; wild boars, beavers and badgers; tree frogs, water snakes and pond turtles; and a rich **flora** of reeds, wild irises, tamarisk, wild rosemary and famous juniper trees, which grow to a height of 6m and form the Bois des Rièges on the islands between the Étang du Vaccarès and the sea, part of the central **National Reserve** to which access is restricted to those with professional research credentials. The whole of the Camargue is a Parc Naturel Régional, with great efforts made to keep an equilibrium between tourism, agriculture, industry and hunting on the one hand, and the indigenous ecosystems on the other.

After World War II, the northern marshes were drained and re-irrigated with fresh water. The main crop planted was rice, established so successfully that by the 1960s the Camargue was providing three-quarters of all French consumption of the grain – although these days the industry is struggling to hold its own against cheaper imports. Vines were also reintroduced, and in the nineteenth century they survived the infestation of phylloxera that devastated every other wine-producing region because their stems were under water. There are other crops – wheat, fruit orchards and the ubiquitous rapeseed – as well as trees in isolated clumps. To the east, along the last stretch of the Grand Rhône, the chief business is the production of salt, first organized in the Camargue by the Romans in the first century AD, and now one of the biggest saltworks in the world. The saltpans and pyramids add an extraterrestrial feel to the Camargue landscape.

Though the Étang du Vaccarès, the Réserve des Impériaux and the central islands are out of bounds, there are paths and sea dykes from which their inhabitants can be watched, and special nature trails (detailed on p.128). The ideal period for bird-watching is the mating season from April to June, with the greatest number of flamingos present between April and September.

industrial complex around the Golfe de Fos. Such villages as are found are little more than hamlets. The rest of the habitations are farmhouses, or *mas*, set well back from the handful of roads, and not within easy walking distance of their neighbours.

There's really no **ideal time** for visiting the Camargue. If you have the sort of skin that attracts **mosquitoes**, then the months from March to November could be unbearable. Staying right beside the sea will be okay, but elsewhere you'll need serious chemical weaponry. Biting flies are also prevalent and can take away much of the pleasure of cycling around this hill-less land. The other problem is the wind, which in autumn and winter can be strong enough to knock you off your bike. Conversely, in summer the weather can be so hot and humid that the slightest movement is an effort. For this reason, it may be better to make Arles your base and visit the Camargue on day-trips.

Transport

There are fairly frequent **bus services** between Arles and Stes-Maries, but fewer between Arles and Salin, and there's no direct service between Stes-Maries and Salin. Timetables are available at the Boutique des Transports at the *halte routière* in Arles. For **drivers and cyclists** the main thing to be wary of is taking your car or bike along the dykes. Maps and road signs show which routes are closed to vehicles and which are accessible only at low tide, but they don't warn you about the surface you'll be driving along. The other

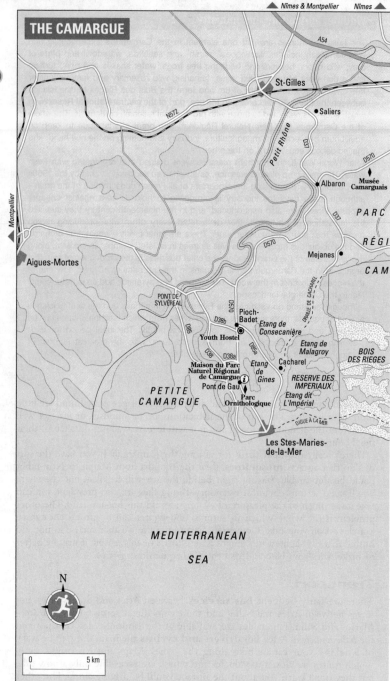

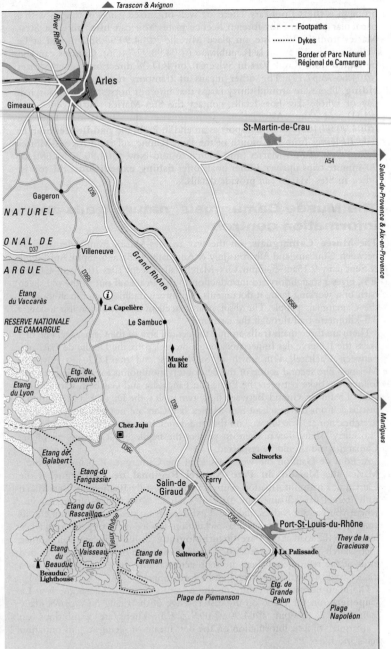

problem is **theft** from cars. There are well-organized gangs of thieves with a particular penchant for foreign licence plates. You can **hire bikes** at Stes-Maries from Le Vélociste, on place Mireille (℡04.90.97.83.26), and at Le Vélo Saintois, 19 av de la République (℡04.90.97.74.56). **Canoes** can also be rented from Kayak Vert in Sylvéréal, on RD 38 direction Aigues-Mortes (℡04.66.73.57.17). The other means of transport to consider is **horse-riding**. There are around thirty farms that hire out horses, by the hour, half day or whole day. For details, contact the Stes-Maries tourist office (see p.131) or the Association Camarguaise du Tourisme Équestre (℡04.90.97.10.40). For transport as an end in itself, the **paddle steamer** *Le Tiki III* leaves from the mouth of the Petit Rhône, off rte d'Aigues-Mortes 2.5km west of Stes-Maries (mid-March to mid-Nov; ℡04.90.97.81.68), for 90-minute trips upriver. Other boats offer **fishing expeditions;** the tourist office in Stes-Maries can provide details.

The Musée Camarguais, nature trails and information centres

The **Musée Camarguais**, on the way to Stes-Maries from Arles, halfway between Gimeaux and Albaron (July & Aug daily 9.15am–6.45pm; April–June & Sept daily 9.15am–5.45pm; Oct–March daily except Tues 10.15am–4.45pm; €5), gives a straightforward introduction to the area. Laid out in the old sheep barn of a working farm, it documents the history, traditions and livelihoods of the Camarguais people. The displays are excellent and you can also follow a 3.5-kilometre trail through the farmland.

There are three main **trails** around the central area of the Camargue. The first skirts the Réserve des Impériaux along a drover's path, the Draille de Cacharel, between Cacharel, 4km north of Ste-Maries, and the D37 just north of Méjanes. The second is one of the best observation points for **flamingoes** and follows the dyke between the Étangs du Fangassier and Galabert, starting 5km west of Salin-de-Giraud. Between these two trails is the Digue à la Mer running just back from the beach of Stes-Maries' bay. Cars are not permitted on these stretches, nor are you allowed on the sand dunes. In fact, you'll see a great many "no entry" signs; they're there to protect the fragile eco-environment of the Camargue and should be respected.

At Pont de Gau, on the western side of the Camargue, 4km north of Stes-Maries, the **Maison du Parc Naturel Régional de Camargue** is the Camargue's main information centre (April–Sept daily 10am–6pm; Oct–March daily except Fri 9.30am–5pm; ℡04.90.97.86.32; ⊛www.parc-camargue.com), where you can see videos, slides and exhibitions on the local environment, its ecosystems and fragility, as well as picking up detailed maps of paths and dykes. Just down the road at the **Parc Ornithologique** (daily: April–Sept 9am–sunset; Oct–March 10am–sunset; €6.50), aviaries house some of the less easily spotted birds of the region, and there are trails across a thirty-acre marsh as well as a longer walk, all with ample signs and information.

The main information centre on the eastern side of the Camargue is at **La Capelière**, on the D36b on the eastern edge of the Étang du Vaccarès (daily 9am–1pm & 2–6pm; ℡04.90.97.00.97; €3). There are exhibitions on Camargue wildlife, information on the best means of seeing it, plus initiation trails and hides.

A short way past Le Sambuc, on the way to Salin, the Domaine Petit Manusclat is home to the **Musée du Riz** (daily 9am–6pm, but call ahead since there is often no one there; ℡04.90.97.29.44 ; €4), a small museum dedicated to rice, with waxwork scenes, tools and other dusty paraphernalia, plus a shop where you can buy the local rice and rice cakes.

Further south, 7km beyond Salin-de-Giraud just off the D36d beside the Grand Rhône, **La Palissade** (daily: mid-June to mid-Sept 9am–6pm; mid-Sept to mid-June 9am–5pm; €3) concentrates on the fauna and flora of its neighbouring lagoons. It has a small and rather dull exhibition, but a good nine-kilometre trail past duck and flamingo nesting grounds, as well as a shorter 1.5-kilometre path. It also offers hour- or two-hour-long guided horseback tours for €15 and €25 per person respectively.

Les Stes-Maries-de-la-Mer

LES STES-MARIES-DE-LA-MER, 36km south of Arles, is the town most people head for in the Camargue. Unlike the rest of the area, this is a built-up (even overdeveloped) seaside resort, with a character and pace much more akin to other beach areas along the French south coast than the wild and empty land that surrounds it. Indeed, Stes-Maries is your archetypal seaside resort, with miles of beaches (always packed with people throughout the summer), a pleasure port with boat trips to the lagoons, horses to ride and water sports. The arenas for bullfights, cavalcades and other entertainment are

---

The legend of Sarah and the gypsy festivals

Sarah was the servant of Mary Jacobé, Jesus's aunt, and Mary Salomé, mother of two of the apostles, who, along with Mary Magdalene and various other New Testament characters, were driven out of Palestine by the Jews and put on a boat without sails and oars – or so the story goes.

The boat subsequently drifted effortlessly to an island in the mouth of the Rhône where the Egyptian god Ra was worshipped. Here Mary Jacobé, Mary Salomé and Sarah, who was herself Egyptian, settled to carry out conversion work while the others headed off for other parts of Provence. In 1448 their relics were "discovered" in the fortress **church** of Stes-Maries on the former island, around the time that the Romanies were migrating into the area from the Balkans and from Spain. It's thought the two strands may have been reunited in Provence.

The gypsies adopted Sarah as their patron saint and have been making their **pilgrimage** to Stes-Maries since the sixteenth century. It's a time for weddings and baptisms as well as music, dancing and fervent religious activities. On May 24, after Mass, the shrines of the saints are lowered from the high chapel to an altar where the faithful stretch out their arms to touch them. Then the statue of Sarah is carried by the gypsies to the sea. On the following day the statues of Mary Jacobé and Mary Salomé, sitting in a wooden boat, follow the same route, accompanied by the mounted *gardians* in full Camargue dress, Arlesians in traditional costume, and all and sundry present. The sea, the Camargue, the pilgrims and the gypsies are blessed by the bishop from a fishing boat, before the procession returns to the church with much bell-ringing, guitar playing, tambourines and singing. Another ceremony in the afternoon sees the shrines lifted back up to their chapel.

In recent years the authorities have considered the event to be getting out of hand and there's now a heavy police presence and the all-night candle-lit vigil in the church has been banned. There is a certain amount of hostility between some townspeople and the *gitans*, though the municipality has actively countered the racism. It's a wonderful event to be part of, but inevitably makes finding accommodation in the town impossible. Another pilgrimage takes place on the Sunday closest to October 22, dedicated solely to Mary Jacobé and Mary Salomé and without the participation of the gypsies.

△ The gypsey pilgrimage of Les Stes-Maries-de-la-Mer

one of the rare features of the town that evoke, albeit in a rather general way, Camarguais culture.

Arrival and accommodation

Buses from Arles arrive at the end of av d'Arles. The **tourist office** is on the seafront at 5 av Van-Gogh (daily: Jan, Feb, Nov & Dec 9am–5pm; March & Oct 9am–6pm; April–June & Sept 9am–7pm; July & Aug 9am–8pm; ☏04.90.97.82.55, ⊛www.saintesmaries.com), five minutes' walk from the bus stop.

From April to October **rooms** in Stes-Maries need to be booked in advance, and for the Romany festival, several months before. Prices go up considerably during the summer and at any time of the year are more expensive than at Arles. Outlying *mas* (farmhouses) renting out rooms tend to be quite expensive. **Camping** on the beach is not officially tolerated, but even at Stes-Maries people sleeping beneath the stars rarely get told to move on. The fifteen-kilometre plage de Piemanson, also known as the plage d'Arles, south of Salin-de-Giraud, 10km east of Stes-Maries, is a favoured venue for *camping sauvage* in summer.

Hotels

Cacharel rte de Cacharel, 4km north on D85a ☏04.90.97.95.44, ⊛www.hotel-cacharel.com. Expensive rooms in one of the Camargue's oldest farms, with chimneys to warm you in winter and a pool to cool off in summer. ❼

Camille 13 av de la Plage ☏04.90.97.80.26, ⊛www.hotel-camille.camargue.fr. Characterless interior, but some rooms have sea views. A/c optional. Closed Nov–Feb. ❸

Le Dauphin Bleu/La Brise de Mer 31 av G-Leroy ☏04.90.97.80.21, ⊛www.hotel-dauphin-bleu.camargue.fr. Rather austere rooms, the better ones with balconies overlooking the sea. ❹

Le Fangassier 12 rte de Cacharel ☏04.90.97.85.02, ⊛www.fangassier.camargue.fr. Pleasant hotel in the centre of town, with friendly staff. Closed mid-Nov to mid-Dec & Jan to Feb. ❸

Le Flamant Rose in Albaron between Arles and Stes-Maries ☏04.90.97.10.18, ⊛www.leflamantrose.camargue.fr. Brightly decorated rooms, some more tastefully done than others, some distance from Stes-Maries. ❸

Mangio Fango rte d'Arles ☏04.90.97.80.56, ⊛www.hotelmangiofango.com. About 600m from Stes-Maries, overlooking the Étang des Launes with pool and patios. Closed mid-Nov to mid-Dec. ❻

Le Mediterranée 4 rue Frédéric-Mistral ☏04.90.97.82.09, ⊛www.mediterraneehotel.com. A very verdant and charming hotel in a good, central location with attractively renovated rooms. Closed Jan. ❸

Hôtel de la Plage 2 rue Victor-Hugo ☏04.90.97.85.09, ℻04.90.97.71.32. Modern hotel 100m from the sea, all rooms with a/c,

en-suite bathrooms and satellite TV. Closed Jan & Feb. ❸

Hostellerie du Pont de Gau rte d'Arles, Pont de Gau, 4km north of Stes-Maries ☏04.90.97.81.53, ⊛www.pointdegau.camargue.fr. Old-fashioned Camarguais decor and a good restaurant close to the Parc Ornithologique. Closed Jan to mid-Feb. ❸

Rièges rte de Cacharel, Stes-Maries ☏04.90.97.85.07, ⊛www.hoteldesrieges.com. Down a track signed off the D85a close to Stes-Maries. An upmarket hotel in an old farmhouse, with swimming pool and garden. Closed mid-Nov to mid-Dec & Jan. ❺

Les Vagues 12 av T-Aubunel ☏ & ℻04.90.97.84.40. A friendly option overlooking the pleasure port on the rte d'Aigues-Mortes. Worth paying a little extra for a balcony. Closed Feb. ❷

Hostel, campsites and chambre d'hôtes

Hostel in Pioch-Badet hamlet, 10km north of Stes-Maries on the Arles–Stes-Maries bus route ☏04.90.97.51.72, ℻04.90.97.54.88. Set in an old school, with rooms holding three to ten beds (€27.30, half board obligatory). Horse rides organized and bikes for rent. Reception 7–10.30am & 5–11pm.

Camping La Brise rue Marcel-Carrière on the east side of Stes-Maries ☏04.90.97.84.67, ℻04.90.97.72.01. On the Arles-Stes-Maries bus route (stop "La Brise"). Three-star site with a pool and laundry facilities, and fridges for hire. €19.80 per tent. Closed mid-Nov to mid-Dec.

Camping Le Clos du Rhône at the mouth of the Petit Rhône, 2km west of Stes-Maries on the rte

d'Aigues-Mortes ℡ 04.90.97.85.99,
℻ 04.90.97.78.85. Busy four-star site with a pool,
laundry and shop. €22.60 per tent. Closed
Oct–March.

Mas de Pioch Pioch-Badet, 10km north of Stes-
Maries ℡ 04.90.97.50.06, ⓦ www.manadecavallini
.com. Chambre d'hôte with a pool and large rooms.
Excellent value but needs booking well in advance. ❸

The Town

Though grossly commercialized, Stes-Maries is still a pretty town with its streets
of white houses and the grey-gold Romanesque **church**, fortified in the
fourteenth century in response to frequent attacks by pirates. Inside, at the back
of the crypt, is the tinselled and sequined statue of Sarah (see box on p.129),
always surrounded by candles and abandoned crutches and calipers. The church
itself has beautifully pure lines and fabulous acoustics, and during the time of
the Saracen raids it provided shelter for all the villagers and even has its own
freshwater well. Some of the best views of the Camargue are from the top of
the church tower (July & Aug 10am–sunset; March–June & Sept to mid-Nov
10am–12.30pm & 2pm–sunset; €2).

The local **Musée Baroncelli**, on rue Victor–Hugo (opening hours vary, check
with tourist office; €1.50), is named after the man who, in 1935, was responsible, along with various *gardians*, for initiating the gypsies' procession down to
the sea with Sarah. This was motivated by a desire to give a special place in the
pilgrimage to the Romanies. The museum covers this event, other Camarguais
traditions and the region's fauna and flora.

Eating and drinking

On summer evenings every other bar and restaurant has flamenco guitarists
playing on the *terrasses* while the streets are full of buskers with a crazy variety
of instruments. The atmosphere can be carnival or tackily artificial, depending
on your mood.

Although there are plenty of **restaurants** to choose from in Stes-Maries, few
are inexpensive: out of season, however, the quality improves, and the prices
come down. The **specialities** of the Camargue include *tellines*, tiny shiny
shellfish served with garlic mayonnaise; *gardianne de taureau*, bull's meat cooked
in wine, vegetables and Provençal herbs; eels from the Vaccarès; rice, asparagus
and wild duck from the district; and *poutargue des Stes-Maries*, a mullet roe dish.
The town **market** takes place on place des Gitans every Monday and Friday.

Restaurants

Belvédère av Gilbert Roy at the corner of av Léon
Gambetta ℡ 04.90.97.92.87. An ordinary menu of
steaks, spaghetti and salads (€7–10), but one of
the few places where you get a sea view while you
eat. Good selection of ice creams. Closed Wed mid-
Nov to mid-Jan.
Bodega Kahlua 8 rue de la République
℡ 04.90.97.98.41. Tapas (€3.50), pizzas (€7–14),
grills (€13-15) and cocktails served on the

terrasse overlooking place des Gitans. Open from
5pm.
Le Delta 1 place Mireille ℡ 04.90.97.81.12. Mostly
seafood, with regional specialities such as *bourride
de baudroie* and *aïoli de morue*, and *tellines* on the
€18.50 menu. Menus €10–26. Closed Mon & Jan.
Les Montilles 2 rue Paul Peyron
℡ 04.90.97.73.83. Inexpensive menus (from €12),
several bull's meat dishes and a friendly atmosphere. Closed Sun in Jan.

Salin-de-Giraud and around

In total contrast to Stes-Maries, **SALIN–DE-GIRAUD**, just west of the Grand
Rhône in the southeastern corner of the Camargue, is an industrial village,
based on the saltworks company and its related chemical factory, with workers'
houses built on a strict grid pattern during the Second Empire.

If you want to take a look at the lunar landscape of the **salt piles**, there's a viewing point with information panels just south of Salin off the D36d. The saltworks here cover an area of 110 square kilometres and produce 800,000 tonnes a year for domestic use and export. Across the Grand Rhône (there's a daily ferry, the bac de Barcarin, at Salin; every 15min; €4.50) and downstream you can see **Port-St-Louis-du-Rhône**, where the rice and salt of the Camargue are loaded onto ships, and where, surprisingly, a small fishing fleet still operates.

There are two reasonable **hotels** in the village: *Les Saladelles*, 4 rue des Arènes (℡04.42.86.83.87, ℻04.42.48.81.89; ❷), a traditional, family-run hotel with a popular restaurant; and *La Camargue*, 58 bd de la Camargue (℡04.42.86.88.52, ℻04.42.86.83.95; closed Jan; ❸), with a little less character, but more spacious rooms.

Between Arles and Salin on the D36c, near the Mas St-Bertrand, the **restaurant** *Chez Juju* (℡04.42.86.83.86; closed Wed eve & Thurs) is worth a visit if you like fish. You select your catch and pay according to its weight (count on spending around €25). Along with the usual fish and seafood, you can try freshly scooped *tellines*, and, while not cheap, it's the best Camarguais dining experience.

Travel details

Trains

Arles to: Avignon (17 daily; 20min); Avignon TGV (2 daily; 20min); Marseille (23 daily; 45min–1hr); Narbonne (5 daily; 2hr); Nîmes (7 daily; 30min); Tarascon (4 daily; 10min).

Buses

Arles to: Aix (4 daily; 1hr 30min); Albaron (7 daily; 30min); Avignon (6 daily; 1hr); Avignon TGV (9 daily; 55min); Les Baux (4 daily; 35min); Le Sambuc (Mon–Sat 3 daily, Sun 2 daily; 35min); Raphèle (11 daily; 15min); Salin (Mon–Sat 3 daily, Sun 2 daily; 1hr 10min); Salon (6 daily; 50min–1hr 15min); Stes-Maries (7 daily; 50min); St-Rémy (4 daily; 50min); Tarascon (10 daily; 20min).

St-Rémy to: Arles (3 daily; 40min); Avignon (7 daily; 40min); Les Baux (4 daily; 15min); Cavaillon (3 daily; 35min).

Tarascon to: Arles (10 daily; 20min); Barbentane (5 daily; 25min); Boulbon (5 daily; 10min).

Avignon and the Vaucluse

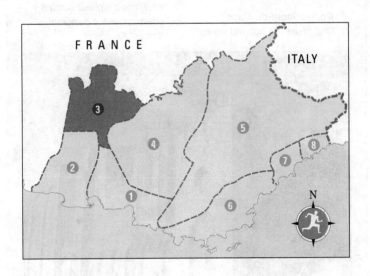

CHAPTER 3 **Highlights**

* **Palais des Papes** Of all Avignon's spectacular monuments and museums, the palace of the popes provides the most imposing backdrop for the Festival d'Avignon, held each July. See p.146

* **Villeneuve-lès-Avignon** More laid back than its bigger cousin across the river, Villeneuve has no shortage of impressive sights. See p.153

* **Châteauneuf-du-Pape** Châteauneuf's rich red wines are some of the most famous in the world. See p.157

* **Vaison's haute ville** Wander through quiet medieval streets up to a ruined cliff-top castle. See p.167

* **Les Dentelles** This region of jagged limestone pinnacles is home to some exceptional and varied wines, as well as plenty of good hiking trails. See p.170

* **Mont Ventoux** Western Provence's highest summit offers unrivalled panoramas. See p.173

△ Palais des Papes, Avignon

Avignon and the Vaucluse

The Rhône winds up through the Bouches du Rhône and, at the point where it meets the River Durance, becomes the western border of the **Vaucluse département**. This was also the erstwhile frontier between Provence and France, with **Avignon** on the Provençal side, the great city of the popes from medieval times until the Revolution, squaring off against the heavily fortified town of **Villeneuve-lès-Avignon** across the river on the French side; to this day Villeneuve remains officially outside Provence in the Languedoc *région*.

As an area with a distinct identity, the Vaucluse dates only from the Revolution. It was created to tidy up all the bits and pieces: the papal territory of the Comtat Venaisson that became part of France in 1791, the principality of Orange won by Louis XIV in 1713, plus parts of Provence that didn't fit happily into the initial three *départements* drawn up in 1791. It's still a bit untidy, with the **Papal Enclave** surrounded by the Drôme *département*, but that apart, it has the natural boundaries of the Rhône, **Mont Ventoux**, the limit of the **Vaucluse plateau** and the **River Durance**. The Durance flows east into the Luberon, the area occupying the southeastern corner of the Vaucluse covered in Chapter 4.

Avignon is the major conurbation of western Provence, attracting thousands of visitors each year by virtue of its rich papal history and longstanding position as one of France's artistic centres. Like Avignon, **Carpentras** was strongly papal, while the other urban centres of **Orange**, **Vaison-la-Romaine** and **Cavaillon** were once part of the imperial Roman belt, with Orange's immaculately preserved Roman theatre as impressive a sight as Avignon's papal palace.

Away from the monuments, museums and ruins, the villages and countryside of this part of Provence are also of great appeal. Just north of Avignon, the vineyards of **Châteauneuf-du-Pape** are the most famous in a green sweep of rich wine-producing country that stretches from the banks of the Rhône northeast past the jagged hills of **the Dentelles** to the bare, imposing slopes of Mont Ventoux. South of here, the **River Sorgue**, with its many channels, flows to its mysterious source at **Fontaine-de-Vaucluse**.

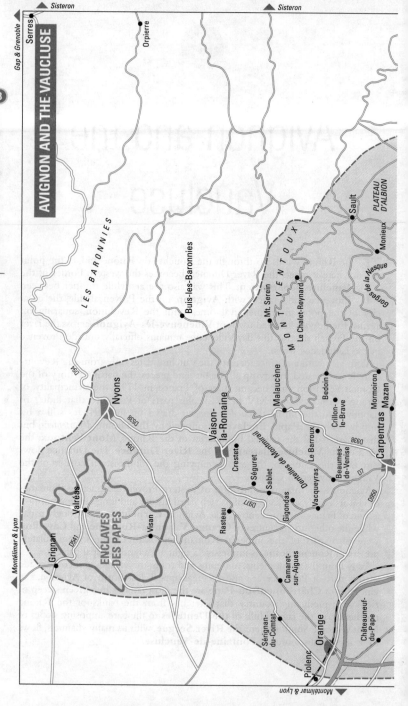

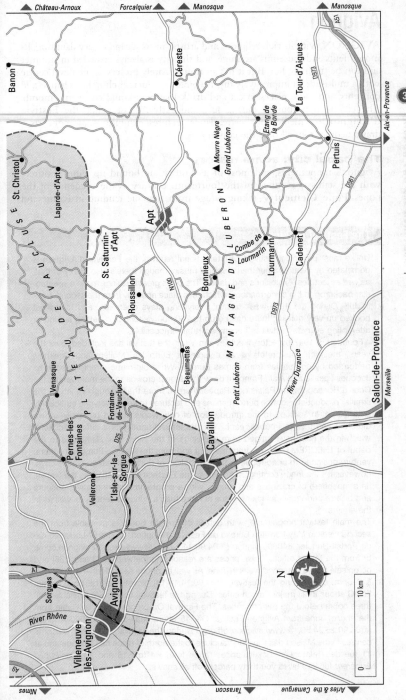

Avignon

AVIGNON, with its rich religious and artistic history, can be very daunting. Its monuments and museums are huge, and the city is always crowded in summer and can be stiflingly hot. But it has an immaculately preserved medieval centre with a multitude of impressively diverse buildings, ancient churches, chapels and convents, and more places to eat and drink than you could cover in a month. The city is at its busiest during July and early August, when the **Festival d'Avignon** – a medley of theatre, dance, lectures, exhibitions and concerts – draws people from all over the country.

The papal city: some history

Avignon's monuments, and most of its history, are bound up almost entirely with the status it acquired in the fourteenth century as the residence of the popes. **Pope Clement V**, taking refuge from anarchic feuding in Rome and

---

The Festival d'Avignon

Unlike most provincial festivals of international renown, the **Festival d'Avignon** is dominated by theatre rather than classical music, though there's also plenty of that, as well as lectures, exhibitions and dance. The city's great buildings make a spectacular backdrop to the performances, which take place annually from the second week in July. During the three-week festival everything stays open late, and things get booked up very quickly; there can be up to 200,000 visitors, and getting around or attempting everyday activities becomes virtually impossible.

Founded in 1947 by actor-director **Jean Vilar**, the festival has included, over the years, theatrical interpretations as diverse as Euripides, Molière and Chekhov, performed by companies from across Europe. While big-name directors (such as Jacques Lasalle and Alain Françon) draw the largest crowds to the main venue, the Cour d'Honneur in the Palais des Papes, there is more than enough variety in the smaller productions, dance performances and lectures to keep everyone sufficiently entertained. In addition to the introduction of new works staged by lesser-known directors and theatre troupes, each year the festival spotlights a different culture, which in the past have ranged from showings of the Hindi epic *Ramayana* to the debut of THEOREM (Theatres from the East and from the West), a European cultural venture designed to bring together the two halves of Europe on stage. These days, however, it's the fringe contingent known as the **Festival Off** which gives the festival its atmosphere of craziness and magic, with a programme of innovative, obscure and bizarre performances taking place in more than a hundred venues as well as in the streets.

The main festival programme, with details of how **to book**, is available from the second week in May from the Bureau du Festival d'Avignon, Cloître St-Louis, 20 rue du Portail-Boquier, 84000 Avignon (℡04.90.14.14.60, ⓦwww.festival-avignon.com), or from the tourist office. Ticket prices are reasonable (between €13 and €36) and go on sale from the second week in June. As well as phone sales (Mon–Fri 9am–1pm & 2–5pm, daily during the festival; ℡04.90.14.14.14), tickets can be bought from FNAC shops in all major French cities. During the festival, tickets are available until three hours before the performances. The Festival Off programme is available from the end of June from Avignon Festival Off, 45 cours Jean-Jaurès, 84000 Avignon (℡04.90.25.24.30, ⓦwww.avignon-off.org). During the festival, there are welcome centres in the Maison des Pays de Vaucluse to the north of place de l'Horloge and at 11 rue des Teinturiers. Tickets prices range from €4 to €16 and a *Carte Public Adhérent* for €10 gives you thirty percent off all shows.

northern Italy, first moved the papal headquarters here in 1309, a temporary act that turned out to last over seventy years – and a few decades longer if you count the city's last flurry in defence of its antipope pretenders.

Though the town, unlike nearby Châteauneuf-du-Pape, did not originally belong to the papacy, it had the advantage of excellent transport links and a good Catholic landlord. Clement was not entirely confident about his security, however, even in France, and shifted his base between here, Vienne and Carpentras. His successor, **Jean XXII**, had previously been bishop of Avignon, so he re-installed himself quite happily in the episcopal palace Clement V had established. The next Supreme Pontiff, **Benoît XII**, acceded in 1335; accepting the impossibility of returning to Rome, he demolished the bishop's palace to replace it with an austere fortress, now known as the **Vieux Palais**.

Number four of the nine Avignon popes, **Clement VI** managed to buy Avignon from Queen Jeanne of Naples and Provence, apparently in return for absolution for any possible involvement she might have had in the assassination of her husband. He also built a **new palace** adjoining the old one, a much more luxurious affair showing distinctly worldly tastes. The fifth and sixth Avignon popes further embellished and fortified the papal palace, before the seventh, **Gregory XI**, after years of diplomacy, and an appeal from Catherine of Siena, moved the Holy See back to Rome in 1377. This did not please the French cardinals who promptly voted in the **Antipope Clement VII** to take up residence in Avignon, thus initiating the division in the Catholic Church known as the Great Schism. The courier business in excommunications and more worldly threats between Rome and Avignon flourished. **Antipope Benoît XIII**, who replaced Clement VII, became justifiably paranoid about the shifting alliances of the Schism. It was he who built the **city walls** and ordered all the houses surrounding the Palais des Papes to be destroyed, creating the space that is now the **place du Palais**. Benoît was hounded out by the French king in 1403 and thereafter Avignon had to be content with mere cardinals, though it remained papal property right up to the Revolution.

The **period of the popes** made a lasting impression on the city's population. Along with the Holy Fathers came a vast entourage of clerks, lawyers, doctors, flatterers, merchants and wheeler-dealers of Italian, French, Catalan, Languedocian and German origin, not to mention pilgrims from all over Europe. Jews were given sanction, and so too, during the Schism, were heretics fleeing papal bulls from Rome. The diverse, multicultural population flourished – as did the criminal community, drawn to the papal enclave to escape prosecution in the neighbouring domains. While the popes entertained visiting monarchs and ambassadors with spectacular candle-lit processions and banquets, every vice flourished. The **Black Death** struck in 1348 and was followed by intermittent periods of plague and famine, and in between times the appalling overcrowding took its toll. But Avignon remained a very lively city – "a sewer where all the filth of the universe has gathered", as Petrarch, a contemporary, described it.

Arrival and information

Both the **gare SNCF**, on place de la République, and the adjacent **gare routière** (☎04.90.82.07.35) on boulevard St-Roch, are close to Porte de la République, on the south side of the old city. In addition, there's a **gare TGV**, 2km south of the city centre, near the hospital, which has cut travelling time to Paris down to two and a half hours. Regular shuttles (daily 6.14am–11.11pm; €1.10) connect the gare TGV with Avignon centre; passengers are picked up or dropped off in front of the main post office, a short walk from the Porte de

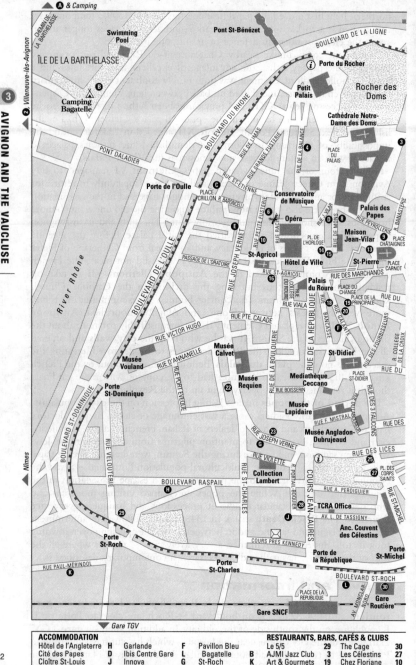

ACCOMMODATION						
Hôtel de l'Angleterre	H	Garlande	F	Pavillon Bleu		
Cité des Papes	D	Ibis Centre Gare	L	Bagatelle	B	
Cloître St-Louis	J	Innova	G	St-Roch	K	
Hôtel d'Europe	C	Le Magnan	I			
La Ferme	A	Mignon	E			

RESTAURANTS, BARS, CAFÉS & CLUBS			
Le 5/5	29	The Cage	30
AJMI Jazz Club	3	Les Célestins	27
Art & Gourmets	19	Chez Floriane	10
Le Belgocargo	12	Christian Étienne	8
Brunel	4	Le Cintra	28

04 90 82 06 01 L'ISLE SONNANTE

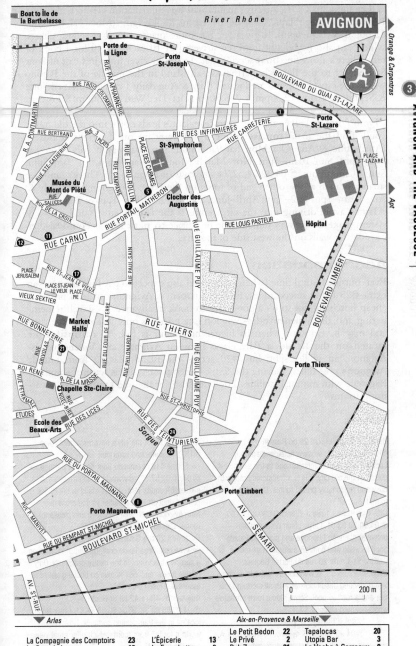

Boat to Île de
la Barthelasse

River Rhône

AVIGNON

Porte de
la Ligne

Porte
St-Joseph

N

Orange & Carpentras

BOULEVARD DU QUAI ST-LAZARE

RUE TROIS COLOMBES

RUE PALAPHIANNERIE

Porte
St-Lazare

R. A. PONTMARTIN

RUE BERTRAND

RUE 3 PLATS

RUE STE-CATHERINE

RUE DES INFIRMIERES

RUE CARRETERIE

PLACE
ST-LAZARE

St-Symphorien

Musée du
Mont de Piété

PLACE DES CARMES

RUE CAMPANE

RUE LEDRU-ROLLIN

St-Symphorien

Clocher des
Augustins

RUE
SALUCES

RUE DE LA CROIX

RUE PORTAIL MATHERON

RUE LOUIS PASTEUR

Hôpital

RUE CARNOT

RUE PAUL-SAIN

RUE GUILLAUME PUY

BOULEVARD LIMBERT

PLACE
JERUSALEM

RUE ST-JEAN LE VIEUX

PLACE ST-JEAN
LE VIEUX

PLACE
PIE

VIEUX SEXTIER

RUE BONNETERIE

Market
Halls

RUE DU FOUR DE LA TERRE

RUE PHILONARDE

RUE THIERS

RUE GUILLAUME PUY

Porte Thiers

RUE
GRIVOLAS

ROI RENE

R. DE LA MASSE

RUE PETRAMALE

RUE
NOEL-BIRET

Chapelle Ste-Claire

RUE ST-CHRISTOPHE

ETUDES

Ecole des
Beaux-Arts

RUE DES LICES

Sorgue

RUE DES TEINTURIERS

RUE DU PORTAIL MAGNANEN

RUE P. MANIVET

Porte Limbert

Porte Magnanen

RUE DU REMPART ST-MICHEL

BOULEVARD ST-MICHEL

AV. P. SÉMARD

AV. ST-RUF

0   200 m

Arles

Aix-en-Provence & Marseille

AVIGNON AND THE VAUCLUSE

3

Apt

La Compagnie des Comptoirs	23	L'Épicerie	13
La Cour du Louvre	16	La Fourchette	6
Couscousserie de l'Horloge	15	D'ici et D'ailleurs	18
L'Empreinte	24	Koala Bar	25
L'Entrée des Artistes	5	Mon Bar	7

Le Petit Bedon	22	Tapalocas	20
Le Privé	2	Utopia Bar	3
Pub Z	21	La Vache à Carreaux	9
The Red Lion	17	Venaissin	14
Le Red Zone	11	La Vieille Fontaine	C
Shakespeare	1	Woolloo Mooloo	26

la République. TCRA, the city's main **local bus** information centre, is also near Porte de la République, at 1 av de Lattre de Tassigny (Mon–Fri 8.30am–12.30pm & 1.30–6pm). It gives out bus route maps, as well as selling tickets, which can also be bought from bus drivers (€1.10 each; €9.40 for a book of ten). There's also a free **boat** service that crosses the river from just east of Pont St-Bénézet to the Île de la Barthelasse, an island in the middle of the Rhône where the city's campsites are located (July & Aug daily 11am–9pm; April–June & Sept daily 10am–12.30pm & 2–6.30pm; Oct–Dec Wed 2–5.30pm, Sat & Sun 10am–noon & 2–5.30pm).

From Porte de la République, cours Jean-Jaurès leads north into the old town; you'll find the main **tourist office** a little way up on the right at no. 41 (April–June & Aug–Oct Mon–Sat 9am–5pm, Sun 10am–5pm; July Mon–Sat 9am–7pm, Sun 10am–5pm; Nov–March Mon–Fri 9am–6pm, Sat 9am–5pm, Sun 10am–noon; ☎04.32.74.32.74, ⓦwww.ot-avignon.fr). There's another smaller branch at the other end of town by the Pont d'Avignon (daily: July & Aug 10am–1pm & 2–7pm; April–June, Sept & Oct 10am–1pm & 2–6pm).

Try to avoid driving into the city centre as the narrow streets and one-way system make things very difficult: the best place **to park** is near Pont Daladier, outside the walls on the west side of the city.

Accommodation

Even outside festival time (when you should also expect to pay higher rates – an extra €25 is not uncommon), finding a **room** in Avignon can be a problem: cheap hotels fill fast so it's a good idea to book in advance. It's worth remembering, too, that Villeneuve-lès-Avignon (see p.153) is only just across the river and may have rooms when its bigger neighbour is full. All **campsites** are located on the Île de la Barthelasse between Avignon and Villeneuve-lès-Avignon, an idyllic spot; bus #20 serves the island, leaving from outside Avignon's post office. During the festival a temporary site is set up behind the Bagatelle with minimal facilities. Look out, also, for the odd **farmhouse** advertising rooms.

Hotels

Hôtel de l'Angleterre 29 bd Raspail ☎04.90.86.34.31, ⓦwww.hoteldangleterre.fr. Located in a quiet neighbourhood in the southwest corner of the old city, this is a traditional hotel with cosy and reasonably priced rooms. Closed mid-Dec to mid-Jan. ❸

Cité des Papes 1 rue J-Vilar ☎04.90.80.93.00, Ⓕ04.90.80.93.01. Large chain hotel located between place de l'Horloge and place du Palais; good location and comfort assured in all rooms. ❻

Cloître St-Louis 20 rue du Portail Boquier ☎04.90.27.55.55, ⓦwww.cloitre-saint-louis.com. In a renovated Jesuit cloister with all modern facilities and a rooftop pool. Some rooms have attractive wood-beamed ceilings. ❽

Hôtel d'Europe 12 place Crillon ☎04.90.14.76.76, ⓦwww.heurope.com. A sixteenth-century town house, unpretentiously classy and set back in a shaded courtyard, where you can enjoy excellent home-made breakfasts and

food from one of the city's best restaurants (see p.151). Peaceful and luxurious. ❽

La Ferme 110 chemin du Bois, Île de la Barthelasse ☎04.90.82.57.53, ⓦwww.hotel-laferme.com. A sixteenth-century farm on the island in the Rhône (signed right off Pont Daladier as you cross over from Avignon), with well-equipped and pleasant rooms. Closed Nov to mid-March. ❺

Garlande 20 rue Galante ☎04.90.85.08.85, ⓦwww.hoteldegarlande.com. Delightful location on a narrow street right in the centre of the city. Only twelve rooms and well known so booking ahead is essential. Closed Jan. ❺

Ibis Centre Gare 42 bd St-Roch ☎04.90.85.38.38, Ⓕ04.90.86.44.81. Chain hotel located in the train station complex. Noisy, but worth it for the front rooms which offer great views over the city. ❻

Innova 100 rue Joseph-Vernet ☎04.90.82.54.10, Ⓔhotel.innova@numericable.fr. Small, friendly, inexpensive and conveniently located: worth booking in advance. ❸

Le Magnan 63 rue Portail Magnanen ☎04.90.86.36.51, ⓦwww.hotel-magnan.com. Just inside the walls by Porte Magnanen a short way east of the station. Quiet, and with a very pleasant shaded garden. ❹

Mignon 12 rue Joseph-Vernet ☎04.90.82.17.30, ⓦwww.hotel-mignon.com. Dated decor but good value and comfortable; reserve well in advance. ❸

St-Roch 9 rue Paul-Mérindol ☎04.90.16.50.00, Ⓕ04.90.82.78.30. Spacious, clean and quiet with a pleasant garden and cable TV in all the rooms. Just outside the city walls. ❸

Hostel and campsites

Camping Bagatelle ☎04.90.86.30.39, ⓦwww.campingbagatelle.com. The closest site to the city centre. A three-star complex, visible as you cross the Daladier bridge from Avignon; bus #20 from the post office to "Bagatelle" stop (or a 15-min walk from place de l'Horloge). There's a hostel here too (see below). €12 per tent. Open all year.

Camping Municipal Pont d'Avignon 10 chemin de la Barthelasse ☎04.90.80.63.50, ⓦwww.camping-avignon.com. Facing Pont St-Bénézet across the river, with a lovely pool and plenty of shade, this four-star site is Avignon's best. Take bus #20 ("Bénézet" stop) or the free boat (see p.144). €17.65 per tent. Closed Nov–March.

Les Deux Rhônes chemin de Bellegarde ☎04.90.85.49.70, ⓦwww.camping2rhone.com. Around 3km from the city and smaller than the other three; bus #20 ("Gravière" stop). €11.66 per tent. Open all year.

Parc des Libertés 4682 rte de l'Islon la Barthelasse ☎04.90.85.17.73, Ⓔparcdeslibertes@free.fr. The cheapest of the four campsites, 4km from the centre. €10.34 per tent. Closed mid-Sept to mid-June.

Pavillon Bleu Bagatelle Camping Bagatelle, Île de la Barthelasse ☎04.90.86.30.39, ⓦwww.campingbagatelle.com. Rather basic hostel facilities in the grounds of the Camping Bagatelle site (see above). Beds in eight-person rooms for €12 (per person), or €16 including breakfast.

The City

Avignon's **walls** still form a complete loop around the city, though they now appear far too low to be a serious defence. In fact half their full height is buried beneath the city, as is the moat – though all the gates and towers were restored during the nineteenth century and there's still a strong sense of being in an enclosed space, or *intra muros*, quite separate from the modern spread of the city.

Running north from the wall gate, **Porte de la République**, cours Jean-Jaurès becomes **rue de la République**, the main axis of the old town, leading straight up to **place de l'Horloge**, the central square. Beyond that is **place du Palais**, the **Rocher des Doms** park and the **Porte du Rocher** overlooking the Rhône by the Pont d'Avignon, or Pont St-Bénézet as it's officially known. Avignon's major monuments occupy a compact quarter inside the northern loop of the walls. The **Palais des Papes**, on the eastern side of place du Palais and home of the medieval popes, is obviously the city's major sight, but there are other palaces dotted about the centre and, as you'd expect, a fair smattering of churches (most with very limited opening hours). The best of the **city's**

Avignon Pass'ion

The tourist offices in Avignon and Villeneuve-lès-Avignon distribute free **Avignon Pass'ion** booklets. After paying the full admission price for the first museum you visit, you and your family receive discounts of 20–50 percent on the entrance fees of all subsequent museums in Avignon and Villeneuve-lès-Avignon. The pass also gives discounts on tourist transport (such as riverboats and bus tours), and is valid for fifteen days after its first use.

museums are the **Petit Palais** and the **Musée Calvet**, while, for a break from the monumental, have a wander around the pedestrian streets east of the papal palace towards place des Carmes, and to the southeast of the centre, the atmospheric **rue des Teinturiers**.

Palais des Papes

Serious sightseeing is bound to start off in the place du Palais, a huge cobbled square dominated by the **Palais des Papes** (daily: mid–March to June & Oct 9am–7pm; July 9am–9pm; Aug & Sept 9am–8pm; Nov to mid-March 9.30am–5.45pm; last ticket 1hr before closing; €9.50 mid-March to Oct, €7.50 Nov to mid-March; ticket includes an audioguide in several languages). The palais is a monster of a building, best viewed from the rue Peyrolerie to its south; inside, so little remains of the original decoration and furnishings that you can be deceived into thinking that all the popes and their retinues were as pious and austere as the last official occupant, Benoît XII. The denuded interior certainly gives sparse indication of the corruption and decadence of fat, feuding cardinals and their mistresses, the thronging purveyors of jewels, velvet and furs, the musicians, chefs and painters competing for patronage, the riotous banquets and corridor schemings which took place here during the period of the popes.

Tours begin in the **Pope's Tower**, otherwise known as the Tower of Angels, entered via the **Treasury**, a vaulted room in the tower. Here, the serious business of the church's deeds and finances went on and, beneath the flagging of the lower treasury, the papal gold and jewels were stored in four large safe holes. The same cunning storage device can be seen in the Chamberlain's quarters, in the **Chambre du Camérier**, just off the Jesus Hall. As the pope's right-hand man, the Chamberlain would originally have had lavishly decorated quarters, but successive occupants have left their mark and what is now visible is a confusion of layers. The other door in this room leads into the **Papal Vestiary**, where the pope would dress before sessions in the consistory. He also had a small library here and could look out onto the gardens below.

A door on the north side of the Jesus Hall leads to the **Consistoire** of the Vieux Palais, where sovereigns and ambassadors were received and the cardinals' council was held. The original flooring and the frescoes were destroyed by fire in 1413 and today it contains fragments of frescoes moved here from the cathedral plus a series of nineteenth-century paintings of the popes, all nine looking remarkably similar – unsurprisingly, given that the artist used the same model for each.

If it's medieval artistry you're after, however, go to the **Chapelle St-Jean**, off the Consistoire, and the **Chapelle St-Martial** on the floor above, reached via the cloisters. Both were richly decorated by the Sienese artist Matteo Giovanetti, and commissioned by Clement VI. The frescoes were damaged in the nineteenth century by soldiers using the building as barracks – they tried to chip off all the heads of the figures in order to sell them.

The **kitchen**, also on this floor, gives an idea of medieval times, and a hint of the scale of papal gluttony – its square walls becoming an octagonal chimney piece for a vast central cooking fire. Major feasts were held in **Le Grand Tinel**, which was also part of the conclave in which the cardinals were locked up in order to elect a new pope; clearly visible are the arches that led to additional rooms in the south and west in which the cardinals conspired and schemed in isolation from the world.

In the adjoining **Palais Neuf**, Clement VI's bedroom and study are further evidence of the pope's secular concerns, with wonderful food-oriented murals and painted ceilings. Beautifully restored, they illustrate in detail fishing, falconry, hunting and other courtly pursuits. However, austerity resumes in the cathedral-like proportions of the Grande Chapelle, or **Chapelle Clementine**, and in the Grande Audience on the floor below.

When you've completed the circuit, which includes a heady walk along the roof terraces, you can watch a glossy but informative film on the history of the palace (English headphones available), or shop for Châteauneuf-du-Pape and other local wines at vineyard prices in the *bouteillerie* as you exit the building. **Concerts** are also held here: programmes are available from the ticket office. During evening visits or concerts the illuminations give the palais a truly Gothic atmosphere.

North to Pont St-Bénézet

Opposite the entrance to the palais is the beautiful seventeenth-century **Hôtel des Monnaies**, the old mint, now the Conservatoire de Musique, with a facade of griffons, cherubs, eagles and swathes of fruit. To the north stands the **Cathédrale Notre-Dame des Doms** (daily: July & Aug 7am–7pm; Sept–June 8am–6pm), which might once have been a luminous Romanesque structure, but the interior has had a bad attack of Baroque. In addition, nineteenth-century fanatics mounted an enormous gilded Virgin on the belfry, which would look silly enough anywhere, but, when dwarfed by the fifty-metre towers of the popes' palace, is absurd. To the west of the square is the redeveloped **quartier de la Balance**, now teeming with souvenir shops, but once home to the gypsies in the nineteenth century.

Behind the cathedral is the **Rocher des Doms park**, a relaxing spot with lovely views over the river to Villeneuve and beyond – the best place in the city for a picnic. To the west of the park is the **Petit Palais** (daily except Tues: June–Sept 10am–1pm & 2–6pm; Oct–May 9.30am–1pm & 2–5.30pm; €6), a former episcopal palace now housing a dauntingly huge gallery. There are almost a thousand paintings and sculptures here and it's easy to get stuck, with more than a dozen rooms still to go, on the mastery of colour and facial expressions of a Simone Martini or Fabriano, or to be fatigued by a surfeit of the Madonna and Child before you've reached Botticelli's masterpiece on the subject or the Niçois painter, Louis Bréa's *Assumption of the Virgin*. Anyone intrigued by labyrinths should look out for *Theseus and the Minotaur*; the labyrinth in the foreground is identical to the one on the floor of Chartres Cathedral, and is thought by some to have mysterious powers of healing.

North of the Petit Palais, and well signposted, is the half-span of **Pont St-Bénézet**, or the Pont d'Avignon of the famous song (same hours as Palais des Papes; last ticket 30min before closing; €4). One theory has it that the lyrics say "*Sous le pont*" (under the bridge) rather than "*Sur le pont*" (on the bridge), and refer to the thief and trickster clientele of a tavern on the Île de la Barthelasse (which the bridge once crossed) dancing with glee at the arrival of more potential victims. Keeping the bridge repaired from the ravages of the Rhône was finally abandoned in 1660, three and a half centuries after it was built, and only four of the original twenty-two arches remain. Despite its limited use, the bridge remained a focus of river boatmen, who constructed a chapel to their patroness on the first of the bridge's bulwarks. Today, the bridge can be walked, danced or sat upon, but if you take small children, beware the precipitous, barely protected drops on either side.

Around place de l'Horloge

South of the Palais des Papes is the busy, café-lined **place de l'Horloge**, site of the city's imposing nineteenth-century **Hôtel de Ville** with its Gothic **clock**

The Festival Provençal

The Palais du Roure is the main Avignon venue for the **Festival Provençal**, which for over two decades has been celebrating the Provençal language and traditions in poetry, theatre, dance and song. It takes place during July and early August, with events in several Vaucluse cities. Details from the Palais du Roure on ☎04.90.80.80.88, or online in Provençal at ⊛www.nouvello.com.

tower, and of the **Opéra**. Just behind the Hôtel de Ville, the restored fourteenth-century **Église St-Agricol** (Sat 4–5pm) is one of Avignon's best Gothic edifices, with a beautifully carved fifteenth-century facade; inside, there's a Renaissance altarpiece of Provençal origin, and paintings by Nicolas Mignard and Pierre Parrocel. Around here lie the most desirable addresses in Avignon. High, heavy facades dripping with cupids, eagles, dragons, fruit and foliage range along **rue Petite-Fusterie** and **rue Joseph-Vernet**, where you'll find the most expensive shops selling chocolate, haute couture and baubles, with restaurants and art galleries to match.

To the south of place de l'Horloge, just behind rue St-Agricol on rue Collège du Roure, is the elegant fifteenth-century **Palais du Roure**, a centre of Provençal culture, whose gateway and courtyard are worth a look. The palais often hosts temporary art exhibitions, or you can take a rambling tour through its attics to see Provençal costumes, publications and presses, photographs of the Camargue in the 1900s and an old stage coach: the tour is on Tuesdays at 3pm (€4.60), or you can make an appointment (☎04.90.80.80.88).

On rue de Mons, to the east of the square, the seventeenth-century Hôtel de Crochans is home to the **Maison Jean Vilar** (July daily 10.30am–6.30pm; Sept–June Tues–Fri 9am–noon & 1.30–5.30pm, Sat 10am–5pm; closed Aug; free; ☎04.90.86.59.64), named after the great theatre director who set up the "Week of Dramatic Art" in 1947, which was to become the Festival d'Avignon (see p.140). The building houses festival memorabilia, an excellent library dedicated to the performing arts, and a collection of videos on everything from Stanislavski to last year's street theatre. These are sometimes shown in the foyer, or at special screenings, but you can also arrange your own viewing, with one day's notice – the catalogue is at the main desk. The maison also puts on temporary exhibitions (separate entrance fees), workshops and public lectures hosted by renowned theatre people.

The Banasterie and Carmes quartiers

The **quartier de la Banasterie**, to the east of the Palais des Papes, is mostly seventeenth- and eighteenth-century. The heavy wooden doors with highly sculptured lintels bear the nameplates of lawyers, psychiatrists and dietary consultants. It's worth poking your nose into the courtyard of the Hôtel de Fonseca, built in 1600 at 17 rue Ste-Catherine, to admire its mullioned windows and old well. Between Banasterie and place des Carmes are a tangle of tiny streets guaranteed to get you lost. Pedestrians have priority over cars on many of them, and there are plenty of tempting cafés and restaurants along the way. At 6 rue Saluces you'll find the peculiar **Musée du Mont de Piété** (Mon 10am–noon & 1.30–5pm, Tues–Fri 8.30–noon & 1.30–5pm; free), an ex-pawnbroker's shop and now the town's archives, which has a small display of papal bulls and painted desiccators for determining the dry weight of what was once the city's chief commodity–silk.

Continuing east, the **Cloitre les Carmes** (Carmelite convent) once spread over the whole of place des Carmes, right down to the bell tower, the **Clocher des Augustins**, on rue Carreterie, built in the 1370s with the bell cage added in the sixteenth century. Today, all that remains of the convent is the **Église St-Symphorien** (Mon–Sat 9.30am–noon & 4–6pm), which contains the stunning painting of *St Éloi* by Nicolas Mignard. The cloisters have become a theatre for Avignon's oldest permanent company, the Théâtre des Carmes, run by André Benedetto.

Further up, at 155 rue Carreterie, you'll find Avignon's **English bookshop** which also serves as a tearoom, meeting place and venue for readings and performances (Tues–Sat 9.30am–noon & 2–6pm).

From place St-Pierre to the rue des Teinturiers

To the south of rue Banasterie, on **place St-Pierre**, stands one of the most spectacular of Avignon's churches, the Renaissance **Église St-Pierre** (Thurs 2–5pm, Fri & Sat 2–7.30pm). Its greatest artwork is the doors, which were carved in 1551, with the Annunciation depicted on the right, and St Jerome and St Michael on the left. Inside, sculpted angels form the base of the nave's ribbed vault, holding up the arches, while beneath the organ loft there's a painting by Nicolas Mignard, *Sainte Famille au Chardonneret*.

To the south is the city's main shopping area, which centres on **place du Change**, and the old **Jewish quarter** around rue du Vieux-Sextier and place Jérusalem, where, during the time of the popes, Jews had to wear yellow caps and were locked in every night. To the east is **place Pie**, site of the ugly modern **market halls** and an open flower market. Just to the south, on rue du Roi-Réné is the **Chapelle Ste-Clare**, where, during the Good Friday service in 1327, the poet Petrarch first saw and fell in love with Laura, as recorded in a note on the pages of the poet's copy of Virgil.

From place Pie, rue Bonneterie heads southeast, becoming **rue des Teinturiers**, the most atmospheric street in Avignon. Its name refers to the eighteenth- and nineteenth-century business of calico printing. The cloth was washed in the Sorgue canal, which still runs alongside the street, turning the wheels of long-gone mills. It's also an excellent street for restaurant- and café-browsing, though the water tends to get a bit smelly as you reach the ramparts.

Place St-Didier and around

A short way south of place de l'Horloge and just east of rue de la République is **place St-Didier**, dominated by the **Église St-Didier** (daily 9am–6.30pm). Check out the altarpiece in the first chapel on the left which depicts Mary's pain with such realism that it has acquired the somewhat uncomfortable name of "Notre-Dame-du-Spasme". There are also some fourteenth-century frescoes in the left-hand chapel.

Between the noisy rue de la République and place St-Didier, on rue du Laboureur, is the impressive fourteenth-century former cardinal's residence, now the municipal library, the **Mediathèque Ceccano** (Mon 1–6pm, Tues–Sat 10am–6pm), where you could easily spend a tranquil afternoon reading in its quiet gardens; occasional exhibitions are also held in the beautifully decorated interior. Opposite, the **Musée Angladon-Dubrujeaud** (mid-April to mid-Nov Tues–Sun 1–6pm; mid-Nov to mid-April Wed–Sun 1–6pm; €6) displays the remains of the private collection of Jacques Doucet. It was once a mighty collection, containing such treasures as Picasso's *Demoiselles d'Avignon* and Douanier-Rousseau's *The Snake Charmer* (now in the Musée d'Orsay), but much of it was either given away or sold bit by bit. Testimony to grander days can be found in the first room, where photographs of Jacques Doucet's house, with rooms decorated according to the style of the paintings therein, reveal a man ahead of his time. The rest of the downstairs room shows what is left of his contemporary collection; *Portrait of Mme Foujita* and a self-portrait by Foujita, Modigliani's *The Pink Blouse*, various Picassos, and Van Gogh's *Railway Wagons*, the only painting from Van Gogh's stay in Provence to be on display in Provence. The theme of decorating rooms around a style has been taken up in the rest of the museum with a room dedicated to the medieval and Renaissance periods, three dedicated to the eighteenth century (Doucet's first passion) and an Oriental room.

Musée Calvet and around

West of rue de la République lies a cluster of museums, a couple of which are well worth checking out. Housed in an impressive eighteenth-century palace, the excellent **Musée Calvet**, at 65 rue Joseph-Vernet (daily except Tues 10am–1pm & 2–6pm; €6), has been undergoing gradual restoration and transformation for the past few years. Although many of the museum's pieces, including the second largest collection of iron work in France, remain in storage while space is found to display them, the current offerings will be enough to satisfy the most avid art and sculpture enthusiast. A visit starts in the **Galerie des Sculptures** with its handful of languorous nineteenth-century marble sculptures, including Bosio's *Young Indian*, perfectly suited to this elegant space. At the end of the gallery, the **Puech Collection** houses a large selection of silverware, Italian and Dutch paintings, and, more unusually, a Flemish curiosities cabinet, painted with scenes from the story of Daniel and full of hidden compartments. Upstairs in the **Vernet Gallery**, the Provençal dynasties of the Vernets and Mignards are well represented: Nicolas Mignard sets off with a fine set of *Seasons*, whilst Joseph Vernet, the most famous of the three painters in the Vernet family, sticks to representing the different times of the day. Also on this floor, look out for Jacques-Louis David's subtle *The Death of Young Barra* as well as Géricault's *Battle of Nazareth*.

The second museum worth visting is the **Musée Vouland**, which lies further west, at the end of rue Victor-Hugo, near Porte St-Dominique (Tues–Sat: May–Oct 10am–noon & 2–6pm; Nov–April 2–6pm; €4). Here you can feast your eyes on the fittings, fixtures and furnishings that French aristocrats once indulged in both before and after the Revolution. There's some brilliant Moustiers faïence, exquisite marquetry and Louis XV ink-pots with silver rats holding the lids.

Avignon's remaining museums are considerably less compelling: next door to the Musée Calvet, the **Musée Requien** (Tues–Sat 9am–noon & 2–6pm; free), is a rather uninspiring natural history museum; the **Musée Lapidaire**, housed in a Baroque chapel at 27 rue de la République (daily except Tues 10am–1pm & 2–6pm; €2), boasts a dull collection of Roman and Gallo-Roman stones; while Avignon's only contemporary art gallery, the **Collection Lambert**, just west of the tourist office, down rue Violette (July & Aug daily 11am–7pm; Sept–June Tues–Sun 11am–6pm; €5.50), houses a disappointing permanent collection, although the temporary exhibitions can sometimes be worthwhile.

Eating and drinking

Good-value midday **meals** are plentiful in Avignon and eating well in the evening needn't break the bank. The large terraced **café-brasseries** on place de l'Horloge, rue de la République and cours Jean-Jaurès serve quick basic meals and are good for people-watching, although the quality of the food is usually quite average. Try the *Venaissin* at 16 place de l'Horloge (℡04.90.86.20.99; menus from €12.50; closed Jan) or *Le Cintra* at 44 cours Jean-Jaurès (℡04.90.82.29.80; menus from €11.50). Rue des Teinturiers and the streets of the Banasterie and Carmes are good places to try if you're on a tight **budget**, and the streets between place Crillon and place du Palais are full of temptation if you're not.

Restaurants

Art & Gourmets 4 place de la Principale ℡04.90.86.81.87. Enjoy duck with fig *laqué* and other tasty dishes at reasonable prices (€11.50–14.50) on a quiet square in the city centre. Closed Sun.

Le Belgocargo 10 place Châtaignes ℡04.90.85.72.99. Inexpensive Belgian restaurant specializing in mussels and beer. Midday menu with drink for €11.80. Closed Sun.

Brunel 46 rue de la Balance ℡04.90.85.24.83. Superb regional dishes, including *bourride*, with menus from €25. Closed Sun & middle two weeks in Aug.

Chez Floriane 2 rue Petite-Fusterie ℡04.90.85.87.12. Well-prepared meat and seafood accompanied by flavoursome sauces – try the scallops with coconut sauce or beef with rocket sauce. Closed Sun lunch.

🏃 **Christian Étienne** 10 rue de Mons ℡04.90.86.16.50. One of Avignon's best restaurants, housed in a twelfth-century mansion and with exotic offerings such as the €60 "tomato" menu featuring tomato *tartare*, *confit* and sorbet. Menus from €30–105. Closed Sun & Mon.

La Compagnie des Comptoirs 83 rue Joseph-Vernet ℡04.90.85.99.04. Appearance reigns supreme in this redecorated Jesuit *cloître*, although the fusion cuisine – Mediterranean and Asian, with vegetarian options as well – isn't far behind. Main dishes around €25. Closed Sun & Mon.

La Cour du Louvre 23 rue St-Agricol ℡04.90.27.12.66. Tucked away at the end of a *cour*, with a romantic atmosphere and good Mediterranean cooking; €34 menu. Closed Sun & Mon.

Couscousserie de l'Horloge 2 rue de Mons ℡04.90.85.84.86. Popular Algerian-run restaurant with a jovial atmosphere and excellent North African food. Try the delicious tagine *aux prunes* at €14.50.

L'Entrée des Artistes 1 place des Carmes ℡04.90.82.46.90. Small, friendly bistro serving traditional French dishes such as beef *tartare*, with a €20 menu. Closed last three weeks in Aug.

L'Épicerie place St-Pierre ℡04.90.82.74.22. A quiet spot, on a cobbled street next to the Église St-Pierre, in which to sample lamb covered with goat's cheese, beef with foie gras moose and other rich and tasty dishes (from €19). Closed Sun.

La Fourchette 17 rue Racine ℡04.90.85.20.93. The basic fixed menu (€30) at this well-regarded restaurant offers marinated sardines, snails and excellent meat stews. Closed Sat, Sun & last two weeks in Aug.

D'ici et D'ailleurs 4 rue Galante ℡04.90.14.63.65. Provençal dishes from "here" mixed with international flavours from "there" – tagines, muffins and suchlike. Lunch for €12, dinner from €16. Closed Sun.

Le Petit Bedon 70 rue Joseph-Vernet ℡04.90.82.33.98. Small, cosy restaurant serving good-quality Provençal dishes (€13–19). Closed Mon lunch & Sun & last two weeks in Aug.

🏃 **La Vache à Carreaux** 14 rue de la Peyrolerie ℡04.90.80.09.05. Goat's cheese roasted in garlic and covered with onion *confiture*, Camembert cooked with caramel, pepper and Calvados, and other delicious and original cheese creations. Good value at €10–12.50 for most main dishes. Reserve ahead.

La Vieille Fontaine at *Hôtel d'Europe*, 12 place Crillon ℡04.90.14.76.76. Gastronomic restaurant with especially good fish and seafood, from lobster to gilt-head bream, served in the sedate surroundings of *Hôtel d'Europe* (see p.144 for review). Most main dishes €35–45.

🏃 **Woolloo Mooloo** 16 bis rue des Teinturiers ℡04.90.85.28.44. An old printshop with all the presses still in place. This hip place now serves dishes from around the world – tagines, *mafé* from West Africa, lasagne – and a good selection of teas. Lunch menus from €13, dinner menus from €21. Closed Mon.

Cafés, bars and salons de thé

Les Célestins 38 place des Corps-Saints. Café-bar with a good mix of young and old customers. Open Mon–Sat 7am–1am.

L'Empreinte 33 rue des Teinturiers. Inexpensive mint tea and Moroccan pastries. Closed Sun eve.

Koala Bar 2 place des Corps-Saints. Loud and popular music emanates from this bar with a bright pink interior. Open daily till 3am.

Mon Bar 17 rue Portail Matheron. Pleasant café with a laid-back atmosphere. Open daily 7am–10pm.

The Red Lion 21–23 rue St-Jean le Vieux. Popular student bar on place Pie. Good beer selection and live music Mon, Wed & Sun. Open daily 10.30am–1.30am.

Shakespeare 155 rue Carreterie. English bookshop and *salon de thé*. Closed evenings and all Sun & Mon.

Tapalocas 15 rue Galante. Cheap drinks, tapas for €2.50 a dish and WiFi connection for Internet users. Daily noon–1am.

Utopia Bar 4 rue Escaliers Ste-Anne. In the shadow of the Palais des Papes, this café has changing exhibitions adorning the walls, live jazz some nights, and is next door to a good cinema. Open daily noon to midnight.

Nightlife and entertainment

Though a lot of the city's energy is saved up for the festival, there's a fair amount of **nightlife and cultural events** in Avignon all year round, particularly café-theatre. For more information, get the free monthly calendar, *Rendez-Vous*, from the tourist office, or the free monthly arts, events and music magazine, *César*, also available from the tourist office and arts centres.

Live music and discos

Le 5/5 1 rempart St-Roch ☎04.90.82.61.32. Mainstream disco, popular with the locals. Tues–Sun from 11pm.

AJMI Jazz Club c/o La Manutention, rue Escalier Ste-Anne ☎04.90.86.08.61, ⓦwww.jazzalajmi .com. Hosts major acts and some adventurous new groups. Check website for programme.

The Cage 5 av Monclar ☎04.90.27.00.84. The city's biggest and best gay and lesbian club, in the *gare routière* building. Thurs–Sat from 11pm.

Le Privé rte de Tavel, Les Angles ☎04.90.25.90.99. Across the Rhône in Les Angles, this club hosts international DJs spinning mainly electronic music. Free entry except for nights hosted by invited DJs. Fri & Sat from 11pm.

Pub Z 58 rue Bonneterie. Rock bar, decorated in black and white in honour of the zebra, DJs at the weekend. Daily till 1am.

Le Red Zone 25 rue Carnot ☎04.90.27.02.44. Trendy bar with DJs playing styles ranging from salsa to electro according to the night. Daily till 3am.

Theatre and cinema

Théâtre du Balcon 38 rue Guillaume-Puy ☎04.90.85.00.80. A venue staging everything from African music and twentieth-century classics to contemporary theatre.

Théâtre des Carmes 6 place des Carmes ☎04.90.82.20.47. Run by one of the founders of Festival Off, this theatre specializes in avant-garde performances.

Théâtre du Chêne Noir 8 bis rue Ste-Catherine ☎04.90.86.58.11. May have mime, a musical or Molière on offer.

Opéra place de l'Horloge ☎04.90.82.81.40. Classical opera and ballet. Oct–June.

Utopia 4 rue Escalier Ste-Anne ☎04.90.82.65.36, ⓦwww.cinemas-utopia.org. Cinema showing art-house, obscure or old-time favourites, always in the original language. The tourist office has programmes, or check the website.

Listings

Airport Aéroport Avignon-Caumont, 8km from centre ☎04.90.81.51.51.

Bike rental Holiday Bikes Provence, 20 bd St-Roch ☎04.32.76.25.88; Provence Bike, 52 bd St-Roch ☎04.90.27.92.61. Both also rent scooters and motorbikes.

Boat trips Grands Bateaux de Provence, allée de l'Oulle ☎04.90.85.62.25, ⓦwww.mireio.net; runs year-round trips upstream towards Châteauneuf-du-Pape and downstream to Arles; two-week advance booking recommended; tickets from €44, meal included. Shorter hour- and two-hour-long cruises from €7.50.

Bookshops Shakespeare, 155 rue Carreterie ℡04.90.27.38.50 (closed Sun & Mon); France Loisirs, 36 cours Jean-Jaurès; FNAC, 19 rue de la République.

Bus Local buses: TCRA, 1 av Lattre de Tassigny ℡04.32.74.18.32, ⊕www.tcra.fr. Buses to other towns: 5 av Montclar ℡04.90.82.07.35.

Car parks Guarded parking (24hr) at 16 bd St-Roch, near the train station; underground car park at place du Palais; free guarded parking with regular shuttles on l'Île de Piot.

Car rental ADA, 23 av St-Ruf ℡04.90.86.18.89; Hertz, bd St-Roch ℡04.90.14.26.90; Rent a Car, 130 av Pierre Sémard ℡04.90.88.08.02; Sixt, 3 av St-Ruf ℡04.90.86.06.61.

Emergencies For doctor/ambulance call: ℡15 or Médecins de Garde ℡04.90.87.75.00. Hospital: Centre Hospitalier H-Duffaut, 305 rue Raoul-Follereau ℡04.32.75.33.33.

Internet Cyber@Net84, 6 place Jerusalem; Webzone 3 rue St-Jean le Vieux.

Laundry Lav'matic: 113 av St-Ruf; 27 rue Portail Magnanen; 66 place des Corps-Saints; 9 rue Chapeau-Rouge; 27 av Montclar; and 48 rue Carreterie.

Markets Antiques: place Crillon (Sat morning). Flea market: place des Carmes (Sun morning). Books and records: cours Jean-Jaurès (July every Sat; rest of year first Sat of the month). Flowers: place des Carmes (Sat morning). Food: in the covered halls on place Pie (Tues–Fri till 1.30pm; Sat & Sun till 2pm) and on rue rempart St-Michel, between portes St-Michel and Magnanen (Sat & Sun till 1pm).

Money exchange 24hr automatic exchange at CIC, 13 rue de la République.

Pharmacy Call police at bd St-Roch on ℡04.90.16.81.00 for addresses of 24-hour pharmacies.

Police Municipale 13 ter bd du Quai St-Lazare ℡08.00.00.84.00 or 04.90.85.13.13.

Post office cours Président Kennedy (Mon–Fri 8.30am–6.30pm, Sat 8.30am–noon).

Swimming pool Privately owned Piscine Olympique des Arènes, Île de la Barthelasse (May–Sept 10am–7pm; €10). Do not attempt to swim in the Rhône.

Taxis place Pie; ℡04.90.82.20.20.

Trains ℡08.92.35.35.35.

Villeneuve-lès-Avignon

VILLENEUVE-LÈS-AVIGNON (also spelled Villeneuve-lez-Avignon) rises up a rocky escarpment above the west bank of the river, looking down upon its older neighbour from behind far more convincing fortifications. In the thirteenth and fourteenth centuries, when its citadel and bridge defences were built, the Rhône at Avignon was the French border, not just with the papal enclave but with the county of Provence, whose allegiances shifted between the many different rivals of the king of France. Despite that, and the French king's habit of claiming land, and therefore taxes, in areas of Avignon that the river flooded, Villeneuve operated largely as a suburb to Avignon, with palatial residences constructed by the cardinals and a great monastery founded by Pope Innocent VI.

To this day Villeneuve is, strictly speaking, part of Languedoc not Provence, and would score better in the hierarchy of towns to visit were it further from Avignon, whose monuments it can almost match for colossal scale and impressiveness. In summer, at least, it benefits, providing venues for the festival, as well as accommodation overspill; during this insanely busy time in Avignon, a trip over the river to the much more sedate Villeneuve provides a welcome respite from the crowds. This said, the town is certainly worth a day of exploring whatever time of year you are visiting.

Arrival, information and accommodation

From the Avignon post office, bus #11 runs every thirty minutes direct to place Charles-David ("Office de Tourisme" stop) in Villeneuve; after 7.45pm you'll have to take a taxi or walk the three kilometres. Villeneuve's **tourist office** is on place Charles-David (July Mon–Fri 10am–7pm, Sat & Sun 10am–1pm & 2.30–7pm; Aug daily 9am–12.30pm & 2–6pm; Sept–June Mon–Sat 9am–12.30pm & 2–6pm;

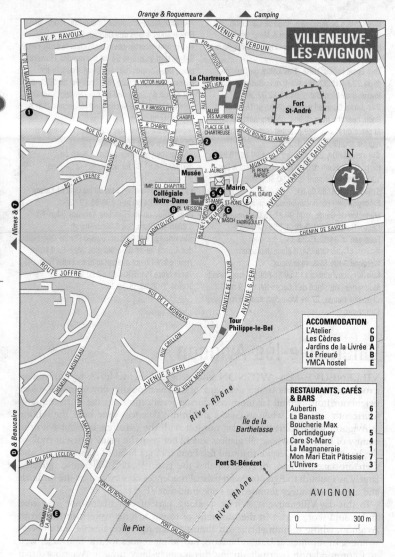

VILLENEUVE-LÈS-AVIGNON

ACCOMMODATION

L'Atelier	C
Les Cèdres	D
Jardins de la Livrée	A B
Le Prieuré	B
YMCA hostel	E

RESTAURANTS, CAFÉS & BARS

Aubertin	6
La Banaste	2
Boucherie Max Dortindeguey	5
Care St-Marc	4
La Magnaneraie	1
Mon Mari Etait Pâtissier	7
L'Univers	3

☎04.90.25.61.33, ⓦwww.villeneuvelezavignon.fr), where there's also a food **market** on Thursday morning and a bric-a-brac market on Saturday morning. The tourist office can help with **accommodation**, as well as providing a list of furnished apartments available for short-term rental on its website. Outside the festival period you shouldn't have too many problems finding your own.

Hotels

L'Atelier 5 rue de la Foire ☎04.90.25.01.84, ⓦwww.hoteldelatelier.com. A sixteenth-century house with huge open fireplaces and a walled garden. Excellent value. Closed Jan. ❹

Les Cèdres 39 av Pasteur ☎04.90.25.43.92, ⓦwww.lescedres-hotel.fr. A converted Louis XIV mansion 2km from the centre with rather ordinary rooms, a pool and restaurant. Closed Nov–Easter. ❹
Jardins de la Livrée 4 bis rue du Camp de Bataille ☎04.90.26.05.05. Bed and breakfast with English-speaking hosts and clean, comfortable

rooms. The only drawback is the noise – all night – of passing trains. No credit cards. ❹
Le Prieuré 7 place du Chapitre ☎04.90.15.90.15, ⓦwww.laprieure.fr. If you fancy being surrounded by tapestries, finely carved doors, old oak ceilings and other baronial trappings, this is indisputably the first choice. Closed Nov to mid-March. ❽

Hostel and campsite

YMCA hostel 7 bis chemin de la Justice ☎04.90.25.46.20, ⓦwww.ymca-avignon.com. Beautifully situated overlooking the river by Pont du Royaume, with balconied rooms for two to four people, and an open-air swimming pool. Bus #10 (direction "Les Angles", stop "Général Leclerc"). ❶

Camping Municipal de la Laune chemin St-Honoré, off the D980 ☎04.90.25.76.06. Near the sports stadium and swimming pools. Pleasant three-star site with plenty of shade, tents for rent and disabled facilities. €15.20 per tent pitch. Closed mid-Oct to Easter.

The Town

Villeneuve clusters around rue de la République which runs north from the Collégiale Notre-Dame church on place St-Marc. The **Fort St-André** lies on a rise to the east.

For a good overview of Villeneuve – and Avignon – make your way south of place St-Marc to the **Tour Philippe-le-Bel** at the bottom of montée de la Tour (bus stop "Philippe-le-Bel"). The tower was built to guard the French end of Pont St-Bénézet, and the views from the top (Tues–Sun: April–Sept 10am–12.30pm & 2–6.30pm; Oct–March 10am–noon & 2–5pm; €1.80) are stunning.

Even more indicative of French distrust of its neighbours is the enormous **Fort St-André** (daily: mid-May to mid-Sept 10am–1pm & 2–6pm; mid-Sept to Oct & April to mid-May 10am–1pm & 2–5.30pm; Oct–March 10am–1pm & 2–5pm; €5), whose bulbous, double-towered gateway and vast white walls loom over the town. Inside, refreshingly, there are no postcard stalls or souvenir shops, just tumbledown houses, and the fort's cliff-face terrace –the classic spot for artists and photographers to compose their views of Avignon. You can reach the approach to the fort, montée du Fort, from place Jean-Jaurès on rue de la République, or by the "rapid slope" of rue Pente Rapide, a cobbled street of tiny houses leading off rue des Recollets on the north side of place Charles-David. Within the fort you can also visit its former **abbey** (Tues–Sun: April–Sept 10am–12.30pm & 2–6pm; Oct–March 10am–12.30pm & 2–5pm; €4), with its gardens of olive trees, ruined chapels, lily ponds and dovecotes. As the abbey is privately owned, the entrance fees for the two sites are separate.

Almost at the top of rue de la République, on the right, allée des Muriers leads from place de la Chartreuse to the entrance of **La Chartreuse du Val du Bénédiction** (daily: April–Sept 9am–6.30pm; Oct–March 9.30am–5.30pm;

Museums and monuments in Villeneuve

A **Passeport Villeneuve** (€6.86) gives you entry to the Fort St-André, Tour Philippe-le-Bel, La Chartreuse du Val de Bénédiction, the Collégiale Notre-Dame and its cloister and the Musée Pierre-de-Luxembourg. The ticket is available from each of the monuments and from the tourist office.

€6.50), one of the largest Charterhouses in France and founded by Innocent VI, the sixth of the Avignon popes, whose sharp profile is outlined on his tomb in the church. The buildings, which were sold off after the Revolution and gradually restored last century, are totally unembellished. With the exception of the Giovanetti frescoes in the chapel beside the refectory, all the paintings and treasures of the monastery have been dispersed, leaving a strong impression of the austerity of the strict practices of the Carthusian order. The only communication allowed was one hour of conversation a week plus the rather less congenial public confessions. Monks left the enclosure for one three-hour walk per week; within, their time was spent as much on manual labour as on prayer, and their diet was strictly vegetarian.

You are free to wander round unguided, through the three cloisters, the church, chapels, cells and communal spaces; there's little to see but plenty of atmosphere to be absorbed. It is one of the best venues in the Festival d'Avignon, along with the fourteenth-century **Église Collégiale Notre-Dame** and its cloister on place St-Marc (Tues–Sun: April–Sept 10am–12.30pm & 2–6.30pm; Oct–March 10am–noon & 2–5pm; free). The church is decorated with paintings by the Avignon School and with caring cupids tending Christ's hands and feet on the altar. However, Notre-Dame's most important treasure, a rare fourteenth-century smiling Madonna and Child made from a single tusk of ivory, supposedly carved by a convert from Islam, is now housed, along with many of the paintings from the Chartreuse, in the **Musée Pierre-de-Luxembourg** just to the north along rue de la République (same hours as Église Collégiale Notre-Dame; €3).

The museum's spacious layout includes a single room given over to the most stunning painting in the collection, *Le Couronnement de la Vierge*, painted in 1453 by Enguerrand Quarton as the altarpiece for the church in the Chartreuse. With fiercely contrasting colours of red, orange, gold, white and blue, the statuesque and symmetrical central figures of the coronation form a powerful and unambiguous subject. To either side of them, in true medieval style, the social hierarchy is defined, using a greater variety of form and colour. Along the bottom of the painting the scale of detail leaps several frames, with flames engulfing sinners, devils and their assistant beasts carrying away victims, walled towns with pin-size figures, and in the distance Mont St-Victoire and the cliffs of Estaque. No other painting in the collection matches Quarton's work and many are too obviously public relations pieces for their patrons, placing the pope, lord or bishop in question beside the Madonna or Christ.

Eating and drinking

Villeneuve's centre has a good choice of **eating** places for those who are ready to spend, but if it's affordable dining you're after, it's best to stick to Avignon. Cave St-Marc on place St-Pons, just up to the right as you approach place St-Marc from place Charles-David (Tues–Sat 6.30pm–midnight; open Mon during July), is a good place for **buying wine** – which you can then drink at the bar (€6 corkage fee).

Aubertin 1 rue de l'Hôpital ☎04.90.25.94.84. Feast on pigs' feet or pigeon risotto with truffles at this sumptuous restaurant in the shade of the old arcades by the Collégiale Notre-Dame (lunch menu €20, dinner menus €35 & €49). Closed Sun & Mon out of season.

La Banaste 28 rue de la République ☎04.90.25 .64.20. Decent Provençal and Languedocian fare, but nicer indoors than on the cramped roadside terrace. Menu at €26. Closed Thurs out of season.

Boucherie Max Dortindeguey 1 place St-Marc ☎04.90.25.13.66. The best meat dishes in town – tartare, mixed grill, prime cuts of beef – are served on a €19 menu at this butcher's shop which operates an evening-only restaurant. Closed Sun & Mon.

La Magnaneraie 37 rue du Camp de Bataille ☎04.90.25.11.11. Excellent, upmarket restaurant five minutes' walk from the centre, serving delicacies such as foie gras marinated in peach wine. Menus €49 & €69; otherwise, most main dishes €30–35. Oct–April closed Sat lunch, Sun eve & Wed.

Mon Mari Etait Pâtissier 3 bd Pasteur ☎04.90.25.52.79. Popular place a little west of the town centre, with some wonderful rabbit, guinea fowl and lamb dishes, as well as excellent desserts, on its €35 menu. Closed Sun & Mon out of season.

L'Univers 5 place Jean-Jaurès. Ordinary café on a picturesque square, in the heart of Villeneuve. Open daily 6am–10pm.

Châteauneuf-du-Pape

Roughly halfway between Avignon and Orange, on the back road linking these two towns, the large village of **CHÂTEAUNEUF-DU-PAPE** takes its name from the ruins of the fourteenth-century Avignon popes' summer château.

△ Wine-tasting in Châteauneuf-du-Pape

However, neither this nor the medieval streets around **place du Portail**, the hub of the village, are why Châteauneuf is a household name. It is, of course, the local **vineyards** that produce the magic, with the grapes warmed at night by large pebbles that cover the ground and soak up the sun's heat by day. Their rich ruby-red wine is one of the most renowned in France, though the lesser-known white, too, is exquisite.

If you can coincide your visit with the first weekend of August you'll find free *dégustation* (tasting) stalls throughout the village, as well as parades, dances, equestrian contests, folklore floats and so forth, all to celebrate the ripening of the grapes in the **Fête de la Véraison**. As well as wine, a good deal of grape liqueur (*marc*) is imbibed.

At other times of the year, several places throughout the village offer free **tastings**: the Cave Brotte, on avenue Bienheureux-Pierre-de-Luxembourg, has its own **Musée du Vin** (daily 9am–1pm & 2–7pm; free), and offers free sampling of its own and other Rhône wines, while the boutique **La Maison des Vins**, at 8 rue du Maréchal Foch (daily: mid-June to mid-Sept 10am–7pm; mid-Sept to mid-June 10.30am–noon & 2–6.30pm), will let you sample its excellent selection of different *domains*. If you'd rather buy direct from a producer, check the lists at the tourist office (see p.144) or the Fédération des Syndicats des Producteurs at 12 av Louis Pasteur (℡04.90.83.72.21). You could also ask for the details of the winner of the previous April 25 competition when the village celebrates the day of Saint Marc, patron saint of wine-growers, with a procession from the church and a tasting by professionals to determine the best wines from the last vintage. Ideally, you'll need your own transport to visit the individual *domains*, since many of them lie outside of the village itself. Unfortunately, there is no one place that sells all of the Châteauneuf-du-Pape wines; the best selection under one roof is at La Maison des Vins (see above).

Practicalities

There are very few **buses** to Châteauneuf-du-Pape. During the school period, you'll find just one or two a day from Orange (arriving at the bottom of av des Bousquets), but these leave late in the afternoon, with no return trip on the same day from Châteauneuf. Services during the school holidays are virtually non-existent. The **tourist office** is on place du Portail (Mon–Sat: July & Aug 9.30am–7pm; Sept–June 9.30am–12.30pm & 2–6pm; ℡04.90.83.71.08, @http://perso.orange.fr/ot-chato9-pape).

Accommodation is confined to four very pleasant but small **hotels**: the cosy, eight-roomed *La Garbure,* 3 rue Joseph-Ducos (℡04.90.83.75.08, @www .la-garbure.com; closed last three weeks in Nov; ❹), whose bright and cheerful rooms all have air conditioning; *La Mère Germaine*, on rue du Cdt Lemaître close to place du Portail (℡04.90.83.54.37, @www.lameregermaine.com; ❸), also with eight welcoming rooms plus a tennis court; the four-star *Hostellerie du Château des Fines Roches*, a ten-minute walk out of town on the route d'Avignon (℡04.90.83.70.23, @www.chateaufinesroches.com; ❾), which has eight very plush rooms featuring four-poster beds and is wonderfully situated with gorgeous views; and the charming *La Sommellerie* on route de Roquemaure (℡04.90.83.50.00, @www.hotel-la-sommellerie.com; ❻), a renovated country house with modern rooms, a pool and superb restaurant. There are also two **chambres d'hôtes** – *Chez Monsieur Melchor*, La Font du Pape (℡04.90.83.73.97; closed Dec–Feb; ❸), and *Chez Mme Dexheimer*, Clos Bimard, route de Roque-maure (℡04.90.83.73.16; closed Dec–Feb; ❸) – and a two-star **campsite**, *Islon St-Luc*, about 2km down chemin de la Calade, south from place Portail

(☎04.32.40.90.49, ⓦwww.campinglislonsaintluc.com; €14 per tent).

You can eat well for around €15 at the **brasserie** *La Mule du Pape* at 2 rue de la République. Alternatively, *La Mère Germaine* (closed Sun eve out of season; menus €16–38) serves well-crafted Provençal dishes and has panoramic views. Top of the range, however, is *La Sommellerie* (closed Sun eve & Mon out of season; menus €29–78), where everything is made on the premises, from the bread to the fine desserts, and the meat is cooked on an outdoor wood fire.

Orange and around

Ten kilometres further north from Châteauneuf-du-Pape, **ORANGE** is best known for its spectacular **Roman theatre** (Théâtre Antique). The city is the former seat of the counts of Orange, a title created by Emperor Charlemagne in the eighth century, and passed to the Dutch crown of Nassau in the sixteenth century. Its most memorable member was the Protestant Prince William, who ascended the English throne with his consort Queen Mary in 1689; the Protestant Orange Order in Ireland was founded to support William's military campaign against his Catholic predecessor, James II, which ended with the Battle of the Boyne. Orange gained recent notoriety with the victory of Jean-Marie Le Pen's Front National in the municipal elections of 1995, and again in 2001 (with a decisive sixty percent of the vote).

The town's medieval street plan, Thursday market, fountained squares and houses with ancient porticoes and courtyards are attractive enough, but aside from the **Théâtre Antique**, the triumphal **Roman arch**, and **museum**, there's not much to detain you. However, just north of Orange, in Sérignan-du-Comtat, there's a surprising treat in the old residence of the nineteenth-century scientist, the **Harmas** of **Jean-Henri Fabre**.

Orange's busiest time is in July, when the city hosts a major **opera festival** (see box on p.161), held in the Théâtre Antique.

Arrival, information and accommodation

The **gare SNCF** is a ten-minute walk east of the centre, at the end of avenue Frédéric-Mistral; and the **gare routière** is just east of the Théâtre Antique (there's undergound **parking** here too). The **tourist office** is on avenue Charles-de-Gaulle (July & Aug Mon–Sat 9.30am–8pm, Sun 10am–1pm & 2–7pm; April–June & Sept Mon–Sat 9.30am–7pm, Sun 10am–1pm & 2–6.30pm; Oct–March Mon–Sat 10am–1pm & 2–5pm; ☎04.90.34.70.88, ⓦwww.otorange.fr), and there's also a **seasonal tourist office** opposite the Théâtre Antique (July & Aug Mon–Sat 10am–1pm & 2–7pm).

For **buying wine**, head to the Palais du Vin, about 3km south of the centre on the N7 (Mon–Sat 9am–7pm; bus #1 to the "Zone Commerciale" stop), where you'll be offered free tastings and a choice of hundreds of different regional wines at fair prices.

You'll have no problem finding **accommodation** in Orange, except during the Chorégies festival in July.

Hotels

Arène Kulm place de Langes ☎04.90.11.40.40, ⓦwww.hotel-arene.com. Spacious rooms with all mod cons, on a quiet, pedestrianized, though not overly attractive, square. ❻

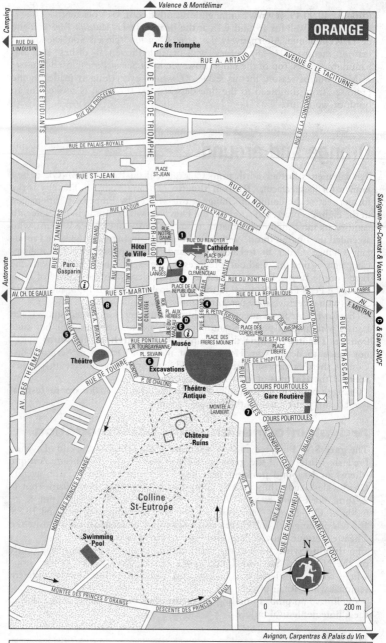

▲ Valence & Montélimar

ORANGE

Camping ◀

Autoroute ◀

Sérignan-du-Comtat & Vaison ▶

G & Gare SNCF ▶

Avignon, Carpentras & Palais du Vin ▶

Arc de Triomphe

RUE DU LIMOUSIN

AVENUE DES ÉTUDIANTS

RUE DES PHOCÉENS

RUE A. ARTAUD

AVENUE G. LE TACITURNE

AV. DE L'ARC DE TRIOMPHE

RUE DE PALAIS-ROYALE

RUE DE LA CONCORDE

RUE ST-JEAN

PLACE ST-JEAN

RUE DU NOBLE

RUE LACOUR

BOULEVARD DALADIER

RUE VICTOR-HUGO

RUE DES TANNEURS

COURS A. BRIAND

RUE PLAISANCE

RUE J. MILLET

RUE NOTRE-DAME

RUE DU RENOYER

Cathédrale

Parc Gasparin

Hôtel de Ville

PL. DE LANGES

PLACE DU CLOITRE

PLACE CLEMENCEAU

PLACE DE LA RÉPUBLIQUE

RUE CARISTIE

RUE DU PONT NEUF

RUE DE LA RÉPUBLIQUE

BOULEVARD DALADIER

AV. J.H. FABRE

AV. F. MISTRAL

RUE CONTRASCARPE

RUE DE L'ANCIEN COLLÈGE

AV. CH. DE GAULLE

RUE ST-MARTIN

RUE GOURMANDE

PL. AUX HERBES

RUE SEGOND WEBER

R. PETITE FUSTERIE

PLACE DES CORDELIERS

RUE DES AVESNES

RUE VIEILLES FOSSES

COURS A. BRIAND

Musée

RUE PONTILLAC

R. TOURGAYRANNE

PL. SILVAIN

PLACE DES FRÈRES MOUNET

RUE ST-FLORENT

PLACE LIBERTÉ

RUE DE L'HOPITAL

Théâtre

Excavations

RUE DE TOURRE

P. DE CHALONS

Théâtre Antique

COURS POURTOULES

Gare Routière

AV. DES THERMES

MONTÉE À LAMBERT

COURS POURTOULES

AV. GÉNÉRAL LECLERC

BD. DALADIER

Château Ruins

MONTÉE DES PRINCES D'ORANGE

Colline St-Eutrope

RUE A. BLANC

RUE GAMBETTA

AV. MARÉCHAL FOCH

Swimming Pool

MONTÉE DES PRINCES D'ORANGE

DESCENTE DES PRINCES D'ORANGE

RUE DE CHATEAUNEUF

N

0   200 m

ACCOMMODATION

Arène Kulm	**A**	Louvre	**C**
Le Glacier	**B**	St-Florent	**E**
L' Herbier d'Orange	**D**		

RESTAURANTS, BARS & CAFÉS

Chez Daniel	**4**	Le Parvis	**7**	Café de l'Univers	**2**
Le Yaca	**6**	Les Négociants	**3**	Café des Thermes	**5**
La Roselière	**1**				

Le Glacier 46 cours Aristide-Briand
☎04.90.34.02.01, ⦿www.le-glacier.com. A
comfortable family-run hotel, offering the best
value in Orange. ❸

🏃 L'Herbier d'Orange 8 place aux Herbes
☎04.90.34.09.23, ⦿www.lherbierdorange
.com. Overlooking the pretty place aux Herbes, this
appealing hotel is a good budget option: it's simple,
clean and quiet. ❷

Louvre 89 av Frédéric-Mistral ☎04.90.34.10.08,
⦿www.hotel-louvre-orange.com. A pleasant three-
star hotel with a garden and a small pool, close to
the train station. ❺

St-Florent 4 rue du Mazeau ☎04.90.34.18.53,
⦿www.hotelsaintflorent.free.fr. Rather kitsch
decor, including four-poster beds in some rooms,
but central and cheap. ❸

Campsite

Le Jonquier 1321 rue Alexis-Carrel
☎04.90.34.49.48, ⦿www.campinglejonquier.com.
Three-star site northwest of the centre, with tennis

courts, pool and mini golf. €22.80 per tent. Closed
Oct–March.

The Town

Orange is not a very big town and can be easily covered on foot. Its old streets
lie north of the enormous Roman theatre which, with the hill of St-Eutrope
behind, is the dominating feature.

Théâtre Antique

Days off in Orange circa 55 AD were spent at the **théâtre**, where an audience
of ten thousand could watch farce, clownish improvisations, song and dance,
and, occasionally, a bit of heavy Greek tragedy, usually in Latin. Today,
although the action is mainly limited to summer music, the theatre (daily:
April, May & Sept 9am–6pm; June–Aug 9am–7pm; Oct & March 9.30am–
5.30pm; Nov–Feb 9.30am–4.30pm; €7.70 including entrance to the Musée
Municipal) is still the focus of the town, an awesome shell at the heart of the
old medieval centre, which survived periods as a fortification, slum and prison
before its careful reconstruction in the nineteenth century. In 1879 the first
performance in 350 years was staged, initiating the Orange **Chorégies**, a
festival of opera performances (see box below).

Said to be the world's best-preserved Roman theatre, Orange's theatre is the
only one with the stage wall still standing – a massive 36m high and 103m
across. The outer face, viewed from place des Frères-Mounet, resembles a
monstrous prison wall, despite the ground-level archways leading into the
backstage areas. Near the top you can see the blocks that held the poles of the
awning which once hung over the stage and the front rows. Those at the back

---

Orange festivals

In July, Orange is packed with opera fanatics, here for the **Chorégies** or **choral
festival**, performed in the Roman theatre. If you're interested in going, you'll need to
make a reservation well in advance; details are available from the Bureau des
Chorégies, 18 place Silvain, 84107 Orange (☎04.90.34.24.24, ⦿www.choregies
.com), and from FNAC shops across the country. Tickets go on sale in October of the
preceding year and prices range from €7.50 to €200, depending on the performance
and your position in the theatre.

The theatre is also used for film, folk and rock concerts. Prices range from €5 to
€30, and some performances are free; details are available from the Service Culturel
de la Ville, place Clemenceau (☎04.90.51.57.57) as well as from FNAC shops.

△ Théâtre Antique

were protected from the sun by the hill of St-Eutrope into which the seats are built. Rows were allocated strictly by rank; an inscription "EQ Gradus III" (third row for knights) is visible near the orchestra pit. The enormous **stage** could accommodate vast numbers of performers, and the acoustics, thanks to the complex projections of the stage wall, allowed a full audience to hear every word. Though missing most of its original decoration, the inner side of the stage wall is an extremely impressive sight. Columned niches, now empty of their statues, run the length of the wall; below them a larger-than-life-size statue of Augustus, raising his arm in imperious fashion, looks down centre stage.

If the spectators grew bored during the day-long performances, they could slip out of the west door to a semicircle complex cut into the rock. According to some archeologists, this contained baths, a stage for combats and a gymnasium equipped with three 180-metre running tracks alongside the wall of rue Pontillac, parts of which still stand. Others say it was the forum, or even a circus. There are widely differing views on how the **excavations** should be interpreted, though all agree that the massive capital was part of a temple.

The best view of the theatre in its entirety, and one for which you don't have to pay, is from **St-Eutrope hill**. You can follow a path up the hill either from the top of cours Aristide-Briand, montée P.-de-Chalons, or from cours Pourtoules, montée Albert-Lambert, until you are looking directly down onto the stage. The **ruins** around your feet are those of the short-lived seventeenth-century **château** of the princes of Orange. Louis XIV had it destroyed and the principality annexed to France, a small setback for William of Orange who was to become William III of Britain and Ireland.

The Musée Municipal and Arc de Triomphe

Orange's **Musée Municipal** (municipal museum) stands across the road from the theatre entrance (same hours as the Théâtre Antique except Nov–Feb daily 9.30am-12.30pm & 1.30–4.30pm; €4.50, or €7.70 including entrance to the theatre). Its various documents concerning the Orange dynasty include a suitably austere portrait of the very first Orangeman, William (Guillaume) the Taciturn, grandfather to William III. The museum also has an interesting – for classical historians at least – property register and land survey of the city in 77 AD, and a display of various bits and pieces from the theatre. The rest of the collection is rotated on a yearly basis, but contains diverse items such as the contents of a seventeenth-century apothecary and a collection of pictures portraying British workers from early last century by Frank Brangwyn, a Welsh painter who learnt his craft with William Morris.

To the north of the centre, on the main road into Orange, stands the town's second major monument, the **Arc de Triomphe**, whose intricate friezes and reliefs celebrate imperial victories against the Gauls. Although highly regarded by classicists as one of the largest, best-preserved and oldest triple-bayed Roman arches in existence, the Arc's position in the middle of a major road detracts somewhat from its appeal.

Eating and drinking

Although **eating out** in Orange is unlikely to prove an exceptional experience, there's no shortage of choice and prices are reasonable. *Chez Daniel*, 12 rue Segond Weber (℡04.90.34.63.48; closed lunchtimes Wed & Sun), serves cheap pizzas and pasta (€8–11) as well as menus from €13 with mussels, while *Le Yaca*, in an old vaulted chamber at 24 place Silvain (℡04.90.34.70.03; closed Tues eve & Wed), boasts a generous choice of Provençal and other French dishes such as *andouillette* and beef bourguignon on menus from €13. Some of Orange's more inventive cooking can be found at *La Roselière*, 4 rue du Renoyer (℡04.90.34.50.42; closed Sat & Sun), a lovely little restaurant by the Hôtel de Ville, where you can sample tasty veal and duck dishes on menus priced from €12 to €15. However, the best food you're likely to get in Orange is at *Le Parvis*, 55 cours des Pourtoules (℡04.90.34.82.00; closed Sun eve & Mon), which serves classic French *haute cuisine*; menus start at €24.50.

For **drinking**, head for the central place de la République, where you'll find *Les Négociants*, with its sunny terrace, and the less expensive *Café de l'Univers*, both lively spots when the shops are open but much quieter at night. A better bet for evening entertainment is the *Café des Thermes* (5pm–1.30am) at 29 rue des Vieux-Fossés, to the west of cours Aristide-Briand, with a good selection of beers, a pool table and a youngish clientele.

Sérignan-du-Comtat

For those with a car, it's an enjoyable drive from Orange to **SÉRIGNAN-DU-COMTAT**, 8km northeast of the city; along the way are beautiful views of the smooth lower slopes of Mont Ventoux. Sérignan-du-Comtat's most celebrated resident is **Jean-Henri Fabre** (1823–1915), who spent the last 36 years of his life here. A remarkable self-taught scientist, Fabre is famous primarily for his insect studies; he also composed poetry, wrote songs and painted his specimens with artistic brilliance as well as scientific accuracy. In his forties, with seven children to support, he was forced to resign from his teaching post at Avignon because parents and priests considered his lectures on the fertilization of flowering plants licentious if not downright pornographic. His friend John Stuart Mill eventually bailed him out with a loan, allowing him to settle in Orange. Darwin was also a friend with whom he had lengthy correspondence, though Fabre was too religious to be an evolutionist.

A **statue of Fabre** stands beside the red-shuttered buildings of the *mairie*, while his actual house, which he named the **Harmas** (Latin for fallow land), is on the edge of the village on the N976 from Orange (mid-May to Oct daily except Tues 10am–12.30pm & 2.30–6pm; €6). Inside, you can look round Fabre's study with its various specimens of insects and other invertebrates and his complete classification of the herbs of France and Corsica. The room gives a strong sense of a person in love with the world he researched, an impression echoed in the selection on the ground floor of Fabre's extraordinary **water-colours** of the fungi of the Vaucluse. The stunning colours and almost halluci-nogenic detail make these pictures seem more like holograms. After visiting the house you're free to wander round the **garden** where over a thousand species, including bamboo, cedar, lilac and a single aleppo pine planted by Fabre himself, grow in wild disorder, exactly as the scientist wanted it.

The Enclave des Papes and Nyons

Heading north from Orange, the **Enclave des Papes**, centred on the town of **Valréas**, is not part of the Drôme *département* that surrounds it, but part of Vaucluse, an anomaly dating back to 1317 when the land was bought by Pope Jean XXII as part of his policy of expanding the papal states around his Holy See at Avignon. When the Vaucluse *département* was drawn up the enclave was allowed to keep its old links and hence remains part of Provence.

Grignan, just outside the western edge of the enclave, and Valréas both have luxurious **châteaux**, and there are many **vineyards**, most edged with roses as an attractive early-warning system of aphid attack. East of the enclave, the pretty, undulating landscape comes to an abrupt end with the arc of mountains around **Nyons**. These are the edge of the **Lower Alps** that curve southeast from Nyons into the **Baronnies range**, forming the border of Provence north of Mont Ventoux. Nyons is not, therefore, a Provençal city but it feels like one and is a delightful place, not least because of its solid protection against northern and eastern winds, including the Mistral.

Valréas

VALRÉAS, at the heart of the enclave, lies 35km northeast of Orange. Here, Mme de Sévigné's granddaughter lived in the Château de Simiane, a mainly eighteenth-century mansion whose arcades, windows and balustrades would look more at home in Paris, though the pantiled roofs are distinctly Provençal. Today, the building is used as the **Hôtel de Ville**; a few rooms can be visited, including the *salon de mariage* and the library (July & Aug daily except Tues 10.30am–noon & 3–6pm; Sept–June Mon, Tues, Thurs–Sat 3–5pm; free), and in July and August the hôtel hosts contemporary art shows (daily except Tues 10.30am–noon & 3–6pm; free). The town's other example of *ancien régime* ornamentation is the painted wooden ceiling of the **Chapelle des Pénitents Blancs** on place Pie (July & Aug guided tours Fri at 9.30am; at other times chapel open for self-guided tours 10am–noon & 3–5pm; free), which stands to the west of the much more subdued eleventh-century **Église Notre-Dame-de-Nazareth**.

Valréas is an important centre of cardboard production and, just outside the town in a warehouse on the road west to Orange, there's a museum dedicated to the use of the product: the **Musée du Cartonnage et de l'Imprimerie** (April–Oct Mon & Wed–Sat 10am–noon & 3–6pm, Sun 3–6pm; Nov–March 10am–noon & 2–5pm; €3.50), a surprisingly intriguing museum of packaging.

Valréas is at its busiest on June 23 and 24, for the night-time procession and show of the **Nuit de Petit St-Jean**, and on the first Sunday in August, when the **Fête des Vins de l'Enclave** takes place. At other times, it's a pleasant, if quiet, place to spend some time. The most interesting diversions lie in buying local **wines**. As well as the Côtes du Rhône *appellation* there's also Valréas Villages and Visan Villages, distinctive enclave wines, with flavours of violet, red fruits and pepper; it's said that these distinctive wines were what persuaded Pope Jean XXII to buy this area in the first place. The **Cave Coopérative** is at the Caveau St-Jean, avenue de l'Enclave des Papes; you can also visit the private cellars (full list from the tourist office).

The **tourist office** is to the north of town on avenue Maréchal Leclerc (July & Aug Mon–Sat 9.15am–12.15pm & 2.30–6.30pm, Sun 9.15am–12.15pm; Sept, Oct & March–June Mon–Sat 9.15am–12.15pm & 2–6pm; Nov–Feb 9.15am–12.15pm & 2–5pm; ☎04.90.35.04.71; ⊛www.ot-valreas.info). The best places **to stay** are the *Grand Hôtel*, 28 av Général-de-Gaulle (☎04.90.35.00.26, ⊕04.90.35.60.93; closed late Dec to Jan; ❹), on the outskirts of town, with a pool and pleasant gardens, and the more moderate *Camargue*, 49 cours Jean-Jaurès (☎04.90.35.01.51; ❷); both have reasonable restaurants. There's also a two-star **campsite**, *Camping de la Couronne*, by the river on route du Pègue (☎04.90.35.03.78; closed Oct–Feb; €15.50 per tent).

A good place **to eat** is *La Ferme Champ-Rond* on chemin des Anthelmes, off route de St-Pierre to the southeast of town (☎04.90.37.31.68); it uses local produce with menus from €18.50. In town, *L'Oustau*, 2 cours Tivoli (☎04.90.35.05.94; closed Thurs eve, Sun eve & Mon), has menus starting from €24 and specializes in seafood à la carte. You can sample the **local wines** at the beautiful *Café de la Paix* on rue de l'Hôtel de Ville. The **market** is held on Wednesday on place Cardinal-Maury and cours du Berteuil on the eastern side of town, with local truffles figuring prominently between November and March.

Grignan

GRIGNAN, on the main route heading west from Valréas out of the enclave, is dominated by its **château** (guided tours: July & Aug daily 9.30–11.30am & 2–6pm; April–June & Sept–Oct daily 9.30–11.30am & 2.30–5.30pm; Nov–March daily except Tues 9.30–11.30am & 2–5.30pm; €5.50). The enormous building takes up all the high ground of the town, rising above the heavy towers and walls of the town's St-Saveur's church and the medieval houses below the southern facade. Though eleventh-century in origin, the château was transformed in the sixteenth century into a Renaissance palace, with tiers of huge windows facing the south and statues lining the roof; the older parts lie to the north.

The château's most famous resident was the writer **Madame de Sévigné**, who came here for long periods to visit her daughter, the countess of Grignan. You can see the comforts and craftsmanship of the contemporary furnishings, plus eighteenth-century additions, in the tour of the *salons*, galleries and grand stairways, Mme de Sévigné's bedroom and the count's apartments.

Four kilometres from Grignan on the Valréas road, just outside the village of Grillon, is the three-room **hotel-restaurant** *Auberge des Papes,* route de Grignan (☎04.90.37.43.67; ⊛www.aubergedespapes.free.fr; half board obligatory July & Aug; closed Sept; ❺), which offers quiet, comfortable rooms and meals in which truffles feature prominently (restaurant closed Wed out of season; menus from €18).

Nyons

After Grignan and Valréas, **NYONS**, on the River Aigues 16km east of Valréas, seems like a metropolis, though its population is well under ten thousand. It is an extremely attractive place, perfect for lazing about in cafés or strolling through, with its medieval centre and aromatic riverside gardens. If Nyons is on your route into Provence, you can begin to appreciate the essentials of the region's cooking here: olives and olive oil, garlic, wild mushrooms, and countless varieties of fruit and vegetables, with seasons quite different to the north. If Nyons is on your way out, then this is the place to do the final shop.

Arrival and accommodation

Nyons has no train links and is served by just one bus a day from Avignon. **Buses** arrive at place Buffaven on the edge of the old town, just northeast of the large central square, place de la Libération, where you'll find the **tourist office** (April–June & Sept Mon–Sat 9.30am–noon & 2.30–6pm, Sun 10am–1pm & 2–5pm; July & Aug Mon–Sat 9am–12.30pm & 2.30–6pm, Sun 10am–1pm & 2–5pm; Oct–March Mon–Sat 9.30am–noon & 2.30–5.45pm; ℡04.75.26.10.35, ⓦwww.nyonstourisme.com).

Nyons has plenty of **hotel** rooms. Moderately priced options include *Au Petit Nice*, 4 av Paul Laurens, just to the west of place de la Libération (℡04.75.26.09.46; closed first two weeks in July & all of Nov; ❸); and *Les Oliviers*, 2 rue A-Escoffier (℡04.75.26.11.44, ⓦwww.les-oliviers-nyons.com; ❹), a small, pleasant hotel with a garden bordering the old town to the north. For a bit more luxury, try the lavish *Une Autre Maison*, on place de la République, with six south-facing rooms overlooking a pretty garden, plus a pool, sauna and Jacuzzi (℡04.75.26.43.09, ⓦwww.uneautremaison.com; ❼); or *La Caravelle*, 8 rue des Antignans (℡04.75.26.07.44, ℗04.75.26.07.40; closed mid-Nov to Jan; ❺), with an attractive riverside location close to the town centre. There are also two excellent **campsites**: the four-star *Camping des Clos*, 1km along the road to Gap (℡04.75.26.29.90, ⓦwww.campinglesclos.com; €18.50 per tent; closed Nov–Feb), which has its own pool, and the two-star *Camping l'Or Vert*, 2km further along the same road (℡04.75.26.24.85, ⓦwww.camping-or-vert.com; €13.30 per tent; closed Oct–March).

The Town

The pavement terraces of **place de la Libération**'s cafés and brasseries are a pleasant place to while away an afternoon, people-watching against a

---

Olive produce

Nyons is famous for its **olives**. Black eating olives are a speciality, as is *tapenade* (a paste of olives, capers and herbs), but the biggest business is making olive oil, a process you can watch between December and February. Among firms that welcome visitors are **Moulin J. Ramade**, avenue P-Laurens (just before place Oliver-de-Serres on the left), who show a video explaining all the subtleties, and **Moulin à Huile Dozol-Autrand**, on avenue de la Digue by the Pont Romain. The tourist office can provide more addresses, and there's also a small **museum** on the subject on rue des Tilleuls (June–Oct Mon–Sat 10–11am & 3–6pm; Nov–May Mon–Sat 3–6pm; €2).

The **Coopérative Agricole du Nyonsais** on place Oliver-de-Serres (July & Aug Mon–Sat 9am–12.30pm & 2–7pm, Sun 10am–12.30pm & 2.30–6.30pm; Sept–June Mon–Sat 9am–12.15pm & 2–6.30pm, Sun 10am–12.30pm & 2.30–6pm) sells a full range of olive products under the trademark "Nyonsolive", as well as nut and chilli oils, wines and honey.

background of fountains, plane trees, palms and curly wrought-iron lampposts, and taking in the views beyond of steep wooded slopes. On Thursdays the square and its neighbour to the northeast, place Buffaven, are taken over by a huge and wonderful **market**. A smaller one takes place on Monday – and in July and August there's a Sunday-morning market in the old town.

East of place de la Libération, the arcaded **place du Dr-Bourdongle** leads into a web of streets, covered passages and stairways running up to the **quartier des Forts**, so named for the now ruined feudal castle; the fourteenth-century Château Delpinal, of which three towers remain; and the extraordinary **Tour Randonne**, which houses a nineteenth-century chapel, with a neo-Gothic pyramid supporting a statue of the Madonna, sitting delicately on the heavy crenellated base of a thirteenth-century keep.

Towards the river, which is crossed by a single-spanned Romanesque bridge, the **Pont Romain**, there are pleasantly untouristy streets, scattered with bars and restaurants. Just beside the bridge, at 4 av de la Digue, is **Les Vieux Moulins** (guided tours: July & Aug Mon–Sat 11.30am, 3pm & 4pm; Sept, Oct & April–June Tues–Sat 11am & 3pm; €4), an old artisanal complex of two eighteenth- and nineteenth-century oil presses, an eighteenth-century soap works, and a traditional Provençal kitchen.

About 500m west of the bridge, along the river, is the small but sensual **Jardin des Arômes**, a garden of aromatic plants from which essential oils are made.

Eating and drinking

One of Nyons' better **restaurants** is *Le Petit Caveau*, 9 rue Victor-Hugo (☎04.75.26.20.21; menus €23–50; closed Sun eve & Mon), which serves very good, classic Provençal food and wines. At *Les Alpes*, 27 rue des Déportés (☎04.75.26.04.99), you can get couscous from €11, while on the same street there's a choice of Tex-Mex dinners at *Le Tex* (from €10) and pizzas at *L'Alicoque* (from €7; closed Mon & Sat lunch). The best place for *steack-frites*, meanwhile, is the *Bar du Pont Roman*, at 10 place Jules Laurent, with great views over the old Pont Romain. For a relaxing **drink**, head for the pavement terraces of the cafés on place de la Libération.

Vaison-la-Romaine and around

Heading south from Nyons back into Provence, you'll soon arrive at charming **VAISON-LA-ROMAINE**. The most dramatic approach, however, is from the southeast along the Malaucène road from Carpentras, from where the first glimpse of the town is of a ruined twelfth-century castle outlined against the sky. As you get closer you see the storeys of old pale stone houses and towers beneath it, and the eighteenth-century town laid around its Roman predecessor. The two are linked by a Roman bridge, spanning the River Ouvèze in a single arch. The original Celtic Voconces, like the late medieval Vaisonnais, chose the high ground for defensive reasons, but their descendants abandoned the citadel and moved back to the right bank in the eighteenth century.

The older generation in Vaison recalls the days when shops were little more than front rooms and you would interrupt the cooking or other household chores when you went in to be served. These days the population of the town and its tourist visitors can keep several dozen bars, hotels and restaurants busy, as well as numerous souvenir shops. Today, its main attractions are the medieval **Haute Ville** with a ruined cliff-top castle, a Roman bridge known as the **Pont**

Romain, a cloistered former cathedral and the exceptional excavated remains of two **Roman districts**.

Arrival, information and accommodation

Buses to and from Avignon, Orange and Carpentras stop at the **gare routière** on avenue des Choralies, near the junction with avenue Victor-Hugo east of the town centre on the north side of the river. Heading down avenue Victor-Hugo you'll come to the main square, **place Montfort**, from where it's a short walk further west to **Grande Rue** which leads left to the **Pont Romain** and right, becoming avenue Général-de-Gaulle, to **place du Chanoine-Sautel**. This is where you'll find the **tourist office** (July & Aug daily 9am–12.30pm & 2–6.45pm; April–June & Sept to mid-Oct Mon–Sat 9am–noon & 2–5.45pm, Sun 9am–noon; mid-Oct to March Mon–Sat 9am–noon & 2–5.45pm; ℡04.90.36.02.11, ⊛www.vaison-la-romaine.com), between the two Roman archeological sites.

Accommodation is thin on the ground and consequently somewhat expensive.

Hotels

Le Beffroi rue de l'Evêché in the Haute Ville ℡04.90.36.04.71, ⊛www.le-beffroi.com. Stylish and expensive lodgings in a sixteenth-century residence; the rooms are furnished in keeping with the building and offer panoramic views. There's also a swimming pool. Closed Feb to mid-March. **❻**

Le Burrhus 2 place Montfort ℡04.90.36.00.11, ⊛www.burrhus.com. The cheapest rooms in town and noisy at weekends as it's above several cafés with terraces. **❸**

La Fête en Provence place du Vieux Marché in the Haute Ville ℡04.90.36.36.43, ⊛www .hotellafete-provence.com. Studios and duplexes, let on a day-to-day basis. Closed Dec to mid-March. **❹**

Le Logis du Château Les Hauts de Vaison ℡04.90.36.09.98, ⊛www.logis-du-chateau.com. Along montée du Château south of the river, and to the west of the Haute Ville; spacious rooms with lovely views. Closed Nov–March. **❸**

Campsite

Camping du Théâtre Romain chemin du Brusquet, off av des Choralies, quartier des Arts ℡04.90.28.78.66, ⊛www.camping-theatre.com. Small, four-star campsite 500m from the centre with good facilities. €19 per tent. Closed mid-Nov to mid-March.

The Town

Of all the distinctive periods in Vaison's history, it is the style and luxuries of the **Roman** population that are the most intriguing. The two excavated Roman residential districts in Vaison lie to either side of avenue Général-de-Gaulle: the **Vestiges de Puymin** to the east (daily: March 10am–12.30pm & 2–5pm; April & May 9.30am–6pm; June–Sept 9.30am–6.30pm; Oct–Feb 10am–noon & 2–5pm; €7.50 includes both sites, plus Puymin museum and cathedral cloisters); and the **Vestiges de la Villasse** to the west (daily except Tues morning: March 10am–12.30pm & 2–6pm; April & May 10am–noon & 2.30–6pm; June–Sept 10am–noon & 2.30–6.30pm; Oct–Feb 10am–noon & 2–5pm).

The Puymin ruins (*vestiges*) contain the theatre, several mansions and houses thought to be for rent, a colonnade known as the *portique de Pompée* and the museum for all the items discovered. The Villasse site reveals a street with pavements and gutters with the layout of a row of arcaded shops running parallel, more patrician houses (some with mosaics still intact), a basilica and the

A taste of Provence

Wholesome yet healthy, the cooking of Provence displays all the benefits of the Mediterranean diet, with superb fish on the coast, excellent lamb from Sisteron and, everywhere, fantastic fresh fruit and vegetables – the rewards of a sunny climate. Although the region is home to some of the world's finest and most expensive restaurants, the true glory of Provençal cuisine lies in honest home cooking based on fresh, locally sourced ingredients: in the countryside, in particular, small, family-run restaurants still serve up tasty *prix-fixe* feasts at traditional prices, while Nice is as good a place as any in Europe to find cheap, simple but delicious street food.

Feasts from the sea

Fish and **seafood** are mainstays of the diet on the Mediterranean coast. At its most sublimely simple this means **oursins** – sea urchins – eaten raw with a sprinkling of lemon juice and a glass of crisp white wine; they're also cooked to make *oursinade* – a fish soup or sauce. But the region's love of fish is best reflected in the celebrated **soups** or **stews**: **bourride**, made with monkfish, where the cooking liquor is thickened with *aïoli* afterwards and served separately as a soup, and the famous **bouillabaisse** of Marseille, originally a humble meal cooked on the beach by fishermen but now quite a grand affair, the high cost of which reflects the quality of the ingredients used – notably *rascasse* or scorpion fish.

Aromatic extras

One of the most distinctive characteristics of Provençal cuisine is the use of strongly flavoured **condiments** derived from a variety of fresh ingredients.

Aïoli

A mayonnaise-like sauce of garlic and olive oil, **aïoli** derives its name from the Provençal for garlic (*ail*) and olive (*oli*). You'll often see *un grand aïoli* on restaurant menus – not a large helping of garlic mayonnaise, but rather an elaborate dish of salt cod, boiled beef, mutton and stewed vegetables, served with *aïoli* and garnished with boiled eggs and snails.

Pistou

The cooking of eastern Provence is closely related to that of Italian Liguria, and **pistou** is the Provençal equivalent of the celebrated Italian pesto sauce. *Pistou* is made with basil, crushed garlic and olive oil, and is most famously added to *soupe au pistou*.

Rouille

A thick, pinky-orange, *aïoli*-like sauce, **rouille** is made with chilli, garlic and saffron, pounded with breadcrumbs or potato, to which are added olive oil and stock. Along with finely-grated cheese, it's one of the classic accompaniments to a Provençal fish soup.

Tapenade

A pungent savoury spread, **tapenade** is made with capers, anchovies and black olives, olive oil and lemon juice, and accompanies fish or crudités or is simply eaten on toast.

Daube de boeuf

This wonderful slow-cooked beef stew is one of the heartiest dishes on any Provençal menu: served piping hot it's a delicious way to keep out the winter chill, though it is also eaten cold. You may encounter variations of it, but **daube de boeuf** commonly contains a curl of orange peel, a few juniper berries, chopped bacon and a great deal of red wine, in which the beef is marinated overnight before cooking, in order develop the rich, deep flavour. It's usually served with fresh *tagliatelles*.

▲ Daube de boeuf

Sweet treats

With such an abundance of fresh produce, **fruit** is the obvious end to a meal in Provence. That doesn't mean that the region lacks in sugary treats: Aix-en-Provence is famous for its **calissons** – lozenge-shaped sweetmeats made from candied melon and ground almonds. Almonds also feature in the deliciously soft, honey-flavoured **nougat** that is found everywhere in the region, though the traditional centre of the industry is in the Rhône valley town of Montélimar just outside Provence. Orange water lends a delicate scent to the **fougassettes** of Grasse, while lavender often adds an exotic flavour to **crème brûlée**. Candied fruit and flowers and the **violet-scented ice cream** of Tourrettes-sur-Loup are among the many other indulgences that Provence has to offer.

▶ Calissons

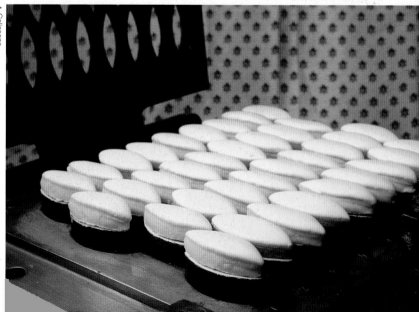

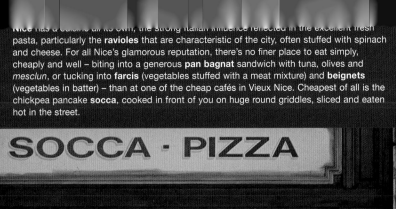

Nice has a cuisine all its own, the strong Italian influence reflected in the excellent fresh pasta, particularly the **ravioles** that are characteristic of the city, often stuffed with spinach and cheese. For all Nice's glamorous reputation, there's no finer place to eat simply, cheaply and well – biting into a generous **pan bagnat** sandwich with tuna, olives and *mesclun*, or tucking into **farcis** (vegetables stuffed with a meat mixture) and **beignets** (vegetables in batter) – than at one of the cheap cafés in Vieux Nice. Cheapest of all is the chickpea pancake **socca**, cooked in front of you on huge round griddles, sliced and eaten hot in the street.

baths. The houses require a certain amount of imagination, but the street plan of La Villasse, the colonnade with its statues in every niche, and the theatre, which still seats seven thousand people during the July **dance festival** (information on ☎04.90.28.74.74 or ⓦwww.vaison-festival.com) make it easy to visualize a comfortable, well-serviced town of the Roman ruling class.

Most of the detail and decoration of the buildings is displayed in the **museum** (closes 15min before the main sites) in the Puymin district. Tiny fragments of painted plaster have been jigsawed together with convincing reconstructions of how whole painted walls would have looked. There are mirrors of silvered bronze, lead water pipes, taps shaped as griffins' feet, dolphin door knobs, weights and measures, plus household and building implements. The busts and statues are particularly impressive: among them a silver head of one of the Villasse villas' owners; the emperor Domitian, under whose reign the conquest of Britain was completed, wearing a breast-plate of Minerva and the Gorgon's head; and a statue of another famous emperor, Hadrian.

The former **Cathédrale Notre-Dame** lies west down chemin Couradou which runs along the south side of La Villasse. The apse of the cathedral is a confusing overlay of sixth-, tenth- and thirteenth-century construction, some of it using pieces quarried from the Roman ruins. The **cloisters** (closes 15min before the main sites) are fairly typical of early medieval workmanship, pretty enough but not wildly exciting. The only surprising feature is the large inscription visible on the north wall of the cathedral, a convoluted instruction to the monks to bring peace upon the house by loving the monastic rule and following God's grace.

Just south of the Roman districts, the **Pont Romain** leads across the river to the *Haute Ville*. The bridge has undergone extensive repair works since 1992, when the River Ouvèze burst its banks, killing thirty people and causing a great deal of material damage. Although the Pont Romain took a battering during the flood, it says a lot for Roman engineering that it fared better than the modern road bridge to the west, which was completely destroyed. Its new casings need weathering to return it to its former beauty, but the grace of the high-arched structure remains.

From the bridge, rue du Pont Romain (pedestrians only during July and Aug) climbs upwards towards place du Poids and the fourteenth-century gateway to the medieval **Haute Ville**. More steep zigzags take you past the Gothic gate and overhanging portcullis of the belfry and into the heart of this sedately quiet, uncommercialized and rich *quartier*. There are fountains and flowers in all the squares, and right at the top, from the twelfth- to sixteenth-century **Castle**, you'll have a great view of Mont Ventoux. In summer the Haute Ville livens up every Tuesday when Vaison's **market** spreads up here.

Eating and drinking

The **restaurant** to head for in Vaison is *Le Bateleur* at 1 place Théodore-Aubanel, downstream from the Pont Romain on the north bank (☎04.90.36.28.04; July–Sept closed Mon & Sat lunch; Oct–June closed Mon, Thurs eve & Sat lunch; menus €28–44): try the guinea fowl stuffed with snails or the roast salmon. Alternatively, *L'Auberge de la Bartavelle*, 12 place Sus-Auze (☎04.90.36.02.16; closed Mon & Fri lunch and Jan & Feb), serves specialities from southwest France – rabbit ravioli, *confit de canard* and the like – on menus from €20. There are several **brasseries** on and around avenue Général-de-Gaulle: *L'Oustal*, at no. 12 (☎04.90.36.05.07; mid-Sept to Easter closed Wed), is good for salads and pizzas as well as traditional *plats* for €12–15.

In the *Haute Ville*, the restaurant at *Le Beffroi* hotel has a surprisingly inexpensive menu (€28), served with stiff formality on a garden terrace with great views. Far less formal is the *Crêperie la Pomme*, at 3 rue du Pont (☎04.90.36.38.80; closed Thurs lunch & Wed out of season; around €5), which also offers fine views.

The **cafés** on place Montfort are the best place to head for **drinks**, while for buying **wine** to take home, the Maison des Vins, in the same building as the tourist office (Tues–Sat 9.30am–12.30pm & 2.30–6.30pm), has several wines from the vineyards of the Dentelles and Ventoux.

The Dentelles

Running northeast to southwest between Vaison and Carpentras, the jagged hilly backdrop of the **DENTELLES DE MONTMIRAIL** is best appreciated from the contrasting landscape of level fields, orchards and vineyards lying to their south and west. The range is named after lace (*dentelles*), its pinnacles slanting, converging, standing parallel or veering away from each other, like the contorted pins on a lace-making board – though the alternative connection with "teeth" (*dents*) is equally appropriate. For geologists, the Dentelles are Jurassic limestone folds, forced upright and then eroded by the wind and rain.

On the western and southern slopes lie the **wine-producing villages** of **Gigondas**, **Beaumes-de-Venise**, **Séguret**, **Vacqueyras** and, across the River Ouzère, **Rasteau**. Several carry the distinction of having their own individual *appellation contrôlée*, within the Côtes du Rhône or Côtes du Rhône Villages areas, meaning their wines are exceptional. If you're in the region over the July 14 holiday, head straight to Vacqueyras for the bacchanalian **Fêtes des Vins**, while at any other time of the year a more sober introduction to the subject is on offer at Rasteau's museum.

Besides wine-tasting and bottle-buying, the Dentelles are good for long **walks**, happening upon mysterious ruins or photogenic panoramas of Mont Ventoux and the Rhône Valley. The jagged hills are also favourite destinations for apprentice **rock-climbers**: the Col de Cayron is one of the favourite pinnacles for serious climbing; the Dent du Turc needs only decent shoes and a head for heights to give a thrill. To the east of the range lies the *village perché* of **Le Barroux**, with a fine twelfth-century château.

Although it's possible to get to the villages by public transport from Vaison or (much less frequently) from Carpentras, having your own transport is a near-necessity if you want to tour from village to village. For **walking and climbing information**, go to the *Gîte d'Etape des Dentelles* in Gigondas (see p.172), whose owner is a serious mountain climber, or pick up a local footpath map (€2.50) from the tourist office in Gigondas (see p.172). Alternatively, Edisud publishes a more detailed guide, *Randonnées au Ventoux et dans les Dentelles* by I. & H. Agresti, which is available from most of the region's tourist offices.

Rasteau

For a good introduction to the art and science of wine-making and the whole business of wine-tasting, head for **RASTEAU** and the **Musée du Vigneron**, on the D975 between Rasteau and Roaix (Mon & Wed–Sat: July & Aug 11am–6pm; April–June & Sept 2pm–6pm; €2), which is owned by the the Domaine de Beaurenard – which also has vineyards in Châteauneuf-du-Pape.

For the serious wine enthusiast, the collection of old bottles, nineteenth-century agricultural implements, pickers' baskets and root injectors for fighting phylloxera is less interesting than the instructive displays on geology, soil, vine types, parasites and wine-growing throughout the world; and a twenty-minute video does a reasonable job of demystifying the incredibly complicated rules for the awarding of *appellation* status. The visit ends with a free tasting with no obligation to buy.

If you want **to stay** in Rasteau, the *Belle Rive* on route Violes (☎04.90.46.10.20, ⊛www.hotel-bellerive.fr; ❼; closed Oct–March) is a quiet hotel with a fine view from its terrace, and serves good food, including *crème brûlées* flavoured with rosemary, chestnut and the like. For walkers, the *Centre Départemental d'Animation* on route du Stade (☎04.90.46.15.48), offers dormitory accommodation for €13 – half board (€32) or full board (€37.50) is obligatory after two nights. The place is often reserved for large groups, so always call in advance.

Séguret and Sablet

The star Dentelles village, **SÉGURET**, whose name means "safe place" in Provençal, is an alluring spot blending into the rocky cliff rising above. With its steep cobbled streets, vine-covered houses and medieval structures, including an old stone laundry and a belfry with a one-handed clock, the village embodies many of Provence's charms. On Christmas Eve, in place of the standard Provençal crib, it hosts a living re-enactment of the Nativity in which people play the parts their grandparents and great-grandparents played before them. The **Fête des Vins et Festival Provençal Bravade** in the last two weeks of August is a relatively recent festival, incorporating processions for the Virgin Mary and the patron saint of wine-growers.

Séguret has two very smart **hotels**, *Domaine de Cabasse*, route de Sablet (☎04.90.46.91.12, ⊛www.domaine-de-cabasse.fr, half board obligatory in July & Aug; closed Nov–March; ❼), and *La Table du Comtat* in the village centre (☎04.90.46.91.49, ⊛www.table-comtat.com; ❻), both with a few well-appointed rooms and good restaurants serving Provençal specialities. A slightly cheaper and a more rustic option is the *Bastide Bleue*, route de Sablet (☎04.90.46.83.43, including breakfast; ❺), 500m from the village on the Vaison road. For **food**, try *Le Mesclun*, rue des Poternes (☎04.90.46.93.43; closed Mon & Nov–Easter), which is renowned for using fresh local ingredients in its dishes; menus start at €25.

Gigondas and Vacqueyras

Known as "Jocunditas" (light-hearted joy) in Roman times, the village of **GIGONDAS** sits at the base of a hill, spreading upwards to the **église Ste-Catherine**. From the church, you get one of the region's best views of limestone pinnacles emerging from the vineyards below. Also in the upper reaches of the village are the vestiges of the old fortifications and château, which have now been transformed into a *Cheminement de Sculptures* (always open; free), a collection of contemporary sculptures and installations.

Gigondas' wine has the best reputation of all the Dentelles *appellations*. It is almost always red, quite strong, has a back taste of spice or nuts and is best aged at least four or five years. Sampling the varieties could not be easier since the **Syndicat des Vins** runs a *caveau des vignerons* (daily 10am–noon & 2–6pm) in place de la Mairie where you can taste and ask advice about the produce from forty different *domaines*. It's also a good place to buy as the bottles cost exactly the same as at the vineyards.

Gigondas' **tourist office** is on place du Portail (July & Aug Mon–Sat 10am–12.30pm & 2.30–6.30pm, Sun 10am–1pm; Sept, Oct & April–June Mon–Sat 10am–12.30pm & 2.30–6pm; Nov–March 10am–noon & 2–5pm ☎04.90.65.85.46, ✉office.tourisme@gigondas-les-dentelles-de-montmirail .fr), and can provide lists of particular *domaines* or *caves* grouping several *vignerons* for the other villages. If you want **to stay**, the *Gîte d'Etape des Dentelles* at the entrance to Gigondas (☎04.90.65.80.85; closed Jan & Feb; ❶), has cheap double rooms, and dormitory accommodation (€12.50 per person). There's also a charming hotel, *Les Florets*, 2km from the village towards the Dentelles (☎04.90.65.85.01, ⓦwww.hotel-lesflorets.com; ❻; closed Jan–March), with an excellent **restaurant** (menus from €25; closed Wed, also Mon eve & Tues out of season, plus Jan to mid-March) with wines from its own vineyard. Alternative food options include *L'Oustalet*, on place du Portail in the village (☎04.90.65.85.30; Nov–April closed Mon), with a pleasant shaded terrace and dinner menus from €27.

Three kilometres to the south, the village of **VACQUEYRAS** is best known as the birthplace of a troubadour poet **Raimbaud**, who wrote love poems to Beatrice in Provençal and died in the Crusades in 1207. Vacqueyras is another of the Dentelles villages with its own *appellation* and is home to an annual **wine festival** (on July 13 & 14) and a wine-tasting competition on the first weekend of June. You'll see plenty of signs for wine producers to visit around the village.

For **accommodation**, there's the upmarket *Montmirail*, just south of the centre (☎04.90.65.84.01, ⓦwww.hotelmontmirail.com; closed Nov to mid-March; ❾), with a good Provençal restaurant (lunch menus from €23, dinner menus from €35).

Beaumes-de-Venise

The most distinctive wine of the region, and elixir for those who like it sweet, is Beaumes-de-Venise muscat. Pale amber in colour and with a hint of roses and lemon following the muscat flavour, it can usually convince the driest palates of its virtue. The place to buy it is at **BEAUMES–DE–VENISE**, at the Cave des Vignerons, in a huge low building on the D7 overlooked by the Romanesque bell tower of **Notre–Dame–d'Aubune** (Mon–Sat 8.30am–12.30pm & 2–7pm, Sun 9am–12.30pm & 2.30–7pm). The *cave* also sells red, rosé and white Côtes du Rhône Villages, and the light Côtes du Ventoux. The **church** in Beaumes reflects the key concern of the area in the trailing vines and classical wine containers sculpted over the door. The **tourist office** (Mon–Sat: June–Sept 9am–noon & 2–7pm; Oct–May 9am–noon & 2–6pm; ☎04.90.62.94.39, ⓦwww.ot-beaumesdevenise.com), near the church, can also provide lists of *domaines* or *caves* for the area.

The village has two quiet, old-fashioned **hotels**, both with good restaurants: the *Auberge St-Roch*, avenue Jules-Ferry (☎04.90.65.08.21; ❸), and, across the street, *Le Relais des Dentelles* (☎04.90.62.95.27; ❹). Both are located on the other side of the river from the old village, but only a short distance away. There's also a **campsite** on route de Lafare, 2km towards Malaucène, the *Roquefiquier* (☎04.90.62.95.07; €6.90 per tent; closed Nov–March).

Le Barroux

To the east of the Dentelles, on the Vaison–Malaucène road, the largely untouristy **LE BARROUX** is a perfect *village perché* with narrow, twisting streets leading up to its château at the top. Dating from the twelfth to eighteenth century, the **château** (July–Spet daily 10am–7pm; April & May Sat & Sun 10am–7pm; June daily 2.30–7pm; Oct daily 2–6pm; €3.50) was restored just before World War II, burnt by the Nazis then restored again from 1960 to 1990, and is now open to the public.

In the heart of the village, on place de la Croix, *Les Géraniums* (℡04.90.62.41.08, ℻04.90.62.56.48; ❹; closed Nov–Jan & first two weeks in March) is a very peaceful, comfortable and unpretentious **hotel** with views of the Dentelles; its popular *terrasse* restaurant serves decent food with lunch and dinner menus for €18 and €28 respectively.

Mont Ventoux and around

From the Rhône, Luberon and Durance, the summit of **MONT VENTOUX**, east of the Dentelles, repeatedly appears on the horizon. White with snow, black with storm-cloud shadow or reflecting myriad shades of blue, the barren pebbles of the final 300m are like a coloured weather vane for all of western Provence. From a distance the mountain looks distinctly alluring: indeed, the fourteenth-century Italian poet Petrarch climbed the heights simply for the experience; the local guides he chartered for the two-and-a-half-day hike considered him completely crazy.

Meteorological information is gathered, along with TV transmissions and Mirage fighter jet movements, from masts and dishes at the top. The tower directing the conglomeration of receptors is in consequence no beauty, its essential design characteristic being to withstand winds from every direction, including the northern Mistral that can accelerate to 250km per hour across Ventoux. Wind, rain, snow and fearsome sub-zero temperatures are the dominant natural accompaniments to this tarmacked mountain top.

The deforestation of Mont Ventoux dates from Roman times, and by the nineteenth century it had got so bad that the entire mountain appeared shaved. Oaks, pines, boxwood, fir and beech have since been replanted and the owls and eagles have returned, but the greenery is unlikely ever to reach the summit again. The road that zigzags up the 1900m and down again with such consummate, if convoluted, ease was built for the purposes of testing prototype cars, an activity that continued up till the mid-1970s. Mont Ventoux is also a sporadic highlight of the Tour de France, hence its appeal in summer for passionately committed cyclists. Around the tree line is a memorial to the great British cyclist Tommy Simpson, who died here from heart failure in 1967 on one of the hottest days ever recorded in the race; legend has it that his last words were: "Put me back on the bloody bike."

Despite the unpromising environment, rest assured that from the summit you have one of the most wonderful **panoramas**, not just in France, but in the whole of Europe. Between **November and May** the road is covered by snow, with only the tops of the black and yellow poles beside the road still visible; then, people ascending Mont Ventoux will be on **skis**, leaving base either at Mont Serein on the north face or from the smaller southern station of Chalet-Reynard.

If you want to make the **ascent on foot** the best path to take is from Les Colombets or Les Fébriers, hamlets off the D974 east of **BEDOIN** whose **tourist office**, on Espace M.L-Gravier (mid–June to Aug Mon–Fri 9am– 12.30pm & 2–6pm, Sat 9.30am–12.30pm & 2–6pm, Sun 9.30am–12.30pm; Sept to mid-June Mon–Fri 9am–12.30pm & 2–6pm, Sat 9.30am–12.30pm; ℡04.90.65.63.95, ⓦwww.bedoin.org), can provide details. It also organizes a weekly **night-time ascent**, in July and August, leaving at 11.30pm on Wednesdays and Fridays to camp near the summit and await the sunrise. Bedoin

△ Mont Ventoux

Location on chemin de la Feraille (☎04.90.65.94.53) rents out **bikes** if you want to join the superfit cyclists in braving the gusts and horribly long steep inclines. It also organizes trips in which you are transported to the summit, and can cycle back down. In **Mont Serein** the Chalet d'Accueil Mt-Serein (☎04.90.63.42.02) can provide info on **ski-rental**, runs and lifts.

Bedoin has several **campsites**, including the two-star *Camping Pastory*, 1km from the village on the Malaucène road (☎04.90.12.85.83; €6.90 per tent; closed Oct–March), and more than a dozen **gîtes ruraux** for anyone considering spending a week or more in the area. Near Bedoin, there's a very good **gîte d'étape**, *Les Écuries de Ventoux*, 2km outside Malaucène, down a track off the road to Beaumont-de-Ventoux (☎04.90.65.29.20; ❶). At the other end of the scale, the *Hostellerie de Crillon le Brave*, place de l'Église (☎04.90.65.61.61, ⓦwww .crillonlebrave.com; ❾), in **Crillon-le-Brave** just west of Bedoin, offers luxurious rooms in seven restored old village houses along with a swimming pool.

Le Chalet-Reynard, on the south face of Mont Ventoux, has a small **restaurant** with a large à la carte choice including truffle omelettes (℡04.90.61.84.55; menu €25), that fills with walkers in the summer and skiers in the winter (ski-rental available).

Gorges de la Nesque

The **GORGES DE LA NESQUE** lies to the south of Ventoux, on the D942 from Carpentras to Sault. The River Nesque is dry most of the year and invisible from most of the road which clings to the rocks above the river – a feat of engineering even more impressive than the geological fault itself. It's a barren area with just one landmark, located on the southern side before the gorge turns northeast again towards the village of Monieux. The 200-metre-high **Rocher du Cire** is coated in wax from numerous hives that wild bees have made, and supposedly provided the men of the nearby village with the reputation-enhancing exploit of abseiling down it to gather honey. This may well be a macho myth; certainly no one does it now. In **MONIEUX**, there's a cheap **gîte d'étape** for walkers, the *Ferme St-Hubert* (℡04.90.64.04.51; call ahead and bring a sleeping bag; ➊), and a little **restaurant**, *Les Lavandes* (℡04.90.64.05.08; menus €24.50 & €30; closed Jan & Feb), serving local specialities such as foie gras in Beaumes-de-Venise muscat and stag terrine.

Sault and the Plateau d'Albion

At **SAULT**, 6km northeast of Monieux, the steep forested rocks give way to fields of lavender, cereals and grazing sheep. Wild products of the woods – lactaire and grisel mushrooms, truffles and game, as well as honey and lavender products – are bought and sold at its Wednesday **market**; autumn is the best time for these local specialities. If you miss the market, La Maison des Producteurs on rue de la République can sell you all the goodies. Sault also has **fairs** on the Wednesday before Palm Sunday, St John's feast day (June 23), August 16 and the end of November.

At the treeless, undulating **PLATEAU D'ALBION**, south of Sault, Mount Ventoux recedes from view and the D30 continues south to St-Christol, passing close to a massive **airforce base** which, until recently, was the base for France's eighteen land-based nuclear missiles, all of which have now been disarmed.

Carpentras and south

Heading west from Sault on the D942 brings you to **CARPENTRAS**, one of the larger towns of the Vaucluse – the population is around thirty thousand – with a history dating back to around 5 BC, when it was the capital of a Celtic tribe. The Greeks, who founded Marseille, came here to buy honey, wheat, goats and skins, but it wasn't until the fourteenth century that the town really flourished – during the period of the popes, it briefly became the papal headquarters and gave protection to Jews expelled from France. Today, despite so many ancient remains, Carpentras lacks the idyllic setting or picturesque castles that have made the names of other Provençal towns and, as such, is not really on the tourist circuit. It is, however, a friendly and laid-back place (perhaps a little *too* quiet, especially in the evenings); and every Friday the town hosts one of the largest and most diverse **markets** in Provence (see box on p.177). Carpentras also makes a good, inexpensive base for exploring Mont Ventoux and the Dentelles.

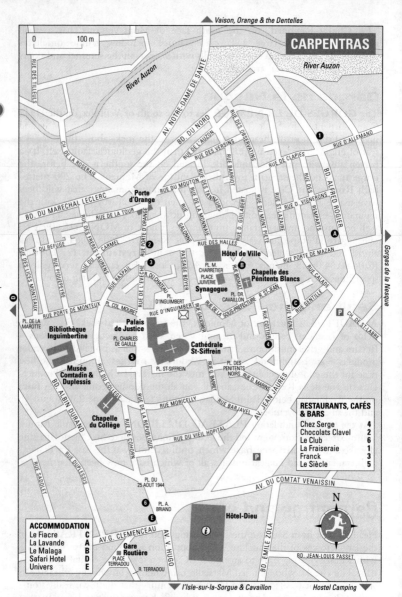

Map labels (clockwise/as shown):

▲ Vaison, Orange & the Dentelles

CARPENTRAS

0   100 m

River Auzon

River Auzon

RUE DES TILLEULS
AV. NOTRE-DAME-DE-SANTÉ
BD. DU NORD
CH. DE LA ROSERAIE
RUE DE L'AUZON
RUE DES OBSERVANTINS
RUE D'ALLEMAND
RUE DES VERSINS
RUE BARRIOT
RUE DE CLAPIÈS
BD. ALFRED ROGIER
RUE DES VIGNERONS
RUE DU MOUTON
RUE DES TANNEURS
RUE DE LA MONNAIE
RUE DU GUILABERT
RUE ST-LAZARE
Porte d'Orange
RUE DES HALLES
Gorges de la Nesque ▶
BD. DU MARÉCHAL LECLERC
RUE DE LA TOUR
RUE DE PORTE D'ORANGE
RUE DU MONT PIETÉ
RUE DES FRÈRES LAURENS
RUE DU REFUGE
CARMEL
GALONNE
Hôtel de Ville
RUE PORTE DE MAZAN
RUE DES LICES MONTEAUX
RUE RASPAIL
RUE DE L'ÉVÊCHÉ
PASSAGE BOYER
PL. M. CHARRETIER
PLACE JUIVERIE
RUE BROAUD
Chapelle des Pénitents Blancs
RUE CALADE
RUE PIQUEPEYRE
RUE DU CHÂTEAU
PL. D'INGUIMBERT
Synagogue
PL. DR CAVAILLON
RUE ST-JEAN
RUE GENTILLE
RUE PORTE DE MONTEUX
PL. COL. MOURET
RUE D'INGUIMBERT
RUE GALOBERT
RUE DE LA SOUS-PRÉFECTURE
RUE VIGNE
P
CH. DE ST-LABRE
PL. DE LA MAROTTE
Bibliothèque Inguimbertine
Palais de Justice
PL. CHARLES DE GAULLE
Cathédrale St-Siffrein
RUE COTTIER
Musée Comtadin & Duplessis
RUE DU COLLÈGE
PL. ST-SIFFREIN
PL. DES PÉNITENTS NOIRS
RUE G. BARRET
RUE D. MARINS
BD. ALBIN DURAND
Chapelle du Collège
RUE DE LA RÉPUBLIQUE
RUE MORICELLY
RUE BARJAVEL
AV. JEAN JAURÈS
RUE DE COHORN
RUE DU VIEIL HOPITAL
P
RUE DUPLESSIS
PL. DU 25 AOUT 1944
AV. DU COMTAT VENAISSIN
N
RUE SADOLET

RESTAURANTS, CAFÉS & BARS

Chez Serge	4
Chocolats Clavel	2
Le Club	6
La Fraiseraie	1
Franck	3
Le Siècle	5

PL. A. BRIAND
Hôtel-Dieu
AV. G. CLEMENCEAU
AV. V. HUGO
BD. ÉMILE ZOLA
BD. JEAN-LOUIS PASSET

ACCOMMODATION

Le Fiacre	C
La Lavande	A
Le Malaga	B
Safari Hotel	D
Univers	E

Gare Routière
PLACE TERRADOU
R. TERRADOU

▼ l'Isle-sur-la-Sorgue & Cavaillon   Hostel Camping ▼

Arrival, information and accommodation

Only freight trains stop at Carpentras, while **buses** arrive either on avenue
Victor-Hugo (from Marseille, Aix and Cavaillon) or at the **gare routière** on
place Terradou (from Avignon, Vaison, and other points north and west). From
the latter it's a short walk to avenue Georges-Clemenceau, which leads to place
Aristide-Briand where the **tourist office** is housed in the Hôtel-Dieu (July &

Carpentras market

Friday is the major **market** day in Carpentras. The local **fruit and vegetables** that appear so early in the lowlands of Vaucluse are available all round the town; **flowers and plants** are sold on avenue Jean-Jaurès; **antiques and bric-a-brac** on rue Porte-de-Monteux and place Colonel-Mouret; while, from the annual St-Siffrein fair (November 24–27) to the beginning of March, place Aristide-Briand and place du 25 Août 1944 are given over to the selling of **truffles**, the rooted not the chocolate kind.

Aug Mon–Sat 9am–1pm & 2–7pm, Sun 9.30am–1pm; Sept–June Mon–Sat 9.30am–12.30pm & 2–6pm; ℡04.90.63.00.78, ⓦwww.ville-carpentras.fr). The town proper is small enough to cover easily on foot, but if you fancy renting a **bike**, try Terzo Sport on avenue du Mont Ventoux (℡04.32.80.26.72).

Most of Carpentras' **hotels** are on the boulevards which circle the old town; there are plenty of bargains to be had, but most places come with few frills. Best of the budget options is the ⚘ *Univers*, 110 place Aristide-Briand (℡04.90.63.00.05, ⓦwww.hotel-univers.com; ❷), in a grand old building with spacious rooms and excellent deals on four-person rooms (❹). The smaller, eight-bed *La Lavande*, 282 bd Alfred-Rogier (℡04.90.63.13.49, ⓦwww.hotel-la-lavande.com; ❷), is basic but clean, while the central *Le Malaga*, on place Maurice-Charretier (℡04.90.60.57.96; ❸) is rather kitsch but perfectly satisfactory. For a bit more luxury, *Le Fiacre*, 153 rue Vigne (℡04.90.63.03.15, ⓦwww.hotel-du-fiacre.com; ❹), offers very nicely decorated rooms, two with terraces, in an old town house with a central courtyard; and there's also *Safari Hotel*, 2km east of the centre at 1 av JH-Fabre (℡04.90.63.35.35, ⓦwww.nid-provencal.com; ❹), with good amenities, including a pool and tennis courts, though rather lacking character.

There is a **hostel**, *Logis des Jeunes du Comtat Venaissin*, 2km from the centre at 200 rue Robert-Lacoste, near the Pierre de Coubertin sports centre (℡04.90.67.13.95, ℱ04.90.67.65.90; dorm beds €11.45), and the local **campsite**, *Lou Comtadou*, is located south of town on avenue Pierre-de-Coubertin (℡04.90.67.03.16, ⓦwww.campingloucomtadou.com; €10.50 per tent; closed Nov–Feb).

The Town

A bird's-eye view of Carpentras shows clearly the perimeter line of the town in the Dark Ages (rues Vigne, des Halles, Raspail, du Collège and Moricelly), enclosed in the ring of boulevards that follow the line of the medieval town wall. Of this only the massive, crenellated **Porte d'Orange** and the odd rampart on rue des Ramparts and rue des Lices-Monteux remain.

At the heart of town on place Charles-de-Gaulle, the **Palais de Justice** (guided tours first & third Mon of the month, April–Sept; check with tourist office for times; €4) was built as an episcopal palace to indulge the dreams, or more likely the realized desires, of a seventeenth-century cardinal of Carpentras. Nicolas Mignard was commissioned to fresco the walls with sexual scenes of satyrs and nymphs, but a later incumbent had all the erotic details effaced.

The palais is attached to the fifteenth-century **Cathédrale St-Siffrein** behind which, almost hidden in the corner, stands a **Roman arch** inscribed with imperial scenes of prisoners in chains. Fifteen hundred years after the cathedral's erection, Jews, coerced, bribed or otherwise persuaded, entered the building in chains to be unshackled as converted Christians. The door they passed through, the **Porte**

Carpentras festivals

The last fortnight in July, Carpentras really comes to life during the **Estivales**, a series of music, theatre and dance performances that are staged in an outdoor auditorium in front of the city's cathedral. The Bureau des Estivales, 64 rue Vigne (℡04.90.60.46.00), has full details. Tickets prices range from €20 to €30.

On August 15, Vaucluse food is celebrated in the **Festival des Saveurs Provençales**, a day of gourmandise in which the minutiae of old-fashioned food production are debated and fêted, with prizes given and plenty of tastings.

Juive, is on the southern side and bears the strange symbolism of rats encircling and devouring a globe. The cathedral stands on the place Charles-de-Gaulle, while to the north is the place d'Inguimbert, lined with plane trees, lanterns and black swan fountains. Running between place d'Inguimbert and rue des Halles is the **Passage Boyer**, a high and beautiful glazed shopping arcade. It was built by the unemployed in a short-lived scheme to generate jobs after the 1848 revolution.

Following rue d'Inguimbert eastwards brings you to the ancient **Jewish ghetto** and a slightly livelier part of the town. The original **synagogue** on place Juiverie was built in the days when the Jews had to pay movement taxes every time they left or entered the ghetto, and when their rights to be in Carpentras at all depended on papal whim. In 1741, when the present synagogue was constructed on the old foundations, Bishop d'Inguimbert would not allow it to be as high as the **Chapelle des Pénitents Blancs** on rue Bidault. The rabbi's response was to paint the ceiling blue with stars, "for then I'll have all the skies". This, along with its low hanging chandeliers, the purification baths (for women after menstruation and for brides) and the bread ovens, can all be visited (Mon–Thurs 10am–noon & 3–5pm, Fri closes 4pm; closed Jewish feast days).

To the west of the centre on boulevard Albert-Durand, the **Musée Comtadin** (daily except Tues: April–Sept 10am–noon & 2–6pm; Oct–March 10am–noon & 2–4pm; €2 combined ticket with Musée Duplessis) contains an unimaginative collection of keys, guns, *santons*, seals, ex-votos, papal bulls, bells and bonnets. The dimly lit pictures are of more interest, among them the portraits of famous Carpentrassiens including François-Vincent Raspail, after whom so many French streets are named. Born just after the Revolution and condemned to death during the White Terror, Raspail was a committed republican all his life, criticizing every brand of nineteenth-century conservatism and dedicating much of his work as a doctor to making medicine available to the poor. The portrait of one of his fellow radical Vaucluse *députés* in the 1876 parliament, Alfred Nacquet, who proposed divorce rights for women, also hangs in these musty rooms. A painting by Denis Bonnet of medieval Carpentras features a nonexistent hill to show the separate Jewish area within the city walls.

On the floor above is the **Musée Duplessis** (same hours and ticket as Musée Comtadin), named after a mediocre eighteenth-century painter from Carpentras whose wealth and influence had much to do with the patronage of the important people he painted. Roman artefacts, an Egyptian tablet with a pharaonic scene captioned in Aramaic, and some very wonderful Renaissance miniatures are also on display. Also in the complex, on the left as you enter the courtyard, is the **Bibliothèque Inguimbertine** (Mon 2–6pm, Tues–Fri 9am–noon & 2–6pm, Sat 9am–noon; free), one of the most important research libraries in the whole of Provence, containing several hundred thousand volumes on the history of Provence, Books of Hours, musical scores and early manuscripts. Contemporary art by mainly local artists is displayed in changing exhibitions at the nearby **Chapelle du Collège** on rue du Collège (Mon–Sat 10am–12.30pm & 2.30–6.30pm; free).

To the south of the centre, just beyond place Aristide-Briand, is the huge eighteenth-century **Hôtel Dieu** building, which still functions as a hospital. Be sure to visit its original opulent **pharmacy** (Tues–Sat: July & Aug 9.30am–noon & 2.30–6.30pm; June & Sept 9am–noon & 2–6pm; free; entrance via the tourist office), where you can feast your eyes on gorgeously decorated vials and boxes containing cat's foot extract, Saturn salt, deer antler shavings and dragon blood; the painted lower cupboards tell a very "Age of Reason" moral tale of wild and happy monkeys ending up as tame and dutiful labourers.

Eating, drinking and entertainment

One of the best and most popular places to **eat** in Carpentras is *Chez Serge*, 90 rue Cottier (℡04.90.63.21.24; closed Sun), whose wide selection of pizzas (around €10) or well-prepared local dishes (€15–18.50) are best enjoyed on the tree-shaded terrace. *Franck*, 30 place de l'Horloge (℡04.90.60.75.00; menus from €20; closed Tues & Wed), offers more gastronomic cuisine, including white truffles, on its €35 menu, while *La Fraiseraie*, 125 bd Alfred-Rogier (℡04.90.67.06.39; menus €16–46; closed Wed), also has truffles in season, and tasty Provençal fare at other times. If you have a sweet tooth, stop at *Chocolats Clavel*, 33 rue Porte d'Orange (℡04.90.63.07.59; closed Wed), to try some *berlingots*, a local sweet flavoured with orange, lemon, aniseed or mint. Magnificent nougat models of space rockets and churches are displayed in the front window, while in the back sits the world's largest *berlingot*. The taciturn owner is no Willy Wonka, but if you have children in tow, he might let you have a look at it.

For **drinking**, *Le Siècle* on place Charles-de-Gaulle offers a shady spot right in front of the cathedral. Virtually the only place to stay open late, however, is *Le Club*, a piano bar at 106 place Aristide-Briand.

Pernes-les-Fontaines

South of Carpentras, on the road to L'Isle-sur-la-Sorgue, lies the exquisite small town of **PERNES-LES-FONTAINES**. The fountains for which it's named (36 in all) – and which give the town its special charm – plus the ramparts, gateways, castle, towers, covered market hall, Renaissance streets and half a dozen chapels all blend into a single complex structure, and the passages between its squares feel more like corridors between rooms.

Approaching from Carpentras, you cross the River Nesque before reaching place Gabriel-Moutte on the left, the site of Pernes' Saturday market and tourist office; from here avenue Jean-Jaurès follows the line of the fourteenth-century ramparts, of which only three gates now remain. Second on the left is the Porte Villeneuve, dating from 1550 and flanked by two imposing round towers, which leads to rue Gambetta and the old town. At the end of rue Gambetta is the **Tour Ferrande** (guided tours arranged by the tourist office) which contains the town's great medieval artwork – immaculately preserved **frescoes** dating from the era of the Bayeux tapestry and similar in style; they portray religious scenes of the Virgin and Child as well as scenes from the legend of William of Orange and the life of Charles of Anjou.

Heading down rue Victor-Hugo and along rue de la Halle brings you to the sixteenth-century Porte Notre-Dame and the elegant **cormorant fountain** with the seventeenth-century market hall. From this gateway, rue Raspail heads south past the fifteenth-century **reboul fountain**, the oldest of Pernes' fountains, and onto the other remaining gate, the Porte St-Gilles.

Practicalities

The **tourist office** is on place Gabriel-Moutte (July & Aug Mon–Fri 9am–12.30pm & 2.30–7pm, Sat 9am–12.30pm & 2.30–6pm, Sun 9.30am–12.30pm; Sept & Oct Mon–Fri 9am–noon & 2–6pm, Sat 9am–12.30pm; Nov–March Mon–Fri 9am–noon & 2–5pm, Sat 9am–noon; April–June Mon–Fri 9am–noon & 2–6pm, Sat 9am–noon & 2–5pm; ☎04.90.61.31.04, ⓦwww .ville-pernes-les-fontaines.fr). An afternoon's wander may well be enough to sample Pernes-les-Fontaines' charms, but if you find yourself seduced, some **hotel** possibilities include *La Margelle*, place Aristide-Briand, on the boulevard ring to the south of the village (☎04.90.61.25.83; ③), with a rambling back garden and inexpensive menus; or *Prato-Plage* (☎04.90.61.37.75, ⓦwww .pratoplage.com; ④), just outside the town on the Carpentras road overlooking an artificial lake. The municipal **campsite** is in the quartier Coucourelles (☎04.90.66.45.55; €10.20 per tent; closed Oct–March;); campervans can park overnight on quai de Verdon (not Fri).

There's a delightful **restaurant** at 73 place L-Giraud, *Au Fil de Temps* (☎04.90.66.48.61; closed Sat lunch & Wed; €32–70), which serves exquisite food: the *millefeuille de boeuf* is outstanding.

Venasque

VENASQUE, 9km east of Pernes just before the road starts to wind over the Plateau de Vaucluse towards Apt (see Chapter 4), is a perfectly contained village on a spur of rock. At its highest end are three round towers and a curtain wall; at its lowest end a sixth-century baptistry, built on the site of a Roman temple which is thought to have been dedicated to Venus. Like most Provençal villages it swings between a sleepy winter state and a tourist honey pot in summer. The best time to visit is in May and June, before the main tourist season begins, and when the daily **market** concentrates exclusively on the sale of local cherries.

Besides its location, Venasque's attractions lie in its food. **Haute cuisine**, with all the ingredients fresh from the market, can be sampled at the *Auberge de la Fontaine*, on place de la Fontaine (☎04.90.66.02.96; menus from €38; closed Wed eve; bookings recommended). The hotel-restaurant *Les Remparts*, at the top of the main street, rue Haute (☎04.90.66.02.79; lunch menus from €18, dinner menus from €24; closed mid-Nov to early March), also has an excellent restaurant – the rabbit *confit* with red wine caramel is particularly good.

The **tourist office**, on Grande Rue (July & Aug Mon, Tues & Thurs–Sat 10am–12.30pm & 3–7pm, Wed & Sun 3–7pm; April–June, Sept & Oct Mon, Tues & Thurs–Sat 10am–noon & 2–6pm, Wed & Sun 2–6pm; ☎04.90.66.11.66, ⓦwww.venasque.fr), can help with **accommodation**, which is fairly thin on the ground: aside from rooms at the *Auberge* (☎04.90.66.02.96, ⓕ04.90.66.13.14; ③) and *Les Remparts* (☎04.90.66.02.79, ⓦwww.hotellesremparts.com; ③, breakfast included; closed mid-Nov to early March), the only other **hotel** in town is *La Garrigue*, route de l'Appiè (☎04.90.66.03.40, ⓕ04.90.66.61.43; ③; closed mid-Oct to mid-March).

L'Isle-sur-la-Sorgue

Halfway between Carpentras and Cavaillon to the south, and 23km east of Avignon, lies **L'ISLE-SUR-LA-SORGUE**, not to be confused with Sorgues on the Rhône. The town straddles five branches of the River Sorgue, its waters once full of otters and beavers, eels, trout and crayfish, and its currents turning the power wheels of a **medieval cloth industry**. Tanneries, dyeing works, and, in the eighteenth century, silk production, all ensured considerable prosperity for "the Island".

Nowadays, the huge blackened wheels of the cloth industry turn only as mementoes, and the mills and tanneries stand empty, plants growing through the crumbling brickwork. But in summer, fishing punts continue to crowd the streams and L'Isle is a cheerful place, particularly on Sundays, when people arrive for its well-known **antiques market** which centres on the Village des Antiquaires on avenue de l'Égalité and spills out onto the boulevards.

Arrival, information and accommodation

Trains from Avignon and Cavaillon arrive at the **gare SNCF**, southwest of the town centre, and **buses** arrive by pont Gambetta, next to the post office. The **tourist office** is in the former granary on place de l'Église (July & Aug Mon–Sat 9am–12.30pm & 2–6pm, Sun 9.30am–1pm; Sept–June Mon–Sat 9am–12.30pm & 2.30–6pm, Sun 9am–12.30pm; ☏04.90.38.04.78, ⓦwww.ot-islesurlasorgue.fr). **Bikes** can be rented from Loca'Bike, at 1081 chemin de la Muscadelle (☏04.90.38.65.99), and Idal Mipi at 3 quai Clovis-Hughes has **Internet** access.

L'Isle-sur-la-Sorgue is not a major tourist destination and there are few **rooms** right in the town centre. The best of these are to be found at *La Prévoté*, behind the church at 4 rue Jean-Jacques-Rousseau (☏04.90.38.57.29, ⓦwww.la-prevote.fr; ❼), whose five luxurious and elegantly furnished rooms complement its excellent restaurant perfectly. Fifteen hundred metres upstream of the town, *Le Pescador* in Partages-des-Eaux – follow signs to Carpentras and turn right immediately after crossing the main branch of the river – (☏04.90.38.09.69, ⓦwww.lepescador.info; closed Wed & mid-Nov to mid-March; ❸), is in an idyllic spot at the point where the waters divide (but watch out for water-loving midges). Alternatively, try the eighteenth-century coach house out in the countryside 3km southwest of town signed left off the D25 to Caumont (the continuation of av de l'Égalité), *Le Mas de Cure Bourse*, 120 chemin de la Serre (☏04.90.38.16.58, ⓦwww.masdecurebourse.com; ❻), where the rooms are decorated in traditional Provençal style.

The municipal three-star **campsite**, *La Sorguette*, 41 Les Grandes Sorgues (☏04.90.38.05.71, ⓦwww.camping-sorguette.com; €19.20 per tent; closed mid-Oct to mid-March), is by the river on the Apt road.

The Town

Though L'Isle-sur-la-Sorgue's claim to be the Venice of Provence stretches a point, it is a pleasant waterside location in which to spend an afternoon. There are few sights to head for, but the central **place de l'Église** and **place de la Liberté** do provide reminders of past prosperity, most obviously in the Baroque seventeenth-century **church** (July & Aug Tues–Sat 10am–noon & 3–6pm, Sun 3–6pm; Sept–June Tues–Sat 10am–noon & 3–5pm), by far the richest religious edifice for miles around. Each column in the nave supports a sculpted Virtue: whips and turtledoves are Chastity's props, a unicorn accompanies Virginity, and medallions and inscriptions carry the adornment down to the floor.

Every year the Isle fishermen retain their medieval guild tradition of crowning a king of the Sorgue, whose job is to oversee the rights of catch and sale. The **Festival de la Sorgue** at the end of July sees them out in traditional gear, with two teams battling from boats in an ancient jousting tournament. On the **spring equinox** the people of Velleron, 5km downstream, process down to the river and launch a fleet of tiny luminous rafts to celebrate the start of spring. If you want to get on the river yourself Canoë Evasion (☎06.86.67.65.74), signed right off the D25 towards Fontaine-de-Vaucluse, organizes **canoe trips**.

Eating and drinking

The town's best **restaurant** is *La Prévoté* (see "Arrival"; closed Sun eve & Mon), with weekday lunchtime menus for €25 and a superb gastronomic evening menu (€43) featuring stuffed crab and a *râble de lapin* with black olives. *Le Pescador* hotel in Partages-des-Eaux (see "Arrival"; menus from €21.50; closed Wed) serves good fish dishes, and the *Mas de Cure Bourse* hotel (see "Arrival"; menu around €26; closed Mon & Tues lunch;) also has a reputable restaurant. For a lighter meal, *Bistro de l'Industrie* on quai de la Charité by place E-Char, offers decent *plats du jour* for €10, rounded off with excellent coffee; or there's the busy brasserie, *Café de la Sorgue*, on quai Jean-Jaurès beside pont Gambetta, with tables right by the water. Good ice cream can be found at *Gelateria Isabella* on 2 esplanade Robert-Vasse. The best place to head for a **drink** is place de l'Église, where you'll find the *Bar Le César* with its faded mirrors, and the swish fin-de-siècle *Café de France*.

Thursday is **market** day but the best place to buy food is at nearby Velleron where producers sell their goods direct at a busy *marché paysan* (April–Sept Mon–Sat 6–8pm; Oct–March Tues, Fri & Sat 4.30–6pm). For inexpensive **wine**, Le Caveau de la Tour de l'Isle at 12 rue de la République is the place to go (closed Sun afternoon & Mon).

Fontaine-de-Vaucluse

The diverging streams of L'Isle-sur-la-Sorgue have their source only 6km to the east in a mysterious tapering fissure deep below the sheer 230-metre cliffs at the top of a gorge above **FONTAINE-DE-VAUCLUSE**. Fascination with the **source**, one of the most powerful natural springs in the world, coupled with the beauty of the ancient riverside village where the fourteenth-century poet Petrarch pined for his Laura, makes this a very popular tourist spot – well over a million visitors a year converge here. But despite the crowds, Fontaine is still a fairly romantic place.

The source and the village

In spring, the waters of the Sorgue often appear in spectacular fashion, bursting down the gorge; at other times they seep stealthily through subterranean channels to meet the riverbed further down. The best time to admire them is in the early morning before the crowds arrive.

If you're intrigued by the source, and understand French, visit the **Ecomusée du Gouffre** in the underground commercial centre alongside chemin de la Fontaine (daily: July & Aug 10am–12.30pm & 2–7.30pm; Sept–Nov & Feb–June 10am–noon & 2–6pm; closed Dec & Jan; hourly 40-minute tours in French; €5.50). It's run by volunteers eager to communicate their passion for crawling about in the bowels of the earth, who lead the tour through a series of mock-up caves and passages. The museum winds up with a collection of underworld concretions gathered by Casteret, one of France's most renowned cavers, ranging from huge, jewellery-like crystals to pieces resembling fibre optics. Displays also document the intriguing history of the exploration of the spring, from the first 23-metre descent in 1878 to the robotic camera that reached the bottom a few years ago, its blurry pictures apparently showing a horizontal passage disappearing into the rock. It's thought that water seeping through a vast plateau of chalk (stretching as far north as Banon) hits an impermeable base that slopes down to Fontaine.

However the water arrives, it has long been put to use in turning the wheels of manufacturing. The first paper mill was built at Fontaine in 1522, and the last, built in 1862, ceased operations in 1968. The medieval method of pulping rags to paper has been re-created in the **Moulin à papier Vallis Clausa**, 500m beyond the Ecomusée du Gouffre alongside the river (daily: July & Aug 9am–7pm; Sept–June 9am–12.20pm & 2–6.55pm; free). Here, flowers are added to the pulp and the resulting paper is printed with all manner of drawings, poems and prose, from Churchill's "Blood, Sweat and Tears" speech to the legend of how God created Provence, on sale in the vast Vallis Clausa shop. There are other quality craft shops in the complex, including one selling household objects carved in olive wood, and an exhibition of *santons* (nativity figures).

A little further along chemin de la Fontaine is the impressive and intense **Musée d'Histoire 1939–1945** (March, Nov & Dec Sat & Sun 10am–noon & 2–6pm; April, May & Oct daily except Tues 10am–noon & 2–6pm; June–Sept daily except Tues 10am–6pm; €3.50, or €4.50 with the Musée de Pétrarque). The overriding purpose of the museum is not to judge or apologize, but to remind people of the humanity of resistance. In so doing it acknowledges the extent to which the war period still perturbs the collective memory of the French. The museum looks at Marshall Pétain's anti-Semitic laws, which were not instructions from Berlin, and stresses how many French people must have opposed them since three-quarters of the French Jewish population escaped deportation. The re-created classroom and other displays of daily life bring home the authoritarian, anti-intellectual and patriarchal nature of France's fascist regime, its insistence on work, family and *patrie*, and the military cult of Pétain. A section is dedicated to the artists who refused to collaborate, another to the German Resistance.

Across the river, through an alleyway just past the bridge, the **Musée de Pétrarque**, on quai du Château Vieux (same hours and admission as the Musée d'Histoire 1939–1945), is home to a collection of beautiful old books dating back to the fifteenth century, and some pictures of Petrarch, his beloved Laura and of Fontaine where he passed sixteen years of his unrequited passion. The museum also hosts temporary art exhibitions.

Practicalities

Buses from L'Isle-sur-la-Sorgue drop you by the car park just before the church. The **tourist office** is on chemin de la Fontaine, off to the left towards the source (July & Aug daily 9.30am–12.30pm & 2–5.30pm; Sept–June Tues–Sat 9.30am–12.30pm & 2–5.30pm; ℡04.90.20.32.22; ℮officetourisme .vaucluse@wanadoo.fr).

The few **rooms** that exist in Fontaine are likely to be full in summer, so booking ahead is advisable: alternatively, you could base yourself in Cavaillon and visit on a day-trip. Fontaine's **place de la Colonne** is a particularly pleasant spot to stay, with balconies, terraced restaurants and cafés overhanging the river: there is a characterful **hotel** here, the *Des Sources* (℡04.90.20.31.84, Ⓦwww.hoteldessources.com; ❹), with a whole variety of *vieille France* rooms. About 1.5km out of the village on the road back to L'Isle, down a track to the right, the *Font de Lauro* (℡ & ℻04.90.20.31.49; closed Oct–March; ❷) is a more basic, but excellent-value, option. About 1km from the village, on chemin de la Vignasse, there's a very pleasant HI **youth hostel** (reception 5.30–9pm;

☎04.90.20.31.65, ✉fontaine@fuaj.org; €15.65 including breakfast; closed mid-Nov to Jan), while the year-round *Les Prés* **campsite** is 500m downstream from the village (☎04.90.20.32.38; €12.50 per tent).

Fontaine has a choice of several reasonably priced **restaurants** including *Lou Fanau* on place de la Colonne (☎04.90.20.31.90), which has menus of solid regional food from €15.70. Slightly more expensive is *Le Château* on quai du Château Vieux (☎04.90.20.31.54; closed Sun & Mon evenings out of season), where menus cost €28 and €48. If you arrive early, the *boulangerie Le Moulin de la Fontaine* near the church does breakfasts, and a few doors down there's a crêperie. **Market** day is on Tuesday.

On the north side of the river, above the aqueduct, you can rent **fishing** rods and lines from the little hut called *Pêche de la Truite*, while Kayak Vert, just upstream (☎04.90.20.35.44), rents **canoes** for a half-hour or hour's paddling, or for a fairly effortless eight-kilometre trip down to L'Isle-sur-la-Sorgue (where the canoes can be left).

Cavaillon

Approaches to **CAVAILLON**, directly south of L'Isle-sur-la-Sorgue and 25km southeast of Avignon, pass through fields of fruit and vegetables, watered by the Durance and Coulon rivers. Market gardening is the major business of the city and to the French, Cavaillon, its Roman origins notwithstanding, is known simply as a melon town. The **melon** in question is the Charentais, a small pale green ball with dark green stripes and brilliant orange flesh, in season from May to September. Together with asparagus and early spring vegetables, they are sold every weekday morning at one of the largest **wholesale markets** in Europe; and the fruit is honoured every year in mid-July during the town's **melon festival**. It must be said, however, that Cavaillon is not a wildly alluring place and, apart from a good choice of hotels that may persuade you to use the town as a base for exploring the surrounding area, there is no reason to linger for too long.

Arrival, information and accommodation

Cavaillon is well served by public transport, with trains and buses from all over stopping at the **gare SNCF** and the **gare routière,** both on avenue P-Semard on the east side of town. The **tourist office**, meanwhile, is on the opposite side of town on place François-Tourel (Mon–Sat 9am–12.30pm & 2–6.30pm, Sun 9am–12.30pm; ☎04.90.71.32.01, ⓦwww.cavaillon-luberon .com). **Internet** access is available at Centre Multimedia de Cavaillon, 189 cours Sadi-Carnot.

In the centre of town, the most attractive budget **hotel** is *Le Toppin*, 70 cours Gambetta (☎04.90.71.30.42, ⓦwww.hotel-toppin.com; ❸), with warmly decorated, comfortable rooms, while the pricier *Le Parc*, a former *maison bourgeoise* at 183 place F-Tourel (☎04.90.71.57.78, ⓦwww.hotelduparccavaillon .com; ❹), is also very agreeable: its flamboyant decor suits the building, though the rooms themselves are more subdued. If these are full, there a couple of basic but cheap options near the tourist office – the clean, quiet *Le Forum*, 68 place du Clos (☎04.90.78.37.55, ⓦwww.hotelforum.fr.st; ❸), and *Le Provence*, at 9 cours Bournissac (☎04.90.78.22.25; ❷), with simple rooms above a bar. At the top end of the scale, the *Mercure*, 601 av Boscodomini, quartier Bosco-domini (☎04.90.71.07.79, ⓕ04.90.78.27.94; ❼), is a modern, luxurious hotel overlooking the Durance, with pool and tennis courts.

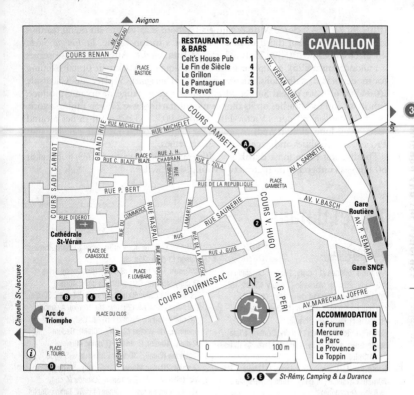

Avignon

CAVAILLON

RESTAURANTS, CAFÉS
& BARS

Celt's House Pub	1
Le Fin de Siècle	4
Le Grillon	2
Le Pantagruel	3
Le Prevot	5

Apt

Cathédrale
St-Véran

Chapelle St-Jacques

Arc de
Triomphe

Gare
Routière

Gare SNCF

N

0   100 m

ACCOMMODATION

Le Forum	B
Mercure	E
Le Parc	D
Le Provence	C
Le Toppin	A

5, E ▼ St-Rémy, Camping & La Durance

For **camping**, there's the three-star *Camping de la Durance*, 495 av Boscodomini, in the direction of the autoroute (☎04.90.71.11.78; €11.10 per tent; closed Oct–March), though it invariably gets crowded in the summer months.

The Town

All that remains of Roman Cavaillon is the **Arc de Triomphe** on place du Clos, which on Mondays is surrounded by the weekly **market**. The **Cathédrale St-Véran**, due north of place du Clos (April–Sept Mon–Sat 8.30am–noon & 2–6pm; Oct–March Mon–Sat 9am–noon & 2–5pm), is an archaic-looking building, on the south side of which God appears above a sundial looking like a winged and battered Neptune. Inside, in the St-Véran chapel above the altar, there's a painting of Saint Véran hauling off a slithery reptile known as Couloubre, who terrorized the locality in 6 AD.

For a panoramic view of the surrounding countryside, you can climb the steep path from behind the Roman arch to the **Chapelle Saint-Jacques**. Built on the site of a temple to Jupiter, it was a regular outpost for hermits whom the peasants would pay to warn them of impending storms (or Couloubre appearances) by ringing the chapel bell.

Eating and drinking

For all its fresh produce, **eating** in Cavaillon isn't all that spectacular. To sample the local speciality, head to *Le Prevot*, at 353 av de Verdon on the road out to St-Rémy

(℡04.90.71.32.43; closed Mon & Sun eve), whose €35 vegetarian menu features an imaginative use of the fruit in the form of a melon tagine. *Le Fin de Siècle*, 46 place du Clos (℡04.90.71.12.27; closed Tues, Wed & Aug lunch), also serves a melon menu (€25), complete with melon liqueur, in a kitsch upstairs dining room decorated with dolls. Alternatively, *Le Pantagruel*, 5 place de Cabassole (℡04.90.76.11.98; closed Sun & Mon), offers a good range of organic produce, fish stews and meat dishes on its dinner menus starting at €27. For a more exotic meal, *Le Grillon*, 50 cours Victor-Hugo (℡04.90.71.33.87; main dishes around €15; Sept–June closed Wed), is good for tagines, couscous and *pastillas*, plus Provençal specialities and excellent Algerian wines.

The liveliest place for a **drink** is *Celt's House Pub*, next to *Le Toppin* hotel at 60 cours Gambetta, which attracts a youngish crowd.

Travel details

Ordinary trains

Avignon to: Arles (17 daily; 20min); Cavaillon (13 daily; 25min); Marseille (7 every 45min; 1hr 20min); Montpellier (14 daily; 1hr); Orange (16 daily; 15min); Tarascon (16 daily; 10min); Toulouse (1 daily; 3hr 50min).
Cavaillon to: Avignon (11 daily; 30min); L'Isle-sur-la-Sorgue (11 daily; 10min); Marseille (3 daily; 1hr 10min).
L'Isle-sur-la-Sorgue to: Avignon (11 daily; 30min); Cavaillon (11 daily; 10min); Marseille (3 daily; 1hr 20min).
Orange to: Avignon (21 daily; 15min), Cavaillon (13 daily; 25min); L'Isle-sur-la-Sorgue (13 daily; 20min).

TGV

Avignon to: Aix-en-Provence TGV (11 daily; 20min); Lyon (12 daily; 1hr 10min); Marseille (hourly; 35min); Paris (12 daily; 2hr 40min); Paris CDG Airport (6 daily; 3hr 30min).

Buses

Avignon to: Aix (4 daily; 1hr 15min); Apt (5 daily; 1hr 10min); Arles (6 daily; 1hr 10min); Barbentane (5 daily; 15min); Beaucaire (5 daily; 45min); Boulbon (5 daily; 30min); Carpentras (16 daily; 45min); Cavaillon (10 daily; 35min); Châteauneuf-du-Pape (2 daily; 35min); Châteaurenard (11 daily; 20min); Digne (1 daily; 3hr 20min); Fontaine-de-Vaucluse (4 daily; 55min); L'Isle-sur-la-Sorgue (10 daily; 35min); Lourmarin (2 daily; 1hr 25min); Marseille (1 daily; 1hr 50min); Montélimar (1 daily; 2hr 50min); Nîmes (4 daily; 1hr 20min); Orange (14 daily; 50min); Pertuis (2 daily; 1hr 45min);

St-Rémy (7 daily; 40min); Tarascon (6 daily; 45min); Vaison (3 daily; 35min).
Avignon TGV to: Apt (3 daily; 1hr 30min); Arles (8 daily; 45min); Carpentras (3 daily; 40min); Cavaillon (3 daily; 50min); Tarascon (8 daily; 30min).
Carpentras to: Aix (2 daily; 1hr 40min); Avignon (16 daily; 45min); Avignon TGV (3 daily; 1hr); Beaumes-de-Venise (2 daily; 20min); Bedoin (2 daily; 40min); Cavaillon (7 daily; 40min); Gigondas (2 daily; 30min); L'Isle-sur-la-Sorgue (7 daily; 20min); Malaucène (2 daily; 30min); Marseille (3 daily; 2hr 15min); Orange (4 daily; 45min); Pernes-les-Fontaines (4 daily; 5min); Sablet (2 daily; 45min); Sault (1 daily; 1hr 15min); Vacqueyras (2 daily; 25min); Vaison (2 daily; 45min).
Cavaillon to: Aix (2 daily; 1hr); Avignon (10 daily; 35min); Avignon TGV (3 daily; 50min); Carpentras (7 daily; 45min); Gordes (3 daily; 30min); L'Isle-sur-la-Sorgue (7 daily; 15min); Marseille (3 daily; 1hr 25min); Pernes-les-Fontaines (7 daily; 35min).
L'Isle-sur-la-Sorgue to: Avignon (15 daily; 45min); Carpentras (7 daily; 15min); Cavaillon (6 daily; 20min); Fontaine-de-Vaucluse (5 daily; 15min); Velleron (4 daily; 10min).
Nyons to: Avignon (1 daily; 1hr 50min); Grignan (4 daily; 40min); Vaison (6 daily; 30min); Valréas (3 daily; 20min).
Orange to: Avignon (14 daily; 50min); Carpentras (4 daily; 40min); Châteauneuf-du-Pape (2 daily; 25min); Sérignan (3 daily; 20min); Vaison (5 daily; 45min).
Vaison to: Avignon (2 daily; 1hr 20min); Carpentras (2 daily; 45min); Nyons (4 daily; 30min); Orange (5 daily; 45min); Séguret (7 daily; 20min); Sablet (7 daily; 25min).
Valréas to: Avignon (3 daily; 1hr 30min); Grignan (4 daily; 20min); Nyons (3 daily; 20min); Orange (3 daily; 45min).

4

Aix-en-Provence, the Durance and the Luberon

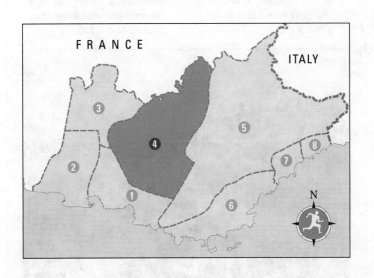

CHAPTER 4   # Highlights

* **Cézanne's Aix** Visit his atelier then explore a living Cézanne landscape in the country around the Mont Ste-Victoire. See p.203 & p.205

* **Forcalquier** Explore this once grand, now slumbering, historic town, and its beautiful, unspoilt *pays*. See p.219

* **Medieval hilltop villages** Though Gordes is the best known, Lacoste, Saignon and Simiane-la-Rotonde are equally picturesque and much less busy. See p.229, p.234, p.225 & p.223

* **Ochre in the Luberon** Brilliantly-coloured landscapes enfold the friendly villages of Rustrel and Roussillon. See p.229

* **Abbaye de Sénanque** The ancient Cistercian monastery is as much a symbol of Provence as the lavender fields surrounding it. See p.231

* **Abandoned hilltop ruins** Quiet and crumbling, Oppède-le-Vieux and the Fort de Buoux provide an atmospheric insight into life in the medieval *villages perchés*. See p.233 & p.225

△ Hilltop village, the Luberon

Aix-en-Provence, the Durance and the Luberon

A wide, rushing torrent in winter that reduces to a dribble in summer, the **Durance** is one of the great alpine rivers of France, slashing 320km southwest from its source near Briançon to its confluence with the Rhône near **Avignon**. No fewer than four *départements* converge on it at the point where it meets the Verdon, a few kilometres northeast of the Pont Mirabeau. Three of the four – the Alpes de Haute Provence, the Vaucluse and the Bouches du Rhône – are at their most atypical here. The portion of the Alpes de Haute Provence, west of the Durance, lacks the genuine alpine terrain of much of the region to the east; the **Luberon**'s history of dissent during the Wars of Religion distinguishes it from the papal tradition of the Vaucluse as a whole; and the pastoral charms of the Coteaux d'Aix and grandeur of the Mont Ste-Victoire stand in stark contrast to the industrialized, metropolitan feel of the Marseille conurbation. But though unrepresentative of their *départements*, together these regions offer a distillation of all that, for visitors, seems most typically Provençal – of lavender and honey, crumbling hilltop villages and ancient abbeys, lively markets and excellent cuisine rooted in the *terroir*.

The charms of **Aix-en-Provence** – the only real city in the region – are commonly sung. With a historic core as perfect as any in France, it glories in the medieval period of independent Provence, the riches of its seventeenth- and eighteenth-century growth and the memory of its most famous sons, Zola and Cézanne.

To the north of Aix, the transition between Mediterranean and Alpine France becomes clear along the valley of the Durance. Downstream, the fruitful countryside between sleepy **Cadenet** and bustling **Pertuis** is classically Provençal, but east of Pertuis, the landscape becomes wilder, the valley narrowing to a rocky gorge at the Défilé de Mirabeau. To the north, **Manosque** offers a rare taste of urban life, while dramatic **Sisteron** acts as a gateway to the Alps and as the northern point of departure from Provence. West of the Durance, the delights of the **Pays de Forcalquier** include the venerable town

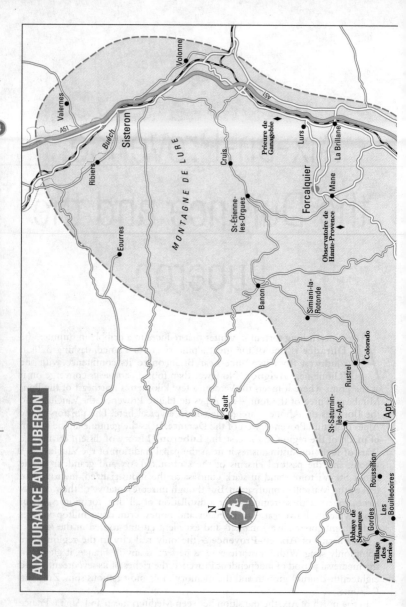

of **Forcalquier** itself and the remote and beautiful hilltop village of **Simiane-la-Rotonde**.

Sweeping further to the west, the great green surge of the **Luberon** massif is as lauded as any landscape in Provence, not least in the books of Peter Mayle, and its beautiful villages nowadays have a distinctly chic edge. Its principal centre, **Apt**, is a lively market town slowly evolving in the face of

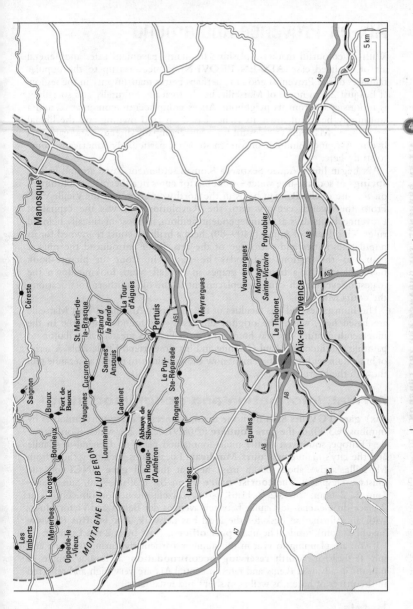

the transformation that the influx of wealthy Parisians and foreigners has wrought on the surrounding districts. The attractions of the countryside are diverse: the multi-hued ochre mines of **Rustrel** and **Roussillon**, the abandoned villages at **Buoux** and **Oppède-le-Vieux**, the immaculate village of **Gordes** and the twelfth-century Cistercian monasteries at **Sénanque** and **Silvacane**.

Aix-en-Provence and around

With its colourful markets, splashing fountains, pavement cafés and general air of civilized ease, **AIX-EN-PROVENCE** measures up to the popular fantasies of the Provençal good life perhaps better than any city in the region. It lies just 25km north of Marseille, but historically, culturally and socially it is moons apart from its neighbour. Aix is complacently conservative, and a stunningly beautiful town, its riches based on land owning and the liberal professions. Marseille's successful financiers, company directors and gangsters live in Aix, and hundreds of foreign students, particularly Americans, come to study here.

Aix began life as Aquae Sextiae, a Roman settlement based around its **hot springs** of sodium-free water – still used for cures in a thermal establishment on the site of the Roman baths in the northwest corner of the Vieille Ville. From the twelfth century until the Revolution Aix was the capital of Provence. In its days as an independent fiefdom, its most mythically beloved ruler, King René of Anjou (1409–80), held a brilliant court renowned for its popular festivities and patronage of the arts. René introduced the muscat grape to the region, and today he stands in stone in picture-book medieval fashion, a bunch of grapes in his left hand, looking down the majestic seventeenth-century replacement to the old southern fortifications, the cours Mirabeau.

The humanities and arts faculties of the university Aix shares with Marseille are based here, where the original university was founded in 1409. In the nineteenth century Aix was home to two of France's greatest contributors to painting and literature, Paul Cézanne and his close friend Émile Zola. A series of brass studs set into the pavement now allows visitors to follow a Cézanne trail through the heart of the city.

Arrival, information and accommodation

Aix's **gare TGV** lies 8km from the town, connected every thirty minutes by minibus (€3.90) to the **gare routière** (℡08.91.02.40.25), which is on avenue de l'Europe, southwest of the multi-fountained place du Général-de-Gaulle and the city's main drag, **cours Mirabeau**. Local trains, including those from Marseille, arrive about 500m from here at the old **gare SNCF** on rue Gustave-Desplaces. The **tourist office** (Mon–Sat 8.30am–7pm, Sun 10am–1pm & 2–6pm; ℡04.42.16.11.61, Ⓦwww.aixenprovencetourism.com) is at 2 place du Général-de-Gaulle, between avenues des Belges and Victor-Hugo, with an information desk for the local bus network, **Aix en Bus** (Ⓦwww.aixenbus.com), inside. The main **post office** is close by at 2 rue Lapierre.

If you are planning to visit in the summer, particularly during the June and July festivals, it's worth **reserving accommodation** at least a couple of months in advance. Rents and rates in central Aix are very high and reflected in the prices of hotels, as well as in shops and restaurants.

Hotels

Hôtel des Arts 69 bd Carnot ℡04.42.38.11.77, Ⓕ04.42.26.77.31. The cheapest rooms in the centre of Aix – a bit noisy, but very welcoming. You can't book ahead, so turn up early. ❷
Hôtel des Augustins 3 rue de la Masse ℡04.42.27.28.59, Ⓦwww.hotel-augustins.com.

Atmospheric, smart hotel in a converted medieval monastery, just off the cours Mirabeau. ❻
La Caravelle 29 bd Roi-René ℡04.42.21.53.05, Ⓦwww.lacaravelle-hotel.com. Well maintained, friendly and soundproofed hotel set back slightly from the boulevards ringing Vieil

Aix. The more expensive rooms overlook courtyard gardens. ④

Hôtel Cardinal 24 rue Cardinale ☎04.42.38.32.30, ⓕ04.42.26.39.05. A clean, peaceful and welcoming hotel in the quartier Mazarin, with classically furnished rooms. ④

Hôtel de France 63 rue Espariat ☎04.42.27.90.15, ⓦwww.hoteldefrance-aix.com. Right in the centre, fronting onto a pretty little *place* and with very comfortable rooms. ④

Hôtel du Globe 74 cours Sextius ☎04.42.26.03.58, ⓦwww.hotelduglobe.com. Modern, unfussy, non-smoking place, with a roof terrace overlooking Vieil Aix. Popular with clients from the nearby baths. ④

Grand Hôtel Nègre Coste 33 cours Mirabeau ☎04.42.27.74.22, ⓦwww.hotelnegrecoste.com. Splendidly situated hotel in a handsome eighteenth-century house with a/c, refurbished bathrooms and comfortable, soundproofed, high-ceilinged rooms. ⑥

Le Manoir 8 rue d'Entrecasteaux ☎04.42.26.27.20, ⓦwww.hotelmanoir.com. Tucked away on a pretty courtyard off a quiet but central street, with agreeable rooms furnished with antiques. Closed Jan. ④

Hôtel Paul 10 av Pasteur ☎04.42.23.23.89, ⓔhotel.paul@orange.fr. Good value for Aix, and with its own leafy garden, though on a busy road. ②

Hôtel le Pigonnet 5 av du Pigonnet ☎04.42.59.02.90, ⓦwww.hotelpigonnet.com. Five-star luxury in the beautiful setting of an eighteenth-century *bastide* surrounded by lush gardens, 10min on foot from the quartier Mazarin. ⑨

Hôtel des Quatre Dauphins 54 rue Roux-Alphéran ☎04.42.38.16.39, ⓔlesquatredauphins@orange.fr. Warm, old-world charm in the quartier Mazarin, with small, prettily furnished rooms. ⑤

St-Christophe 2 av Victor-Hugo ☎04.42.26.01.24, ⓦwww.hotel-saintcristophe.com. Comfortable, a/c, soundproofed rooms above a smart Art Deco brasserie close to the tourist office and cours Mirabeau. ⑤

Hostel and campsites

Airotel Camping Chanteclerc rte de Nice, Val St-André ☎04.42.26.12.98, ⓦwww.aixenprovencetourism.com/aix-chanteclerc.htm#. Four-star site 3km from the centre; take bus #3. Expensive, but the facilities are excellent and include a pool. €18.30 per tent. Open year-round.

Camping Arc-en-Ciel rte de Nice, Pont des Trois Sautets ☎04.42.26.14.28. Four-star site 3km southeast of town; take bus #3. Not particularly cheap, but with very good facilities. Open April–Sept.

HI youth hostel 3 av Marcel-Pagnol ☎04.42.20.15.99, ⓦwww.fuaj.org. Two kilometres west of the centre, next to the Fondation Vasarely; take bus #4 (direction "la Mayanalle", stop "Vasarely Auberge de la Jeunesse"). Reception 7am–1pm & 5pm–midnight. Completely renovated in 2002, with a dining room, bar, washing facilities, TV, table tennis, basketball and volleyball courts. Closed mid-Dec to early Feb.

The City

The old city of Aix, clearly defined by its ring of boulevards and the majestic cours Mirabeau, is in its entirety the great monument here, far more compelling than any one single building or museum within it. With so many streets alive with people, so many tempting restaurants, cafés and shops, plus the best markets in Provence, it's easy to pass several days wandering around without needing any itinerary or destination. Beyond **Vieil Aix**, there are a few museums in the **quartier Mazarin** south of **cours Mirabeau** and, further out, the **Vaserely Foundation**, **Cézanne's studio** and the Cézanne family home, **Jas de Bouffan**. The **Cité du Livre** cultural complex is part of a major regeneration across the entire west side of Vieil Aix.

Aix for less

Aix's excellent-value **Visa** card (€2) gives discounted admission to the principal museums, plus half-price guided tours and reduced-rate travel on the city's buses.

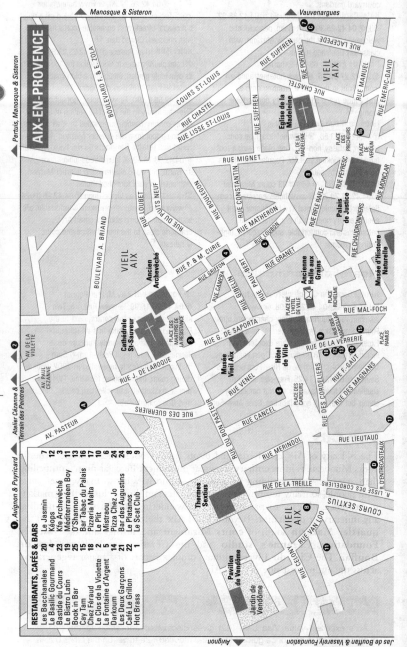

AIX-EN-PROVENCE

▲ Manosque & Sisteron   ▲ Vauvenargues

◀ Pertuis, Manosque & Sisteron

◀ Atelier Cézanne &
Terrain des Peintres

◀ Avignon & Puyricard

AIX-EN-PROVENCE, THE DURANCE AND THE LUBERON

4

194

▼ Avignon   ▼ Jas de Bouffan & Vasarely Foundation

RESTAURANTS, CAFÉS & BARS	
Les Bacchanales	20
Le Basilic Gourmand	4
Bastide du Cours	23
Le Bistro Latin	19
Book in Bar	25
Cay Tam	15
Chez Féraud	18
Le Clos de la Violette	2
La Fontaine d'Argent	5
Darkoum	14
Les Deux Garçons	21
Café Le Grillon	22
Hot Brass	1
Le Jasmin	7
Kēops	12
Kfe Archevéché	3
Méditerranéen Boy	11
O'Shannon	13
Bar Tabac du Palais	16
Pizzeria Malta	17
Le Plit	10
Mistraou	6
Pizza Chez Jo	24
Bar des Augustins	8
Le Platanos	9
Le Scat Club	1

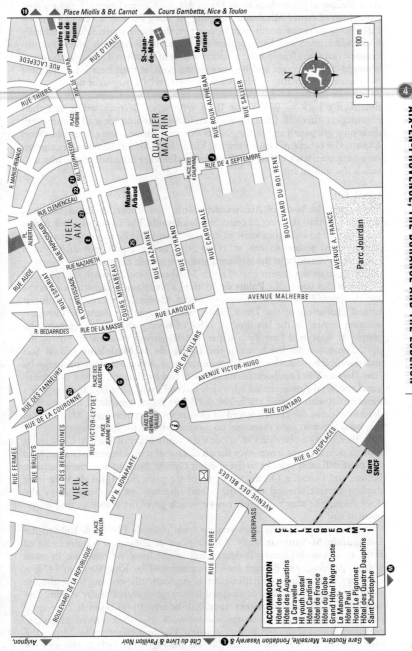

Place Miollis & Bd. Carnot   Cours Gambetta, Nice & Toulon

Theatre du Jeu de Paume

RUE LACEPEDE

RUE D'ITALIE

St-Jean-de-Malte

Musée Granet

RUE THIERS

RUE DE L'OPERA

PLACE FORBIN

RUE ROUX-ALPHERAN

RUE SALLIER

N

100 m

0

R. MARIUS-REYNAUD

RUE TOURNEFORT

QUARTIER MAZARIN

PLACE DES 4 DAUPHINS

RUE DE 4 SEPTEMBRE

RUE CLEMENCEAU

BOULEVARD DU ROI RENE

PL. ALBERTAS

RUE PARASSANDI

VIEIL AIX

Musée Arbaud

RUE MAZARINE

RUE GOYRAND

RUE CARDINALE

AVENUE A. FRANCE

Parc Jourdan

RUE AUDE

RUE ESPARIAT

RUE NAZARETH

R. COURTEISSADE

COURS MIRABEAU

AVENUE MALHERBE

R. BEDARRIDES

RUE DE LA MASSE

RUE LAROQUE

RUE DE VILLARS

RUE DES TANNEURS

RUE DE LA COURONNE

PLACE DES AUGUSTINS

AVENUE VICTOR-HUGO

RUE FERMEE

RUE BRUEYS

RUE VICTOR-LEYDET

RUE DES BERNARDINES

PLACE JEANNE D'ARC

PLACE DU GENERAL DE GAULLE

RUE GONTARD

VIEIL AIX

AV N. BONAPARTE

RUE G.-DESPLACES

PLACE NIOLLON

BOULEVARD DE LA REPUBLIQUE

RUE LAPIERRE

AVENUE DES BELGES

UNDERPASS

Gare SNCF

ACCOMMODATION

Hôtel des Arts   C
Hôtel des Augustins   F
La Caravelle   K
HI youth hostel   L
Hôtel Cardinal   H
Hôtel de France   G
Hôtel du Globe   B
Grand Hôtel Nègre Coste   E
Le Manoir   D
Hôtel Paul   A
Hotel Le Pigonnet   M
Hôtel des Quatre Dauphins   J
Saint Christophe   I

Gare Routière, Marseille, Fondation Vasarely & Cité du Livre, Pavillon Noir

Avignon,

Cours Mirabeau

As a preliminary introduction to life in Aix, take a stroll beneath the gigantic plane trees of **cours Mirabeau**, stopping off along the way at one of the many cafés along its sunny north side. In contrast, the shady south side is decidedly businesslike, lined with banks and offices lodged in seventeenth- to eighteenth-century mansions. These have a uniform hue of weathered stone, with ornate wrought-iron balconies and Baroque decorations, at their heaviest in the tired old musclemen holding up the porch of the *Hôtel d'Espargnet* at no. 38.

Opposite the hotel is Aix's most famous café, *Les Deux Garçons*, with a reputation dating back to World War II of serving intellectuals, artists and their entourage; earlier still, Cézanne was a customer. The interior is all mirrors with darkening gilt panels and reading lights that might have come off the old *Orient Express*. The other cafés have a shifting hierarchy of kudos. All are pricey, though very tempting, with cocktails, ice creams and wicker armchairs from which to watch the milling street.

Vieil Aix

To explore the heart of Aix, wander north from cours Mirabeau and then anywhere within the ring of cours and boulevards. The layout of **Vieil Aix** is not designed to assist your sense of direction, but it hardly matters when there's a fountained square to rest at every 50m and a continuous architectural backdrop of treats from the sixteenth and seventeenth centuries.

Starting from the eastern end of cours Mirabeau, heading north into place de Verdun brings you to the **Palais de Justice**, a Neoclassical construction on the site of the old counts of Provence's palace. Count Mirabeau, the aristocrat turned champion of the Third Estate, who accused the États de Provence, meeting in Aix for the last time in 1789, of having no right to represent the people, is honoured here by a statue and allegorical monument. Just to the north, on place des Prêcheurs, is the **Église de la Madeleine** (closed Sun afternoon). The church's crumbling interior is decorated with paintings by Jean-Baptiste Van Loo, born in Aix in 1684, and by Rubens, as well as a three-panel medieval Annunciation in which Gabriel's wings are owl feathers and a monkey sits with its head just below the deity's ray of light. Sadly, the structural deterioration of the church forced its closure for safety reasons in May 2006; as this book went to press there was no confirmed date for its reopening.

Further west, in place de l'Hôtel de Ville at the heart of Vieil Aix, a massive, though delicate, foot hangs over the architrave of the old corn exchange, now the **post office**. It belongs to the goddess Cybele, dallying with the masculine Rhône and Durance. On the west side of the *place*, the **Hôtel de Ville** itself displays perfect classical proportions and filigreed wrought iron above the door. Alongside stands a **clock tower** which gives the season as well as the hour of day.

Rue Gaston-de-Saporta takes you up from place de l'Hôtel de Ville to the **Cathédrale St-Sauveur** (daily 7.30am–noon & 2–6pm), a conglomerate of fifth- to sixteenth-century buildings, full of medieval art treasures. Its most notable painting, *The Burning Bush*, commissioned by King René in 1475, is currently undergoing restoration and is consequently not on show, though there's an English-language audiovisual lecture on it each Tuesday at 3pm. The beautiful Romanesque **cloisters** (tours half-hourly: 10–11.30am & 2.30–5pm) have recently emerged from restoration work and their carved pillars are perhaps the best sculptures in the cathedral. The four corner pillars depict the four beasts of the Revelation: man, the lion, the eagle and the bull. Also remarkable are the cathedral's west doors, carved by Toulon carpenter Jean Guiramand

△ Cours Mirabeau

in the early sixteenth century to depict four Old Testament prophets and twelve sybils, the wise women of antiquity who supposedly prophesied Christ's birth, death and resurrection.

Close by, across place des Martyrs de la Résistance at the side of the cathedral, is the former bishop's palace, the **Ancien Archevêché**, the setting, each July, for part of Aix's grandiose music festival. It also houses the **Musée des Tapisseries** (Mon & Wed–Sun 10am–12.30pm & 1.30–4.45pm; €2.50), a collection of wonderful tapestries. Highlights include the musicians, dancers and animals in a 1689 series of grotesques; nine scenes from the life of Don Quixote, woven in the 1730s, including one with a club-footed cat being divested of its armour by various *demoiselles*; and four superbly detailed *Jeux Russiens* (*Russian Games*) from a few decades later. A contemporary section hosts temporary exhibitions, and there's also a section given over to the costumes, stage designs and history of the music festival.

The **Musée du Vieil Aix**, at 17 rue Gaston-de-Saporta (Tues–Sun 10am–noon & 2.30–6pm; €4), is worth a glance while you're in this part of town. It devotes a whole section to the old Fête-Dieu religious procession, which originally took place here each June and was last held in 1851. Traditionally associated with King René, the procession became less regular and more secular over the centuries, with much attendant practical jokery. The depictions of the procession here include Bontoux's wooden marionettes dating from 1836 and a wonderful eighteenth-century painted screen. Among the other odds and ends are the Talking Crib – a set of complex nineteenth-century mechanical marionettes by Benoît d'Aix which together create a nativity scene – along with some Moustiers faïence and various maps of Aix through the ages.

South of the l'Hôtel de Ville is the elegant, cobbled eighteenth-century Rococo **place d'Albertas**, which hosts occasional concerts on summer evenings. The square is just off rue Espariat, which runs west to place du Général-de-Gaulle and has a distinctly Parisian style. Many of Aix's classiest couturier shops cluster in this area: Escada is on rue Marius-Reinaud, and Yohiji Yamamoto on rue Fabrot.

At 6 rue Espariat, the impressive seventeenth-century *Hôtel Boyer d'Eguilles* houses the **Musée de l'Histoire Naturelle** (daily 10am–noon & 1–5pm; €2.50), where the cherubs and garlands decorating the ceilings are slightly at odds with the stuffed birds and beetles, ammonites and dinosaur eggs below. Nonetheless, it makes for a good rainy day – or sunstroke – refuge.

Quartier Mazarin

Taking rue Clemenceau south over cours Mirabeau brings you into the heart of the **quartier Mazarin**, built in five years in the mid-seventeenth century by the archbishop brother of the cardinal who ran France when Louis XIV was a baby. It's a very dignified district, and very quiet.

Before you reach the beautiful place des Quatre Dauphins with its four-dolphin fountain, you'll pass **Musée Paul Arbaud**, at 2 rue du 4 Septembre, a dark, musty old house, to which you are grudgingly granted admission after ringing the bell (Mon–Sat 2–5pm; €3). The museum's main collection is of Marseillais and Moustiers ceramics, but there are more interesting items tucked away in the claustrophobic rooms of leather-bound books, silk wallpaper and painted and panelled ceilings. The best is a portrait by Pierre Puget of his mother. There are also portraits of Mirabeau, and family and royalist trinkets such as nobles' rings offered as bail for Louis XVI while he was imprisoned in Paris.

A couple of blocks east of the dolphin fountain, on place St-Jean-de-Malte in the former priory of the Knights of Malta, is the most substantial of Aix's museums, the **Musée Granet** (Mon & Wed–Sun 11am–6pm; €10), which reopened in the summer of 2006 after extensive rebuilding with a major exhibition marking the centenary of Cézanne's death. Covering art and archeology, the museum exhibits the ever-growing finds from the Oppidum d'Entremont (see p.203), a Celto-Légurian township 3km north of Aix, which flourished for about a hundred years, along with the remains of the Romans who routed them in 124 BC. Its paintings are a mixed bag: Italian, Dutch and French, mostly seventeenth- to nineteenth-century. François Granet (1775–1849), whose collection initiated the museum, was an Aixois painter; his portrait by Ingres hangs here but his own works are better represented in the Musée Paul Arbaud (see above). The portraits of Diane de Poiters by Jean Capassin and Marie Mancini by Nicolas Mignard are an interesting contrast and there is also a self-portrait by Rembrandt. The most famous Aixois painter, Paul Cézanne, studied on the ground floor of the building, which once held the city's art school. Two of his student drawings are here as well as a handful of canvases, including *Bathsheba, The Bathers* and *Portrait of a Woman*.

West of Vieil Aix: Jas de Bouffan, Vasarely Foundation and the Cité du Livre

The man who came to be regarded as the father of modern painting cut a lonely figure for much of his life, spurned by the Parisian art establishment and happier away from the capital in his beloved Aix. Paul Cézanne was born in Vieil Aix at 28 rue de l'Opéra, the son of a hatter of Italian descent turned prosperous banker, but he grew up in a grand eighteenth-century house to the southwest of the city. The house, known as **Jas de Bouffan** (daily 10am–12.30pm & 2–6.30pm; visitable only on a pre-booked tour from Aix tourist information office; €5.50), opened for guided visits to mark the centenary of Cézanne's death in 2006 but was scheduled to close again temporarily for further refurbishment as this book went to press. For many years Cézanne was able to use the elegant salon here as his studio, and at the start of the tour an impressive audiovisual presentation projects many of the canvases originally painted in the room onto its white-painted walls, including *Les Jouers de Cartes*, whose subjects were the simple agricultural folk who were his father's clients, and *Le Bassin du Jas de Bouffan en hiver*. The tour continues in the lovely garden, where you can see the basin itself.

In Cézanne's day this area was still outside the city, but today Aix has spread far beyond the family home. The hill of Jas de Bouffan is now dominated by the **Fondation Vasarely**, 1 av Marcel-Pagnol (Mon–Sat 10am–6pm; €7), a building in black and white geometric shapes created by the Hungarian-born artist in 1976. To get there take bus #4 (stop "V. Vasarely"). The seven hexagonal spaces of the ground floor are hung with Vasarely's monumental kinetic tapestries and paintings, while the rest of the museum hosts large-scale temporary exhibitions. The Fondation's messy history stands in stark contrast to Vasarely's clean, boldly geometric art. In 1995, the artist's daughter-in-law obtained a court order to remove the bulk of the exhibits donated to the Fondation, leaving just the monumental works, a decision disputed by Vasarely's grandson, who has since battled to regain control. Then, in 2005, the Fondation's erstwhile director, Charles Debbasch, was convicted of selling off works privately and pocketing the cash during his tenure from 1981 to 1993; he has thus far escaped prison by settling in Togo. After a long period of closure, the Fondation reopened, but its troubles persist – the bailiffs are an ever-present threat, the building leaks, some of the artworks have been damaged or vandalized, and staffing levels are cut to the bone.

Calmer cultural waters are to be found at the **Cité du Livre**, a delightful arts centre a little closer to the centre of Aix in the old match-making factory at 8–10 rue des Allumettes (Tues, Thurs & Fri noon–6pm; Wed & Sat 10am–6pm; free), a short way south of the *gare routière*. It includes libraries, a cinema, theatre space, and a *videothèque d'art lyrique* where you can watch just about any French opera performance. A little to the north along rue des Allumettes is one of the jewels in Aix's contemporary artistic crown, the **Pavillon Noir**, home to the internationally renowned Ballet Preljocaj (ⓦ www.preljocaj.org). The new building is a startling web of black concrete columns designed by the Algerian-born Provençal architect Rudi Ricciotti and housing rehearsal studios and a 378-seat theatre.

The Atelier Paul Cézanne and the Terrain des Peintres

Cézanne used many studios in and around Aix, but at the turn of the twentieth century, four years before his death, he had a house built for the purpose at what is now 9 av Paul-Cézanne, overlooking Aix from the north. By this stage in his life Cézanne had achieved both financial security and the recognition that had so long eluded him. It was here that he painted the *Grandes Baigneuses*, the *Jardinier Vallier* and some of his greatest still lifes. The **Atelier Paul Cézanne** (daily: April & May 10am–noon & 2–6pm; June–Sept 10am–7pm; Oct–March 10am–noon & 2–5pm; €5.50; timed admission, with film show while you wait) has been left exactly as it was at the time of his death in 1906: coat, hat, wine glass and easel, the objects he liked to paint, his pipe, a few letters and drawings – everything save the man himself, who would probably have been horrified at the thought of it being public. The guides are true enthusiasts, and provided the atelier isn't too busy a visit is a real joy. To get to the house, take bus #1 or #20 (stop "Cézanne"); otherwise it's a ten-minute walk or so uphill from the north end of the Vieille Ville.

Two kilometres further north up the hill of Les Lauves at Chemin de Marguerite (bus #20; stop "Marguerite") is the **Terrain des Peintres** (free access), an informal Mediterranean garden on the spot where, towards the end of his life, Cézanne painted Mont Ste-Victoire over and over again. Despite the suburban development that has covered Les Lauves since Cézanne's day, the view remains miraculously intact, and this is still the highest vantage point in Aix from which to view the mountain. At the top of the garden plaques depict several of the Mont Ste-Victoire canvasses, though they're scarcely necessary, as it would be impossible to imagine this now as anything other than Cézanne's landscape.

Eating and drinking

Aix is stuffed full of **restaurants** of every price and ethnic origin. Place des Cardeurs, just west of the Hôtel de Ville, is filled with restaurant, brasserie and café tables, while rue de la Verrerie, running south from rue des Cordeliers, is good for ethnic choices – Vietnamese, Egyptian and Tunisian, in particular. Rue des Tanneurs is also good for those who don't want to pay gourmet prices, with a mix of ethnic and Provençal options. The elegant **café-brasseries** on cours Mirabeau, though occasionally pricey, are also tempting. That said, Aix's restaurant scene repays careful exploration, as some of the most tempting places are away from these tourist hotspots.

Restaurants

Les Bacchanales 10 rue Couronne
ⓣ 04.42.27.21.06. Inventive cooking, featuring dishes such as rolled shoulder of lamb rolled in a vegetable *mousseline* or snails on a bed of tomatoes, wild mushrooms and creamy garlic; menus from €30 upwards. Closed all day Tues & Wed eve.

Le Basilic Gourmand 6 rue du Griffon
☎04.42.96.08.58. Classic Provençal food in an
appealing dining room decked out with old adver-
tisements and paraphernalia. Occasional live music
too. Evenings only; closed Sun & Mon in winter.

Le Bistro Latin 18 rue Couronne
☎04.42.38.22.88. Chickpea terrine with cheese
and tapenade, tartar of lentils with marinated
smoked trout, and fillet of perch pan-fried with
lemon butter are among the delicacies here. Menus
at €16 and €21. Closed for lunch Sat–Mon.

Cay Tam 29 rue Verrerie ☎04.42.27.28.11. Smart,
well-regarded Vietnamese restaurant with menus
at €15.50 and €20.50 and a few Chinese, Thai
and Korean dishes. Closed all day Mon & lunch
Tues–Thurs & Sun.

🏃 **Chez Féraud** 8 rue du Puits Juif
☎04.42.63.07.27. Classy, romantic
Provençal restaurant in a quiet corner near the
Hôtel de Ville, with *croquant* of *chèvre* and auber-
gines, loin of pork with dauphinoise potatoes and
crème caramel *aux calissons* on a superb €26.50
menu. Closed Sun & Mon.

Le Clos de la Violette 10 av de la Violette
☎04.42.23.30.71. Aix's most renowned restaurant
with dishes that might not sound too seductive –
stuffed lamb's feet and *pieds et paquets* – but are
in fact gastronomic delights. More obviously alluring
are the puddings: a clafoutis of greengages and
pistachios with peach sauce, and a tart of melting
dark chocolate. Lunch menu at €54, otherwise
€90. Closed Sun, plus Mon & Wed lunchtimes.

Darkoum 31/33 rue Félibre-Gaut
☎04.42.91.38.98. Plush Moroccan restaurant with
tagines, couscous and *brik de framboises* on a
€21 menu. Closed Sun lunch & Mon.

Le Jasmin 6 rue de la Fonderie
☎04.42.38.05.89. Iranian food on €16.50 and
€22 menus. Closed Sun.

Kéops 28 rue de la Verrerie ☎04.42.96.59.05.
Egyptian cuisine featuring falafel, stuffed pigeon
and delicious milk-based desserts. Menus
from €8.

Kfe Archevéché 25 rue Gaston de Saporta
☎04.42.21.43.57. Smart place with good midday
salads from €10.60, plus meat, fish & pasta on an
€18 menu. Closed Sun in winter.

Mistraou 38 place des Cardeurs
☎04.42.96.98.69. Provençal restaurant in an
atmospheric if rather damp cellar, with veggie and
non-veggie menus from €25 – watch out for the
anchovies if you are veggie, though.

Pizza Chez Jo/Bar des Augustins 59 rue
Espariat ☎04.42.26.12.47. Cheap pizzas and
traditional *plats du jour* from €12 upwards; usually
packed, but you won't have to wait long for a table.
Closed Sun.

Pizzeria Malta 28 place des Tanneurs
☎04.42.26.15.43. Nice atmosphere and cheap
plonk to accompany the pizzas or pasta. Menu
€17. Closed Sun lunch & Mon.

Le Platanos 13 rue Rifle-Rafle ☎04.42.21.33.19.
Very cheap and popular Greek restaurant with a
€14 menu.

Cafés & bars

Bastide du Cours 41–47 cours Mirabeau
☎04.42.26.10.06. A fashionable, big, expensive
café on the cours. Open daily.

🏃 **Les Deux Garçons** 53 cours Mirabeau
☎04.42.26.00.51. The erstwhile haunt of
Albert Camus is done up in faded 1900s style
and still attracts a motley assortment of literati.
Good brasserie food, but not especially cheap,
with *plats* from €16.80 up. Open daily.

Café Le Grillon 49 cours Mirabeau
☎04.42.27.58.81. One of the best of the

brasseries on the cours, with light meals from
around €8.50. Open daily.

Méditerranéen Boy 6 rue Paix ☎04.42.27.21.47.
Aix's most established gay bar is small and
discreet but frequently packed.

O'Shannon 30 rue de la Verrerie ☎04.42.23.44.61.
Boisterous Irish pub that's just about the liveliest
spot for serious beer drinking in Aix.

Bar Tabac du Palais cnr rue Manuel/place des
Prêcheurs. Small, pleasant bar from which to view
the market.

Nightlife and entertainment

A much smaller city than its southern neighbour, Aix unsurprisingly lacks the
sheer variety of theatre that you can find in Marseille, though for its size it is
lively enough, and is also home to the internationally renowned contemporary
dance company, Ballet Preljocaj. There are also some good **pubs** with **live
music**, excellent **jazz** venues, and **classical concerts** given in the city's
churches. If you fancy a trip to the **cinema**, try Le Mazarin, 6 rue Laroque

(℡08.92.68.72.70) or Le Renoir, 24 cours Mirabeau (same number), two independent cinemas where most foreign films are shown in their original language.

A selection of concerts and other mainstream cultural events is listed in *Le Mois à Aix*, available free from the tourist office, where you can also book tickets for events in Aix and elsewhere. The best time for Aix nightlife is during the summer **festivals** when much of the entertainment happens in the street.

Book in Bar 1 bis rue Cabassol ℡04.42.26.60.07. English café and bookshop with regular book signings, lectures and theme nights.

Cité du Livre 8–10 rue des Allumettes ℡04.42.91.98.88. Concerts, plays, cutting-edge contemporary dance, poetry readings and films.

La Fontaine d'Argent 5 rue de La Fontaine-d'Argent ℡04.42.38.43.80. Café-theatre with a diverse programme including comedy.

Hot Brass 1857 chemin d'Eguilles-Célony ℡04.42.23.13.12. The best jazz club in Aix, open Fri, Sat & evenings before public holidays from 10.30pm.

Le Pavillon Noir 530 av Wolfgang Amadeus Mozart ℡04.42.93.48.00; ⊛www.preljocaj.org. Impressive new home and performance base for the celebrated Ballet Preljocaj.

Le Plit 24 rue de la Verrerie ℡04.42.21.31.58. Mainstream disco with stylish modern decor. Open Tues–Sun from 11pm

Le Scat Club 11 rue de la Verrerie ℡04.42.23.00.23. All kinds of jazz, rock and funk – the best live-music venue in Vieil Aix; reasonable prices. Closed Sun and Mon.

Théâtre du Jeu de Paume 17–21 rue de l'Opéra ℡04.42.99.12.00. Aix's grandest venue for mainstream theatre and music, in opulent and historic Rococo surroundings.

The festivals

For much of June and July, Vieil Aix is taken over by its music festivals and the accompanying street entertainers of the alternative scene; street theatre, rock concerts and impromptu gatherings turn the whole area into one long party. The main events are the **Aix en Musique**, a rock, jazz, experimental and classical music event in June and the **Festival International d'Art Lyrique**, dedicated to opera and classical concerts in July.

Tickets for the festivals' mainstream events average €28 and up, though tickets for the opera can be considerably more expensive. For the Aix en Musique festival, they are available from Espace Forbin, on place John-Rewald (℡04.42.21.69.69); for the Festival International d'Art Lyrique from the festival shop at 11 rue Gaston-de-Saporta (℡04.42.17.34.34).

Shopping and markets

Aix's **markets** provide the greatest retail pleasures, but there are also some very good **specialist shops**. For English-language **books** there's Paradox Bookstore, 15 rue du 4 Septembre, and Book in Bar at 1 bis rue Cabassol, while the best place for French-language books is Vents du Sud, on rue du Maréchal-Foch. **Santons**, the Provençal crib figures, are made and sold at Fouque, 65 cours Gambetta.

Some of the best shops around, however, are those specializing in food. If you like your **bread** fresh and warm, the boulangerie-pâtisserie on rue Tournefort is open around the clock, even on Christmas Day, and sells pizzas, pastries and other snacks as well as bread. Claude Poulain, at 42 rue Espariat, also sells wonderful bread and cakes. Should you want to try the local **Coteaux d'Aix wines**, contact the Maison des Agriculteurs, 22 av Henri-Pontier (℡04.42.23.57.14), where you can also get advice on where to buy **olive oil**. On the last weekend in July, the Coteaux d'Aix **wines** are celebrated with a fair on cours Mirabeau.

The finest **chocolates and sweets** are sold at Puyricard, 7 rue Rifle-Rafle, though they cost around €66 a kilo. If you're really keen, you can visit the famous chocolatier's production laboratory in the quartier Maliverny at Puyricard, north of Aix (av Georges-de-Fabry ☎04.42.28.18.14; July–Aug Tues at 9am, Feb–May & Sept–Oct Wed at 9am; €6). For Aix's speciality **almond and melon sweets**, *calissons*, head to Du Roy René, 10 rue Clémenceau.

Markets

On **Tuesdays, Thursdays** and **Saturdays** the whole of Vieil Aix is taken up with **markets**. Fruit, vegetables and regional specialities are sold on **place des Prêcheurs**: purple, white and copper onions; huge sprigs of herbs; the orange flowers from young courgettes; and, according to season, different forest mushrooms or red fruits in mouthwatering displays. **Place de l'Hôtel de Ville** is filled with lilies, roses and carnations, while around **Palais Monclar** and the law courts to the east and on cours Mirabeau you can buy clothes – new, mass-produced, hand-made or second-hand. Beyond the Palais de Justice, **place de Verdun** hosts its flea market with bric-a-brac and anything from real rabbit hats to plastic earrings. A farmers' market takes place daily in **place Richelme**; an antiquarian book market is held on the first Sunday of each month in place de l'Hôtel de Ville.

Listings

Bike rental Cycles Zammit, 27 rue Mignet ☎04.42.23.19.53; closed Sun & Mon.
Car rental AGL Thrifty, 34 rue Irma-Moreau ☎04.42.64.64.64; Avis, 11 bd Gambetta ☎04.42.21.64.16; Europcar, 55 bd de la République ☎08.25.89.69.76; National Citer, gare TGV ☎04.42.69.06.63.
Emergencies SAMU ☎15; Centre Hospitalier, av de Tamaris ☎04.42.33.90.28; SOS Médecins ☎04.42.26.24.00.
Laundry 60 rue Boulégon; 36 cours Sextius; 11 rue des Bernardines; 5 rue de la Fontaine.
Money exchange L'Agence, 15 cours Mirabeau

☎04.42.26.84.77; Change Nazareth, 7 rue de Nazareth ☎04.42.38.28.28; La Poste, 2 rue Lapierre. There are cash machines at most banks, but since the introduction of the euro fewer ordinary commercial banks exchange foreign currency.
Police Av de l'Europe ☎04.42.93.97.00; emergency ☎17.
Post office 2 rue Lapierre.
Taxis Taxi Radio Aixois 24hr service ☎04.42.27.71.11; Aix Taxi ☎06.78.77.69.40; Taxi François ☎06.12.48.24.08; Taxi Mirabeau ☎04.42.21.61.61.

Around Aix

If city life begins to pall, there is gorgeous countryside to be explored around Aix, particularly to the east, where you'll find **Cézanne**'s favourite local subject, the **Mont Ste-Victoire**, which he painted over fifty times. In addition, there are the ancient sites at **Oppidum d'Entremont** and a strange artist's château in **Vauvenargues**. North of the city, the vineyards of the **Coteaux d'Aix** stretch towards the **Abbaye de Silvacane** and the river Durance itself.

Oppidum d'Entremont

Three kilometres north of Vieil Aix is the archeological site of the **Oppidum d'Entremont** (Mon & Wed–Sun 9–11.30am & 2–5pm; free; bus #21 or 24, stop "Entremont"), once the chief settlement of one of the strongest confederations of indigenous people in Provence. Built in the second century BC, it was divided into two parts: the upper town, where the leading fighters were thought to have lived; and the lower town, for artisans and traders. The site lay on an important trade crossroads from Marseille to the Durance Valley and from Fréjus to the Rhône and was protected by curtain walls and towers, within which the streets were laid out on a grid pattern. It was the Marseille merchants who finally persuaded the Romans to dispose of this irritant to their expanding business (see Musée Granet on p.199).

The plateau on which this Celtic-Ligurian stronghold was built is as interesting for its views over Aix and across to the dramatic Mont Ste-Victoire, as for the ancient layout marked by truncated walls but denuded of all other objects.

Vauvenargues

Leaving Aix via boulevard des Poilus, the D10 road east to Vauvenargues passes the lake and barrage of Bimont from where you can walk south past Mont Ste-Victoire to Le Tholonet (see p.205). If you want to drive, the sixty-kilometre circuit round the mountain offers wonderful views. At peaceful **VAUVENARGUES**, 14km from Aix, a perfect, weather-beaten, red-shuttered fourteenth-century **château**, bought by Picasso in 1958, stands just outside the village with nothing between it and the slopes of the mountain. **Picasso** lived there till his death in 1973, and is buried in the gardens, his grave adorned with his sculpture *Woman with a Vase*. The château, still owned by his stepdaughter, is strictly private, and the otherwise friendly locals are taciturn when it comes to discussing the connection. If the village appeals, you can stay at the pleasant, small **hotel**, *Le Moulin de Provence*, 33 av des Maquisards (☎04.42.66.02.22, ⓦwww.lemoulinedeprovence.com; ❷), with views over Mont Ste-Victoire and Picasso's château, a terrace restaurant, and friendly owners.

Mont Ste-Victoire

If you're interested in **climbing Mont Ste-Victoire**, 8km east of Aix, the northern approach is a little easier than that of the southern face, which has a sheer 500-metre drop, though it'll still require some determination. Don't underestimate the fierce sun either: avoid attempting the walk between about 11am and 3pm, especially in the summer months when you should always wear a hat, and bring suncream and a minimum of two litres of water per person. The path leaves the D10 just before Vauvenargues, after a parking bay called Les Cabassols. The round trip to the monumental **Cross of Provence** and back takes around three to four hours, depending on fitness, and the path is steep and poorly marked towards the top. Once at the top of the ridge, at 945m – marked by a chapel and a cross that doesn't figure in any of Cézanne's pictures – serious hikers can follow the path east to the summit of the Sainte-Victoire massif at **Pic des Mouches** (1011m), along some breathtakingly vertiginous cliff faces. Just beneath the Pic des Mouches, on the north side, is the **Gouffre du Garagaï** chasm, that was once rumoured, among other things, to be the bottomless pit into hell. The path branches to the north about 200m past the summit, and after about fifty minutes rejoins the road at the **Col des Portes** pass (a good alternative starting point for climbing the massif). Otherwise stay on the ridge and descend southwards to **Puyloubier** (about 15km from the cross).

Le Tholonet and Puyloubier

The D17 south of Mont Ste-Victoire skirts the edge of woods leading up to the defensive face of the mountain. There are two parking places with confusing maps of paths. Heading upwards towards Le Tholonet you soon get views of Sainte-Victoire, from this angle looking like a wave with surf about to break. This was yet another of the vantage points Cézanne used to paint the mountain, and for some years he rented a room at the *Château Noir* just off the D17 in order to be close to it. Modern aqueducts pass overhead, the responsibility of the Société du Canal de Provence which has its headquarters in the Italianate seventeenth-century château in **LE THOLONET**; the château is not open to the public. On the east side of the village, an old windmill, the **Moulin de Cézanne**, has been converted into an exhibition space for art and sculpture, with a bronze relief of Cézanne on a stele outside. The Le Tholonet region also has its own tiny AOC, the Vins de Palette, comprising just 23 hectares and a handful of producers, notably the Château Simone at Meyreuil, 2km southwest of Le Tholonet, which can't be visited.

At the main crossroads there's a popular **restaurant**, *Chez Thome* (T04.42.66.90.43), with outdoor tables under the trees and menus starting at €24. For those with lots of cash to blow, there's the modern, swish **hotel-restaurant** *Relais Sainte-Victoire* in Beaurecueil, roughly 4km east of Le Tholonet (T04.42.66.94.98, Wwww.relais-sainte-victoire.com; restaurant closed Mon, Fri lunch & Sun eve; menus from €25; rooms ❾). Also in Beaurecueil is the two-star *Sainte-Victoire* **campsite** (T04.42.66.91.31, Wwww.campingsaintevictoire.com; €11.60 for tent and two persons), which can be reached by the "Victorine" bus from Aix's tourist office.

East of Le Tholonet, the D17 takes you beneath the mighty face of the massif, past the **Maison du Parc** (April–June & Sept–Oct Mon–Fri 9.30am–6pm, Sat & Sun 10.15am–7pm; July–Aug Mon–Fri 10am–6.30pm, Sat & Sun 10.15am–7pm; Nov–March daily 9.30am–6pm; T04.42.66.84.40), a tourist centre with information and hiking maps as well as a shop, and on to **PUYLOUBIER**. Here military enthusiasts can visit the French Foreign Legion's Pensioners' Château, which is 1.5km from the crossroads in Puyloubier at the end of the chemin de la Pallière and sits in a magnificent landscape surrounded by vineyards. Its small **museum** (Tues–Sun 10am–noon & 2–5pm; free) is really only for devotees of the Legion with its collection of uniforms and ceramics, metalworking and bookbinding workshops. A shop sells Legion sweatshirts, books and souvenirs. From Puyloubier, the road continues through vineyards towards **Pourrières**, before twisting up a marvellous wooded road, and looping back round to Col des Portes and Vauvenargues.

Towards the Durance: the Route des Vins and the Abbaye de Silvacane

North of Aix, the vineyards of the **Coteaux d'Aix** fan out across a broad belt of countryside between the city and the river Durance. At 35sqkm, this is the second largest AOC in Provence after the Côtes de Provence itself, and one which is still forging its reputation. The soil is particularly suited to the production of great red wines, with Grenache, Syrah, Cabernet Sauvignon and Vermentino the main grape varieties grown. The rosés are rich and fruity and go well with Provençal dishes like *bourride*; white wines are much less common, but are fresh and fragrant. Some of the best Coteaux d'Aix wines are produced around the isolated village of **Rians**, well to the east of Aix, where the Château Vignelaure is particularly renowned. Much more accessible, however, is the signposted **Route des Vins**, which follows a circuit through the heart of the AOC, beginning and ending in the village of **Éguilles**, 9.5km west of Aix on the D17; along the circuit the opportunities to stop and try the wines are fairly frequent. One of the better places to linger is **Le Puy Ste-Réparade**, just to the north of the Route des Vins on the D13. Here, southeast of the village, the well-regarded *vignoble* of Fonscolombe (rte de St-Canadet; Mon–Fri 9am–noon & 2–6pm, Sat 9am–noon & 2–7pm; Wwww.fonscolombe.com) produces

Coteaux d'Aix wines on an estate surrounding the splendid eighteenth-century **Château de Fonscolombe**, which stands in a deer park. The equally handsome **Château de Beaulieu** (Mon–Sat 8.30am–noon & 2.30–7pm; closes 6.30pm in winter; Ⓦwww.chateaubeaulieu.fr) on the D14c southeast of **Rognes**, once belonged to the grandest Provençal families and nestles in the crater of an extinct volcano. The vineyard, which was only re-established in 2002, produces limited quantities of fine Cuvée Bérengère wines plus a variety of *vin cuit*, a Provençal curiosity that is heated during maturation.

Six kilometres north of Rognes, the D543 intersects with the D561 on the south bank of the Durance. A little to the west of the junction along the D561 stands the **Abbaye de Silvacane**, built by the same order and in the same period as the abbeys of Sénanque (see p.231) and Le Thoronet (see p.249), although the "wood of rushes" from which the name Silvacane derives had already been cleared by Benedictine monks before the Cistercians arrived in 1144. As at the other two great monasteries, the architecture of Silvacane reflects the no-nonsense rule of Saint Benedict (Benoît) in which manual work, intellectual work and worship comprised the three equal elements of the day.

You can still visit the stark, pale-stoned church and its surrounding buildings and cloisters (May–Sept daily 10am–6pm; Oct–April daily except Tues 10am–1pm & 2–5pm; closed public hols; last entry 30min before closing; €6.50). The buildings look pretty much as they did seven hundred years ago, with the exception of the refectory, rebuilt in 1423 and given Gothic ornamentation that the earlier monks would never have tolerated. The windows in the church would not have had stained glass either. The only heated room would have been the *salle des monies* where the work of copying manuscripts was carried out, and the only areas where conversation would have been allowed were the *salle capitulaire*, where the daily reading of "the Rule" and the hearing of confessions took place, and the *parloir* (literally, a room for talking in).

Along the Durance

Twenty-six kilometres from Aix and just east of the Abbaye de Silvacane the D543 reaches the broad River Durance at the **Pont de Cadenet**, an incongruously impressive structure – particularly in summer, when the mighty Alpine river it crosses is often reduced to a pathetic dribble. The countryside on the river's north bank shelters below the massifs of the Grand and Petit Luberon and is Mediterranean in climate – hot and dry, fragrant with pines and wild thyme, ablaze with yellow and gold honeysuckle and immortelle, and alive with the quick movements and long stillnesses of sun-basking reptiles. The Durance Valley is highly fertile and yields the region's classic crops, including all the ingredients for ratatouille, while the lower slopes of the Luberon massifs are dotted with cherry trees and vines, grown both for wine and grapes. Because of the importance of agriculture, the villages here are still very Provençal in character, with far fewer Parisians and other foreigners than in the northern Luberon.

As a touring base **Cadenet** has its charms, while the market town of **Pertuis** has the best transport links in the area. The beautiful villages of **Lourmarin**, **Vaugines** and **Cucuron** sit amidst vineyards and the unspoilt countryside of the Grand Luberon foothills, while **La Tour d'Aigues** and **Ansouis** boast elegant châteaux.

East of the dramatically narrow Défilé de Mirabeau and north of its confluence with the Verdon, the Durance has a somewhat different character. The Alps are close here, the river itself is exploited for electricity generation and the valley is busier and more urbanized. The major centres here are **Manosque**, a bustling market town, and **Sisteron**, dominated by its splendid citadel. Between the two, the A51 Marseille-Grenoble autoroute speeds along the River Durance, bypassing the industrial town of **St-Auban** and its older neighbour **Château-Arnoux**, renowned for its superb restaurant, *La Bonne Étape*. The views from the fashionable little village of **Lurs** and the ancient **Prieuré de Ganagobie** have not been affected, nor has their isolation. **Volx** is the site of an impressive new museum devoted to the olive, while La Brillane is the nearest gare SNCF to Lurs.

Cadenet

The main road heading north to Lourmarin detours round **CADENET**, lending the place a sleepy charm with none of the chi-chi airs of the villages to the north. The town has a small museum, the **Musée de la Vannerie** on avenue Philippe-de-Girard (April–Oct Mon & Thurs–Sat 10am–noon & 2.30–6.30pm; €3.50) set in a former atelier and devoted to basket-weaving, which is a traditional industry in the area. In the central place du Tambour d'Arcole there stands a statue of a manic drummer-boy, hair and coat-tails flying as he runs. The monument commemorates André Étienne for his inspired one-man diversion that confused the Austrians and allowed Napoleon's army to cross the River Durance in 1796. Also on the square is Cadenet's **tourist office** (July–Aug Mon–Sat 10am–12.30pm & 1.30–6pm; Sept–June Mon–Sat 9.30am–12.30pm & 1.30–5.30pm; ☎04.90.68.38.21). There's an excellent lakeside **campsite** southwest of the village off chemin de Pile, the four-star *Val de Durance* (☎04.90.68.37.75, ⓦwww.homair-vacances.com; €30 for a car, tent and two people in high season; open April–Sept), and a **restaurant**, *Le Cinq Sens*, 35 rue Gambetta (☎04.90.68.07.14; closed eves Mon, Tues & Sun), with menus from €10.50. **Market** day is Monday.

Otherwise, there's not a great deal to detain you here, though a short but energetic climb from the centre of the village brings you to the remains of Cadenet's château, from which there are wonderful views over the surrounding countryside. There are various routes on foot, though chemin des Rougettes off cours Voltaire is the easiest for car users and has a small parking area.

Lourmarin

LOURMARIN stands at the bottom of a *combe* 4km north of Cadenet, its Renaissance **château** guarding with nonchalant ease a small rise to the west. A fortress once defended this strategic vantage point but the current edifice dates from the sixteenth century when comfort was beginning to outplay defence; hence the generous windows.

Since 1929 the château has belonged to the University of Aix, who use it to give summer sabbaticals to artists and intellectuals of various scientific and philosophical persuasions. Many have left behind works of art, which you can see on a 45-minute **guided tour** (Jan Sat & Sun only 2.30–4.30pm; Feb–Dec daily 10–11.30am plus afternoons as follows: Feb & Nov–Dec 2.30–4pm; March & April 2.30–4.30pm; May & June 2.30–5.30pm; July & Aug 2.30–6pm; Sept 2.30–5.30pm; Oct 10.30–11.30am & 2.30–4.45pm; €5.50) through vast rooms with intricate wooden ceilings, massive fireplaces and beautifully tiled floors where the favoured cultural workers socialize. **Concerts** are held in the château during July and August, and throughout the spring, summer and autumn art **exhibitions** of all sorts are staged (contact the tourist office for more information).

The most famous literary figure associated with Lourmarin is the writer Albert Camus, who spent the last years of his life here and is buried in the cemetery. Nowadays the village is extremely chic, and often overrun with visitors in summer.

Practicalities

Lourmarin's **tourist office** is at 9 av Philippe-de-Girard (Mon–Sat 10am–12.30pm & 3–6pm; ☎04.90.68.10.77, ⓦwww.lourmarin.com), and organizes Camus-themed literary walks. In the village, the glamorous *Moulin de Lourmarin* (☎04.90.68.06.69, ⓦwww.moulindelourmarin.com; ❼) is the luxury place **to stay**, with stylish modern decor and a restaurant; for something more secluded the best option is the wonderfully situated *Hostellerie Le Paradou* on the D943 at the start of the *combe* (☎04.90.68.04.05, ⓦwww.leparadou-lourmarin.com; *demi-pension* only April–Sept, otherwise ❹). Alternatively, back towards Lourmarin, the gîte *Le Four à Chaux* (☎04.90.68.24.28, ⓦwww.le-four-a-chaux.com) has dormitory beds (€11) and a few rooms (❶). There's a three-star **campsite**, *Les Hautes Prairies*, on route de Vaugines (☎04.90.68.02.89, ⓦcampinghautesprairies.com), with two pools, a bar and restaurant.

There are several **restaurants** around the fountained squares of the village, including *La Récréation*, 15 rue Philippe de Girard (☎04.90.68.23.73; closed Wed), which serves good and reasonably priced organic dishes, with menus from €22.50. Further out of town, the expensive but excellent hotel-restaurant *L'Auberge de la Fenière* on route de Cadenet (☎04.90.68.11.79; menus from €46; closed Mon, Tues lunch, and mid-Nov to mid-Dec) uses absolutely fresh ingredients to create seriously gourmet concoctions and has a few stylish, individually designed **rooms** (❻).

East to Pertuis

East from Lourmarin, the first place along the minor D56 road is **VAUGINES**, a gorgeous little village with a charming café, *Café de la Fontaine*, opposite the *mairie*, and a **hotel** with great views, the *Hostellerie du Luberon* (☎04.90.77.27.19, ⓦwww.hostellerieduluberon.com; ❼). Vaugines is the meeting point of the GR97 from the Petit Luberon and the GR9 which crosses the Grand Luberon to Buoux in one direction and in the other loops above Cucuron and skirts the Mourre-Nègre summit before running along the eastern end of the ridge.

The neighbouring village of **CUCURON** is a bit larger and almost as fetching, with some of its ancient ramparts and gateways still standing and a bell tower with a delicate campanile on the central place de l'Horloge. Cucuron had a glimpse of fame when it was taken over by the film industry for the shooting of Rappeneau's 1995 movie *The Horseman on the Roof*, based on a Giono novel, and, at the time, the most expensive French film made; the village has been revisited by film location crews many times since. The village's main business, however, is olive oil and it has a sixteenth-century mill in a hollow of the rock face on rue Moulin à l'Huile that is still used to press olives. At the top of the rock a **park** surrounds the surviving *donjon* of the citadel; the journey up to the castle above the Tour de l'Horloge takes you through some of the oldest and most beautiful parts of the village. At the other end of Cucuron is the **Église Notre-Dame-de-Beaulieu**, which contains a seventeenth-century altarpiece in coloured marble originally commissioned for the Chapelle de la Visitation in Aix. From the end of May to the middle of August a huge felled poplar leans against the church, a tradition dating back to 1720 when Cucuron was spared the plague. On rue de l'Église, a short way from the church, is a small **museum** (10.30am–noon & 2–5.30pm; closed Tues morning; ring the bell in the hallway to gain entry; free) on local traditions and early history, with a collection of daguerreotypes.

On the north side of the village, by the reservoir bordered by plane trees, the **hotel-restaurant** *L'Étang* (T04.90.77.21.25, Wwww.hoteldeletang.com; ❹) serves very pleasant food (menus from €22). There are two **campsites**: *Lou Badareu* at La Rasparine, southeast of the village towards La Tour d'Aigues (T04.90.77.21.46, Wwww.loubadareu.com; €9.60 per tent; open April to mid-Oct) next to a rather expensive *gîte d'étape*; and *Le Moulin à Vent* on chemin de Gastoule off the D182 to Villelaure (T04.90.77.25.77, Wavignon-et-provence .com/campings/moulin-vent; €11.50 per tent; closed Oct–March). A Tuesday **market** is held on place de l'Étang.

Halfway between Cucuron and Pertuis, the hilltop village of **ANSOUIS** has a **château** (July–Sept daily 2.30–6pm; Easter–June & Oct Mon & Wed–Sun 2.30-6pm; Nov–Dec & Feb–Easter Sun 2.30–6pm; closed Jan; €6), lived in since the twelfth century by the same family; the mother of the current ducal resident wrote a bestseller called *Bon Sang Ne Peut Mentir* (Good Blood Cannot Lie). The real attraction of this superb castle, however, is its remarkably rich furnishings, from Flemish tapestries and silver chandeliers to kitchen pots and pans. In the village below, the **Musée Extraordinaire** (daily: 2–6pm; €3.50) is dedicated to underwater life and has some extremely kitsch touches. The village **market** is held on Thursday.

Pertuis and La Tour d'Aigues

The one sizeable place this side of the Durance is **PERTUIS**, likeable enough but of interest primarily as a transport hub and potential touring base. Like so many towns in the area, it only really comes to life on **market** day, Friday in this case. In July, the Festival de l'Enclos brings rock, ragga, reggae and world music to Pertuis and a month later there's a big-band festival.

Pertuis is served by the TER (regional train network) on the Marseille to Aix line. However, the **train station** is a kilometre to the south of town, whereas buses stop at the **gare routière**, on place Garcin, within easy walking distance of the centre: leave the square on the opposite side from the bus station and turn left up rue Henri-Silvy. The town centres around place Parmentier, where you'll find flowers for sale on Friday, rue Colbert, the main clothes shopping street leading up to place Jean-Jaurès, and place du 4 Septembre and the more historic place Mirabeau just to the north. The **tourist office** is on place Mirabeau (July–Aug Mon 10am–12.30pm & 2–6.30pm, Tues–Fri 9am–12.30pm & 2–6.30pm, Sat 9.30am–12.30pm & 2.30–6.30pm; Sept–June Mon 10am–noon & 2–6pm, Tues–Fri 9am–noon & 2–6pm, Sat 9.30am–noon & 2.30–6pm; T04.90.79.15.56, Wwww.vivreleluberon.com) in the old keep, all that remains of Pertuis' castle. The narrow streets of the Vieille Ville to the north are, for the most part, low-lit and lifeless.

Of the **places to stay**, the only central option is the *Hôtel du Cours*, place Jean-Jaurès (T04.90.79.00.68, Wwww.hotelducours.com; ❸), which is small and friendly, if nothing special. The alternatives are both chain hotels on the outskirts: for budget travellers, there's a spanking new *Etap* in an industrial zone on route d'Aix south of the town (T08.92.68.30.87, Wwww.etaphotel .com; ❸), while the more expensive option is the *Sévan*, on avenue de Verdon on the way out towards Manosque (☎04.90.79.19.30, ⓦwww.hotelsevan .com; ❼); it is rather unappealing from the outside, though the rooms and the swimming pools are pleasant enough. The three-star municipal **campsite**, *Les Pinèdes*, east of town on the Manosque road (☎04.90.79.10.98, ⓦwww .campinglespinedes.com; €10.80 per tent; closed mid-Oct to mid-March), has excellent facilities.

You'll find plenty of inexpensive **bars, cafés** and **brasseries** on the main squares and streets, but nothing wildly special: more ambitious meals using organic produce can be found at *Le Boulevard*, 50 bd Pécout (☎04.90.09.69.31; menus €18 & €35; closed Sun, Tues eve & Wed), midway between the town centre and the *gare SNCF*. **Bikes** can be rented at Cycles Genin (☎04.90.79.49.43), on avenue des Jardins, and there's also a smoke-filled **Internet** café, *La Cave aux Loups*, at 31 rue Murette.

Just west of Pertuis along the D973, the gardens and winery of **Val Joanis** (April–Oct daily 10am–7pm; free) surrounding the sixteenth-century *bastide* of the same name are very much a work in progress. Re-established in 1978 by Cécile Chancel, the gardens are an attempt to recreate an eighteenth-century garden with both ornamental and productive elements, including a traditional kitchen garden and a beautiful long arbour planted with rambling roses. In addition to the gardens there's a vineyard producing increasingly respected Côtes du Luberon wines, and there are opportunities to taste these and the estate's olive oil.

Heading northeast from Pertuis towards Grambois brings you to **LA TOUR D'AIGUES** where a vast shell of a **château** dominates the village centre. The castle was half destroyed during the Revolution but the most finely detailed Renaissance decoration, based on classical designs including Grecian helmets, angels, bows and arrows and Olympic torches, has survived on the gateway arch. You can admire most of the ruins' glories from the outside but there's also a **Musée de Faïence** and a small exhibit on the rural habitat of the area inside (July & Aug daily 10am–1pm & 2.30–6.30pm; April–June, Sept & Oct Sun & Mon 2.30-6pm, Tues 10am–1pm, Wed–Sat 10am–1pm & 2.30–6pm; Nov–March Mon 2–5pm, Tues 10am–noon, Wed–Sat 10am–noon & 2–5pm, Sun 2–5pm; €4.50), covering local archeological finds, the development of traditional rural homes (*mas*) in the area, plus temporary exhibitions. The château is also a popular venue for year-round music and dance concerts (☎04.90.07.50.33, ⓦwww.chateau-latourdaigues.com). There's a shaded **café** on the far side of the main road from the castle and one **hotel**, *Le Petit Mas de Marie*, not far from the centre on the Pertuis road (☎04.90.07.48.22, ⓦwww.lepetitmasdemarie.com; ❹).

Manosque and around

MANOSQUE, 36km northeast of Pertuis, is an ancient town, strategically positioned just above the right bank of the River Durance. Its small old quarter is surrounded by nondescript tower blocks and beyond them by ever-spreading industrial units and superstores. It is a major population centre in the *département* of Alpes de Haute Provence and busy profiting from the new corridor of affluence that follows the river. Many of its residents work at the Cadarache atomic centre, or in Aix, or even in Marseille now that the highway gives speedy access.

Manosque is also home of the phenomenally successful soap and oil retailer L'**Occitane en Provence**, founded in 1976 by Olivier Baussan, and thus is as responsible as anywhere for propagating the idyllic image of Provence internationally. For the French, however, it is most famous as the home town of the

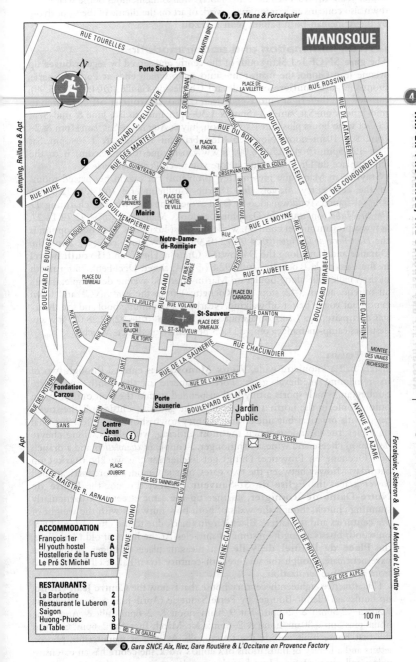

MANOSQUE

Ⓐ Ⓑ, Mane & Forcalquier

RUE TOURELLES

Porte Soubeyran

PLACE DE LA VILLETTE

RUE ROSSINI

RUE DE LATANNERIE

BD. MARTIN BRET

R. SOUBEYRAN

RUE MONTAGU

BOULEVARD C. PELLOUTIER

RUE DU BON REPOS

BOULEVARD DES TILLEULS

BD. DES COUGOURDELLES

RUE DES MARTELS

PLACE M. PAGNOL

RUE D. ECOLES

PL. OBSERVANTINS

R. QUINTRAND

RUE D. MARCHANDS

❶

RUE MURE

❷

PL. DE GRENIERS

PLACE DE L'HOTEL DE VILLE

RUE VOLTAIRE

RUE REPUBLIQUE

RUE LE MOYNE

RUE LE MOYNE

❸ Ⓒ

Mairie

RUE GUILHEMPIERRE

RUE ROUGE DE L'ISLE

RUE DESANGE

RUE ROBERT

RUE DU PALAIS

Notre-Dame-de-Romigier

RUE J. J. ROUSSEAU

❹

BOULEVARD E. BOURGES

PLACE DU TERREAU

PL. ET RUE DU CONTROLE

RUE D'AUBETTE

PLACE DU CARAGOU

BOULEVARD MIRABEAU

RUE DAUPHINE

RUE 14 JUILLET

RUE GRAND

RUE VOLAND

St-Sauveur

PLACE DES ORMEAUX

RUE DANTON

RUE KLEBER

RUE ROCHE

PL. D'EN GAUCH

PL. ST-SAUVEUR

RUE CHACUNDIER

MONTEE DES VRAIES RICHESSES

RUE TORTE

RUE TORTE

RUE DE LA SAUNERIE

RUE DES PRUNIERS

RUE DE L'ARMISTICE

Fondation Carzou

RUE DES POTIERS

Porte Saunerie

BOULEVARD DE LA PLAINE

Jardin Public

AVENUE ST. LAZARE

RUE SANS NOM

RUE RAFFIN

Centre Jean Giono ⓘ

RUE DE L'EDEN

PLACE JOUBERT

RUE DES TANNEURS

RUE DU TRIBUNAL

ALLEE MAISTRE R. ARNAUD

AVENUE J. GIONO

RUE RENE-CLAIR

ALLEE DE PROVENCE

RUE DES ALPES

BD. C. DE GAULLE

N

Camping, Reillane & Apt

Apt

Forcalquier, Sisteron & Le Moulin de l'Olivette

Ⓓ, Gare SNCF, Aix, Riez, Gare Routière & L'Occitane en Provence Factory

0   100 m

ACCOMMODATION

François 1er	C
HI youth hostel	A
Hostellerie de la Fuste	D
Le Pré St Michel	B

RESTAURANTS

La Barbotine	2
Restaurant le Luberon	4
Saigon	1
Huong-Phuoc	3
La Table	B

author **Jean Giono**, born here in 1895. As well as mementoes of the writer, the town also contains an extraordinary work of art on the theme of the Apocalypse by the Armenian-born painter **Jean Carzou**.

Arrival, information and accommodation

The **gare SNCF** is 1.5km south of the centre and served by regular **buses** up avenue Jean Giono, the main route into town which ends at Porte Saunerie. From the **gare routière** on boulevard Charles-de-Gaulle (℡04.92.87.55.99), turn left and then right onto avenue Jean Giono. The **tourist office** (March to mid-June Mon–Sat 9am–12.15pm & 1.30–6pm; mid- to late June & mid-Sept to Oct same hours plus Sun 10am–noon; July & Aug Mon–Sat 9am–1pm & 2–7pm, Sun 10am–noon; Nov–Feb Mon–Fri 9am–12.15pm & 1.30–6pm, Sat 9am–12.15pm; ℡04.92.72.16.00, ⓦwww.manosque-tourisme.com) is to the left on place du Dr-Joubert just before you reach Porte Saunerie.

Staying in Manosque presents few problems. For reasonably priced rooms in the centre, try *François 1er*, 18 rue Guilhempierre (℡04.92.72.07.99, ⓔhotel-francois1er@wanadoo.fr; ❹). Further out of town, the charming *Le Pré St Michel* on route de Dauphin overlooks Manosque (℡04.92.72.14.27, ⓦwww.presaintmichel.com; ❺), while the most luxurious, and costly, option is the *Hostellerie de la Fuste* (℡04.92.72.05.95, ⓦwww.lafuste.com; ❼), across the Durance and 1km along the D4 towards Oraison. There's an **HI youth hostel** in the Parc de la Rochette (℡04.92.87.57.44; closed Dec–Feb), 750m north of the Vieille Ville along boulevard Martin-Bret and avenue de l'Argile; there's an infrequent bus (#2; stop "La Rochette") from the *gare SNCF* and town centre but you're better off walking. Nearby is a swimming pool and the three-star **campsite**, *Les Ubacs*, on avenue de la Repasse (℡04.92.72.28.08, ⓦwww.lesubacs.camp-in-france.com; €11.65 per tent; closed Oct–March).

The Town

Barely half a kilometre wide, **Vieux Manosque** is entered through two of its remaining medieval gates: Porte Saunerie in the south and Porte Soubeyran, which sports a tiny bell suspended within the iron outline of an onion dome, in the north. Once through the gates it's a little dull, the streets lined with practical but unexciting country-town shops and a few national multiples; rue Grande is much the most enticing, with shops selling chèvre de Banon cheese and wine, a fishmonger, a couple of *chocolatiers* and a branch of L'Occitane en Provence. Things get livelier for the weekly **market** on Saturday. Midway between the two gates, on rue Grand, a more intricate bell tower graces the **Église de St-Sauveur**. Neither this nor the **Église de Notre-Dame-de-Romigier**, further up the same street, is a particularly stunning church, though the walls of both bow outwards with the weight of the centuries and the latter's Black Virgin (black due to the effect of gold leaf on wood) boasts a lengthy resumé of miracles. At the heart of old Manosque, the **Place de l'Hôtel de Ville** is a pleasant place to linger awhile at a pavement café, though the seventeenth-century town hall itself has suffered from bland modernization.

The attractive eighteenth-century house that is now the **Centre Jean Giono**, on boulevard Elémir-Bourges by Porte Saunerie (April–June & Sept Tues–Fri 9.30am–12.30pm & 2–6pm, Sat 9.30am–noon & 2–6pm; July & Aug same hours plus Sun 9.30am–noon & 2–6pm; Oct–March Tues–Sat 2–6pm; €4), was the first house built outside the town walls. As well as manuscripts, photos, letters and a library of translations of Giono's work, the centre has an extensive video collection of films based on his novels, interviews and documentaries.

Giono himself did not live here, but at **Le Paraïs** (guided tours on Fridays by arrangement only: call ☎04.92.87.73.03; free), off montée des Vrais Richesses 1.5km north of the Vieille Ville.

Giono was imprisoned at the start of World War II for his pacifism, and again after liberation because the Vichy government had promoted his belief in the superiority of nature and peasant life over culture and urban civilization, as supporting the Nazi cause. In truth, far from being a fascist, Giono was a passionate ecologist, and the countryside around Manosque plays as strong a part in his novels as do the characters. World War II embittered him, and his later novels are less idealistic. Giono never left Manosque and died here in 1970.

Giono's contemporary, **Jean Carzou**, confronts the issues of war, technology, dehumanization and the environmental destruction of the planet head on in his extraordinary, monumental **L'Apocalypse**. The work is composed of painted panels and stained-glass windows in the former church of the Couvent de la Présentation, now the **Fondation Carzou**, on boulevard Elémir-Bourges just up from the Centre Jean Giono (June & Sept Tues–Sat 2.30–6.30pm; July–Aug Tues–Sun 10am–noon & 2.30–6.30pm; Oct–May Wed–Sat 2.30–6.30pm; €4). Everything from the French Revolution to Pol Pot's massacres is portrayed here, in nightmarish detail.

On the far side of the A51 autoroute in the industrial quarter of Saint-Maurice is the **L'Occitane en Provence** factory, forty-minute guided tours of which (by appointment only via Manosque tourist office; free) are followed by a film on the ingredients used in the products, and workshops on massage and the use of essential oils. There's also the chance to buy the products in the factory store. Another place worth heading out to for high-quality souvenirs of the region is **Le Moulin de l'Olivette** on place de l'Olivette, approximately 750m northeast of Vieux Manosque along avenue Saint Lazare (Mon–Sat 8am–noon & 2–6.30pm; ☎04.92.72.00.99) which produces and sells AOC cold pressed extra virgin olive oil.

Eating and drinking

The **restaurants** in the Vieille Ville are generally good value. *La Barbotine* on place de l'Hôtel de Ville (☎04.92.72.57.15; closed Sun) offers simple but satisfying meals from around €25, with a veggie menu at €17, while *Restaurant le Luberon*, at 21 bis place du Terreau (☎04.92.72.03.09; closed Mon & Sun eve out of season), has menus from €27.50. If you want a change from Provençal cuisine, try one of the town's excellent Vietnamese/Chinese restaurants, such as the expensive *Saigon*, 7 bd Casimir-Pelloutier (☎04.92.87.36.83), or *Huong-Phuoc*, 38 bd Elémir-Bourges (☎04.92.72.84.96; menus from €11.50). For something a bit more upmarket, *La Table* at the hotel *Le Pré St Michel*, on route de Dauphin (☎04.92.72.12.79; menus €22–39; closed Mon & Sat lunchtimes), has a broad terrace, and serves a wonderful chocolate pudding.

The Écomusée l'Olivier at Volx

Just over 8km north of Manosque on the busy N96, the village of **Volx** is the site of the new **Écomusée l'Olivier** (daily Feb–Dec 10am–6.30pm; €4) which opened in the summer of 2006 to tell, with the help of attractively laid out interactive exhibits and audiovisual displays, the story of the olive – the "gift of the Mediterranean" – and the cultures that have nurtured it, from Provence to the eastern Mediterranean, with tasting and shopping opportunities on site.

Lurs and around

Perched on a narrow ridge above the west bank of the Durance some 20km north of Manosque, **LURS** is a *village de caractère*, undeniably charming yet extremely conscious of its picturesque status. Immaculately restored houses stand amid immaculately maintained ruins; there's a tiny, Roman-style theatre, but little commerce. From the top of the village, you can see across the wide, multi-branching river to the abrupt step up to the Plateau de Valensole, with the snowy peaks beyond; to the south the land drops before rising again in another high ridge along the river; while to the west and north the views are just as extensive, from the rolling hills around Forcalquier to the Montagne de Lure.

The best way to appreciate this geography is to follow the paths to the small chapel of **Notre-Dame-de-Vie** along the narrowing escarpment. The right-hand path goes through the woods and is practically overgrown; the eastern path, the **Promenade des Evêques**, is marked by fifteen small oratories.

By the late 1940s Lurs was deserted save for the odd passing bandit, but it gained international notoriety in 1952 when the British scientist Sir Jack Drummond and his family were murdered while camping alongside the Durance below the village. The case was never satisfactorily solved: the man convicted of the murder was spared execution and ultimately released from custody, and in recent years it has been suggested that Sir Jack was a victim of the Cold War, assassinated because he was a British spy.

In recent years, the village has become a centre for **graphic artists and printers**, including the author of the universal nomenclature for typefaces, and it is they who have brought life back to Lurs. They even hold an annual conference here, the Rencontres Internationales de Lurs, which brings in practitioners of the graphic arts from calligraphers to computer-aided-design consultants for the last week in August.

For somewhere **to stay**, there's the hotel-restaurant, *Le Séminaire*, near the car park on place de la Fontaine (℡04.92.79.94.19, Ⓦwww.hotel-leseminaire.com; ❼; menus €19–26.50), housed in the old summer residence of the bishops of Sisteron. Alternative eating options include the nearby *La Bello Visto* **restaurant** on rue de la Mairie (℡04.92.79.95.09; menus from €16; closed Wed), and *Chez Justine*, on the way into the village from the car park.

The Prieuré de Ganagobie

About 7km north of Lurs, in the twelfth-century **Prieuré de Ganagobie** (Tues–Sun 3–5pm; free), you'll find some fine examples of complex design skills that far predate the invention of printing. The floor of the priory church is covered with mosaics composed of red, black and white tiles: they depict fabulous beasts whose tails loop through their bodies, and the four elements represented by an elephant (Earth), a fish (Water), a griffon (Air) and a lion (Fire). Interlocking and repeating patterns show a strong Byzantine influence, and there's a dragon slain by a St George in Crusader armour. The porch of the church is also an unusual sight, its arches carved to a bubbly pattern that's thought to be an imitation of medieval bunting.

If you're not in a hurry, you can pass the time walking through the oaks and broom, pines and lavender eastwards along the allée des Moines to the edge of the Plateau de Ganagobie on which the priory stands, 350m above the Durance, or westwards following the allée de Forcalquier for views to the Montagne de Lure and beyond Forcalquier to the Luberon.

The Pénitents des Mées and Château-Arnoux

North of the priory, the impending confluence of the Durance and Bléone is announced by the **Pénitents des Mées**, a long line of pointed rocks on the east bank, said to be the remains of cowled monks, literally petrified for desiring the women slaves a local lord brought back from the Crusades. Beyond here, the landscape is not very promising, with industry covering the right bank of the Durance at **St-Auban**, a dull suburb laid out in 1916.

Once you reach **CHÂTEAU-ARNOUX**, the hills once more close in and the river takes on a smoother and more majestic prospect, as a seven-kilometre-long artificial lake ending at the barrage just south of the town. Dominating the centre of Château-Arnoux – the pounding traffic on the main road through the town aside – is an imposing Renaissance **castle**, with five towers and multicoloured tiles on its roof. You can't visit the castle, but you can wander in its **park**, which has the best and most diverse collection of trees in Haute-Provence. The main reason to visit Château-Arnoux, however, is to eat at *La Bonne Étape* (℡04.92.64.00.09; menus €42–100; Oct–April closed Mon & Tues), just across the road from the château and renowned as one of the best **restaurants** in Provence, where the cooking celebrates the produce of the region without trendy foreign influences. If your budget won't stretch to this, the simpler *Au Gout du Jour* next door is part of the same concern, with menus at €18 to €24.

Sisteron and around

The last Provençal stretch of the Route Napoleon (see p.393) runs from Château-Arnoux to **SISTERON**. The most picturesque approach is to follow Napoleon's footsteps via the D4 on the left bank of the Durance. The first sight of Sisteron reveals its strategic significance as the major mountain gateway of Provence. The site, fortified since ancient times, was half-destroyed by the Anglo-American bombardment of 1944, but its **citadel** still stands as a fearsome sentinel over the city and the solitary bridge across the river. After heavy rains the Durance, the colour of *café au lait*, becomes a raging torrent pushing through the narrow Sisteron gap.

Sisteron gave Napoleon something of a headache. Its mayor and the majority of its population were royalist, and given the fortifications and geography of the town, it was impossible for him to pass undetected. However, luck was still with the Corsican in those days, as the military commander of the *département* was a sympathizer and removed all ammunition from Sisteron's arsenal. Contemporary accounts say Napoleon sat nonchalantly on the bridge, contemplating the citadel above and the tumultuous waters below, while his men reassembled and the town's notables, ordered to keep their pistols under wraps, looked on impotently. Eventually Napoleon entered the city, took some refreshment at a tavern and received a tricolour from a courageous peasant woman before rejoining his band and taking leave of Provence.

Sisteron today is a lively place, its prosperity based as much on the extensive industrial zone that has grown up to the north along the N75 as it is on tourism. The truth of the town's claim to be a gateway to the mountains, however, is effectively demonstrated if you try to use a mobile phone: reception is terrible.

Arrival, information and accommodation

From Sisteron's **gare SNCF** turn right and head along avenue de la Libération until you reach place de la République. Here you'll find the **gare**

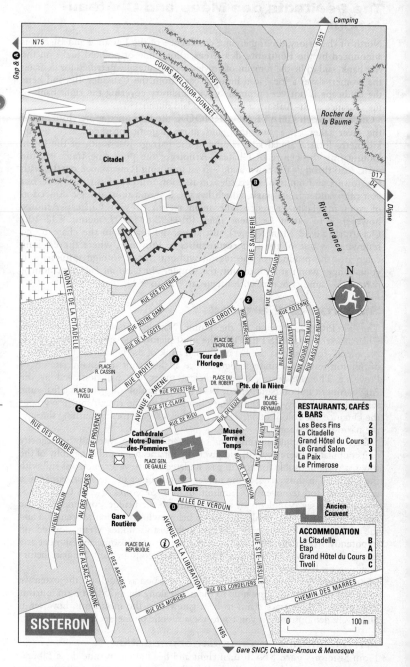

Camping

N75

Gap & A

D951

COURS MELCHIOR-DONNET

N85ST

Rocher de
la Baume

Citadel

D17
D4

Digne

River Durance

RUE SAUNERIE

B

N

RUE DE FONT-CHAUDE

1

RUE DES POTERIES

2

RUE MERCERIE

RUE POTERNE

RUE NOTRE DAME

RUE DROITE

RUE CHAPUZIE

RUE GRAND-COUVERT

RUE BOURG-REYNAUD

RUE BASSE-DES-REMPARTS

RUE DE LA COSTE

PLACE DE
L'HORLOGE

3

MONTEE DE LA CITADELLE

Tour de
l'Horloge

PLACE
R. CASSIN

RUE DROITE

4

PLACE DU
DR. ROBERT

PLACE DU
TIVOLI

AVENUE P. ARENE

RUE POUSTERIE

Pte. de la Nière

PLACE
BOURG-
REYNAUD

C

RUE STE-CLAIRE

RUE DES COMBES

RUE DE PROVENCE

RUE DE RIEU

RUE DELEUZE

RUE PORTE SAUVE

RUE CHAPUZIE

**RESTAURANTS, CAFÉS
& BARS**

Les Becs Fins   2
La Citadelle   B
Grand Hôtel du Cours D
Le Grand Salon   3
La Paix   1
Le Primerose   4

Cathédrale
Notre-Dame-
des-Pommiers

Musée
Terre et
Temps

RUE DE LA MISSION

PLACE GEN.
DE GAULLE

AVENUE MOULIN

AV DES ARCADES

Les Tours

D

ALLÉE DE VERDUN

Ancien
Couvent

Gare
Routière

AVENUE DE LA LIBERATION

PLACE DE LA
REPUBLIQUE

i

RUE STE-URSULE

ACCOMMODATION

La Citadelle   B
Etap   A
Grand Hôtel du Cours D
Tivoli   C

AVENUE ALSACE-LORRAINE

RUE DES ARCADES

RUE DES CORDELIERS

CHEMIN DES MARRES

RUE DES MURIERS

N85

0   100 m

SISTERON

Gare SNCF, Château-Arnoux & Manosque

routière, post office and **tourist office** (Sept–June Mon–Sat 9am–noon & 2–5pm; July & Aug Mon–Sat 9am–7pm, Sun 10am–1pm; ☎04.92.61.36.50, ⓦwww.sisteron.fr), which can provide details of good walks and advise on **bike rental**.

For somewhere central to **stay**, try *La Citadelle*, overlooking the river at the end of rue Saunerie (☎04.92.61.13.52; ❸); the *Tivoli*, 21 place René Cassin (☎04.92.61.15.16, ⓦwww.hotel-tivoli.net, ❸), or the genteel, air-conditioned three-star *Grand Hôtel du Cours*, allée de Verdon (☎04.92.61.04.51, ⓦhotel-lecours.com; ❹). Further out, there's a modern, well-equipped *Etap* hotel (☎04.92.68.07.55, ⓦwww.etaphotel.com; ❸) at the autoroute exit, 4km north of town on the N75, and the four-star **campsite**, *Les Prés-Hauts*, with a pool (☎04.92.61.19.69, ⓔcamping.sisteron@orange.fr; €13.50 per tent; closed Nov–Feb); it's over the river, and 3km along the D951 to the left.

The Town

To do the **citadel** justice (daily: July & Aug 9am–7.30pm; April, May & Oct to mid-Nov 9am–6pm; June & Sept 9am–7pm; mid-Nov to March by appointment; ☎92.61.27.57; €4) can easily take up half a day as you scramble from the highest ramparts to the lowest subterranean passage. There is a leaflet in English but no guides, just tape recordings in French attempting to recreate historic moments, such as Napoleon's march and the imprisonment in 1639 of Jan Kazimierz, the future king of Poland. Most of the extant defences were constructed after the Wars of Religion, and added to a century later by Vauban when Sisteron was a frontline fort against neighbouring Savoy. No traces remain of the first Ligurian fortification nor of its Roman successor, and the eleventh-century castle was destroyed in the mid-thirteenth century during a pogrom against the local Jewish population.

As you climb up to the fortress, there seems no end to the gateways, courtyards and other defences. The outcrop on which the fortress sits abruptly stops at the lookout post, **Guérite du Diable**, 500m above the narrow passage of the Durance, and affording the best views. On the other side of the ravine, the vertical folds of the **Rocher de la Baume** provide a favourite training ground for local mountaineers.

In the fortress grounds, a **festival** known as *Nuits de la Citadelle* takes place in late July and early August, with open-air concerts and performances of opera, drama and dance. There is also a **museum** on the history of the citadel with a room dedicated to Napoleon, and temporary art exhibitions in the vertiginous late medieval chapel, **Notre-Dame-du-Château**, restored to its Gothic glory and given very beautiful subdued stained-glass windows in the 1970s.

Outside the citadel, perhaps the most striking features of Sisteron are the three huge **towers** which belonged to the ramparts built around the expanding town in 1370. Though one still has its spiralling staircase, only ravens use them now. Beside them is the much older former **Cathédrale Notre-Dame-des-Pommiers**, whose strictly rectangular interior contrasts with its riot of stepped roofs and an octagonal gallery adjoining a square belfry topped by a pyramidal spire. The altarpiece incorporates a Mignard painting; other seventeenth-century works adorn the chapels.

At the rear of the cathedral, a former convent of the Visitandine order houses the **Musée Terre et Temps** (April–June & Sept–Oct Mon & Thurs–Sun 9.30am–12.30pm & 2–6pm; July & Aug daily except Tues 10am–1pm & 3–7pm; €3), which charts the measurement of time from ancient sundials

△ Sisteron's citadel

through calendars to the latest atomic clocks, in parallel with the measurement of geological time, though frankly after the thrills of the citadel it's all a little dry and best saved for a rainy day. From the museum, you can follow a signposted route through the lower town, past tall houses enclosing narrow passages with steep steps and ramps that interconnect through vaulted archways, known here as **andrônes**. Houses on the downslope side of rue Saunerie, overlooking the river, often descend at the back a further three or four storeys to the lanes far below. In the troubled days of 1568 (during the Wars of Religion) sixty lanterns were put in place to light the alleyways and deter conspiracies and plots; there's no such luxury today, and Old Sisteron can take on a sinister aspect at night. In the upper town, on the other side of rue Saunerie and rue Droite, the houses, like the citadel above them, follow the curves of the rock.

Place de l'Horloge, at the other end of rue Deleuze from the church, is the site for the Wednesday and Saturday **market**, where stalls congregate to sell sweet and savoury *fougasse*, lavender honey, nougat and almond-paste *calissons* that rival those from Aix. On the second Saturday of every month the market becomes a **fair**, and there are likely to be flocks of sheep and lambs, and cages of pigeons as well as stalls selling clothes and bric-a-brac.

Eating and drinking

Sisteron has no outstanding **restaurants**, though you can certainly have a filling meal at a reasonable price. Of the hotel-restaurants, *La Citadelle* has menus from €13, plenty of salads, and a terrace above the river where you can eat; while the *Grand Hôtel du Cours* serves copious meals including the renowned *gigot d'agneau de Sisteron* (menus at €13.50–28). *Les Becs Fins*, in rue Saunerie (℡04.92.61.12.04), specializes in delicious seasonal ingredients like *trompettes de* *mort*, with menus from €16 all the way up to €53. Alternatively, there's no shortage of crêperies, brasseries, Tex-Mex and pizzerias along rue Saunerie and on the squares around the Tour de l'Horloge – the pizzeria *La Paix*, at 41 rue Saunerie (℡04.92.62.62.29), does particularly good pizzas at €9.50 as well as more elaborate dishes. The best nougat and *calissons* come from Canteperdrix on place Paul-Arène, which also runs *Le Grand Salon*, a *salon de thé* serving salads, cakes and ice creams. For anchovy *fougasse* head to Boulangerie Bernaudon, 37 rue Droite, and for *charcuterie* to Traiteur des Gourmets, 136 rue de Provence. Sisteron doesn't really have a bar scene to speak of; the best bet for relaxed drinking is one of the bigger brasseries.

Vilhosc and Vaumeilh

If you're staying in Sisteron for several days there are some worthwhile expeditions into the wilds. To the east along the D17 you come to **VILHOSC** whose priory has an eleventh-century crypt hidden in its walls (ask the owner for access); a few kilometres further on is the graceful fourteenth-century **Pont de la Reine Jeanne**, which crosses the River Vançon. It's a lovely spot, but the roads end here, the tracks that continue on either side of the bridge being currently impassable in places and in a dangerous state due to the risk of landslides.

If you're keen on **flying**, the Aérodrome de Sisteron (℡04.92.62.17.45) can arrange for you to go up in a glider or microlight. It's 10km to the north of Sisteron, through Valernes off the D951 in the village of **VAUMEILH**.

From the Durance to the Luberon

Bounded in the east by the valley of the Durance, to the north by the **Montagne de Lure** and shading to the south and west into the **Parc Naturel Régional du Luberon** (see box, p.227), the **Pays de Forcalquier** is a beguiling mix of agrarian plenty and scenic beauty, with honey, fruit aperitifs, olive oil and cheese to savour and clear skies and pure air to enjoy. It's a region far removed from urban centres, and even the venerable capital, **Forcalquier,** has a sleepy, rural feel to it. The countryside, gentle enough around Forcalquier and the neighbouring village of **Mane**, becomes progressively wilder towards the Plateau d'Albion in the west. Here, remote villages such as **Simiane-la-Rotonde** and **Banon** have a particular charm, not yet as smart as the villages of the Luberon but easily their equal for beauty and history. It's in the more northerly villages of the Pays de Forcalquier, including Banon, that you're likely to hear Provençal being spoken and see aspects of rural life that have hardly changed over centuries. It was in a tiny place, on the Lure foothills due north of Banon called Le Contadour, that Jean Giono (see p.212) set up his summer commune in the 1930s to expostulate the themes of peace, ecology and the return to nature. But it's not all bucolic and timeless, for the pristine atmospheric conditions have also attracted the attentions of astronomers, whose **Observatoire de Haute-Provence** sits in splendid isolation close to the village of **St-Michel-l'Observatoire**.

Forcalquier

Mellow **FORCALQUIER**, 11km west of the Durance on the D12, dominates the surrounding countryside, its distinctive hilly outline visible for miles around.

Not that Forcalquier is any kind of urban blot: it's not on any rail line, the surrounding industrial development is very modest and the masonry of its ancient houses is frayed gently at the edges. The glories of its history are there for all to see, and consequently Forcalquier is as appealing as the gentle, hilly surrounding countryside. That said, things are a good deal livelier on Monday, when it's **market day**.

Arrival, information and accommodation

Buses drop you off at place Martial Sicard, one block back from the main place du Bourguet, where you'll find the **tourist office** at no. 13 (mid-June to mid-Sept Mon–Sat 9am–12.30pm & 2.30–6.30pm, Sun 10am–noon; mid-Sept to mid-June Mon–Sat 9am–noon & 2–6pm; ℡04.92.75.10.02, Ⓦwww.forcalquier .com). You can **rent bikes** from Forcalquier Motocycle on boulevard de la République (℡04.92.75.12.47).

The best place **to stay** is the attractive *Auberge Charembeau* (℡04.92.70.91.70, Ⓦwww.charembeau.com; closed mid-Nov to mid-Feb; ❺), 2km out of town, at the end of a long drive signed off the road to Niozelles. *Le Colombier* (℡04.92.75.03.71, Ⓦwww.lecolombier.fr; July & Aug *demi-pension* compulsory from €70 per person, otherwise ❹) is another pleasant countryside retreat, 3km south of Forcalquier off the D16. In town, the *Hostellerie des Deux Lions*, close to the tourist office at 11 place du Bourguet (℡04.92.75.25.30, Ⓦwww .lesdeuxlions.com; closed Dec; ❹), is a seventeenth-century coach house, with comfortable rooms and an excellent restaurant serving game and fowl dishes flavoured with all the herbs of Provence. The three-star *Camping Indigo* (℡04.92.75.27.94; Ⓦwww.camping-indigo.com; €18.30 per tent; closed Nov–March) is 500m out of town on the road to Sigonce, past the cemetery; it also rents out caravans.

The Town

Despite its slumbering air, Forcalquier was once a place of some significance, as its **public buildings** betray. In the twelfth century the counts of Forcalquier rivalled those of Provence, with dominions spreading south and east to the Durance and north to the Drôme. Gap, Embrun, Sisteron, Manosque and Apt were all ruled from the **citadel** of Forcalquier, which even minted its own currency. When this separate power base came to an end, Forcalquier was still renowned as the *Cité des Quatre Reines*, since the four daughters of Raimond Béranger V, who united Forcalquier and Provence, all married kings. One of them, Eleanor, became the wife of Henry III of England, a fact commemorated by a modern plaque on the Gothic fountain of place Bourguet.

Not much remains of the ancient citadel at the summit of the rounded, wooded hill that dominates the town. Beside the ruins of a tower, sole vestige of the counts of Forcalquier's castle, and the half-buried walls of the original cathedral, stands a neo-Byzantine nineteenth-century chapel, **Notre-Dame-de-Provence,** visible for miles from the surrounding countryside.

Looming over the central place du Bourguet, the former **Cathédrale Notre-Dame** has an asymmetric and defensive exterior, a finely wrought Gothic porch and a Romanesque nave which has recently been restored. Behind the cathedral you enter the **Vieille Ville** where the houses date from the thirteenth to the eighteenth century. From place Vieille or rue Mercière you can bear right for place St-Michel and the ancient street fronts of Grande Rue, rue Béranger, place du Palais and rue du Collège. Place St-Michel has another fountain, whose decorative figures are embroiled in activities currently banned under biblical sanction in half the states of the USA.

At the top and to the left of rue Passère, running south off place Vieille, and with more crumbling historic facades, you reach the start of montée St-Mari, which leads up to the citadel. East of place Vieille on rue des Cordeliers stands the old **synagogue**, which marks the site of the former Jewish quarter; just beyond it is the one remaining gateway to the Vieille Ville, the Porte des Cordeliers. The superior power of the Roman Catholic Church is represented by the **Couvent des Cordeliers** at the end of boulevard des Martyrs. Built between the twelfth and fourteenth centuries, it bears the scars of wars and revolutions but preserves a beautifully vaulted scriptorium and a library with its original wooden ceiling, though sadly the interior is no longer open to the public.

Eating and drinking

Place du Bourguet has a few decent places to eat: the *Deux Lions* (☎04.92.75.25.30; menus from €22; closed Sun & Tue eves plus Wed), offers traditional fare; *Le Commerce* (☎04.92.75.00.08; *menu du marché* €16) is a good place to try the wonderful local lamb; and *L'Estable*, behind *Le Commerce* at no. 4 (☎04.92.75.39.82), serves Provençal cuisine with menus starting at €22. *Oliviers & Co*, on rue des Cordeliers (☎04.92.75.00.75), specializes in more modern creations, with a tempting array of olive oils and other local produce on sale; it's one of the small number of restaurants belonging to the olive oil company owned by the founder of L'Occitane en Provence (see p.221). *La Crêperie*, at 4 rue des Cordeliers, does great salads, grills, ice creams and crêpes, with menus from €16.

Another product of the town, based on fruits and nuts from further south, is **exotic alcohol**. The Distillerie et Domaines de Provence has its shop on avenue St-Promasse just down from the tourist office, where you can buy cherries, pears and mixes of different fruits and nuts pickled in liqueur. Of its fruit wines, the *de brut de pêche*, a sparkling peach aperitif, needs to be tasted to be believed. For ordinary **café drinking**, the *Brasserie La Fontaine* on place St-Michel is a friendly locals' watering hole, or there's the very central *Café L'Hôtel de Ville*, on place du Bourguet.

Mane

The village of **MANE**, 4km south of Forcalquier at the junction of the roads from Apt and Manosque, still has its feudal citadel – now a private residence and closed to the public – and Renaissance churches, chapels and mansions remarkably intact. The most impressive building is a former Benedictine priory, **Notre-Dame-de-Salagon**, half a kilometre out of Mane off the Apt road (Feb–April & Oct daily 2–5pm; May & Sept daily 10am–12.30pm & 2–6.30pm; June–Aug daily 10am–7.30pm; Nov–Dec Sun only 2–5pm; closed Jan; €6). It comprises fifteenth-century monks' quarters, seventeenth-century stables and farm buildings, and an enormous fortified twelfth-century Romanesque church with traces of fourteenth-century frescoes and sculpted scenes of rural life. Archeological digs in the choir have revealed the remnants of an earlier, sixth-century church. Three stunning **gardens**, one of aromatic plants, another of medicinal plants, and a third cultivated as the medieval monks would have used it, have been recreated to illustrate the way in which the monks used the land; there are also modern and ecological gardens. A number of exhibitions and activities, including themed guided tours, are organized each year by the Conservatoire du Patrimoine Ethnologique of the Alpes de Haute Provence *département* which runs the site, and you can buy plants.

Further along the Apt road, past a medieval bridge over the River Laye, you come to a palatial residence that has been called the Trianon of Provence. The pure eighteenth-century ease and luxury of the **Château de Sauvan** (guided tours at 3.30pm, otherwise by appointment on ☎04.92.75.05.64: mid-Jan to March Sun & public holidays; April–June & Sept to mid-Nov Thurs, Sun & public holidays; July–Aug daily except Sat; closed mid-Nov to mid-Jan; €5.60) come as a surprise in this harsh territory, leagues from any courtly city. Though there are hundreds of mansions like it around Paris and along the Loire, the residences of the rich and powerful in Haute Provence tend towards the moat and dungeon, not to French windows giving onto lawns and lake. The furnishings are predictably grand and the hall and stairway would take some beating for light and spaciousness, but what's best is the setting: the swans and geese on the square lake, the peacocks strutting by the drive, the views around and the delicate solidity of the aristocratic house.

L'Observatoire de Haute Provence

The tourist literature promoting the pure air of Haute Provence is not just hype. Proof of the fact is the National Centre for Scientific Research **observatory** on the wooded slopes 2.5km north of the village of St-Michel-l'Observatoire, southwest of Mane, sited here because it has the fewest clouds, the least fog and the lowest industrial pollution in all France. Visible from miles around, it presents a peculiar picture of domes of gleaming white mega-mushrooms pushing up between the oaks. It's open for **guided tours** (July–Aug Wed & Thurs 1.15–4.15pm; April–June & Sept Wed 2–4pm; Oct–March Wed 3pm; €4), so you get to see some telescopes and blank monitors, and the mechanism that opens up the domes and aims the lens. More exciting, however, are the night-time sky-watching vigils at the associated **Centre d'Astronomie**, just east of St-Michel-l'Observatoire (July & Aug only Tues–Fri 9.30pm; €9). A museum displaying part of the observatory's collections is scheduled to open in the village in 2007.

Banon

The houses of the tiny Haute Ville of **BANON,** 25km northwest of Forcalquier on the D950, form a guarding wall. Within the impressive fourteenth-century fortified gate, the **Portail à Machicoulis**, the bustle of the modern village below disappears and all is peaceful and immaculate; the houses of the rue des Arcades arch across the roadway and the village peters out just beyond the former chapel of the château at the top of the slope, with only a few stretches of ruined masonry beyond.

Banon is famous above all for its **cheese**. The *plateau des fromages* of any half-decent Provence restaurant will include a round goats' cheese marinaded in brandy and wrapped in sweet chestnut leaves, but there's nothing like tasting different ages of the untravelled cheese, sliced off for you by the *fromager* at a market stall on place de la République. As well as ensuring that you taste the very young and the well-matured varieties, they may give you an accompaniment in the form of a sprig of savory, an aromatic local plant of the mint family.

Accommodation options in Banon are limited, as there's no hotel. You could enquire about *chambres d'hôtes* at the **Point d'Information** on place de la République (Mon–Sat 9.30am–12.30pm & 2–5pm, Sun 10am–noon, ☎04.92.72.19.40, ⓦwww.village-banon.fr). Otherwise there's a **campsite,** *L'Épi Bleu*, just outside the village (☎04.92.73.30.30, ⓦwww.campingepibleu.com;

€16 per tent; closed Nov–March), with a pool and organized children's activities. For meals or snacks, there's the *Bar-Restaurant Les Voyageurs,* the *Café de France* on the main street, or *La Braserade* pizzeria.

The Montagne de Lure

Roads north of Banon peter out at the lower slopes of the **Montagne de Lure**. To reach the summit of the Lure, by road or the GR6, you have to head east to **St-Étienne-les-Orgues**, 12km north of Forcalquier. The footpath avoids the snaking road for most of the way, but you're walking through relentless pine plantation and it's a long way without a change of scenery (about 15km). Just below the summit you'll see the **ski lifts**.

When the trees stop you find yourself on sharp stones without a single softening blade of grass. The summit itself is a mass of telecommunications aerials and dishes; a grimmer high-perched desert would be hard to find. That said, the point of the climb is that the Lure has no close neighbours, giving you 360 degrees of mountainscape, as if you were airborne. The view of the distant snowy peaks to the north is the best; those with excessive stamina can keep walking towards them along the GR6 to Sisteron. If you feel like lingering in the area, you could stay in the appealing little village of **CRUIS**, 5km northeast of St-Éienne-les-Orgues, at the *Auberge de l'Abbaye* (①04.92.77.01.93, closed last two weeks Nov & all Jan; ❹) with a well-regarded restaurant serving refined creations using local produce on its €48 menu.

Simiane-la-Rotonde

The spiralling cone of **SIMIANE-LA-ROTONDE,** 9.5km southwest of Banon on the D51, marks the horizon with an emphasis greater than its size would warrant. However many *villages de caractère* (Simiane's official classification) you may have seen, this is one to re-seduce you. Neither over-spruce nor on the verge of ruin, Simiane feels like a place that people love and are prepared to work for.

The modern village and much of the commerce – what there is of it – lies in the plain by the D51, cleanly separated from the old village's winding streets of honey-coloured stone in which each house is part of the medieval defensive system. The zigzags end at the **Rotonde** (April to mid-May & Sept Mon & Wed–Sun 2–6pm; mid-May to Aug daily 10am–1pm & 3–7.30pm; Oct–March groups only, by appointment ①04.92.73.11.34; €4), a large domed building that was once the chapel of the castle but looks more like a keep. Nineteenth-century restoration work added smooth limestone to its rough-hewn fortress stones, but the peculiar feature is the asymmetry between its interior and exterior, being hexagonal on the outside and irregularly dodecagonal on the inside. The set of the stones on the domes is wonderfully wonky and no one knows what once hung from or covered the hole at the top. In August the Rotonde is a venue for the annual international **festival of ancient music** (Ⓦ www.festival-simiane.com).

Beyond the Rotonde there's a path to the chapel of **Notre-Dame-de-Pieté**, which stands amongst old windmills. As you head back down through the village you pass all sorts of architectural details which catch the eye: heavy carved doors with stone lintels in exact proportion, wrought-iron street lamps, the scrolling on the dark wooden shutters of the building opposite the **covered hall of the old market**, Simiane's most stunning building. With its columns framing open sky, the hall almost overhangs the hillside on the steepest section of the village; no longer used as a marketplace, it's where people stop on their daily rounds to pass the time of day or stare into the middle distance, where cats stretch out in the sun, and where, each July 14, the **village dance** is held.

Practicalities

Tourism is not Simiane's main preoccupation, but it does have a **tourist office**, housed in the Rotonde (same hours; T04.92.73.11.34, W www .simiane-la-rotonde.com). There's only one simple **hotel**, the *Auberge du Faubourg* (T04.92.75.92.43; closed Nov–Easter; ❸), with just eight rooms. There are, however, several **gîtes** and **chambres d'hôtes** in and around Simiane, including *Le Chaloux*, (T04.92.75.99.13, W www.chaloux.free.fr; ❸; closed Jan–Feb): it's off the D51 about 3km south of the village, and right on the GR4 footpath. There's also a two-star **campsite**, *Camping de Valsaintes*, on the main road (T04.92.75.91.46, W www.valsaintes.com; closed late Oct to March). Simiane isn't richly endowed with places to **eat** or **drink**: there's a *bar-tabac*, *Le Chapeau Rouge*, and a *salon de thé*, *Aux Plaisir des Yeux*, where you can also buy honey, liqueurs and *crème de marrons*.

The Luberon

The great fold of rock of the Luberon runs for fifty-odd kilometres between the Coulon and the Durance valleys, and sits at the heart of the **Parc Naturel Régional du Luberon**. The massif is divided by the **Combe de Lourmarin**, a narrow gorge through which a lone metalled road gives access south to Cadenet and Aix. The **Grand Luberon** is the portion of the massif to the east of the Combe de Lourmarin, while the **Petit Luberon** is the section to the west. Though many forestry tracks cross the ridge, they are barred to cars (and too rough for bikes), and where the ridge isn't forested it opens into tableland pastures where sheep graze in summer. The northern slopes have Alpine rather than Mediterranean leanings: the trees are oak, beech and maple, and cowslips and buttercups announce the summer. But it is still very hot and there are plenty of vines on the lower slopes. North of the massifs, the lively market town of **Apt** is the chief urban centre of the Luberon: close to it the remnants of ochre extraction have created the extraordinary **Colorado Provençal** and the vibrant orange-red landscapes of **Roussillon**. The most beguiling of the Luberon's **villages** stand on high ground overlooking the vale of the Calavon: **Saignon**, **Bonnieux**, **Lacoste**, **Ménerbes** and, to the north, **Gordes**. Equally beguiling – and mysterious – are the ruined villages of Buoux and Oppède le Vieux.

The Colorado Provençal and the Grand Luberon

RUSTREL, 13km southwest of Simiane-la-Rotonde, is a sweet little village with a small and welcoming **hotel**, the *Auberge de Rustréou*, 3 place de la Fête (T04.90.04.90.90, F04.90.04.98.06; ❸), and a convivial **bar**, *Les Platanes* (T04.90.04.96.26), which serves good beers and has live music most Friday nights. It is home, too to a series of dramatic ochre quarries, known as the **Colorado Provençal** (daily 9am–5.30pm; parking €2.50), signed off the D22 towards Gignac. The track round the quarries begins at the car park entrance.

Having passed the remains of old settling tanks that look like unearthed foundations and a small ruined building, take the track on the right marked with white. The full, circular, route takes about an hour and a half to walk and the **map** (€3.50), available from the snack bar in the car park, will prove useful, as the route can be quite hard to follow – particularly when the stream meanders onto the creamy ochre sand of the path. Persevere and you will end up in an amphitheatre of coffee, vanilla and strawberry ice-cream-coloured rock, whipped into pinnacles and curving walls. If you continue up above a little waterfall, you can turn left, then left again onto a wider path, which soon brings you to the gods' seats over the quarry. Continue and you'll end up on the same route leading back to the settling tanks.

Saignon

Fourteen kilometres south of Rustrel, **SAIGNON** is 4km from Apt but sits high enough to have an eagle-eye view not just of the town, but of the whole region. From below, the village rises like an immense fort with natural turrets of rock; on closer inspection it has an almost troglodyte charm, its houses – some exquisitely preserved, others still in a semi-ruinous state – set among the rocky outcrops on which the village's castle once stood. The very best of the views are from the pulpit-like **Rocher de Bellevue** at the far end of the village. The panorama here is almost 360°; you climb the uneven steps at your own risk, and given the exposed, windy vantage point, the experience is properly breathtaking.

There's a pleasant **hotel** in the centre of the village, the *Auberge du Presbytère*, place de la Fontaine (℡04.90.74.11.50, ⓦwww.auberge-presbytere.com; ❹), with pretty and individually styled rooms, some with beams.

Fort de Buoux

From Saignon the D232 heads 5.5km west towards the D113 and the village of **Buoux**, from where a minor road leads the short distance to the fortified, abandoned hilltop village known as the **Fort de Buoux**. It stands on the northern flank of the Grand Luberon massif, overlooking a canyon forged by the once powerful River Aiguebrun at the start of its passage through the Luberon. To reach the fort follow the road signed off the D113 to the gateway at the end, beyond which it's a ten- to fifteen-minute walk to the entrance (March to mid-Nov daily sunrise till sunset; mid-Nov to Feb weekends only; €3).

Numerous relics of prehistoric life have been found in the Buoux Valley, and in the earliest Christian days anchorite monks survived against all odds in tiny caves and niches in the vertical cliff face. In the 1660s, Fort de Buoux was demolished by command of Richelieu for being a centre of Protestantism, but the remains of old Buoux – including water cisterns, storage cellars with thick stone lids, arrow-slitted ramparts, the lower half of a Romanesque chapel and a pretty much intact keep – still give a good impression of life here over the centuries. Today, the spot is popular with **climbers**, many of whom can be seen clinging to the cliff face as you approach the fort. Most of them will be denizens of the corporate or municipal holiday homes that cluster round the road into the valley.

Back at the junction with the D113, a left turn takes you past the slender Romanesque tower of the former Prieuré de St-Symphorien to the Lourmarin road, while a right turn brings you back to the present-day village of **BUOUX** (the "x", by the way, is pronounced). Just outside the village, the *Auberge de la Loube* **restaurant** (℡04.90.74.19.58; no credit cards; closed Sun eve, Mon &

Thurs) has a considerable local reputation: some say it's pretentious and overpriced, others that it's *génial* and serves delicious food. You can judge for yourself with the midday €21 menu. For **accommodation** try the *Auberge des Seguins* (☎04.90.74.16.37, ℻04.90.74.03.26; *demi-pension* or full *pension* only; ❻; closed mid-Nov to March), tucked away in the spectacular canyon not far from the Fort de Buoux.

From Buoux there are fabulous views west from the road to the Combe de Luberon; in the gorge itself you can stop off by the river, at its most spectacular in spring.

Apt and around

APT, the main settlement in the Luberon, lies northeast of the Combe de Lourmarin, nestling beneath the northern slopes of the Grand Luberon on the banks of the River Coulon. Best known for its crystallized fruit and preserves, Apt, like so many of the surrounding villages, is gentrifying rapidly as foreigners and wealthy Parisians move in. For now, though, the balance between timeless market town and newly fashionable urban oasis is about right, and Apt is a likeable and bustling little place with one of the oldest cathedrals in Provence, excellent shops and a lively Saturday **market**. In July *Les Tréteaux de Nuit* **festival** provides a choice of shows with concerts, plays, café-theatre and exhibitions. If you have your own transport, Apt also makes a useful base for visiting the villages of the Grand Luberon – Saignon and Buoux – and the ochre-mining village of **Roussillon** to the west.

Arrival, information and accommodation

Buses drop you off either at the main **place de la Bouquerie** or at the **gare routière** (☎04.90.74.20.21) on avenue de la Libération at the eastern end of the town; the train station is for freight only. The **tourist office** is at 20 av Philippe-de-Girard (July & Aug Mon–Sat 9am–7pm, Sun 9.30am–12.30pm; May–June & Sept Mon–Sat 9am–noon & 2–6pm, Sun

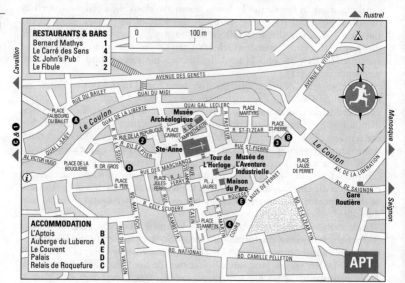

9.30am–12.30pm; Oct–April Mon–Sat 9am–noon & 2–6pm; ☎ 04.90.74.03.18, ⓦ wwwt.ot-apt.fr), just to your left as you face the river from place de la Bouquerie. Arriving by **car**, you may have to park along the quays or in one of the larger car parks to the east of the town centre, but place de la Bouquerie is still the focal point to head for. You can **rent bikes** from Guy Agnel, 27 quai Général-Leclerc (☎ 04.90.74.17.16), or Gassou Shop, 422 av Victor-Hugo (☎ 04.90.74.61.66). Infotelec, at 44 quai de la Liberté, has **Internet** access.

There's a reasonable choice of **accommodation** in and around Apt; hotels in the town are less likely to be booked up here than in the more scenic hilltop villages.

Hotels

L'Aptois 289 cours Lauze-de-Perret ☎ 04.90.74.02.02, ⓦ www.aptois.fr.st. Overlooking place Lauze-de-Perret and the Saturday market, this clean, basic hotel is reasonably priced, and most rooms have TVs. ❸

Auberge du Luberon 8 place Faubourg du Ballet ☎ 04.90.74.12.50, ⓦ www.auberge-luberon-peuzin .com. Directly across the river, with pleasant rooms and a quiet setting. ❹

🏃 **Le Couvent** 36 rue Louis-Rousset ☎ 04.90.04.55.36, ⓦ www.loucouvent.com. Stylish *maison d'hôtes* in a seventeenth-century convent in the centre of the town, with simple but spacious rooms. ❻

Palais 24 bis place Gabriel-Péri ☎ 04.90.04.89.32, ⓔ hotel-le-palais@orange.fr. Cheap option bang in the centre of town, above a rather uninspired pizzeria. Closed mid-Nov to April. ❸

Relais de Roquefure Le Chêne, 6km from Apt on the N100 towards Avignon ☎ 04.90.04.88.88, ⓦ www.relaisderoquefure.com. A large renovated country house with a pool, and ochre-tinted rooms with en-suite bathrooms. Closed Dec & Jan. ❹

Campsites

Camping les Cèdres av de Viton ☎ 04.90.74.14.61, ⓦ www.francecamping.fr. A two-star site within easy walking distance of the town, across the bridge from place St-Pierre. €13 per tent. Closed mid-Nov to Feb.

Camping le Luberon rte de Saignon ☎ 04.90.04.85.40, ⓦ www.campingleluberon.com. Three-star site, less than 2km from town, with swimming pool, restaurant and disabled facilities. €18.65 per tent. Closed Oct–March.

The Town

Saturday is the best day to visit Apt, when cars are barred from the town centre to allow artisans and cultivators from the surrounding countryside to set up stalls. As well as featuring every imaginable Provençal edible, the **market** is accompanied by barrel organs, jazz musicians, stand-up comics,

---

Parc Naturel Régional du Luberon

The **Parc Naturel Régional du Luberon** is administered by the Maison du Parc in Apt at 60 place Jean-Jaurès (April–Sept Mon–Fri 8.30am–noon & 1.30–6pm, Sat 9am–noon & 1.30-6pm; Oct–March closed Sat; ☎ 04.90.04.42.00, ⓦ www.parcduluberon .fr). It's a centre of activity with laudable aims – nature conservation and the provision of environmentally friendly tourist facilities – though many people have misgivings about the practicalities of the project. Be that as it may, the Maison du Parc is the place to go for information about the fauna and flora of the Luberon, footpaths, cycle routes, pony-trekking, gîtes and campsites. The centre also houses a small Musée de la Paléontologie (€1.50), designed for children. A submarine-type "time capsule" door leads down to push-button displays that include magnified views of insect fossils and their modern descendants.

aged hippies and notorious local characters. Everyone, from successful Parisian artists with summer studios here, to military types from the St-Christol base, serious ecologists, rich foreigners and local Aptois, can be found milling around the central **rue des Marchands** for this weekly social commerce.

The great local speciality of fruits – crystallized, pickled, preserved in alcohol or turned into jam – features at the market, but during the rest of the week you can go to La Bonbonnière on the corner of rue de la Sous-Préfecture and rue de la République for every sort of sweet and chocolate and the Provençal speciality *tourron*, an almond paste flavoured with coffee, pistachio, pine kernels or cherries. If you're really keen on sticky sweets you can ring Aptunion, the **confectionery factory**, in quartier Salignan, 2km from Apt on the Avignon road, for a free tour (July & Aug 10.30am & 2pm; ☎04.90.76.31.43) or just to visit the shop (Mon–Sat 9am–noon & 2–6pm).

Other **shops** worth looking at are Tamisier, on rue du Docteur-Gros, selling kitchenware and the traditional fly-proof open boxes for storing cheese and sausage; Station Peintre, on place de la Bouquerie, with artists' materials at very good prices; the Atelier du Vieil Apt for faïence on place Carnot; and the Librarie Majuscule, on the corner of rue des Marchands and place G-Péri, with some English books for sale.

While window-shopping along rue des Marchands, you'll see the **Tour de L'Horloge** (bell tower) spanning the street, and the **Cathédrale de Ste-Anne** (July & Aug Mon–Sat 8.30am–6pm; Sept–June Mon–Fri 8.30am–noon & 2–5.30pm, Sat 8.30am–noon & 3–5.30pm), one of the oldest cathedrals in Provence if scarcely the most coherent architecturally, though it's an agreeable enough mish-mash of styles. The very oldest parts of the cathedral include a beautiful fourth-century carved stone ceiling in the *crypte inferieure*; elsewhere slabs dating from the eighth and ninth centuries were reused in the twelfth. The cathedral's chief relic is a veil said to have belonged to St Anne herself.

Elsewhere in town, the **Musée Archéologique** at 4 rue de l'Amphithéâtre (groups only, by appointment), is not wildly exciting, with a few remains of a Roman theatre in the basement. Apt's industrial heritage is the subject of a spanking new museum, the **Musée de l'Aventure Industrielle**, 14 place du Postel (June–Sept Mon–Fri 10am–noon & 3–6.30pm, Sun 3–7pm; rest of year Mon & Wed–Sat 10am–noon & 2–5.30pm; €4), laid out over three floors and covering the three major industries of the town and surrounding area – ochre, candied fruits and the production of fine faïence. Exhibits include the recreation of a potter's studio, plus works by the sculptor Alexis Poitevin, who was inspired by industrial themes. The adjacent **Atelier d'Art Fernand Bourgeois** (Mon & Wed–Sat 2–5.30pm; free) is the occasional venue for temporary art exhibitions

Eating and drinking

One of the best **restaurants** in Apt is *Le Carré des Sens*, on place St-Martin at the top of cours Lauze-de-Perret (☎04.90.74.74.00; closed Mon & Tues lunch), with a €26 menu featuring such exquisite dishes as *millefeuille* of tuna, gravadlax and *jamón serrano* or tian of *rascasse* in pimentade with *imam biyaldi* and red pesto; for similar fare at lower prices, nip round the back to the affiliated *bar à vins* on rue St-Martin, where you'll also find a *salon de thé*, wine shop and delicatessen. For more traditional cuisine, and a superb choice of desserts, try the *Auberge du Luberon*, (see p.227; closed Mon & Tue lunch out of season), with menus from €29. Five kilometres out of town at Le Chêne (off the Avignon road), *Bernard*

Mathys on chemin des Platanes (☎04.90.04.84.64; closed Tues & Wed) offers more good food on menus from €30, and a chance to try a wide selection of local goats' cheeses, plus a delicious lavender *crème brûlée*. The best places for a **drink** are the brasseries on place de la Bouquerie, or *St John's Pub* on place St-Pierre.

Roussillon

Perching precariously above soft-rock cliffs 10km northwest of Apt, the buildings of **ROUSSILLON** radiate all the different shades of the seventeen ochre tints once quarried here. A spiralling road leads past potteries, antique shops and restaurants up to the summit of the village, which is worth the effort for the views over the Luberon and Ventoux. If you want to see the **ochre quarries** themselves, a well-signed footpath leads from the car park on place de la Poste, where you'll also find the **tourist office** (Easter–Nov Tues–Fri 9am–noon & 1.30–6.30pm, Sat & Mon 10am–noon & 2–5.30pm; Dec–Easter Mon-Sat 10am–noon & 2–5.30pm; ☎04.90.05.60.25, Ⓦwww .roussillon-provence.com) and a Centre Social et Culturel with occasional art exhibitions. Just outside Roussillon, on the Apt road, an old **ochre factory**, the Usine Mathieu, has been renovated and you can look round the various washing, draining, settling and drying areas, though you probably won't get much out of a visit without joining one of the guided tours (daily except Mon morning: July & Aug every 30min from 9am–7pm; March–June & Sept–Nov 11am & hourly 2–5pm; €5). It also hosts excellent exhibitions on themes related to the use and production of ochre, with accompanying workshops for both adults and children.

If you need somewhere to stay, the *Rêves d'Ocres* **hotel**, on route de Gordes (☎04.90.05.60.50, Ⓦwww.hotel-revesdocres.com; Ⓢ), is warm, welcoming and has some rooms with good views of the Luberon. There's also a very pleasant two-star **campsite**, *Camping L'Arc en Ciel*, in pine woods, 2km along the D104 to Goult (☎04.90.05.73.96; Ⓔcampingarcenciel@orange.fr; €13.24 per tent; closed Nov to mid-March). For **meals**, try Roussillon's *La Treille*, 1 rue du Four (☎04.90.05.64.47), which serves a mixture of North African, Turkish and Scandinavian specialities with menus from €21, or you can get a crêpe at *La Gourmandine* on place l'Abbé-Avon.

Gordes and around

GORDES, west of Roussillon and 6km north of the main Apt-Avignon road (but only as the crow flies), tumbles to spectacular effect down a steep hillside to create one of the most photographed views in all Provence. The village is popular with film directors, media personalities, musicians and

---

Ochre quarrying

Ochre quarrying has been practised in the Vaucluse since prehistoric times, producing the natural dye that gives a range of colours, which don't fade in sunlight, from pale yellow to a blood red. By the nineteenth century the business had really taken off, with overloaded donkeys, then, by the 1880s, trains, carrying truckloads of the dust to Marseille to be shipped round the world. At its peak, in 1929, forty thousand tonnes of ochre were exported from the region. Twenty years later it was down to 11,500 tonnes, and in 1958 production was finally stopped, in part because of reduced demand with competition from synthetic dyes, but also because the foundations of Roussillon were being undermined.

painters, many of whom have added a Gordes address to their main Paris residence. As a result, the place is full of expensive restaurants, cafés and art and craft shops.

There are good reasons for its popularity with the rich and famous. The approach at sunset is particularly memorable as the ancient stone turns gold. In addition, in the vicinity, you can see a superb array of dry-stone architecture in **Village des Bories**, as well as the **Abbaye de Sénanque**, and a couple of museums dedicated to glass and olive oil. There's also a festival, **Les Soirées d'Été de Gordes,** in the first two weeks of August when the village is awash with theatrical performances, jazz and classical music concerts.

The village

In the past, near-vertical staircases hewn into the rock gave the only access to the summit of the village, where the church and houses surround a twelfth- to sixteenth-century **castle** with few aesthetic concessions to the business of fortification. By the beginning of the 20th century most of Gordes' villagers had abandoned the old defensive site and the place was in ruins. A centre of resistance during World War II, Gordes was rediscovered by various artists, including Chagall and the Hungarian scientist of art and design, Victor Vasarely.

Vasarely undertook the restoration of Gordes castle and, in 1970, opened his Didactic Museum within its Renaissance interior. However, on his death in 1995, the collection was reclaimed by his family (although the Aix-en-Provence collection remains in situ) and the space devoted to the very different and less accessible **Musée Pol Mara** (daily 10am–noon & 2–6pm; €4). The career of the Belgian artist, also seduced by the beauty of Gordes, moves from Post-Expressionism to Pop Art with one dominant theme – the female body.

Practicalities

Gordes does not lie on any major public transport routes and it's likely you will arrive under your own steam. Infrequent **buses** connecting it with Cavaillon, 16km to the west, arrive at place du Château. Gordes' helpful **tourist office**, in the Salle des Gardes of the castle (Mon–Sat 9am–noon & 2–6pm, Sun 10am–noon & 2–6pm; ℡04.90.72.02.75, ⓦwww.gordes-village.com), has lists of accommodation and details of local events. One of the best value **hotels** in the village is the reasonably priced *Le Provençal*, on place du Château (℡04.90.72.10.01, Ⓔazort@tiscali.fr; ❹), with just seven rooms. Overlooking the village, the old country house *Les Romarins*, on the route de Sénanque (℡04.90.72.12.13; ⓦwww.hoteldesromarins.com; ❻), has traditionally styled comfortable rooms. *Domaine de l'Enclos*, on the route de Sénanque (℡04.90.72.71.00, ⓦwww.avignon-et-provence.com/domaine-enclos/index .html; ❼), is set in a terraced garden with spacious rooms and a heated pool. The most luxurious option in the village itself is *La Bastide de Gordes* (℡04.90.72.12.12, ⓦwww.bastide-de-gordes.com; ❾) with spacious, traditionally furnished rooms and stunning views over the Luberon from its pool and terrace. Halfway between Gordes and Murs on the D15 is a very pleasant two-star **campsite**, *Camping des Sources* (℡04.90.72.12.48, Ⓕ04.90.72.09.43; €17.30 per night, closed Oct–March); early booking is advisable.

Five kilometres south of Gordes in Les Imberts, *Le Mas Tourteron*, chemin de St-Blaise (℡04.90.72.00.16; menu €57; closed Nov–Feb & Mon & Tues, eves only Wed–Sat, lunch only Sun), is an excellent and pretty non-smoking **restaurant** where you can eat gorgeous Provençal specialities in a shaded garden. On Grande rue in Cabrières d'Avignon, 7km along the winding road to Fontaine, *Le Vieux Bistrot* (Tues–Sat; ℡04.90.76.82.08; lunch menu €16, evening €33) dishes up the likes of *filet de daurade* with white asparagus and a cream morel sauce on a shady terrace or in the handsome, red-painted dining room. In Gordes itself, the most popular place to eat is the *Comptoir des Arts*, close to the château on place Genty-Pantaly (℡04.90.72.01.31; closed Mon eve & Tues out of season; *plats* around €24), which is always full of Parisians in summer. Alternatively, the neighbouring *L'Artégal* (℡04.90.72.02.54; closed Sun eve & Mon) has a €32 menu with ravioli of *chèvre* with a spaghetti of courgettes and filet mignon of pork with fresh garlic *jus*. *Le Jardin*, on route de Murs (℡04.90.72.12.34, closed Mon out of season), is a gay-friendly café-gallery with a pretty terrace and salads at €10. If you simply want a cheap snack, *L'Encas*, on place du Château, is central if plain and sells very acceptable panini for €4.

Village des Bories

About 4km east of Gordes, signed off the D2 to Cavaillon, is an unusual rural agglomeration, the **Village des Bories** (daily 9am–sunset; €5.50). This walled enclosure contains dry-stone houses, barns, bread ovens, wine stores and workshops constructed in a mix of unusual shapes: curving pyramids and cones, some rounded at the top, some truncated and the base almost rectangular or square. They are cleverly designed so that rain runs off their exteriors and the temperature inside remains constant whatever the season. To look at them, you might think they were prehistoric, and Neolithic rings and a hatchet have been found on the site, but most of these buildings in fact date from the eighteenth century and were lived in until the early nineteenth century. Some may well have been adapted from or rebuilt over earlier constructions, and there are extraordinary likenesses with a seventh- or eighth-century oratory in Ireland, and with huts and dwellings as far apart as the Orkneys and South Africa.

Abbaye de Sénanque

About 4km north of Gordes, **Abbaye de Sénanque** (guided tours only: Jan & mid-Nov to Dec two daily at 2.50 pm & 4.20pm; Feb–March & Oct to mid-Nov four daily 10.30am–4.35pm; April–May & Sept 5 daily 10.10am–4.35pm; June seven daily 10.10am-4.35pm; July–Aug 11 daily 9.50am–4.35pm; closed Sun am and certain religious festivals; €6) is one of a trio of twelfth-century monasteries established by the Cistercian order in Provence, and predates both the *bories* and the castle. It stands alone, amid fields of lavender in a hollow of the hills, its weathered stone sighing with age and immutability. Though it has become one of the most familiar Provençal views, visitor numbers are tightly regulated and visitors are asked to dress modestly and to respect the silence to which the abbey is consecrated. The shop at the end of the visit sells the monks' produce, including liqueur, as well as honey and lavender essence.

From the abbey, the loop back to Gordes via the D177 and D15 reveals the northern Luberon in all its glory.

Les Bouilladoires

The area around Gordes was famous for its olive oil before severe frosts killed off many of the trees. A still-functioning Gallo-Roman press, made from a single slice of oak two metres in diameter, as well as ancient oil lamps, jars and soap-making equipment, can be seen at the **Moulin des Bouillons** (April–Oct daily except Tues 10am–noon & 2–6pm; €7) in **LES BOUILLADOIRES**, on

△ Abbaye de Sénanque

the D148 just west of St-Pantaléon, 3.5km south of Gordes, and well signed from every junction.

The ticket for the Moulin also gives you access to the **Musée du Vitrail Frédérique Duran** (same hours), signalled by a huge and rather gross sculpture by Duran and housed in a semi-submerged bunker next to the Moulin. Duran's contemporary stained-glass creations are extremely garish, but if you want to learn about the long history of stained glass, you can, though perhaps the most attractive items are the gorgeous, strutting fowl and hedges of rosemary in the gardens around the two museums.

Musée de la Lavande

If you've travelled through Provence in high summer you will have seen, smelled and probably tasted lavender. The **Musée de la Lavande** (daily: July–Aug 9am–7pm; June & Sept 9am–noon & 2–7pm; Feb–May & Oct–Dec 10am–noon & 2–6pm; closed Jan; €5), on the route de Gordes near the hamlet of Coustellet, offers a chance to learn more about lavender and its uses. Exhibits include copper stills dating back to the sixteenth century; there's a film show and free English-language audio guide, plus the inevitable shop. In July and August there are also daily demonstrations of harvesting and outdoor distillation.

The Petit Luberon

The **Petit Luberon** has long been popular as a country escape for Parisians, Germans, the Dutch and the British – it was the setting for Peter Mayle's *A Year in Provence* – and *résidences secondaires* are everywhere. It remains a beguiling pastoral idyll, though these day's it's a rich man's retreat, its hilltop villages increasingly chic and its ruins, like **de Sade**'s **château** in **Lacoste** and the **Abbaye de St-Hilaire** near Bonnieux, being restored by their private owners.

There are few **hotels** in these parts, and, as a consequence, those that there are, are fairly expensive. Basing yourself at Cavaillon (covered in Chapter Three) or Apt may be the most sensible option.

Oppède-le-Vieux

OPPÈDE-LE-VIEUX, above the vines on the steeper slopes of the Petit Luberon, remains relatively free of the yuppie invasion, and ravishingly beautiful. There are a couple of cafés, the *Petit Café* on place de la Croix (℡04.90.76.74.01, ⓦwww.oppidum-oppede.com; dinner €25, rooms ❺) being the most pleasant, and a shop selling classy pottery. With its Renaissance gateway, the square in front of the ramparts suggests a monumental town within. But behind the line of restored sixteenth-century houses there are only the romantic, overgrown ruins that stretch up to the remains of the medieval **castle;** here and there isolated new homes have been crafted from restored fragments of the complex. Take care when exploring the ruins, as there are no fences or warning signs, steps break off above gaping holes, paths lead straight to precipitous edges and at the highest point of the castle you can sit on a foot-wide ledge with a drop of ten or more metres below you. The views at the very top are every bit as lovely as the castle itself.

Ménerbes

Heading east from Oppède-le-Vieux, **MÉNERBES** is the next hilltop village you come to. Shaped like a ship, its best site, on the prow as it were, is given over to the dead. From this cemetery you look down onto an odd jigsaw of fortified

4

The wars of religion in the Luberon

During five days in April 1545 a great swathe of the Petit Luberon, between **Lourmarin** and **Mérindol**, was burnt and put to the sword. Three thousand people were massacred and six hundred sent to the galleys. Their crime was having Protestant tendencies in the years leading up to the devastating Wars of Religion. Despite the complicity of King Henri II, the ensuing scandal forced him to order an enquiry which then absolved those responsible – the Catholic aristocrats from Aix.

Lourmarin (see p.207) itself suffered minor damage but the castle in Mérindol was violently dismantled, along with every single house. Mérindol's remains, on the hill above the current village on the south side of the Petit Luberon, are a visible monument to those events, and to this day the south face of the Petit Luberon remains sparsely populated.

buildings and mansions, old and new. In the other direction houses with exquisitely tended terraces and gardens, all shuttered up outside holiday time, ascend to the mammoth wall of the citadel, now another *résidence secondaire*.

Outside Ménerbes, left off the D103 towards Beaumettes, is the wine-producing Domaine de la Citadelle's **Musée de Tire-Bouchon** (Museum of Corkscrews; April–Oct daily 10am–noon & 2–7pm; Nov–March Mon–Sat 10am–noon & 2–5pm; €4), housed in a château dating back to the seventeenth century. The intriguing collection includes a Cézar compression, a corkscrew combined with pistol and dagger, others with erotic themes and many with beautifully sculpted and engraved handles. You can also visit the wine cellars for a free tasting. Between Ménerbes and Lacoste, on the D109, is the **Abbaye de St-Hilaire** (daily: April–Sept 10am–7pm; Oct–March 10am–5pm), with its fine seventeeth-century cloisters, exquisite Renaissance stairway and ancient dovecotes, though it's currently undergoing restoration and parts of the abbey may be off limits.

If you're looking **to stay** in Ménerbes itself, your best option is the welcoming *Le Galoubet* in the centre of the village, at 104 rue Marcellin-Poncet (T & F 04.90.72.36.08; closed mid Jan & late Feb–early March; ❹). It has charming but small rooms and a very pleasant **restaurant** serving classic Provençal cuisine on the terrace (menus at €17–29; closed Wed). Alternatively, there's the quiet and very agreeable *Hostellerie Le Roy Soleil* (T 04.90.72.25.61, W www.roy-soleil.com; ❾), just outside Ménerbes, on route des Baumettes, with a restaurant serving Provençal fare on its €55 menu. For cheap snacks and drinks head for the friendly *Café du Progrès*, featured in *A Year in Provence*, which has superb views over the surrounding countryside and a newsstand selling *The Financial Times*.

Lacoste

LACOSTE and its **château** can be seen from all the neighbouring villages, and are particularly enticing in moonlight while a wind rocks the hanging lanterns on the narrow cobbled approaches to the château, and the castle itself is a floodlit beacon, visible from miles around. Its most famous owner was the Marquis de Sade, who retreated here when the reaction to his writings got too hot, but in 1778, after seven years here, he was locked up in the Bastille and the castle destroyed soon after. Semi-derelict, the château now belongs to *couturier* Pierre Cardin, and is closed to the public. These days you're as likely to hear American as French voices in Lacoste, since much of the village forms an outpost of the Savannah College of Art and Design.

For **accommodation**, there are eight rooms above the excellent *Café de France* (℡04.90.75.82.25; ❷), which also provides inexpensive sandwiches, quiches and pizzas; the alternative pit stop is the pretty *Café de Sade*. **Market** day is on Tuesday.

Bonnieux and around

From the *terrasse* by the old church on the heights of the steep village of **BONNIEUX** you can see Gordes, Roussillon and neighbouring Lacoste, 5km away. Halfway down the village, on rue de la République, there's a museum of traditional bread-making, the **Musée de la Boulangerie** (July & Aug daily except Tues 10am–1pm & 3–6.30pm; April–June & Sept–Oct Mon & Wed-Sun 10am–12.30pm & 2.30–6pm; closed Nov–March; €3.50), and on avenue des Tilleuls the **Église Neuve** exhibits four fifteenth-century wood paintings.

From Bonnieux the D149 joins the Apt–Avignon road just after the triple-arched **Pont Julien** over the Coulon, which dates back to the time when Apt was the Roman base of Apta Julia. Well before you reach the bridge you'll see signs for the **Château La Canorgue**, a good place to sample the light and very palatable Côtes de Luberon wines (Mon–Fri 9am–7pm, Sat 9am–noon & 2–7pm).

The best **accommodation** option in Bonnieux is *La Bouquière*, quartier St-Pierre (℡04.90.75.87.17, ⓦwww.labouquiere.com; ❼), though it's very popular, so you'll need to book months in advance. Failing that, there are a couple of unexceptional options – the *César*, on place de la Liberté at the top of the village (℡04.90.75.96.35, ⓦwww.hotel-cesar.com; ❷) is nice enough, with classy furnishings in the lobby and wonderful views from some of the rooms, or the central but rather snooty *Hotel le Prieuré* on rue Jean-Baptiste-Aurard (℡04.90.75.80.78, ⓦwww.hotelprieure.com; ❼). For **eating**, try *Le Fournil*, overlooking the fountain in place Carnot (℡04.90.75.83.62; lunch menu €20; dinner from €38.50; closed Mon, Tues lunch & Sat lunch), which serves lovely Provençal dishes laced with olive oil and garlic. Friday is **market** day.

Travel details

Trains

Aix TGV to: Paris (8 daily; 2 hr 5min).
Aix to: Briançon (4 daily; 3hr 50min); Château-Arnoux-St Auban (4–5 daily; 1hr 10min); Marseille (hourly; 45min); Manosque/Gréoux Bains (4–5 daily; 40–45min); Meyrargues (4–9 daily; 20min); Sisteron (4 daily; 1hr 15min–1hr 25min).

Buses

Aix TGV to: Aix (every 30min; 15min); Digne-les-Bains (2–3 daily; 1hr 55min).
Aix to: Aix TGV (every 30min; 15 min); Apt (2 daily; 1hr 50min); Arles (6 daily; 1hr 20min); Avignon (6–8 daily; 1hr 15min); Brignoles (2 daily; 55min–1hr 5min); La Ciotat (6 daily; 1hr

5min–1hr 45min); Martigue (8 daily; 1hr 15min–1hr 45min); Marseille (every 5min at peak times; 30min); Marseille-Provence Airport (every 30min; 30min); Nice (3–5 daily; 2hr 15min–3hr 40min); St-Maximin (2 daily; 30min); Salon (16 daily; 35–45min); Sisteron (2–4 daily; 1hr 30min–2hr); Toulon (2–6 daily; 1hr 15min).
Apt to: Aix (2 daily; 2hr 35 min); Avignon (4–6 daily; 1hr 10min); Avignon TGV (2–4 daily; 1hr 30min); Bonnieux (2 daily; 20min); Cadenet (2 daily; 55min); Digne (1–4 daily; 2hr); Lourmarin (2 daily; 50min); Marseille (1–2 daily; 2hr 15min–2hr 35min); Pertuis (2 daily; 1hr 20min); Rustrel (2–6 weekly; 35min); Sault (1 weekly; 1hr–1hr 30min).
Banon to: Aix (1–2 daily; 2hr–2hr 15min); Marseille (1–2 daily; 2hr 50min); Simiane (1 daily; 10min).

Forcalquier to: Apt (1–2 daily; 50min); Avignon (1–2 daily; 2hr 20min); Digne (1 daily; 1hr 15min); Lurs (1 daily; 15min); Mane (9–10 daily; 5min); Manosque (2–10 daily; 30min); Marseille (1–4 daily; 1hr 50min–2hr); St Michel l'Observatoire (1–2 daily; 10min); Sisteron (1 daily; 1hr).

Manosque to: Aix TGV (2–3 daily; 1hr); Aix (8 daily; 55min); Château-Arnoux (1 daily; 40min); Digne (2–3 daily; 1hr 5min); Forcalquier (1–8 daily; 30–45 min); Marseille (8 daily; 1hr 20min); St-Auban (2–3 daily; 35min); Sisteron (3–4 daily; 50min–1hr).

Pertuis to: Aix (5 daily; 30min); Ansouis (1 daily; 10min); Apt (2 daily; 1hr 20min); Avignon (2–4 daily; 1hr 45min); Cadenet (2–4 daily; 15min); Cavaillon (2–4 daily; 1hr 10min); Cucuron (2 daily; 20–45min); Lourmarin (2–4 daily; 20 min).

Sisteron to: Aix (3–4 daily; 1hr 30min–1hr 55min); Château-Arnoux (2–3 daily; 20min); Digne (2 daily; 1hr); Forcalquier (1 daily; 1hr); Manosque (3–4 daily; 50min–1hr); Marseille (3–4 daily; 2hr 10min–2hr 25min); Nice (1 daily; 4hr 40min).

The Haut Var and Haute Provence

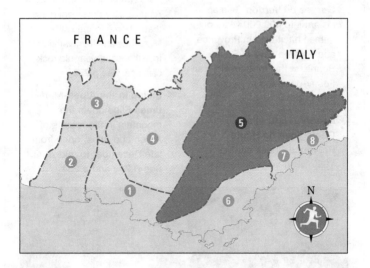

CHAPTER 5

Highlights

✳ Abbaye du Thoronet An exquisite rose-coloured monastic complex, and the oldest of Provence's three great Cistercian monasteries. **See p.249**

✳ Grand Canyon du Verdon Walk, drive, cycle, raft or bungee, but whatever you do, don't miss Europe's largest and most spectacular gorge. **See p.259**

✳ Musée de Préhistoire des Gorges du Verdon Gain an insight into 400,000 years of human habitation in Provence, and visit the cave of Baume Bonne, at this modern Norman Foster-designed museum. **See p.265**

✳ Réserve Naturelle Géologique de Haute Provence Check out the 185-million-year-old fossils in Europe's largest protected geological area. **See p.271**

✳ Entrevaux and Colmars These picturesque towns both retain beautifully preserved fortifications designed by Vauban. **See p.276 and p.285**

✳ The Clues of Haute Provence A hidden landscape of rocky gorges, tiny villages and rural tranquillity, a mere 40km from the Riviera. **See pp.278–280**

✳ Parc National du Mercantour An unspoilt alpine wilderness that is home to the Vallée des Merveilles and its mysterious four-thousand-year-old rock carvings. **See p.282**

✳ Skiing in the Alpes-Maritimes Slide down the mountain in the resorts of Auron and Allos, open from late December to mid-April. **See p.289 and p.284**

△ Grand Canyon du Verdon

The Haut Var and Haute Provence

Stretching from the **Chaîne de la Ste-Baume** up to the **Alpes-de-Haute-Provence**, the unspoilt geographical heartland of Provence is characterised by deep valleys and snowcapped mountains in the north, the source of the rivers **Var, Bléone, Tinée, Vésubie** and **Verdon**, flowing down to the gentle undulating fields of vines, lavender, sunflowers and poppies in the south. Small towns and villages such as **Aups**, **Riez**, **Cotignac**, **Forcalquier** and **Simiane-la-Rotonde** still thrive on their traditional industries of making honey, tending sheep, digging for truffles and pressing olive oil; and in isolated places like **Banon** and the hamlets around **Sisteron**, it's hard to believe this is the same country, never mind province, as the Côte d'Azur.

True, foreigners have bought second homes in the idyllic **Haut Var villages**, but the tidal wave of new-house building does not yet extend north of the Autoroute Provençale (A8). Nor has the Marseille-Gap highway, which follows the **River Durance**, encouraged major industrialization, aside from an industrial park north of Sisteron. Prices here remain much lower than on the coast or in western Provence.

Landscapes are exceptional, from the gentle countryside of the Haut Var or Pays de Forcalquier to the rolling plains and wide horizons of the **Plateau de Valensole** and the high harshness of the **Montagne de Lure**; the wild emptiness of the **Plateau de Canjuers**, the untrammelled forests east of Draguignan and, most spectacularly of all, Europe's largest ravine, the **Grand Canyon du Verdon**.

Food is fundamentally Provençal: lamb from the high summer pastures, goats' cheese, honey, almonds, olives and wild herbs. The soil is poor and water scarce, but the Côtes de Provence **wine** *appellation* extends to the Upper Var.

The towns, like busy but workaday **Draguignan**, are not the prime appeal. First and foremost, this is an area for **walking** and **climbing**, or **canoeing** and **windsurfing** on the countless dammed lakes that provide power and irrigation. The Grand Canyon du Verdon is a must, even if only seen from a car or bus. The best way of discovering the area, however, is just to stay in a village that takes your fancy, eating, dawdling and letting yourself drift into the rhythms of local life.

The mountainous northeastern corner of Provence, Haute Provence, is a different world from season to season. In **spring** the fruit trees in the narrow

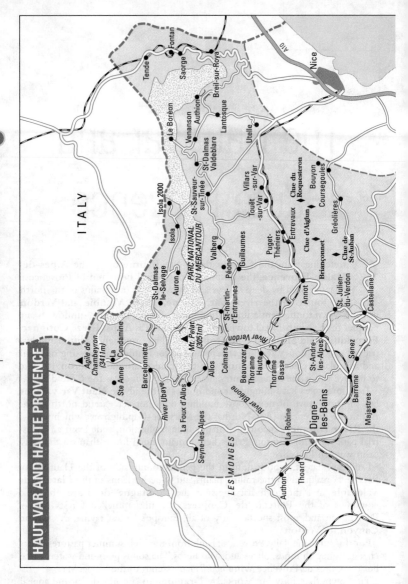

HAUT VAR AND HAUTE PROVENCE

valleys blossom, and melting waters swell the Verdon, the Vésubie, the Var, the Tinée and the Roya, sometimes flooding villages and carrying whole streets away. In the foothills, the groves of chestnut and olive trees bear fruit in **summer** and **autumn**, while higher up the pine forests are edged with wild raspberries and bilberries, and the moors and grassy slopes with white and gold alpine flowers. Above the line where vegetation ceases there are rocks with eagles' nests and snowcaps that never melt.

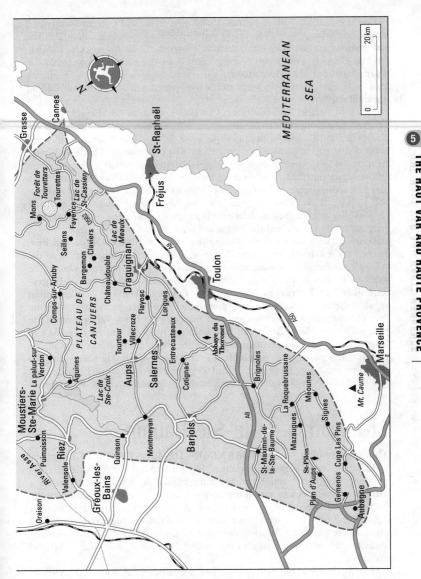

In **winter** the sheep and shepherds retreat to warmer pastures, leaving the snowy heights to antlered mouflons and chamois, and the perfectly camouflaged ermine. The villages, where the shepherds came to summer markets, are battened down for the long cold haul, while modern conglomerations of Swiss-style chalet houses, sports shops and discotheques come to life around the ski lifts. From November to April many of the mountain passes are closed, cutting off the dreamy northern town of **Barçelonnette** from its lower neighbours.

This is not an easy place to live. Abandoned farms and overgrown terraced slopes bear witness to the declining viability of mountain agriculture. But the **ski resorts** bring in money and summer brings the dedicated trekkers, naturalists and climbers. One area, covering 75km from east to west, protected as the **Parc National du Mercantour**, has no permanent inhabitants at all. It's crossed by numerous paths, with refuge huts providing basic food and bedding for trekkers.

For centuries the border between Provence and Savoy ran through this part of France, a political divide embodied by the impressive fortifications of Entrevaux and **Colmars**, the principal town of the Haut Verdon. To this day, most of the region is not considered to be part of Provence. The French refer to it by the geographical term, the **Alpes-Maritimes**, which is also the name of the *département* that stretches from between the Haut Var and Verdon valleys and just above the source of the Tinée Valley to the Italian border, and includes the Riviera. Where Provence ends and the Alps begin is debatable, with the Tinée Valley usually cited as definitely belonging to the latter – the mountains here are pretty serious and the Italian influence becomes noticeable.

Running along the southern limit of the Alps is the **Nice–Digne rail line**, known as the Chemin de Fer de Provence, the only remaining segment of the region's nineteenth- and twentieth-century narrow-gauge network. One of the great train rides of the country, it takes in the isolated Var towns of **Puget-Théniers** and **Entrevaux**, and ends at **Digne**, a low-key but intriguing regional capital that serves as the centre of the lavender industry. Away from the Nice–Digne line, transport is a problem except in the **Roya Valley**, over in the east, where the **Nice–Turin rail line** links the Italianate towns of **Tende** and **Sospel**. Buses are infrequent and many of the best starting points for walks or the far-flung pilgrimage chapels are off the main roads. If you have your own transport, you'll face tough climbs and long stretches with no fuel supplies, but you'll be free to explore the most exhilaratingly beautiful corner of Provence.

St-Maximin-de-la-Ste-Baume

The attractive old town of **ST-MAXIMIN-DE-LA-STE-BAUME** is where, in 1279, the count of Provence claimed to have found the crypt with the relics of Mary Magdalene and Saint Maximin hidden by local people during a Saracen raid. The count started the construction of a basilica and **monastery** on place de l'Hôtel-de-Ville, which took their present shape in the fifteenth century, and have since seen lavish decoration of stone, wood, gold, silk and oil paint added, particularly during the reign of Louis XIV, one of many French kings to make the pilgrimage to the nearby Ste-Baume *grotte* (see p.244) and the crypt.

There is, therefore, plenty to look at in the **basilica** (daily 8am–6pm), with its beautifully detailed wood panelling in the choir and the paintings on the nave walls, as well as Ronzen's lovely *Retable de la Passion* (1520), with its eighteen scenes from the Passion. Also look out for the wonderfully sculptured fourth-century sarcophagi and the grotesque skull once venerated as that of Mary Magdalene, encased in a glass helmet framed by a gold neck and hair, in the **crypt**. The building itself is a substantial Gothic affair, unusual for Provence, but the thirteenth-century **cloisters** and chapterhouse of the monastery (access through the *Couvent Royal* on av de la Libération; free) are much more delicate. Look down the well to see the escape route that the Dominican friars used on several occasions in the sixteenth century when the monastery was placed under siege. Today, the monastery is the setting for classical concerts (call ☎04.94.59.84.59 for details).

To the south of the church a covered passageway leads into the beautiful arcaded rue Colbert, a **former Jewish ghetto**. All the medieval streets of St-Maximin, with their uniform tiled roofs at anything but uniform heights, have considerable charm, and there's a reasonable choice of restaurants, and shops selling the work of local artisans.

Practicalities

The **tourist office** is in the Hôtel de Ville next to the basilica (daily 9am–12.30pm & 2–6pm; ☎04.94.59.84.59; ⑩www.ville-stmaximin.com). If you walk west from the basilica along rue Général-de-Gaulle, the well-run, friendly **hotel**, *Plaisance*, at 20 place Malherbe (☎04.94.78.16.74, ⓕ04.94.78.18.39; ❹), is a grand town house with spacious rooms, while the newly expanded ⚓ *Couvent Royal* on place Jean-Salusse (☎04.94.86.55.66, ⑩www.hotelfp-saintmaximin.com; ❺) is a particularly atmospheric option, with clean, excellent-value rooms, some looking out over the cloister itself. The local three-star **campsite**, *Provençal* (☎04.94.78.16.97; €15 per tent), is 3km out along the chemin de Mazaugues, the road to Marseille. **Cafés** and **brasseries** congregate on place Malherbe, the present-day hub of St-Maximin, but for a more formal meal, the restaurant in the former chapterhouse at the *Couvent Royal* has an elegant ambience, with menus from €26 (closed Sun eve, Mon & Tues). There's also a *Maison des Vins de Pays du Var* within the *Couvent* complex, if you'd like to taste the local **wines**.

The Chaîne de la Ste-Baume

Marseille's suburbs extend relentlessly east along the highway and N8 corridor north of the Chaîne de St-Cyr. The range to the east is the **Chaîne de la Ste-Baume**, a sparsely populated region of rich forests and one of the most unspoilt areas in the district. Once you're up on the plateau to the north, it's a wonderful territory for walking and bike riding with a profusion of woods, flowers and wildlife on the northern face, which is rare in these hot latitudes. All of the area north to St-Maximin, south to **Signes**, west to **Gémenos** and east to **La Roquebrussanne** is protected. You are not allowed to camp in the woods or light fires, and a still extant royal edict forbids the picking of orchids.

For details of the numerous **footpaths**, including the GR9, GR98 and GR99, the best guide is Josianne Alor-Trebootte and Alexis Lucchesi's *Rando-Sainte Baume à pied et à VTT*, one of Edisud's series of French-only walking and cycling guides (⑩www.edisud.com; €13).

Gémenos to Plan-d'Aups

GÉMENOS, 3km east of Aubagne, has a beautiful seventeenth-century château as its Hôtel de Ville and is a tempting place to stop. The area around the château has several **cafés**, **bars** and good **pâtisseries**, in particular the *Pain Doré* on place Georges-Clémenceau, and the **restaurant** *Le Fer à Cheval* on place de la Mairie (☎04.42.32.20.97), with menus from around €15. For **accommodation**, there's a wonderful luxury hotel, the *Relais de la Magdeleine* (☎04.42.32.20.16, ⑩www.relais-magdeleine.com; lunch menu €30, otherwise €42 & €55; ❼; closed Dec to mid-March), set in a lovely, vine-covered eighteenth-century manor house in a park designed by Le Nôtre; it lies just off the Rond Point de la Fontaine on the N396 route d'Aix on the way out of town. Two minutes' walk further along the N396 is a less expensive option, the friendly *Le Provence* (☎04.42.32.20.55, ⊕www.hotel-leprovence-gemenos.com; ❶), which also has family rooms for up to four people.

From Gémenos the D2 follows the narrow valley of St-Pons, past an open-air municipal theatre cut into the rock and the **Parc Naturel de St-Pons** with beech, hornbean, ash and maple trees around the ruins of a thirteenth-century Cistercian abbey, before beginning the zigzagging ascent to the Espigoulier pass. A footpath beyond the park soon links to the GR98, which climbs directly up the Ste-Baume and then follows the ridge with breathtaking views.

At **PLAN-D'AUPS** the dramatic climb levels out to a forested plateau running parallel to the ridge of Ste-Baume, which cuts across the sky like a massively fortified wall. A comfortable small **hotel**, *Lou Pèbre d'Aï*, in the quartier Ste-Madeleine (☎04.42.04.50.42, ⊕www.loupebredai.com; menus from €25; ❸), offers one of the very few **restaurants** in this scattered settlement. There's a tiny Romanesque church and a **tourist office** next to the *mairie* (Mon, Tues, Thurs & Fri 9.15–11.45am & 4–5.30pm; Wed & Sat 9.15–11.45am; ☎04.42.62.57.57).

Four kilometres on from Plan-d'Aups is the starting point for a **pilgrimage** based on Provençal mythology, or simply a walk up to the peaks. The myth takes over from the sea-voyage arrival in Stes-Maries-de-la-Mer of Mary Magdalene, Mary Salomé, Mary Jacobé and St-Maximin (see p.129). **Mary Magdalene**, for some unexplained reason completely at odds with the mission of spreading the gospel, gets transported by angels to a cave just below the summit of Ste-Baume. There she spends 33 years, with occasional angel-powered outings up to the summit, before being flown to St-Maximin-de-la-Ste-Baume (see p.242) to die.

The difficult **paths** up from the *Hôtellerie*, a roadside pilgrimage centre run by Dominican friars and open for prayers, information, food and accommodation (☎04.42.04.54.84; ❶), are dotted with oratories, calvaries and crosses, before reaching the fabled *grotte*, where mass is held daily at 10.30am. The *grotte* is suitably sombre, while the path beyond to the **St-Pilon summit** makes you wish for some of Mary's winged pilots. For further information enquire at the *Hôtellerie* or at the **Écomusée de la Sainte Baume** opposite (daily mid-April to Oct 9am–noon & 2–6pm; Nov to mid-April 2–5pm; €3), which has exhibitions on the cultural and natural heritage of the Ste-Baume and organizes seasonal events.

East to La Roquebrussanne

The road east from Plan-d'Aups crosses the range through miles of unspoiled forest. The groves of spindly, stunted oaks and beeches have exerted a mystical pull since ancient times, and it is believed they were once a sacred Druidical forest. Around the village of **MAZAUGUES**, just before you reach La Roquebrussanne, you pass huge, nineteenth-century covered stone wells, built to hold ice which could then be transported on early summer nights down to Marseille or Toulon; an industry which once gave livelihoods to many an inhabitant of the Ste-Baume. There's a small **tourist office** (Sat & Sun 9am-noon & 2-5pm) while next door, surrounded by lavender bushes teaming with butterflies, is the **Musée de la Glace** (June-Sept Tues-Sun 9am-noon & 2-6pm, Oct-May Sun only 9am-noon & 2-5pm; €2.30), which traces the history of ice-making in Provence and worldwide. From Mazaugues the GR99 takes you, after an initial steep climb, on a gentle three- to four-hour walk down to Signes (it also links halfway with the GR98 from Ste-Baume); while continuing east by road will bring you to **LA ROQUEBRUSSANNE**, and its **gliding-school**, Fly Azur, in quartier Le Riolet (☎04.94.86.97.52, ⓦwww.flyazur.com). The village itself is attractive, with a large Saturday food **market** and a pleasant **hotel**, *La Loube* (☎04.94.86.81.36, ⓕ04.94.86.86.79; ❹; menus from €26).

Méounes-les-Montrieux and Signes

Continuing south on the D5 you pass through **MÉOUNES-LES-MONTRIEUX**, a tiny village with an astonishing eleven fountains, a couple of **hotels**, including the small, welcoming *Hôtel de France* on place de L'Église (☎04.94.33.95.92; closed mid-Oct to Feb, ❸), and a Sunday market. There are also two **campsites**, of which the best equipped is *Camping Blue Garden* (☎04.94.48.95.34, ⓦwww.chateau-gavaudan.com; €23 per tent), 1.5km from the village at the Château de Gavaudan.

From Méounes you can follow the lovely Gapeau stream west, which has its source just before **SIGNES**. This is yet another appealing little village, a place where palm trees and white roses grow around the war memorial, where the clock tower is more than 400 years old, and where the people make their living from wine, olives, cereals and market gardening, or, in the case of two small enterprises, biscuits and nougat. At Lou Goustetto on the main road as you leave the village westwards, you can sample biscuits in a multitude of natural flavours that include Provençal herbs and nuts, lemon, cinnamon, cocoa and honey. They are hard and unsweetened and excellent to munch as you climb the Ste-Baume. The edible treat comes from Nougat Fouque, 2 rue Louis-Lumière, whose seasonal black or white nougat provides a honey overdose that manages not to stick to your teeth (Oct–Dec only).

The village has a Thursday **market** on place Marcel-Pagnol, and a *médiathèque* which provides **tourist information** on rue Frédéric-Mistral (Wed–Sat 10am–noon & 2–6.30pm; ☎04.94.98.87.80; ⓦwww.signes.com), which has details of local **gîtes d'étape**. Alternatively, the Garcia family's wonderful **chambres d'hôtes** at the *Chateau de Cancerilles* is an old stone farm surrounded by vines on the route de Belgentier, (☎04.94.90.81.45; ⓦwww.chateaudecancerilles. com; ❻). Rue Bourgade has a couple of places to **eat**, *La Marmite de Mathilde* (☎04.94.90.83.21) and *Pizzeria Chez Pat* (☎04.94.90.82.11).

Brignoles

BRIGNOLES, 18km east of St-Maximin, is a good base for a night or two's stay. For years the town made a living from mining bauxite for the aluminium works in Marseille and Gardanne. The mine closed in 1969, and today Brignoles is ringed with modern commercial zones much like those of any other sizeable French town and, to the north of the Vieille Ville, suffers from lorries thundering through on the N7. But there's plenty of life in its centre, with piped music in the main shopping streets adding a surreal touch to the recently gentrified, warren-like medieval quarter full of quiet, shaded squares and old facades with faded painted adverts and flowering window boxes.

At the southern end of the old quarter is a thirteenth-century summer residence of the counts of Provence, now adapted as the **Musée du Pays Brignolais** (April–Sept Wed–Sat 9am–noon & 2.30–6pm, Sun 9am–noon & 3–6pm; Oct–March Wed–Sat 10am–noon & 2.30–5pm, Sun 10am–noon & 3–5pm; €4). This fascinating, old-style museum dips into every aspect of local life that the town is proud of: from one of the oldest palaeo-Christian sarcophagi ever found to a reinforced concrete boat made by the inventor of concrete in 1840. There's a statue of a saint whose navel has been visibly deepened by the hopeful hands of infertile women, a reconstruction of a bauxite mine, a crèche of *santons*, a fine collection of *ex voto* paintings, some Impressionist Provençal landscapes by Frédéric Montenard and the chapel of the palace, cluttered with ancient religious statuary from around the area. Climb the tower for the best view of the town and its surroundings. Next door to the main museum is the **Office de la Culture**, an elegantly converted space hosting contemporary art shows (Mon–Fri 10am–noon & 3–6pm, Sun 3–6pm; free).

Rue des Lanciers, with fine old houses where the rich Brignolais used to live, leads up from place des Comtes-de-Provence to **St-Sauveur**, a twelfth-century church in which, on the left-hand side, you can see the remains of an older church. Behind St-Sauveur the stepped street of rue Saint-Esprit runs down to rue Cavaillon and place Carami, the café-lined central square of the modern town.

Practicalities

Buses stop at place St-Louis. The excellent modern **tourist office** (Mon–Fri 9.30am–noon & 2–5.30pm; ℡04.94.72.04.21, ⓦwww.la-provence-verte.net) is on the north side of the River Carami by the carrefour de l'Europe roundabout. The only **hotel** in the centre of Brignoles is *Le Provence*, on place du Palais de Justice (℡04.94.69.01.18; ❸), a better option than the *Formule I* in the Ratan industrial quarter (℡04.94.69.45.05; ❶) and the *Ibis* on chemin du Val, north of the town centre (℡04.94.69.19.29; ❹), is the **Chambres d'hôtes** *La Bastide de Messine* 2km north west on chemin de Cante Perdrix (℡04.94.72.09.06, ⓦwww.bastide-messine.com; ❺), a renovated old farm with a pool run by Nelly and Bruno. The two-star municipal **campsite** is 1km down the route de Nice (℡ & ℻04.94.69.20.10; €12.50 per tent; closed mid-Oct to mid-March).

There's also a profusion of places to **eat** and **drink**, none of them very expensive. On place Carami, you can get meals or snacks at *Le Central* bar-brasserie (plats du jour from €8.20) and the *Café de l'Univers* - being refurbished at the time of writing. *Le Pourquoi Pas* on rue Cavaillon (℡04.94.69.00.76; closed lunchtimes & Mon) serves couscous, steaks and *moules frites* from around €10, while *La Gousse d'Ail*, at 7 rue Louis-Maître (℡04.94.59.28.92; menu at €14), offers good value Provençal dishes. In the heart of the Vieille Ville, *Les Romarins*, at 5 rue St-Esprit (℡04.94.59.20.99; closed lunchtimes & Wed), serves pizzas from €8 and grills, while *Lou Crespeu*, across the bridge from the **tourist office** at 56 rue Barbaroux (closed Sun & Mon lunch; ℡04.94.69.33.43), makes delicious, inexpensive crêpes from €2 – try the buckwheat *galettes de sarrasin* with any of the fillings.

The Haut Var

Brignoles administrative influence reaches northwards to the rocky Haut Var and the picturesque medieval villages of **Cotignac** and **Entrecasteaux** while the neighbouring villages of **Flayosc** and **Lorgues** are closer to the garrison town of **Draguignan** in the east. Further north, the **Argens Valley** to the **Verdon Gorge**, is the true heart of Provence, with soft enveloping countryside of woods, vines, lakes and waterfalls, streaked with rocky ridges before the high

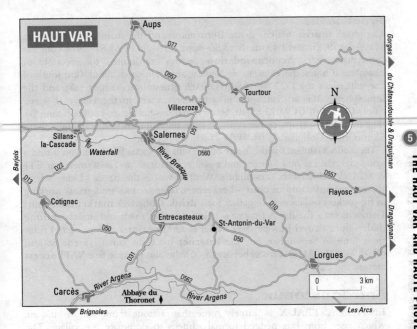

plateaux and mountains. To the outsider, the picturesque villages merge together; to know them properly you'd have to live here for winter after winter, limiting your world to just a few square miles. For, despite the proliferation of *résidences secondaires*, they hold on to their identity, however guarded it is from the casual eyes of visitors. The region is also home to the **Abbaye du Thoronet**, the oldest of Provence's three surviving Cistercian monasteries.

Cotignac

North of Brignoles, along the quiet D22, is **COTIGNAC**, the most beautiful of all the Haut Var villages and one of the most upmarket. From its utterly photogenic place de la Mairie, rue de l'Horloge leads under the clock tower and up to the church; from here, a path takes you to the foot of the eighty-metre cliff that forms the village's back wall, a troglodyte mass of passages and odd little structures. At the summit stand two ruined towers of a long-abandoned castle, between which the rock is riddled with caves and subterranean passages of white rock and stalactite formations. You can ascend the nerve-racking cliff pathway from Easter to mid-October (€2).

Centre stage in the history of Cotignac are the now defunct tanning works, once a major industry of the Haut Var, and the miraculous Virgin in the **Chapelle de Notre-Dame-des-Grâces**, on the summit across the valley to the south. Long venerated as a saviour from the plague, this Virgin finally hit the big time in 1638 when Louis XIII and Anne of Austria – married for 22 childless years – made their supplications to her. Nine months after the royal visit, the future Sun King let out his first demanding squall.

If you want to sample some of Cotignac's local produce, head for Les Ruchers du Bessillon, on rue Victoire, which sells an exceptional variety of **honey**, and the Vignerons de Cotignac, 100m out of town on the Salernes road (D13), for **wine**.

Cotignac's **tourist office,** 2 rue Bonaventure, off the main cours Gambetta (Tues–Sat 9.45am–12.45pm & 3.30–6pm; ☎04.94.04.61.87, ⓦot-cotignac .provenceverte.fr). **Accommodation** options are limited to a couple of chambres d'hôtes: the *Domaine de Nestuby*, amid vineyards about 4km south of the village on the D22 (☎04.94.04.60.02, ⓔnestuby@orange.fr; ❹), and the atmospheric *Maison Gonzagues*, in a former tannery in the village at 9 rue Lúon-Gúrard (☎04.94.72.85.40, ⓦwww.maison-gonzagues-cotignac.com; ❻). The municipal **campsite** *Les Pouverels* is on the Aups road on your right about 3km outside Cotignac (☎04.94.04.71.91; €9 per tent).

The cours Gambetta is the heart of the village's social life: here, you'll find a good pizzeria, *Les Trois Marches,* and a posher restaurant, *du Cours* (menus at €11 & €28, closed Jan–Feb, Tues night & Wed), as well as the *Bar de l'Union,* where the community's various clans – beekeepers, *vignerons* and immigrants working as fig-packers or labourers – gather for a **drink**. Cotignac's **market** is on cours Gambetta on a Tuesday. A *brocante* is held four times a year and attracts **antique** dealers from all over Europe; the earthier *marché paysane* takes place every Friday from June to September. For the **Internet** try Cyberia.net, 18 rue St-Jean (☎04.94.80.09.31, ⓦwww.cyberianet.net) who also provide free **WiFi access** around the café.

Entrecasteaux

ENTRECASTEAUX is scarcely more than a stone frame for its château, which rises from box-hedged formal gardens to dominate the village. The château owes its current condition to a Scottish painter, Ian McGarvie-Munn (1919–81), who trained as a naval architect after World War II and later became the head of the National Workshops for Applied Arts in Colombia. Soon after his wife's father became president of Guatemala, McGarvie-Munn took over as head of the Guatemalan navy, following that with a stint as the country's ambassador to London. In 1974, by now retired, he bought the ruined shell of Entrecasteaux's seventeenth-century château, and spent the rest of his life and wealth on the massive restoration job. His family continued the work after his death, but sold up in 1995. The château is still privately owned.

You can visit the **château** (Easter–Nov daily except Sat, guided visits at 4pm; Dec–Easter, groups only by appointment; ☎04.94.04.43.95; €7), and the publicly owned **Le Nôtre** gardens (dawn–dusk; free), which separate it from the village. Its interior is spacious, light and charmingly rustic, typified by the terracotta tiles, a style that was all the rage when the Count and Countess of Grignan used the château as their summer residence; the opulence of the countess's bedroom, however, gives some idea of the status of the one-time inhabitants. Exhibitions on the first floor relate to later occupants, including Raymond Bruny, who charted part of the coast of western Australia and Tasmania, and photos of the sorry state in which McGarvie-Munn first found the château.

Practicalities

New **chambres d'hotes** are popping up every year. The terracotta *Bastide Notre Dame* (☎04.94.04.45.63, ⓦbastidenotredame.free.fr; ❺) started by Marie-Thé and Thierry has pretty rooms and a shaded garden just west of the village in Adrech de Sainte Anne, while the welcoming **hotel-restaurant** *Lou Cigaloun* in St-Antonin-du-Var, Entrecasteaux's even smaller neighbour to the east (☎04.94.04.42.67, Ⓕ04.94.04.48.19; closed Nov–Feb; ❹), is also a good bet; its restaurant (closed Wed; menu from €17–35) offers simple but fine cooking. Decent food can also be found in Entrecasteaux at *La Forchette*, up beyond the château entrance (☎04.94.04.42.78; menus from €18 to €26; closed all day Mon, Tue & Sun eve out of season). For a **snack**, head to *la Crêperie â l'Atelier* on le Collet.

The Abbaye du Thoronet

Sixteen kilometres south of Entrecasteaux, via Carcés, deep in the forest of La Daboussière, is one of Provence's three great Cistercian monasteries, the austere, rose-coloured **Abbaye du Thoronet** (April–Sept Mon–Sat 9am–7pm, Sun 10am–noon & 2–7pm; Oct–March 10am–1pm & 2–5pm, Sun 10am–noon & 2–5pm; €6.50). Like Silvacane and Sénanque (see p.206 & p.231), it was founded in the first half of the twelfth century, but Thoronet is the oldest of the three and the one that was completed in the shortest time, giving it an aesthetic coherence that transcends its relatively modest size. Finally abandoned in 1791, it was kept intact during the Revolutionary era as an historic monument. Restoration started in the 1850s, and a more recent campaign has brought it to graceful, melancholy perfection. The *abbaye* is off the D79, between the hamlet of Le Thoronet and Cabasse; there are no buses, so you'll need your own transport to get there.

Flayosc and Lorgues

Fifteen kilometres east of the Abbaye, across the River Argens, is **LORGUES** and a little further north, **FLAYOSC**, both of which make excellent stops for **food**. *L'Oustaou* on place Brémond, the main square of Flayosc (☎04.94.70.42.69; menus from €34; closed all day Mon, plus Thurs & Sun eves), serves delicious local specialities accompanied by a rare genuine Provençal atmosphere. *Chez Bruno*, on route de Vidauban in Lorgues (☎04.94.85.93.93, ⓦwww.restaurantbruno.com; menus at €59 and €120; closed all day Mon plus Sun eve out of season), is considerably more expensive, but if you're prepared to pay the extra money, you can try wonderful wild local ingredients in a chestnut and *chanterelle* soup and in the truffle and game dishes, followed by *crème brûlée* with figs in wine. The restaurant also has a few rooms attached (❺), but it's worth pointing out that the chef, M Bruno, is one of France's celebrity chefs and may well be away cooking dinners for presidents, royalty or other distinguished diners.

Salernes and Sillans

Compared with Cotignac, **SALERNES**, 13km northeast, is quite a metropolis, with a thriving tile-making industry and enough near-level irrigated land for productive agriculture. Sunday and Wednesday are the best days to visit the **market** beneath the ubiquitous plane trees on the *cours*. There are also twenty or so **pottery and tile workshops**, selling a mix of designs you'd find in any home improvement shop as well as items with more local flair. In the nineteenth century the workshops churned out the hexagonal terracotta floor tiles that have been reproduced in various synthetic materials ever since. You'll find shops in the centre of the town and larger *ateliers-magasins* on the outskirts: Maurice Emphoux, Jacques Polidori and Pierre Boutal on the road to Draguignan; Alain Vagh on the road to Entrecasteaux; and Ateliers de la Baume 4km east on the D560. Remember, if you do want to take home some originals, these are artisans' artefacts and are priced accordingly.

Salernes' **tourist office** is on place Gabriel-Péri (July–Aug Mon–Sat 9am–7pm; Sept–June Tues–Sat 9.30am–12.30pm & 2–6pm ℡04.94.70.69.02, ⓦwww.ville-salernes.fr). For somewhere **to stay**, there's a fourteenth-century farmhouse, *La Bastide Rose*, across the River Bresque towards La Colle Riforan (℡04.94.70.63.30, ⓦwww.bastide-rose.com; ❹), and a four-star campsite, *Les Arnauds*, just outside the town on the Sillans road (℡04.94.67.51.95, ⓦwww.village-vacances-lesarnauds.com; €22.55 per tent; closed Oct–April). **Places to eat** in Salernes include *Tout en Passent Chez Giles* 20 rue Victor-Hugo (℡04.94.70.72.80), with menus between €15 and €30, and *La Cuillère*, on rue Pierre-Blanc (closed Mon), with decent pizzas from €9. There's a range of cafés on the *cours* serving light meals and snacks, and a **bar** with a good selection of beers opposite the tourist office.

Located six kilometres west of Salernes, tiny **SILLANS** is not in itself overtly picturesque, but its **waterfall** is stunning, gushing down into a turquoise pool that makes for a brilliant swim. It's signed down a delightful path from the main road (a 20min walk from the car park). If you want to **stay** in Sillans, there's *Les Pins* hotel-restaurant (℡04.94.04.63.26, ℻04.94.04.72.71; menus €16–34; ❷), or the three-star **campsite**, *Le Relais de la Bresque* (℡04.94.04.64.89, ⓦwww.lerelaisdelabresque.com), 1km out along the road to Aups.

Villecroze

Five kilometres northeast of Salernes, **VILLECROZE**, like Cotignac, sits beneath a water-burrowed cliff, whose intriguing grottoes can be visited in summer (daily 10am–noon & 2.30–7pm; €2). The gardens around the base are delightfully un-Gallic and the same lack of formality extends throughout the town. It's an appealing place, with lovely vaulted arcades down rue des Arcades and rue de France, and a Romanesque church with a wall of bells.

Aside from its attractiveness, Villecroze is of interest as home to the early radical ecologist, Jean Pain, who in the 1970s ran his heating, lighting and 2CV on compost made from the undergrowth of the surrounding woods, material otherwise destroyed to avoid the risk of fire. Pain's compost gave back nutrients to the forest soil and agricultural land of this harsh terrain, and his methods of generating power from compost have been taken up as far afield as Canada, California and Senegal.

If Villecroze tempts you to **stay**, one of the best deals in the region can be found at the seven-roomed *Auberge des Lavandes* on place du Général-de-Gaulle (℡04.94.70.76.00, ℻04.94.67.56.45; closed Jan & Feb; ❸). Failing that, the secluded and very comfortable *Au Bien Être*, in quartier Les Cadenières, 3.5km south along the D557 (℡04.94.70.67.57; ⓦwww.aubienetre.com; ❹), is also a good bet. **Campsites** include *Les Cadenières* (℡04.94.67.59.66, ⓦwww.camping-les-cadenieres.com; €25 for two people and a tent; closed Nov–March) on the D560 towards Flayosc. For food, the **restaurant** at the *Au Bien Être* has menus at €26 and €36 (out of season closed all day Mon, Tues & Wed lunchtimes), while the well-reputed *Le Colombier* on route de Draguignan (℡04.94.70.63.23, ⓦwww.lecolombier-var.com; menus from €27; closed Mon, plus Sun eve out of season), has a truffle menu from December to March, and a few rooms (❺).

Tourtour

TOURTOUR sits 300m higher than Villecroze, atop a ridge from where the view extends to the massifs of Maures, Ste-Baume and Ste-Victoire. The village has a seemingly organic unity, soft-coloured stone growing into stairways and curving streets, branching to form arches, fountains and towers. The ruin of an old mill looks as if it has always been like this; the elephant-leg towers of the sixteenth-century bastion stand around the *mairie* and the post office as if of their own volition, while the twelfth-century **Tour du Grimaldi** might have erupted spontaneously from the ground. The two elms on the main square, planted when Anne of Austria and Louis XIII visited Cotignac, are almost as enormous as the bastion towers, but are beginning to show signs of decrepitude.

Having said this, Tourtour is all a bit unreal, full of *résidences secondaires* and *salons de thé* selling expensive fruit-juice cocktails. It also has the region's most upmarket **hotel-restaurant**, the *Bastide de Tourtour* (℡04.98.10.54.20, ⓦwww.verdon.net/tourtour; menus from €27.50; ⓨ), specializing in classic local cuisine, and with Jacuzzis, tennis courts and a gym to accompany the lavish rooms.

Aups

For those with their own transport, the village of **AUPS**, 10km north of Salernes, makes an ideal base for visiting the villages of the Haut Var or the Grand Canyon du Verdon. Though only 500m or so above sea level, it was considered by the ancients to be the beginning of the Alps; the Romans called it Alpibus which became Alps then Aups. The chief town of one of the Ligurian tribes and the location for a Roman army hospital, it then thrived in the Middle Ages, and by the eighteenth century its prosperity was inducing delusions of grandeur in the local abbot. Having mathematically proved Aups to be at the centre of Europe, he drew a map of the continent on the tiles of his house to illustrate the fact. He also erected a column in his garden inscribed with the scientific knowledge of his day and was responsible for one of the seven sundials that decorate the village.

Arrival, information and accommodation

Coming from Sillans, Salernes or Villecroze, you enter Aups along avenue Georges-Clemenceau ending up at place Frédéric-Mistral and place Martin-Bidouré. The very helpful **tourist office** is to your left in the former town hall (Mon–Sat April–June & Sept 9am–noon & 2.30–5.30pm; July–Aug 9am–12.30pm & 3–6.30pm; Oct–May 9.30am–noon & 2–5.30pm; ℡04.94.84.00.69, ⓦmembres.lycos.fr/otsiaups/), and has details of local walks. The Vieille Ville is in front of you with the church to the right.

The **hotels** in Aups itself are good value: the basic but pretty *Grand Hôtel* on place Duchâtel (℡04.94.70.10.82, ⓦwww.grand-hotel-aups.com; closed Feb–March, ❸) is a good example. Outside town, about 3km along the road to Moustiers-Ste-Marie, *Bastide de l'Estré* (℡04.94.84.00.45, ⓦwww.estre.com; ❹) provides bed and breakfast accommodation, a gîte to rent, and a camping barn for walkers and cyclists, in an attractive rural location. For more luxury, try *La Bastide du Calalou* in the village of Moissac-Bellevue, 5km from Aups on the D9 (℡04.94.70.17.91, ⓦwww.bastide-du-calalou.com; closed mid-Nov to March; ❼). There are two **campsites** close to town: the two-star *Camping Les Prés*, to the right off allée Charles-Boyer towards Tourtour (℡04.94.70.00.93; €12 per tent); and the three-star *Saint Lazare*, 2km along the Moissac road (℡04.94.70.12.86; €12 per tent; closed Oct–March), which has a pool. The big three-star *International Camping* (℡04.94.70.06.80; €17.20 per tent; closed Oct–March) is 500m out of town, on the road to Fox-Amphoux.

The Town

On **place Martin-Bidouré** a monument commemorates a period of republican resistance all too rarely honoured in France. Its inscription reads: "To the memory of citizens who died in 1851 defending the Republic and its laws", the year being that of Louis Napoleon's coup d'état. Peasant and artisan defiance was strongest in Provence, and the defeat of the insurgents, who flew the red flag because the tricolour had been appropriated by the usurper, was followed by a massacre of men and women alike. At Aups, the badly wounded Martin Bidouré escaped, but was found soon afterwards being succoured by a peasant and shot dead on the spot.

This event might explain the strident "République Française, Liberté, Egalité, Fraternité" sign on the **Église St-Pancrace**, proclaiming the supremacy of state before religion – a common feature of French churches, though it's usually more discreet. The church was designed by an English architect five hundred years ago and has had its doors restored in the last ten years by two resident British carpenters. The Renaissance portal is in good shape, there are some altarpieces inside and the attractive nineteenth-century stained-glass windows have been cleaned and repaired.

Another plus for Aups is its **museum of modern art** – the Musée Simon Segal, in the former convent chapel on avenue Albert-1er (mid-June to mid-Sept 10am–noon & 4–7pm; €2.50). The best works are by the Russian-born painter Simon Segal, but there are interesting local scenes in the other paintings, such as the Roman bridge at Aiguines, now drowned beneath the artificial lake of Ste-Croix.

Unfortunately La Fabrique, the former abbot's house, is a private residence and can't be visited. But the old streets, the sixteenth-century clock tower with its campanile, and the Wednesday and Saturday morning **market** which fills place Martin-Bidouré, all make this a very appealing place to be. Aups has become more geared to tourism in recent years but its living still comes from agriculture and there's fresh local produce on sale in the shops. Along with honey, the Aups speciality is truffles, and if you're here on a Thursday between November and the end of February you'll witness the **truffle market**. The local lamb has a gourmet reputation: marinaded and roasted with thyme is the traditional preparation. Other delicacies include small birds cooked with juniper berries; the gun shop in the main street explains the ready supply. For food shopping, Bernard Georges sells **honey** from his farm, Mas du Vieux Moulin, on rue de la Piscine east of place Martin-Bidouré; the Pâtisserie Brunet à la Claire Fontaine sells **nougat** and other local sweets; and, at 7 rue Maréchal-Foch, L'Herbier sells soaps, **liqueurs** and dried flowers. The best place for bread and cakes (olive oil *fougasses*, in particular) is the Boulangerie-Pâtisserie Canut on place du Marché, while the Domaine Valmoisine, on the avenue Albert-1er, is the place to go for **wine** *en vrac*.

Eating, drinking and entertainment

For **meals**, your first choice should be the hotel-restaurant *St-Marc* (☎04.94.70.06.08 ⓦwww.lesaintmarc.com; closed Tues, Wed & middle two weeks of June; ❷), a nineteenth-century mill on rue Aloisi. Serving local dishes, truffles and boar in season, it offers menus from €16 to €30. For snacks try the *boulangerie-pâtisserie* at 12 av Albert-1er (closed Dec–April) while the **bar** opposite the church is the place to sip *pastis*. The tourist office has details of the theatre, film and other **entertainment** that takes place in the Centre Culturel, on chemin des Prés.

Barjols

Fountains are the chief attraction of **BARJOLS**, 16km west of Cotignac; there are no fewer than 28 of the mossy water features dotted around the village. They are mostly concentrated in its older, eastern half, the **Quartier du Réal**: the **tourist office** on boulevard Grisolle, one block east of the broad place Rouguière (Mon–Sat 10am–noon & 2–6pm; ☎04.94.77.20.01, ⊛www.ville-barjols.fr), can provide a map to follow the circuit of fountains. The glum, rickety buildings of the town's now-defunct local tanning industry have been taken over by artists and craft workers; you can visit their studios (follow signs to Art-Artisanal) down the old road to Brignoles, east of the Vieille Ville. Looking back upwards from here at the industrial ruins is a good spooky night-time experience.

In January, a strange **festival** takes place which commemorates the miraculous arrival of an ox during a famine, but is in honour of the town's patron saint, St-Marcel: the cow gets killed and roasted to the accompaniment of flutes and tambourines and the refrain "Saint Marcel, Saint Marcel, the little tripe, the little tripe".

The **hotel-restaurant** *Le Pont d'Or* on route de St-Maximin (☎04.94.77.05.23, ⊛www.hotel-pontdor.com; closed mid-Nov to mid-Jan; ❸;) serves the best **food** in town with menus from €20-35. Nightlife, such as it is, centres around the bars and cafés in place Capitaine-Vincens and along avenue Eugène-Payan.

Draguignan and around

DRAGUIGNAN, in the southeast of the region and the main settlement of the inland Var, is a military town. Reminders of this are everywhere, from the monuments to the resistance and the Allied war cemetery on boulevard John Kennedy, to the barracks and artillery schools that use the beautiful, desolate **Plateau de Canjuers** to the north as a firing range. It's a bustling place, if not particularly exciting; one of the few truly urban spots in this region, with a lively **market** on Wednesdays and Saturdays in and around place du Marché, and a striking **theatre**, which combines 1970s modernism with a Neoclassical portico dating from 1838. The town also has a couple of worthwhile **museums**, of art and of social history. More practically, its boulevards and compact medieval centre have enough moderately priced hotels and restaurants to make it a viable touring base, especially out of season when much of the rest of the inland Var shuts down.

Arrival, information and accommodation

The **gare routière** and the redundant **gare SNCF**, from where shuttle buses connect with the main line at Les Arcs, are at the bottom of boulevard Gabriel-Péri, south of the town centre. At the top of the boulevard, turn left to find the modern **tourist office** at 2 bd Lazare Carnot (Sept-June Mon–Sat 9am–6pm; July & Aug Mon–Sat 9am–7pm & Sun 9am–1pm; ☎04.98.10.51.05, ⊛www.ot-draguignan.fr), which serves not just Draguignan but the surrounding *pays* as well.

For **hotels** a cheap cheerful option with a garden is *La Pergola* on avenue du 4 Septembre (☎04.94.19.18.54; ❸), just ten minutes' walk from the centre, or the *Hôtel du Parc*, 21 bd de Liberté (☎04.98.10.14.50, ⊛www.hotel-duparc.fr; ❹), which has rooms overlooking a courtyard. Slightly grander, *Le Victoria*, 52 bd Lazare-Carnot (☎04.94.47.24.12, ⊛www.hotelrestaurantvictoria.fr; ❹), is in a *belle époque* building close to the centre with a garden, though its decor is slightly staid. The two-star *La Foux* **campsite** is 2km along the road towards Les Arcs (℡04.94.68.18.27; closed Nov–March; €13.50 for two people and a tent).

The Town

Draguignan's compact old town is dominated by its distinctive seventeenth-century **Tour d'Horloge** (July & Aug guided tours only; free; contact tourist office for details), which stands next to the twelfth-century Chapelle Saint-Sauveur atop a small hill just north of place du Marché. Southwest of the market, the **Musée des Arts et Traditions Populaires de Moyenne Provence**, 15 rue Joseph-Roumanille (Tues–Sun 9am–noon & 2–6pm; €3.50), beautifully showcases the old industries of the Var. Nineteenth-century farming techniques and the manufacturing processes for silk, honey, cork, wine, olive oil and tiles are presented within the context of daily working lives – though some scenes are spoilt by rather dire wax models. There are early photographs of Var villages, many of them unaltered today, except for the loss of trees: the mulberry, on which the silk industry once depended, is now one of the region's rarest species.

On rue de la République, the **Musée Municipal** (Mon–Sat 9am–noon & 2–6pm; free) is housed in a former bishop's palace. Its highlights include a delicate marble sculpture by Camille Claudel; Greuze's *Portrait of a Young Girl*; two paintings of Venice by Ziem; a Renoir; and upstairs in the library, a copy of the *Romance of the Rose* and early Bibles and maps. *Child with a Soap Bubble* by Rembrandt was stolen from the museum in 1999, thieves broke down a back door on the eve of Bastille day; the police still have no leads.

Eating and drinking

There's a wide choice of inexpensive **places to eat** in the Vieille Ville and surrounding boulevards, though nothing really stands out. If you've come from the coast, however, you'll be relieved to be in **cafés** charging under €2 for a sit-down terrace coffee. A couple of good choices for a meal are the *Bar de Négociants* amidst the flower stalls on place du Marché, and the excellent *Les Mille Colonnes*, on place aux Herbes, with a decent *plats* around €16. If sugary things are your passion, seek out the De Neuville *confiserie* at 191 rue du Combat. There's an **Internet** café at 18 rue Pierre-Clement called VIP (℡04.94.68.44.92; Mon–Sat 9.30am-7pm).

Towards Lac de St-Cassien

If you're heading east towards Grasse from Draguignan a number of medieval villages north of the main Draguignan–Grasse road (the D562) may detain you. Sheltering below the inhospitable wilderness of the plateau of Canjuers to the north, the settlements of **Callas**, **Claviers**, **Bargemon**, **Seillans**, **Mons**, **Fayence**, **Tourettes** and **Montauroux** were all virtually inaccessible less than a hundred years ago. Not so now, though they retain their charm, despite a nasty rash of commercial development along the main D562. South of it is a wonderful, almost uninhabited expanse of forest where, between January and June, you may see untended cattle with bells round their necks and sheep chewing away at the undergrowth. After a long period of campaigning, farmers have managed to persuade the authorities to allow the animals to roam some of the old pasturing grounds of the transhumance routes, which has great ecological benefits in maintaining the diversity of the forest fauna.

Callas and Bargemon

Twelve kilometres northeast of Draguignan, **CALLAS** is a pleasant place to stop, with a lovely square by the church at the top of the village and a very reasonable **hotel-restaurant**, the *Hôtel de France*, further down on the shaded place Georges-Clemenceau (℡04.94.76.61.02, ℻04.94.39.11.63; menu at €16.70; ❷). For somewhere much grander, the *Hostellerie des Gorges de Pennafort* overlooks Pennafort waterfalls, with its own pool, lake and olive grove (℡04.94.76.66.51, ⓦwww.hostellerie-pennafort.com; ❹): it's still in the *commune* of Callas, but 7km south of the village, below the Draguignan-Grasse road on the D25.

Continuing north from the village of Callas, the steep narrow D25 leads through luscious valleys for 6km, to **BARGEMON**, tucked behind fortified gates. With its fountained squares shaded by towering plane trees, the village is particularly picturesque in spring, when its streets are filled with orange petals and mimosa blossom. The little **Chapelle St-Étienne**, which forms part of the defences, is now home to the **musée-galerie Honoré Camos** and hosts exhibitions of local painters (daily: May–Sept 3–6pm; Oct–April 2.30–5.30pm; free). The two angel heads on the high altar are attributed to the great Marseillais sculptor Pierre Puget.

For **food** and **accommodation**, there's the excellent *L'Oustaloun*, 12 av Pasteur (℡04.94.76.60.36, ⓦwww.oustaloun.fr; menus from €24–28; restaurant closed Wed eve & Thurs out of season; ❺).

Seillans

Heading east from Bargemon to **SEILLANS**, 13km away, the long-distance view suddenly opens out to the mountains. As you approach the village you'll see the effects of Côte-style property development in an ugly rash of white villas, while the Vieux Village, where the painter Max Ernst spent his last years, hides behind medieval walls. A small **collection** of lesser-known lithographs by Ernst, as well as some by his companion Dorothea Tanning, is on display a few doors down from the tourist office on rue de l'Église (Tues–Sat: summer 3–7pm; winter 2–6pm; €2). Seillans' most spectacular piece of artistry, however, lies 1km beyond the village on the road to Fayence. A Renaissance retable, attributed to an inspired Italian monk, is housed in the Romanesque **Chapelle de Notre-Dame-de-l'Ormeau** (Thurs 11am–noon; guided tours July & Aug Tues at 5.30pm). To book guided tours of the chapel, contact Seillans' **tourist office** at 1 rue du Valat (April–Sept Mon–Sat 9.30am–12.30pm & 2.30–6.30pm; Oct–March closes at 6pm; ℡04.94.76.85.91, ⓦwww.seillans-var.com).

The best place to **stay** or **eat** in Seillans is *Les Deux Rocs*, an exquisitely restored town house with beautiful antiques and warm decor, on the fountained place Font-d'Amont by the old wash house (℡04.94.76.87.32, ⓦwww.hoteldeuxrocs.com; closed Tues & Nov–March; ❹).

Fayence and around

FAYENCE, called Favienta Loca (favourable place) by the Romans, is today better known as one of the main centres for **gliding** in France. Larger and livelier than most of its neighbours, it makes a good base for exploring the surrounding countryside. Fayence's charm lies in the contrast between its small-town bustle and the peaceful traffic-free side streets spilling over with flowers. Its Vieille Ville curls tightly around the steep slopes of a hill, with the imposing porchway of the *mairie* guarding the entrance to it; within the Vieille Ville, stands a fourteenth-century gateway, the **Porte Sarrazine**. There's a market on place de l'Église on Tuesdays, Thursdays and Saturdays, as well as the inevitable ateliers and souvenir shops, and great views over the countryside.

For information, there's the **tourist office** on place Léon-Roux (mid-June to mid-Sept Mon–Sat 9.15am–12.15pm & 2.30–6.30pm, Sun 9.30am–noon; mid-Sept to mid-June Mon–Sat 9am–12.10pm & 2–6pm; ☎04.94.76.20.08, ⓦwww.mairiedefayence.com), and the Castle bookshop, at 1 rue St-Pierre (Mon 2.30–7pm; Tues–Sat 9am–12.30pm & 2.30–7pm), near the car park, which sells a reasonable selection of local guides and maps in English. The **gliding school**, the Association Aéronautique Provence Côte d'Azur, is based at Fayence-Tourettes aerodrome, just south of the village (☎04.94.76.00.68, ⓦwww.aapca.net; temporary membership €70 or €35 for under-25s).

Fayence's **accommodation** options include *La Sousto* on rue du Paty (☎04.94.76.02.16, ⓔhotel.sousto@orange.fr; ❸), in the peaceful old heart of the village, with five well-equipped studio rooms for two to four people; and *Les Oliviers*, just below the village on the D19 (☎04.94.76.13.12; ❺), with a pool. Alternatively, try the *Auberge de la Fontaine*, 3km away on the road to Fréjus, beyond the junction with the main Draguignan–Grasse road (☎04.94.76.07.59; ❸); here, Provençal cooking, adds to the attraction of its isolation. For really special surroundings, however, book in at *Le Moulin de la Camandoule*, a converted mill 1km from town on the road out to Notre-Dame-des-Cyprès (☎04.94.76.00.84, ⓦwww.camandoule.com; ❼); it's run by an English couple, but the meals (menus from €30) are prepared by a skilled and inventive French chef. Options for **camping** include the three-star *Lou Cantaire*, 7km out on the road to Draguignan (☎04.94.76.23.77, ⓦwww.camping-lou-cantaire.fr; €17 for a tent and two people; closed Oct–March), and the four-star *Le Parc*, in the quartier Trestaure (☎04.94.76.15.35; closed Oct–March).

In addition to the hotel **restaurants**, there are a few places on place Léon-Roux; the *Entracte* is open for light lunches, and snacks all day. For a quieter place and more substantial meal, try *La Farigoulette*, at the top of the village (☎04.94.84.10.49), or the *Patin Couffin*, placette de l'Olivier (☎04.94.76.29.96; menu at €25; closed Mon), which is known for its large portions of good food. For a gourmet treat, try *Le Castellaras*, signed off the Seillans road (☎04.94.76.13.80; menus from €43-58; closed Mon & Tues out of season), where you can eat lobster, wild mushrooms, pigeon and courgette flowers by a rose garden.

Tourettes and Mons

The distinctly un-medieval **château** in **TOURETTES**, Fayence's neighbour 1km to the east, is a copy of an early nineteenth-century cadet school set up in St Petersburg for Tsar Nicholas I by a French colonel. He built this replica for his retirement and it's still a private residence and is not open to the public.

For an energetic ten-kilometre walk from Fayence, take the GR49 (off the D563 just north of town) through the Fôret de Tourettes, across the valley of La Siagnole River and up to the truly perched village of **MONS**. Once there, you can reward yourself with a drink at one of the cafés on place St-Sébastien and the tremendous views, which sometimes extend as far as Corsica and Italy.

Callian, Montauroux and the Lac de St-Cassien

CALLIAN, 9km east of Fayence, and **MONTAUROUX**, its larger neighbour, have merged together, with just a short stretch of forest to the east separating them from the suburbs of Grasse. Callian is more obviously picturesque but Montauroux is livelier, and its large open place du Clos makes a change from narrow, twisting medievalism, as does the grassy summit of the village with its fig tree, church and little chapel of St-Barthélemy whose ceiling and walls are covered in painted panels.

The **Lac de St-Cassien** reservoir lies 4km to the south of here. You can swim here (best access is from the D37 after you've crossed the lake), and go sailing or rowing; pizzas, grilled food and ice creams are available from the various lakeside establishments. No motor boats are allowed and the water is very clean.

Châteaudouble, Comps-sur-Artuby and Castellane

About 5km northwest of Draguignan along avenue de Montferrat is **Rebouillon**, an exquisitely peaceful village built around an oval field on the banks of the River Nartuby. Beyond here, the scenery changes dramatically with the start of the **Gorges du Châteaudouble**. Though a mere scratch compared to the great Verdon gorge, it has some impressive sites, not least the village of **CHÂTEAUDOUBLE** which hangs high above the cliffs. Nostradamus predicted that the river would grind away at the base until the village fell; he is yet to be proved right. Almost deserted except during the summer holidays, Châteaudouble consists of little more than a couple of churches; a handful of houses; a potter's workshop; a beekeeper and his hives; *La Tour* restaurant (☎04.94.70.93.08; menus at €22.50 and €32) with a terrace overlooking the gorge; and a ruined tower and ramparts, which you can reach from a path beside the *Bar du Château* (☎04.94.70.90.05; menus at €25 and €50).

North of Châteaudouble, the D955 crosses the increasingly bleak military camp of Canjuers before reaching the isolated settlement of **Comps-sur-Artuby**, after 20km. There are few specific sights here, other than the fortified chapel of **St André**, and the magnificent scenery surrounding the village, but there's a pleasant **hotel-restaurant**, the *Grand Hotel Bain*, on avenue de Fayet (☎04.94.76.90.06, ⓦwww.grand-hotel-bain.fr; ❹), with menus from €15-35 and a sunny garden.

Castellane

Few towns can have as dramatic a site as **CASTELLANE**, dominated by a 180m cliff that looms over the Vieille Ville and is topped by the chapel of **Notre Dame du Roc**. Billed as the "gateway" to the Gorges du Verdon, some 17km away (see p.259), Castellane has long been a major tourist camp, and your reason for stopping is likely to be for the range of restaurants, hotels and cafés which in summer gives the town an animation rare in these parts. The place where Napoleon stopped to dine on March 3, 1815 is now the **Musée des Arts et Traditions Populaires de Castellane et Moyen Verdon**, 34 rue Nationale (late May, June & Oct Tues–Sat 9am–noon & 2–6pm; July–Sept daily 10am–1pm & 2.30–6.30pm; €2), which has temporary exhibitions of variable interest.

Houses in Castellane's old quarter are packed close together, as if huddling for protection from the sheer violence of the surrounding landscape; some of the lanes are barely shoulder wide. The path up to the chapel of Notre Dame du Roc starts behind the parish church at the head of place de l'Église, winding its way up past the Vieille Ville and the machicolated **Tour Pentagonal**, standing uselessly on the lower slopes. Twenty to thirty minutes should see you at the top, from where you can't actually see the gorge, but you do get a pretty good view of the river disappearing into it and the mountains circling the town.

Practicalities

There are two **buses** a day in July and August into the Gorges du Verdon (1hr 20min to La Maline). The **tourist office** is at the top of rue Nationale (July & Aug Mon–Sat 9am–12.30pm & 1.30–7pm, Sun 10am–1pm; Sept–June Mon–Fri 9am–noon & 2–6pm; ℡04.92.83.61.14, ⓦwww.castellane.org) and can provide a full list of hotels and campsites.

The best **hotel** deals in Castellane are the *Hostellerie du Roc*, place de l'Église (℡04.92.83.62.65, ℻04.92.83.73.76; closed Mon, Nov & Dec; ❸), *Les Canyons du Verdon*, boulevard de la République (℡04.92.83.62.02, ⓦwww.studi-hotel .com; ❸), and the *Auberge Bon Accueil*, place Marcel-Sauvaire (℡04.92.83.62.01, ⓦwww.auberge-du-bon-accueil.com; closed Oct to mid-April; ❷). The *Hôtel du Commerce* in place de l'Église (℡04.92.83.61.00, ⓦwww.hotel-fradet.com; menus from €20; closed Nov–Feb; ❹) is the most upmarket, with questionable decor but wonderful **food** served in the 🍴 restaurant garden. You can get pasta dishes for around €9 at *La Main à la Pâte* on rue de la Fontaine and there's a pleasant ice-cream bar at the end of the same street. Wednesday and Saturday are **market** days and there's a good wine shop on rue Nationale. Seven kilometres towards la Palud is a small turning right, to Chasteuil; a steep road with eleven switchback bends takes you to a hamlet of stone houses and the beautiful, recently opened **chambres d'hôte** 🍴 *Gite Chasteuil* (℡04.92.83.72.45, ⓦwww.gitedechasteuil.com; ❹) with spectacular mountain views.

There are eleven **campsites** within 3km of the town. The closest is *Le Frédéric-Mistral* (℡04.92.83.62.27), by the river on the route des Gorges du Verdon. Further on down the same road you'll see the caravans and bungalows of the *Camping Notre-Dame* (℡04.92.83.63.02; closed mid-Sept to April), and 1.5km out of town the four-star *Camp du Verdon* (℡04.92.83.61.29, ⓦwww .camp-du-verdon.com; €30 per tent; closed mid-Sept to mid-May). In summer all the sites along this road are likely to be full. A good one to try that's further afield and away from the gorge is *La Colle* on the GR4 off the route des Gorges (℡04.92.83.61.57, ⓦwww.campinglacolle.com; €15 for a tent and two people; closed Nov–March).

For **canoeing** and **rafting** on Lac de Castillon and the Gorges du Verdon, Aqua-Verdon at 9 rue Nationale (℡04.92.83.72.75), and Aboard Rafting, at 8 place de l'Eglise (℡04.92.83.76.11, ⓦwww.aboard-rafting.com), are the places to get information. It's easy enough to rent a mountain **bike** in Castellane: try Aboard Rafting or Aqua Viva Est, 12 bd de la République (℡04.92.83.75.74).

Along the Route Napoléon

North of Castellane the barren scrubby rocks lining the Route Napoléon need the evening light to turn them a more becoming pinkish hue. The town's landmark remains visible all the way up the zigzags to the **Col de Leque**, from where the Route Napoléon traverses the **Clue de Taulanne**, then opens out onto a marvellous northward view of a circle of crests. To either side of the road lie some of the most obscure and empty quarters of Provence. The populations of villages such as **Blieux** and **Majastres**, on the slopes of the Mourre ridge to the west, have dwindled close to the point of desertion. Life here is a picture of rural poverty at its starkest, for all the seeming promise of the springtime or early summer land to the amateur's eye.

Back on the only significant road, the village of **SENEZ** speaks of the same decline, with its barn-like Romanesque former cathedral that could easily accommodate ten times the present number of residents. The episcopal see established here in the fourth century, one of the earliest in France, was throughout the centuries one of the poorest bishoprics in the country. The church is only open on Sunday, but at other times the key is available from Mme Mestre on place de la Fontaine behind the cathedral.

The Grand Canyon du Verdon

North of Aups, the D957 skirts the military Camp de Canjuers and crosses the River Verdon at the bottom of the gorge, just before it enters the vast Lac de Ste-Croix. This is the quickest approach from the south to Europe's widest and deepest gorge, the **Grand Canyon du Verdon**, though not the most dramatic. For that you must approach from Draguignan via the Gorges de Châteaudouble and Comps-sur-Artuby, following one of the few public roads through the

Information and guides: a checklist

There are plenty of organizations and individual guides with whom you can arrange expeditions on foot, horseback, raft, canoe or by air, especially in La Palud, Castellane, Moustiers and Aiguines. The Bureau des Guides and Le Perroquet Vert in La Palud will also give advice if you don't want to be part of a group. Prices vary with the season and the number of people taking part, but they are generally reasonable.

Aboard Rafting Castellane, ☎04.92.83.76.11, ⓦwww.aboard-rafting.com. Masses of water-based activities including rafting, canoeing, canyoning, hydrospeed, water rambling, and mountain biking.

Bureau des Guides La Palud, ☎04.92.77.30.50. Association of professional guides for walks, canyoning and rock-climbing.

Bruno Potié La Palud, ☎04.92.77.32.07. Professional walking guide and rock-climber.

Parc Naturel Région du Verdon Domaine de Valx, Moustiers, ☎04.92.74.68.00, ⓦwww.parcduverdon.fr. National park authority.

Le Perroquet Vert La Palud, ☎04.92.77.33.39, ⓦwww.leperroquetvert.com. Climbing shop & chambres d'hôtes.

Ranch Les Pioneers La Palud, ☎04.92.77.38.30. Horse-rides with your own guide.

UCPA La Palud, ☎04.92.77.31.66, ⓦwww.ucpa-vacances.com. Climbing, walking, canoeing and nautical trekking with a trained guide.

Verdon Passion Moustiers, ☎04.92.74.69.77, ⓦwww.verdon-passion.com. Canyoning, climbing and paragliding.

Latitude Challenge Marseille, ☎04.91.09.04.10, ⓦwww.latitude-challenge.fr. Bungee jumps from the Pont de l'Artuby.

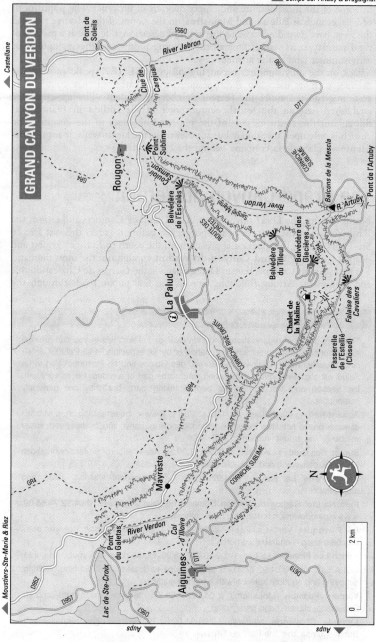

GRAND CANYON DU VERDON

Comps-sur-Artuby & Draguignan

Castellane

Moustiers-Ste-Marie & Riez

Pont de Soleils

River Jabron

D955

Clue de Carejuan

Pont Sublime

Rougon

GR4

Couloir Samson

Belvédère de l'Escalès

ROUTE DES CRÊTES

Sentier Martel

River Verdon

Belvédère des Glaciers

Belvédère du Tilleul

CORNICHE SUBLIME

Balcons de la Mescla

R. Artuby

Pont de l'Artuby

D71

D90

la Palud

CORNICHE RIVE DROITE

Chalet de la Maline

Passerelle de l'Estellié (Closed)

Falaise des Cavaliers

GR4

Mayreste

CORNICHE SUBLIME

N

2 km

0

GR4

Pont du Galetas

River Verdon

Col d'Illoire

Aiguines

D71

Lac de Ste-Croix

D952

D957

D957

D619

Aups

Aups

5

Camp de Canjuers. After Comps the road turns westwards through 16km of end-of-the-earth heath and hills, with each successive horizon higher than the last. When you reach the canyon, it is as if a silent earthquake had taken place while you journeyed.

Approached from Comps, the first vantage point, the **Balcons de la Mescla**, is a memorable *coup de théâtre*, with the view withheld until you are almost upon it. Nothing prepares you for the 250-metre drop to the base of the V-shaped, 21km-long gorge incised by the Verdon through piled strata of limestone. Ever-changing in its volume and energy, the river falls from **Rougon** to the east of the gorge, decelerating for shallow languid moments and finally exiting in full steady flow at the **Pont de Galetas** to fill the huge reservoir of the **Lac de Ste-Croix**.

Running west from the Balcons is the **Corniche Sublime**, built expressly to give the most breathtaking and hair-raising views. On the north side, the **Route des Crêtes** serves the same function, at some points looking down a sheer 800-metre drop to the sliver of water below, though the views are not as consistently good. The entire circuit is 130km long and it's cycling country solely for the preternaturally fit. Even for drivers it's hard work, as the hidden bends and hairpins in the road are perilous and, in July and August, so is the traffic.

Public transport around the canyon is poor. There's one **bus** between Marseille, Aix, Moustiers, La Palud, Rougon and Castellane (July to mid-Sept on Mon, Wed & Sat; mid-Sept to June on Sat only); and one other bus twice daily between La Palud, Rougon and Castellane (July & Aug Mon–Sat; Easter–June & Sept Sat & Sun only, plus public hols). **Drivers** should note that petrol stations are few and far between, so fill up whenever you see one.

By far the best way to explore the canyon, if your legs are strong enough, is to descend to the river and follow it by foot; to **walk** from La Maline to the Point Sublime on the **Sentier Martel** takes seven hours, and is best undertaken as part of a guided group (see box above). You can do it independently, but beware of the sudden changes in water levels, caused by the Verdon's hydroelectric activity – drownings can and do occur. Unaccompanied shorter excursions into the canyon include the **Sentier du Lézard**, a relatively easy marked walk from the **Point Sublime**, with various routes from 30 minutes to four hours, passing though the **Couloir Samson**, a 670-metre tunnel with occasional "windows" and a stairway down to the chaotic sculpture of the river banks.

Canoeing or **rafting** the entire length of the gorge should not be attempted unless you are very experienced and strong, as you will have to carry your craft for long stretches. However, you can pay (quite a lot) to join a group and tackle certain stretches of the river. Because of the electricity board's operations these trips aren't always possible, so be prepared for disappointment. A cheaper, though less exciting option, is to paddle about on the last stretch of the gorge: you can rent canoes and pedalos at the Pont du Galetas. **Rock-climbing** is also possible, as is **horse-riding** on the less precipitous slopes around the gorge. For the ultimate buzz, you can **paraglide**, or **bungee jump** from the 182-metre-high **Pont de l'Artuby**.

La Palud-sur-Verdon

LA PALUD-SUR-VERDON is the closest village to the gorge and makes a good base for exploring the area. There's not much to the village itself, which all but closes down out of season, though it does have a certain bleak appeal.

Housed in La Palud's château, the **Maison des Gorges du Verdon** is a centre for environmental tourism that includes the **tourist office** and an exhibition on the gorge (mid-March to mid-Nov Wed–Mon 10am–noon & 4–6pm; ☏04.92.77.32.02, ⓦwww.lapaludsurverdon.com; entrance to exhibition €4). The tourist office can help with accommodation and information on **walking tours** of the area and there is **Internet** access in the *mairie* opposite. Before setting out on any walk in the gorge, always get details of the route and advice on **weather conditions** (recorded information ☏08.36.68.02.04, ⓦwww.meteoconsult.fr). You'll also need drinking water, a torch/flashlight (for the tunnels), and a jumper for the cold shadows of the narrow corridors of rock. Always stick to the path and don't cross the river except at the *passerelles* as the EDF (electricity board; ☏04.92.83.62.68 for recorded information) may be opening dams upstream.

There is plenty of **accommodation** in and around the village. Of the hotels, *Le Provence*, route de la Maline (☏04.92.77.38.88, ⓦwww.hotel-le-provence-lapaludsurverdon.com; closed Nov to late March; ❸), has the most stunning position, just below the village, while *Les Gorges du Verdon*, 500m from the start of the route des Crêtes and a few minutes' walk from the trails down into the gorge (☏04.92.77.38.26, ⓦwww.hotel-des-gorges-du-verdon.fr; closed Oct–April; ❻), has all mod cons and is beautifully isolated. In La Palud itself, *Le Panoramic*, route de Moustiers, (☏04.92.77.35.07, ⓦwww.hrpanoramic.com; ❹; closed Nov–March), may not have such good views, but it's an agreeable enough place, and there's also the small *Auberge des Crêtes*, 1km east of La Palud (☏04.92.77.38.47, ⓦwww.provenceweb.fr/04/aubergedescretes; closed Oct–March; ❸), with just twelve rooms. There's a two-star **campsite** on the route de Castellane (☏04.92.77.38.13).

The centre of La Palud's social life is *Lou Cafetie* **bar-café** where conversation is inevitably thick with stories of near-falls, near-drownings and near-death from exposure. Most people eat at the hotel **restaurants**, but there's also a pizzeria, *Pépino*, and a crêperie, *Les Tilleuls*. The **market** is on Sunday.

Aiguines

AIGUINES, at the western end of the Corniche Sublime, is perched high above the Lac de Ste-Croix, with an enticing château (closed to the public) of pepperpot towers that dazzle with their coloured tiles. The town was formerly a wood-turning centre, with its speciality being the crafting of boules for pétanque from ancient boxwood roots; in the 1940s the industry sustained a population of six hundred people. Women would bang the little nails into the boules to give them their metal finish, inventing intricate and personalized designs. There's a tiny **Musée des Tourneurs sur Bois** (mid-June to mid-Sept Tues–Sun 9am–noon & 2–6pm; €2), devoted to the intricate art of wood-turning, while the **Galerie d'Art**, opposite the tourist office, sells some very expensive and beautiful woodwork, as well as pottery and faïence.

Every conceivable **water sport** is practised on the nearby **Lac de Ste-Croix**, and you should find gear available for rent at Les Salles-sur-Verdon or Ste-Croix-du-Verdon and at other outlets around this enormous reservoir. **Swimming** is good, with easy access from the D957 between Aups and Moustiers, though sometimes when the water levels are low it's a bit muddy round the edges.

There are plenty of places to stay around Aiguines. For central **hotels**, try *Le Vieux Château*, on the main road (☏04.94.70.22.95, ⓦwww.hotelvieuxchateau.fr; closed mid-Oct to March; ❹), or *Altitudes 823*, just below the main road (☏04.98.10.22.17, ⓦwww.aiguines.com/alt823; closed Nov–March; ❸). Alternatively, there's chambre d'hôtes accommodation in the *Château de Chanteraine*, signposted off the D19 1km out of Aiguines on the Lac de Ste-Croix road

(☎04.94.70.21.01, ⓦwww.chanteraine.net; ❹ per person half board only). For a bit more style and comfort, *Le Grand Canyon* on the Corniche Sublime, halfway between Aiguines and Comps (☎04.94.76.91.31, ❺04.94.76.92.29; closed mid-Oct to mid-April; ❹), has comfortable rooms, balconies and a dining terrace teetering on the edge of a 300-metre drop. There's also a two-star **campsite**, *Le Galetas*, on the D957 (☎04.94.70.20.48; closed Nov–March), almost within diving distance of the lake, a long way down from the village.

Moustiers-Ste-Marie

The 800 or so car-parking spaces tell you all you need to know about the summer popularity of **MOUSTIERS-STE-MARIE**, 17km north of Aiguines. Glutted with *ateliers* making and selling glazed pottery – Moustiers' traditional speciality – the village amounts to little more than a picturesque location for a shopping spree. But it is *very* picturesque, almost absurdly so; the backdrop of sheer cliffs with a star slung between them will be familiar from a thousand calendars. There's rather more appeal out of season, and if you want to escape the commercialism you can at least puff your way uphill to the aptly-named chapel of **Notre Dame de Beavoir**, high above the village proper. If, however, plates and jugs are your thing, this is the place to buy them: the pottery, like the village, is pastel and pretty. There's also a small **Musée de la Faience** (April–Oct Mon & Wed–Sun 9am–noon & 2–6pm; July–Aug closes at 7pm; €1) in the hôtel de ville.

The **tourist office** is on place de L'eglise at the top of the village (daily: May, June & Sept 10.30am–12.30pm & 2–6.30pm; July & Aug 9.30am–12.30pm & 2–7.30pm; Oct–April 2–5pm; ☎04.92.74.67.84, ⓦwww.moustiers.fr). If you want to **stay**, the *Hotel-Café du Relais* is right in the heart of the village (☎04.92.74.66.10, ⓦwww.lerelais-moustiers.com; ❹), with menus at €21 and €28. The **chambres d'hôtes** above the colourful *Clerissy* pizzeria, place du Chevalier du Blacas (☎04.92.74.62.67, ⓦwww.clerissy.fr; ❸) are simple, clean and full of character despite the white walls and proliferation of Ikea furniture. You may want to splash out on the rather more luxurious *La Bastide de Moustiers*, on the main road just below the village (☎04.92.70.47.47, ⓦwww.bastide-moustiers .com; ❸), run by celebrity chef Alain Ducasse. Each of the rooms has its own theme, there's a herb garden and a helicopter pad in the grounds and the **restaurant** offers weekday set menus at a (relatively) modest €57. If that's too much, the *Bar-Resto le Bellevue*, next to the lower of the two bridges in the heart of the village, lives up to its name with a plum riverside site.

Riez and around

Fourteen kilometres south west of Moustiers, and in total contrast to its commercialism, **RIEZ** is one of the least spoilt small towns of inland Provence. Its main business comes from the lavender fields that cover this part of the region. Just over the river, about a kilometre away on the road south, is a **lavender distillery**, a building strangely reminiscent of 1950s Soviet architecture, which produces essence for the perfume industry.

Information and accommodation

The **tourist office** is at place de la Mairie (July–Aug daily 9am–12.30pm & 3–7pm; Sept–June Mon–Sat 8.30am–noon & 1.30–5pm; ☎04.92.77.99.09, ⓦwww.ville-riez.fr). **Accommodation** options are limited to the modern, executive-style *Carina*, across the river in the quartier St-Jean (℡04.92.77.85.43, ℻04.92.77.74.93; closed mid-Nov to March; ❸), with views back across to the town, or the out-of-town *Hôtel Cigalou* (℡04.92.77.75.60; ❸) on the route de Roumoules, and the *Château de Pontfrac* (℡04.92.77.78.77, ⓦ www.chateaudepontfrac.com; ❹) on the route de Valensole. There's a two-star **campsite** on rue Edouard-Dauphin, across the river (℡04.92.77.75.45, ⓦ www.rose-de-provence.com; €12.95 for two people and a tent; closed mid-Oct to March).

❺ The Town

Although today Riez is more village than town, a brief stroll around will soon uncover its grander past. Some of the houses on Grande rue and rue du Marché – the two streets above the main allées Louis-Gardiol – have rich Renaissance facades, and the former hôtel de ville on place Quinconces was once an episcopal palace. The cathedral, which was abandoned four hundred years ago, has been excavated just across the river from allées Louis-Gardiol. Beside it is a **baptistry** (mid-June to Sept Tues & Fri 6pm only; Oct to mid-June by arrangement with the tourist office; €2), originally constructed, like the cathedral, around 600 AD and restored in the nineteenth century. If you recross the river and follow it downstream you'll find the even older and more startling relics of four **Roman columns** standing in a field.

A rather more strenuous **walk** – head first for the clock tower above Grande rue, then take the path up past the cemetery (on the left) – brings you to a cedar-shaded platform at the summit of the hill. This is the site of the Roman town, though the only building remaining is the eighteenth-century **Chapelle St-Maxime**, with a patterned interior that is gaudy or gorgeous, depending on your taste.

The **Maison de l'Abeille**, 1km out of the village along the road to Digne (daily 10am–12.30pm & 2.30–7pm; closed Jan & Feb; free), is a fascinating research and visitors' centre where you can buy various **honeys** as well as hydromel, or mead – the honey alcohol of antiquity. The enthusiastic staff are very keen to share their knowledge of all aspects of a bee's life, from anthropology, to sexuality and physiology, and may even show you the bees themselves.

Eating and drinking

Rue du Marché and the open squares along allées Louis-Gardiol are where you'll find most of Riez's **eating** and **drinking** options. *L'Arts des Mets* in allées Louis-Gardiol (℡04.92.77.82.60) has menus at €18 and €22, while the restaurant *Le Rempart* on rue du Marché (℡04.92.77.89.54) serves Italian and Provençal dishes, with menus from €21. The pleasant *Bar Central* is on the corner of allées Louis-Gardiol and place Maxime Javelly.

The Plateau de Valensole

Riez lies to the south of the **Plateau de Valensole**, bordered by the Bléone and Durance rivers and cut in two by the wide, stony course of the River Asse. Roads and villages north of the river are sparse. It's a beautiful landscape: a wide, uninterrupted tableland whose horizons are the sharp, high edges of mountains.

The most distinctive sight of the plateau is row upon row of **lavender** bushes, green in early summer, turning purple in July. Every farm advertises *lavandin* (a hybrid of lavender used for perfume essence) and *miel de lavande* (lavender honey). There are fields of golden grain, of almond trees blossoming white in early spring, and the gnarled and silvery trunks of olive trees. Even for Provence, the warm quality of the light is exceptional: the ancient town of Valensole, midway between Riez and Manosque, the village of Puimoisson on the road to Dignes, and the tiny hamlets along the Asse exude warmth from it even on wintry days.

This region is well off the beaten track, and there are few hotels. For campers, there's a two-star municipal **campsite**, *Les Lavandes* (☎04.92.74.86.14), on the road to Puimoisson, and most farmers hereabouts won't mind you camping on their land, provided you ask first.

Fourteen kilometres west of Riez, the village of **VALENSOLE** itself is a photogenic huddle of stone houses piling up to an eleventh-century hilltop church. It has its own **Maison de l'Abeille**, on the edge of the village on the Manosque road (Tues–Sat 8–11.30am & 1.30–5pm; free), where they will be happy to sell you as much of the sweet stuff as you can stomach.

The Lower Verdon

Southwest of Riez, along the Colostre and the last stretch of the Verdon, the land is richer and more populated. People commute to the Cadarache nuclear research centre at the confluence of the Durance and the Verdon, or to the new high-tech industries that are very gradually following the wake of the Marseille-Grenoble autoroute. The main reason to head this way is to visit the well-preseved **château** at Allemagne en Provence (tours July to mid-Sept Wed–Sun at 4 and 5pm; April–June & mid-Sept to Oct Sat & Sun at 4 & 5pm; €6), halfway between Riez and the long-established but rather dull spa town of Gréoux-Les-Bains. Built in the twelfth century and converted into a Renaissance residence during the sixteenth century, the château now boasts an impressive mix of warlike battlements and delicate stone pinnacles.

Quinson and the Musée de Préhistoire des Gorges du Verdon

On the far more attractive route south from Riez towards Barjols, **QUINSON** sits at the head of the **Basses Gorges du Verdon**. If you have not yet explored the Grand Canyon du Verdon, these 500-metre depths will strike you as quite dramatic, although, unfortunately, they are quite difficult to get to. The GR99 makes a short detour to the south side of the gorge a couple of kilometres downstream from Quinson, and there are paths from the road between Quinson and Esparron that lead to the gorge's edge.

The chief attraction hereabouts, however, is Quinson's **Musée de Préhistoire des Gorges du Verdon**, route de Montmeyan (Ⓦwww.museeprehistoire.com; April–June & Sept Mon & Wed–Sun 10am–7pm; July & Aug daily 10am–8pm; Oct to mid-Dec, Feb & March Mon & Wed–Sun 10am–6pm; €7), designed by the British architect Norman Foster in a clean and sympathetic modern style. Opened in 2001, it's the largest museum of human prehistory in Europe, and uses the latest audiovisual techniques to chart one million years of human habitation in Provence. There is a multimedia presentation of the cave of Baume Bonne and a fifteen-metre long reconstruction of the caves of the canyon of Baudinard, with their six-thousand-year-old red sun paintings.

△ Musée de Préhistoire

A themed path leads from the museum past reconstructed prehistoric homes and through a Neolithic garden to the most important of the sixty or so archaeological sites in and around Quinson, the cave of **Baume Bonne** itself, where excavations over the last fifty years or so have traced human occupation back 400,000 years.

There's a pleasant, old-fashioned **hotel**, the *Relais Notre-Dame* (☏04.92.74.40.01; ❷; menus at €15 and €39; closed mid-Dec to Jan), on the main road just south of Quinson, close to the river before it enters the gorge.

Digne-les-Bains and around

The retirement spa town of **DIGNE-LES-BAINS** is the capital of the Alpes-de-Haute-Provence *département*, and by far the largest town in northeastern Provence, with about 17,000 inhabitants. Yet despite the almost metropolitan swank of the main street, boulevard Gassendi, and its superb position between the Durance Valley and the start of the real mountains, it can be a dull place to explore. Aside from the crumbling Vieille Ville with its tasteful modern infill, the town is principally a centre for administration and functional shopping, particularly in the vast retail park southwest of the town along the N85.

Digne does, however, have a busy calendar of festivals, including a "lavender month" in summer (see p.271), a couple of interesting museums, and a Tibetan foundation that has been visited by the Dalai Lama. It also has a good range of affordable places to stay, and, if you have your own transport, makes a decent base for trips into the surrounding mountains. This is serious walking country, much of which is protected by the **Réserve Naturelle Géologique de Haute Provence**, which encompasses a huge area surrounding the town.

Arrival, information and accommodation

From the Durance Valley the Route Napoléon enters Digne along the west bank of the Bléone, arriving at the rond-point du 4 Septembre, with the **gares SNCF** (bus connection to St-Auban and Aix TGV; ☎04.92.31.50.00) and **Chemin de Fer de Provence** (☎04.92.31.01.58) just to the west, along avenue Paul-Sémard. Avenue de Verdon continues to Grand Pont, the main bridge, over which is the rond-point du 11 Novembre 1918, where you'll find the **tourist office** (Sept–June Mon–Fri 8.45am–noon & 2–6pm, Sat 10am–noon; July & Aug Mon–Sat 9.30am–12.30pm & 1.30–7pm, Sun 10am–noon & 3–6pm; ☎04.92.36.62.62, ⓦwww.ot-dignelesbains.fr), the **gîtes de France** office and the **gare routière**. From the south the Route Napoléon comes in along the east bank of the river to the rond-point du 11 Novembre 1918. From the rond-point, the main street, boulevard Gassendi, leads northeast up to place du Gal-de-Gaulle, while boulevard Thiers, which becomes avenue du 8 mai 1945, leads east towards the Établissement Thermal, 3km from the centre. The **old town** lies between these two. **Bikes** can be rented from GB Sports Cycles, 8 cours des Arès (☎04.92.31.05.29).

The best-value **hotel** in Dignes is the basic *Origan*, 6 rue Pied-de-la-Ville (☎04.92.31.62.13, ⓕ04.92.31.68.31; ❶), which also serves good food (menus from €18; closed Mon); and the comfortable *Central*, 26 bd Gassendi (☎04.92.31.31.91, ⓦwww.lhotel-central.com; ❷). For those on a larger budget, *Le Grand Paris*, 19 bd Thiers (☎04.92.31.11.15, ⓦwww.hotel-grand-paris.com; closed Dec–Feb; ❺), provides considerably more luxury in a seventeenth-century former convent with tastefully decorated large rooms and Digne's top gourmet restaurant (menus from €25–68; closed Dec–Feb). Eleven kilometres west of Digne, in the fifteenth-century hilltop village of Aiglun, is the pretty **chambre d'hôtes** *Le Vieil Aiglun* (☎04.92.34.67.00, ⓦwww.vieil-aiglun.com; ❻) with an inviting pool, vaulted stone ceilings and charming hosts Charles & Annick.

The two-star municipal **campsite** *du Bourg* is 2km out from the centre along the D900 to Seynes-les-Alpes (☎04.92.31.04.87; €11.50 per tent; closed Nov–March); take avenue Ste-Douceline left from the top of boulevard Gassendi and then turn right into avenue du Camping. Alternatively, the three-star *Camping des Eaux Chaudes*, avenue des Thermes (☎04.92.32.31.04; €13.70 per tent; closed Nov–March), is more pleasantly situated, 1.5km out of town towards the Établissement Thermal.

The City

Late medieval Digne had **two centres**: the area to the north around Notre-Dame du Bourg, where pre-Roman Digne developed; and the existing Haute Ville where the Cathédrale St-Jérôme was built as a small church at the end of the fifteenth century, to be successively enlarged as it took over the functions of Notre-Dame.

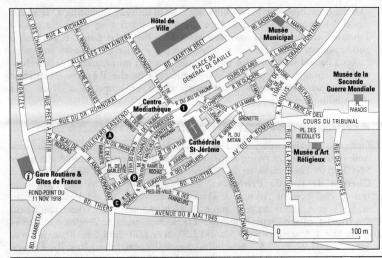

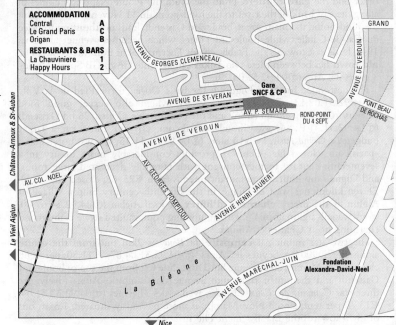

ACCOMMODATION
Central   A
Le Grand Paris   C
Origan   B
RESTAURANTS & BARS
La Chauviniere   1
Happy Hours   2

Standing in splendid isolation on placette du Prévat, **Notre-Dame du Bourg** (June–Oct daily 3–6pm) is typical of Provençal Romanesque architecture, save for its relative bulk and the lightness of its yellowy stone. Built between 1200 and 1330, it contains fragments of early medallions and late medieval murals, the least faded illustrating the Last Judgement. Archaeological digs have revealed a first-century construction and a fifth-century

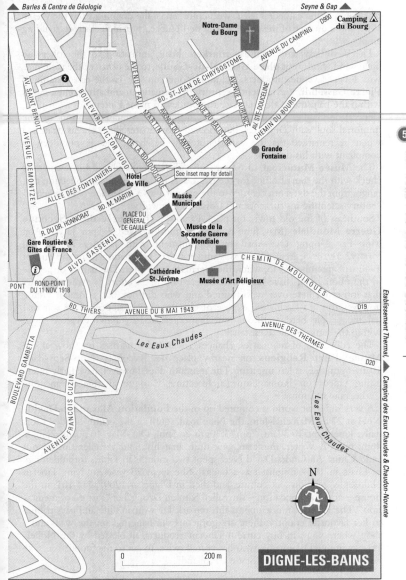

church from which a Merovingian altar and a mosaic floor remain.

In contrast, the fifteenth-century **Cathédrale St-Jérôme** in the *Haute Ville* (June–Oct Tues, Wed, Thurs & Sat 3–6pm) stands weed-encrusted and dilapidated. Its Gothic facade is still impressive and the features inside, in particular the Gothic stained-glass windows, clearly indicate that this was once an awesome place of worship. Sadly, some of the surrounding streets remain as

269

run-down as the cathedral itself, with commercial life draining from the Vieille Ville, and a quarter of the shops in rue de l'Hubac, its principal street, standing empty.

The Wednesday and Saturday **markets** bring animation to the otherwise lifeless and windswept **place Général-de-Gaulle**, to the north of the cathedral, with lots of lavender products, including honey, on sale. To the east, a statue of **Pierre Gassendi**, a seventeenth-century mathematician and astronomer, stands within the balustrades that separate the boulevard named after him from place Général-de-Gaulle. Gassendi used to dispute the precise location of the immortal soul with Descartes, but showed more materialism on his deathbed when he remarked that he would not now be dying had he not been so compliant with his doctors.

The **Musée Municipal**, at 64 bd Gassendi (currently closed for restoration; check with the tourist office for the latest details), has a good art collection that ranges from the sixteenth century to the present, plus a collection of nineteenth-century scientific instruments and Gassendi mementoes.

Southeast of the old town, on place Paradis, is the **Musée de la Seconde Guerre Mondiale** (May, June & Sept to mid-Oct Wed 2–5pm; July & Aug Mon–Fri 2–6pm; Oct–April by appointment with Jacques Teyssier on ☏04.92.31.28.95; free). Digne was under Italian occupation from the end of 1942 to September 1943, when the Germans took over. The names of people in the photographs have had to be covered up in an effort to avoid the rows that still erupt here over who resisted and who did not. For a foreign visitor, however, this is a fascinating exposé of one town's experience of the war that left the people here, as throughout France, scarred by bitter divisions, even within the ranks of the Resistance.

The collection of reliquaries, chalices, robes and crucifixes on show at the **Musée d'Art Religieux** on nearby place des Récollets (June–Sept daily 10am–6pm; free) is less inspiring. The museum does, however, have fairly interesting videos on Romanesque architecture, Baroque altarpieces, and the Cathédrale St-Jérôme.

A very different world is conjured up in the **Fondation Alexandra-David-Neel** at 27 av Maréchal-Juin, the Nice road, south of the centre (guided tours daily: June–Sept 10.30am, 2pm, 3.30pm & 5pm; Oct–May 10.30am, 2pm & 4pm; free). A writer, musician, one-time anarchist, and traveller throughout Indo-China, Alexandra David Neel spent two months in Tibet's forbidden city of Lhasa in 1924, disguised as a beggar. She spent 25 years studying Tibetan philosophy, religion and culture, and died in Digne in 1969, aged 101, in the house – now the Fondation – she called Samten Dzong, her "fortress of meditation". The Fondation documents this remarkable woman's life and pays tribute to her favourite country; there are gorgeous silk hangings on the walls and a shop where you can buy current Tibetan products, all blessed by the Nobel-Prize-winning Dalai Lama, who has visited twice. To get to the foundation, take bus #2 and get off at stop "Stade J. Rolland".

Eating, drinking and entertainment

Some of the best **food** to be had in Digne is at the hotels, with *Le Grand Paris* (☏04.92.31.11.15; menus from €25) and the *Origan* (☏04.92.31.62.13; menus from €18) both serving good-quality Provençal dishes using local ingredients. Alternatively, *La Chauvinière*, 54 rue de l'Hubac (☏04.92.31.40.03; menus from around €21; closed Mon), is a more intimate spot in the Vieille Ville, also serving traditional Provençal dishes. Whilst boulevard Gassendi and place Général-de-Gaulle both have plenty of **cafés** and **brasseries** to choose from, none of them is particularly special, and you're better off heading north to the lively café, *Happy Hours*, at 43 bd Victor-Hugo (℡04.92.31.23.37; closed Sun) which also has **WiFi** internet access.

Out of season Digne can be very quiet in the evening, with **entertainment** limited to the Centre Culturel Pierre Gassendi, 45 av du 8 Mai 1945 (℡04.92.30.87.10), which puts on shows, concerts and films year-round, and also has a cybercafé. If you want to dance, head out towards Aiglun, 12km west from Digne along the N85 on route de Marseille, where there are two **discos**, *Meteore* (℡04.92.34.75.89) and *Les Douze Chênes* (℡04.92.34.65.10).

The first weekend in August sees the **Corso de la Lavande**, a jamboree with parades of floats celebrating the lavender crop and its two key products, honey and perfume. The **Foire-Exposition de la Lavande** at the end of August and the beginning of September is more commercially minded but excellent for buying pots of goodies to take back home. In September the **Journées Tibétaines** celebrate all things Tibetan; and there are special **film** seasons in March, July and November.

The Réserve Naturelle Géologique de Haute Provence

On the northern outskirts of Digne, at the end of the road off to the left after the Pont des Arches, the **Centre de Géologie** (April–Oct daily 9am–noon & 2–5.30pm; Nov–March Mon–Fri 9am–noon & 2–5.30pm; €4.60) has extremely good videos, workshops, exhibitions and aquarium explaining the **Réserve Naturelle Géologique de Haute Provence**, the biggest protected geological area in Europe, covering an area of 150 square kilometres and stretching north of Digne and south to the Gorges du Verdon. The reserve's sites include imprints and fossils of various Miocene creatures – crabs, oysters, ammonites, an ichthyosaurus – which record the time before the Alps had forced the sea southwards. In spring the Centre runs guided walks to various sites in the Réserve (℡04.92.36.70.70). To get to the Centre, take bus #2 from Dignes' *gare routière*, and get off at stop "Champourcin". If you're driving, note that it's a fifteen-minute walk from the car park to the Centre.

Close to the Centre, on the road to Barles, you can see on the left of the road a wall of ammonites, the fossils of shells whose creatures lived off these rocks 185 million years ago. Beyond here, the road forks left to **LA ROBINE**, starting point for a one-hour walk to the extraordinarily well-preserved fossilized skeleton of an ichthyosaurus, a 4.5-metre-long reptile that was swimming around these parts while dinosaurs lumbered about on land. The walk starts from the car park near La Robine's school at the far end of the village, and the path is well signed with the logo of an ichthyosaurus.

Along the Eaux Chaudes

The sulphurous water (29–49°C), whose health-giving properties have been known since antiquity, spouts out of the Falaise St-Pancrace just east of the town above avenue des Thermes; the stream called Eaux Chaudes, which runs alongside the avenue, however, is actually no warmer than any mountain stream. If you want to take a cure, the **Établissement Thermal**, where Edith Piaf howls out of a gramophone from the retirement holiday camp window whilst the residents scowl down from the balcony above (℡04.92.32.32.92), will be only too happy to oblige. If you're not sure what it entails there's a guided tour (March–Aug & Nov Thurs 2pm; bus #1, stop "Thermes").

If you're more interested in stunning landscapes, the D20 along the Eaux Chaudes, which meets the Route Napoléon at Chaudon-Norante, is a great route to follow. Meadows contrast with the great wall of mountain to the north; acacia trees give way to larch forests as you climb to the Col du Corobin where the views open up to a vast expanse southwards. Near Digne you may notice women wearing floral scarves and long skirts of a distinctly un-Provençal style. They are likely to be Albanians, one of several foreign communities who have settled in this harsh and marginalized environment.

East to St-André-les-Alpes and the Lac de Castillon

From Annot, the Chemin de Fer de Provence heads due north before tunnelling through to the Verdon Valley and **Thorame-Haute**'s station, where you can take buses further north up the Verdon. Here, the rail line turns south again, with the next major stop at **St-André-les-Alpes**. St-André stands at the head of the **Lac de Castillon**, one of the Verdon's many artificial lakes, stretching a good 10km southwards to the Barrage de Castillon and the smaller Lac de Chaudanne from where the Verdon descends dramatically into **Castellane**, the second most significant town on the **Route Napoléon** after Grasse.

The main road along the Var Valley, the N202 from Entrevaux, skirts Annot and heads west through the Clue de Rouaine to the Lac de Castillon at **St-Julien-du-Verdon**, then takes over from the D955 as the lakeside corniche up to St-André. The road and rail line run parallel again west from St-André along a beautiful stretch of rock, river and forest to meet the Route Napoléon at **Barrême**.

With good train and road access, plenty of accommodation and well-organized facilities for outdoor activities, particularly water and airborne sports, this is an easy corner of Haute Provence to explore. Castellane and St-Julien can feel a bit too subservient to entrepreneurial tourism, but traditional Provence is never far away, as the sight of sheep taking over the roads on their way to or from their summer pastures may well remind you.

St-André-les-Alpes

Unlike so many tightly huddled Provençal villages, **ST-ANDRÉ-LES-ALPES** has a straggly feel, with its streets and squares open to the magnificent views of the surrounding mountains and the lake. Accommodation and food are cheap; the only difficulty is choosing which of the beautiful routes out from St-André to explore. However, the choice is made easier by the helpful free guide, in English, to walks & mountain biking trails in the area which is given out by the **tourist office** on place Marcel-Pastorelli (mid-June to mid-Sept Mon–Sat 9am–noon & 2–6pm, Sun 10am–12.30pm; mid-April to mid-June & mid-Sept to mid-Oct Mon–Fri 9am–noon & 2–5.30pm, Sat 10am–noon & 4–6pm; mid-Oct to mid-April Mon–Fri 9am–noon & 2–5pm; ☎04.92.89.02.39, ⊛www .ot-st-andre-les-alpes.fr). As well as offering information on the surrounding area, including St-Julien, Thorame and Moriez the office also provides **Internet access.** Northeast of the village centre across the N202 is the **gare Chemin de Fer de Provence** with trains towards Dignes and Nice.

Of the seven **hotels** in and around St-André, the *Lac et Forêt* on the road to St-Julien (☎04.92.89.07.38, ⊛www.lacforet.com; closed Nov–Feb; ❸) rents

bikes and has the best views over the lake, while the *France*, on place de l'Église (☎04.92.89.02.09; ❶), is the cheapest, with budget rooms right in the centre of the village. The two-star municipal **campsite**, *Les Iscles*, by the confluence of the Verdon and the Issole on the road to St-Julien (☎04.92.89.02.29, ⓦwww.saint-andre-les-alpes.fr; €10.40 for two people and a tent; closed Oct–April), has good facilities. If you prefer a **gîte d'étape**, try the one in Moriez, the next stop on the Chemin de Fer de Provence or a five-minute drive west of St-André (☎04.92.89.13.20, ⓦwww.verdon-provence.com/gitemoriez; closed mid-Nov to Feb). Several of the hotels have their own **restaurants**, or try *La Table de Marie*, place Charles-Bron (☎04.92.89.16.10). There's a good choice of beers available at *Le Commerce* **bar** on place de l'Église.

Paragliding and **hang-gliding** are popular here, around Mont Chalvet to the west of the village. It's very well organized and regulated by the École de Vol Libre 'Aerogliss' at the Base de Loisirs des Iscles to the south of the village (☎04.92.89.11.30, ⓦwww.aerogliss.com). Short flights for the less experienced take place in the morning, and a five-day beginners' course starts at €445. *Natur Elements* (☎04.92.89.13.26, ⓦwww.naturelements.com) organize **walks**, and **rafting**, **canyoning** and **canoeing** on the Lac de Castillon and Gorges du Verdon.

North to Château-Garnier and Thorame

From St-André, following the River Issole along the D2 brings you to Château-Garnier, 15km north. The narrow road stays close to the banks most of the time, and well-signed footpaths lead off into the wooded hills, which are prone to landslides, as the frequent boulder-strewn scars on the slopes show. After 8km you can turn left towards **TARTONNE** where there's a pleasant gîte d'étape with a good restaurant, *Les Robines* (c/o Mme Pascale Reybaud; ☎04.92.34.26.07; menus from €13; ❷), or keep going to La Bâtie where the valley opens out into meadows ringed by hills. Between La Bâtie and Château-Garnier, along the footpath to Tartonne, is the twelfth-century **Chapelle St-Thomas**, decorated with medieval frescoes (the key is available from the *miellerie* in Château-Garnier).

The main reason to stop in **CHÂTEAU-GARNIER**, however, is to visit the serious and dedicated **honey** business Miellerie Chailan at the far end of the village on the left (Mon–Fri 8am–noon & 1.30–6pm, Sat 9am–noon & 2–5pm; ⓦwww.miels-chailan.com). Though only groups are given tours of the hives, you may see the gleaming machinery in action, and you can certainly buy superb honey with such flavours as rosemary, acacia, "thousand flowers", sunflower, pine and lavender, plus nougat, sweets, candles and medicinal derivatives.

From Château-Garnier the road veers east through **THORAME BASSE**, where the church has an unlikely clock on the spire and the *Café du Vallée* serves inexpensive *plats du jour*. The road then continues through wide open meadows to **THORAME HAUTE** where the landscape is scarred by gravel extraction. There's a **hotel-restaurant** here, *Au Bon Accueil* (☎04.92.83.90.79; ❸–❹), a *charcuterie* and a one-star municipal **campsite** *Fontchaude* (☎04.92.83.47.37; €8 for two people and a tent), down by the river.

South along the Lac de Castillon

Slightly milky and an unearthly shade of aquamarine, the hundred-metre-deep **Lac de Castillon** is a popular bathing spot in high summer, with closely-supervised **beaches** and **boats** for rent, south of St-André along the N202. The landscape gets more dramatic after the road crosses over the lake and the hills start to close in.

ST-JULIEN-DU-VERDON was a casualty of the creation of the lake. Today it's a tiny place with a two-star **campsite**, *Camping du Lac* (℡04.92.89.07.93, ⓦcampdulac.monsite.orange.fr; €10 for two people and a tent; open mid-June to mid-Sept), and a **hotel**, *Lou Pidanoux* (℡04.92.89.05.87, ⓦwww.verdon-provence.com/pidanoux.htm; ❷), but nothing to suggest that this was once Sanctus Julienetus, on the Roman road from Nice to Digne. Still, it's a pleasant, quiet spot if you just want to laze about by calm water with a gorgeous backdrop of mountains.

The main road east to Annot from St-Julien leads through the dramatic *clues* of Vergons and Rouaine, and past the exquisite Romanesque chapel of Notre-Dame de Valvert. The road south to Castellane follows the lake, with plenty of opportunities for **water-skiing**. The gleam of gold up in the hills on the opposite bank is the Buddhist centre of Mandaron. At the southern tip of the lake, the road crosses the awe-inspiring **Barrage de Castillon**, where there's a small parking area if you want to stop for a closer look, though bathing is forbidden.

The Lower Var Valley

From Nice, both the Chemin de Fer de Provence and the road stick to the left bank of the Var, which is wide, turbulent and not greatly scenic downstream of its confluence with the Esteron. Past the confluence with the Vésubie, a short way further north, you enter the **Défilé de Chaudan**, a long gorge between vertical cliffs through which the rail line and road have to tunnel. At the northern extremity of the gorge, the River Tinée comes rushing out of the **Gorges de la Mescla** to join the Var in a twisted, semi-subterranean junction of rock and water. From here the course of the Var runs almost due west for 40km, passing tiny medieval villages and the towns of **Puget-Théniers** and **Entrevaux**. The main road and the rail line then continue west along the River Vaïre to **Annot**.

Villars-sur-Var

VILLARS-SUR-VAR, 11km west of the Gorges de la Mescla, may have the northernmost vineyards of the Côtes de Provence *appellation*, but the quantity of wine produced is only just sufficient for local consumption, so you'll be lucky to get a glass of it in one of the two cafés.

The reason for stopping here – apart from the charm of a *village perché* with stepped streets – is to see the **Église de St-Jean-Baptiste**. The carefully restored Baroque church is decorated with trompe-l'oeil frescoes and an eighteenth-century ex-votive painting to Saint Patron de la Bonne Mort, thanking him for killing off only 66 residents in the previous year's plague. The main altar has a striking retable, with another on the left wall from the Nice School.

Touët-sur-Var and the Gorges du Cians

Crammed against a cliff 10km west of Villars-sur-Var, **TOUËT-SUR-VAR** also has a church that's rather special, though for a very different reason: it's built over a small torrent, visible through a grille in the floor of the nave. The village's highest houses look as if they are falling apart, but in fact the gaps between the beams are open galleries where the midday sun can reach the rows of drying figs.

There's nowhere to stay in Touët, but it has a good **restaurant**, the *Auberge des Chasseurs*, on the main road (☎04.93.05.71.11; menus at €19 & €27; closed Tues), serving local fare which in autumn involves game and wild mushrooms. The specialities of the area are squash ravioli with nut sauce and *tartes des blettes* (Swiss chard tarts).

The River Cians joins the Var just west of Touët. The road along this tributary, the D28, leads to the ski resort of Beuil, passing first through the Gorges Inférieures du Cians, close to the confluence, and then the **Gorges du Cians** proper, an ominous chaos of water tumbling between looming red schist cliffs. Much of the route is tunnelled. This and the Gorges de Daluis to the west (see p.286) are well-signed tourist routes, so be prepared for traffic.

Puget-Théniers

Arriving by train at **PUGET-THÉNIERS**, the first monument you see, on the *cours* below the old town, is a statue of a woman with bound hands. Sculpted by Maillol and titled *L'Action Enchaînée*, it commemorates **Auguste Blanqui**, born here in 1805. Blanqui was one of the leaders of the Paris Commune of 1871, and spent forty years in prison for – as the inscription states – "fidelity to the sacred cause of workers' emancipation". There are few French revolutionaries for whom the description "heroic defender of the proletariat" is so true, and none who came from a more isolated, unindustrialized region.

To some extent, dilapidated Puget-Théniers is the ugly duckling of the *pays*, though its **Vieille Ville**, on the right bank of the River Roudoule, is full of thirteenth-century houses, some with symbols of their original owners' trades on the lintels. The left bank is dominated by the great semicircular apse of the Romanesque **church**, outreaching even the ancient cedar alongside, and suggesting a fort or prison more than a place of worship. It's not a pretty structure, but it does contain a brilliantly realistic Flemish *Entombment*, painted in the 1500s, and an expressive calvary sculpted in wood.

Practicalities

The **tourist office** (June–Aug daily 9am–12.30pm & 3–7pm; Sept–May daily 9am–noon and 2–5.30pm; ☎04.93.05.05.05; ⊛www.provence-val-dazur.com) is on the main road by the gare Chemin de Fer de Provence and has information on walks, canoeing and the steam trains that run between Puget-Théniers and Annot.

The *Laugier*, at 1 place A-Conil (☎04.93.05.01.00; ❷), is the best place to **stay**; alternatively, try the modern *Alizé* (☎04.93.05.06.20; ❸), which is by the busy N202, but has its own swimming pool. Puget's two-star municipal **campsite** is by the river (☎04.93.05.10.53; closed Oct–Feb).

On summer evenings the **cafés** and **restaurants** on place A-Conil in the Vieille Ville and down along the Roudoule towards the Var are livelier than you'd expect from a small *haut-pays* town. The restaurant in the *Laugier* hotel is a good bet in the centre of town, but first choice for food is *Les Acacias* (☎04.93.05.05.25; closed Wed), 1km east of Puget-Théniers on the main road, where *cuisine de terroir* using the local produce can be enjoyed on a €20 lunch menu, or for €26 in the evenings. Excellent old-fashioned *boulangeries*, *charcuteries* and *fromageries* can be found in the old quarter and, if you happen to be here at Pentecost, nearby La Croix-Sur-Redoule has a communal feast of bean soup cooked in a vast cauldron.

Entrevaux

Upstream from Puget-Théniers the valley widens, allowing space for pear, apple and cherry orchards. After 13km you reach the absurdly photogenic **ENTREVAUX**, whose most striking feature is its fortified old town on the north bank of the river. Built on the site of a Roman settlement, this was once a key border town between France and Savoy.

△ The old town of Entrevaux

The single-arched drawbridge across the rushing Var – the only access – was fortified by Vauban, and it is Vauban's linking of the town with the ruined **château** (access at any time; €3) that gives the site its menacing character. Perched 135m above the river at the top of a steep spur, the château originally could only be reached by scrambling up the rock. By the seventeenth century this had become unacceptable, perhaps because soldiers leaving the garrison on their hands and knees did not do much for the army's image. Consequently, Vauban built the double-walled ramp, plus attendant bastions, that zigzags up the rock in ferocious determination.

The former **cathedral** (summer 9am–7pm; winter 9am–5pm), in the lower part of the old town, is well integrated into the military defences, with one wall forming part of the ramparts and its belfry a fortified tower. The interior, however, is all twirling Louis Quinze, with misericords, side altars and organ as over decorated as they could possibly be. Just beyond the church, through the **Porte d'Italie**, you can escape from Baroque opulence and military might alike.

Practicalities

The **gare Chemin de Fer de Provence** is just downstream from the bridge on the south bank, and the **tourist office** (July–Aug daily 9am–7pm; March–June & Sept daily 9am–noon & 2–5pm; Oct–Feb Tues–Sat 10am–noon & 2–5pm; ☎04.93.05.46.73, ⓦwww.entrevaux.info) is in the left-hand tower of the drawbridge; it organizes guided tours of the town (July–Aug; €3.80) in medieval costume.

For places to stay, there's the rudimentary **hotel** *Hostellerie Vauban*, 4 place Moreau (☎04.93.05.42.40, ⓦwww.hotel-le-vauban.com; ❸), south of the river, and two **gîtes d'étapes**: the *Gîte des Moulins* (❶) and the *Gîte de Plan* (❶), both bookable through the tourist office.

For **food and drink** try the *Bar au Pont-Levis* opposite Vauban's bridge, where English-speaking tourists congregate. The *Hostellerie Vauban* has a restaurant specializing in trout, pasta and the local dry beef sausage (*secca de boeuf*) with menus from €16.50, and *Le Planet* snack bar, serving omelettes, *pan bagnat* and pizzas. The Lovera *charcuterie* (closed Mon & Thurs), two doors from *Le Planet*, sells *secca de boeuf* to take away, though it's best seasoned with lemon and olive oil.

Annot

Surrounded by hills, **ANNOT** is primarily a holiday centre for its climate, pure health-giving waters and clean air. The Vieille Ville, if not outstanding, does have some pretty arcades and a Renaissance clock tower on its church; the modern town is grouped around its *cours*, a large open space lined by plane trees to the south of the medieval quarter. It is an excellent base for walks, up past strange sandstone formations to rocky outcrops with names like *Chambre du Roi* (the King's Chamber) and *Dent du Diable* (the Devil's Tooth).

The **gare Chemin de Fer de Provence** is to the southeast of the town, at the end of avenue de la Gare, which leads to the main *cours*. The helpful **tourist office** on boulevard St-Pierre (March-Oct Mon-Sat 9am-noon & 3-6pm, Sun 9am-noon; Nov-April Mon-Sat 9am-noon & 3-5pm; ☎04.92.83.23.03, ⓦwww.annot.fr) has plenty of details on walks, rides, sports facilities, the steam train to Puget-Théniers, exhibitions and local festivities. It also organizes guided tours of the Vieille Ville on Tuesdays in season.

Accommodation is easy to come by and reasonably priced. Of the **hotels**, budget options include *La Cigale* to the north on boulevard St-Pierre (☎ & ⓕ04.92.83.33.37; ❷) and the *Beau Séjour*, by the entrance to the Vieille Ville on place du Revelly (℡04.92.83.21.08, ⓦwww.hotelbeausejourannot.com; ❸). The hotel on avenue de la Gare, *L'Avenue* (℡04.92.83.22.07; ⓦwww.hotel-avenue .com; closed Nov–March; ❹), has small cosy rooms and the best **restaurant** in town (menus at €16 & €25). For **campers** there's a very pleasant two-star site, *La Ribière*, on the road to Fugeret (℡04.92.83.21.44, ⓦwww.la-ribiere.com; €9.60 for two people and a tent; mid-Feb to mid-Nov) just north of the town.

Clues de Haute Provence

To the west of the River Var, north of Vence and the Route Napoléon in the Pre-Alpes de Grasse, lies the area known as the **Clues de Haute Provence**, *clues* being the word for the gorges cut through the limestone mountain ranges by their torrential rivers. This is an arid, sparsely populated region, its seclusion disturbed only by the winter influx of skiers from the coastal cities to the 1777-metre summit of the **Montagne du Cheiron**, and the car rallies along the route des Crêtes, which follows the contours of the Montagne de Charamel and the Montagne St-Martin between the Cols de Bleine and Roquestéron.

Each claustrophobic and seemingly collapsible *clue* opens onto a wide and empty landscape of white and grey rocks with a tattered carpet of thick oak and pine forest. The horizons are always closed off by mountains, some erupting in a space of their own, others looking like coastal cliffs trailing the **Cheiron**, the **Charamel** or the 1664-metre-high **Montagne de Thorenc**. It's the sort of scenery that fantasy films take place in, with wizards throwing laser bolts from the mountains.

To appreciate it, though, you really need your own **transport**. Not all the passes are open in winter – notices on the roads forewarn you of closures – and you should keep an eye on your fuel gauge and plan your route accordingly as garages are scarce. Routes that go through the *clues* rather than over passes are manageable for cyclists: this is gorgeous, clean-air, long-freewheeling and panoramic terrain. There are plenty of footpaths, with the **GR4** as the main through-route for walkers from Gréolières to Aiglun across the Cheiron. The Conseil Général des Alpes Maritimes produces an excellent series of walking guides for the region, available online (ⓦwww.cg06.fr), and the *Guide Rand Oxygène Moyen Pays* covers the Esteron.

Accommodation isn't plentiful. What hotels there are tend to be very small, with a faithful clientele booking them up each year. Campsites are also thin on the ground, but there are a variety of gîtes scattered about. Even winter accommodation at **Gréolières** and **Gréolières-les-Neiges** is fairly minimal, as people tend to come up for a day's skiing or have their own weekend places. Most of the villages offer tourist information at the *mairie*. If you get stuck, the towns of Vence, Grasse, Puget-Théniers, Castellane or Nice are not far away.

Coursegoules and Gréolières

Coming from Vence you approach the *clues* via the Col de Vence, which brings you down to **Coursegoules**. Approaching from Grasse and the Loup Valley, the road north leads to **Gréolières**, 11km west of Coursegoules.

Coursegoules

The bare white rocks that surround **COURSEGOULES** are not the most hospitable of sites for a working village, so it's no surprise that many of the smartly restored houses here are now second homes. The population has steadily declined to around three hundred or so people who don't need to eke out a living from the soil-scoured terrain. **Accommodation** possibilities here, all of which have superb views, include a chambre d'hôte, 400m from the village (M et Mme Durand, *L'Hébergerie*; ☎04.93.59.10.53; ❸), and the hotel *L'Auberge de l'Escaou* on the lovely place des Tilleuls in the old village (☎04.93.59.11.28, ⓦwww.hotel-escaou.com; ❹). The hotel has a perfectly good **restaurant** and there's also a crêperie and small bistro in the village.

Gréolières and around

GRÉOLIÈRES, 10km west, seems an equally unpromising site for habitation. Originally a stopping point on the Roman road from Vence to Castellane, it's now surrounded by ruins, of Haut-Gréolières to the north and a fortress to the south. The church, opposite the fortress, has a Romanesque facade and a fifteenth-century retable of St Stephen. The village is liveliest during the winter, but passes as a summer resort as well; it's a popular site for paragliding.

The **tourist office**, at 21 Grande rue (Mon–Fri 9am–noon & 2–6pm; ☎04.93.59.97.94, ⓦwww.greolieres.fr), has plenty of information on sports and activities in Gréolières and its neighbouring villages. For **hotel-restaurants** the only choice is the very reasonable *La Vieille Auberge*, on place Pierre-Merle (☎04.93.59.95.07; ❷), in the centre of the village. A good and inexpensive place to **eat** in the village is *La Barricade* pizzeria (menus at €12– 21; closed Mon & Tues).

Heading west around the mountains from Gréolières brings you through the Clue de Gréolières, carved by a tributary of the Loup, to the ski station **GRÉOLIÈRES-LES-NEIGES**, 18km by road from Gréolières. This is the closest ski resort to the Mediterranean and a centre for **cross-country skiing** (information on ☎04.93.59.70.57). Fourteen lifts ascend Mont Cheiron in winter, and in July and August a single chairlift operates for summer panoramas. There are no **hotels** here, accommodation being in the form of furnished apartments (information from tourist office in Gréolières), but there is a handful of **cafés** and **restaurants**, mostly open year-round.

Thorenc, St-Auban and Briançonnet

Thirteen kilometres west of Gréolières, off the D2, **THORENC** is now a popular paragliding and cross-country-skiing resort, originally founded by English and Russians at the beginning of the twentieth century. The dense woods and style of the older buildings give it an almost Central European atmosphere. It's a lively spot in both winter and summer, and has a very pleasant small **hotel-restaurant** *Les Merisiers*, 24 av du Belvédère (☎04.93.60.00.23, ⓦwww.aubergelesmerisiers.com; menus at €23 & €29; closed Tues; ❷).

To the north, the narrow and rough D5 crosses the Montagne de Thorenc by the Col de Bleine, then the D10 takes over for the ascent of Charamel, without a moment's pause in the twisting climb. The D10 leads to Aiglun while the D5 takes the easier westward route to **ST-AUBAN** and its *clue*. Tiny St-Auban rises above the grassy valley with its back to the mountain-side, its wide southern views making up for the plainness of the village itself. The gash made by the River Esteron has left a jumble of rocks through which the water tumbles beneath overhanging cliffs riddled with caves and fissures. In summer, rock-climbing and canyoning are possible in the narrow *clue*. St-Auban's only **hotel-restaurant** is *Le Tracastel* (☎04.93.60.43.06, ⓦwww.auberge-tracastel.com; closed Nov–Easter; ❸), but there's also a *gîte* *equestre* where you can rent horses (reservations through the *mairie*; ☎04.93.60.41.23 or 04.93.60.43.20; ❷).

Further downstream, **BRIANÇONNET** has one of the most stunning positions in the whole of inland Provence. This is best appreciated at the cemetery, from where the views stretch southwards past the edge of the Montagne de Charamel across miles of uninhabited space. The Romans had a settlement here and the present houses are built with stones from the ancient ruins, with odd bits of Latin still decipherable in the walls. There's just one street with a *boulangerie*, a *tabac*, a small museum of local history, the church – which contains a retable of *The Madonna of the Rosary* by Louis Bréa, showing Mary protecting the ecclesiastical and secular potentates in her cloak – and one tiny **hotel-restaurant**, *Le Chanan* (☎04.93.60.46.75; ❶).

From here you can head north across the **Col de Buis** (usually closed Nov to mid-April) to Entrevaux or Annot, or east towards the Clue d'Aiglun and the Clue de Riolan.

The Route des Crêtes

Clinging to the steep southern slope of the Montagne de Charamel, the switch-back **Route des Crêtes** (D10) requires concentration and nerve. For long stretches there are no distracting views, only thick forest matted with mistletoe. After Le Mas, which hangs on the edge of a precipitous spur below the road, trees can no longer get a root-hold in the near-vertical golden and silver cliffs; the narrowing road crosses high-arched bridges over cascading streams which fall to smoothly moulded pools of aquamarine.

Just before Aiglun you cross the Esteron as it shoots out from the high-pressure passage (too narrow for a road) that splits the Charamel and the Montagne St-Martin. This is the most formidable of all the *clues* and is impossible to explore. You can, however, walk along the GR4 southwards from the D10, 1.5km west of the *clue*, to the **Vegay waterfall**, halfway between Aiglun and Gréolières-les-Neiges (a distance of about 3km), where water destined for the Esteron plummets down a vertical cliff face.

In the village of **AIGLUN** you can **stay**, if you're lucky, in one of the six rooms at the *Auberge de Calendal* (☎04.93.05.82.32; closed Feb & first week of March; ❷), which also manages a dormitory-style *gîte communale* on the GR4 (enquiries to the tourist office at Gréolières; ☎04.93.59.97.94). East from Aiglun, the campanile and silvery olive groves of the ancient fortified village of La Sigale flicker into view.

Beyond La Sigale, midway to Roquesteron, the **Chapelle Notre-Dame d'Entrevignes** has preserved fragments of fifteenth-century frescoes including the unusual scene of Mary, ready to give birth, with Joseph expressing deep suspicion. To visit, apply to La Sigale's *mairie* (Mon–Fri 8.30am–noon & 2.30–5pm; ☎04.93.05.83.52) for keys: you will have to leave a passport behind as security.

ROQUESTERON, about 10km east of St-Aiglun, was divided for a hundred years by the France–Savoy border, which followed the course of the Esteron. There's one **hotel** here, the *Passeron* at 25 bd Salvago (☎04.93.05.91.01; ❷). From Roquesteron you have the choice of following the D17 above the Esteron to the river's confluence with the Var, or taking the tangled D1, through passages of rock seamed in thin vertical bands to **BOUYON**, from where the D8 takes you back to Coursegoules. Both routes take you through a succession of eagle's-nest villages. At Bouyon you'll find an excellent **hotel-restaurant**, the *Catounière* in place de la Mairie (☎ & ℱ04.93.59.07.15; closed Oct–Easter; ❷).

Massif les Monges and Seyne

North of Digne, the mountains that reach their highest peak at Les Monges (2115m) form an impassable barrier, as far as roads go, between the valleys running down to Sisteron and the Durance and those of the Bléone's tributaries. There are footpaths for serious **walkers** (which begin at Digne on the west bank of the Bléone north of the Grand Pont), and just one road loops south of Les Monges linking Digne and Sisteron via **Thoard** and **Authon** across the **Col de Font-Belle**. Fantastic forested paths lead off past vertical rocks from the pass.

The D900a, which follows first the course of the Bléone, and then the Bès torrent, before joining the main D900 and continuing north to **Seyne-les-Alpes**, passes many of the protected sites of the **Réserve Naturelle Géologique de Haute Provence**, where shrubs, flowers and butterflies are now the sole visible wildlife. After heavy rain the waters tear through the **Clues de Barles and Verdaches** like a boiling soup of mud in which it's hard to imagine fish finding sustenance.

Making any decent livelihood from the land here is difficult. A lot of "*marginaux*" (hippies or anyone into alternative lifestyles) manage to survive, making goats' cheese and doing seasonal work; the indigenous *paysans* are more likely to be opening gîtes and servicing the increasing numbers of city dwellers who come for **trekking** or **skiing** trips. But it's still very wild and deserted, with little accommodation other than gîtes and chambres d'hôtes; petrol stations are also few and far between.

Seyne-les-Alpes

SEYNE-LES-ALPES lies in a distinctly alpine landscape some 40km north of Digne, its highest point topped by a Vauban fort. The town's main influx is in winter, when its three skiing stations, **St-Jean, Chabanon** and **Le Grand Puy**, are in operation. The rest of the year Seyne is quieter, but still has plenty of accommodation on offer and scope for walking and riding into the mountains. It also has the only surviving horse fair in southeast France – held on the second Saturday of October – and a mule breeder's competition at the beginning of August.

The **tourist office** off the Grande rue on place d'Armes, the road past the church (Mon–Fri 9am–noon & 2–5pm; ☎04.92.35.11.00, ⓦwww.vallee-de-la -blanche.com), provides information about **skiing**, **walking** and **horse-riding**. For **accommodation**, there's *La Chaumière* hotel-restaurant, also on Grande rue (☎04.92.35.00.48, ⓦwww.hotel-seyne.com; ❸), and *Au Vieux Tilleul* (☎04.92.35.00.04, ⓦwww.vieux-tilleul.fr; ❷), 1km from the town centre at Les Auches, with its own pool/skating rink and a restaurant with menus from €13. Below the town, on either side of the river, are two **campsites**, the three-star *Les Prairies* (☎04.92.35.10.21, ⓦwww.campinglesprairies.com; €18 for two people and a tent; closed Oct–March) and the two-star *Camping la Blanche* (☎04.92.35.02.55, ⓦwww.campinglablanche.com). There are a couple of **bars** on Grande rue and one pizzeria, *La Bugade* (menus from €7).

Along the Ubaye to Barçelonnette

From the northern border of Provence at the Lac de Serre-Ponçon, the D900 follows the River Ubaye to **Barçelonnette**. It passes through a dramatic landscape of tiny, irregular fields backed by the jagged silhouettes of the mountains at the head of the valley, looking like something out of a vampire movie. There are **campsites** on the river bank in each village, and **canoeing**, **rafting**, **canyoning** and **hydrospeed** bases at Le Lauzet-sur-Ubaye and Meolans-Revel. The Aérodrome de Barçelonnette-St-Pons is announced by a grounded aeroplane transformed into a restaurant.

Barçelonnette

Snow falls on **BARÇELONNETTE** around Christmas and stays till Easter, yet, despite the proximity of several ski resorts, summer is the main tourist season. The town is immaculate, with sunny squares where old men wearing berets play pétanque, backed by views of snowcapped mountains. The houses all have tall gables and deep eaves, and a more ideal spot for doing nothing would be hard to find. The central square, place Manuel, has a white clock tower commemorating the centenary of the 1848 revolution. The Spanish association of the town's name, "Little Barcelona", is due to its foundation in the thirteenth century by Raimond Béranger IV, count of Provence, whose family came from the Catalan city.

Some of the larger houses on avenue de la Libération are particularly opulent, having been built by Barçelonette's sheep farmers and wool merchants who emigrated to Latin America in the nineteenth century to make their fortunes, before returning home to build their dream houses. One of these grand villas, *La Sapinière*, at 10 av de la Libération, houses the **Musée de la Vallée** (Jan–May & Oct to mid-Nov Wed–Sat 2.30-6pm; June to mid-July & Sept Tues–Sat 3– 6pm; mid-Jul to Aug daily 10am–noon & 3–7pm; €3.30), which details the life and times of the people of the Ubaye Valley, the emigration to Mexico and the travels of a nineteenth-century explorer from the town. In summer, the ground floor becomes an information centre for the **Parc National du Mercantour** (mid-June to mid-Sept daily 10am–noon & 3–7pm; ℡04.92.81.21.31), a national reserve stretching from the mountain passes south of Barçelonnette almost to **Sospel**. They can provide maps, advise on walks and mountain refuges, and tell you about the fauna and flora of the area.

Practicalities

Barçelonnette is very small. **Buses** from Marseille or Gap arrive on place Aimé-Gassier, three blocks south of the main street, rue Manuel, which leads to place F-Mistral. In a small courtyard just off place F-Mistral you'll find the **tourist office** (July & Aug daily 9am–7pm; Sept–June Mon–Sat 9am–noon & 2–6pm; ℡04.92.81.04.71, ⊛www.barcelonnette.com). **Bikes** can be rented from Bouticycle Granphi Sports, 51 avenue des Trois Freres Arnaud (℡04.92.81.23.69) and Rando Passion/Maison de la Montagne, 31 rue Jules-Béraud (℡04.92.81.43.34, ⊛www.rando-passion.com), who can also provide guiding and instruction for **walks** and **VTT** in summer and **snow-shoeing** and **igloo**

Skiing

The tourist office in Barçelonnette has brochures for all the local **ski resorts**, which can also be contacted direct: Pra-Loup (℡04.92.84.10.04, ⊛www.praloup.com); Ste-Anne/La Condamine (℡04.92.84.30.30, ⊛www.sainte-anne.com); Jausiers (℡04.92.81.21.45, ⊛www.jausiers.com); Le Sauze/Super-Sauze (℡04.92.81.05.61, ⊛www.sauze.com). During the skiing season a **free bus** does the rounds of the resorts from Barçelonnette. Pra-Loup's pistes link up with La Foux d'Allos (see p.284).

building in winter. More than a dozen companies offer every conceivable white-water activity from **canyoning** and **hydrospeed** to **canoeing** and **rafting;** try Alligator, Pont Long (☎04.92.81.06.06; Open April–Oct).

The best budget **places to stay** in the centre of town are the cosy *Touring*, 4 rue Jules-Béraud (☎04.92.81.07.57; ❶), or the old-fashioned and comfortable *Grand Hôtel*, 6 place Manuel (June to mid-Oct & Jan to mid-May; ☎04.92.81.03.14, ✉grandhotelbarcelonnette@hotmail.com; closed mid-Oct to Jan and first two weeks of May; ❷). Slightly more upmarket are the excellent-value *Grande Éperviére* at 18 rue des Trois Freres Arnaud (☎04.92.81.00.70, ⓦwww.hotel-grande-eperviere.com; ❹), surrounded by its own park, and *L'Azteca*, 3 rue François-Arnaud (☎04.92.81.46.36, ⓦwww.hotel-azteca.fr.st; ❹), an extremely pleasant hotel in a Mexican-style house, with superb views of the mountains. There are two **campsites** on avenue Émile-Aubert, the D902 leading to the Col de la Cayolle: the closer, three-star *Camping du Plan* (☎04.92.81.08.11, ⓦwww.campingduplan.com; closed Oct to mid-May) is 500m out of town; the two-star *Le Tampico* (☎04.92.81.02.55; €12 for two people and a tent) is 1km further out.

The best **restaurant** in the area is 9km east in **Jausiers**, *Villa Morelia* (☎04.92.84.67.78, ⓦwww.villa-morelia.com) is a neo-Mexican folly housing a gastronomic restaurant serving a nouvelle cuisine menu from €60. Back in Barce-lonnette, and continuing the South American theme, try *l'Argentine* for grilled meats in a small atmospheric restaurant, 4 place St-Pierre (☎06.22.81.44.35; a la carte from €15). Pizza is available at *Le Coco-Loco*, place Manuel (☎04.92.81.50.72; closed in winter). Whilst in town be sure also to try the local juniper liquor, *Génépi*, produced by the distiller La Maison Rousseau at La Fresquiere, 10km from Barçelonnette, but generally available in the town on market days. **Nightlife** is limited to the bars *St Tropez* and *Chocas* on place Manuel. For **Internet** access head to *Le Cyber Truc*, rue Saint Domineque (☎04.92.81.57.50) though the whole village is due to become a free **WiFi** zone in 2007.

Wednesday and Saturday are **market** days on place Aimé-Gassier and place St-Pierre, where you'll find all manner of sweets, jams and alcohol made from locally picked bilberries, pâtés made from local birds – thrush, partridge, pheasant – and the favourite liqueurs of this part of the world, distilled from alpine plants and nuts. There are also farmers' markets in summer on place de la Mairie, and in November, December, February, April and May on place Manuel.

Moving on from Barçelonnette: the mountain valleys

From Barçelonnette there are four routes across the watershed of Mont Pelat, La Bonette, Chambeyron and their high gneiss and granite extensions. The Col d'Allos leads into the **Haut-Verdon** Valley; the Col de la Cayolle into the **Haut-Var** Valley; the road across the summit of La Bonette to the **Tinée** Valley; and the Col de Larche into Italy. All but the last are snowed up between November and April, and can sometimes be closed as late as June. Further east the **Vésubie** rises just below the Italian border; like the Tinée and the Verdon it runs into the Var.

The Haut-Verdon Valley

The most westerly route from Barçelonnette crosses the **Col d'Allos** (closed Nov–May) at 2250m to join the River Verdon just a few kilometres from its source. A mountain refuge, *Col d'Allos* (☎04.92.83.85.14; closed Sept–July), on the pass, marks the junction with the GR56, which leads west to the Ubaye Valley and Seyne-les-Alpes, and east to the Col de Larche and the Tinée Valley. In late June pale wild pansies and deep blue gentians flower between patches of ice. The panorama is magnificent, though once you start backstitching your way down the side of the pass to the Verdon, the hideous vast hotels of **La Foux d'Allos** come into view.

La Foux d'Allos

If you're going to **ski** or snowboard, scruffy **LA FOUX D'ALLOS** is probably the cheapest Provençal resort in which to do it. The 50 lifts and 180km of pistes are open from late December to mid-April. The area joins up with Pra-Loup to the north, and the resort is quite high (1800–2600m) with over 250 snow cannons, so melting shouldn't be a problem. A day pass is €27 and skis/snowboards can be rented in season at Lantelme Sports, Le Centre (☎04.92.83.80.09) who for the rest of the year rent out **VTT bikes**.

La Foux d'Allos and its neighbours are also keen to promote themselves as summer resorts, with all kinds of activities on offer at the Parc de Loisirs in Allos, from trampolining to horse-riding, archery, courses in wildlife photography and water sports. During July and August a handful of lifts are open to transport VTT bikers to the well-marked trails around the mountain. The **tourist office** in the Maison de la Foux (July, Aug & 20 Dec to April daily 9am–noon & 2–6.30pm; ☎04.92.83.80.70) can provide details.

The best-value place to stay is the **youth hostel**, *HI La Foux d'Allos* (☎04.92.83.81.08, ⓦwww.val-dallos.fuaj.org; closed mid-Sept to Nov & mid-May to mid-June), which must be booked well in advance. Other options include the **hotels** *Le Sestrière* (☎04.92.83.81.70, ⓦwww.lesestriere .com; closed May, Oct & Nov; ❸) and *Le Toukal* (☎04.92.83.82.76, ⓦwww .hotel-letoukal.com; closed May to late June & mid-Sept to Nov; ❹).

Allos and its lake

The medieval village of **ALLOS**, 9km south of La Foux d'Allos, was all but destroyed by fire in the eighteenth century; one tower of the ramparts half - survived and was turned into the current clock tower. The old livelihoods of tending sheep and weaving woollen sheets only just made it past the turn of the twentieth century when tourism began with the discovery of the **Lac d'Allos**, 13km east and 800m above Allos. Once skiing became an established pastime the agricultural days of Allos were numbered. But for all its *résidences secondaires*, it's not a bad place to spend a day or two.

From Allos an uneven, single track road weaves up 46 bends in 6km through a dense forest of larch trees to a busy car park. From here it is a 45-minute walk to reach what was once the head of a glacier. If you want to walk the whole way from Allos, follow the path which starts by the church. At 2228m the round and impossibly blue surface reflects the high amphitheatre half-circling it. The lake nourishes trout and char in its pure cold waters and bounding around its banks are mouflon and chamois. Looking in the direction of the one-time glacier flow, you can just see the peak of **Mont Pelat**, the highest mountain in the Parc National du Mercantour.

Practicalities

For information on paths, weather conditions and so forth, the Parc National du Mercantour has an office (☎04.92.83.04.18) in the same building as the **tourist**

office (July, Aug & mid-Dec to mid-April Mon–Sat 8.30am–noon & 2–6.30pm, Sun 9am–noon & 3–6.30pm; Sept to mid-Dec and mid-April to June Mon–Sat 9am–noon & 2–5pm, Sun 9am–noon; ☎04.92.83.02.81, ⓦwww.valdallos.com), at the northern end of the old village. Note that the only **bank** in this stretch of the valley is the Crédit Agricole opposite (Tues–Sat).

Hotels include the *Hotel Les Gentianes* (☎04.92.83.03.50; ❸) in the old village, and the more upmarket but characterless *Plein Soleil* (☎04.92.83.02.16, ⓔhotel .pleinsoleil@laposte.net; ❸) in Super-Allos, the modern extension northeast of the village. There's a very comfortable **chambre d'hôte**, *La Ferme Girerd-Potin*, on route de la Foux (☎04.92.83.04.76, ⓦwww.chambredhotes-valdallos.com; ❸), and a **gîte d'étape**, the *Chalet Auberge L'Autapie* (☎04.92.83.06.31, ⓦwww .lautapie.com; half board only €30 per person). Walkers can also stay at the *Refuge du Lac d'Allos* on the lake itself (☎04.92.83.00.24; closed Oct–June; ❶), but will have to book well in advance.

The choice of places to **eat** in Allos is limited. You can get pasta and fondue at *Le Bercail*, 1 Grand rue (☎04.92.83.07.53; menus from €14), while upmarket picnic food can be bought from *La Ferme Gourmande* opposite the tourist office. A useful place to shop, for food and anything else you might need, is the Shopi supermarket on the main road (Mon–Sat 8.45am–12.15pm & 3.30–7pm; closed Wed pm). **Skis** and **VTT bikes** can be rented from Au Petit Allossard, rue du Pré de Foire (☎04.92.83.14.62).

Colmars-les-Alpes

The next town downstream from Allos is **COLMARS-LES-ALPES**, an extraordinarily well-preserved stronghold, whose name comes from a temple to Mars built by the Romans on the hill above the town. The sixteenth-century ramparts with their arrow slits and small square towers are complete; and though the two main entrances, the Porte de France and Porte de Savoie, have been reduced to just gateways, the impression is still that this is a perfect historical model. The ramparts were constructed on the orders of François I of France to reinforce the defences that had existed since 1381, when Colmars became a border town between Provence and Savoy. When Savoy declared war on France, in 1690, Vauban was called in to make the town even more secure. He designed the **Fort de Savoie** and the **Fort de France** at either end of the town.

Having passed through the Porte de France, the Porte de Savoie or the smaller Porte de Lance halfway between them – all adorned with climbing roses – you find yourself in an exquisite old and quiet Provençal town with cobbled streets and fountained squares. The Fort de Savoie is open for guided tours in July and August (daily 10am; €4; tickets from the tourist office), when exhibitions of art or local traditions are set up beneath the magnificent larch-timbered ceilings. All in all, there's not a lot to do in Colmars except wander around and soak up the atmosphere, or you could take a twenty-minute walk east of the town to the Lance waterfall.

The **tourist office** is by Porte de la Lance (July & Aug daily 8am–7pm; Sept–June Mon–Sat 9am–12.15pm & 2–5.45pm; ☎04.92.83.41.92, ⓦwww .colmars-les-alpes.fr). There is one **hotel**, *Le Chamois*, just off the D908 opposite the walled town (☎04.92.83.43.29; closed mid-Nov to Dec; ❸); a **gîte d'étape**, the *Gassendi*, rue St Joseph, eight dorms with ten beds each, housed in a twelfth-century Templar hospice (☎04.92.83.42.25; ❶); and a very scenic **campsite**, *Le Bois Joly*, by the river (☎04.92.83.40.40; closed Oct–April). For **food** there's *Le Lézard* restaurant and *salon de thé*, on the corner of Grande rue and place Neuve, which serves *raclette*, and the *Café Rétro* on place

J-Girieud by the *mairie*. For picnic supplies, there's a *boulangerie*, *charcuterie* and wine shop, all on Grande rue.

Colmars lies at the junction of the Verdon Valley road with the D78 which climbs up between the Frema and Encombrette mountains and descends to the Var Valley at St-Martin-d'Entraunes. Six kilometres along the road, signed left, is the **Ratery ski-station** (☎04.92.83.40.92), which rents out **bikes** in summer. You can **trek** from here over the Encombrette to the Lac d'Allos or east across the Col des Champs (closed mid-Nov to mid-May) to the Var at Entraunes.

Beauvezer

If you're heading south towards Thorame, Annot or St-André (see pp.272–277), you can follow the D908 for 5km to **BEAUVEZER** – experienced cross-country skiers can take a looping route there through the Forêt de Monier and across the summit of the Laupon. The road sticks to the Verdon, a wide dramatic torrent in winter or spring, a wide messy track of scattered boulders and branches in summer. Beauvezer perches high above its right bank, a wonderful ancient village smelling of old timbers whose ancient stone wash basins give away the villages linen making past. Beside the beautiful ochre church is one of the prettiest **hotel-restaurants** in Haute Provence, *Le Bellevue*, place de l'Église (☎04.92.83.51.60, ⓦwww.hotellebellevue.org; ❸).

The Haut-Var Valley

The route to the **Haut-Var Valley** from Barçelonnette first follows the River Bachelard through its gorge, then east, following its course between Mont Pelat to the south and the ridge of peaks to the north, whose shapes have given them the names Pain de Sucre (Sugarloaf), Chapeau de Gendarme (Gendarme's Hat) and Chevalier (Horseman). At the *Bayasse* refuge (☎04.92.81.07.31, ⓦrefuge.bayasse.free.fr; ❶), the main road turns south towards the **Col de la Cayolle**, while a track and the GR56 continue east towards La Bonette and the Tinée Valley.

The Var makes its appearance below the Col de la Cayolle and pours southwards through Entraunes and St-Martin-d'Entraunes to Guillaumes and on down through the **Gorges de Daluis** to Entrevaux. Its banks are punctuated with chapels built before and after disasters of avalanches, floods, landslides and devastating storms. Many are superbly decorated, like the Renaissance Chapelle de St-Sébastien, just north of Entraunes and the church at St-Martin-d'Entraunes, with its Bréa retable.

Tucked beneath the ruined Château de la Reine Jeanne, **GUILLAUMES**, the valley's minor metropolis and a favourite with cyclists in summer, is a traditional resting place for sheep on their way between the Haut-Var summer pastures and Nice. Though most flocks now travel by lorry, the old **sheep fairs** on September 16 and the second Saturday of October are still held. Winter sees a migration in the opposite direction, as the residents of the Côte d'Azur flock to the ski resorts of Valberg and Beuil, to the east of Guillaumes, on the fabulous road that climbs over to the Tinée Valley.

The biggest **tourist office** in the area is in Valberg (daily 9am–noon & 2–6pm; ☎04.93.23.24.25, ⓦwww.valberg.com), although Guillaumes has a "chalet du tourisme" on the main road opposite the town hall (☎04.93.05.57.76; daily 10am–12.30pm & 1.30–5pm). For **accommodation** in Guillaumes, there's the *Les Chaudrons* hotel on the main road (☎04.93.05.50.01; ❷), and *La Renaissance*, an old-fashioned establishment 100m up on the right just past the bridge (☎04.93.05.59.89, ⓦwww.hotelrenaissance.fr; ❸), whose restaurant has menus at €14, €17 and €24.

About 5km south of Guillaumes, the Var enters the dramatic red-rocked **Gorges de Daluis**. The Pont de la Mariée across the gorge is a popular spot for bungee-jumpers. It's worth noting that the road upstream has the better view while the downstream carriageway is in tunnels much of the way. Walkers can get a closer look at the gorge by following the 2km *Sentier du Point Sublime* from Pont de Berthèou on the D2202 to the Point Sublime itself.

The Tinée Valley

The longest of the Var's tributaries, the Tinée rises just below the 2800-metre summit of **La Bonette**. The mountains on its left bank – under whose shadow **St-Étienne** and **Auron** nestle – rise up to the Italian border, while the river heads south to cut a steep, narrow valley before joining the Var 30km from the sea.

Across La Bonette

Claiming to be the highest stretch of tarmac in Europe, the road across **La Bonette** gives a feast of high-altitude views. The summit of the mountain, a ten-minute scrabble up scree from the road, is not particularly exciting, and is made more ugly by its military training camp. But the green and silent spaces of the approach, circled by barren peaks, are magical.

Before the hairpins begin for the southern descent, at Camp des Fourches, you can abandon your wheels and take the **GR5/56** north and parallel with the Italian border to the Col de Larche, then northwest towards Larche, where there's a gîte (☎04.92.84.30.80; ❷). It's not exactly a stroll, but once you've climbed to the Col de la Cavale (after 5km or so) it's more or less

△ Parc National du Mercantour

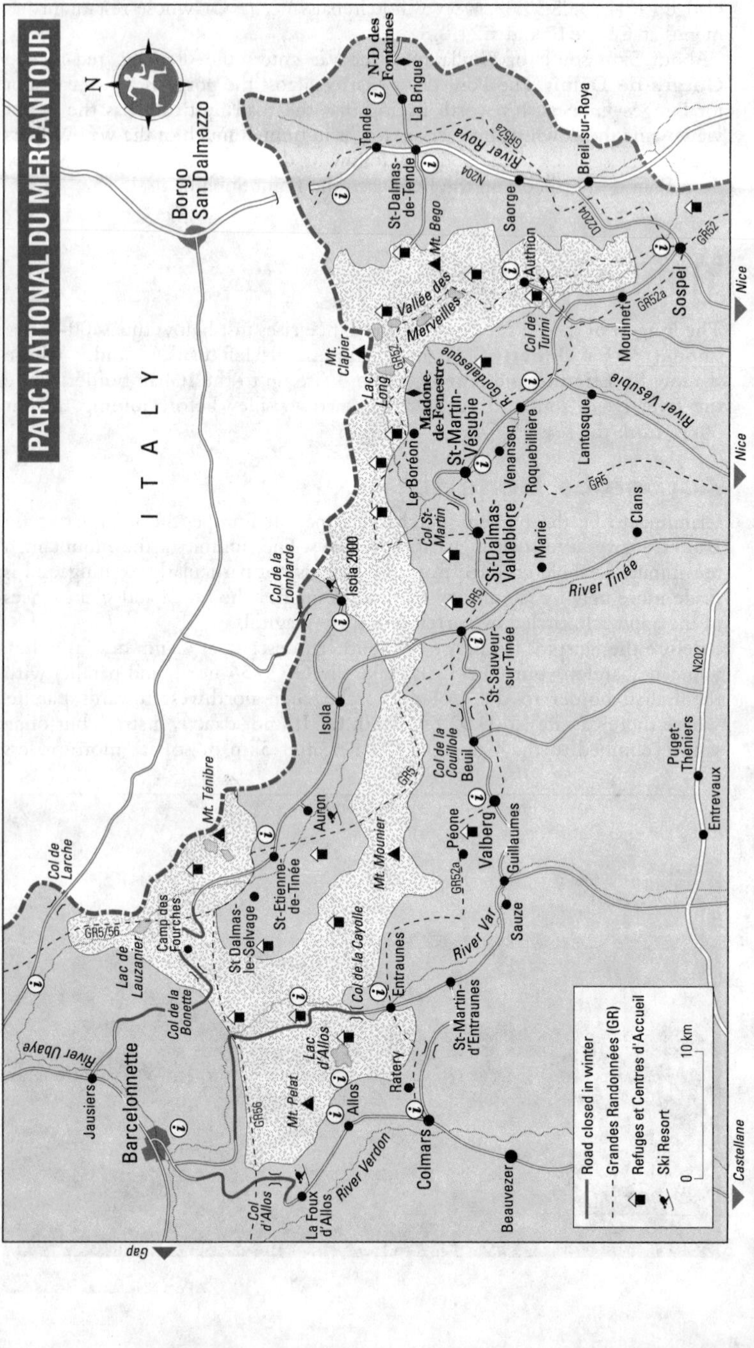

PARC NATIONAL DU MERCANTOUR
N
ITALY
Borgo San Dalmazzo
Col de Larche
Jausiers
River Ubaye
Barcelonnette
Gap
Lac de Lauzanier
GR5/56
Camp des Fourches
Col de la Bonette
Mt. Ténibre
St Dalmas-le-Selvage
Col d'Allos
GR56
St-Etienne-de-Tinée
Col de la Lombarde
Mt. Pelat
La Foux d'Allos
Lac d'Allos
Auron
Isola
Isola 2000
Allos
Col de la Cayolle
River Verdon
Mt. Mounier
Mt. Clapier
Lac Long
Ratery
Entraunes
GR5
GR52
Vallée des Merveilles
Tende
N-D des Fontaines
St-Dalmas-de-Tende
La Brigue
Colmars
Le Boréon
Madone-de-Fenestre
Mt. Bego
Col St-Martin
St-Martin-Vésubie
Col de la Couillole
GR52a
Péone
St-Martin-d'Entraunes
Beuil
River Var
Valberg
St-Sauveur-sur-Tinée
St-Dalmas-Valdeblore
Venanson
R. Gordalesque
N204
River Roya
Saorge
Beauvezer
Sauze
Guillaumes
Roquebillière
Authion
Col de Turini
Marie
Lantosque
River Tinée
D2204
Breil-sur-Roya
Moulinet
River Vésubie
Clans
Road closed in winter
Grandes Randonnées (GR)
Refuges et Centres d'Accueil
Ski Resort
0
10 km
Puget-Théniers
N202
Entrevaux
Sospel
Castellane
Nice
Nice

downhill all the way, with the Ubayette torrent as your guide, and the **Lac de Lauzanier**, 5km on from the Col de la Cavale, a spot you may never want to leave.

A short way down from the Camp des Fourches is the *Gîte de Bousiéyas* (℡04.93.02.42.20; closed mid-Sept to mid-June). About 5km on, a track on the left to the tiny hamlet of **Vens** leads to a footpath that follows the Vens torrent to the Lacs de Vens and a refuge at 2380m (℡04.93.02.44.87; closed mid-Sept to mid-June).

St-Étienne-de-Tinée and Auron

Continuing on the road, with the Tinée alongside, you descend to the small, isolated town of **ST-ÉTIENNE-DE-TINÉE** that comes to life only during its sheep fairs, held twice every summer, and the Fête de la Transhumance at the end of June. The **tourist office** at 1 rue des Communes-de-France (daily 9am–noon & 2–5pm; ℡04.93.02.41.96, ⓦwww.auron.com), organizes tours (€3.10) of the town's chapels, the museums of milk-making and traditional crafts and of the old school. Just up from the Pont St-Antoine, at the northern end of the village, is the **Maison du Parc National du Mercantour** (daily 2–5.30pm; ℡04.93.02.42.27), with displays and information about the park.

There are two **hotel-restaurants** in town – the *Regalivou*, boulevard d'Auron (℡ & ⓕ04.93.02.49.00; ❹), and *Des Amis*, 1 rue Val Gélé (℡04.93.02.40.30; ❷) – as well as a few alpine-style restaurants. The *Café Autheman*, on the corner of the main square, has a good selection of beers.

On the west side of the town off boulevard d'Auron, a cable-car then chairlift climb to the summit of **La Pinatelle** (€6.90), linking the village to the ski resort of **AURON**. In **summer** a handful of the lifts are open to hikers and mountain bikers (July-Aug; €8.30 day) while in **winter** the 21 lifts and 135km of pistes are used by skiers (Dec-April; €26.30 day). Georges Sports 2000, in St-Étienne-de-Tinée (℡04.93.02.45.95) **rents** bikes in summer and ski equipment in winter. By road, Auron is 7km south of St-Étienne, on a dead-end spur from the main road.

The next stretch downstream from St-Étienne has nothing but white quartz and heather, with only the silvery sound of crickets competing with the water's roar before reaching **Isola**, an uneventful village at the bottom of the climb to the purpose-built ski resort of **ISOLA 2000** (ⓦwww.isola2000.com), a jumble of concrete apartment blocks high in the mountain, just below the tree line, built to accommodate the skiers using the 22 lifts and 120km of piste (Dec-Apr; €26.30 day).

St-Sauveur-sur-Tinée

On the road south towards **ST-SAUVEUR-SUR-TINÉE**, the drop in altitude is marked by sweet chestnut trees taking over from the pines. St-Sauveur is dominated by its medieval needle belfry, which perches above the river in Mediterranean rather than Alpine fashion. The adornments of the Romanesque gargoyled church include a rather fine fifteenth-century retable, behind the bloodied crucifix, and a fifteenth-century statue of St Paul above the side door outside.

There's not a lot to do here other than sit in the sun above the river or head off along the GR52A, but it's an attractive place to stop. There's a small **café**, the *Café du Village*, on the main road through the village, while the *boulangerie* on the corner of place de la Mairie sells basic provisions as well as scrumptious *tourtes de blettes* (closed Tues). For **accommodation**, try the *Auberge de la Gare* at the southern end of the village (℡04.93.02.00.67; ❶), or the *Relais d'Auron*,

18 av des Blavets (☎04.93.02.00.03, ℻04.93.02.10.89; ❷). The two-star municipal **campsite** is in quartier Les Plans (☎04.93.02.03.20; closed mid-Sept to mid-June).

From St-Sauveur, you can either head west along the D30 towards Valberg and the Haut-Var Valley, a dramatically precipitous climb, or follow the Tinée south, passing far below the charming perched villages of Marie, Clans and La Tour, all of which have medieval decorations in their churches.

The Vésubie valley

A few kilometres south of St-Sauveur-sur-Tinée, the D2565 heads off east to climb abruptly to the scattered **Commune of Valdeblore**, with its ancient village of **St-Dalmas**. The road then descends to **St-Martin-Vésubie** standing at the head of the **Vésubie Valley**, and at the junction of two torrents, Le Boréon and La Madone de la Fenestre, descending from the north and east. South from St-Martin, road and river head towards the Var, passing the flood-prone *commune* of **Roquebillière**, the perched village of **Lantosque**, and the approach to the pilgrimage chapel of **Madonne d'Utelle**. An alternative southern route from the valley crosses east to the **Col de Turini** and down the **River Bévéra** towards Sospel.

The Commune de Valdeblore and St-Dalmas

Straddling the Col St-Martin between the Tinée and Vésubie valleys, the **COMMUNE DE VALDEBLORE** consists of a series of settlements strung along the D2565, starting with La Bolline and La Roche, then the ancient village of St-Dalmas, finishing, on the eastern side of the col, with the ski resort of **La Colmiane**, where you can take a chairlift for stunning views from the **Pic de Colmiane** (Christmas–March daily 10am–4.50pm; July & Aug daily 10am–6pm; €2.50). The **tourist office** is in La Roche (daily 9am–noon & 2–6pm; ☎04.93.23.25.90, ⓦ www.colmiane.com).

The most interesting of Valdeblore's villages is **ST-DALMAS**, which was built on the remains of a Roman outpost, and lies at the strategic crossroads between the most accessible southern route across the lower Alps, linking Piedmont with Provence, and a north–south route linking Savoy with the sea. The former importance of this region is clear from the dimensions of the **Église Prieurale Bénédictine** (mid-June to mid-Sept afternoons only; mornings and mid-Sept to mid-June by request; call Jean Alcoy on ☎04.93.02.82.29), parts of which are thought to date from the tenth century. A gruesome glazed tomb reveals a 900-year-old skeleton; more appealing are the fragments of fourteenth-century frescoes in the north chapel. The present structure is Romanesque, plain and fierce with its typically Alpine bell tower and rounded apsidal chapels on which eleventh-century Lombardian decoration is still visible. If your French is good it's worth getting a guided tour from Jean Alcoy, who can be found at the **Musée du Terroir** just up from the church (same hours as the church; €3), which displays traditional agricultural tools, household items, and a large model train set.

St-Martin-Vésubie and around

Eleven kilometres east of St-Dalmas, **ST-MARTIN-VÉSUBIE** is at its busiest in July and August, though even at the height of the season, it's not jam-packed.

In late spring and early autumn it's a perfect base for exploring the surrounding mountains, and in winter you can go for wonderful walks in snowshoes, or tackle some of the cross-country skiing routes that pass through the town.

The main artery of the old quarter, the **rue du Docteur-Cagnoli**, is a single-file cobbled street of Gothic houses with overhanging roofs and balconies, through which flows a channelled stream designed in the fifteenth century for sewage and now charged with rainwater or melting snow. Halfway down on the left is the **Chapelle des Pénitents Blancs**, decorated with eighteenth-century paintings. At the end of the street is St-Martin's **church**, with works attributed to Louis Bréa, a mirror on the high altar reflecting the stained-glass window above the door, and a venerated polychrome wooden statue of the Madonna that is taken up to the Chapelle de Madone de Fenestre (see p.292) at the beginning of July and brought back towards the end of September. Southeast of the church you can look down at the Madone de Fenestre torrent from place de la Frairie. In the opposite direction a narrow lane leads to the junction of rue Kellerman and the main road, beyond which is the old wash house and **Le Vieux Moulin**, the town's one museum (June & Sept Fri, Sat & Sun 2.30–6.30pm; July & Aug daily 2.30–6.30pm; Oct–May Sat & Sun 2.30–6.30pm; €3), which illustrates the traditional way of life of the Vésubiens.

The **fountain** on allées de Verdun, the *cours* in front of place Félix-Fauré, has a placard detailing its mineral contents and citing the ministerial declaration of 1913 that claims the water has negative pathogenic germs. *Alpha* (Ⓦ www.alpha-loup .com; daily 10am-5pm; €9) is a new **wolf reserve**, 8km north at **Le Boréon**, which despite its lack of information and signage in English, makes an interesting visit, particularly in spring when you can see the new born puppies from the three observation points; minibuses depart from outside the tourist office.

Practicalities

St-Martin's **gare routière** is on place de la Gare, where avenue de la Gare loops south into avenue de Caqueray, while the **tourist office** is on place Félix-Fauré (July-Aug daily 9am-7pm; Sept–June daily 9am–noon & 2–6pm; Oct–May Mon–Sat 9am–noon & 2.30–5.30pm, Sun 10am–noon; ℡04.93.03.21.28, Ⓦ www.saintmartinvesubie.fr) along with the *mairie*, post office and a bank.

The tourist office has lists of gîtes and mountain refuges for St-Martin and the surrounding area posted up outside, plus lists of walking guides and weather information. On rue du Dr-Cagnoli, just below place du Marché, the Bureau des Guides et Accompagnateurs de la Haute Vésubie (℡04.93.03.26.60) can organize **walks** - including winter expeditions with snowshoe rental, and give advice for your own expeditions. The Guides du Mercantour, on place de Marché (℡04.93.03.31.32), can arrange **canoeing**, **climbing**, **horse rides**, **walks** and **skiing**. Maps, compasses and the like can be purchased from Aux Milles Articles, 50 rue du Dr Cagnoli. La Librairie de Mercantour, 56 rue du Dr Cagnoli, is another excellent source of **books and maps** on the national park.

Accommodation is plentiful. The least expensive of the town's five **hotels** is the *Hotel des Alpes* on place Félix-Fauré (℡04.93.03.21.06; ❷), while *La Bonne Auberge*, a short way up the allées de Verdun (℡04.93.03.20.49, Ⓦ www .labonneauberge06.fr; closed mid-Nov to Jan; ❷), and the *La Châtaigneraie*, also on the allées de Verdun (℡04.93.03.21.22, Ⓕ 04.93.03.33.99; closed Oct–May; ❺), offer slightly more comfort. The closest **campsite** is the two-star *Ferme St-Joseph* on the route de Nice by the lower bridge over La Madone (℡04.93.03.20.14; Ⓦ www.camping-alafermestjoseph.com; €10 per tent). In the opposite direction 1.5km out of town, on the route de la Colmiane, there's *La Mério* (℡ 04.93.03.30.38, Ⓦ www.univers-nature.com/la-merio; €14 per tent; open June to mid-Sept) and, to the southwest, on the route de Venanson, the two-star *Le Champouns* (☎04.93.03.23.72, @www.champouns.com; €11.70 for two people & a tent), which also has apartments to let and dormitory accommodation.

The nicest **restaurant** in town is *La Trappa* on place du Marché (closed Mon in term time), which offers a four-course meal from €17–22, and the restaurant in *La Bonne Auberge* is also worth trying. For snacks, *La Mavorine café-boulangerie* on place Félix-Fauré serves *bruschettas* for around €6, plus ice creams, crêpes and cakes.

Finally, there's an après-ski **disco**, *Le Croque Montagne*, off rue du Dr Cagnoli on the east slope of the old town.

Around St-Martin: Le Boréon and Madone de Fenestre

Asides from *Alpha*, the wolf park (see p.291), the other reason for visiting **LE BORÉON**, 10km north of St-Martin and just inside the Parc du Mercantour,

Wildlife of the Mercantour

The least shy of the mammal inhabitants of these mountains is the **marmot**, a cream-coloured, badger-sized creature that is often seen sitting on its haunches in the sun. Chamois, mouflon and ibex are almost equally unwary of humans, even though it was not so long ago that they were hunted here. The male **ibex** is a wonderful, big, solid beast with curving, ribbed horns that grow to a metre long; the species very nearly became extinct, and it is one of the successes of the park that the population is now stable. Another species of goat, the **chamois**, is also on the increase. The male is recognizable by the shorter, grappling-hook horns and white beard. The **mouflon**, introduced to the Mercantour in the 1950s, is the ancestor of domestic sheep. Other animals that you might see include **stoats**, rare species of **hare**, and **foxes** which are now the most abundant predator since bears and lynxes became extinct in the region. The most problematic predator, however, is the **wolf**, once extinct, but stalking the region again since 1992, having crossed the border from Italy. With eight hundred sheep killed by wolves in a single year, sheep farmers are not happy, and the predators have been found killed despite their protected status.

The Mercantour is a perfect habitat for **eagles**, which have any number of crags on which to build their nests, and plenty to eat – including marmots. Pairs of **golden eagles** are now breeding, and a rare vulture, the **lammergeier**, has been successfully reintro-duced to the region. Other birds of prey, **kestrels**, **falcons** and **buzzards**, wing their way down from the scree to the Alpine lawn and its torrents to swoop on lizards, mice and snakes. The **great spotted woodpecker** and the black and orange **hoopoe** are the most colourful inhabitants of the park. **Ptarmigan**, which turn snowy-white in winter, can sometimes be seen in June parading to their would-be mates on the higher slopes in the north. **Blackcocks**, known in French as *tétras-lyre* for their lyre-shaped white tails, burrow into the snow at night and fly out in a flurry of snowflakes when the sun rises.

The **flowers** of the Mercantour are an unmissable glory, with over two thousand species represented, about forty of which are unique to the region. The moment the snow melts, the lawn between the rocky crags and the tree line begins to dot with golds, pinks and blues. Rare species of **lily** and **orchid** grow here, as do the elusive **edelweiss** and the wild ancestors of various cultivated flowers – pansies, geraniums, tulips and gentian violets. Rarest of all is the **multi-flowering saxifrage** (*saxifraga florulenta*), a big spiky flower that looks as if it must be cultivated, though it would hardly be popular in suburban gardens since it flowers just once every ten years. Wild strawberries, raspberries and bilberries tempt you into the woods.

Camping, lighting fires, picking flowers, playing loud music or doing anything else that might disturb the delicate environment is strictly outlawed.

is to eat trout, either caught yourself or by those who supply the clutch of **restaurants** and **hotels** at this small, scenic mountain retreat. During the fishing season, from mid-March to early September, you can get a licence from the hotels here or from most of the bars in St-Martin. The two **hotel-restaurants** are *Le Boréon*, quartier du Cascade (☎04.93.03.20.35, Ⓦwww.hotelboreon .com; menus from €18-€29; closed mid-Nov to Dec; ❹), and *Le Cavalet*, Lac du Boréon (☎04.93.03.21.46, Ⓕ04.93.03.34.34; half-board only, €65 per person). There's also a **gîte** at 248 rte de Salése (☎04.93.03.27.27; ❶).

Returning to St-Martin then heading east for 11.5km along the D94 will bring you to the **Chapelle de Madone de Fenestre** standing above the tree line in a setting of barren rocks, also just within the borders of the Parc du Mercantour. Half a dozen gloomy, rough-hewn stone buildings, one of them housing a refuge and restaurant, surround the chapel, named after the hole in the rock above it through which you can see the sky. The main purpose for coming up here is to **trek** along the GR52, which passes by the sanctuary and leads eastwards to the Vallée des Merveilles (see p.298). This is not the shortest route but it's a very dramatic path that rarely descends below 2000m.

In summer there is a weekly **bus** on Thursdays from St-Martin to Le Boréon, and one, on Sunday, to Madone de Fenestre.

Downstream to Madone d'Utelle

South from St-Martin on the other side of the valley, but approached by a circuitous route that heads north out of the town, is the little village of **VENANSON**, which dubs itself, appropriately, a "zone of silence". It has just one **hotel-restaurant**, the *Bella-Vista* on place St Jean (☎04.93.03.25.11, Ⓕ04.93.64.45.60; half-board only; ❷), a dark **chapel** with Baleison frescoes, and an excellent view over St-Martin.

Back on the left bank you come to the old village of **ROQUEBILLIÈRE**, which has been rebuilt six times since the Dark Ages after catastrophic landslides and floods. The last major disaster was in 1926 when half the old village disappeared under mud; a new village was created high above the right bank of the Vésubie. The planned, wide, tree-lined avenues of 1940's and 1950's houses of the nouveux village lie in stark contrast to the crumpling, leaning, medieval houses bearing down over narrow passageways in the dark and sad *vieux village* which lies deep in the valley on the left bank. Apart from the archaeological interest of the various superseded settlements and the beauty of the frequently rebuilt church, the new village has a wonderful *boulangerie*, Chez Somiani (closed Sun pm) on the main street, avenue C-Moulinie.

The road along the **Gordolesque Valley** above old Roquebillière heads north for 16km with paths leading off eastwards towards the Vallée des Merveilles. Where the road ends you can continue upstream past waterfalls and high crags to Lac de la Fous where you meet the GR52 running west to Madone de Fenestre and east to the northern end of the Vallée des Merveilles (see p.298). This triangle between Mont Clapier on the Italian border (3045m), Mont Bego (2873m) to the east and Mont Neiglier (2785m) to the west is a fabulous area for walking, but not to be taken lightly. All the **mountain refuges** here belong to the Club Alpin Français (☎04.93.62.59.99) and may well be unsympathetic if you turn up unannounced.

South of Roquebillière, the D70 leaves the Vésubie Valley to head east through the chic resort of La-Bollène-Vésubie to the Col de Turini (see below). Staying with the Vésubie, you reach **LANTOSQUE**, which, like Roquebillière, has had its share of earth tremors and was badly flooded in 1993. Yet it survives in picturesque form, a pyramid of winding, stepped streets full of nervous cats, with a wonderful café-brasserie, the *Bar des Tilleuls*, on the lower *place*, serving copious and delicious *plats du jour* for around €12. The village has one swish **hotel** on the other side of the river, the *Hostellerie de L'Ancienne Gendarmerie*, in quartier Rivet (℡04.93.03.00.65, Ⓦwww.hotel-lantosque.com; closed mid-Nov to Feb; ⑤), with an excellent restaurant.

Just before the river starts to pick up speed through the gorge leading to its confluence with the Var, you can detour upwards to yet another far-flung **chapel**, dedicated to **La Madone d'Utelle**. It stands on a plateau above the village of Utelle, high enough to be visible from the sea at Nice. According to legend, two Portuguese sailors lost in a storm in the year 850 navigated safely into port by a light they saw gleaming from Utelle. They erected a chapel here to give thanks, though the current one dates from 1806. Pilgrimages still take place on Easter Monday, the Monday of Pentecost, August 15 and September 8, and are concluded with a communal feast on the grassy summit. You'll find reasonable fare in the village at *La Bellevue* on route de la Madone (℡04.93.03.17.19; menus from €12; closed Jan).

The Col de Turini

At the **Col de Turini**, 15km east of Roquebillière, you know you're in a popular spot from the litter and snack bars. Four roads and two tracks meet at the pass, all giving access to the **Forêt de Turini**, which covers the area between the Vésubie and Bévéra valleys. Larches grow in the highest reaches of the forest, giving way further down to firs, spruce, beech, maples and sweet chestnuts.

The road north from the col through the small ski resort of **Camp d'Argent** to L'Aution gives a strong impression of limitless space, following the curved ridge between the two valleys and overlooking a hollow of pastures. There are plenty of walks hereabouts, but the sun, the flowers and the wild strawberries and raspberries are so pleasant you might just want to stop in a field and listen to the cowbells. The nicest place **to stay** is *Le Relais du Camp d'Argent*, Camp d'Argent, Turini (℡04.93.91.57.58; half-board only, at €48 per person), which serves decent **meals** from €20.

Sospel and the Roya Valley

From the Col de Turini the D2566 follows the valley of the River Bévéra southeast to **Sospel**, which straddles the main road and rail links from the French coast to the **Roya Valley**. Though it's the most easterly valley of Provence, the Roya is also the most accessible, being served by train lines from Nice, via Sospel, and from Ventimiglia in Italy: the lines converge just south of **Breil-sur-Roya**. When Nice became part of France in 1860, the upper Roya Valley was kept by the newly appointed King Victor Emmanuel II of Italy to indulge his passion for hunting, despite a plebiscite in which only one person in Tende and La Brigue voted for the Italian option. It was not until 1947 that the valley was finally incorporated into France. As you would expect from the result of the vote, everyone speaks French, though they do so with a distinctly Italian intonation.

Sospel

The ruggedness of the surrounding terrain only serves to emphasize the placid idyll of **SOSPEL**, a dreamy Italianate town spanning the gentle River Bévéra.

Its main street, avenue Jean-Médecin, follows the river on its southern bank before crossing the most easterly of the three bridges to become boulevard de Verdun heading for the Roya Valley. The central bridge, the **Vieux Pont** with its tower between the two spans for collecting tolls, was built in the early eleventh century to link the town centre on the south bank with its suburb across the river. Impossibly picturesque, it's the architectural lynchpin of Sospel's townscape. The scene is made yet more alluring by the balconied houses along the north bank which back on to the grimy rue de la République. The banks are lush with flowering shrubs and trees, and one house even has a trompe-l'oeil street facade. Viewed from the eastern end of avenue Jean-Médecin, with the hills to the west and the bridge tower reflected in the water, this scene would be hard to improve.

Yet there's another vista in the town that rivals the river scene. For maximum effect, it's best approached down rue St-Pierre from the eastern place St-Pierre. The street, which is deeply shadowed and gloomy with equally uninviting alleyways running off it, suddenly opens onto **place St-Michel** and you have before you one of the most beautiful series of peaches-and-cream Baroque facades in all Provence. In front of you is the **Église St-Michel** with its separate austere Romanesque clock tower. To the left are the **Chapelle des Pénitents Gris** and the **Chapelle des Pénitents Rouges**, and to the right are the medieval arcades and trompe-l'oeil decoration of the **Palais Ricci**. St-Michel contains an altarpiece by François Bréa in which the background to the red and gold robes of the Madonna is a bewitching river landscape of mountains, monasteries and dark citadels. On the right-hand panel Saint Martha has the snarling *Tarasque* well under control on a lead.

The road behind the church, rue de l'Abbaye, which you can reach via the steps between the two chapels, leads up to an ivy-covered **castle ruin**, from where you get a good view of the town. Further up, along chemin de St-Roch, an even better view can be had from the **Fort St-Roch**, part of the ignominious interwar Maginot line, which houses the **Musée de la Résistance** (April–June Sat & Sun 2–6pm; July–Sept Tues–Sun 2–6pm; €5), illustrating the courageous local resistance movement during World War II. Although under Italian occupation after June 1940, the town hall continued to fly the French flag; when the Germans took over in 1943, however, life became much harsher, and only a few of the Jews who had taken refuge here managed to escape south to Monaco. After Menton was liberated in September 1944, the Allied force advanced north carrying out airborne attacks on Sospel, but stopped 5km short of the town. Sospel, therefore, was left to the mercy of the Germans, but with Allied artillery attacks adding to the casualties. At the end of October the Germans were forced to retreat, but not far enough, and the battle for Sospel continued until April 1945.

Practicalities

The **gare SNCF** is southeast of the town on avenue A-Borriglione, which becomes avenue des Martyrs-de-la-Résistance, before leading down to the riverside place des Platanes. Sospel's **tourist office** is at 19 av Jean-Médecin (Mon 2.30–6.30pm, Tues–Sat 9.30am–12.30pm & 2.30–6.30pm, Sun 9.30am–12.30pm; ☎04.93.04.15.80, ⓦ www.sospel-tourisme.com).

The *Auberge du Pont-Vieux*, 3 av Jean-Médecin (☎04.93.04.00.73; ❸), is Sospel's cheapest **hotel**. The *Hôtel des Étrangers* at 7 bd de Verdun (☎04.93.04.00.09, ⓦ www.sospel.net; closed Nov–Feb; ❻) has good service, the use of a pool and can arrange **bike** rental, while the *Hôtel de France* next door (☎04.93.04.00.01, ⓦ www.hoteldefrance-sospel.com; closed mid-Nov to mid-Dec, **⑤**) is pleasant and welcoming. For more comfort, the *Auberge Provençale*, on route du Col de Castillon 1.5km uphill from the town (℡04.93.04.00.31, Ⓦwww.aubergeprovencale.fr; **⑦**), has a pleasant garden and terrace from which to admire the town. There are four **campsites** around the town, the closest of which is the one-star *Le Mas Fleuri* in quartier La Vasta (℡04.93.04.14.94; €16 per tent; closed Oct–Feb), with its own pool, 2km along the D2566 to Moulinet following the river upstream.

There are various **eating places** along avenue Jean-Médecin including the *Bistrot Sospellois* which serves *plats du jour* for around €9. At *Le Relais du Sel*, 3 rue de Verdun (℡04.93.04.00.43; closed Tues), just across the eastern bridge, you can eat for between €20 and €30 on a terrace above the river, while the restaurant of the *Hôtel des Étrangers* next door has menus from €21-€31. A Thursday **market** is held on place des Platanes, and on Sunday local produce is sold on place du Marché. There's a wonderful *boulangerie/pâtisserie/chocolatier*, Papasergio, at 13 bis avenue Jean-Médecin. *Bar Modern* (℡04.97.00.00.42), 17 av Jean-Médecin, doubles as an **Internet café** and is a pleasant early evening drinking spot next to the river.

Breil-sur-Roya

Twenty-three kilometres north of Sospel, over the Col de Brouis, the town of **BREIL-SUR-ROYA** sits in a deep, narrow valley, 8km from the Italian border. Here, the River Roya has picked up enough volume to justify a barrage, behind which a placid and aquamarine lake makes a perfect location for canoeing. A town of modest industries – leather, olives and dairy products – Breil spreads back from both banks, with the old town on the eastern edge. A Renaissance chapel, with a golden angel blowing a trumpet from its rooftop cross, faces place Biancheri, while the vast eighteenth-century **Église Santa-Maria-in-Albis**, by the pont Charabot, is topped by a belfry with shiny multicoloured tiles, and has an impressive organ loft.

Several good **walks** are signed from the village; if you just want a short stroll, follow the river downstream past the barrage and the wash houses, then fork upwards through an olive grove to a tiny chapel and an old Italian gatehouse. The path eventually leads up to the summit of the Arpette, which stands between Breil and the Italian border. Alternatively, if you want to do some white-water **canoeing** or **rafting** up through the Gorges de Saorge, or simply paddle more gently through the village, Roya Evasion, at 1 rue Pasteur (℡04.93.04.91.46, Ⓦwww.royaevasion.com), rents out all the equipment, and organizes guided trips.

Of the three **hotels** in town, the *Castel du Roy*, chemin de l'Aigara, off the route de Tende (℡04.93.04.43.66, Ⓦwww.castelduroy.com; closed Nov–Mar; **⑤**), is the most luxurious and has a very good **restaurant** (menus from €25), though the other two – *La Bonne Auberge*, 52 rue Pasteur (℡04.93.04.41.50, Ⓕ04.93.04.92.70; **③**), or the more pleasant *Le Roya* on place Biancheri (℡04.93.04.48.10; **③**) – are more central. The municipal two-star **campsite** (℡04.93.04.46.66; €16 for two people & a tent) is by the river, just upstream from the village.

Saorge and Fontan

Seven kilometres north of Breil, the pretty village of **SAORGE** consists of a clutter of houses in grey and mismatched shades of red tumbling across a hillside, brightened by its church and chapel towers shimmering with gold Niçois tiles. Almost nothing in the village is level: vertical stairways turn into paths lined with bramble, and there's just one near-horizontal main street, and even that goes up and down flights of steps and through arches formed by the houses. At the end of the street a path leads across the cultivated terraces to **La Madone del Poggio**, an eleventh-century chapel guarded by an impossibly high bell tower topped by an octagonal spire; the chapel is private property and can't be visited. Back in the village, there's a seventeenth-century **Franciscan convent** (daily except Tues: April–Oct 10am–noon & 2–6pm, Nov–March 10am–noon & 2-5pm; €4.60) with rustic murals around its cloisters, and the **Église St-Sauveur** (daily 9am–5pm), with its rich examples of ecclesiastical art.

The **gare SNCF**, which it shares with Fontan, is 1.5km below the village in the valley, while for **food**, there's a pizzeria, *Lou Pountin*, rue Revelli (closed Mon & Tues lunch & Wed eve), and one *bar-tabac, Chez Gilou*.

FONTAN, 2km upstream and with another shining Niçois-tiled belfry, has one **hotel** to fall back on; the *Terminus* (℡04.93.04.34.00, ⓦwww.hoterminus.fr; ❸), overlooking the Roya at the north end of the village, was named after the large abandoned station opposite which was built by Mussolini to transport rock salt from the mountains. The hotel's restaurant has some decent menus starting at €19, and a beautifully painted ceiling. Here and at the **restaurant** *Les Platanes*, at the other end of the village, the speciality is fresh trout from the river.

La Brigue and Notre-Dame-des-Fontaines

The very appealing village of **LA BRIGUE**, 8km northeast of Fontan, lies on an eastern tributary of the Roya, just south of Tende, surrounded by pastures and with the perennial snowcap of Mont Bego visible to the west. Its Romanesque church, the **Église St-Martin**, is full of medieval paintings, including several by Louis Bréa, most of them depicting hideous scenes of torture and death. But the church, and the octagonal seventeenth-century **Chapelle St-Michel** alongside it, pale into insignificance compared with the sanctuary of **Notre-Dame-des-Fontaines**, 4km east of the village.

From the exterior this seems to be a plain, graceful place of retreat, but inside it's something more akin to an arcade of video nasties. Painted in the fifteenth century by Jean Baleison (the ones above the altar) and Jean Canavesio (all the rest), the sequence of restored **frescoes** contains 38 episodes. Each one, from Christ's flagellation, through the torment on the Cross to devils claiming their victims, and, ultimate gore, Judas's disembowelment, is full of violent movement and colour. The chapel is open daily in summer (9.30am–7pm; €1.50; guided tours organized by the tourist office; €1.20; ℡04.93.04.36.07). There's no bus, but it's a very pleasant walk up the D43 for 2km, then turning right over the Pont du Coq, built, like the chapel, in the fifteenth century. Next to the **tourist information** 26 av Général-de-Gaulle (℡04.93.04.60.04; Jun-Sep Mon & Wed-Sat 10am-noon & 2-5pm) is the **Maison du Patrimoine** a museum dedicated to farming history and tradition in the region (same hours as tourist information; €3).

If you want **to stay** in La Brigue, place St-Martin by the church has a couple of options – the *Auberge St-Martin* (℡04.93.04.62.17, ⓦwww.auberge-st-martin.fr; closed mid-Nov to Feb; ❸) and the *Fleurs des Alpes* (℡04.93.04.61.05, ℻04.93.04.69.58; closed Dec–Feb; ❸) – both with **restaurants** serving very satisfying meals for less than €15. The more upmarket *Le Mirval* (℡04.93.04.63.71, ⓦwww.lemirval.com; closed Nov–March; ❸), downstream from place St-Martin on rue Vincent-Ferrier, has rooms overlooking the Levenza stream.

The Vallée des Merveilles

The **Vallée des Merveilles** lies between two lakes over 2000m up on the western flank of Mont Bego. The first person to record his experience of this high valley of lakes and bare rock was a fifteenth-century traveller who had lost his way. He described it as "an infernal place with figures of the devil and thousands of demons scratched on the rocks". What his contemporary readers must have imagined to be delusions brought on by the terror of the place were no imaginings. The rocks of the valley are carved with thousands of images, of animals, tools, people working and mysterious symbols, dating from some time in the second millennium BC. More are to be found in the **Vallée de Fontanable** on the northern flank of Mont Bego, and west from the Vallée des Merveilles across the southern slopes of Mont des Merveilles. Very little is known about them and the instruments that fashioned them have never been found.

Over the centuries other travellers, shepherds and eventually tourists have added their own engravings to the collection. As a result explorations of the Vallée de Fontanable, and the Mont des Merveilles area, are restricted to one path unless accompanied by an official Mercantour guide.

The easiest route to the Vallée des Merveilles is the ten-kilometre trek (6–8hr) that starts at *Les Mesces* refuge, about 8km west of St-Dalmas-de-Tende on the D91. The first part of the climb is through woods full of wild raspberries, mushrooms and bilberries, not all of it steeply uphill. Eventually you rise above the tree line and **Lac Long** comes into view. A few pines still manage to grow around the lake, and in spring the grass is full of flowers, but encircling you is a mountain wilderness. From the *Refuge des Merveilles* by the lake, you continue up through a fearsome valley where the rocks turn from black to green according to the light. From here to just beyond the **Lac des Merveilles** you can start searching for the engravings. For the Vallée de Fontanable the path starts 4.5km further up the D91 from the *Le Mesces* refuge, just before the Casterino information point.

Several companies organize **guided walks** in the area: the Association Merveilles Gravures et Découverte, 18 rue A.-Operto in Tende (June Sat & Sun; July & Aug daily; Sept Fri–Mon; ☎06.86.03.90.13), the Bureau des Guides in St-Martin-Vésubie (see p.290; ☎04.93.03.26.60), and Destination Merveilles in Villeneuve-Loubet (☎04.93.73.09.07, ⓦwww.destination-merveilles.com) are all recommended. Going alone, it's perfectly possible to miss the engravings altogether, and blue skies and sun can quickly turn into violent hailstorms and lightning.

Tende

TENDE, the highest town on the Roya, guards the access to the Col de Tende, which connects Provence with Piedmont but is now bypassed by a road tunnel. Though not especially attractive, Tende is fairly busy, with plenty of cheap accommodation, places to eat, bars to lounge around in and shops to browse round.

The town's old and gloomy houses are built with green and purple schist, but blackened by fumes from the heavy trucks that cross to and from Italy. Above the houses rise the cherry-coloured belfry of the **collegiate church**, the peachy-orange towers and belfries of various **chapels**, and a twenty-metre needle of wall which is all that remains of a château destroyed by the French in the seventeenth century. Tende's main attraction is the **Musée des Merveilles** at the northern end of town on avenue du 16 Septembre 1947

(May to mid-Oct daily 10am–6.30pm; mid-Oct to April Mon & Wed–Sun 10am–5pm; €4.55), which details the geology, archaeology and traditions of the areas where engravings have been found. Scenes from the daily lives of Copper- and Bronze-Age man have been set up, and reproductions of the rock designs are on display along with attempts to decipher the beliefs and myths that inspired them. Whether you've been to the Vallée des Merveilles or not, the museum is an invaluable insight into an intriguing subject.

The **Vieille Ville** is fun to wander through, looking at the symbols of old trades on the door lintels, the overhanging roofs and the balconies on every floor. On place de l'Église, the **Collégiale Notre-Dame de l'Assumption** is more a repository of the town's wealth than a place of contemplation, with Baroque excess throughout, though the Apostles wearing their halos like lids on the Renaissance porch and the lions supporting the two Doric columns are a nice touch. At the other end of town near the station, the seventeenth-century **Église St-Michel**, on place du Grande Marché, was entirely remodelled in the 1960s, when its *chevet* was replaced by a wall of glass looking onto the trees and shrubs of the former convent gardens. It was decorated by a local artist, some of whose dream-inspired paintings of a semi-symbolist, semi-surrealist nature, are dreadful, while others strike an eerily appropriate note.

Practicalities

The **gare SNCF** is set back from the top of the main street, avenue du 16 Septembre (becoming avenue Aimable-Gastaud and avenue Georges-Bidault as it runs southwards), at the end of avenue Vassalo. Turning left out of the station you'll see the **tourist office** 103 av du 16 Septembre 1947 (Tues–Sat: May–Sept 9am–12.30pm & 2–6pm; Oct–April 9am–noon & 2–5.30pm; ☎04.93.04.73.71, ⊛www.tendemerveilles.com). This central axis leads down left towards place de la République; the Vieille Ville is further down on your right to either side of the Roya's tributary.

Hotels in Tende are inexpensive: there's the *Miramonti* at 5–7 av Vassalo (☎04.93.04.61.82, ℻04.93.04.61.82; closed Nov; ❸), just by the station, or the *Hôtel du Centre*, 12 place de la République (☎04.93.04.62.19; closed Nov–March; ❷). If you follow chemin Ste-Catherine, off rue St-Jean past the cathedral, you'll come to the edge of the town and the **gîte d'étape** *Les Carlines* (☎04.93.04.62.74; closed Oct to mid-April; ❶), which has gorgeous views down the valley. The one-star municipal **campsite** *Saint Jacques* is 500m down a path to the left of the *gare SNCF* (☎04.93.04.76.08; June–Aug only).

There's no shortage of **restaurants** to be found on avenue du 16 Septembre and rue de France: although there's nothing very special, there are plenty of Italian dishes to choose from. *La Margueria* pizzeria, on avenue du 16 Septembre, with beams strung with dried herbs and garlic, and stuffed foxes on the walls, is the most popular. For the **Internet** try the médiatheque on avenue M. Barrucchi across the river.

Travel details

Trains

Chemin de Fer de Provence (Nice–Digne)
Nice to: Annot (4–5 daily; 2hr); Barrême (4–5
daily; 1hr 45min); Digne (4–5 daily; 3hr 15min);
Entrevaux (4–5 daily; 1hr 30min); Puget-Théniers
(4–5 daily; 1hr 30min); St-André-des-Alpes (4–5
daily; 2hr 25min); Thorame-Gare (4–5 daily; 2hr
15min); Touët-sur-Var (4–5 daily; 1hr 10min);
Villars-sur-Var (4–5 daily; 1hr).
From **Digne** a regular SNCF bus links the Chemin
de Fer de Provence with the SNCF Marseille–
Sisteron line at St-Auban–Château-Arnoux (30min).
From **Thorame-Gare** a bus meets 3 trains daily
(during the ski season, July and Aug) for connections to: Beauvezer (20min); Colmars-les-Alpes
(30min); Allos (45min); La Foux d'Allos (1hr
10min).

SNCF line

Nice to: Breil-sur-Roya direct (5 daily; 55min); La
Brigue (3 daily; 1hr 35min); St-Dalmas-de-Tende
direct (3 daily; 1hr 50min); via Ventimiglia (4–5
daily; 1hr 40min); Saorge-Fontan (3 daily; 1hr
15min–1hr 40min); Sospel (6 daily; 45min);
Tende (3 daily; 1hr 40min–2hr 30min).

Buses

Barçelonette to: Digne (1 daily; 1hr 45min); Gap
(3 daily; 1hr 20min); Marseille (2–4 daily; 3hr 50min).
Digne to: Aix (4 daily; 2hr); Aups (2 daily; 30–
40min); Avignon (3 daily; 3hr 15min); Barçelonnette
(1 daily; 1hr 30min); Castellane (1 daily; 1hr
10min); Grenoble (1 daily; 4hr 50min); Manosque
(4 daily; 1hr 15min); Marseille (4 daily; 2hr–2hr
30min); Moustiers-Ste-Marie (1 daily; 1hr 20min);
Nice (4 daily; 3hr 15 min); Puget-Théniers (1 daily;
2hr); Pra-Loup (1 daily; 1hr 50min); St-André-les-
Alpes (2–3 daily; 1 hr); Seyne-les-Alpes (1 daily;
40min); Sisteron (2–3 daily; 1hr).

Draguignan to: Aix (3 daily; 2hr 30min); Aups
(1 daily; 1hr–1hr 20min); Bargemon (5 daily;
45min); Barjols (1 daily; 1hr 10min); Brignoles
(3 daily; 1hr); Callas (3 daily; 40min); Entrecasteaux
(2 weekly; 45min); Fayence (4 daily: 1hr 40min);
Grasse (2 daily; 2hr 45min); Les Arcs (frequent;
20min); Lorgues (4 daily; 20min); St-Raphaël
(12 daily; 1hr 15min–1hr 30min); Salernes (3 daily;
1 hr 15min–1hr 45min); Seillans (3 daily; 1hr
20min); Toulon (4 daily; 2hr 15min); Tourtour
(1 daily; 50 min); Villecroze (2 weekly; 1hr).
Fayence to: Draguignan (Mon–Sat 3 daily; 1hr
30min); Grasse (Mon–Sat 3 daily; 1hr); St Raphaël
(Mon–Sat 4 daily; 1hr 20min).
Gréolières to: Grasse (1–2 daily; 35–50min).
Puget-Théniers to: Annot (1 daily; 20min);
Barrême (1 daily; 1hr 10min); Digne (1 daily; 2hr);
Entraunes (1 daily; 1hr 30min); Entrevaux (1 daily;
10min); St-André-les-Alpes (1 daily; 1hr); St-
Martin-d'Entraunes (1 daily; 1hr 20min).
Riez to: Barjols (1 daily; 45min); Digne (1 daily;
1hr 15min); Manosque (1 daily; 1hr); Marseille
(1–2 daily; 2hr); Moustiers-Ste-Marie (1–4 daily;
15min).
St-André-les-Alpes to: Allos (1–3 daily in high
season; 1hr); Barrême (1 daily; 10min); Digne
(1 daily; 1hr); La Foux d'Allos (1–3 daily; 1hr
15min); Nice (1 daily; 2hr).
St-Étienne-de-Tinée to: Auron (1–5 daily; 15min);
Isola (1–4 daily; 15min); La Tour (1–4 daily; 1hr
5min); Nice (1–4 daily; 2hr 30min); St-Sauveur-de-
Tinée (1–4 daily; 45min).
St-Martin-Vésubie to: Lantosque (3 daily; 30min);
Nice (3 daily; 1hr 45min); Roquebillière (3 daily;
15min); St-Dalmas (1 weekly; 20min).
Sospel to: Menton (9 daily; 35min–1hr); Moulinet
(2 daily; 40min).
Thorame-Gare to: Allos (3 daily; 45min);
Beauvezer (3 daily; 20min); Colmars-les-Alpes
(3 daily; 30min); La Foux d'Allos (3 daily; 1hr
10min).

Toulon and the southern Var

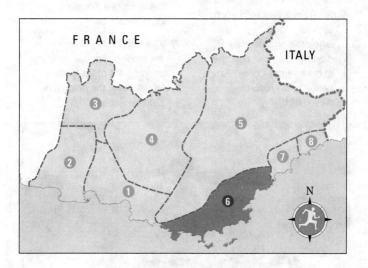

CHAPTER 6

Highlights

✳ **Bandol Appellation Controlée** Sample the fine wines and explore the peaceful wine-growing country a little way inland from the bustle of the coast. See p.306

✳ **The island of Port-Cros** Take a glass-bottomed boat to explore the fascinating marine life off France's smallest national park. See p.323

✳ **St-Tropez** Suspend your cynicism for a day and enjoy the art, the absurdity, the glamour and sheer excess of the Côte d'Azur's best-known resort. See p.331

✳ **Massif des Maures** Escape the glitz and development of the coast to explore the sombre wooded hills, and the unspoilt country towns of Collobrières and La Garde Freinet. See p.338 & p.342

✳ **Fréjus** Founded by Julius Caesar as a naval base, Fréjus has some of the best-preserved Roman remains along this coast, including a theatre, an amphitheatre and the ruins of a Roman aqueduct. See p.348

✳ **The Esterel** Drive or walk in the most distinctive, rugged and ancient of the coast's landscapes, the craggy, red Esterel. See p.355

△ Beach bar, St-Tropez

Toulon and the southern Var

Winding east, from the urban sprawl of **Toulon** through the glitz of **St-Tropez** to the wild **Esterel**, the **Côte d'Azur** is the most desirable and, at times, the most detestable stretch of Mediterranean coast. The glimmering rocks along its shore and the translucent sea, the February mimosa blossom, the springtime scents of pine and eucalyptus or the golden autumn chestnut crop and reddening vines all combine with the Mediterranean light to create a sensual magic landscape. It can still cast the spell that attracted the Impressionist and Post impressionist painters over a hundred years ago – whose work can be seen at St-Tropez – as well as their bohemian successors, and the 1950s film world. But in summer it also has the worst traffic jams and public transport, the most crowded quaysides, campsites and hitching queues, the most short-tempered locals – and outrageous prices.

The westernmost part of this stretch of coastal road boasts minor attractions in Roman **Les Lecques** and neighbouring **St-Cyr**, before reaching the wine-producing town of **Bandol**. The sweeping vineyards gradually give way to the outskirts of **Toulon**, a bustling port that's home to the French navy's Mediterranean fleet. The city's turbulent past resulted in poor redevelopment, but a dramatic position and atmospheric streets are its salvation. Continuing eastwards **Hyères**, which attracted foreign visitors in the eighteenth century, thrives on its horticulture as much as on tourism and is an affordable place to stay. The crystal-clear waters and scented eucalyptus trees of **Îles de Hyères**'s northern beaches look across to the **Corniche des Maures** – a tangle of small fishing villages turned resorts hard to distinguish one from another. At **Cavalière**, **Pramousquier**, **Le Rayol** with its fabulous **garden**, and **Le Trayas** you can get glimpses of how this coast all once looked. There are even stretches which have held out against the construction mania altogether, including the section west of **Cap Bregançon**, the southern end of **St-Tropez**'s **peninsula**. However **St-Tropez** itself, or "St-Trop" as its aficionados like to call it, is the region's pre-eminent resort, a brand name for sea, sun, celebrity and sex. Looking across the bay in envy **Ste-Maxime** tries to compete. Further east **Fréjus** is the most historical of the major towns, dating back to Roman times; its neighbour **St-Raphaël** ignores its ancient origins, and dedicates itself to holiday-makers, with rooms and food for every budget. For real coastal wilderness though, you need to head out along the **Corniche d'Esterel** west of Le

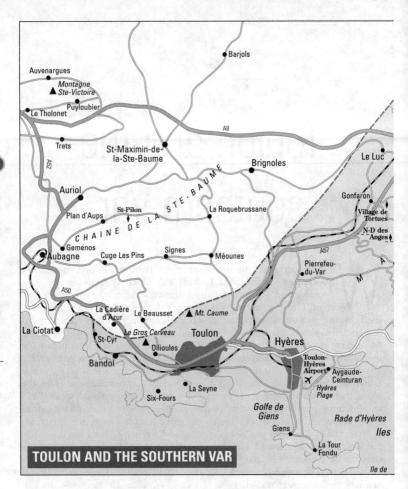

TOULON AND THE SOUTHERN VAR

Trayas, below the dramatic red volcanic crags of the **Massif d'Esterel.** Inland, the dark wooded hills of the **Massif des Maures** form a backdrop east to St-Raphaël. Hidden amid the sweet-chestnut trees and cork oaks are ancient monasteries and medieval villages. **Collobrières** and **La Garde-Freinet** have not forsaken traditional livelihoods and carry on their wine, cork and chestnut businesses beyond the tourist season, while on the Massif's eastern edge **Grimaud** and **Rocquebrune** provide exclusive second homes for the more discerning Côte clientele.

Les Lecques and St-Cyr

Before reaching Toulon and Bandol, there are a couple of worthwhile stops along the coastal road. Although today no more than a cluster of tourist

shops and eateries around fine sand and shingle beaches, **LES LECQUES** claims to have been the Ancient Greek trading post of Taureontum, site of a decisive naval battle between Caesar (the eventual victor) and Pompey for the control of Marseille. The remains of a **Roman villa**, now the **Musée de Taureontum** (June–Sept Mon & Wed–Sun 3–7pm; Oct–May Sat & Sun 2–5pm; €3) on the route de la Madrague at the east end of the bay, dated first century AD, boasts three extant mosaics, patches of frescoes, a couple of interesting sarcophagi, numerous beautiful Greek and Roman vases and other household paraphernalia.

Les Lecques gradually merges into the inland village of **ST-CYR-SUR-MER**. St-Cyr has a few sites to detain you briefly: the small **Centre d'Art Sébastien** on boulevard Jean-Jaurès (Mon & Wed–Sun 9am–noon & 2–6pm; €1) displays the paintings and tender terracotta statues of this Parisian-born artist and friend of Picasso in a beautifully restored former caper storehouse, while the **Espace Provence**, next door (Tues–Sat 9am–noon & 3–6pm), exhibits local crafts and produce. On place de Portalis is a miniature, golden **Statue of Liberty**, sculpted by Bartholdi, the artist who created its better-known sister. Beyond these, St-Cyr's main attraction is its **vineyards**, which belong to the excellent Bandol *appellation*. One of the best reds comes from the Château des Baumelles, a seventeenth-century manor house just out of St-Cyr to the right off the Bandol road, which can be visited by appointment only (℡04.94.32.63.20), while the Domaine du Cagueloup on the D66 towards La Cadière d'Azur (Mon–Fri 9am–noon & 2.30–6pm; ℡04.94.26.15.70) has open *dégustations*. St-Cyr also has a food **market** on Sunday in the G Péri car park in the Vieille Ville.

The **gare SNCF** lies midway between St-Cyr-sur-Mer and Les Lecques; from the station it is a twenty-minute walk down to Les Lecques. The **tourist office**, which caters for both towns, is on place de l'Appel du 18 Juin, off avenue du Port in Les Lecques (June & Sept Mon–Sat 9am–6pm; July & Aug Mon–Sat 9am–7pm, Sun 10am–1pm & 4–7pm; Oct–May Mon–Fri 9am–6pm, Sat 9am–noon & 2–6pm; ℡04.94.26.73.73, ⓌWww.saintcyrsurmer.com).

Of the Les Lecques **hotels**, the very small *Beau Séjour*, 34 av de la Mer (℡04.94.26.54.06, Ⓕ04.94.26.63.78; ❷; closed Jan), is a reasonably priced option close to the sea, or there's the comfortable *Grand Hôtel*, 24 av du Port (℡04.94.26.23.01, Ⓦwww.lecques-hotel.com; ❽; closed mid-Nov to March), set in a large garden. Les Lecques also has a large three-star **campsite**, *Les Baumelles* (℡04.94.26.21.27, Ⓦwww.campinglesbaumelles.net; €20 per tent; closed Nov–Feb), on the beach right in the centre of the resort.

The widest choice of **restaurants** in Les Lecques is along avenue du Port on the seafront. Alternatively, head along the coastal path, which runs from La Madrague at the east end of Les Lecques' beach down to the Pointe du Déffend – east of here, on the calanque de Port-d'Alon, there's a snack bar *La Calanque* (℡04.94.26.20.08; salads around €10; closed Sun eve, Mon & Oct–Jan). If you'd rather **picnic**, the coastal path offers plenty of secluded spots, and continues on to Bandol (3hr 30min).

Bandol and around

Continuing southeast on the coastal road to Toulon, the next stop is **BANDOL**, an unpretentious coastal resort fringed by unappealing apartment complexes. It bustles with day-trippers attracted by the cheap clothes shops, and with yachties milling around the vast marina, which obliterates most of the town's sea view. The town is rightly proud of its wines, which have their own, distinct Bandol *Appellation Controlée*. As well as all the usual casinos, discos, cocktail bars and water sports, Bandol has some cheap accommodation so makes a good coastal base from which to explore Toulon. Along the coast, the wines and the hinterland are the main attractions, along with the **Île de Bendor**, which aptly houses France's largest exposition of wines, spirits and alcohols.

Arrival, information and accommodation

From Bandol's **train station**, head straight downhill and you'll reach the town centre above the port. The **tourist office** is on allées Vivien by the quayside (mid-June to mid-Sept daily 9am–7pm; mid-Sept to mid-June Mon–Fri 9am–noon & 2–6pm, Sat 9am–noon; ℡04.94.29.41.35, Ⓦwww.bandol.fr). You can rent **bikes**, motorized or not, at Holiday Bikes, 127 rte de Marseille (℡04.94.32.21.89), west down avenue Loste on the other side of the rail lines from the station. A smart new *mediatheque* is due to open in 2008; in the meantime there's **Internet access** at Boss Cyber Café, 9 rue des Ecoles.

A couple of the cheaper **hotels** worth considering are *Le Bandolia*, 231 av du 11 Novembre (℡04.94.29.41.05; ❹), a 1900s town house with a large garden surrounded by palm trees, and the slightly more upmarket *L'Oasis*, 15 rue des Écoles (℡04.94.29.41.69, Ⓦwww.oasisbandol.com; ❺; closed mid-Oct to mid-April), in a residential area between the town centre and Rènecros, and the very pleasant good-value *Golf Hôtel*, right on Rènecros beach (℡04.94.29.45.83, Ⓦwww.golfhotel.fr; ❼). Bandol's top hotel, *Île Rousse*, 17 bd Louis Lumière (℡04.94.29.33.00, Ⓦwww.ile-rousse.com; ❾), has a terrace leading down to the beach from the west of the port, vast light rooms and a choice of restaurants. If you're **camping**, try the three-star *Vallongue* (℡04.94.29.49.55, Ⓦwww.campingvar.com; €16 per tent; closed Oct–March), 2.5km out of town on the route de Marseille.

There are also a couple of hotels on **Île de Bendor**, both aimed at the company expense account market: *Le Delos Palais* (℡04.94.25.06.06, Ⓦwww.hoteldelos.com; ❺; closed Oct–March) at the far end of the island is the best bet, but you'd still have to book months in advance.

The Town

Bandol's charms are based principally on wine, in particular the town's own *appellation* produced in the area encompassing St-Cyr (see p.306). The reds have the best reputation, maturing for over ten years on a good harvest, with bouquets sliding between pepper, cinnamon, vanilla and black cherries; the rosé is equally wonderful. Back from the port on allées Vivien, the **Maison des Vins du Bandol** (℡04.94.29.45.03) sells its own selection of wines and will give you lists of local *propriétaires* to visit. For cheese, sausages and the like to accompany your wine, there's a Tuesday morning **market** on the quayside, supplemented in summer by a regular evening crafts market at the same place.

Bandol's most scenic sandy **beach** is around the **Anse de Rènecros**, an almost circular inlet just over the hill west of the port, reached via boulevard Louis-Lumière. Better still are the coves and beaches along the coastal path to Les Lecques which you reach from avenue du Maréchal-Foch on the western side of the Anse de Rènecros (signed in yellow).

The Île de Bendor

ÎLE DE BENDOR was an uninhabited rocky island when it was bought by the rags-to-riches *pastis* man **Paul Ricard** in the 1950s, and today the atmosphere is somewhat surreal, with unlikely statues, an uneasy discrepancy between the people and the place, and a 1950s architectural style severely stamped on most of its buildings. Ricard himself died in 1997, but his family still owns the place, and there's an exhibition on the island covering his life and works (Mon & Wed–Sun 10am–noon & 2–6pm). Boats leave for the seven-minute crossing to Bendor from Bandol's quai de l'Hôtel-de-Ville on the port (April to mid-June & mid-Sept to Oct daily 7am–11pm; mid-June to mid-Sept daily 7am–2am; Nov–Mar 7am–5pm; €8 return).

For most of the year, activities on the island revolve around the **Club International de Plongée** (℡04.94.29.55.12, Ⓔcipbendor@hotmail.com), which offers diving training from beginner to instructor level, and has a sea school for 8- to 12-year-olds, and the **Club Nautique** (℡04.94.29.52.91), which runs a sailing school and rents catamarans, dinghies and windsurf boards. Inland, there's also the cavernous **Exposition Universelle des Vins et Spiritueux** (April–Sept Mon & Wed–Sat 10am–noon & 2–6pm; free) to the west of the port. Decorated with murals by art-school students, the hall has a comprehensive display of French wines and liquors and a slowly expanding selection of liquid intoxicants from around the world. The exposition's claim that no culture has ever failed to produce alcohol has yet to be refuted, and there are some weird and wonderful items, including an evil bottle of Chinese spirit in which a large gecko floats.

Eating and drinking

In the centre of Bandol, you'll find plenty of **restaurants** along rue de la République and allée Jean-Moulin, running parallel to the port side promenade. The *Auberge du Port*, 7 allée Jean-Moulin (℡04.94.29.42.63; à la carte around €40), has classic fish dishes, while the elegant restaurant *Les Oliviers* at the hotel *Île Rousse* (℡04.94.29.33.00; see p.307) is the place for braised knuckle of veal with truffles and confit of shallots, plus elaborate desserts including a peppermint chocolate *gratinée*; menus start at €34.50. Arguably as good is *Le Clocher*, 1 rue de la Paroisse (℡04.94.32.47.65; menus from €24, à la carte €17–21; closed Nov), with specialities including home-made foie gras and pesto.

Bandol's **bars** tend towards the sophisticated: *Le Bistro* at 6 av Jean-Moulin is chic and modern, with a long cocktail list and light meals from €14, while *Le 38 Caffe*, *Poupoune* and *L'Escale*, all along quai Charles-de-Gaulle above the beach, are similarly fashionable cocktail-sipping spots.

Around Bandol

Despite the creeping suburbanization, the countryside north of Bandol makes good **cycling** country: you could head for the perched medieval village of **La Cadière d'Azur** (take the road above the station, left on the D559, then right), and then across the valley to the more touristy fortified hamlet of **Le Castellet** with its vast car parks, gloomy, crypt-like bastion of a twelfth-century church, perfumed boutiques and wonderful panorama of the vineyards below.

Approximately 6km southeast of Le Castellet, south of Le Beausset, is **Le Vieux Beausset**, whose Romanesque **Chapelle Notre-Dame** (Mon, Tues, Thurs, Fri 2–5.30pm, Sat 9am–5.30pm, Wed & Sun 9.30am–5.30pm) rewards the long and winding approach with a suberb panoramic view.

The Cap Sicié peninsula and Ollioules

The coastal approach to Toulon from Marseille takes you via the congested neck of the **Cap Sicié peninsula**. On the western side, **Six-Fours-les-Plages** sprawls between Bandol's neighbour **Sanary-sur-Mer** and **Le Brusc** on the western tip where you can get boats to another Ricard-owned island, **Île des Embiez**. The eastern side of the peninsula merges with Toulon's former shipbuilding suburb of **La Seyne-sur-Mer**, while at the southern end a semi-wilderness of high cliffs and forest reigns.

Approaching Toulon on the Aubagne road, you'll pass through the twisting **gorge d'Ollioules**, where the heights of **Le Gros Cerveau** and **Mont Caume** above it are well worth visiting.

Sanary-sur-Mer and around

The little fishing harbour of **SANARY-SUR-MER** is approximately 5km east of Bandol on the Cap Sicié peninsula. With its palm trees, nineteenth-century church spire, pastel pink and yellow facades along the seafront, and fountains with statues representing agriculture and fishery, the harbour retains its charm despite the urban conglomoration it's now immersed in. It hasn't sold its soul to the yachting crowd as much as Bandol, either. Housed in the thirteenth-century **Tour Romane** by the port is a small **diving museum** (July & Aug daily 9am–noon & 4–8pm; Sept–June Sat & Sun 9am–12.30pm & 3–6.30pm; free), based around the collection of one of the pioneers of the modern sport, Frédéric Dumas, who worked with Jacques Cousteau. Also by the port in the Jardin de la Ville is a plaque commemorating the German-speaking artistic community that made Sanary its base in the 1930s, having fled from the strictures of Hitler's NSDAP party: the exiles included Thomas, Golo and Heinrich Mann, Erwin Piscator and Arthur Koestler.

Practicalities

Buses run frequently from Bandol's quai de l'Hôtel-de-Ville to Sanary. The town's **train station**, which it shares with Ollioules (see p.310), is 2.5km north of the centre, but the buses into town don't always link up with train arrivals. The **tourist office** is by the port in the Jardin de la Ville (July & Aug Mon–Sat 9am–12.30pm & 2–7pm, Sun 9.30am–12.30pm; May, June, Sept & Oct Mon–Fri 9am–noon & 2–6pm, Sat 9am–noon & 2–5pm; Nov–April Mon–Fri 9am–noon & 2–5.30pm, Sat 9am–noon & 2–5pm; ☎04.94.74.01.04, ⓦwww .sanarysurmer.com).

If you want **to stay**, the *Centre Azur* hostel, 149 av du Nid (☎04.94.74.18.87, ⓦwww.ymca-sanary.org; ❶), is between Portissol and La Cride, a little west of the centre, or there's the attractive *Hôtel de la Tour*, 24 quai Général-de-Gaulle (☎04.94.74.10.10, ⓦwww.sanary-hoteldelatour.com; ❺), with a perfect location right on the port. There's also a good three-star **campsite**, *Les Girelles*, on the chemin de Beaucours, by the sea on the Bandol road (☎04.94.74.13.18, ⓦwww.lesgirelles.com; €23.90 per tent; closed Oct–Easter).

The **restaurant** *Bonj-Sen*, on place Chanoine-Arnaldi (☎04.94.74.22.20; lunch buffet €12.50; closed Tues), serves Asiatic fusion cuisine, while *L'enK*, on 13 rue Louis-Blanc (☎04.94.74.66.57; menu €27), does Provençal cuisine with a modern edge.

Around Sanary

From Sanary, the D559 and D63 head towards Toulon through **Six-Fours-les-Plages**, which seems nothing but sprawling suburbs littered with hoardings, though its shingly beaches are well kept. A small road off the D63, to the north, however, takes you up to **Notre-Dame-de-la-Pépiole** (open Mon & Wed–Sat 3–6pm; mass Sundays at 9.30am; free), a stunning sixth-century chapel in the midst of pines, cypresses and olive trees.

The southeast reaches of the peninsula are not exactly wilderness, but the sturdy sentinel of **Notre-Dame-de-Mai** (Oct–April every first Sat of the month; throughout May for pilgrimages, plus 15 Aug & 14 Sept), once a primitive lighthouse, provides a reason to **hike** for an hour or two up the pretty backroads towards Cap Sicié. The local tourist map marks several routes, some starting in the midst of Six-Fours' traffic-choked suburban sprawl, but the best one is *sentier du littoral*, starting from chemin des Cargadoux, which runs east from the quay in **Le Brusc** and follows the coast. It's a walk of several kilometres, worth it for the heady views in every direction; it can get pretty windy up here, and even on a calm day exploring the cliffs should be done with a certain amount of caution. Back in Le Brusc, you can reward yourself with a generous fish dinner at *Le St-Pierre*, 47 rue de la Citadelle (☎04.94.34.02.52; menus at €18, €25.50 and €35.50; closed Tues eve & Wed out of season).

Île des Embiez

Paul Ricard's second island, the **Île des Embiez** (ⓦwww.ile-des-embiez
.com), greets visitors with mock classical goddesses on pillars around its large
pleasure port and scattered Greco-Roman picnic tables. The **Institut
Océanographique Paul Ricard** (daily 10am–noon & 2–5pm; ⓦwww
.institut-paul-ricard.org; €5) has aquariums and exhibitions on underwater
matter. There are pony and go-kart rides for the under-12s and in summer a
miniature road-train does a circuit of the island (adult €5; child over 6 €3),
all great fun for pre-teens. Away from the paying attractions, much of the
island has been laid waste by various "works". In spring the more or less
untrammelled south-facing cliffs are a riot of yellow flowers but the rest of
the year they're covered in dull scrub and, with the exception of a few
pocket-handkerchief-sized beaches of fine gravel and crystal water, there's
not much to induce a lengthy stay.

There are frequent **ferry crossings** from Le Brusc (daily: mid-June to
mid-Sept 7am–12.45am; mid-March to mid-June & mid-Sept to mid-Nov
7am–10.45pm; mid-Nov to mid-March 7am–8.20pm; journey time 10min;
€10). If you want to stay, there's a small **hostel** (no membership needed but
book well in advance; ☎04.94.88.08.30), and a couple of **hotels** – the de
luxe *Hélios* (☎04.94.10.66.10, ⓦwww.helios-embiez.com; ⑨), and the more
modest *Le Canoubié* (☎04.94.74.94.94, ⓦwww.lecanoubie.com; ⑦) – plus a
few rented apartments.

Ollioules

OLLIOULES, north of the peninsula, derives its name from "olive", and it's
one of those small Provençal towns that, despite a ruined medieval castle,
arcaded streets, fountains and a Romanesque church, still manages to have an
economy not totally dependent on tourism. Much of this rests on its floral
wholesale and export market, the biggest in France, though open to the public
only during the *Foire aux Plantes* at the end of April, on the central place Jean-
Jaurès. Small-scale artisans are also much in evidence, earning their keep making
barrels, pots, nougat or reeds for musical instruments, as well as wine and olive
oil. On the cultural front, the *commune* contains the **Centre National de
Création et de Diffusion Culturelles** in the château of Châteauvallon (off
the D92 towards Toulon), with an impressive calendar of arts events including
music, theatre, circus and film. It also hosts an **international dance festival**
every July (details from the centre ☎08.00.08.90.90, or from Ollioules or
Toulon tourist offices).

Practicalities

Ollioules shares its **gare SNCF** with Sanary; it lies between the two, about
3.5km south of Ollioules. There's a regular bus (#120) between the town
and the station, and you can also catch a bus (#12) from place de la Liberté
in the centre of Toulon. Ollioules' **tourist office** is in the Espace Culturel
at 116 rue Ph De Hautecloque (Mon–Fri 9am–noon & 2–6pm, Sat 9am–
noon; ☎04.94.63.11.74, ⓦwww.ollioules.com). **Bikes** can be rented at Oki
Bike, 18 av Georges-Clémenceau, across the bridge from the tourist office
(☎04.94.63.46.37). A **market** takes place on place Jean-Jaurès on Thursday
and Saturday mornings.

Good **places to stay** in Ollioules are thin on the ground; better to head past
the chain hotels along the N8 to **Seyne-sur-Mer** where the *chambre d'hote La
Lézardière,* a nineteenth-century mansion on allée des Tamaris (☎04.94.30.08.89,

W www.villa-la-lezardiere.com; ⑤), is a more appealing option. For **meals** *Restaurant les Temps des Copains* on place Henri-Duprat is popular and jolly, with a *brochette*-dominated menu at €26. For some very special Bandol AOC **wine**, head for the Domaine de Terrebrune, 724 chemin de la Tourelle, signed off the route du Gros Cerveau (Mon–Sat 9am–12.30pm & 2–6.30pm), which produces a wonderful deep and dusky red wine and has an expensive but very good Provençal restaurant, *Le Table du Vigneron*, with menu at €47 (☎04.94.88.36.19; closed Sun eve & Mon).

Mont Caume and Le Gros Cerveau

Though less dramatic in their inclines than the Cap Sicié cliffs, the mountain ranges to the north of the peninsula give the best panorama of this complex coast. **Mont Caume** to the east is, at 804m, by far the highest point in the locality. Access at the top is restricted by the military, but you can get a view northwards across acres of forest to the Chaîne de la Ste-Baume and the distinctively sharp drop of the Mont de la Loube by La Roquebrussanne.

The road between Mont Caume and the gorges takes in the villages of **Le Broussan** and **Evenos**, the latter perched up in the winds around a ruined castle.

West of the gorges, the **Gros Cerveau** ridge reveals the islands of Embiez and Bendor, the Toulon roadstead, Cap Sicié and La Ciotat's shipbuilding yards. From an abandoned military barracks you can look down northwards onto the strange rock forms. This is good walking country, though watch out in the hunting season for *chasse gardée* signs.

Toulon

Viewed from the distant heights of Mont Caume or Notre-Dame-du-Mai, it's clear why **TOULON** had to be a major port. The heart-shaped bay of the Petite Rade gives over 15km of shoreline around Toulon and its suburb **La Seyne-sur-Mer** to the west. Facing the city, about 3km out to sea, is **St-Mandrier**, a virtual island, connected to the Cap Sicié peninsula by the isthmus of Les Sablettes and protecting the Grande Rade both northwards and eastwards. All in all it's a magnificent natural harbour, deserving of a Rio or Hong Kong to grace its shores. But that, the cynics might say, is the trouble: instead of Rio, they built Toulon.

The city was half-destroyed in World War II and its rebuilt whole is dominated by the military and associated industries. The arsenal that Louis XIV created is one of the major employers of southeast France and the port is home to the French Navy's Mediterranean fleet. The shipbuilding yards of La Seyne have, however, been axed, closing the book on a centuries-old and at times notorious industry. Up until the eighteenth century, slaves and convicts were still powering the king's galleys and, following the Revolution, convicts were sent to Toulon with iron collars round their necks for sentences of hard labour. After 1854 convicts were deported to the colonies that Toulon's ships had played a major part in winning.

Toulon gained notoriety in 1995 when local elections returned a *Front National* administration to the town hall with a policy of 'preference for the French', which left French nationals of non-European origin facing the threat of second-class treatment in housing and provision of local services. Now returned to mainstream right-of-centre (RPR) control, it faces an uphill task in rebuilding its image.

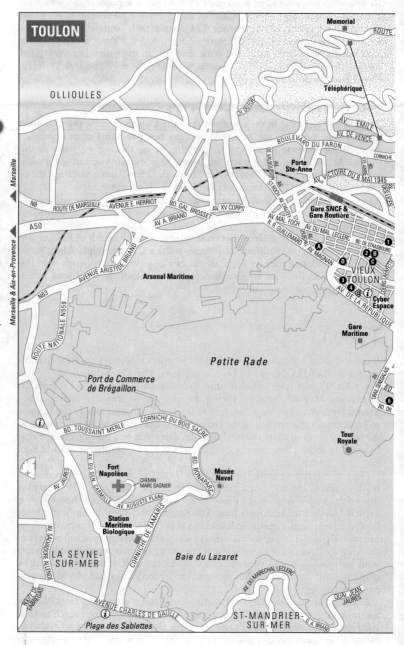

TOULON

OLLIOULES

Memorial
ROUTE

Téléphérique

Porte
Ste-Anne

BOULEVARD DU FARON

AV. EMILE
AV. DE VENCE

CORNICHE

AV. VICTOIRE DU 8 MAI 1945

N8
ROUTE DE MARSEILLE
AVENUE E. HERRIOT
BD. GAL. BROSSET
AV. XV CORPS

A50
AV. A. BRIAND

Gare SNCF &
Gare Routière

AV. DU MAL LECLERC

BD. DE STRASBOURG

R. R. GUILLEMARD
AV. MAGNAN

AV. MAL. FOCH

VIEUX
TOULON

AVENUE ARISTIDE BRIAND

Arsenal Maritime

N63

ROUTE NATIONALE N559

Cyber
Espace

AV. DE LA RÉPUBLIQUE

Gare
Maritime

Petite Rade

Port de Commerce
de Brégaillon

BD. TOUSSAINT MERLE
CORNICHE DU BOIS SACRE

BD. BONAPARTE

Tour
Royale

AV. DU GEN. CAMILLE
CHEMIN
MARC SAGNIER
AV. AUGUSTE PLANE

Fort
Napoléon

Musée
Naval

AV. JAURES

Station
Maritime
Biologique

CORNICHE DE TAMARIS

Baie du Lazaret

LA SEYNE-
SUR-MER

AV. SALVADORE ALLENDE

ROUTE DE FABREGAS

AV. DU MARECHAL LECLERC

AVENUE CHARLES DE GAULLE

QUAI JEAN
JAURES

Plage des Sablettes

ST-MANDRIER-
SUR-MER

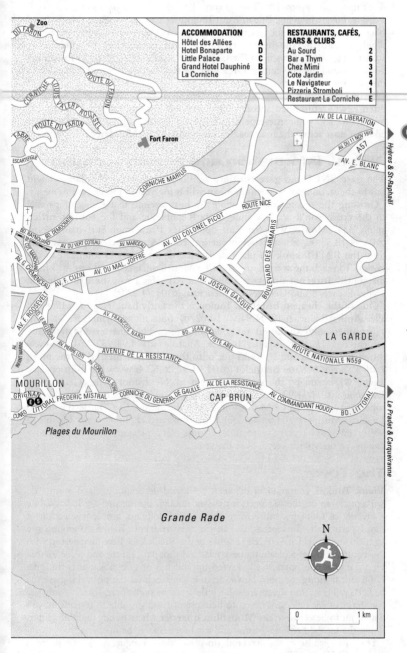

ACCOMMODATION

Hôtel des Allées	A
Hotel Bonaparte	D
Little Palace	C
Grand Hotel Dauphiné	B
La Corniche	E

RESTAURANTS, CAFÉS, BARS & CLUBS

Au Sourd	2
Bar a Thym	6
Chez Mimi	3
Cote Jardin	5
Le Navigateur	4
Pizzeria Stromboli	1
Restaurant La Corniche	E

Zoo

DU FARON

CORNICHE LOUIS VALERY ROUSSEL

ROUTE DU FARON

ROUTE DU FARON

CABRE

ESCARTEFIGUE

Fort Faron

CORNICHE MARIUS

AV. DE LA LIBERATION

AV. DU 11 NOV 1918

A57

AV. E. BLANC

ROUTE NICE

BD. RAYNOUARD

BD. DEMOCRATIE

AV. DU VERT COTEAU

AV. MARCEAU

AV. DU COLONEL PICOT

BOULEVARD DES ARMARIS

COT MARCHAND

AV. G. CLEMENCEAU

AV. F. CUZIN

AV. DU MAL JOFFRE

AV. JOSEPH GASQUET

AV. F. ROOSEVELT

LECLERCU

AV. FRANÇOIS NARDI

BD. JEAN BAPTISTE ABEL

LA GARDE

ROUTE NATIONALE N559

AV. PIERRE LOTI

AVENUE DE LA RESISTANCE

INFANT MARINE

AV. CORONAT AL SOREL

MOURILLON

GRIGNAN

E 5

CORNICHE DU GENERAL DE GAULLE

AV. DE LA RESISTANCE

CAP BRUN

AV. COMMANDANT HOUOT

BD. LITTORAL

CUNEO

LITTORAL FREDERIC MISTRAL

Plages du Mourillon

Grande Rade

N

0   1 km

The high apartment buildings and wide highways slicing through the centre don't make the approach to Toulon very alluring, and its reputation for sleaze is a disincentive to staying. But in truth Toulon feels no more seedy than parts of Nice or Marseille, and the city is fighting back, with a gentrification programme slowly beautifying the inner city and a smart new gallery of modern art attracting touring shows from Paris. There are also no fewer than 25 **fountains** dotted around the city centre; a free walking map from the tourist office details the position and age of each one.

If you do choose to stay in Toulon, there is at least a choice of good-value, often newly-refurbished accommodation, good markets and cheap shops and restaurants, and you can escape the city centre by heading up **Mont Faron** or taking a boat across the roadstead to **La Seyne** or **St-Mandrier**.

Arrival, information and accommodation

The **gare SNCF** and **gare routière** are on place Albert-1ᵉʳ. Walking straight out of the station down avenue Vauban will bring you to the place d'Armes.

Crossing the square and following the busy avenue that runs east parallel to the coast, you'll reach avenue de la République and the **tourist office** at no. 334 (Mon & Wed–Sat 9am–6pm, Tues 10am–6pm, Sun 10am–noon; ☏04.94.18.53.00, ⓦwww.toulontourisme.com). A city **bus map** is available from the RMTT kiosk on place de la Liberté, three blocks southeast of the station. To reach the seaside suburb of Le Mourillon, take bus #3 or #13 from the centre. **Internet access** is available at ten cafés across the city, including Cyber Espace, 88 bd Georges-Clémenceau, (☏04.94.22.93.11).

One of the cheapest **hotels** in Toulon is the fairly basic *Hôtel des Allées*, 18 allée Amiral-Courbet (☏04.94.91.10.02, ⓔcontact@hoteljaures.fr; ❷), with a (summer-only) studio to rent, sleeping four. The smarter and tastefully refurbished *Hôtel Bonaparte*, 16 rue Anatole (☏04.94.93.07.51, ⓦwww .hotel-bonaparte.com; ❹) looks out onto the place d'Armes, while the plush *Little Palace*, at 6–8 rue Berthelot (☏04.94.92.26.62, ⓦwww.hotel-littlepalace .com; ❹), is run by the same management. Next door is the *Grand Hôtel Dauphiné* (☏04.94.92.20.28, ⓦwww.grandhoteldauphine.com; ❹), another superior two-star. In Le Mourillon, east of the centre, *La Corniche*, 17 littoral Frédéric-Mistral (☏04.94.41.35.12, ⓦwww.cornichehotel.com; ❺), has a lovely enclosed terrace garden and some very pleasant rooms, the more expensive ones with views over the sea.

The Town

Vieux Toulon, crammed in between boulevard de Strasbourg and avenue de la République on the old port, is pleasant enough during the day. It has a fine scattering of fountains, more often than not of dolphins, a decent selection of shops, particularly for clothes, and an excellent **market** (Tues–Sun) around rue Landrin and cours Lafayette. Big chunks of the Vieille Ville have disappeared with the construction of a gleaming new *lycée* and shopping centre, and place Victor-Hugo around the opera is all cleaned up and full of café tables, as is the quai Cronstadt fronting the port. However, one block behind the port, along avenue de la République, the streets are still a little seedy by night; here, Toulon's only gay bar, *Texas*, offers a pleasant haven to heterosexual and gay alike. Alternatively, you may want to head east to the **Mourillon quartier** where trendy nightlife glitters down the littoral Frédéric-Mistral and the beaches face the open sea.

The vast expanse of the **Arsenal**, on place Monsenergue, marks the western end of the Vieille Ville, with its grandiose eighteenth-century gateway leading

△ Mont Faron cablecar, Toulon

to the **Musée de la Marine** (Mon & Wed–Sun 10am–noon & 2–7pm; €5), where French and English visitors alike are greeted by Pierre-Louis Ganne's depiction of the battle of Trafalgar. The museum displays figureheads, statues of admirals, an extensive collection of model ships and an enormous fresco showing the old arsenal before it was burnt by the British (see below), as well as stark black-and-white photos showing the aftereffects of the scuttling of the French fleet in Toulon harbour during World War II. To the north, beyond the rather scruffy formal gardens of **place d'Armes** and up the main boulevard, the grandiose **Musée d'Art**, 113 bd Maréchal-Leclerc (currently closed for refurbishment; check opening times with tourist office), has a collection spanning seventeenth- and eighteenth-century Provençal artists, the Provençal Fauves and more modern works including some from the *Support-Surfaces* movement. It shares a building with the **Muséum d'Histoire Naturelle** (Mon–Fri 9.30am–noon & 2–6pm, Sat & Sun 1–6pm; free), whose musty collection of mineral and dinosaur displays outshine the stuffed animals and mounted butterflies.

Further east, at 236 bd Maréchal-Leclerc, is the handsome **Hôtel des Arts** (daily 11am–6pm; free), housed in the Beaux Arts, former Conseil General building and intended as a home for touring exhibitions of modern art. The building itself is architecturally conservative, but the gallery pulls in shows from the major Parisian galleries, and it's always worth a look to see what's on. The most impressive public artwork in the city, however, is Pierre Puget's sculptures of **Atlantes**, holding up all that is left of the old town hall on avenue de la République. It's thought that Puget, working in 1657, modelled these immensely strong, tragic figures on galley slaves as allegories of might and fatigue.

Around the Petite Rade

Several companies offer **boat tours** with commentary around both the Grande and Petite Rade, but a much cheaper option is to take one of the public transport **boats** from quai Stalingrad, along the avenue de la République, across the Petite Rade to **La Seyne** (#8M; 20 min); **St-Mandrier** (#28M; 20min); or **Les Sablettes**, the isthmus between them, which stops at Tamaris on the way (#18M; 20 min).

Although it now has the merchant shipping port, the loss of **LA SEYNE**'s naval shipyards at the end of the 1980s took a heavy toll on this industrial working-class community. However, it reverted to its old red colours by electing a communist mayor when Toulon voted for the *Front National*. The **Musée Naval du Fort Balaguier** on boulevard Bonaparte (mid-June to mid-Sept Tues–Sun 10am–noon & 3–7pm; mid-Sept to mid-June Tues–Sun 10am–noon & 2–6pm; €3) explores La Seyne's long association with naval history. In 1793, after Royalists had handed Toulon over to the British and Spanish fleet, the British set up a line of immensely secure fortifications between this fort and the fort now known as **Fort Napoleon**, a kilometre or so inland from the museum on chemin Marc-Sangnier. Despite its ability to rain down artillery on any attacker, Fort Balaguier was taken by a Captain Bonaparte with a bunch of volunteers, who sent the enemies of revolutionary France packing, though not before they burnt the arsenal, the remaining French ships and part of the town. Fort Napoleon now houses a cultural centre and gallery, which occasionally hosts excellent contemporary art exhibitions; for details, check with La Seyne's **tourist office**, on corniche Georges-Pompidou in Les Sablettes (summer Mon–Sat 9am–7pm, Sun 10am–12.30pm & 3.30–7pm; winter Mon–Sat 9am–12.30pm & 2–6pm; ☎04.98.00.25.70, ⓦwww.ot-la-seyne-sur-mer.fr).

Between Fort Balaguier and the sand spit of Les Sablettes is the shoreline of the peaceful former resort of **Tamaris**, with its rickety wooden jetties and fishing huts on stilts overlooking the mussel beds of the Baie du Lazaret. The beautiful oriental building on the front, now the Institut Michel Pacha Marine Physiology Institute, was constructed in the nineteenth century by a local who had made his fortune in Turkey.

At **Les Sablettes** you can lounge on the south-facing beach; beyond the neck of sand is the little port of **ST-MANDRIER-SUR-MER**, sandwiched between the high walls of *terrain militaire*, where you can look across the harbour, past all the battleships, to the grim metropolis.

Mont Faron

Aside from the harbour boat trips, the best way to pass an afternoon in Toulon is to leave the town 542m below you and ascend to the summit of **Mont Faron**. By road, avenue Emile-Fabre to the northwest of the centre becomes route du Faron, snaking up to the top and descending again from the northeast, a journey of 18km in all. The road is a one-way, narrow slip of tarmac with no barriers on the cliff-edge hairpin bends, looping up and down through luscious vegetation. To reach the summit as the crow flies, take bus #40 (direction "Super Toulon" or "Mas du Faron"; stop "Téléphérique") to boulevard Amiral-Vence where a **cable car** operates (daily 9.30am–noon & 2–6.45pm; ☎04.94.92.68.25; €6.10 return; closed mid-Nov to early Feb and in poor weather); it's a bit pricey but a treat.

At the top of Mont Faron there's a **memorial museum** to the Allied landings in Provence of August 1944 (May & June Tues–Sun 10am–noon & 2–5.30pm; €3.80), with screenings of original newsreel footage. In the surrounding park are two restaurants, and a little further up to the right, a **zoo** (Mon–Sat 2–6pm, Sun 10am–6pm; ☎04.94.88.07.89; €8) specializing in big cats. Beyond the zoo you can walk up the hillside to an abandoned fort and revel in the cleanliness of the air, the smell of the flowers and the views beyond the city way below.

Eating, drinking and nightlife

Toulon's best rewards are mainly in **eating**. There are plenty of brasseries, cafés and restaurants along the quayside, some selling just sandwiches, others offering seafood-based fixed menus for under €10. Toulon's oldest restaurant, *Au Sourd*, 10 rue Molière, in the Vieille Ville (T04.94.92.28.52; closed Mon, Sun eve & most of July), specializes in fish dishes including bouillabaisse, and has a good menu at €28, with main courses à la carte around €35. Good couscous can be enjoyed at *Chez Mimi*, 83 av de la République (T04.94.24.97.42; closed Wed), on a €15.50 menu. North of boulevard Strasbourg, close to the opera and in an area with several pizza restaurants, the *Pizzeria Stromboli*, 40 rue Picot (T04.94.62.44.02; closed Sun), stands out, serving pizzas and pasta, from €10, until midnight. The littoral Frédéric-Mistral in Le Mourillon is chock-a-block with restaurants; the one at *Hôtel La Corniche* (T04.94.41.10.04; closed Sat, Sun eve & Mon), serves *plateaux de fruits de mer* and Bandol wines, with menus from €27.80 to €53.

Toulon's **nightlife** scene is lively and student-orientated; pick up the free *Le Petit Bavard* **listings guide** from the tourist office to see what's going on. *Bar à Thym*, 32 bd Dr-Cuneo (T04.94.41.90.10), is a good spot for an after-beach beer, with tapas and occasional live music, while *Le Navigateur*, 128 av de la République (T04.94.92.34.65) is a glitzy bar with 150 different beers and DJ Manix to heat up the pre-club set. *Côte Jardin,* 437 littoral Frédéric-Mistral, offers free WiFi access when you buy a drink.

East towards Hyères

Beyond Le Mourillon to the east, Toulon merges with **LE PRADET** where old houses with lovely gardens are shaded by pines above the cliffs leading to the **Pointe de Carqueiranne**. A path follows the coast all the way round the headland to Carqueiranne and steep steps lead down to beaches which are crowded during the day but lovely in the evening as they catch the sun setting over Toulon's harbour. At **Carqueiranne**, 10km east of Toulon, the modern, beach-hut/terrace **restaurant** *L'Adventure* (T04.94.21.72.27) serves up fish specialities accompanied by panoramic sea views (*moules frites* €11).

Past Pointe de Carqueiranne, between Pointe du Bau Rouge and the D559, the chemin du Bau Rouge crosses the side of a hill guarded by two old forts with views of the Presqu'Île de Giens and the Île de Porquerolles (see p.324). Along this road you'll also find the **Musée de la Mine de Cap Garonne** (July & Aug daily 2–5.30pm; Sept–June Wed, Sat & Sun 2–5pm; Wwww .mine-capgaronne.fr; €6.20), with its treasure trove of semi-precious minerals, including malachite, azurite and cyanotrichite. There's also an exhibition on the history of the miners themselves.

If you're **cycling** from Toulon to Hyères there's a proper track running beside the D559.

Hyères

HYÈRES is the oldest resort of the Côte d'Azur, listing among its pre-twentieth-century admirers Empress Joséphine, Queen Victoria, Tolstoy and Robert Louis Stevenson. It was particularly popular with the British, being

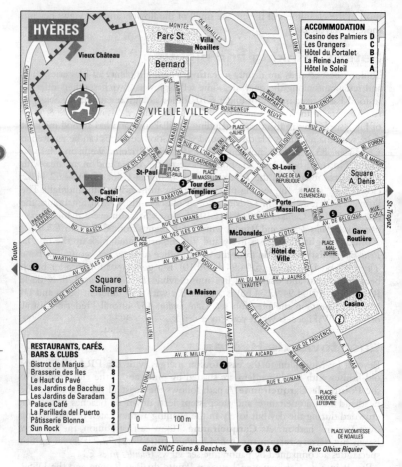

HYÈRES

Vieux Château

Parc St
Bernard

Villa
Noailles

MONTÉE DE NOAILLES

N

Castel
Ste-Claire

VIEILLE VILLE

RUE BARRUC

RUE ST-BERNARD

RUE PARADIS

RUE DE L'ORATOIRE

RUE BARBACANE

RUE ST-CATHERINE

RUE STE-CLAIRE

CHEMIN DU VIEUX CHÂTEAU

1

St-Paul   PLACE
         ST-PAUL

3 Tour des
Templiers

PLACE
MASSILLON

RUE RABATON

RUE DE LIMANS

B

RUE DU TEMPLE

RUE FRANKLIN

RUE NEUVE

RUE BOURGNEUF

RUE DES RAMPARTS

A

PLACE
ALHET

RUE MASSILLON

St-Louis

PLACE DE LA
RÉPUBLIQUE

2

CRS STRASBOURG

RUE DE LA RÉPUBLIQUE

BD. MATIGNON

RUE DE VERDUN

BD. D'ORIENT

AV. G. MANGIN

Square
A. Denis

PLACE G.
CLEMENCEAU

Porte
Massillon

AV. A. DENIS

5 **4**

RUE
CURIE

AV. DE BELGIQUE

Gare
Routière

RUE DES ILES D'OR

AV. GÉN. DE GAULLE

AV. DU PORTALET

McDonalds

AV. J. CLOTIS

AV. DU MAL FOCH

PLACE
MAL-
JOFFRE

PLACE
G. PÉRI

RUE P. PÉRON

AV. DR. J. J. PÉRON

MOULIS

Hôtel de
Ville

6

PASSAGE
A. SAMARON

BD. V. BASCH

AV. DES ILES D'OR

R. WARTHON

C

R. SÈRE DE RIVIÈRES

Square
Stalingrad

AV. GALLIENI

La Maison
@

AV. DU MAL
LYAUTEY

AV. J. JAURES

RUE DE BREST

Casino

D

i

AV. VICTORIA

AV. E. MILLET

AV. GAMBETTA

RUE DE PROVENCE

AV. AICARD

RUE DE BREST

AV. A. THOMAS

7

RUE E. DUNAN

PLACE
THÉODORE
LEFEBVRE

PLACE VICOMTESSE
DE NOAILLES

Toulon

St-Tropez

ACCOMMODATION
Casino des Palmiers   D
Les Orangers   C
Hôtel du Portalet   B
La Reine Jane   E
Hôtel le Soleil   A

**RESTAURANTS, CAFÉS,
BARS & CLUBS**
Bistrot de Marius   3
Brasserie des Iles   8
Le Haut du Pavé   1
Les Jardins de Bacchus   7
Les Jardins de Saradam   5
Palace Café   6
La Parillada del Puerto   9
Pâtisserie Blonna   2
Sun Rock   4

0   100 m

Gare SNCF, Giens & Beaches, ▼ **E**, **8** & **9**   *Parc Olbius Riquier* ▼

closer, and more southerly, than its rival Nice. To winter at Hyères in style
one needed one's own villa, hence the expansive gardened residences that
spread seawards from the Vieille Ville, giving the town something of the
atmosphere of a spa. By the early twentieth century, however, Nice and
Cannes began to upstage Hyères, and when the foreign rich switched from
winter convalescents to summer sunbathers Hyères, with no central seafront,
lost out.

Today it has the unique distinction on the Côte of not being totally dependent
on the summer influx. The town exports cut flowers and exotic plants, the most
important being the date palm, which graces every street in the city. The
orchards, nursery gardens, vineyards and fields of vegetables, taking up land
which elsewhere would have been developed into a rash of holiday units, are
crucial to its economy. Even the saltworks are still going. Hyères is consequently
rather appealing: the Vieille Ville is neither a sanitized tourist trap nor a slum
and the locals aren't out to squeeze maximum profit from the minimum
number of months.

Arrival and information

Walled and medieval **old Hyères** lies on the slopes of Casteou hill, 5km from the sea. Avenue des Îles d'Or and its continuation avenue Général-de-Gaulle mark the border with the **modern town** with avenue Gambetta the main north-south axis. At the coast the peculiar **Presqu'Île de Giens** is leashed to the mainland by an isthmus, known as **La Capte**, and a parallel sand bar enclosing the salt marshes and a lake. **La Tour Fondue** port at Giens is the closest embarkation point to the Île de Porquerolles (see Îles d'Hyères on p.323); Hyères' **main port** is at **Hyères-Plages** at the top of La Capte. **Le Ceinturon**, **Ayguade** and **Les Salins d'Hyères** are the village-cum-resorts along the coast northeast from Hyères-Plages; **L'Almanarre** is to the west where the sand bar starts.

The **gare SNCF** is on place de l'Europe, 1.5km south of the town centre; frequent buses connect the station with the **gare routière** on place Mal-Joffre. The modern Hyères-Toulon **airport** is between Hyères and Hyères-Plage, 3km from the centre with a regular shuttle to the centre.

The **tourist office** is in the Forum du Casino complex at 3 av Ambroise-Thomas (July & Aug daily 8.30am–7.30pm; Sept–June Mon–Fri 9am–6pm, Sat 10am–4pm; ☎04.94.01.84.50, ⊛www.ot-hyeres.fr). Its map of Hyères and the surrounding resorts is very useful and it can provide information on everything from archery and karate clubs to fishing and surfing competitions. **Bikes** and mopeds can be rented from Holiday Bikes on rue Jean-d'Agrève close to the port (☎04.94.38.79.45). For **Internet** access try Geni Web, 4 av Brossolette (☎04.94.33.43.86), or La Maison Internet, rue Soldat Bellon (☎04.94.65.92.82), while the local McDonald's on avenue Gambetta offers free **WiFi**.

Accommodation

With a few exceptions, hotels in Hyères are not that expensive, nor very memorable. There are only three in the Vieille Ville, but more in the modern town and even more on La Capte and along the seafront between Hyères-Plage and L'Ayguade. The hotels in central Hyères stay open all year, while those at the coast tend to close for the winter.

Hotels

Hotel BOR 3 allée Emile-Gérard, Les Presquiers ☎04.94.58.02.73, ⊛www.larosedesmers.com. A small new designer hotel right on the beach, with large areas of decking under palm trees. ❼

Casino des Palmiers 1 av Ambroise-Thomas ☎04.94.12.80.80, ⊕04.94.12.80.94. Staying at the casino itself may be fun and it is the swishest hotel in town, though it's a modern building and rather lacking in atmosphere. ❼

Les Citronniers 1134 bd du Front de Mer, L'Ayguade ☎ 04.94.66.41.81, ⊛www.hotelcitronnier.com. With just seven rooms the hotel is a labour of love for M. "Fredo" Pellegrino and his family who rescued it from ruin. ❺

Les Orangers 64 av des Îles d'Or ☎04.94.00.55.11, ✉orangers@9business.fr. This pleasant small hotel is situated in an attractive villa district, west of the modern centre, and has an attractive garden and terrace. ❸

Hôtel du Portalet 4 rue de Limans ☎04.94.65.39.40, ⊛www.hotel-portalet.com. In the lower, and busier, part of the old town, this hotel has TVs in all the rooms and accepts pets. ❸

La Reine Jane le port de l'Ayguade ☎04.94.66.32.64, ⊛www.reinejane.com. Overlooking the port at Ayguade, this is a friendly place with a restaurant, bar and terrace to make up for its out-of-town location. Closed Jan. ❷

Hôtel le Soleil rue du Rempart ☎04.94.65.16.26, ⊛www.hoteldusoleil.com. Well positioned in the Vieille Ville, high up at the foot of parc St-Bernard, this popular hotel is not particularly cheap in summer, but offers better value outside high season. ❺

Semaine Olympique de Voiles

Thanks to its idyllic waters and consistently strong winds, the Hyères bay is one of the world's best-known sailing centres, bustling year-round with windsurfers, kit surfers and sailors alike. Each April, for the last 40-odd years, the town has hosted the **Semaine Olympique de Voiles**, a major six-day competition when some fifty national teams and more than a thousand ships descend on the bay in what amounts to a rehearsal for the Olympic Games, with many countries using the competition to select their future teams. With sponsors, support teams and around a thousand sailors thronging the streets and bars, a festive atmosphere prevails in town, with flags of all nations hanging from balconies and windows, while down by the port crowds brace the weather for glimpses of boats off shore. During the event hotels around the port are at a premium and although there is more in the Vieille Ville are easier to come by it is advisable to book at least three months in advance.

If watching the event inspires you to try out sailing yourself, the International Yacht Club de Hyères (IYCH), 61 av du Docteur-Robin (℡04.94.57.00.07, ⊛www.iych.com), will point you in the right direction for local sailing schools and equipment rental.

Campsites

There are plenty of **campsites** on Presqu'Île de Giens, La Capte and all along the coast, some of them housing over a thousand pitches. Some of the smaller, more pleasant ones include the two-star *Camping-Bernard*, close to the beach in Le Ceinturon (℡04.94.66.30.54, ℻04.94.66.48.30; closed Oct–Easter); *Le Capricorne* on route des Vieux Salins, 1.5km from the beach at Les Salins (℡04.94.66.40.94, ⊛site.voila.fr/capricorne; closed Oct–March), also a two-star; and *Clair de Lune*, avenue du Clair de Lune (℡04.94.58.20.19, ⊛www.campingclairdelune.com; closed mid-Nov to Jan), a three-star on Giens with facilities for divers and windsurfers.

The Vieille Ville

To the west of place Clemenceau a medieval gatehouse, **Porte Massillon**, opens onto rue Massillon and the Vieille Ville. At **place Massillon**, you encounter a perfect Provençal square, with terraced cafés looking onto the twelfth-century **Tour des Templiers** (opening hours depend on exhibitions, contact tourist office; free), the remnant of a Knights Templar lodge. The tower now houses contemporary art exhibitions, though these are frequently less impressive than their dramatic setting: don't miss the narrow staircase that leads up onto the roof for a bird's-eye view of the medieval centre. Behind the tower, rue Ste-Catherine leads uphill to place St-Paul, from where you have another panoramic view over a section of medieval town wall to Costabelle hill and the Golfe de Giens. It is round here, where the crumbly lanes are festooned with bougainvillea, wisteria and yuccas, that the real charm of the Vieille Ville begins to be apparent.

Dominating the square is the former collegiate church of **St-Paul** (under restoration; due to reopen late 2007), whose wide steps fan out from a Renaissance door. Its distinctive belfry is pure Romanesque, as is the choir, though the simplicity of the design is masked by the collection of votive offerings hung inside. The decoration also includes some splendid wrought-iron candelabras and a Christmas crib with over-life-size *santos*. Today – when it's open – the church is used only for special services – the main place of worship is the mid-thirteenth-century former monastery church of **St-Louis** on place de la République.

To the right of St-Paul's, a Renaissance house bridges rue St-Paul, its turret supported by a pillar rising beside the steps. Through this arch you can reach rue St-Claire which leads past the neo-Gothic Porte des Princes to the entrance of **parc Ste-Claire** (daily 8am–dusk; free), the exotic gardens around **Castel Ste-Clair**. Now housing the offices of the Parc National de Port Cros, the castle was originally owned by the French archeologist Olivier Voutier (who discovered the Venus de Milo), before becoming home to the American writer Edith Wharton.

Back at St-Paul's church, if you follow rue Paradis north, you'll pass an exquisite Romanesque house at no. 6, before reaching the **Porte Barruc**. At the side of the *porte* you can ascend to **parc St-Bernard** (8am–dusk; free), an enjoyable warren full of almost every Mediterranean flower known. At the top of the park, along montée des Noailles – which can be reached by car from cours de Strasbourg and rue Long – is the **Villa Noailles**, an angular Cubist mansion designed by Mallet-Stevens in the 1920s, with gardens enclosed by part of the old citadel walls. All the luminaries of Dada and Surrealism stayed here and left their mark, including Man Ray who used it as the setting for one of his most inarticulate films, *Le Mystère du Château de Dé*. The villa was recently restored, and is only open to the public during the various exhibitions that it hosts throughout the year (opening hours vary according to exhibition, contact tourist office for information).

To the west of the park and further up the hill you come to the remains of Hyères' **Vieux Château** (always open) whose keep and ivy-clad towers outreach the oak and lotus trees and give stunning views out to the Îles d'Hyères and east to the Massif des Maures.

The modern town

The switch from medieval to eighteenth- and nineteenth-century Hyères is particularly abrupt, with wide boulevards and open spaces, opulent villas, waving palm fronds and stuccoed walls marking the modern town. Most of the former aristocratic residences and grand hotels now have more prosaic functions, though the **casino** (daily 10am–4am), south of the *gare routière*, is still in use. Unfortunately its elegant Beaux Arts exterior and interior have lost much of their original character due to some crude modernization, and the current gloomy interior will disappoint all but the most hardened gamblers.

South of the casino, at the bottom of avenue Olbius-Riquier, is Hyères' botanic garden, the **Parc Olbius Riquier** (Jan–March 7.30am–6pm; April, May & Sept 7.30am–7pm; June–Aug 7.30am–8pm; Nov & Dec 7.30am–5pm; free), which opened in 1868. Pride of place is given to the palms, of which there are 28 varieties, plus yuccas, agaves and bamboos. There's a hothouse full of exotics including banana, strelitzia, hibiscus and orchids, and a small zoo and miniature train to keep children amused.

Down to the coast

There are plenty of beaches around Hyères' coastal suburbs, though mosquitoes can be a problem, so bring insect repellent just in case. The eastern side of La Capte, the built-up isthmus of the **Presqu'Île de Giens**, is one long sand beach, with very warm and shallow water, and gets packed out in summer. To the northeast, traffic fumes and proximity to the airport detract from the charms of the seaside between Hyères-Plage and Le Ceinturon, despite the pines and ubiquitous palms. It's far more pleasant further up by the little fishing port of **Les Salins d'Hyères**. East of Les Salins, where the coastal road finally turns inland, you can follow a path between abandoned salt flats and the sea to a naturist beach.

Alternatively, there's the less sheltered **L'Almanarre** beach to the west of the Presqu'Île de Giens, where you can swim from a narrow crescent of sand: the French sailing championships are sometimes held here, and it's a popular surfers' hangout, too. L'Almanarre is also the site of the ancient Greek town of **Olbia**, whose ruins you can wander round today (April–Sept Tues & Sat 3–6pm, Thurs & Fri 9.30am–12.30pm & 3–6pm; €6). Founded in the fourth century BC on a small knoll by the sea, Olbia was a maritime trading post, and excavations here have revealed Greek and Roman remains, including baths, temples and homes, plus parts of the medieval abbey of St-Pierre de L'Almanarre.

South of L'Almanarre, the route du Sel (closed to cars mid-Nov to mid-April) leads down the sand bar on the western side of the Presqu'Île, giving you glimpses of the saltworks and the lake with its flamingoes, that lies between the sand bar and the built-up La Capte. At the far end of the sand bar sits the placid suburban seaside resort of Giens, with its **Tour Fondue**, a Richelieu construction on the eastern side, overlooking the small port that serves the Îles d'Hyères.

Regular **buses** from Hyères' *gare routière* run to Giens, L'Almanarre, Hyères-Plage and Le Ceinturon.

Eating, drinking and markets

The best places to eat and drink in Hyères are the terraced **café-brasseries** in and around place Massillon, where you'll also find a good choice of crêperies, pizzerias and little bistros that serve *plats du jour* for €10–15. There's a food **market** on place de la République on Tuesday and Thursday mornings and along avenue Gambetta on Saturday morning, while organic produce is sold on place Vicomtesse-de-Noailles on Tuesday, Thursday and Saturday mornings. There's also a food market at Giens on Tuesdays, at Ayguade on Wednesday mornings, at Les Salins on Thursdays, La Capte on Friday mornings and at the port on Sundays. Back in Hyères, there's a flea market along avenue des Îles d'Or on Saturday mornings.

Restaurants, cafés, bars and clubs

Bistrot de Marius 1 place Massillon ℡04.94.35.88.38; closed Mon and Tues. Upmarket little place serving an excellent *soupe de poisson*, Menus €17–60.

Brasserie des Îles ℡04.94.57.49.75. A swish brasserie at the port serving a big *plateau de fruits de mer*, with menus from €26 to €40. Closed Mon.

Le Carré Port St Pierre ℡04.94.48.84.53. A popular, young pre-club bar down on the port with a huge, lively terrace.

Le Haut du Pavé 2 rue du Temple ℡04.94.35.20.98. Provençal and Mediterranean-style cooking, with live jazz in the basement. Menus €25 & €32. Closed Mon (& Tues out of season).

Les Jardins de Bacchus 32 av Gambetta, on the edge of the new town ℡04.94.65.77.63. Try novel concoctions such as caramelized pears on salmon

with prawns and bacon on menus from €28.80 to €48.80. Closed Mon.

Les Jardins de Saradam 35 av de Belgique ℡04.94.65.97.53. A pretty North African restaurant serving reasonable *brik*, tagines and couscous opposite the *gare routière*. À la carte around €20. Closed Mon out of season.

Palace Café 8 av Jean-Jacques-Perron ℡04.94.65.09.42. Uber-designed bar with a modern menu. À la carte from €12. Closed Sun.

La Parillada del Puerto ℡04.94.57.44.82. Down at the port, this place specializes in Spanish dishes based on fresh fish. À la carte from €19. Closed Nov to mid-March & Tues.

Pâtisserie Blonna 1 place Clemenceau. The best cakes and ice creams in town. Closed Mon.

Sun Rock 20 av de Belgique ℡04.94.65.02.48. Home to *L'Aréna Club*, which is as lively midweek as weekends.

The Îles d'Hyères

Originally a haven from tempests in ancient times, then the peaceful habitat of monks and farmers, in the Middle Ages the **Îles d'Hyères** (also known as the Îles d'Or) became a base for piracy and coastal attacks by a relentless succession of aggressors, against whom the few islanders were powerless. In 1550, Henri II tried to solve the problem by turning the islands into penal colonies, but unfortunately the convicts themselves turned to piracy, even attempting to capture a ship of the royal fleet from Toulon. Forts were built all over the islands from the sixteenth century onwards, when François I started a trend of underfunded fort building, to the twentieth century, when the German gun positions on Port-Cros and Levant were knocked out by the Americans. Some of the forts exist to this day, with a few having been rebuilt, others left half-destroyed or abandoned.

The military presence remains, too, thanks to the habit of the French armed forces of acquiring prime beauty sites for their bases. This has at least prevented the otherwise inevitable development, and in the non-military areas the Parc National de Port-Cros and the Conservatoire Botanique de **Porquerolles** have been protecting and documenting the islands' rare species of wild flowers. **Port-Cros** and its small neighbour Bagaud are just about uninhabited, so the main problem there is controlling the flower-picking and litter-dropping habits of visitors. On **Levant**, the military rule all but a tiny morsel of the island.

Overall, the Îles d'Hyères are a very fragile environment, with their wild, scented greenery and fine sand beaches contrasting with the overpopulated, over developed coastline nearby. A host of measures protect the islands, and in hot, dry weather some of the forest areas may well be out of bounds due to the fire risk. If you want to **stay**, the only reasonably priced options are on Levant, and then you need to book months in advance. Accommodation on Porquerolles is limited to pricey hotels and rented apartments; on Port-Cros it is almost nonexistent.

Getting to the islands

There are ferries to the Îles d'Hyères, from seven ports along the Côte d'Azur, though some services only operate in summer. Departures are from **Cavalaire**

△ Îles d'Hyères

(summer only; ℡04.94.71.01.02) to Port-Cros (45min) and Porquerolles (1hr 5min); **La Croix Valmer** (summer only; ℡04.94.71.01.02) to Port-Cros (1hr) and Porquerolles (45min); **La Londe** Port de Miramar (summer only; ℡04.94.05.21.14) to Port-Cros (45min) and Porquerolles (30min); **Le Lavandou** *gare maritime* (℡04.94.71.01.02) to Île de Levant (35min–1hr), Port-Cros (35min–1hr) and Porquerolles (50min); **Port d'Hyères** (℡04.94 .57.44.07) to Île de Levant (1hr 30min), Port-Cros (30min) and Porquerolles (summer only; 1hr 15min); **Toulon** quai Stalingrad (summer only; ℡04.94 .92.96.82) to Porquerolles (1hr 15min); and **La Tour Fondue** Presqu'Île de Giens (℡04.94.58.21.81; bus #67 from the Port d'Hyères) to Porquerolles (20min; €15.50 return), plus 35-minute cruises, summer-only, in a glass-bottomed catamaran around La Tour Fondue (4 daily; €12). Parking at the ferry in La Tour Fondue costs €10 daily; cheaper car parking is available further back from the port.

Porquerolles

PORQUEROLLES is the most easily accessible of the islands and has a permanent village around the port, with a few hotels and restaurants, and plenty of cafés. In summer, the island's population expands dramatically, but there is some activity year-round. This is the only cultivated island and it has its own wine, with three Côte de Provence *domaines* which can be visited. During hot spells much of the island may be closed to minimize the risk of forest fire.

The **village of Porquerolles** began life as a nineteenth-century military settlement, with its central square, the place d'Armes, being the old parade ground. It achieved notoriety of the non-military kind in the 1960s, when Jean-Luc Godard filmed the bewildering finale of his film *Pierrot le Fou* here, as well as at the calanque de la Treille, at the far end of the plage de Notre-Dame. Overlooking the village is the ancient **Fort Ste-Agathe**, whose origins are unknown, though evidence suggests it was already in existence by 1200, and was refortified in the sixteenth century by François I, who built a tower with five-metre-thick walls to resist cannon fire. The fort has a small **museum** (May–Sept daily 10am–noon & 2–5.30pm; €3), which traces the history of the island and the work of the national park.

Five minutes south of the village, in Le Hameau, the **Conservatoire Botanique National Méditerranéen de Porquerolles** (May–Sept 9.30am–12.30pm & 1.30–5pm; free) opens its gardens and orchards to the public to wander around. The orchards are particularly interesting, as the Conservatoire is concerned with preserving biodiversity through protecting traditional and local varieties of fruit trees. If you prefer a wilder environment, however, you're better off heading south to the **lighthouse** (July & Aug 10am–noon & 2–4pm; Sept–June by appointment with the information centre; see below) and the **calanques** to its east, both of which make good destinations for an hour's walk. Be aware, though, that it's not safe to swim on this side of the island, as the southern shoreline is all cliffs with scary paths meandering close to the edge through exuberant Provençal vegetation. The best swimming is to be found at the sandy **beaches** on either side of the village: the closest is the **plage d'Argent**, a 500-metre strip of white sand around a curving bay, backed by pine forests and a single restaurant; the longest and most beautiful beach is the **plage de Notre-Dame**, 3km northeast of the village, while the **plage de la Courtade** and the **plage d'Argent** are closer to the port. The rocky exposed southern coast through the forest is very wild and has no beaches.

Practicalities

There's a small **information centre** by the harbour (daily: April–Sept 9am–5.30pm; Oct–March 9am–12.30pm; ☎04.94.58.33.76, ⓦwww.porquerolles .com), where you can pick up basic maps of the island (€1.50). The nearby Banque Société Marseillaise de Credit has an ATM. **Hotels** in Porquerolles cost upwards of €100 a night and need to be booked months in advance. The most luxurious is *Le Mas du Langoustier* (☎04.94.58.30.09, ⓦwww.langoustier.com; closed Oct–April) at the western end of the island, which insists on either full or half board, at €208 per person. More reasonable, though still pricey, are *Les Medes* (☎04.94.12.41.24, ⓦwww.hotel-les-medes.fr; ❸) on the edge of the village, and *Auberge l'Arché de Noé* (☎04.94.58.33.71, ⓦwww.arche-de-noe.com; ❸) on place d'Armes. There is no **campsite** and *camping sauvage* is strictly forbidden.

Most of the **cafés** and **restaurants** in the village cater for wealthier tourists, who can snack on lobster at *Le Mas du Langoustier* (lunch menus from €55 to €88). Slightly more affordable is the grilled fish at the *Auberge des Glycines* on place d'Armes (☎04.94.58.30.36; menus from €21.90), while *La Plage d'Argent* (☎04.94.58.32.48; closed Oct–March), overlooking the beach, serves decent fish lunches for €14 to €21. *Cocofrio,* on rue de la Ferme, offers 53 flavours of the most delicious home-made ice cream.

Gravel roads form a network of bike tracks around the island, and you can rent **bikes** from one of nine outlets in the village: *L'Indien* on the central place d'Armes (☎04.94.58.30.39) will give a ten-percent discount when you show your Rough Guide.

Port-Cros

The dense vegetation and mini mountains of **PORT-CROS** make exploring this island considerably harder going than Porquerolles, even though it is less than half the size. Aside from ruined forts and a handful of buildings around the port, the only intervention on the island's wildlife is the classification labels on some of the plants and the extensive network of paths. You are not supposed to stray from these and it would be difficult to, given the thickness of the undergrowth.

With just 35 permanent residents, the island is France's smallest national park and a protected zone – smoking is forbidden outside the port area, as is picking any flowers. It's the only one of the islands with natural springs, and boasts the richest **fauna and flora**: kestrels, eagles and sparrowhawks nest here; there are shrubs that flower and bear fruit at the same time, while more common species such as broom, lavender, rosemary and heather flourish in abundance. If you come armed with a botanical dictionary, and the leaflet provided by the **Maison du Parc** (☎04.94.01.40.72) at the port, you'll have no problem spotting all the different species.

One kilometre northeast of the port is the nearest beach, the **plage de la Palud**, backed by dense vegetation. On the way to the beach, you'll find the **Fort de L'Estissac** (July–Sept 10am–6pm; free), housing an exhibition on the national park and the island's protected marine life. The best way to see some of the marine life for yourself is to take a glass-bottomed boat-trip from La Tour Fondue (see p.319 for details), though more serious divers will want to head for the island's southern shore to explore the waters round the **Ilot de la Gabinière**.

Walkers will enjoy the paths that cross the island from the port via the **Vallon de la Solitude** and **Vallon de la Fausse-Monnaie** to the cliff-bound south coast; alternatively, there's a signed ten-kilometre **circuit of the island**.

Staying on Port-Cros is, sadly, not much of an option: the only hotel, *Le Manoir d'Hélène* (☎04.94.05.90.52, ⓦmonsite.orange.fr/hotelmanoirportcros; half board only, €160 per person; closed mid-Oct to mid-April), is prohibitively expensive, as are the five rooms at the *Hostellerie Provencale* (☎04.94.05.90.43, ⓦwww.hostellerie-provencale.com; half board only, €105 per person; closed Nov–Easter). The island's **restaurants** are not cheap either, though there are a few places where you can pick up a sandwich or a slice of pizza. Camping is forbidden.

Île de Levant

Ninety percent military reserve, the **ÎLE DE LEVANT** is almost always humid and sunny. Cultivated plant life goes wild with the result that giant geraniums and nasturtiums climb three-metre hedges, overhung by gigantic eucalyptus trees and yucca plants.

The tiny bit of the island spared by the military is dominated by the **nudist colony** of **Héliopolis,** founded in the early 1930s, and nudity is compulsory on the beaches of Bain de Diane and Les Grottes. About sixty people live here year-round, joined by thousands of summer visitors and many more day-trippers. The residents' preferred street dress is "*les plus petits costumes en Europe*", on sale as you get off the boat.

Visitors who come just for a few hours tend to be treated as voyeurs. If you stay, even for one night, you'll generally receive a much friendlier reception, but in summer without advance booking you'd be lucky to find a room or camping pitch. **Hotel** rooms need to be reserved well in advance. The cheapest place is the nine-roomed *La Source* (☎04.94.05.91.36, ⓕ04.94.05.93.47; ❺; closed Nov–March). Slightly more upmarket is the small and very charming *La Brise Marine*, in the centre of the village (☎04.94.05.91.15, ⓦwww.labrisemarine.fr; ❼). For total luxury, try the cliff-top *Le Ponant* (☎04.94.05.90.41, ⓦwww.ponant.fr; half board only, €87.50 per person; closed Oct–May), with stunning views from its terrace, or the very smart *Héliotel* (☎04.94.00.44.88, ⓦwww.heliotel.info; ❽; closed Nov–Easter), near the centre of the village, with luxuriant gardens. In addition, there are two naturist **campsites**: *Le Colombero* (☎04.94.05.90.29; €14 per tent; closed Oct–March) and *La Pinède* (☎04.94.05.92.81; €17 per tent).

Levant has a better choice of **places to eat** than the other islands, with the hotel restaurants being the best bet: *La Source* offers decent *plats du jour* from €10, while *La Brise Marine* has a menu at €23, served on an attractive Andalucian-style patio complete with fountain.

The Corniche des Maures

The Côte d'Azur really gets going to the east of Hyères, with the resorts of the **Corniche des Maures**, a twenty-kilometre stretch of coast from Le Lavandou to the Baie de Cavalaire; multi-million-dollar residences lurk in the hills, pricey yachts in the bays, and seafront prices start edging up. This is where the rich and famous go to seed: Douglas Fairbanks Jr (a house in Bormes) and the late grand duke of Luxembourg to name but two, plus a whole host of titled names familiar to readers of *Tatler*. And though aristos and celebrities are not always known for their good taste, when it comes to living in the best locations, they can usually be relied upon.

The Corniche des Maures has beaches that shine silver from the mica crystals in the sand, shaded by tall dark pines, oaks and eucalyptus; glittering rocks of purple, green and reddish hue; and chestnut-forested hills keeping winds away. There are even unspoilt stretches where it's possible to imagine what all this coast looked like in bygone years, notably around **Cap de Brégançon**, at the **Domaine de Rayol gardens**, and between **Le Rayol** and the resort of **Cavalaire**.

Transport around the Corniche is the biggest problem. The coast road is narrow and littered with hairpin bends: it's served by regular buses year-round, though they are very slow, as are the cars that follow. Cycling is strenuous and hair-raising until you get east of Le Lavandou, when a decent bridleway follows much of the coast. There are no trains.

Bormes-les-Mimosas

You can almost smell the money as you spiral uphill from the D559 into immaculate **BORMES-LES-MIMOSAS**, 20km east of Hyères. It's indisputably medieval, with a restored castle at the top, protected by spiralling lines of pantiled houses backing onto short-cut flights of steps. The castle is private, but there is a public terrace alongside it with attractive views. The winding alleys of the village are oddly named, with addresses such as "alleyway of lovers", "street of brigands", "gossipers' way", and "arse-breaker street". They're stuffed full of arts and crafts ateliers, and there's a small **Musée d'Art et d'Histoire**, at 103 rue Carnot (Mon & Wed–Sat 10am–noon & 2.30–5pm; Sun 10am–noon; free), displaying early twentieth-century regional painting.

Although it only dates from 1968, Bormes-les-Mimosas' name is apt, particularly in February when you'll see a spectacular display of the tiny yellow pom-poms. Despite their popularity along the whole of the Côte d'Azur, mimosa are no more indigenous to the region than Porsches, having been introduced from Mexico in the 1860s.

Bormes' ugly pleasure port at **La Favière** is flanked by spot-the-spare-foot-of-sand beaches. To the south the tip of **Cap Bénat** can be reached on foot along a coastal path from La Favière's beach. From Cap Bénat westwards to the bland modern seaside extension of **La Londe**, vineyards and private woods will block your way, as well as the security arrangements around the château at **Cap de Brégançon**, which is the holiday home of the president of the Republic. In summer you will have to pay for parking if you want to use the public tracks down to the shore from the La Londe-Cabasson road (cars around €7). However, once you've reached the water you can wander along the gorgeous beaches as far as you like, with no apartment buildings amongst the pine trees, not even villas, just the odd mansion in the distance surrounded by its vineyards.

Practicalities

In July and August Bormes-les-Mimosas is served by a **minibus** from Le Lavandou (6 daily; 30min); otherwise, it's a two-kilometre walk uphill from Le-Pin-de-Bormes on the main Hyères-Le Lavandou road. Minibuses arrive at the top of the village, near place Gambetta, where you'll also find the **tourist office** (June & Sept daily 9am–12.30pm & 2.30–6.30pm; July & Aug daily 9am–12.30pm & 3–8.30pm; Sept–March Mon–Sat 9am–12.30pm & 3–5.30pm; ☎04.94.01.38.39, ⓦwww.bormeslesmimosas.com). If you want **to stay** overnight the most basic, but clean and pleasant, option is the *Bellevue* on place Gambetta in old Bormes (☎04.94.71.15.15, ⓦwww.bellevuebormes .fr.st; ❸). A little more special is the wonderful *Hostellerie du Cigalou*, place Gambetta (☎04.94.41.51.27, ⓦwww.hostellerieducigalou.com; ❻). In nearby

Cabasson there's a very attractive and peaceful hotel, *Les Palmiers*, at 240 chemin du Petit Fort (℡04.94.64.81.94, Ⓦwww.hotellespalmiers.com; ❼; closed mid-Nov to Feb), with its own path to the beach. There are several **campsites** in the vicinity, all of which need to be booked in advance in high season. These include the four-star *Camp du Domaine* right by the sea on the route de Bénat in La Favière (℡04.94.71.03.12, Ⓦwww.campdudomaine.com; €27 per tent; closed Nov–March); a much smaller four-star site, *Clos-Mar-Jo*, 895 chemin de Bénat, between the D559 and the port (℡04.94.71.53.39, Ⓦwww.camping-clau-mar-jo.fr; €27 per tent; closed Oct–March); the two-star *La Célinette*, 30 impasse du Houx, just off the main route de Bénat south of the port (℡04.94.71.07.98; closed Oct–March); and the two-star *Les Cyprès* on avenue de la Mer, close to the port in La Favière (℡04.94.64.86.50; closed Oct–March).

This being the Côte proper, there's no shortage of interesting, if costly, **restaurants**. A reasonably priced and excellent quality option is *La Tonnelle*, on place Gambetta (℡04.94.71.34.84; closed Wed & Sun eve), with menus from €27 to €42. *Pâtes…et Pâtes*, on place du Bazar, serves the best pasta in town from around €12, while more run-of-the-mill meals including pizzas can be had at *La Pastourelle*, 41 rue Carnot (℡04.94.71.57.78), with menus from €16 to €29.

Le Lavandou

Five kilometres from Bormes, **LE LAVANDOU** is an out-and-out seaside resort, with sandy beaches, a scattering of high-rise hotels and an unpretentious holiday atmosphere. Its origins as a Mediterranean fishing village are betrayed by the dozen or so remaining fishing vessels, which are kept in business by the region's upmarket seafood restaurants. Merging with Bormes to the west and St-Clair to the east, Le Lavandou concentrates its charm in the tiny area between avenue du Général-de-Gaulle and quai Gabriel-Péri where café tables overlook the boules pitch and the traffic of the seafront road. Three narrow stairways lead back from here to rue Patron–Ravello, place Argaud and rue Abbé Helin, each lined with specialist shops and cafés.

However, it's the coast that is the real attraction, and there's no shortage of water sports and boat trips on offer: the Centre International de Plongée diving school offers initiation **dives** (℡04.94.71.54.57, Ⓦwww.cip-lavandou.com; €40) while Cap Sud on quai Gabriel-Péri (℡04.94.71.59.33) rents out **motor boats**. **Ferries** to the Îles d'Hyères (daily), to St-Tropez (April–Sept; every Tues), and to Brégançon (April–June & Sept; every Mon), leave from the *gare maritime* in front of the tourist office (see below). For escaping into the hills or hunting out secluded beaches, you can rent **bikes** from Holiday Bikes, avenue Vincent Auriol (℡04.94.15.19.99). For **beaches**, St-Clair, just to the east of town, is pleasant enough, but if you're after the fabled silver stretches of sand you need to carry on east to any of the string of villages between here and Cavalaire-sur-Mer.

Practicalities

Buses stop on the avenue de Provence, close to the Shopi supermarket and a short walk west of the **tourist office** on quai Gabriel-Péri (June–Sept daily 9am–12.30pm & 2.30–7pm; Oct–May Mon–Sat 9am–noon & 3–6pm; ℡04.94.00.40.50, Ⓦwww.lelavandou.com).

In summer your chances of finding a **hotel** room are pretty slim. Prices are similar to Bormes, but with rather less charm at the bottom end of the range. A

La Provence sportive

Forget for a moment Provence's seductive scenery, tranquil villages and relaxing beaches; thanks to its varied geography and distinct seasons, the region provides the perfect canvas for a vivid palette of sports and outdoor activities, from cycling along country lanes or schussing down the pristine pistes of the Alpes Maritimes and Haut Var to enjoying a traditional game of pétanque in a leafy village square.

Cycling and mountain biking

Cycling is the French national sport and there is no better region in which to pedal than Provence, blessed with warm weather, stunning coastal scenery, mountain passes and smooth, well-maintained roads. Whether breezing past lavender fields in the Luberon or riding around the streets of Aix or Avignon, cyclists are well catered for, with plenty of bike shops in the towns, and sympathetic drivers out on the roads. Cyclists are by no means confined to the asphalt, though. Many ski resorts in the Alpes Maritime and around the Parc National du Mercantour have signposted – and mapped – tracks for *VTT* (*Vélo Tout Terrain*) **mountain bikes**; in summer, riders can use the ski lifts to whisk them up to new heights, previously only accessible to walkers, before thundering back down marked mountain tracks.

Tour de France

Every year, the **Tour de France** – Le Tour – whizzes through Provence, its riders climbing the heights of the Alpine passes before sweeping down to the Riviera along routes filled with rapturous supporters. First scaled in Le Tour over a half-century ago, **Le Mont-Ventoux**, the Giant of Provence, awaits the cyclists at the end of one of the stages – this extremely difficult, 21-kilometre mountaintop finish famously claimed the life of British cyclist Tim Simpson, whose last words are rumoured to be "put me back on the bloody bike!"

Winter sports

From December to April, the resorts and villages in the northeast of the region, in the Alpes Maritimes and Haut Var, are covered in a thick blanket of snow. The once cut-off agricultural villages of Allos, Pra Loup and Isola have developed world-class **alpine ski** areas. New hotels cling to the mountainside in clusters linked by high-tech ski lifts and wide pistes. In the shady valleys at Ratery, **cross-country skiing** trails pick their way between the tall firs and larches, while **ski-touring** and **snow-shoeing** have experienced a renaissance in the sunny valley around Colmars-les-Alpes as people seek to get off the beaten track and closer to nature.

Semaine Olympic des Voiles

Thanks to its predominantly warm and sunny climate and consistently strong winds, Hyères bay is one of the best sailing centres in the world. Every spring, some fifty national teams and more than a thousand ships descend on the town to prove themselves at the six-day Semaine Olympique des Voiles, a major sailing event and a rehearsal for the Olympics themselves – all the Olympic classes are in attendance and many countries use the week to select their team for the games.

Watersports

Inland, especially in spring, when the ice and snow melts and the waters course with torrents, the region's rivers provide a mass of adrenalin-pumping white-water sports, from **rafting** in the Grand Canyon du Verdon to **canoeing** on the Roya River. On the Côte d'Azur, particularly in Estrel and Hyères, **windsurfing**, **kite-surfing** and **sailing** have mushroomed. thanks to the Mistral wind that funnels down the Rhône Valley to the coast. Less strenuous watersports can be enjoyed on the lakes of Sainte-Croix and De Esparron, where fleets of pedalos and small sailing boats drift across the tranquil, cobalt-coloured waters.

Pétanque: a game for old hands

Most village life centres round the pétanque square, for what the game lacks in motion it more than makes up for in interest, passion and dedication. A variation of *boules*, *pétanque* starts with a small wooden ball, called a *cochonnet* (piglet), being tossed approximately 10m from the throwing end: the goal is to throw your three *boules* (metal balls) as close as possible to the *cochonnet*. The bowlers' restricted throwing position – "*pétanque*" is derived from the term "*pieds tanqués*", which means "stuck feet" in the Marseilles dialect – results in a game of strategy and skill rather than physical exertion; indeed, youth and strength are no match for age and judgment on a lazy Sunday afternoon.

◀ Playing Pétanque

Monaco Grand Prix

Arguably the most important – and without doubt, the classiest – event in the grand prix season, the **Monaco Grand Prix** is the only street circuit in the Formula 1 calendar, run on the very real roads of the principality's city centre; indeed, hearing the sound of F1 cars screaming around its tight corners is one of the most thrilling motor-racing experiences in the world. Held each May, the three-day event culminates in the grand prix itself, on the Sunday – always full of glamour and excitement, and set against an unbelievably beautiful harbour backdrop.

few central options worth trying are *L'Îlot Fleurie*, boulevard Front de Mer, right next to the beach but also to a rather loud disco (℡04.94.71.14.82, ⓦwww.lilotfleuri.com; ❹); *Hôtel l'Oustaou*, 20 av Général-de-Gaulle (℡04.94.71.12.18, ⓦwww.lavandou-hotel-oustaou.com; ❸); and *L'Auberge Provençale*, 11 rue Patron-Ravello (℡04.94.71.00.44, ⓔaubprovencal@aol.com; ❹). Far nicer, however, are the upmarket *Auberge de la Calanque*, 62 av du Général-de-Gaulle (℡04.94.71.05.96, ⓦperso.orange.fr/aubergelacalanque; ❾; closed Nov–March), with rooms from €155, and the *Belle-Vue*, chemin du Four des Maures in St-Clair (℡04.94.00.45.00, ℉04.94.00.45.25; ❾; closed Nov–March), which has charming rooms overlooking the sea. If you really want to push the boat out, *Les Roches*, on avenue des Trois Dauphins in Aiguebelle (℡04.94.71.05.07, ⓦwww.hotelroches.com; ❾), is the place to go for – it stands right on the water's edge, has stunning views from its restaurant (menus from €50) and a list of illustrious former guests that includes Churchill and Bogart; rooms cost from €280, while suites with sea view start at €880. For **campsites**, there's *Caravaning St-Clair*, avenue André-Gide in St-Clair (℡04.94.01.30.20; closed Nov to mid-March), though it only takes campervans and caravans.

For gastronomy with a sea view, *L'Algue Bleue* in the *Auberge de la Calanque* (℡04.94.71.05.96; closed mid-Oct to March) is a good, if pricey, choice, while the busy **restaurant** at *L'Auberge Provençale* (menus from €29; closed all day Mon, Tues plus Wed lunch) may not have sea views, but the food is excellent if a touch expensive à la carte. For fresh fish caught by the restaurant's owner, *Le Pêcheur*, on quai des Pêcheurs (℡04.94.71.58.01; menus €22.80 & €31.50; closed Sun), is a good bet. As for **café** lounging, you can take your pick along quai Gabriel-Péri: *Le Rhumerie La Rade* has live music at weekends and the most comfy terrace chairs, while *Chez Mimi* has good beers and perhaps the edge on the ice cream front. For cocktails in a stylish setting, try the *Brasserie du Centre* on place Ernest-Reyer.

Along the corniche

The D559 east from Le Lavandou is lined with pink oleander interspersed with purple bougainvillea, a classic feature of the Côte d'Azur corniche as it curves its way through the steep wooded hills that reach down to the sea. This, along with the St-Tropez peninsula it leads to, is the most beautiful part of the Côte d'Azur, boasting silvery beaches and sections of unspoiled tree-backed coastline.

The first **beaches** you come to, between Aiguebelle and Cavalière, are the tiny, secluded *calanques*, either side of **Pointe du Layet**, at Plage du Rossignol and the naturist Plage du Layet. **CAVALIÈRE** itself has a long, wide beach and hill horizons that easily outreach the highest houses, while a couple of kilometres further on at **PRAMOUSQUIER**, you can look up from the turquoise water to woods undisturbed by roads and buildings. A further 4km east, the villages of **LE CANADEL** and **LE RAYOL** have gradually merged and colonized the hills behind them. At Le Canadel, the sinuous D27 to La Môle (see p.340) leaves the coast road and quickly spirals up past cork-oak woodland to the **Col du Canadel**, giving unbeatable views en route.

Le Rayol, however, is best known as home to the huge and stunning **Domaine du Rayol gardens** (daily: Feb–June & Sept to mid-Nov 9.30am–12.30pm & 2.30–6.30pm; July & Aug 9.30am–12.30pm & 3–8pm; €7.20), which extend down to the Figuier bay and headland. The land originally belonged to a banker who, before going bust at Monte Carlo in the 1930s, built the Art Nouveau mansion through which you enter the gardens, the Art Deco villa, farmhouse and classical pergola to which a later owner added the dramatic long flight of steps lined with cypresses. Areas of the garden are dedicated to plants from different parts of the world that share the climate of the Mediterranean: Chile, South Africa, China, California, Central America, Australia and New Zealand. Apart from the extraordinary diversity of the vegetation, some of which is left alone to spread and colonize at will, there's sheer brilliance in the landscaping that entices you to explore, to retrace your steps and get to know every path and every vista. In July and August, you can take a snorkelling tour of the "Jardin Marine" (book at least a week in advance; ☎04.98.04.44.00; €15). There are also highly informative and engaging guided tours of the garden (French only: July & Aug 10.15am, 4.30pm & 5pm; Sept–June 3pm), given by professional gardeners.

East from Le Rayol, the corniche climbs away from the coast through 3km of open countryside, sadly scarred most years by fire, before ending with the sprawl of **CAVALAIRE-SUR-MER**. Here the tiny *calanques* give way to a long stretch of sand and flat land that has been exploited for the maximum rentable space. In its favour, Cavalaire is very much a family resort and not too stuck on glamour.

Practicalities

In Le Rayol, the helpful **tourist office**, on place Michel-Goy (Mon, Wed & Fri 9.30am–12.30pm & 2.30–4.30pm; Tues, Thurs & Sat 9.30am–2.30pm; closed mid-Nov to early Dec; ☎04.94.05.65.69), has details of possible walks including the *Ex-Voie Férée*, a former railway track. Cavalaire-sur-Mer's **tourist office**, in the Maison de la Mer (mid-June to mid-Sept daily 9am–7pm; mid-Sept to mid-June Mon–Fri 9am–12.30pm & 2–6pm; Sat 9am–12.30pm; ☎04.94.01.92.10), is prominently sited where avenue des Alliés meets promenade de la Mer, and has lists of hotels and campsites. **Bikes** can be rented nearby at Holiday Bikes, les Régates, rue du Port (☎04.94.64.18.17).

Finding **rooms** in this area outside July and August should not present a problem; if you get stuck there are a number of hotels in Cavalaire-sur-Mer, with first choice being the small, upmarket *La Calanque*, rue de la Calanque (☎04.94.00.49.00, Ⓦwww.hotel-la-calanque.com; Ⓞ); it's beautifully perched on a low cliff overlooking the sea, a little way out of town; rooms start at €180. In Pramousquier, *Le Mas*, 9 av Capitaine-Ducourneau, above the main road (☎04.94.05 .80.43, Ⓦwww.hotel-lemas.com; Ⓞ), is a good option with a pool and great views.

The place to **eat and drink** is *Le Maurin des Maures* on the main road at Le Rayol (☎04.94.05.60.11; Mon–Sat lunchtime menu €13.50, otherwise €22.50), serving fresh grilled fish, *bourride* and *aioli*. In Cavalaire, *Le Quai des Moules* on the Nouveau Port (☎04.94.15.44.63; closed Dec–Jan) serves *moules-frites* in all its variety, for around €9, while *La Crêperie Bretonne* on rue du Port (☎04.94.64.16.98; April–Oct only) serves decent crêpes from €4. For **nightlife**, *Le Tropicana* **disco** on Le Canadel's beach (July & Aug Thurs, Fri & Sat; ☎04.94.05.61.50) stays open until the early hours.

La Croix-Valmer

At the eastern end of Cavalaire-sur-Mer's bay lies another exceptional stretch of wooded coastline, the **Domaine de Cap Lardier**. This pristine coastal conservation area snakes around the southern tip of the St-Tropez peninsula, and is best accessed from **LA CROIX-VALMER**, even though the village centre is some 2.5km from the sea. Being slightly inland, however, adds charm, since some of the land between is taken up by vineyards that produce a decent wine. Local legend maintains that Emperor Constantine stopped here with his troops on his way to Rome and had his famous vision of the sun's rays forming a cross over the sea which converted him, and therefore ultimately all of Europe, to the new religion; hence the "cross" in the name of the village which only came into existence in 1934.

To reach the best **beach** in the vicinity, Plage du Gigaro, and the start of the paths to Cap Lardier, you need to take boulevard Georges-Selliez from place des Palmiers (the D93), turn right into boulevard de Sylvabelle, then left along boulevard de la Mer. It's a four-kilometre walk, so you may prefer to catch the *navette* or **shuttle bus** (15 June–15 Sept; 9 daily) from outside the tourist office (see below) to the beach.

Practicalities

La Croix-Valmer's **tourist office** (mid-June to mid-Sept Mon–Sat 9.15am–12.30pm & 2.30–7pm, Sun 9am–1pm; mid-Sept to mid-June Mon–Fri 9.15am–noon & 2–6pm, Sat & Sun 9am–noon; ☎04.94.55.12.12, ⓦwww.lacroixvalmer.fr) is in Les Jardins de la Gare, just up from the central junction place des Palmiers, and has a list of walks in the area. **Bikes** and scooters can be rented from Holiday Bikes on boulevard Georges-Selliez, east of the village centre; ☎04.94.79.75.12). One of the cheapest places **to stay** in La Croix-Valmer is *La Bienvenue* on rue L-Martin (☎04.94.79.60.23, ⓦwww.hotel-la-bienvenue.com; ❸; closed Nov–Easter), right in the centre of the village, while the small, family-run *Hostellerie La Ricarde*, quartier de la Plage du Débarquement (☎04.94.79.64.07, ⓦwww.golfe-infos.com /la-ricarde; ❸; closed Oct–March), is a good option near the beach. At the other end of the scale, *Le Château de Valmer* on route de Gigaro (☎04.94.79.60.10, ⓦwww.chateau-valmer.com; ❾; closed Nov–March) is a seriously luxurious old Provençal manor house within walking distance of the sea; rooms start at €231. There's one **campsite**, the pricey four-star *Sélection* on boulevard de la Mer, just 400m from the sea and with excellent facilities (☎04.94.55.10.30, ⓦwww.selectioncamping.com; €31.50 per tent; closed mid-Oct to mid-March; booking essential in summer); it's 2.5km southwest of the village on the main road towards Cavalaire.

There are some tempting **restaurants** along the beach, though none is particularly cheap; the best is *Souleias* (☎04.94.55.10.55; closed mid-Oct to March), with menus from €48 to €82, while good, inexpensive pizzas are guaranteed at *Le Coin de l'Italien – Pepe le Pirate,* on Plage de Gigaro (☎04.94.79.67.16), the last restaurant before the conservation area.

The St-Tropez peninsula

The origins of **ST-TROPEZ** are not unusual for this stretch of coast: a fishing village that grew up around a port founded by the Greeks of Marseille, it was destroyed by the Saracens in 739 and finally fortified in the late Middle Ages. Its sole distinction was its inaccessibility. Stuck out on a peninsula that never warranted real roads, St-Tropez could only really be easily reached by boat. This was the case as late as the 1880s, when the novelist **Guy de Maupassant** sailed his yacht into the port during his final high-living binge before the onset of syphilitic insanity. The Tropeziens were a little shocked but it was the beginning of their induction to bizarre strangers seeking paradise in their home.

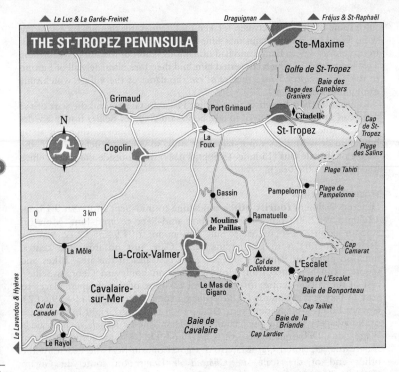

Map labels:
THE ST-TROPEZ PENINSULA

Le Luc & La Garde-Freinet · Draguignan · Fréjus & St-Raphaël

Ste-Maxime

Golfe de St-Tropez

Baie des Canebiers

Plage des Graniers

Citadelle

Cap de St-Tropez

St-Tropez

Plage des Salins

Grimaud

Port Grimaud

La Foux

Cogolin

N

Plage Tahiti

Gassin

Pampelonne

Plage de Pampelonne

Moulins de Paillas

Ramatuelle

0   3 km

La Môle

La-Croix-Valmer

Col de Collebasse

Cap Camarat

L'Escalet

Plage de L'Escalet

Baie de Bonporteau

Cavalaire-sur-Mer

Le Mas de Gigaro

Cap Taillat

Col du Canadel

Baie de Cavalaire

Baie de la Briande

Cap Lardier

Le Rayol

Left margin:

6

TOULON AND THE SOUTHERN VAR | The St-Tropez peninsula

Le Lavandou & Hyères

Soon after Maupassant's visit, the painter and leader of the Neo-Impressionists, **Paul Signac**, sailed down the coast in his boat named after Manet's notorious painting *L'Olympia*. Bad weather forced him to moor in St-Tropez and, being rich and impulsive, he decided to have a house built there – *La Hune*, on what is now rue Paul-Signac, was designed by fellow painter Henri van de Velde. Signac opened his doors to impoverished friends who could benefit from the light, the beauty and the distance from the respectable convalescent world of Cannes and Nice. **Matisse** was one of the first to take up his offer; the locals were shocked again, this time by Madame Matisse modelling in a kimono. **Bonnard**, **Marquet**, **Dufy**, **Derain**, **Vlaminck**, **Seurat**, **Van Dongen** and others followed, and by the eve of World War I, St-Tropez was fairly well established as a hang-out for bohemians.

The 1930s saw a further artistic influx, this time of writers as much as painters: **Jean Cocteau** came here; **Colette** lived for fourteen years in a villa outside the village, describing her main concerns as "whether to go walking or swimming, whether to have rosé or white, whether to have a long day or a long night"; while **Anaïs Nin**'s journal records "girls riding bare-breasted on the back of open cars; an intensity of pleasure" and undressing between bamboo bushes that rustled with concealed lovers.

But it wasn't until after World War II that St-Tropez achieved international celebrity. In 1955, Roger Vadim arrived to film **Brigitte Bardot** in *Et Dieu Créa La Femme*, and the cult of Tropezian sun, sex and celebrities took off, creating a tourist boom which continues to this day. Recent celebrity visitors include Puff Daddy, Robbie Williams and David and Victoria Beckham, while the elite list of St-Tropez property owners numbers George Michael and Jean-Paul Belmondo, as well as Harrods owner Mohamed Al-Fayed. Bardot, for decades the very icon of the place, finally left in the late 1990s, some years after famously denouncing the "black tide of human filth" that was physically and morally polluting her beloved village. When questioned about Bardot's criticisms, the mayor agreed: "It's true that St-Tropez is a dying village, but who brought all this vice and indecency here in the first place?"

In 1991 the village was dealt a further blow, with the discovery that the hundred-year-old **plane trees** on place des Lices were rotting. Several had to be cut down; the remainder underwent intensive surgery and their hollow trunks are now propped up with metal crutches. They are perhaps a fitting metaphor for St-Tropez itself: a recent report suggests the village's permanent population is shrinking, with many locals fleeing to neighbouring communes where essential shops are still plentiful and prices are more reasonable.

Arrival, information and accommodation

On entering St-Tropez, the road from La Foux divides into avenue Général-Leclerc and avenue Général-de-Gaulle, which itself quickly becomes avenue 8 du Mai 1945 at the **gare routière**, and runs parallel to a vast port-side car park before becoming avenue du 11 Novembre 1918. The harbour here is the **Nouveau Port** for yacht overspill. Follow avenue du 11 Novembre 1918 past the **post office** and you'll hit the **Vieux Port**, with the Vieille Ville rising above the eastern quay. The **tourist office** is opposite you on the Vieux Port at the start of quai Jean-Jaurès (April–June, Sept & Oct 9.30am–12.30pm & 2–7pm; July & Aug daily 9.30am–8.30pm; Nov–March 9.30am–12.30pm & 2–6pm; ℡04.94.97.45.21, ⓦwww.ot-saint-tropez.com). You can rent **bikes** from Holiday Bikes, 12 av Général-Leclerc (℡04.94.97.09.39).

The tourist office can help with **hotel** reservations, although with ever more people wanting to pay homage to St-Tropez, accommodation is a problem. Between April and September you won't find a room unless you've booked months in advance and are prepared to pay exorbitant prices. If you have your own transport, you may be better off staying in La Croix-Valmer or even Cavalaire-sur-Mer (see p.330). Out of season you may be luckier, though in winter few hotels stay open.

Camping near St-Tropez can be just as difficult as finding a room. The nearest two sites are on the plage du Pampelonne, though both charge extortionate rates and are massively crowded in high summer. In summer it's worth checking out the signs for **camping à la ferme** that you'll see along the D93. Pitching on a farm can be more pleasant than the overcrowded official sites, but make sure you know the charges first.

Hotels

Le Baron 23 rue de l'Aïoli ℡04.94.97.06.57, ⓦwww.hotel-le-baron.com. A comfortable hotel overlooking the citadel, and a bit quieter than those in the centre. It's small and cosy with just ten rooms and a restaurant. ❻

L'Ermitage av Paul-Signac ℡04.94.97.52.33, ℉04.94.97.10.43. Above place des Lices, charming and very comfortable, and away from the bustle of the village centre. Closed mid-Nov to mid-March. ❻

Les Lauriers rue du Temple ℡04.94.97.04.88, ℉04.94.97.21.87. Small and very good value, with its own garden. Close to place des Lices. Closed Jan. ❹

Lou Cagnard 18 av Paul-Roussel ℡04.94.97.04.24, ⓦwww.hotel-lou-cagnard.com. Dreary-looking from the outside, but with a decent garden and quiet at night time. Closed Nov & Dec. ❹

Maison Blanche place des Lices ℡04.94.97.52.66, ⓦwww.hotellamaisonblanche .com. Gorgeous white designer hotel in a fine bourgeois villa, with an elegant garden and lots of quirky touches. Rooms start at €240 in high season. ❾

La Ponche 3 rue des Remparts ☎04.94.97.02.53, ⓦwww.laponche.com An old block of fishermen's houses, luxuriously furnished and with a host of famous names in its guest book. Rooms start at €245. Closed Nov to mid-Feb. ⑨

Le Sube 15 quai Suffren ☎04.94.97.30.04, ⓦwww.hotel-sube.com. Unique views over the port, and decor to make you think you're in a yacht with mirrors everywhere. ⑥

Campsites

La Croix du Sud route des Plages ☎04.94.55.51.23, ⓦwww.camping-saint-tropez .com; A four-star site 3km from Ramatuelle towards the Plage de Pampelonne (see p.336). €35 per tent. Closed Oct–March.

Parc St James Montana off the road to Bourrian near Gassin ☎04.94.55.20.20,

ⓦwww.camping-parcsaintjames.com. A pricey four-star site. €32.50 per tent. Closed Dec.

Les Tournels on rte de Camarat ☎04.94.55.90.90, ⓦwww.tournels.com. Vast site but well situated, 1km from the sea. €33 per tent.

The Town

Beware of coming to St-Tropez in high summer, unless by yacht and with limitless funds. The 5km of road from La Foux is an unpleasant introduction, lined with out-of-town superstores, fast-food restaurants and interminable traffic jams in summer. The pedestrian jams in the port are not much better, while the hotels and restaurants are full and expensive, and the beaches are not that clean, having lost their Blue Flag award for water quality in 2000, due to oil pollution and smelly drains. That said, if you can time your trip for a spring or autumn day, you'll understand why this place has charmed so many for so long.

The **Vieux Port** is where you get the classic St-Tropez experience: the quayside café clientele eyeing the yacht-deck Martini-sippers, with the latest fashions parading in between, defining the French word *frimer* (derived from sham) which means exactly this – to stroll ostentatiously in places like St-Tropez. You may well be surprised at just how entertaining this spectacle can be, especially when accompanied by the jugglers, fire-eaters and mimics who ply their trade in the streets. The oversized yachts pretty much obliterate the views across the port, though the owners are as likely to be bankers as aristocrats or celebrities. They tend to be registered in Britain, the US, the Caribbean or France, with Union Jacks predominating.

The other pole of St-Trop's life is **place des Lices**, southeast of the Vieux Port, with its sad but surviving plane trees and the benches and boules games underneath. The café-brasseries have become a bit too Champs-Elysées in style, and a new commercial block has been added near the northern corner, but you can still sit down for free and ponder the unchanged dusty surface that is so essential for the momentum of Provence's favourite pastime. In the streets between place des Lices and the port – rue Sibilli and rue Clemenceau – and the smaller lanes in the heart of the old village you can window-shop or buy haute couture, antiques, *objets d'art* and classy trinkets to your heart's content.

Heading east from the port, from the top end of quai Jean-Jaurès, you pass the **Tour Suffren**, originally built in 980 by Count Guillaume 1er of Provence, and enter place de l'Hôtel-de-Ville where the *mairie* with its attractive earthy pink facade and dark green shutters is one of the few reminders that this is a real town. A street to the left takes you down to the tiny, rocky **Baie de la Glaye**; straight ahead, rue de la Ponche passes through an ancient gateway to place du Revelin above the lovely **fishing port** with its tiny beach. Turning inland and upwards, struggling past shop fronts, stalls and café tables, you can finally reach the open space around the sixteenth-century **citadel** (daily except bank holidays: mid-July to Sept 10am–8pm; Oct to mid-July 10am– 6.30pm; €5.50), which houses a small museum of local history. Far more interesting, however, is to take a walk round the ramparts, whose excellent views of the gulf and the back of the town have not changed since their translation into oil on canvas in the early twentieth century.

These paintings can be seen at the **Musée de l'Annonciade** (June–Sept Mon & Wed–Sun 10am–noon & 3–7pm; Oct & Dec–May Mon & Wed–Sun 10am–noon & 2–6pm; €5.50), reason in itself for a visit to St-Tropez. It was originally Signac's idea to have a permanent exhibition space for the Neo-Impressionists and Fauves who painted here, though it was not until 1955 that collections owned by various individuals were put together in the deconsecrated sixteenth-century chapel on place Georges-Grammont just west of the port. The museum features representative works by Signac, Matisse and most of the other artists who worked in St-Tropez: grey, grim, northern scenes of Paris, Boulogne and Westminster, and then local, brilliantly sunlit scenes by the same brush. Two winter scenes of the village by Dufy contrast with Camille Camoin's springtime *Place des Lices* and Bonnard's boilingly hot summer view. The museum is a real delight for its contents, unrivalled outside Paris for the 1890 to 1940 period, for the way it displays them, and for the fact that it can sometimes be the least crowded place in town.

Eating and drinking

There are **restaurants** for every budget in St-Tropez, as well as plenty of **snack bars** and takeaway joints, particularly on rue Georges-Clemenceau and place des Lices. Almost all are open daily from June to September; many close altogether in the winter months. Place aux Herbes has a daily (except Mondays in winter) fish **market** with some fruit and veg also on sale, though the main food market takes place on place des Lices on Tuesday and Saturday mornings.

Cafés and snack bars

Bar du Port Vieux Port. With its stylish retro-Sixties decor, this bar is the epitome of St-Tropez idling.

Le Café (formerly Café des Arts) place des Lices. The number-one café-brasserie on the square, with old-timers still gathering in the bar at the back. Menus €30–40.

Le Gorille quai Suffren. Straightforward quayside fare, where you can get a brasserie-style meal for under €16. July & Aug open 24hr.

Rotisserie Tropezienne bd Vasserot and rue F-Sibille. One of a series of snack stalls in a complex on the edge of place des Lices; this one sells the ubiquitous roast chicken on a spit, the others include an Asian fast-food stall, a crêperie and a kebab stall.

Café Sénéquier on the port. The top quayside café: it's horribly expensive, but sells sensational nougat (also available from the shop at the back).

La Tarte Tropezienne place des Lices and 36 rue G-Clemenceau. A celebrated pâtisserie which claims to have invented this eponymous sponge and cream custard cake.

Restaurants

Auberge des Maures 4 rue du Dr-Boutin, off rue Aillard ☎04.94.97.01.50. Specializes in chargrilled fish and meat from around €30, with a menu at €45. Evenings only; closed mid-Dec to mid-Dec & Jan.

Café de Paris quai de Suffren ☎04.94.97.00.56. Pizzas, salads, sashimi and light meals at round €30, all served in elegant port-side surroundings.

Joseph 1 place de l'Hôtel de Ville ☎04.94.97.01.66. Good bouillabaisse, *bourride* and desserts; around €50 à la carte.

Le Petit Charron 6 rue des Charrons ☎04.94.97.73.78. Tiny terrace and dining room serving beautifully cooked Provençal specialities, for around €40. Closed mid-Nov to mid-Feb.

Regis 19 rue de la Citadelle ☏ 04.94.97.15.53.
Small, friendly bistro and snack bar; around €20 à
la carte.
Spoon Byblos av du Maréchal-Foch
☏ 04.94.56.68.20. It's all about presentation
here – and that goes for the food, restaurant
and patrons. Celebrity chef Alan Ducasse marks

the zigzags on a lemon tart so precisely that it
has to taste good – and it does. Menu
around €60.
La Table du Marché 38 rue Clemenceau
☏ 04.94.97.85.20. Hard to get a table here but
worth the wait for true bistro-style gourmandise;
menus at €18 and €26.

Nightlife

In season St-Tropez stays up late, as you'd expect. The **boules games** on place des Lices continue till well after dusk; the portside spectacle doesn't falter till the early hours; and even the shops stay open well after dinner. If you have pots of cash and want to sample the infamous St-Tropez **nightlife**, head for *La Bodega du Papagayo* in the Résidence du Nouveau Port, with world music and theme nights; the glitzy *VIP Room* at the same location; or *Les Caves du Roy* in the flashy *Hôtel Byblos* on rue Paul-Signac, which is the most expensive and probably the tackiest. Alternatively, there's the **gay** disco *L'Esquinade*, 2 rue du Four, a long-standing St-Tropez institution, popular with gays and straights alike. All the clubs open every night in summer, and usually Saturday only in winter, though your chances of getting in will depend on who's on the door, and whether they think you look the part.

The beaches

The nearest beach to St-Tropez, within easy walking distance, is **Les Graniers** below the citadel just beyond the Port des Pêcheurs along rue Cavaillon. From here a path follows the coast around the **Baie des Canebiers**, which has a small beach, to Cap St-Pierre, Cap St-Tropez, the very crowded **Salins** beach and right round to **Plage Tahiti**, 12.5km from St-Tropez. This eastern area of the peninsula is where the rich and famous have their vast villas with helipads and artificial lakes in acres of heavily guarded grounds.

Tahiti-Plage is at the top end of the almost straight five-kilometre north-south **Plage de Pampelonne**, famous bronzing belt of St-Tropez and initiator of the topless bathing cult. The water is shallow for 50m or so and exposed to the wind, and it's sometimes scourged by dried sea vegetation, not to mention slicks of industrial pollutants. But spotless glitter comes from the rash of beach bars and restaurants built out over the coarse sand, all with patios and sofas, all serving cocktails and ice creams (as well as full-blown meals), and all renting out beach mattresses and matching parasols. Though you'll see people naked on all stretches of the beach, only some of the bars welcome visitors carrying wallets and nothing else. *Club 55*, named after the year when Vadim's film crew scrounged food from what was then a family beach hut, is supposed to be a favourite with the celebrities (à la carte from €56; closes at sundown).

The beach ends with the headland of **Cap Camarat**, beyond which the private residential settlement of **Villa Bergès** grudgingly allows public access to the **Plage de l'Escalet**. Another coastal path leads to the next bay, the **Baie de la Briande**, where you'll find the least populated beach of the whole peninsula. Beyond here the villas end and you can continue to **Cap Lardier** with a choice of paths upwards and downwards and along the gorgeous shore all the way round to La Croix-Valmer.

To **get to the beaches** from St-Tropez, there's a frequent minibus service from place des Lices to Salins, and an infrequent **bus** from the *gare routière* to Ramatuelle, the nearest you'll get to any of the beaches by bus. Alternatively, you could rent **bikes** in St-Tropez (see p.331) and cycle out to the beaches. For **drivers**, if you want to avoid the high parking fees that all the beaches charge, you'll need to leave your car some distance from the sea and risk being prey to thieves.

The interior of the peninsula

Though the coast of the St-Tropez peninsula continues to sprout holiday homes and even golf courses, the **interior** is almost uninhabited, thanks to government intervention, complex ownerships and the value of some local wines. The best view of this richly green, wooded and flowering countryside is from the hilltop village of **Gassin**, its lower neighbour **Ramatuelle**, or the tiny road between them, the beautiful route des Moulins de Paillas where three ruined windmills could once catch every wind.

Gassin

The highly chic village of **GASSIN** gives the impression of a small ship perched on a summit. Once a Moorish stronghold, it is now best known as the birthplace of French soccer idol David Ginola and the place where Mick and Bianca Jagger married. It's a perfect place for a blow-out dinner, sitting outside by the village wall with a spectacular panorama east over the peninsula. Of the handful of restaurants, *Bello Visto*, 9 place des Barrys (℡04.94.56.17.30, Ⓦwww.bello-visto.com; restaurant closed Tues & Nov–Easter; ❹), serves decent Provençal specialities, with menus from €27, and also has nine good-value rooms. The nearby *Au Vieux Gassin* (℡04.94.56.14.26; closed mid-Oct to late March) also serves good Provençal dishes, as well as lobster, and has menus from €24 to €55.

Ramatuelle

RAMATUELLE is bigger than its neighbour, though just as old, and is surrounded by some of the best Côte de Provence vineyards (the top selection of wines can be tasted at Les Maîtres Vignerons de la Presqu'île de St-Tropez by the La Foux junction on the N98). The twisting and arcaded streets are inevitably full of arts and crafts shops selling works of dubious talent, but the village itself is very pleasant nonetheless. The central Romanesque **Église Notre-Dame** that formed part of the old defences has heavy gilded furnishings from the Chartreuse de la Verne (see p.339) and an impressive early-seventeenth-century door carved out of serpentine.

Opposite the church, on place de l'Ormeau, the small **tourist office** (April–June, Sept & Oct Mon–Sat 9am–1pm & 3–7pm; July & Aug daily 9am–1pm & 3–7.30pm; Nov–March Mon–Fri 9am–12.30pm & 2–6pm; ℡04.98.12.64.00) has a good list of *campings à la ferme*. Of the few **hotels** in the village, try the fairly basic *Chez Tony*, 31 rue Clemenceau (℡04.94.79.20.46; ❷), or *L'Ecurie du Castellas* (℡04.94.79.20.67, Ⓦwww.lecurieducastellas.com; ❻), just outside the village on the road to Gassin, with panoramic views and its own restaurant. At the foot of the old village towards the beach, there's the luxurious *Ferme Augustin* (℡04.98.55.97.00, Ⓦwww.fermeaugustin.com; ❽; closed mid-Oct to mid April), surrounded by beautiful gardens and very close to the stunning Pampelonne bay. For **chambre d'hôte** try *Leï Souco*, at Le Plan (℡04.94.79.80.22, Ⓦwww.leisouco.com; ❻) a handsome Provençal country house set in acres of land filled with eucalyptus and mimosas 4km from the village. The best place to **eat** is *Au Fil à la Pâte*, 7 rue Victor-Léon (℡04.94.79.16.40; à la carte €16–30; closed Nov–Feb), which serves great dishes of fresh pasta as well as a meat or fish special.

The Massif des Maures

The secret of the Côte d'Azur is that despite the gross conglomeration of the coast, Provence is still just behind – old, sparsely populated, village-oriented and dependent on the land for its produce as much as for its value as real estate. Between Marseille and Menton, the most bewitching hinterland is the sombre **Massif des Maures** that stretches from Hyères to Fréjus.

The highest point of these hills stops short of 800m but the quick succession of ridges, the sudden drops and views, and the curling, looping roads are pervasively mountainous. Where the lie of the land gives a wide bowl of sunlit slopes, vines are grown. Elsewhere the hills are thickly forested, with Aleppo and umbrella pines, holly, sweet-chestnut trees, and tremendous gnarled cork oaks, their trunks scarred in great bands where their precious bark has been stripped. On a windy autumn day chestnuts the size of grenades explode upon your head, while water from a thousand springs cascades down each face of rock. In the heat of summer there is always the darkest shade alternating with one-way light – the rocks that compose this massif absorb rather than reflect – and it's hardly surprising that its name derives from the Provençal and Latin words for dark, *mauram* and *mauro*.

Much of the massif is inaccessible even to **walkers**. However, the GR9 follows the most northern and highest ridge from Pignans on the N97 past Notre-Dame-des-Anges, La Sauvette, **La Garde-Freinet** and down to the head of the Golfe de St-Tropez. There are other paths and tracks, such as the one following the Vallon de Tamary from north of La Londe-des-Maures to join one of the roads snaking down from the Col de Babaou to Collobrières. Some of the smaller backroads don't go very far and many are closed to the public in summer for fear of forest fires, but when they are open, this makes exceptional countryside for exploring by mountain bike or on foot. Bear in mind, however, that at certain times of the year the entire Massif is thick with hunters.

For **cyclists**, the D14 that runs through the middle, parallel to the coast, from Pierrefeu-du-Var north of Hyères to **Cogolin** near St-Tropez, is manageable and stunning.

Collobrières and around

At the heart of the massif is the ancient village of **COLLOBRIÈRES**, reputed to have been the first place in France to adopt cork-growing from the Spanish. From the Middle Ages until recent times, **cork** production has been the major business of the village, and it is still the best place in the region to buy items roughly fashioned from raw cork bark such as fruit platters and plant pots, sold from a couple of roadside stalls in the centre of the village by the old men who own the cork-collecting concessions. However, the main industry now is *marrons glacés* and every other confection derived from sweet chestnuts.

From the terrace of the main *bar-tabac* that overlooks the River Collobrier, the forests that surround the village appear to go on for hundreds of miles, while in the village itself, the church, the *mairie* and the houses look like they come straight out of the nineteenth century. Yet on the other side of the river, at the eastern end of the village, a streamlined, no-nonsense, gleaming bright-blue building, the **Confiserie Azurienne**, exudes efficiency and modern business skills. Workers clock in and out, production schedules are met, profits are made, all from the conker's sister fruit. The factory itself can't be visited but there's a shop that sells chestnut ice cream, chestnut jam, chestnut nougat, chestnut purée, chestnut glacées and chestnut bonbons. For the fanatic, there's always the annual

Fête de la Châtaigne, the **chestnut fair**, at the height of the harvest on the last three Sundays of October, with special dishes served in restaurants and roast chestnuts sold in the streets.

Practicalities

Collobrières' welcoming **tourist office** on boulevard Charles-Caminat (June–Sept Mon–Sat 10am–noon & 2–6pm; Oct–May closes 5.30pm; ℡04.94.48.08.00, Ⓦ www.collobrieres.fr) can supply details of various **walks** through the massif and some excellent local *gîtes d'étape* in the surrounding hills. There are two **hotels** in the village, both of them small, so it is advisable to book in advance in summer: *Notre-Dame*, 15 av de la Libération (℡04.94.48.07.13, Ⓕ04.94.48.05.95; ❷), and the excellent-value *Auberge des Maures*, 19 bd Lazare-Carnot (℡04.94.48.07.10, Ⓕ04.94.48.02.73; ❶). There's also a great **chambre d'hôte**: Andrée Cécile de Saleneuve's *La Bastide de La Cabrière*, 6km towards Gonfaron on the D39 (℡04.94.48.04.31, Ⓦ www.saleneuve.com; ❺). The small, one-star municipal **campsite**, the *St-Roch*, is open mid-June to mid-September (℡04.94.13.83.83; €8.10 per tent). *Camping sauvage* is forbidden: you might just get away with pitching up in the woods in late autumn or early spring, but when it's hot and dry don't even consider it – one stray spark and you could be responsible for a thousand acres of burnt forest.

For food, other than chestnuts and the fare at *Auberge des Maures*, the **restaurant** *La Petite Fontaine*, 1 place de la République (℡04.94.48.00.12; closed Sun eve & Mon), is congenial and affordable with menus at €24 and €28, though it books up fast. South of the village, signed off the D41 to Bormes at the Col de Babaou, the *Ferme de Peïgros* (℡04.94.48.03.83; daily lunch only) is an isolated farmhouse in wonderful surroundings serving its own produce on a €22 menu. If you want to buy some local **wines**, head for the Cave Cooperative on avenue de la Libération; the **market** in place de la Libération is on Thursdays (summer only) and Sundays.

Around Collobrières

Writing at the end of the nineteenth century, Maupassant declared that there was nowhere else in the world where his heart had felt such a pressing weight of melancholy as at the ruins of **La Chartreuse de la Verne** (Mon & Wed–Sun: June–Sept 11am–6pm; Oct–Dec & Feb–May 11am–5pm; €5). Since then a great deal of restoration work has been carried out on this Carthusian monastery, abandoned during the Revolution and hidden away in total isolation, 12km east of Collobrières on a winding, partially tarmacked track off the D14 towards Grimaud. It remains a desolate spot; the buildings of this once vast twelfth-century complex, in the dark reddish-brown schist of the Maures, combined for decorative effect with local greenish serpentine, appear gaunt and inhospitable, but the atmosphere is indisputable. However, if the nutty, chocolate-brown olive bread on sale in the shop is anything to go by, life here for the monks couldn't have been that deprived.

Another religious settlement concealed in these hills is **Notre-Dame-des-Anges**, 11km north of Collobrières on the Gonfaron road, almost at the highest point of the Maures (daily: June–Aug 10am–7pm; April & May 10am–5pm; Sept–May Sat & Sun 10am–5pm). As a place of worship it goes back to pagan times, but in its nineteenth-century remodelled form it lacks the atmosphere of La Verne. The main point of a visit for most people is to take in the expansive views stretching from the Alps to the sea.

About 20km north of Collobrières and 2km east of Gonfaron on the D75 to Les Mayons, **Le Village des Tortues** (March–Nov daily 9am–7pm; €8;

@www.villagetortues.com) is not just a tourist attraction but a serious conservation project to repopulate the native Hermann tortoise. A million years ago the tortoises populated a third of France, but now, due to the ever-increasing threat of urbanization, forest fires, theft of eggs and sale as pets, this rare creature only just survives in the Massif des Maures. The tortoises are cared for and protected here, and you can look round their large enclosures where you'll see the tiny babies, "juveniles" and those soon to be released back into the wild. The visit is both relaxed and educational.

La Môle

Southeast of Collobrières, **LA MÔLE** sits on the fast N98 between Bormes and Cogolin in a fabulous bowl of meadows and vineyards, with old farmhouses dotted along the lanes leading into the hills. There are three reasons to stop here: the *Auberge de la Môle* **café** (closed Mon & mid-Nov to mid-March) serving good strong coffee and decked out with wooden fittings, ancient framed posters and a wonderfully old-fashioned petrol pump; the *Relais d'Alsace* **restaurant** (℡04.94.49.57.02; out of season closed Mon, Sat & Sun; menus around €14) with hearty specialities from northeast France; and, best of all, the *Boulangerie de la Môle* (Tues–Sun 8am–1pm & 3.30–7pm), which bakes amazing olive and raisin breads, *pain de campagne* and *pain rustique*, as well as selling its own jam. As you leave La Môle for Cogolin, you'll pass the tiny airport used by St-Tropez-bound celebrities and, more down-to-earth, a one-star **campsite**, *Les Caramagnols* (℡04.94.54.40.06, @www.lescaramagnols.com; €14.50 per tent; closed mid-Sept to mid-June), with caravans to rent in July and August.

Cogolin

Eight kilometres east of La Môle, and a mere 8.5km from St-Tropez, **COGOLIN** is renowned for its craft industries, including reed-making for wind instruments, pipes for smoking, wrought-iron furniture, silk yarn and knotted wool carpets, all offering one-off, made-to-order, high-quality and high-cost goods for the Côte d'Azur market.

It's possible to visit some of the **craft factories**; the helpful tourist office (see opposite) can provide a *guide pratique*, and help with making appointments. Alternatively, you can just wander down avenue Georges-Clemenceau and pop into the retail outlets. For **carpets**, the Manufacture de Tapis, just off avenue Clemenceau on boulevard Louis-Blanc (exhibition room Mon–Thurs 8am–noon & 2–6pm; closed 4–17 Aug), is known for its recreations of designs by famous artists such as Léger and Mondrian. Each carpet is hand-made, taking up to a year to finish, and the order book includes presidential residences, embassies and local palaces. The production of **pipes** from briarwood is on show at Courrieu, 58 av Clemenceau (Mon–Sat 9am–noon & 2–7pm), while world-famous musicians drop in on Rigotti, on rue F. Arago, to replace the reeds of their oboes, bassoons and clarinets; unfortunately, they open their doors only to professionals.

On the way out of town, before joining the N98 heading west, the **Cave des Vignerons**, on rue Marceau (summer Mon–Sat 8.30am–12.30pm & 2.30–7.30pm, Sun 9am–12.30pm; winter Mon–Sat 8.30am–12.30pm & 2–6pm), is worth a visit to sample some of the local wines, which are said to have particularly impressed Julius Caesar.

Practicalities

From the **gare routière** on avenue Georges-Clemenceau head upwards to the central place de la République, where you'll find the **tourist office**

(July & Aug Mon–Sat 9am–1pm & 2–6.30pm; Sept–June Mon–Sat 9am–12.30pm & 2–6pm; ☎04.94.55.01.10, ⓦwww.cogolin-provence.com).

Hotels in Cogolin are reasonable and are a viable alternative to staying in congested St-Tropez: the best-value option is the comfortable and amiable *Le Coq* on place de la Mairie (☎04.94.54.13.71, ⓕ04.94.54.03.06; ❹), while *La Maison du Monde*, at 63 rue Carnot (☎04.94.54.77.54, ⓦlamaisondumonde.fr; ❻), an ochre-coloured Provençal house and artist's studio transformed into a funky small hotel, is more upmarket. For **food**, try *La Grange*, 7 rue du 11 Novembre (☎04.94.54.60.97; closed Mon), with menus at €15 and €28, or *Careé des Oliviers*, 16 rue Carnot (☎04.94.54.64.21; menus from €29, with a lunchtime *plat du jour* from €13; closed Mon) which uses market produce on its *carte gastronomique*.

Grimaud and around

Four kilometres north of Cogolin, **GRIMAUD** is a film set of a *village perché*, where the cone of houses enclosing the twelfth-century church, culminating in the spectacular ruins of a medieval castle, appears as a single, perfectly unified entity, decorated by its trees and flowers. The most vaunted street in this ensemble is the narrow **rue des Templiers**, which leads up past the arcaded Gothic house of the Knights Templars to the pure Romanesque **Église St-Michel**. The views from the château ruins (currently undergoing restoration) are superb, and the monumental, sharply cut serpentine window frames of the shattered edifice stand in mute testimony to its former glory.

These days Grimaud is an exclusive little village whose "corner shop" sells antiques and contemporary art. There's a small **tourist office** at 1 bd des Aliziers, just off the main road passing the village (Mon–Sat: July & Aug 9am–12.30pm & 3–7pm; April–June & Sept 9am–noon & 2.30–6.15pm; Oct–March 9am–12.30pm & 2.15–5.30pm; ☎04.94.55.43.83, ⓦwww.grimaud-provence .com). If you're on a budget and need a place to stay it's worth carrying on to La Garde-Freinet (see p.342), although *Le Coteau Fleuri* (☎04.94.43.20.17, ⓦwww .coteaufleuri.fr; menu from €45; ❺), on place des Pénitents at the western edge of the village, offers a few reasonable **rooms** above its good restaurant. **Campers** should head for the *Camping Charlemagne* (☎04.94.43.22.90), at le Pont de Bois, 2km outside the village on the road to Collobrières. For food, you can get crêpes and omelettes at *Le Boubou* on the fountained place du Cros (closed Oct–March), or decent *plats du jour* at *L'Écurie de la Marquise*, 3 rue du Gacharel (☎04.94.43.27.26; menu from €16.50). For more serious fare, settle down on the vine-covered terrace of the ☘ *Café de France* on place Neuve (☎04.94.43.20.05; €22 menu; closed Nov–Feb). On the lower side of place Neuve, the *Pâtisserie du Château* tearoom sells wonderful cakes and fresh nutty breads. The village **market** is held on Thursdays.

Port Grimaud

Avoiding the St-Tropez traffic chaos is tricky if you're visiting **PORT GRIMAUD**, the ultimate Côte d'Azur property development, half standing, half floating at the head of the Golfe de St-Tropez just north of La Foux.

It was created in the 1960s by developer François Spoerry – whose tomb is in the village church – as a private pleasure lagoon with waterways for roads and yachts parked at every door. The houses are in exquisitely tasteful old Provençal style and their owners, amongst them Joan Collins, are more than a little well heeled. The development is not wired off, and anyone can wander in for a gawp: the main visitors' entrance is 800m up the well-signed road off the

N98, surrounded by vast (and distinctly unpicturesque) parking areas. You don't pay to get in, but you can't explore all the islands without renting a boat or taking a crowded boat tour (around €4). Even access to the church tower costs €1. There are plenty of places to **eat** and **drink**, though they are clearly aimed at visitors rather than the residents, and are not particularly good value, though affordable enough.

La Garde-Freinet

The attractive village of **LA GARDE-FREINET**, 10km north of Grimaud, was founded in the late twelfth century by people from the nearby villages of Saint Clément and Miremer. The original fortified settlement sat further up the hillside, and the foundations of its **fort** are visible above the present-day village beside the ruins of a fifteenth-century castle. To explore the ancient fort, it's a steep one-kilometre clamber along a path signposted "Aire de la Planète", leading from the tourist office car park. The fort can also be reached from La Croix des Maures car park.

During the insurrectionary days of Louis Napoleon's coup d'état, La Garde-Freinet played a radical role. Not only did its cork workers form a successful cooperative in 1851, but in their struggle with the landowners women played as strong a role as men. So much so that the prosecuting magistrate of Aix wrote to the minister of justice warning him that La Garde-Freinet, with its new form of socialism in which women took part, would encourage other villagers to abandon public morals and descend into debauchery.

Although today La Garde-Freinet's residents include Oxbridge professors and other Anglos with time on their hands, the village still feels like it belongs to the locals, thanks to the regeneration of the cork and chestnut forestry business, and the number of young local children around. It also has top-notch medieval charm; easy walks to stunning panoramas; markets each Wednesday and Sunday; a sweet-chestnut cooperative on the main road as you leave the village heading north; and tempting food shops such as *La Voute*, 38 rue St-Jacques, selling organic produce and good local wines. For hikers, the 21-kilometre GR9 **route des Crêtes** to the west of the village passes along a tremendously scenic forested ridge. The going is good as it used to be open to vehicles, and half the route is surfaced, though traffic has now been banned due to fire risk.

Practicalities

The helpful **tourist office** operates from La Chapelle St-Jean on place de la Mairie (Easter–Oct Mon–Sat 10am–12.30pm & 3–6pm, Sun 10am–12.30pm; Nov–Easter closed Sun; ☎04.94.43.67.41, ⓦwww.lagardefreinet-tourisme .com), and provides information on all the Maures region, including suggested walks. Above it, a small **museum** (same hours as tourist office) displays archeological finds from the fortifications.

Accommodation prospects are reasonable: *Hôtel Longo Mai*, 14 rte National, on the D588 after it turns west at the top of the village (☎04.94.55.59.60, ⓦwww.hotel-longomai.com; ⑤), has pleasant rooms to rent, while *La Claire Fontaine* on place Vieille (☎04.94.43.60.36, Ⓕ04.94.43.63.76; ③) and *Le Fraxinois* on rue François-Pelletier (reception at the *Tabac-Presse*; ☎04.94.43.62.84, ⓦwww .hotelfraxinois.com; ③) are incredibly good value for this part of the world. There is a **campsite** close at hand: *La Ferme de Bérard* (☎04.94.43.21.23; €11.60 per tent closed Nov–Feb) 5km along the D558 towards Grimaud, with its own pool and restaurant. **Walkers** can stay at a **gîte d'étape**, the *Hameau de La Cour Basse*, on the GR51 towards the coast (☎04.94.43.64.63; €15.50 for a dorm bed).

In the evenings, *Le Carnotzet* **restaurant** and **bar** on the exquisite place du Marché is the place to be (☎04.94.43.62.73; lunch menu €13, evening menu €20), with regular jazz and blues concerts. More elaborate food is served up in the rampant garden of *La Faucado* on the main road to the south (☎04.94.43.60.41; lunch menu €36 otherwise à la carte around €28; booking essential; closed Jan & Feb & Tues out of season). Pigeon fanciers, in the culinary sense, should try *La Colombe Joyeuse* on the place Vieille (☎04.94.43.65.24; menu €26; closed Mon & Nov–Jan) for its game and pigeon in honey and red wine.

Ste-Maxime and around

STE-MAXIME, which faces St-Tropez across the gulf, is an archetypal Côte resort: palmed corniche and enormous pleasure-boat harbour, beaches crowded with confident, bronzed windsurfers and waterskiers, a local history museum in a defensive tower that no one goes to, and a proliferation of estate agents. It sprawls a little too far – like many of the towns along this coast – but the magnetic appeal of the water's edge is hard to deny. Compared to its more famous neighbour, though, it's all rather lacking in atmosphere.

Its **beaches**, however, have the Blue Flags for cleanliness that St-Tropez's lack, and **Cherry Beach** or its neighbours on the east-facing Plage de la Nartelle, 2km from the centre round the Pointe des Sardinaux towards Les Issambres, is the strip of sand to head for. As well as paying for shaded, cushioned comfort, you can enter the water on a variety of different vehicles, eat grilled fish, have drinks brought to your mattress, and listen to a piano player as dusk falls. Four kilometres further on, with much the same facilities, is **Plage des Eléphants**, named after the cartoons of Jean de Brunhoff, creator of Babar the elephant, who had a holiday home in Ste-Maxime.

In addition to the beaches, Ste-Maxime's Vieille Ville has several good **markets**: there's a covered flower and food market on rue Fernand-Bessy (July & Aug Mon–Sat 7am–1pm & 4–8pm, Sun 7am–1pm; Sept–June Tues–Sun 7am–1pm); a Thursday morning food market on and around place du Marché; a bric-a-brac market every Friday morning (9am–noon) on place Jean-Mermoz; and arts and crafts in the pedestrian streets daily (mid-June to mid-Sept 10am–11pm).

Ten kilometres north of town on the road to Le Muy, the **Musée du Phonographe et de la Musique Mécanique** at parc St-Donat (Easter–Oct Wed–Sun 10am–noon & 3–6pm; €3) is the result of one woman's forty-year obsession with collecting audio equipment. This marvellous museum's facade resembles Hansel and Gretel's fantastical biscuit house but is actually modelled on an eighteenth-century Limonaire mechanical music machine. Inside, the owner has on display one of Thomas Edison's "talking machines" of 1878, the first recording machines of the 1890s and an amplified lyre (1903). One of the first saucer-shaped amplifiers, made of paper, is still in remarkably good condition, along with a 1913 audiovisual language-teaching aid and the wonderfully neat portable record players of the 1920s. In addition, there's an extraordinarily wide selection of automata, musical boxes and pianolas. Almost half the exhibits still work, and you may find yourself listening to the magical, crackling sounds of an original wax cylinder recording from the 1880s played on the equipment it was made for.

Practicalities

Buses arrive in town along the seafront and stop in front of the **tourist office** on the promenade Simon Lorière (June & Sept daily 9am–noon & 2–7pm; July

& Aug Mon–Sat 9am–8pm; Oct–May Mon–Sat 9am–noon & 2–6pm; ☎04.94.55.75.55, ⓦwww.ste-maxime.com). If you're heading for St-Tropez it's a good idea to do the journey by **boat**; the service from Ste-Maxime's **gare maritime** on the quai L-Condroyer runs daily all year round, with crossings every thirty minutes in July and August (☎04.94.49.29.39; €11.50). **Bikes** and **mopeds** can be rented at Rent Bike, 13 rue Magali (☎04.94.43.98.07), or Holiday Bikes, 10 rte du Plan de la Tour (☎04.94.43.90.19).

The tourist office can advise on **hotel** vacancies, which are very rare in summer. Among the less expensive options are the welcoming *Auberge Provençale*, 49 rue Aristide-Briand (☎04.94.55.76.90, ⓕ04.94.55.76.91; ❹), which has a decent restaurant attached, or the small *Castellamar*, 21 av G-Pompidou (☎04.94.96.19.97; ❸; closed Oct–March), on the west side of the river but still close to the centre and the sea. Slightly further out, the *Marie-Louise*, 2km west in the Hameau de Guerre-Vieille (☎04.94.96.06.05, ⓦwww.hotel-marielouise.com; ❹), is tucked away in greenery but within sight of the sea. Pricier alternatives include the smart *Hôtellerie de la Poste*, 11 bd Frédéric-Mistral (☎04.94.96.18.33, ⓦwww.hotelleriedusoleil.com; ❼), which has very nice rooms and is right in the centre, and the pleasant *Hostellerie de la Croisette*, 2 bd des Romarins (☎04.94.96.17.75, ⓦwww.hotel-la-croisette.com; ❻). For **campers**, there's *Les Cigalons*, in quartier de la Nartelle, a two-star seaside site (☎04.94.96.05.51, ⓦwww.campingcigalon.com; €20 per tent; closed Nov–March), or *La Baumette*, route du Plan de la Tour (☎04.94.96.14.35, ⓕ04.94.96.35.38; €20 per tent; closed Oct–March), 2km out of town, up in the hills off the D74.

There's plenty of choice for places **to eat**, with the pedestrian streets jam-packed with restaurants – one way of choosing from those on rue Hoche is to check them from the kitchen side along rue Fernand-Bessy. The *Hostellerie de la Belle Aurore*, 4 bd Jean-Moulin (☎04.94.96.02.45; menu at €35; closed Wed lunch & mid-Oct to mid-March), serves gourmet dishes on a sea-view terrace, while *L'Hermitage*, 118 av Général-de-Gaulle (☎04.94.96.04.05; à la carte from €15), specializes in fish dishes at around half the price.

Along the coast to St-Aygulf

Beyond Ste-Maxime, its suburb **Val d'Esquières** merges with **Les Issambres**, the seaside extension of Roquebrune, and **St-Aygulf**, belonging to the *commune* of Fréjus, along the fast and rather dangerous coast road. For all that, this stretch has its attractions, revealing traditional colour-washed, pantiled Provençal architecture amid the filing-cabinet condominiums, and a shoreline of rocky coves and *calanques* alternating with golden crescents of sand. In Les Issambres there's even a narrow band of pines that almost lets you pretend that the corniche apartments and villas don't exist. If the seaside development gets too much, you can always head up and away into the empty eastern extremity of the Massif des Maures.

Practicalities

Hotels worth trying in Les Issambres include *La Quiétude*, set back from the corniche (☎04.94.96.94.34, ⓦwww.hotel-laquietude.com; ❺; closed mid-Oct to late Feb), and *La Bonne Auberge*, on the N98 at Calanque des Issambres (☎04.94.96.90.74; ❷; closed Nov–Feb), overlooking the sea. In St-Aygulf, *Le Catalogne*, avenue de la Corniche d'Azur (☎04.94.81.01.44, ⓦwww.hotelcatalogne.com; ❼; closed mid-Oct to Easter), has a pleasant, shaded garden. There's no shortage of **campsites** along this stretch, all well signed off the corniche. **Bikes** can be rented from Holiday Bikes, at 595 av Corniche d'Azur, the main road through St-Aygulf (T04.94.81.35.94).

The *Villa St-Elme* is the fancy **restaurant** on the corniche des Issambres, where elaborate and delicate fish dishes can be consumed overlooking the Golfe de St-Tropez: it also has a few rooms for well-heeled guests (T04.94.49.52.52; menu at €62 and a blow-out *menu gastronomique* at €100; ⑨). At the other end of the scale, *Le Pointu*, on place de la Galiote in St-Aygulf, dishes up a brilliant *moules marinières* for €11. St-Aygulf has a good daily market, too, and great *poulets rôtis* from a permanent stall overlooking the main square on boulevard Honoré-de-Balzac.

Inland: the Argens Valley

The **River Argens** meets the Mediterranean in unspectacular style between St-Aygulf and St-Raphaël. It is an important source of irrigation for orchards and vines, but as a waterway it has little appeal, being sluggish, full of breeding mosquitoes and on the whole inaccessible. The geographical feature that dominates the lower Argens Valley, and acts as an almost mystical pole of attraction, is the **Rocher de Roquebrune** between the village of **Roquebrune-sur-Argens** and the town of **Le Muy**.

Roquebrune-sur-Argens and the Rocher de Roquebrune

The village of **ROQUEBRUNE-SUR-ARGENS** lies on the edge of the Massif des Maures, 12km from the sea, facing the flat valley of the Argens opening to the northeast. Some of its sixteenth-century defensive towers and ramparts remain, and almost every house within them is four hundred years old or more, joined together by vaulted passageways and tiny cobbled streets. The central square is a satisfying slice of small-town France, with graceful ironwork balconies and shady arcades.

To sample some of the delicious local red and rosé **wines** (phone first), visit the Domaine de Marchandise, route des Marchandises (T04.94.45.42.91), or the Domaine des Planes on the D7 to St-Aygulf (T04.98.11.49.00). Alternatively, you can fill up with quality plonk at the Coopérative Vinicole, at rond point St Pierre, on the D7 just east of the village centre. Delicious nougat and chocolate can be bought from Courreau, 2 montée St-Michel, and there's a **market** on Tuesday on place Germain-Ollier, and Friday morning on place Alfred-Perrin.

The **tourist office**, on avenue Gabriel-Péri (Feb to mid-June & mid-Sept to Oct Mon–Fri 9am–noon & 2–6pm; mid-June to mid-Sept Mon–Sat 9am–noon & 2–6pm; Nov–Jan Mon–Fri 9am–noon & 2–5pm; T04.94.19.89.89, Wwww.roquebrunesurargens.fr), can provide addresses for accommodation, as well as information on walks and sports.

The only real option for **accommodation** in the village is *La Maurette Roquebrune*, in La Maurette just outside the village (T04.98.11.43.53, Wwww .lamaurette.fr; ⑥), a beautiful stone house with a spectacular view of the Rocher de Roquebrune. Otherwise it's a choice between the unappealing budget chain hotels of *Formule I* on rond point des 4 Chemins (T04.94.81.61.61; ①), between Roquebrune and Le Muy, and the *Villages Hôtel*, at La Garillans on the D7 (T04.94.45.45.00; ②). Between the village and St-Aygulf the road is lined with mega **campsites**, but more pleasant pitches can be found on local farms;

ask at the tourist office. Of the **restaurants**, *Le Gaspacho*, 21 av Général-de-Gaulle (☎04.94.45.49.59; closed Nov), serves Provençal specialities with menus from €11.50 to €19.

Rocher de Roquebrune

Three kilometres west of Roquebrune, the rust-red mass of the **Roquebrune rock** erupts unexpectedly out of nothing, as if to some purpose. Even the Autoroute du Soleil thundering past its foot fails to bring it into line with the rest of the coastal scenery glimpsed from the fast lane. To reach it, coming from Roquebrune, take the left fork just after the village, signed to La Roquette; at the next fork you can go left or right depending on which side of the mountain you want to skirt. The right-hand route runs alongside the highway towards **Notre-Dame-de-la-Roquette**, an erstwhile place of pilgrimage (now closed to the public), while the left-hand fork takes you round the quieter, steeper southern side.

The rock itself is private property and casual visitors are far from welcome. However, the tourist office in Le Muy (in whose *commune* the rock actually stands) can organize guided visits, usually on a Tuesday.

Le Muy and around

Although not a wildly exciting place, **LE MUY** is interesting politically, having had one of the sole surviving communist mayors of the Côte d'Azur in the 1980s, before switching to a coalition of right-wing and *Front National* in 1989, and shifting in the late 1990s to a centrist administration who created the 1000 parking spaces boldly advertised as you enter the village.

The town's political history and ideological leanings are often mirrored in the names of its streets, its buildings and architecture. One street is named after Maurice Lachâtre, a revolutionary writer, publisher and printer who escaped from the 1871 Paris Commune and was sheltered in Le Muy. The *Provençal* **bar** that surrounds and hides the apse of the town's church was built during the 1930s period of militantly atheist socialism, while no fewer than sixty pastel-hued *HLM*s (council blocks) radiating in neat avenues from the pretty central square, are the legacy of its communist mayor.

The **tour Charles-Quint** takes its name from the attempted assassination of the Emperor Charles V in 1536 by the people of Le Muy. Unfortunately for the Le Muy natives, the king was aware of his unpopularity and had paid a Spanish poet, Garcilaso de la Vega, to masquerade as him. Consequently the Muyoise killed the Spaniard, retreated to the tower, were told by the invader that they would be spared if they surrendered, came out with their hands up and were promptly massacred; the tower was renamed after their arch enemy. Today, the tower houses a **Musée de la Libération** (April–June Sun 10am–noon; July & Aug Thurs & Sun 10am–noon; Sept–April by appointment at the tourist office), commemorating 1944's Operation Dragoon, which opened a second front in the south of France against the Germans.

If you want to **stay** in the village, try the *Hôtel les Allées*, 2 allée Victor-Hugo (☎04.94.45.08.30, ℉04.94.45.95.25; ❷), a fairly basic place in the centre of the village. For **food**, *Le Vieux Piano*, 7 bis av Cavalier (☎04.94.45.83.86), has a €18 menu, and theatrical portraits on the walls. Le Muy's Sunday morning **market** is one of the largest in the region.

Chapelle de Ste-Roseline

A short way up the road to Draguignan (see p.253) from Le Muy, the D91 leads left to the **Chapelle de Ste-Roseline** (Tues–Sun: March–May 2–6pm;

June–Sept 3–7pm; Oct–Feb 2–5pm; free). The old abbey buildings of which the chapel is part are a private residence belonging to a wine grower, and you can also visit the cellars and taste the *cru classé* named after the chapel (Mon–Fri 9am–noon & 2–6.30pm, Sat & Sun 10am–noon & 2–6pm).

The chapel's interior is really rather ghoulish. Saint Roseline was born in 1263 and spent her adolescence disobeying her father by giving food to the poor. On one occasion he caught her and demanded to see the contents of her basket; the food miraculously turned into rose petals. She became the prioress of the abbey and when she died her body refused to decay. It was paraded around Provence until it got lost. A blind man found it and it now, supposedly, lies in a glass case in the chapel, shrivelled and brown but not quite a skeleton. What's worse are her eyes – one lifeless, the other staring at you – displayed in a gaudy frame on a wall. Louis XIV is said to be responsible for the dead eye. On a pilgrimage here he reckoned the eyes smacked of sorcery so he had his surgeon pierce one. Life immediately left it. Horror objects apart, the chapel has a fabulous mosaic by **Chagall** showing angels laying a table for the saint; some beautifully carved seventeenth-century choir stalls; and an impressive Renaissance rood-loft in which peculiar things happen to the legs of the decorative figures.

Les Arcs-sur-Argens and beyond

Eight kilometres west of Le Muy, the picturesque medieval village of **LES ARCS** has been carefully restored, with its skyline dominated by a Saracen lookout tower, the sole remnant of a thirteenth-century castle. Les Arcs is one of the centres for the Var wine industry, and at the **Maison des Vins** (daily 10am–1pm & 1.30–7pm; July–Aug until 8pm) you can taste and buy wine and cheeses and pick up details of local *vignerons* to visit and *routes du vin* to follow: it's on the main road from Le Muy, past the turning to the village and the bridge across the Argens.

The **tourist office** on place Général-de-Gaulle (July & Aug Mon–Sat 9.15am–12.15pm & 2.45–7pm; Sept–June Mon–Fri 9.15am–12.15pm & 1.45–6pm; ☎04.94.73.37.30, ⓦwww.ville-lesarcs.com) has plenty of information on the surrounding area. The nicest place to **stay**, if your budget will stretch, is the exclusive hotel *Le Logis du Guetteur* on place du Château (☎04.94.99.51.10, ⓦwww.logisduguetteur.com; ❻), with panoramic views of the Saracen tower. Less expensive rooms are available at *L'Avenir*, avenue de la Gare (☎04.94.73.30.58; ❷), by the *gare SNCF*, halfway between the village and the N7. The **restaurant** in *Le Logis* is good (menus €37–76), as is *Le Bacchus Gourmand* (☎04.94.47.48.47; menus from €34; closed Sun eve out of season, and Mon), the Maison des Vins' very beautiful restaurant (☎04.94.99.50.20), which serves Provençal specialities. The best day to visit Les Arcs is Thursday when a busy **market** is held on the central square.

Vidauban

Following the road west from Les Arcs, after 8km you'll come to the village of **VIDAUBAN**, as attractive as its neighbour, particularly at night when its old-fashioned lamps are lit. The village has a charming **restaurant**, *Le Concorde*, 9 place Clemenceau (☎04.94.73.01.19; menus €29–55; closed Wed), and some interesting wine *domaines*, including the Vieux Château d'Astros (to arrange an appointment, call ☎04.94.73.02.56) and the Château St-Julien d'Aille (to arrange an appointment, call ☎04.94.73.02.89).

St-Raphaël and Fréjus

The major conurbation of **St-Raphaël** on the coast and **Fréjus**, centred 3km inland, has a history dating back to the Romans. Fréjus was established as a naval base under Julius Caesar and Augustus, St-Raphaël as a resort for its veterans. The ancient port at Fréjus, or Forum Julii, had 2km of quays and was connected by a walled canal to the sea, which was considerably closer back then. After the battle of Actium in 31 AD, the ships of Antony and Cleopatra's defeated fleet were brought here.

The area between Fréjus and the sea is now the suburb of **Fréjus-Plage** with a glitzy 1980s marina, **Port-Fréjus**. St-Raphaël merges with Fréjus and Fréjus-Plage, which in turn merge with **Boulouris** to the east. West of Fréjus a vast modern out-of-town shopping strip – amongst the largest in the South of France – spreads west as far as the A8 autoroute.

Despite the obsession with facilities for the seaborne rich – there were already two pleasure ports at St-Raphaël before Port-Fréjus was built – this is no bad place for a stopover. There's a wide range of hotels and restaurants, some interesting sightseeing in Fréjus, and good transport links with inland Provence and the coast eastwards along the Corniche d'Esterel.

Fréjus

The population of **FRÉJUS**, remarkably, was greater in the first century BC than it is today if you count only the residents of the town centre, which lies well within the Roman perimeter. But very little remains of the original Roman walls that once circled the city, and the harbour that made Fréjus an important Mediterranean port silted up early on and was finally filled in after the Revolution. It is instead the medieval centre, with its lively shopping and cafés and intimate, small-town side streets full of tiny houses, that evokes a feel for this ancient town.

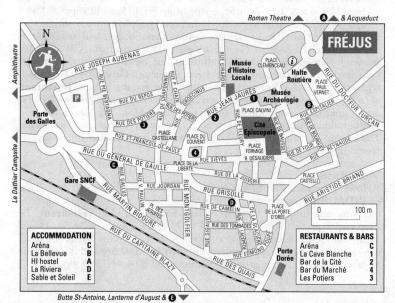

ACCOMMODATION
Aréna — C
La Bellevue — B
HI hostel — A
La Riviera — D
Sable et Soleil — E

RESTAURANTS & BARS
Aréna — C
La Cave Blanche — 1
Bar de la Cité — 2
Bar du Marché — 4
Les Potiers — 3

Arrival and information

Around a dozen trains a day from St-Raphaël stop at **Fréjus gare SNCF**, a journey of between three and six minutes. Buses between the two towns are much more frequent and take fifteen minutes, arriving at the Fréjus **halte routière** on place Paul-Vernet on the east side of the town centre, opposite the small **tourist office**, 325 rue Jean-Jaurès (Mon–Sat 9am–noon & 2–6pm, Sun 10am–noon & 3–6pm; ☎04.94.51.83.83, ⊛www.frejus.fr). Here, you can buy the useful Fréjus Pass (see p.350) and pick up a helpful street map of the entire Fréjus-St Raphaël conurbation. **Bikes** can be rented from Holiday Bikes, rond point des Moulins (☎04.94.51.35.94).

Accommodation

Hotels are not as plentiful in Fréjus as in St-Raphaël, but it's generally a quieter place to stay. There's a **youth hostel** a couple of kilometres from the centre, and plenty of **campsites** along the route des Combattants d'Afrique du Nord west of the town. These are mostly on a vast scale, however – the largest has almost 800 pitches – and only a few are especially close to the sea.

Hotels

Aréna 145 av Général-de-Gaulle ☎04.94.17.09.40, ⊛www.arena-hotel.com. Rather elegant, with pretty rooms, if a bit small, in a converted bank in Fréjus centre. Roman columns surround the pleasant swimming pool. ❼

La Bellevue place Paul-Vernet ☎04.94.17.27.05, ⓕ04.94.51.32.25. Right in town so not the quietest location, but convenient and inexpensive. ❹

La Riviera 90 rue Grisolle ☎04.94.51.31.46, ⓕ04.94.17.18.34. Very small hotel in the centre of Fréjus. Not very modern, but clean and perfectly acceptable. ❶

Sable et Soleil 158 rue Paul-Arène, Fréjus-Plage ☎04.94.51.08.70, ⊛sableetsoleil.site.voila.fr. A pleasant, small, modern hotel, 300m from the sea. ❹

Hostel and campsites

HI hostel Auberge de Jeunesse de Fréjus, chemin du Counillier ☎04.94.53.18.75, ⓔfrejus-st-raphael@fuaj.org. Located in a small pine grove, 2km from Fréjus centre; take bus #4, #8 or #9 from St-Raphaël or Fréjus (direction "L'Hôpital", stop "Les Chênes") and walk up av du Gal d'Armée Jean-Calliès – the chemin du Counillier is the first left. In the mornings a minibus departs from the hostel for the station and the beach. Reception closed 10am–6pm; 11pm curfew (10pm in winter). From €13 for a dorm bed.

Le Dattier rte des Combattants d'Afrique du Nord ☎04.94.40.88.93, ⊛www.camping-le-dattier.com. A four-star site 3.5km north of Fréjus. €24 per tent. Closed Oct–Easter.

Site de Gorge Vent quartier de Bellevue ☎04.94.52.90.37, ⊛www.frejus.com/gorge-vent. A two-star site off the N7 towards Cannes, 3km from the town centre. €20 per tent.

The Roman town

Taking a tour of the **Roman remains** gives you a good idea of the extent of Forum Julii, but they are scattered throughout and beyond the town centre and to see them all would take a full day. Turning right out of the *gare SNCF* and then right down boulevard Séverin-Decuers brings you to the **Butte St-Antoine**, against whose east wall the waters of the port would have lapped, and which once was capped by a fort. It was one of the port's defences, and one of the ruined towers may have been a lighthouse. A path around the southern wall follows the quayside (odd stretches are visible) to the medieval **Lanterne d'Auguste**, built on the Roman foundations of a structure marking the entrance of the canal into the ancient harbour.

Le Fréjus Pass

Available from the tourist office, the **Le Fréjus Pass**, is valid for seven days and gives access to the amphitheatre, the Roman theatre, the Cité Episcopale, the Musée Archéologique Municipal, Pagode Hong Hien and the Musée d'Histoire Locale as well as other monuments across the city. Adults €4.60; concession €3.10; under 12s €2. To visit any one of the sights individually costs €2.

Heading in the other direction from the station, past the Roman **Porte des Gaules** and along rue Henri-Vadon, leads you to the **amphitheatre** (April–Oct Mon & Wed–Sun 10am–1pm & 2.30–6.30pm; Nov–March Mon–Fri 10am–noon & 1–5.30pm, Sat 9.30am–12.30pm & 1.30–5.30pm; €2), smaller than those at Arles and Nîmes, but still able to seat around ten thousand. Its upper tiers have been reconstructed in the same greenish local stone used by the Romans, but the vaulted galleries on the ground floor are largely original. Today, it's still used for bullfights and rock concerts.

North of the town, along avenue du Théâtre-Romain, stands the Roman **theatre** (April–Oct Mon & Wed–Sun 10am–1pm & 2.30–6.30pm; Nov–March Mon–Fri 10am–noon & 1–5.30pm, Sat 9.30am–12.30pm & 1.30–5.30pm; €2). Although its original seats are long gone, it still sometimes hosts outdoor spectacles. Northeast of the theatre, at the end of avenue du XV Corps-d'Armée, a few arches are visible of the forty-kilometre **aqueduct**, which was once as high as the ramparts. The remains stand in the parc Aurelien (daily, dawn–dusk; €2), also home to the large Beaux-Arts Villa Aurélienne, which hosts cultural events and exhibitions. Closer to the centre, where boulevard Aristide-Briand meets rue des Quais, are the arcades of the **Porte d'Orée,** positioned on the former harbour's edge, the only remaining monumental arch of what was probably a bath complex.

The medieval town

The **Cité Episcopale**, or cathedral close, takes up two sides of **place Formigé**, the marketplace and heart of both contemporary and medieval Fréjus. It comprises the cathedral, flanked by the fourteenth-century bishop's palace, now the Hôtel de Ville, the baptistry, chapterhouse, cloisters and archeological museum. Visits to the cloisters and baptistry are guided and leave approximately every hour (April–Sept Mon & Wed–Sun 9am–7pm; Oct–March Mon & Wed–Sun 9am–noon & 2–5pm; €2); access to the cathedral is free (daily 9am–noon & 2.30–6.30pm), but you'll have to peer through a glass partition to see the baptistry and will miss the fascinating seventeenth-century carved wooden portals with their depictions of a Saracen massacre unless you take the tour.

The oldest part of the complex is the **baptistry**, one of France's most ancient buildings, built in the fourth or fifth century and, as such, contemporary with the decline and fall of the city's Roman founders. Its two doorways are of different heights, signifying the enlarged spiritual stature of the baptized, and it was used in the days of early Christianity when adult baptism was still the norm. Parts of the early Gothic **cathedral** may belong to a tenth-century church, but its best features, apart from the coloured diamond-shaped tiles on the spire, are Renaissance: the choir stalls, a wooden crucifix on the left of the entrance, and the intricately carved doors with scenes of a Saracen massacre. By far the most beautiful and engaging component of the whole ensemble, however, is the **cloisters**. Slender marble columns, carved in the twelfth century, support a fourteenth-century ceiling of wooden panels painted with apocalyptic creatures. Out of the original 1200 pictures, 400 remain, each about the size of this page. The subjects include multiheaded monsters, mermaids, satyrs and scenes of bacchanalian debauchery. The **Musée Archéologique** (April–Oct Mon & Wed–Sat 10am–1pm & 2–6.30pm; Nov–March Mon–Fri 10am–noon & 1.30–5.30pm, Sat 9.30am–12.30pm, Sun 1.30–5.30pm; €2) on the upper storey of the cloisters has as its star pieces a complete Roman mosaic of a leopard and a copy of a renowned double-headed bust of Hermes. You can wander through the modern courtyard of the Hôtel de Ville, but you get a better view of the orange Esterel stone walls of the episcopal palace from rue de Beausset.

Close by, in an old bourgeois town house at 153 av Jean-Jaurès, is the small **Musée d'Histoire Locale** (mid-June to mid-Sept Tues–Sat 9am–noon & 3–7pm; mid-Sept to mid-June Tues–Sat 9am–noon & 2–6pm; €2), with reconstructions of past life including an old school classroom, plus displays on traditional local trades.

Around Fréjus

The environs of Fréjus hold several reminders of France's colonial past. About 2km north of town, there's a Vietnamese pagoda and a Sudanese mosque, both built by French colonial troops. The **Pagode Hong Hien** (daily: June–Sept 9am–7pm; Oct–May 9am–5pm; €2), at the crossroads of the N7 to Cannes and rue Henri-Giraud (bus #L13), is still maintained as a Buddhist temple. There's also a **memorial** to the Indochina wars close by. About 4km north of Fréjus, the **Mosquée Missiri de Djenné** is on rue des Combattants d'Afrique du Nord, off the D4 to Bagnols 2km from the RN7 junction. It's a strange, guava-coloured, fort-like building in typical West African style, and decorated inside with fading murals of desert journeys gracefully sketched in white on the dark pink walls.

There are plenty of activities for children around Fréjus, including a **zoo** at Le Capitou, 5km north of the town (daily: March–May & Sept 10am–5pm; June–Aug 10am–6pm; Nov–Feb 10am–4pm; €12; @www.zoo-frejus.com;), and the **Aqualand water park**, off the RN98 to St-Aygulf (July & Aug daily 10am–7pm; June & Sept daily 10am–6pm; €22, children €18; bus #L9), complete with Europe's biggest wave pool, paddle boats, galleons and other water-based attractions, plus an 18-hole miniature-golf course. Next door, Fréjus' **Base Nature** (℡04.94.51.91.10) offers a vast range of sporting activities including sand-yachting, skateboarding and rollerblading, while more gentle pursuits, such as walking and bird-spotting, can be indulged at the **Étangs de Villepey** wetland nature reserve (dawn–dusk; free), off the RN98 between Fréjus and St-Aygulf.

Eating, drinking and nightlife

Fréjus is not a bad place for menu-browsing and café-lounging, with the cheaper **eateries** found on place Agricola, place de la Liberté and the main shopping streets. At Fréjus-Plage there's a string of eating houses to choose from, with more upmarket seafood outlets at Port-Fréjus. For **nightlife**, the port and beach are the places to aim for, with Fréjus' two discos, *L'Odysée* and *La Playa*, both on the seafront boulevard de la Libération.

Aréna 145 av Général-de-Gaulle ℡04.94.17.09.40. Attached to the hotel of the same name (see p.349), this decent restaurant serves excellent fish dishes; menus start at €25. Closed Sat lunch & all day Mon.

La Cave Blanche on place Calvini above the Cité Episcopale ℡04.94.51.25.40. Offers *rascasse*; menus €20, €25 & €36. Closed Sun eve and all day Mon.

Bar de la Cité 152 rue Jean-Jaurès. A pleasant, ordinary bar.

Bar du Marché place de la Liberté. A classic café for snacks and sipping beers under the shade of plane trees.

Les Potiers 135 rue des Potiers ☎04.94.51.33.74. Charmingly located in a tiny backstreet, this is one of the best restaurants in Fréjus; it serves dishes of fresh seasonal ingredients, with menus from €23 to €34 Closed Tues lunch & all day Wed.

St-Raphaël

A large resort and now one of the richest towns on the Côte, **ST-RAPHAËL** became fashionable at the turn of the twentieth century. It lost many of its *Belle Époque* mansions and hotels in the bombardments of World War II; some, like the *Continental*, have been rebuilt virtually from scratch in a modern style, others have undergone more gradual restoration. Meanwhile, the tiny **old quarter** (*vieux quartier*) beyond place Carnot on the other side of the rail line is pleasantly low-key, no longer the town's major commercial focus but one of the better places to stroll and browse.

Arrival and information

St-Raphaël's gare SNCF, on rue Waldeck-Rousseau in the centre of the town, is the main station on the Marseille–Ventigmilia line; the **gare routière** is just across the rail line from the *gare SNCF*, on place du Dr-Régis. The **tourist office** is by the coast on quai Albert 1er (July & Aug daily 9am–7pm; Sept–June Mon–Sat 9am–12.30pm & 2–6.30pm, Sun hours vary; ☎04.94.19.52.52, ⓦwww.saint-raphael.com).

Accommodation

There are plenty of **hotels** in St-Raphaël, from seafront palaces to backstreet budget options. They can all get extremely busy in summer, however, so it's worth booking in advance. If you prefer **camping**, head for the area east of St-Raphaël along the Esterel coast – the large three-star *International de L'Ile d'Or*, above the N98 at Boulouris (☎04.94.95.52.13), is a good bet with sea views.

Beau Séjour promenade René-Coty ☎04.94.95.03.75, ⓦwww.hotelbeausejour.fr. One of the less expensive seafront hotels with a pleasant terrace. Closed Nov–March. ❺

Bellevue 22 bd Félix-Martin ☎04.94.19.90.10, ⓦww.hotelbellevue.150m.com. Excellent value for its central location, but book well in advance. ❹

La Bonne Auberge 54 rue de la Garonne ☎04.94.95.69.72. Close to the old port, half board only in summer (€39 per person). Closed mid-Nov to Feb. ❺

Continental promenade René-Coty ☎04.94.83.87.87, ⓦwww.hotelcontinental.fr. A modern, a/c seafront hotel with private parking and light, spacious rooms, rebuilt on the site of its illustrious predecessor in 1993. ❻

Hôtel de France 25 place Galliéni ☎04.94.95.19.20, ⓦwww.hoteldefrance-saintraphael.com. A plain and simple option, but not seedy, in a potentially noisy location, opposite the station. ❹

Nouvel Hôtel 6 av Henri-Vadon ☎04.94.95.23.30, ⓦwww.nouvelhotel.net. A cheerful and reasonably smart tourist hotel, near the station. ❻

Hôtel du Soleil 47 bd du Domaine de Soleil, off bd Christian-Lafon ☎04.94.83.10.00, ⓦwww.perso .orange.fr/hotel-du-soleil. A small, pretty villa with its own garden to the east of the centre. The hotel also has studios to rent. ❺

Le Touring 1 quai Albert 1er ☎04.94.95.01.72, ℮letouring@orange.fr. Portside location, so not that quiet, but you can't get more central than this. Closed mid-Nov to mid-Dec. ❹

The Town

On rue des Templiers, to the north of the stations, in the courtyard of a crumbling fortified Romanesque church, you'll find fragments of the Roman aqueduct that brought water from Fréjus. Further along rue des Templiers,

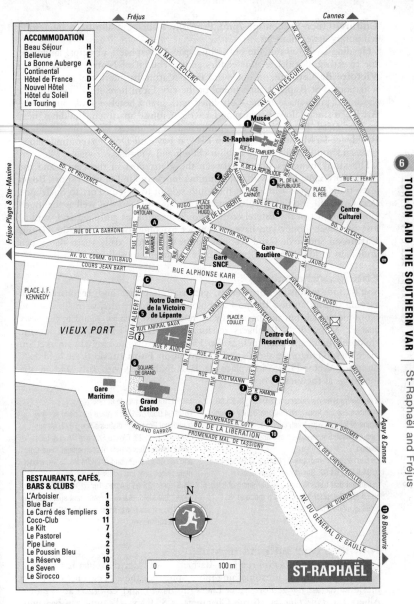

▲ *Fréjus*   *Cannes* ▲

AV. DU MAL. LECLERC

AV. DE VALESCURE

AV. DE VERDON

RUE L'ISNARD

RUE JOSEPH PIERRUGUES

Musée ①

AV. DE ISCLES

AV. DE VALESCURE

St-Raphaël

RUE DES REMPARTS

RUE CHATEAUDUN

BD. DE PROVENCE

RUE CHARABOIS

RUE DES TEMPLIERS

RUE DE LA RÉPUBLIQUE

RUE ALLONGUE

RUE DU PÉTRON

③ PL. DE LA
RÉPUBLIQUE

RUE J. FERRY

② RUE V. HUGO

PLACE
VICTOR
HUGO

PLACE
CARNOT

PLACE
G. PERI

PLACE
ORTOLAN

RUE DE LA LIBERTÉ

④

RUE DE LA LIBERTÉ

**Centre
Culturel**

RUE DE LA GARRONE

RUE THIERS

Ⓐ

IMP. DE LA
MARINE

RUE SUFFREN

RUE VAUBAN

RUE L. GAMBETTA

RUE L. BASSO

AV. VICTOR HUGO

BD. D'ALSACE

**Gare
Routière**

RUE J.

RUE A. FRANCE

AV. A. JAURES

AV. DU COMM. GUILBAUD

COURS JEAN BART

RUE ALPHONSE KARR

**Gare
SNCF**

Ⓓ

AVENUE VICTOR HUGO

RUE ROGER TANDINI

PLACE J. F.
KENNEDY

Ⓒ

QUAI ALBERT 1ER

**Notre Dame
de la Victoire
de Lépante** ⑤

Ⓔ

RUE AMIRAL BAUX

R. AMIRAL BAUX

RUE W. ROUSSEAU

PLACE P.
COULLET

VIEUX PORT

ⓘ

RUE AMIRAL BAUX

RUE P. AUBLE

BD. FELIX MARTIN

RUE J. AICARD

**Centre de
Reservation**

AV. F. MISTRAL

⑥

SQUARE
DE GRAND

RUE CH. GOUNOD

RUE
BOETMANN

RUE JULES BARBIER

RUE H. VADON

Ⓕ

**Gare
Maritime**

**Grand
Casino**

⑦

R. HAMON

Ⓑ

⑨

PROMENADE R. COTY

Ⓖ

Ⓗ

CORNICHE ROLAND GARROS

BD. DE LA LIBERATION

⑩

AV. P. DOUMER

PROMENADE MAL. DE TASSIGNY

AV. DES CHEVREFEUILLES

N

AV. DU GENERAL DE GAULLE

AV. DUMONT

0   100 m

ST-RAPHAËL

◄ *Fréjus-Plage & Ste-Maxime*

▼ *Agay & Cannes*

① *& Boulouris*

6

TOULON AND THE SOUTHERN VAR | St-Raphaël and Fréjus

there's a local history and underwater archeology **museum** (Tues–Sat: June–
Sept 10am–noon & 3–6.30pm; Oct–May 10am–noon & 2–5.30pm; free),
which contains Neolithic, Paleolithic and Bronze Age artefacts and a large
collection of amphorae. The streets in this *vieux quartier* are home to some of
St-Raphaël's more interesting and sophisticated restaurants and bars, while just
to the east, on place Gabriel-Péri, stands the town's contemporary **Centre**

Culturel (Tues–Sat 8.30am–7pm). Primarily a library, it also hosts interesting temporary art exhibitions.

Heading back towards the port, you'll pass St Raphaël's principal landmark, the towering, florid late-nineteenth-century church of **Notre Dame de la Victoire de Lépante**, on boulevard Félix-Martin. Its interior houses a representation of St Raphaël, the symbol of the city. From here, it's a brief stroll to the broad promenade René-Coty lined with grand hotels – look out for the Art Deco stucco flowers adorning La Rocquerousse apartment buildings, next to the *Hôtel Beau Séjour*. The promenade culminates with the grandiose Résidence La Méditerranée, built in 1914, at 1 av Paul-Doumer: continue along here, and you'll find a pretty English church and a *fin-de-siècle* villa.

The sandy **beaches** stretch between the Vieux Port in the centre and the newer Port Santa Lucia, with opportunities for every kind of water sport. **Boats** leave from the *gare maritime* on the south side of the Vieux Port to St-Tropez, Port Grimaud, the Îles d'Hyères and the islands off Cannes as well as the much closer *calanques* of the Esterel coast. If you're tired of sea and sand and want to lose whatever money you have left on slot machines or blackjack, the **Grand Casino** on Square de Gand overlooking the Vieux Port (daily 10am–4am; open until 5am in July & August) will be only too happy to oblige.

Eating and drinking

You'll find reasonable **brasseries**, pizzerias, crêperies and **restaurants** of varying quality around the port and along the promenades, with smaller and more individual (but not necessarily more expensive) places inland in the *vieux quartier*. Many of St-Raphaël's restaurants are family-friendly with specific children's menus. **Cafés** such as *Bar Victor-Hugo*, overlooking the market on place Victor-Hugo, are also a good, cheap option. **Food markets** are held daily on place Victor-Hugo and place de la République, with fish sold in the mornings at the Vieux Port.

L'Arboisier 6 av de Valescure ℡04.94.95.25.00. Inventive cuisine from chef Philippe Troncy includes tagine of lobster with fresh coconut. €27 lunch menu. Closed Sun eve, Wed eve and Mon out of season.

Le Carré des Templiers 2 place de la République ℡04.94.83.64.07. Smart new *vieux quartier* restaurant that turns into a cigar bar and nightclub on Fri and Sat, after 11pm. Lunch menu at €17, evening menu from €26.

Le Pastorel 54 rue de la Liberté ℡04.94.95.02.36. This place has been serving traditional Provençal dishes since 1922. Menus start around €28. Closed Sun eve, Mon & Tues.

Le Poussin Bleu corner of promenade René-Coty and rue Charles-Gounod ℡04.94.95.25.14. Moderately priced seafront brasserie.

Le Sirocco 35 quai Albert 1er ℡04.94 95 39.99. Smart, but staid, sea view restaurant specializing in fish. The menus range from €16.50–46, but the wine is expensive.

Nightlife and entertainment

For **drinking**, *Blue Bar* on rue Jules-Barbier above Plage du Veillat has a decent selection of beers, or, for something more upmarket, there's cocktails and piano music at *Coco-Club* at Port Santa Lucia (till dawn), and *Le Seven*, at 171 quai Albert 1er. *Pipe Line*, at 16 rue Charabois, is St Raphaël's only gay bar, with regular cabaret (weekends only out of season). *La Réserve*, on promenade René-Coty, is the stereotypical Côte d'Azur **disco** (open from 11pm), with ladies' nights and popular hits, while *Le Kilt*, at 130 rue Jules-Barbier, bills itself as the disco for the over-30s.

If you're in St-Raphaël in early July, try to catch some of the bands playing in the international competition of New Orleans **jazz** bands: ask at the tourist office for details of venues.

Listings

Bike rental Atout Cycles, 330 bd Jean-Moulin ℡04.94.95.56.91.

Boat rental Club Nautique, at the western end of Port Santa Lucia ℡04.94.95.11.66.

Car rental Most are in or near the *gare SNCF*: Avis is on place de la Gare ℡04.94.95.60.42; Budget is on rue Waldeck-Rousseau ℡04.94.82.24.44; and Europcar at 274 place Pierre-Coullet ℡04.94.95.56.87.

Diving Club Sous l'Eau, at Port Santa Lucia to the east of the town centre (℡04.94.95.90.33, ⓦwww.clubsousleau.com), takes divers out to the numerous wartime wrecks and underwater archeological sites off the coast; Club Subaquatique de Cachan, 56 rue de la Garonne (℡04.94.19.33.70, ⓦcscasso.free.fr/straphael .htm), specializes in night-diving.

Emergency ℡15; Hôpital Intercommunal Bonnet, av André-Léotard, Fréjus ℡04.94.40.21.21; SOS Médecins ℡04.94.95.15.25.

Laundry Top Pressing, 34 av Général-Leclerc; Lav'Matic, Port Santa Lucia.

Money exchange Most banks have cashpoint machines, or try the Crédit Agricole Change Service, 26 av du Commandant-Guilbaud, on the Vieux Port.

Pharmacy For the name of an emergency pharmacy, call the Police Municipale in St-Raphaël by day ℡04.94.95.00.17; or in Fréjus by night ℡04.94.51.90.00.

Police Commissariat, av Amiral-Baux, St-Raphaël ℡04.94.95.00.17.

Post office Poste Principale, av Victor-Hugo.

Taxi ℡04.94.95.04.25 or 04.94.83.24.24.

The Esterel

The 32-kilometre **Corniche de l'Esterel**, the sole stretch of wild coast between St-Raphaël and the Italian border, remains untouched by property development – at least between **Anthéor** and **Le Trayas** – its backdrop a 250-million-year-old arc of brilliant red volcanic rock tumbling down to the sea from the harsh crags of the **Massif de l'Esterel**. From the two major routes between Fréjus and **La Napoule**, the coastal N98 and rail line, and the inland N7, minor roads lead into this steeply contoured and once deeply wooded wild terrain. The **shoreline**, meanwhile, is a mass of little beaches, some sand, some shingle, cut by rocky promontories.

The inland route

The high, hairpin **inland route** is a dramatic but sometimes heart-rending drive; for every 2km of undisturbed ancient olive trees and gravity-defying rock formations, you have to suffer 1km of new motels and "residential parks" with real-estate hoardings. The Esterel is – or was – one of the most beautiful areas on the planet, with an interior uninhabited for centuries, save for reclusive saints, escaped convicts from Toulon, and Resistance fighters. It has no water and the topsoil is too shallow for cultivation. Prior to the twentieth-century creation of the corniche, the coastal communities were linked only by sea. The inland route (N7), however, is ancient, following in parts the Roman Via Aurelia.

Because of the fire risk many of the minor roads are barred to vehicles and even bicycles during the summer months, and some are closed throughout the year between 9am and 6pm: call the information line on ℡04.98.10.55.41 for details. All fires, and even cigarettes, are banned all year round. This makes **walking** even more enjoyable, though camping is strictly forbidden. The tourist office in St-Raphaël (see p.352) can provide details of paths and of the peaks that are the most obvious destinations. The highest point is **Mont Vinaigre**, which you can almost reach by road on the N7; a short, signposted footpath leads up to the summit. At 618m it's hardly a mountain, but the view from the top is spectacular.

The corniche

With half a dozen train stations and ten buses a day between St-Raphaël and Le Trayas, this is a very accessible coastal stretch for non-drivers. Boats also run along the coast from St-Raphaël's *gare maritime*. Along the stretch between Anthéor and Le Trayas, each easily reached beach has its summer snack-van, but by clambering over rocks you can usually find a near-deserted cove.

Le Dramont, Agay and Anthéor

The merest snatch of clear hillside and brasserie-less beach distinguishes Boulouris from **LE DRAMONT**, 7km east of St-Raphaël, where the landing

△ Cycling the corniche de l'Esterel

of the 36th American division in August 1944 is commemorated. A clifftop path around the **Cap du Dramont** headland gives fine views out to sea, though looking inland the most severe and recent encroachment on the Esterel is revealed – the tasteful but utterly unreal "designer village" of **Cap Esterel**, squatting smugly on the ridge between Le Dramont and Agay.

In contrast, Le Dramont's close neighbour **AGAY** is one of the least pretentious resorts of the Côte d'Azur, and beautifully situated around a deep horseshoe bay edged by sand beaches, red porphyry cliffs and pines. Both Agay and its eastern neighbour **ANTHÉOR** suffer a little from the creeping contagion of housing estates with rural names like Mas and Hameaux edging ever higher up their hills, but once you get above the concrete line, at the **Sommet du Rastel**, for example (signed up Agay's av du Bourg or bd du Rastel), you can begin to appreciate this wonderful terrain.

There are at least ten **campsites** in this area: along the Valescure road near the River Agay you'll find the four-star *Les Rives de L'Agay* (T04.94.82.02.74, W www.lesrivesdelagay.fr; €31 per tent; closed Nov–Feb), and the three-star *Agay-Soleil*, by the beach at 1152 bd de la Plage (T04.94.82.00.79, W www.agay-soleil.com; €26.50 per tent; closed mid-Nov to mid-March); or there's the three-star *Azur Rivage*, around the headland in Anthéor-Plage (T04.94.44.83.12, W www.camping-azur-rivage.com; €17 per tent; closed Nov–Feb). There's also no shortage of hotels: both Agay's *Le Relais d'Agay* on boulevard de la Plage (T04.94.82.78.20, W www.relaisdagay.com; ⑤; closed Nov–Easter) and *Sol e Mar*, on the N98 in Le Dramont (T04.94.95.25.60, W www.saint-raphael.com/solemar; ⑥), have sea views. Less expensive options include *Hôtel l'Esterella* on boulevard de la Plage in Agay (T04.94.82.00.58, W www.hotelesterella.com; ④), and *Les Flots Bleus* on boulevard Eugène Brieux in Anthéor (T04.94.44.80.21, W www.hotel-cote-azur.com; ④; closed mid-Nov to late March). Agay's **sailing school**, Ecole Française de Voile, based in a modern hut at the eastern end of the beach (T04.94.82.08.08, W www.ffvoile.org), offers lessons for many types of boat including catamarans and windsurfers.

Le Trayas

LE TRAYAS is on the highest point of the corniche and its shoreline is the most ragged, with wonderful inlets to explore. You can also trek to the Pic de l'Ours from here (about 3hr; the path is signed from the *gare SNCF*).

The **hotel** *Relais des Calanques*, route des Escalles (T04.94.44.14.06, F04.94.44.10.93; ⑦), nestles above a cove, the water almost lapping at its terrace where good sea-fish is served (around €25). Less expensive rooms can be found at *L'Auberge Blanche*, 1061 rte des Calanques/RN98 (T04.94.44.14.04, F04.94.44.17.27; ⑥), where the bus stops.

Travel details

Trains

Les Arcs to: Fréjus (15 daily; 15–20min); Gonfaron (2-4 daily; 20min); St-Raphaël (25 daily; 20–25min); Toulon (20 daily; 35–40min); Vidauban (2 daily; 5min).

Hyères to: Toulon (7–9 daily; 20min).

St-Raphaël to: Agay (10 daily; 10–12min); Anthéor (6 daily; 15min); Boulouris (13 daily; 4min); Cannes (approx every 20min; 25–35min); Les Arcs-Draguignan (21 daily; 15–20min); Le Dramont (9 daily; 10min); Le Trayas (9 daily; 20–25min); La Napoule (13 daily; 20–30min); Marseille (19 daily; 1hr 35min–2hrs); Nice (approx every 20min;

50min–1hr 20min); Théoule-sur-Mer (9 daily; 20–30min); Toulon (25 daily; 45min–1hr 10min). **Toulon** to: Marseille (every 15 min at peak times; 45min–1hr 5min).

Buses (Sundays and holidays reduced services)

Fréjus to: Nice Airport (2 daily: 55min–1hr 20min). **Hyères** to: Bormes (frequent; 25min); La Croix-Valmer (8 daily; 1hr 15min); Le Lavandou (16 daily; 30min); Le Rayol (9 daily; 50min); St-Tropez (7 daily; 1hr 30min); Toulon (13 daily; 35–50min). **Le Lavandou** to: Bormes (14 daily; 5min); Cavalaire-sur-Mer (9 daily; 30min); Cavalière (9 daily; 10min); Hyères (13 daily; 35min); La Croix-Valmer (8 daily; 40min); Le Rayol (9 daily; 20min); St-Tropez (8 daily; 1hr); Toulon (14 daily; 45min–1hr 10min). **Ste-Maxime** to: Cogolin (8 daily; 30min); La Foux (8 daily; 35min); Les Arcs (2 daily; 30–35min); Grimaud (8 daily; 20min); St-Tropez (9 daily; 45min). **St-Raphaël** to: Cogolin (6 daily; 55min–1hr 5min); Grimaud (6 daily; 55min–1hr); La Foux (8 daily; 1hr–1hr 15min); Les Issambres (8 daily; 20–30min); Nice Airport (4 daily; 1hr 15min); Ste-Maxime (8 daily; 30–40min); St-Tropez (8 daily; 1hr 10min–1hr 25min). **St-Tropez** to: Bormes (8 daily; 1hr–1hr 15min); Cavalaire-sur-Mer (8 daily; 25–35min); Cavalière

(8 daily; 45–55min); Cogolin (10 daily; 15min); Gassin (2 weekly; 25min); Grimaud (10 daily; 20–25min); Hyères (8 daily; 1hr 20min–1hr 35min); La Croix-Valmer (8 daily; 15–20min); Le Lavandou (8 daily; 55min–1hr 5min); Le Rayol (8 daily; 35–45min); Les Issambres (8 daily; 50min–1hr); Ramatuelle (2 weekly; 25min); Ste-Maxime (8 daily; 45min); St-Raphaël (8 daily; 1hr 20min–1hr 30min); Toulon (8 daily; 2hr–2hr 15min). **Toulon** to: Aix (4 daily; 1hr 15min); Bandol (every 30min; 1hr); Brignoles (6 daily; 1hr 30min); Draguignan (5 daily; 2hr 10min); Hyères (every 45min; 30–40min); Le Brusc (6–7 daily; 25min); Le Pradet (every 30min; 20min); Méounes (2 daily; 50min); Nice (2 daily; 2hr 30min); Ste-Maxime (1 daily; 1hr 40min); St-Raphaël (4 daily; 2hr); St-Tropez (8 daily; 2hr–2hr 10min); Sanary (every 30min; 35–45min); Signes (2 daily; 1hr 15min); Six-Fours (frequent; 25min).

Ferries

Toulon to: Bastia Corsica (1 daily except Sun; 8hr); Ajaccio (3 weekly; 8hr).

Flights

Hyères/Toulon to: Brest (2 weekly; 1hr 45min); Brussels (3 weekly; 1hr 45min); Paris (Orly) (4 daily; 1hr 25min); Rotterdam (6 weekly; 1hr 50min); and London (Stansted) (6 weekly; 2hr 10min).

Cannes and the western Riviera

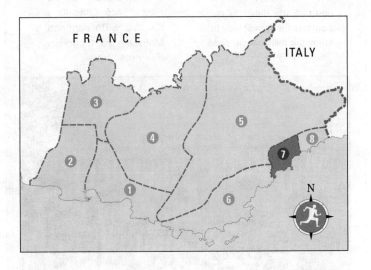

CHAPTER 7

Highlights

✳ **Promenade de la Croisette, Cannes** Pop on your shades, turn on your iPod and rollerblade along the Riviera's most glamorous seafront. See p.357

✳ **Îles des Lérins** Clean, pine-scented air, peaceful walks and shimmering rocks and water, just minutes from the centre of Cannes. See p.371

✳ **Plage de la Salis, Cap d'Antibes** Sandy, beautiful and free, this delightful public beach is the laziest way to enjoy the millionaires' cape. See p.389

✳ **Jazz à Juan** The Riviera's most renowned jazz festival brings some of the biggest names in the business to Juan-les-Pins every summer. See p.390

✳ **Fondation Maeght** Art and architecture fuse with landscape and the dazzling Provençal light to create this astonishing museum, whose building is as stunning as the works of art – by the likes of Miró, Chagall, Kandinsky, Bonnard and Matisse – that it contains. See pp.402–404

△ *Cartton Intercontinental* on the Promenade de la Croisette, Cannes

Cannes and the western Riviera

The stretch of coast between the Massif de l'Esterel and the River Var makes up the **western French Riviera**, a region as much legend as reality and a playground for the rich and famous for the better part of two centuries. The names of Cannes, Juan les Pins or Antibes summon up powerful images, even for those who have never been there: of a fantasy playground where the sparkling blue sea is speckled with boards, bikes and skis, and where extravagant yachts moor tantalizingly out of reach, disgorging their privileged cargo to fill the glamorous bars and restaurants or populate the latest event in the celebrity-studded calendar. There's truth in the legend still, though what was originally a remote and inhospitable shore is now one of the most developed and densely populated stretches of coast in Europe. Resorts that once catered only to the jet set have long since opened their doors to a far wider range of visitors, though the region still has some of the world's best **restaurants**, catering to some of the world's richest clientele. That said, speedy and inexpensive **train connections** make it easy for the less well-heeled to visit all the coastal towns and villages without committing yourself to staying overnight.

Though it shares much in common with the stretch of coast to the east of the Var, the western Riviera has a rather different **history**. Unlike the formerly Savoyard (and strongly Italianate) Nice and Menton, Cannes and Antibes were always Provençal, the latter almost a border town, just a few kilometers west of the frontier on the Var. The fishing village of **Cannes** itself was discovered in the 1830s by a retired British chancellor, Lord Brougham, who couldn't get to Nice because of a cholera epidemic. From the beginning, tourism in the western Riviera had a more exclusive air than in bustling, raffish Nice, and until World War I, aristocrats and royals from across Europe and North America built their opulent mansions here. In the 1920s, as Coco Chanel popularized the suntan and the glamorous Eden Roc on Cap d'Antibes stayed open all through the year for the first time, the season switched from winter to summer and a new kind of élite took centre stage, notably film stars like Charlie Chaplin, Maurice Chevalier and Lilian Harvey; it was an era immortalized in F. Scott Fitzgerald's *Tender is the Night*. Then, in 1936, the socialist government of Léon Blum granted workers paid holidays for the first time, and the democratization of the Riviera began.

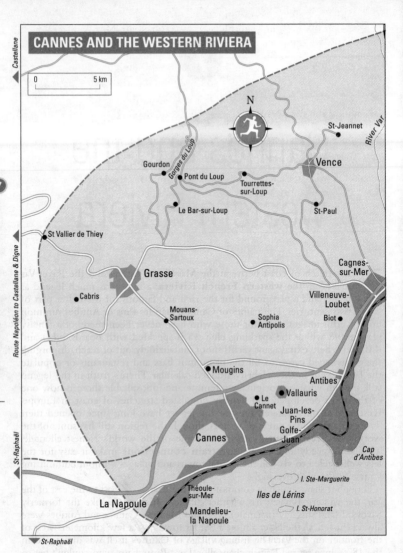

War in 1939 interrupted everything – including the first film festival in Cannes – but by the 1950s **mass tourism** took off in earnest and the real transformation began. Locals quickly realized that servicing the new influx of visitors was far more profitable than working on the land or at sea, and overenthusiastic property development and sheer pressure of numbers have been problems ever since. The coast is now built up all the way from Cannes to Antibes, while inland the hills between the villages are carpeted with disorienting, featureless suburbia that does little for the region's charm but adds greatly to its traffic headaches.

The appeal of the coast, however, is still easy enough to discern, most notably the legacies of the **artists** who stayed here: Picasso in **Antibes** and **Vallauris**;

Léger in **Biot**; Matisse in **Vence**; Renoir in **Cagnes-sur-Mer**; and all of them in **St-Paul-de-Vence** and **Haut-de-Cagnes**.

Cannes and around

If you've got it, **CANNES** is as good a place as any in the south of France to flaunt it. Superficial it may be, but in many ways it's the definitive Riviera resort of popular fantasy, with its immaculate seafront hotels and exclusive beaches, glamorous yachts and glitzy designer boutiques. It's a place where appearances definitely count, especially during the film festival, when the orgy of self-promotion reaches its annual peak. The vast seafront **Palais des Festivals** is the heart of the film festival but also hosts conferences, tournaments and trade shows throughout the rest of the year. Other year-round attractions include people-watching and window-shopping, and these at least are free. Yet Cannes works surprisingly well as an unpretentious beach resort, with plenty of free sandy **beaches** west of the port and hotels and restaurants to suit all pockets. If the present-day glitz gets too much, you can always explore the nineteenth-century glitz of **La Californie** or **La Croix des Gardes**, while further out of town the hilltop village of **Mougins** is home to some of the region's top restaurants, the otherwise unremarkable commune of **Le Cannet** celebrates its link with the painter **Pierre Bonnard**, and **Vallauris** is a centre for ceramics, some designed by Picasso. Above all, for a sublime contrast to the buzz of the city, the peaceful **Îles de Lérins** are just a short boat-ride offshore.

Arrival, orientation, information and city transport

The central **gare SNCF** is on rue Jean-Jaurès, while **buses** from inland towns including Grasse, Mougins, and Mouans-Sartoux arrive at the *gare routière* next door; buses to Vallauris depart from place Vauban north of the station. All other bus services – chiefly the urban routes (which also serve Le Cannet), plus coastal services to Juan-les-Pins, Antibes, Nice, La Napoule and St-Raphaël – arrive at and leave from the main *gare routière* on place B-Cornut Gentille overlooking the Vieux Port.

The central axis of Cannes is **Rue d'Antibes**, halfway between rue Jean-Jaurès and La Croisette, becoming rue Félix-Faure behind the Vieux Port. With just five blocks between rue Jean-Jaurès and the seafront, central Cannes is not particularly big, though it manages to look daunting. **Le Suquet**, the hill overlooking the modern town from the west, is the heart of Old Cannes.

Urban buses run from outside the Hôtel de Ville; you can buy individual tickets for €1.40, a *carnet* of ten for €9.40 and a weekly pass, the *Carte Palm'Hebdo*, for €10.40. A useful and enjoyable service is the open-top #8 bus along the seafront from the quai Laubeuf to Palm Beach Casino on Pointe Croisette, at the other end of the bay. If you prefer to cycle, **bikes** can be hired from Alliance Location, 19 rue des Frères Pradignac (℡04.93.38.62.62) or Holiday Bikes, 32 av du Maréchal-Juin (℡04.93.94.30.34, Ⓦww .holiday-bikes.com/maps/cannes.htm).

There are **tourist offices** at the *gare SNCF* (Mon–Sat 9am ℡04.93.99.19.77); at 1 av Pierre-Sémard in La Bocca (Tues–Sat 9am 2.30–6.30pm; ℡04.93.47.04.12); and at the Palais des Festivals (dail ℡04.92.99.84.22, Ⓦwww.cannes.com).

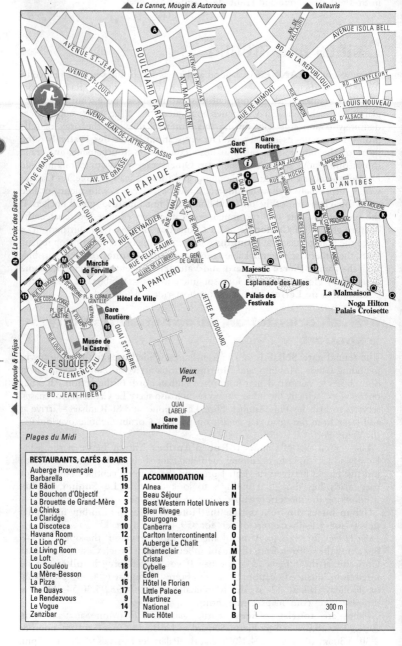

CANNES AND THE WESTERN RIVIERA

Le Cannet, Mougin & Autoroute   Vallauris

RESTAURANTS, CAFÉS & BARS

Auberge Provençale	11
Barbarella	15
Le Bâoli	19
Le Bouchon d'Objectif	2
La Brouette de Grand-Mère	3
Le Chinks	13
Le Claridge	8
La Discoteca	10
Havana Room	12
Le Lion d'Or	1
Le Living Room	5
Le Loft	6
Lou Souléou	18
La Mère-Besson	4
La Pizza	16
The Quays	17
Le Rendezvous	9
Le Vogue	14
Zanzibar	7

ACCOMMODATION

Alnea	H
Beau Séjour	N
Best Western Hotel Univers	I
Bleu Rivage	P
Bourgogne	F
Canberra	G
Carlton Intercontinental	O
Auberge Le Chalit	A
Chanteclair	M
Cristal	K
Cybelle	D
Eden	E
Hôtel le Florian	J
Little Palace	C
Martinez	Q
National	L
Ruc Hôtel	B

0   300 m

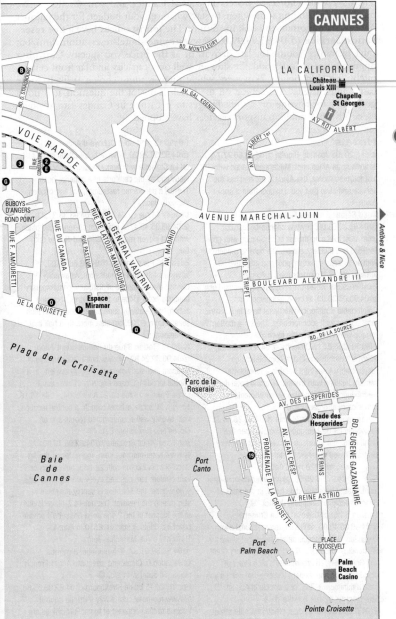

CANNES

BD. MONTFLEURY

LA CALIFORNIE

Château
Louis XIII

Chapelle
St Georges

AV. GAL KOENIG

AV. ROI ALBERT

BD. D. STRASBOURG

VOIE RAPIDE

RUE CONSTANTINE

BUBOYS
D'ANGERS
ROND POINT

RUE F. AMOURETTI

RUE DU CANADA

RUE PASTEUR

BD. GENERAL VAUTRIN

RUE DE LATOUR-MAUBOURGE

AV. MADRID

AVENUE MARECHAL-JUIN

BD. E. TRIPET

BOULEVARD ALEXANDRE III

Antibes & Nice

DE LA CROISETTE

Espace
Miramar

BD. DE LA SOURCE

Plage de la Croisette

Parc de la
Roseraie

AV. DES HESPERIDES

Stade des
Hesperides

BD. EUGENE GAZAGNAIRE

Baie
de
Cannes

Port
Canto

PROMENADE DE LA CROISETTE

AV. JEAN CRESP

AV. DE LERINS

AV. REINE ASTRID

Port
Palm Beach

PLACE
F. ROOSEVELT

Palm
Beach
Casino

Pointe Croisette

Accommodation

There's a wide choice of **hotels** in central Cannes, and you shouldn't have much trouble finding somewhere to stay, whatever your budget; for the cheaper options it's important to book in advance. The tourist offices have a free **reservation service** (℡04.93.99.99.00, Ⓦwww.cannes-hotel-reservation.com), but can't guarantee rooms for late arrivals or at the price you specify. **Camping** opportunities are not good: the sites are well over capacity and far from central; pitching in Mandelieu, 7km west, where there is more choice, is likely to be easier and cheaper. As sleeping on the beach is out of the question, it is not a good idea for anyone on a tight budget to get stuck in Cannes late at night, especially after public transport services have stopped.

Hotels

Alnea 20 rue Jean-de-Riouffe ℡04.93.68.77.77, Ⓦwww.hotel-alnea.com. Moderately priced with just fourteen rooms, the *Alnea* is a/c and has the service and style that you'd expect from a pricier place. ⑤

Beau Séjour 5 rue des Fauvettes ℡04.93.39.63.00, Ⓦwww.cannes-beausejour .com. Just to the northwest of Le Suquet, with good facilities and a quiet location. The hotel is modern with an extensive garden, pool and attractive terrace, and all the rooms have balconies. ⑨

Best Western Hôtel Univers 2 rue Maréchal-Foch ℡04.93.06.30.00, Ⓦbw-hotelunivers.com. Comfortable if rather conventional hotel in a central location, but well soundproofed. There's a rooftop terrace with views over the town. ⑦

Bleu Rivage 61 La Croisette ℡04.93.94.24.25, Ⓦwww.frenchriviera-online.com/bleurivage /accueil.htm. A seafront hotel in a nineteenth-century building with traditional grand hotel decor, neighbouring all the deluxe establishments but rather more affordable. ⑨

Bourgogne 11 rue du 24 Août ℡04.93.38.36.73, Ⓦwww.hotel-de-bourgogne.com. Inexpensive small hotel, not luxurious but well-kept and very central. Closed mid-Nov to mid-Dec. ③

Canberra 120 rue d'Antibes ℡04.97.06.95.00, Ⓦwww.hotels-ocre-azur .com. Classy boutique-style hotel, in the thick of Cannes' designer shopping district. ⑦

Carlton Intercontinental 58 La Croisette ℡04.93.06.40.06, Ⓦwww.intercontinental.com. Legendary Belle Époque palace hotel that starred in Hitchcock's *To Catch a Thief*, along with Cary Grant and Grace Kelly. The rooms are a nice blend of grand tradition and modern touches, but will set you back a minimum €335 for a double in August. ⑨

Chanteclair 12 rue Forville ℡ & Ⓕ04.93.39.68.88. Budget place in a side street close to Le Suquet, with quiet rooms and no TVs. ③

Cristal 13 rond-point Duboys-d'Angers ℡04.92.59.29.29, Ⓦwww.hotel-cristal.com. Just off La Croisette with funky modern decor in the lobby and all the comforts of a superior hotel. There's a panoramic restaurant, bar and pool on the sixth floor. ⑨

Cybelle 14 rue du 24 Août ℡04.93.38.31.33, Ⓕ04.93.38.43.47. A small, much-renovated place, with just eleven rooms. Closed mid-Nov to mid-Dec. ⑤

Eden 133 rue d'Antibes ℡04.93.68.78.00, Ⓦwww.eden-hotel-cannes.com. As swanky Cannes places go, this stylish, airy, contemporary boutique hotel, close to the designer shopping action, has relatively sane prices: doubles in high season from €200, but little more than half that off-season. ⑨

Hôtel le Florian 8 rue du Commandant-André ℡04.93.39.24.82, Ⓦwww.hotel-leflorian.com. A pleasant two-star hotel with friendly owners, in a central location. Closed end Nov to mid-Jan. ⑤

Little Palace 18 rue du 24 Août ℡04.92.98.18.18, Ⓦwww.littlepalace-hotel.com. In a central location with twenty well-soundproofed rooms and a/c. Closed late Nov to late Dec. ④

Martinez 73 La Croisette ℡04.92.98.73.00, Ⓦwww.hotel-martinez.com. Top suites at the Art Deco *Martinez* come with 24-hour butler service, vast outdoor terraces and eye-watering price tags – no wonder the *Martinez* is simply *the* place to stay during the Festival. The hotel's Z-plage is one of the hippest of the Plage de la Croisette's private beaches. Doubles start at €510 in Aug. ⑨

National 8 rue Maréchal-Joffre ℡04.93.39.91.92, Ⓔhotelnationalcannes @wanadoo.fr. Clean and adequate Anglo-French managed hotel with a/c. ④

Ruc Hôtel 15 bd de Strasbourg ℡04.92.98.33.60, Ⓦwww.ruc-hotel.com. Away from the central hubbub to the northeast of town. Furnishings are elegant but old-fashioned and slightly faded; there are tennis courts nearby. ⑤

Hostels and campsites

Auberge Le Chalit 27 av Maréchal-Galliéni
☏04.93.99.22.11, ✉le-chalit@orange.fr. Five
minutes' walk from the train station, Cannes' only
hostel has 4-, 5-, and 8-bed dorms for €16-22 a
night. There's no curfew. Closed mid to end Nov.
Camping Bellevue 67 av Maurice-Chevalier
☏04.93.47.28.97, ⦿www.parcbellevue.com.
Three-star campsite 3km northwest of the centre

in the suburb of Ranguin; bus #2 from Hôtel de
Ville (stop "Sainte-Jeanne"). €24 per tent. Closed
Oct–March.
Le Ranch Camping chemin St-Joseph, l'Aubarède
☏04.93.46.00.11, ⦿www.leranchcamping.fr.
Three-star site 2km out in Le Cannet, and very
close to the A8 autoroute; bus #10 from the Hôtel
de Ville (direction "Les Pins Parasols", stop "Le
Ranch"). €19 per tent. Closed Nov–March.

The Town

Though the centre of Cannes is neatly defined by the loop of the rail line
tunnelled beneath the Voie Rapide and the sea, the town's urban sprawl
stretches west to **Mandelieu-La-Napoule**, north past **Le Cannet**, **Mougins**
and **Mouans-Sartoux** more or less to **Grasse**, and east to **Vallauris** and
Juan-les-Pins. If you're just popping into Cannes for a quick look, the seafront
La Croisette is the bit to experience. An afternoon's visit could take in **Le
Suquet**, the old town to the west of the Vieux Port, and if you have any longer,
head straight out to the wonderful **Îles de Lérins** before taking a stroll around
the aristocratic suburbs of **La Croix des Gardes** and **La Californie**.

The beaches and town centre

You'll find extensive free sandy beaches to the west of Le Suquet towards La
Bocca along the **boulevard du Midi**, and though the boulevard is backed by
a distinctly unglamorous railway line and the water isn't always the cleanest, the
atmosphere is unpretentious and family-oriented, and there are regular kiosks
selling simple snacks and ice creams to compensate for the lack of more
elaborate facilities. In complete contrast, there are only a few meagre scraps of
free sand at both extremities of the celebrated, swanky **Plage de la Croisette**,
which otherwise disappears in summer beneath the many chic (and expensive)
private beach concessions. The stretches of beach owned by the deluxe palace-
hotels are where you're most likely to spot a face familiar from celluloid,
especially during the film festival, though you'll be lucky to see further than the
backs of the paparazzi buzzing around them. If you can't get onto the beach,
you can at least take advantage of the little blue chairs provided free along the
elegant **boulevard de la Croisette**, the broad promenade which curves all the
way from the Vieux Port to the Cap de la Croisette. Here you can watch the
endless display of rollerbladers, rubbernecking visitors and genteel retired folk
with tiny dogs.

Much of the original nineteenth-century architectural swank of central
Cannes has fallen victim to redevelopment, though the buildings lining La
Croisette still include a few palatial hotels from the town's golden age, notably
the **Carlton Intercontinental**, whose cupolas were inspired by the breasts of
a famous courtesan, and the Art Deco **Martinez**. But there are also a few
monstrosities, such as the **Noga Hilton**. Rather overshadowed by the seafront
glitz is the beautiful **La Malmaison** at no. 47, the former tea room of the now-
vanished *Grand Hotel*, built in 1863 and demolished a century later. This is the
home of the city's cultural affairs department, where temporary exhibitions of
modern and contemporary art are often staged (July to mid-Sept Tues–Sun
11am–8pm; mid-Sept to June Tues–Sun 10am–1pm & 2.30–6.30pm; €3).
Further east, the **Espace Mirarar** (June–Sept Tues–Sun 2–7pm; Oct–May
Tues–Sun 1–6pm; free) also hosts temporary exhibitions.

Each May Cannes hosts the most famous of all movie media events, the **Festival International du Film** (@ www.festival-cannes.com). It was first conceived as a rival to the Venice film festival, then under Mussolini's influence. Since only pro-fascist films had any chance of winning prizes, an alternative competition was planned for 1939 in Cannes. World War II dictated otherwise and it was not until 1946 that the first Cannes festival took place.

Winning the top prize, the **Palme d'Or**, can't compete with Oscars for box-office effect, but within the movie world it is unrivalled. Some years it seems as if the big names are all too busy talking finance in LA to come to Cannes; the next they are all begging for the accolades. Even if the Hollywood moguls keep their new block-busters under wraps, they still send minions to wheel and deal.

The festival is strictly an event for film professionals and the associated media, and without proper accreditation you won't get into to the Palais des Festivals. However, it is possible to gain entry to the open-air *Cinéma de la Plage*, which screens certain official selections to the public. Invitations for these screenings are available at the main Cannes tourist information office.

In contrast to the attendant glitz and froth of the event, the Festival has lately cultivated a reputation for rewarding politically committed (and at times controversial) film-makers: the 2004 Palme d'Or went to Michael Moore's documentary *Fahrenheit 9/11*, while the 2006 prize went to Ken Loach's historical drama about Irish independence, *The Wind That Shakes The Barley*.

Walking around town in swimming gear or bikini bottoms used to be the norm in Cannes, but since the 1990s there's been a legal ban on swimsuits in museums and the town centre, and the style these days is to dress up, not down. And no wonder: the western end of La Croisette, the mid-section of **rue d'Antibes** and the streets between them form the South of France's most extensive luxury shopping district, stuffed with designer names, such as Bulgari, Cartier, Chanel, Lacroix and Vuitton. The grid of streets bounded by rue Macé, rue V.-Cousin, rue Dr G.-Monod and rue des Frères-Pradignacs is also the focus for some of Cannes' most stylish nightlife.

This part of town looks its best in the weeks leading up to Christmas, when the streets glitter with tasteful white lights and the crowds of summer are long forgotten. A small Christmas market takes place on the **Vieux Port**, while in summer you can watch the millionaires eating meals served by white-frocked crew on enormous yacht decks. Between here and La Croisette stands the ugly **Palais des Festivals**, which resembles a misplaced concrete missile silo. Here, you can compare hand sizes with the imprints of those of film stars that have, Hollywood-style, been set in tiles on the pavement in front of the main entrance. Opposite stands a phone booth in the shape of a reel of film, paying witty tribute to the importance of the film industry to Cannes' economy.

Le Suquet

The old town is known as **Le Suquet** after the hill on which it stands. Back in the eleventh century it became the property of the Îles de Lérins monks, and a castle built by the *abbé* in 1088 still stands. Alongside it is the white stone twelfth-century Romanesque **Chapelle de Ste-Anne**. After several centuries in which a small town took root around the religious settlement, a dispute arose between the monks and the townsfolk who wanted their own parish and priest. Two hundred years after their initial demand in 1648, **Notre-Dame de**

l'Espérance was finally built beside the Chapelle de Ste-Anne, in Gothic style as if to emphasize just how overdue it was.

Inside the castle and the chapel is the **Musée de la Castre** (Tues–Sun; April, May & Sept 10am–1pm & 2–6pm; June–Aug 10am–1pm & 3–7pm; Oct–March 10am–1pm & 2–5pm; €3), which has some interesting pictures and prints of old Cannes and strong ethnology and archeology displays. Its highlight, however, is the brilliant collection of musical instruments from all over the world, including Congolese bell bracelets, an Ethiopian ten-string lyre, an Asian "lute" with a snakeskin box and an extraordinary selection of drums. Climb the medieval tower in the museum courtyard for the best view of Le Suquet and the town below.

Although Le Suquet started out as home to the city's poorer residents, the streets leading to the summit are now gentrified, and the various places to **eat** and **drink** increasingly tourist-oriented and chic, if (for the most part) less overtly trendy than in the streets behind La Croisette. From the top, the panorama across La Croisette is superb.

La Croix des Gardes and La Californie

If much of the nineteenth-century elegance of central Cannes disappeared in a frenzy of postwar redevelopment, the same certainly isn't true of the leafy suburbs of La Croix des Gardes and La Californie. From the very outset, Cannes' aristocratic visitors preferred to build their own villas, and many of these survive, though some have been adapted for other uses and still others are hidden behind high walls, the preserve to this day of the discreetly rich. **La Croix des Gardes** is the closest to the centre, lying just a few hundred metres west of Le Suquet. Here, Lord Brougham's elegant **Château Eléonore** still stands on avenue du Dr Raymond-Picaud on the plot he bought after his enforced sojourn in the then-unknown village of Cannes in 1834. Close by, on the opposite side of the road, is the **Villa Victoria**, built in an unmistakably English Victorian Gothic style in 1852-3 by the developer Sir Thomas Woolfield, who built and sold around 30 villas in the town, and whose landscape gardener, John Taylor, went on to found one of the Riviera's best known estate agencies. Neither of these houses is open to the public, but you can visit the opulent **Villa Maria Thérèse**, 1 av Jean-de-Noailles, just around the corner from Lord Brougham's villa. The Beaux-Arts mansion was built in 1881 for the Dowager Baroness Rothschild. It now houses the Cannes **multimedia library** (Tues–Sat 9.30am-6pm), which in addition to the usual books, CDs and videos also contains the Cannes archive. The house is set in a lovely garden with winding paths and waterfalls.

Some 2km east of the centre of Cannes, **La Californie** is harder to get to grips with – it's hilly and spread out, and the roads wind in haphazard fashion around the hill. But it is, if anything, even more redolent of the Riviera's opulent past, since it was the holiday home of members of both the British and Russian royal families. The architecture here is especially eclectic and flamboyant, though some of the biggest and most impressive piles – such as the **Château Scott** on avenue du Maréchal-Juin or the turreted **Château Louis XIII** high above Cannes on avenue de la Tropicale - are hidden behind high walls and therefore rather hard to see. More easily visible are the gorgeous stained glass structure at the **Villa Soligny** on av Roi Albert, and the incongruous Surrey stockbroker Tudor of the **Villa Rose Lawn** on the corner of avenue de la Favorite at 42 avenue Roi-Albert, complete with towering red brick chimneys. Further west along avenue Roi-Albert, the **Chapelle St-Georges**, formerly the town's Anglican church, is one of the best examples of English Victorian church architecture on the Riviera. It was built as a memorial to Edward VIII's brother, the Duke of Albany, who

died young in Cannes as a result of an accident in 1884. The church was consecrated on February 12, 1887, with the future king in attendance. A fountain,
erected by the people of Cannes in the Duke's memory, stands close to the **Villa
Nevada** on boulevard des Pins, where he died. Higher vantage points in La
Californie – on **boulevard Superieur** and up towards the former observatory
– offer tantalizing views over the **Îles des Lérins**.

Eating and drinking

Cannes' **restaurants** tend to stay open very late, and getting a meal after midnight
is no great problem. There are hundreds of places to eat, covering the whole range
from €12 lunchtime menus to €100–plus blowouts, though quality across the
board can be patchy. The vigour of the Forville **market**, two blocks north of the
Vieux Port, however, means that every chef in town has access to the finest and
freshest ingredients. The best areas for less expensive dining are **rue Meynadier**,
Le Suquet and **quai St-Pierre** on the Vieux Port, lined with **brasseries** and
cafés. Reserving a table is advisable at almost all the restaurants listed below.

Restaurants

Auberge Provençale 10 rue Saint-Antoine
℡04.92.99.27.17. Generous portions of Provençal
cooking in a rustic setting at Cannes' oldest
restaurant. Menus from €27. Open daily all year.

Barbarella 16 rue Saint-Dizier
℡04.92.99.17.33. Philippe Starck *Ghost*
chairs and Japanese-influenced food contrast with
the quiet location of this gay-friendly restaurant in
Le Suquet. The sushi of fruits is a must. Menus
from €29. Open Tues-Sun, eves only (daily during
Festival).

Le Bouchon d'Objectif 10 rue de Constantine
℡04.93.99.21.76. An excellent local bistro
serving *aïoli*, *magret de canard* and other staple
dishes with admirable simplicity. Menus at €17
and €28.

La Brouette de Grand-Mère 9 bis rue d'Oran
℡04.93.39.12.10. A single menu (around €35)
that includes an aperitif and wine, with filling
dishes such as a *cuisse de lapin* or grilled
andouillettes. Fun and good value. Closed at
lunchtime, Sun & late June to mid-July.

Le Claridge 2 place du Général-de-Gaulle
℡04.93.39.05.86. Fashionable bar/ice cream
parlour with a broad terrace, in a grandstand
location opposite the Palais des Festivals – wear
your shades. It serves generous panini from
€6.50, and sandwiches at around €5.50. Open
daily all year.

Lou Souléou 16 bd Jean-Hibert ℡04.93.39.85.55.
A fish specialist serving a good range of seafood
on very reasonably priced menus in view of the sea
west of Le Suquet. Menus from €23. Closed Mon
& Wed evenings.

La Mère-Besson 13 rue des Frères-Pradignacs
℡04.93.39.59.24. Each day has a different speciality: *filet de rascasse*, *aïoli* and *lottes à la provençale*
(tiny fried monkfish) among them. Menus at €27 and
€32. Evenings only. Closed Sun and Christmas.

La Palme d'Or *Hôtel Martinez*, 73 La Croisette
℡04.92.98.74.14. A renowned temple of taste,
where the stars celebrate their film festival prizes
with some of the most exquisite and original food
this coast has to offer. Menus at €75, €98 and
€145 without drinks, à la carte €125 without
wine. Closed Sun & Mon (except during Festival),
second week of Nov & first half of Feb.

La Pizza 3 quai St-Pierre ℡04.93.39.22.56.
Bustling, if not particularly cheap Vieux Port
stalwart serving reliable Italian food. The fresh
ravioli are excellent, helpings are generous, and
they write your tab on the paper tablecloths. Three
courses with wine around €48. Open until late.

Le Rendezvous 35 rue Félix-Faure
℡04.93.68.55.10. Big, slightly old-fashioned
brasserie facing the port, one of a number where
comfort levels are high and fish is to the fore. The
€28.90 menu includes the likes of ravioli with cep
mushrooms and fillet of daurade.

Nightlife

As you'd expect, Cannes abounds with trendy, exclusive **bars** and **clubs,**
nowhere more so than in the tight little grid of streets bounded by rue Macé,
rue V. Cousin, rue Dr G.-Monod and rue des Frères-Pradignacs. As is so often
the case in the south of France, the boundaries between restaurant, bar and club

are somewhat blurred, so that you can frequently dine, drink and dance – at a price – in the same venue. After a night out at even the cheapest **bars** and **clubs** you're unlikely to have much change from €50, and if your tastes run to cocktails or exotic spirits you won't find it too difficult to spend more.

Cannes' **lesbian and gay** bar scene is smaller than that in Nice, but smart and a good deal more relaxed, and some venues attract hetero as well as gay visitors. If you are determined to lose money in Cannes, choose from **casinos** at the Palais des Festivals, at the Palm Beach at the eastern end of La Croisette or in the *Noga Hilton Hotel*. There's also a fairly lively year-round **theatre, dance** and **music** scene, centred on the Palais des Festivals, the Théâtre Palais Croisette in the *Noga Hilton*, and the Théâtre La Licorne in La Bocca. The **Stade des Hespérides** in the district of La Croisette is the venue for occasional concerts as well as major sporting events.

Bars and clubs

Le Baôli Port Pierre Canto, bd de la Croisette. Spectacular luxury restaurant/disco with Asian food, an "exotic" outdoor setting with palms and tented pavilions, and no shortage of VIP visitors, from Paris Hilton to Ivana Trump. Open Fri & Sat 8pm-5am. Closed Nov-April.

Le Chinks 88 rue Meynadier. Tiny but trendy lounge & cocktail bar close to the Vieux Port and Le Suquet, playing jazz, swing and salsa and with rather overpriced Thai food.

La Discoteca 22 rue Macé. Fashionable, central disco just off La Croisette. Open Thurs-Sun from midnight, daily in high season.

Le Havana Room 42 La Croisette. Champagne and cocktail bar with a garden terrace in a prime seafront location. Open 10am-3pm & 7-11pm

Le Living Room 17 rue Dr Gérard-Monod. DJ bar-restaurant with a jazz and soul soundtrack and simple, slick modern decor. Open Thurs-Sat from 6.30pm until 2.30am.

Le Loft 13 rue Dr Gérard-Monod. Cool modern lounge bar above a trendy Asian fusion restaurant. Open daily 10pm-2.30am.

The Quays 17 quai St Pierre. The inevitable Irish pub, opposite the swanky yachts of the Vieux Port. Open until 2.30am.

Lesbian and gay bars

Le Vogue 20 rue du Suquet. Smart, rather pricey Le Suquet bar where the champagne is always on ice and the atmosphere usually chilled. Mixed gay and hetero crowd. Open Tues-Sun 8pm-6am

Le Zanzibar 85 rue Félix-Faure. Dance music meets matelot chic at this long-established gay bar. Open 6pm-4am.

Listings

Airport Cannes-Mandelieu, 6km from the centre of town ☎04.93.90.40.40.

Banks Most banks on rue d'Antibes have cash dispensers.

Bookshop Cannes English Bookshop, 11 rue Bivouac-Napoleon ☎04.93.99.40.08; sells English-language books.

Car rental Avis, 69 La Croisette ☎04.93.94.15.86, and at the *gare SNCF* ☎04.93.39.26.38; Budget Comeback, 160 rue d'Antibes ☎04.93.99.44.04; Europcar, 3 rue du Commandant-Vidal ☎04.93.06.26.30, Hertz, 147 rue d'Antibes ☎04.93.99.04.20.

Emergencies ☎18 or ☎15; SOS médecins ☎08.25.00.50.04; Hôpital de Cannes, av des Broussailles ☎04.93.69.71.50.

Lost property 1 av St Louis ☎04.97.06.40.00.

Parking Palais des Festivals, *gare SNCF*, Forville (rue Pastour).

Pharmacy Call ☎04.93.06.22.22 for address of emergency pharmacy after 7.30pm.

Police Commissariat Central de Police, 1 av de Grasse ☎04.93.06.22.22.

Post office 22 rue Bivouac-Napoleon.

Taxis Cannes Allo Taxi ☎04.92.99.27.27.

Îles de Lérins

The **Îles de Lérins** would be lovely anywhere, but at only a fifteen-minute ferry ride from Cannes, they're a haven away from the madness of the modern city. Known as Lerina, or Lero, in ancient times, the two islands have a long historical pedigree and today offer the gentle pace and tranquility the Riviera so often lacks.

Getting to the islands

Boats for both islands leave from the quai des Îles at the seaward end of the quai Max-Laubeuf. There are regular services to **Ste-Marguerite** run by two companies, S.A.R.L Horizon (hourly; winter 9am-4.15pm, spring 9am-5.15pm, summer until 6.15pm; ℡04.92.98.71.36; €11), and Trans Côte d'Azur (℡04.92.98.71.30, ⓦwww.trans-cote-azur.com; up to 16 departures 9am-5pm; €11): the last boats back to Cannes leave Ste-Marguerite at 5.15pm, 6pm or 7pm, depending on the operator and season. **St-Honorat** is served by Compagnie Planaria, run by the Abbaye de Lérins (℡04.92.98.71.38, ⓦwww.abbayedelerins.com; summer 10 daily; winter 7 daily; €11): the last boat back to Cannes leaves at 5pm in winter and 6pm in summer.

Ste-Marguerite

Of the two islands, **STE-MARGUERITE** is the more animated, with plenty of day trippers and a working boatyard, though it still has clear water and beautiful scenery, and is large enough for visitors to find seclusion if they're prepared to leave the crowded port and follow paths through the thick woods of Aleppo pines and evergreen oaks. The quickest way to the peaceful southern shore is to take the **allée des Eucalyptus**, which crosses the island from the Fort. Narrow rocky beaches along the southern shore provide good bathing points, though as the channel between Ste-Marguerite and St-Honorat is a popular anchorage for motor yachts you're unlikely to find real solitude. This side of the island is also dotted with stone-built picnic tables. The **Chemin de la Ceinture** follows the shore for about 3km to the battery on the eastern headland. Returning via the northern shore provides you with views back to Cannes.

The dominating structure and crowd puller of the island is the **Fort Ste-Marguerite** (Jan-March & Oct-Dec Tues-Sun 10.30am-1.15pm & 2.15-4.45pm, April to mid-June & mid to late Sept Tues-Sun 10.30am-1.15pm & 2.15-5.45pm, mid-June to mid-Sept daily 10.30am-5.45pm; €3), a Richelieu commission that failed to prevent the Spanish occupying both Lérins islands between 1635 and 1637. Later, Vauban rounded it off, presumably for Louis XIV's glory, since the strategic value of greatly enlarging a fort facing the mainland without upgrading the one facing the sea is pretty minimal. The main interest in the Fort Ste-Marguerite today is the identification of one cell as having held the **Man in the Iron Mask**, a mythical character given credence by Alexandre Dumas – author of *The Three Musketeers* and *The Count of Monte Cristo* – and by Hollywood. Other cells undoubtedly held the prisoners attributed to them, mostly Huguenots imprisoned for refusing to submit to Louis XIV's vicious suppression of Protestantism. A series of modern wall paintings by Jean le Gac, commissioned in 1992, covers the cell walls and depicts the painter as prisoner. Also housed in the fort is the **Musée de la Mer**, containing amphorae from a Roman shipwreck discovered in 50m of water close to the islet of Tradelière in 1971 as well as ceramics from a tenth-century Arab ship discovered off the western tip of the island in 1973. The fort contains three Roman **cisterns**; Ste-Marguerite has no natural springs and water supply has been a problem since the island was first occupied.

These days, getting something to **eat and drink** shouldn't be a problem on Ste-Marguerite during the summer months, as in addition to the **restaurant** *l'Escale* there are a couple of snack stalls just up from the port selling filling and reasonably priced *pan bagnats*. From November to March options are more limited, however, and at any time of the year it's worth bringing a bottle of water at least.

St-Honorat

ST-HONORAT, the smaller southern island, has been owned by monks almost continuously since its namesake and patron founded a monastery here in 410 AD. Honoratus, a Roman noble turned good, is said to have chosen the isle of Lerina because of its reputation for being haunted, full of snakes and scorpions, and lacking any fresh water. Quickly divining a spring and gradually exterminating all the vipers, the saint and his two companions found themselves with precisely the peace and isolation they sought. In time, visitors started to increase in frequency and numbers; the monastic order was established to structure a growing community. By the end of Honoratus's life the Lérins monks had monasteries all over France, held bishoprics in cities such as Arles and Lyon, and were renowned throughout the Catholic world for their contributions to theology. St Patrick was one of the products of the seminary, training here for seven years before setting out for Ireland.

The present **abbey** buildings are mostly nineteenth-century, though vestiges of medieval and earlier construction survive in the church and cloisters. You can visit the austere church, but there is no access to the residential part of the monastery unless you're staying there on a spiritual retreat. Today, 28 Cistercian monks live and work here, tending an apiary and a vineyard that produces a sought-after white wine, as well as making liqueurs, all of which are on sale in the abbey's shop. Behind this complex, on the sea's edge, stands an eleventh-century **fortress**, a monastic bolthole that was connected to the original abbey by a tunnel, and used to guard against the threat of invaders, especially the Saracens. Of all the protective forts built along this coast, this is the only one that looks as if it could still serve its original function.

The other buildings on St-Honorat are the churches and chapels that served as retreats. **St-Pierre**, beside the modern monastery, **La Trinité**, in the east of the island, and **St-Sauveur**, west of the harbour, remain more or less unchanged. By **St-Cabrais**, on the eastern shore, is a furnace with a chute for making cannonballs, evidence that the monks were not without worldly defensive skills.

Today, the main attraction of the island is its tranquillity. There is just one small restaurant by the landing stage (open April-Oct only), and no cars or hotels: just the cultivated vines, lavender, herbs and olive trees mingled with wild poppies and daisies; and pine and eucalyptus trees shading the paths beside the white rock shore and mixing with the scent of rosemary, thyme and wild honeysuckle. Visitors should respect the abbey's silence, and note that nudity is not permitted on the island.

West of Cannes: La Napoule, Miramar and Théoule-sur-Mer

A fantasy castle, built onto the three towers and gateway of a fourteenth-century fort, dominates **LA NAPOULE**, 8km from Cannes at the western end of the Riviera (bus #20 from *gare SNCF* or Hôtel de Ville). The **castle** ranks high amongst the classic pre-World War I follies built by foreigners on the Côte; the creators, in this instance, being the American sculptor Henry Clews and his wife. The castle and its lovely gardens can be visited (7 Feb-7 Nov gardens daily

10am–6pm, castle tours at 11.30am, 2.30pm, 3.30pm & 4.30pm; 8 Nov–6 Feb gardens Mon–Fri 2–6pm, Sat & Sun 10am–6pm, castle tours Mon–Fri 2.30pm, 3.30pm & 4.30pm, Sat & Sun 11.30am, 2.30pm, 3.30pm & 4.30pm; gardens €3.50, castle tour €6), with their collection of Clews' odd and gloomy works, represented on the outside by the grotesques on the gateway.

The **tourist office** on avenue Henri-Clews opposite La Napoule's port (April–June and Sept–Oct Mon–Fri 9.30am–12.30pm & 2–6pm; July–Aug daily 10am–12.30pm & 2.30–7pm; closed rest of year except during February mimosa festival; ☎04.92.97.99.27, Ⓦwww.ot-mandelieu.fr) can help with **accommodation**. There are two hotels worth trying: *La Calanque*, on boulevard Henri-Clews (☎04.93.49.95.11, Ⓕ04.93.49.67.44; ❻), has a pretty restaurant and rooms with views of the castle and the sea; and the better-value and more peaceful *Villa Parisiana*, on rue de l'Argentière (☎04.93.49.93.02, Ⓦwww.villaparisiana.com; ❸). If you get stuck, the characterless inland golfing resort of Mandelieu-La Napoule has plenty of hotels, though little appeal to non-golfers.

If you have the money to splash out on a special meal, head for the gourmet **restaurant** *L'Oasis*, on rue Jean-Honoré-Carle (book in advance; ☎04.93.49.95.52; closed Mon); evening menus range from €75–155, but there is also a good lunch menu at €54. For something more down-to-earth, the restaurant at *La Calanque* (see above) serves some fine Provençal fish dishes, with *aïoli* around €11.

At **THÉOULE** and neighbouring **MIRAMAR**, the Corniche de l'Esterel begins, and the ruggedly picturesque setting is the chief attraction. Théoule is a quiet, rather low-key place with a sandy beach, large marina and a small castle that can't be visited; the coast gets wilder and more dramatic to the south. From the Pointe de l'Esquillon between Théoule and Miramar you get an unhindered view of the private residential estate designed by Jacques Couelle at Porte-La-Galère on the neighbouring headland.

If you want **to stay**, *La Tour de l'Esquillon*, on the N98 coast road in Miramar (☎04.93.75.41.51, Ⓦwww.esquillon.com; ❼), is worth splashing out on, with breathtaking views from high up on the corniche, its own beach and a good restaurant. Théoule's **tourist office**, at 1 corniche d'Or (Mon–Sat 9am–7pm, Sun 9am–2pm; ☎04.93.49.28.28, Ⓦwww.theoule-sur-mer.org), provides the usual local information.

North of Cannes: Le Cannet, Mougins and Mouans-Sartoux

To the north, Cannes merges imperceptibly with **Le Cannet** along the busy boulevard Sadi-Carnot. Although the town's built-up area is indistinguishable from Cannes' sprawl, Le Cannet's old part, along rue St-Sauveur, preserves some villagey charm. The original town was built on land belonging to the Îles de Lérins monks to house 140 families summoned from Liguria to cultivate the orange trees. These original 'Le Cannois' are commemorated by the mural and orange trees on **place Bellevue**. If you approach the *place* from the south you'll pass the tiny fifteenth-century **Chapelle de St-Sauveur** on rue St-Sauveur (guided visits Fri–Mon & Wed 2–6pm; free), exuberantly decorated by the contemporary artist Tobiasse. Le Cannet's main claim to artistic fame, however, is as the home from 1939 until his death in 1947 of **Pierre Bonnard**, perhaps the most private of the Riviera's great artists; he is buried in the town's Notre Dame des Anges cemetery. Born in the suburbs of Paris in 1867, Bonnard found fame early as a member of the Nabis, followers of Gauguin. He subsequently created his own style, distinguished by intense colour and a highly domestic choice of subject matter, frequently featuring his wife Marthe, most particularly in a late series of *baignoires* on which he worked long after her death at the age of 73 in 1942. It was just a year after their marriage in 1925 that Bonnard bought the Villa le Bosquet in Le Cannet. As part of a project to open a Bonnard museum in the town, the **Espace Bonnard** (daily 2-7pm during exhibitions) in the Jardins de Tivoli regularly attracts interesting temporary art shows.

It's an easy journey to Le Cannet: **buses** #1A or #4 from the Hôtel de Ville in Cannes stop at place Leclerc at the foot of the old village. The **tourist office** is at 20 bd Sadi-Carnot (☎04.93.46.74.00).

Mougins and around

If **MOUGINS**, 8km north of Cannes, is your first experience of a Provençal village, you're likely to be charmed by its hilltop site, exquisitely preserved lanes and associations with Man Ray and with Picasso, who had his last studio here and who died here in 1973. If, however, you arrive with images of Cotignac, Simiane la Rotonde or even St-Paul de Vence fresh in mind, Mougins may strike you as rather over-praised, a pretty bauble lost in the sea of bland suburbia that has engulfed much of the surrounding countryside and robbed the village of any real rural character. The most compelling reasons to visit Mougins are in any case culinary, for it was at the **Moulin de Mougins**, on the opposite side of the Cannes-Grasse highway from the old village on avenue Notre Dame de Vie, that legendary chef Roger Vergé perfected his *Cuisine of the Sun*, a modern reworking of Provençal cooking that won him (and Mougins) international acclaim in the 1970s. Vergé retired in 2004, but his hand-picked successor Alain Llorca has maintained the Moulin's culinary fame and it remains a firm favourite with Hollywood stars attending the Cannes Film Festival.

In the village itself there's an excellent **photography museum** (July–Aug daily 10am–8pm; Sept-Oct & Dec-June Mon-Fri 10am–6pm, Sat & Sun 11am–6pm, closed Nov; free), just beyond the Porte Sarrazine, which hosts changing exhibitions and has its own small collection that includes some pictures of Jacques Lartigue (who lived in the neighbouring village of Opio) – and rather too many portraits of Picasso. At the top end of the village, the old wash house, **Le Lavoir**, on avenue J.C.-Mallet (March–Oct daily 11am–7pm; free), forms another exhibition space for the visual arts, its wide basin of water playing reflecting games with the images and the light, though if there's no exhibition on the building is locked. The **Espace Culturel & Musée Gottlob**, on place du Commandant-Lamy (Dec to Oct Mon–Fri 9am–5pm; weekends 11am–6pm; free), holds classy exhibitions of art and design, and the old village's winding lanes are thick with ateliers and small galleries.

Three kilometres southeast of Mougins, just off the D3 slip road and alongside the A8 autoroute to Nice, is a museum that will delight even those who don't share the passion for its subject, the **Musée de l'Automobiliste** (June-Sept daily 10am-6pm; Dec–May Tues–Sun 10am–1pm & 2–6pm; €7). No expense has been spared on this indulgent dedication to the motorcar and its two-wheeled relations. Sculptures made of shiny, tangled exhaust pipes line the pathway to the hangar-like exhibition space. Inside, the exhibits include glamorous vintage cars, such as a 1933 Hispano-Suiza; German army vehicles; record-breaking racing cars and a large collection of miniature motors. The museum shop sells reproductions of historic posters from the Monaco Grand Prix, car badges and models.

The frequent #600 **bus** service from Cannes to Grasse stops at Mougins. If money is no object you should **stay** at *Le Mas Candille* boulevard Clément-Rebuffel (℡04.92.28.43.43, Ⓦwww.lemascandille.com; ⑨), a deluxe spa amid olive groves and cypresses, where the tastefully decorated rooms start at around €300 a night, or at the *Moulin de Mougins* itself (℡04.93.75.78.24, Ⓦwww.moulindemougins.com; ⑨), where the simple but handsome rooms start at a more modest €140. For smaller budgets, there's *Les Liserons de Mougins*, 608 av St-Martin (℡04.93.75.50.31, Ⓦwww.hotel-liserons-mougins .com; ⑤), a pleasant two-star place with its own pool.

Mougins has some very fine **restaurants**, none of them cheap. If your budget doesn't stretch as far as the *Moulin de Mougins* (℡04.93.75.78.24; closed Mon; menus €48-170), you can try its pretty former cooking school, *L'Amandier*, place des Patriotes (℡04.93.90.00.91; lunch menu €25, otherwise from €34), though Alain Llorca has now established his own school in the village. The restaurant at *Le Mas Candille* (℡04.92.28.43.43; menus €75 and €105) also serves inventive modern Mediterranean cuisine. Place du Commandant-Lamy is home to a trio of less grand but still pleasant and dependable options: the congenial *Bistrot de Mougins* (℡04.93.75.78.34; lunch menu €19.85, other menus from €31.50), serving Provençal specialities; the *Brasserie de la Méditeranée* (℡04.93.90.03.47; menus from €24); and *Le Feu Follet* (℡04.93.90.15.78; menus from €25).

Mouans-Sartoux

Three kilometres northwest of Mougins, the village of **MOUANS-SARTOUX** lies to the north of the Cannes-Grasse highway (N85), the modern village straggling along the traffic-choked avenue de Cannes but the pretty, peaceful old quarter laid out on a neat grid system. The #600 **bus** between Cannes, Mougins and Grasse stops here.

The main focus for a visit to Mouans-Sartoux is the exquisite little v-shaped **château**, just north of the old village centre between chemin des Bastions and avenue de Grasse. Rebuilt to its medieval design in the nineteenth century, and chosen by the Socialist former minister for culture, Jack Lang, to be one of twenty provincial venues for modern and contemporary art, it opened in 1990 to house **L'Espace de l'Art Concret** (daily: July-Aug 11am–7pm; Sept–June Tues–Sun 11am–6pm; €3). The gallery concentrates on the rationalist form of art defined by Théo Van Doesburg as "concrete rather than abstract because nothing is more real than a line, a colour or a surface". Staff are keen and welcoming, so it's sad to note that the gallery is at times woefully under-visited. The striking lime green structure adjacent to the château opened in 2004 to house the **Donation Albers-Honegger** (same ticket and hours), which displays fine and applied arts by a diverse selection of artists and designers including Eileen Gray, Charles Eames, Joseph Beuys and Augusto Giacometti. Mouans-Sartoux also has a **Centre Culturel**, 27 allée des Cèdres (Mon–Thurs 9am–noon & 2–6pm), boasting one of the biggest collections of literature in the Provençal language, though you have to contact the **Mediathèque** (201 av de Cannes, ℡04.92.92.43.75; Tues 3-7pm, Wed 10am-6pm, Fri 2-6pm & Sat 10am-5pm) to gain access to it.

Vallauris

Pottery and Picasso are the attractions of **VALLAURIS**, an otherwise unremarkable town in the hills above Golfe-Juan, 6km east of Cannes. Vallauris's association with ceramics dates from Roman times, but it was in the early sixteenth century, after the Plague had decimated the population, that **pottery** became the major industry. The bishop of Grasse rebuilt the village from its infested ruins and settled Genoese potters to exploit the clay soil and the fuel from the surrounding forests, and the industry flourished. By the end of World War II, however, aluminium had become a much cheaper and easier material to use for pots and plates, and the pottery began rapidly to lose its popularity.

△ Pottery in Vallauris

It took the intervention of Picasso to reverse this decline. In 1946, while installed in the castle at Antibes, the artist met some of the town's few remaining potters, and was invited to Vallauris by the owner of a ceramics studio, Georges Ramié. Picasso got hooked on clay and spent the next two years working at Ramié's **Madoura workshop**. The result, apart from adding pages to the catalogue of the Picasso *oeuvre*, was a rekindling of the local industry. Today the main street, avenue Georges-Clemenceau, sells nothing but pottery, much of it garish and indifferent. The Madoura pottery is on avenue Suzanne-et-Georges-Ramié, to the left as you ascend avenue Georges-Clemenceau from the foot of the village, and still has sole rights on reproducing Picasso's designs, which are on sale, at a price, in its shop (Mon-Fri 10am-12.30pm & 3-6pm; closed Sat, Sun & November). Other classy commercial galleries include the **Sassi-Milici** at 65 bis, avenue Georges-Clemenceau (open daily: July-Aug 10.30am-7pm, rest of year 10.30am-1pm & 2-6.30pm)

A bronze **Man with a Sheep**, Picasso's gift to the town, stands in the main square, place Paul-Isnard, beside the church and castle. The municipality had some misgivings about the sculpture but decided that the possible affront to their conservative tastes was outweighed by the benefits to tourism of Picasso's international reputation. They needn't have worried; the statue looks quite simply like a shepherd boy and sheep.

The local authorities then offered Picasso the task of decorating the early medieval deconsecrated **chapel** in the castle courtyard (Mon & Wed–Sun: mid-June to mid-Sept 10am–12.15pm & 2–6pm; mid-Sept to mid-June 10am–12.15pm & 2–5pm; €3.20), which he finally did in 1952. The space is tiny and, with the painted panels covering the vault, has the architectural simplicity of an air-raid shelter. Picasso's subject is *War and Peace*. At first glance it's easy to be unimpressed (as many critics still are) – it looks mucky and slapdash with paint runs on the unyielding plywood surfaces. Stay a while, however, and the passion of this violently drawn pacifism slowly emerges. On the *War* panel a music score is trampled by hooves and about to be engulfed in flames; a fighter's lance tenuously holds the scales of justice and a shield bears the outline of a dove, while from a deathly chariot skeletons escape. *Peace* is represented by Pegasus; people dancing and suckling babies; trees bearing fruit; owls; books – and the freedom of the spirit to mix up images and concepts with innocent mischief.

The ticket for the chapel also gives admission to the **Musée de la Céramique/Musée Magnelli** (same hours) in the castle, which for some years has exhibited many of the ceramics Picasso made at the Madoura, in addition to several Pre-Columbian pieces and a collection of paintings by Alberto Magnelli.

Buses from Cannes and Golfe-Juan *gare SNCF* arrive at the rear of the castle. The **tourist office** and principal tourist car park is at the bottom of avenue Georges-Clemenceau on place du 8 mai 1945 (July & Aug daily 9am–7pm; Sept–June Mon-Sat 9am–12.15pm & 1.45–6pm; ☏04.93.63.82.58, Ⓦ www.vallauris-golfe-juan.fr). Vallauris's **restaurants** are neither remarkable nor especially cheap, but there's no shortage of snack stops along avenue Georges-Clemenceau.

Grasse and around

With its medieval heart, uninterrupted sea views, and hilly location amongst scented flowers, **GRASSE** has been capital of the **perfume industry** for over two hundred years, though these days suburbia sprouts with rather greater luxuriance than flowers on its fringes. Making perfume is usually presented as a mysterious process, an alchemy, turning the soul of the flower into a liquid of luxury and desire. The reality, including traditional methods of *macération* – mixing the blossoms with heated animal fat – and *enfleurage* – placing the flowers on cold fat, then washing the result with alcohol and finally distilling it into the ultimately refined essence – are far more vividly described in Patrick Süskind's novel *Perfume*, set in the city, than in the perfume factories in Grasse. Since the 1920s synthetic ingredients have been added to the perfumeries' repertoire, but locally grown jasmine and roses are still used, with the industry preferring to keep quiet about modern innovations and techniques.

Arrival, information and accommodation

Grasse's **gare routière** is to the north of the Vieille Ville at the Notre-Dames-des-Fleurs car park. Turning left out of the compound and heading downhill on avenue Thiers, you'll pass an annexe of the tourist office immediately on your right, where avenue Thiers becomes boulevard du Jeu de Ballon. Five minutes' walk further down, on cours Honoré-Cresp, is the old casino, now converted into

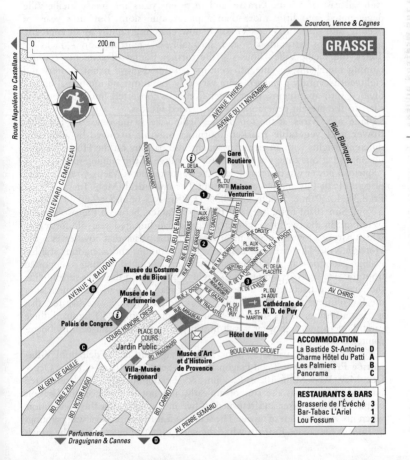

▲ Gourdon, Vence & Cagnes

GRASSE

0   200 m

N

Route Napoléon to Castellane

AVENUE THIERS
AVENUE DU 11 NOVEMBRE
BOULEVARD CLEMENCEAU
BOULEVARD CHARABOT
BD DU JEU DE BALLON
Riou Blanquet
BD GAMBETTA

Gare Routière (A)

(i) PL. DE LA FOUX

PL. DU PATTI
Maison Venturini (1)

PL. AUX AIRES
RUE DE L'ORATOIRE
RUE DU PEYROGOUS
RUE AMIRAL DE GRASSE
RUE DE FONTETTE

(2)
RUE R.M. JOURNET
RUE MOUGINS ROUQUIER
RUE DE LA POISSONNERIE
R. DE LA PLACETTE
RUE DROITE
PL. AUX HERBES
R. DE LA POVOST
PL. DE LA PLACETTE

Musée du Costume et du Bijou
RUE J. OSSOLA
RUE GAZAN
RUE TRACASTEL
R. HPITRE
R. DE LA FOISSONNERIE
(3)
R. DE L'EVÊCHÉ
PL. DU 24 AOUT

AV. CHIRIS

Musée de la Parfumerie
AVENUE Y. BAUDOIN (B)
RUE MIRABEAU
PL. DU PETIT PUY
PL. ST. MARTIN
Cathédrale de N. D. de Puy

(i)
Palais de Congrès (C)
COURS HONORE CRESP
PLACE DU COURS
Jardin Public
BD. FRAGONARD
Musée d'Art et d'Histoire de Provence
Hôtel de Ville
BOULEVARD CROUET

Villa-Musée Fragonard
AV. GEN. DE GAULLE
BD. EMILE ZOLA
BD. VICTOR HUGO
BD. CARNOT
AV. PIERRE SEMARD

Perfumeries,
Draguignan & Cannes ▼ (D)

ACCOMMODATION
La Bastide St-Antoine	**D**
Charme Hôtel du Patti	**A**
Les Palmiers	**B**
Panorama	**C**

RESTAURANTS & BARS
Brasserie de l'Évêché	**3**
Bar-Tabac L'Ariel	**1**
Lou Fossum	**2**

a Palais des Congrès and housing the main **tourist office** (July–Sept Mon–Sat 9am–7pm, Sun 9am–1pm & 2–6pm; Oct–June Mon–Sat 9am–12.30pm & 2–6pm; ☎04.93.36.66.66, ⓦwww.grasse-riviera.com).

Accommodation options in Grasse are relatively limited. Of the budget choices, perhaps the most appealing is *Les Palmiers*, 17 av Y-Baudoin (☎ & ⓕ04.93.36.07.24; ❹), a chambre d'hôte with good views of the surrounding countryside and down to the coast. Rather more central is the *Panorama* on place du Cours (☎04.93.36.80.80, ⓦwww.hotelpanorama-grasse.com; ❹; closed Jan), which offers rooms with a view and all mod cons. Even more comfortable, if less well located, is the *Charme Hôtel du Patti*, place du Patti (☎04.93.36.01.00, ⓦwww .hotelpatti.com; ❺), with pretty, Provençal-style rooms including three adapted for wheelchair users. If it's luxury in country-house surroundings you want, *La Bastide St-Antoine*, 48 av Henri-Dunant (☎04.93.70.94.94, ⓦwww.jacques-chibois.com; ❾), is the finest place in Grasse.

The Town

Even when Grasse was part of the aristocratic tourist boom of the late nineteenth century, the desirable addresses, Queen Victoria's among them, were all east of **Vieux Grasse**, and in recent years the pretty Vieille Ville degenerated into little more than a picturesque slum. But after years of peeling into oblivion, Vieux Grasse is now changing rapidly as an energetic programme of restoration – and, inevitably, of gentrification - kicks in. Today, the Vieille Ville's houses – the former homes of sixteenth-century tanning merchants, seventeenth-century perfumed-glove manufacturers and eighteenth-century *parfumiers* – are variously museums and municipal offices, divided into apartments, their street frontages converted into boutiques to cater to the present generation of well-heeled visitors.

Place aux Aires, at the top of the Vieille Ville, is the venue for the daily **flower and vegetable market** (mornings only). It is ringed by arcades of different heights with an elegant wrought-iron balcony on the Hôtel Isnard at no. 33, and at one time was the exclusive preserve of the tanning industry.

Spiritual power was concentrated at the opposite end of Vieux Grasse, around place du Petit-Puy and place du 24 Août. The **cathedral** (Mon–Tues & Thurs–Fri 8.30–11.30am & 3–6pm, Wed 9.30–11.30am & 3–6pm, Sat 9.30–11.30am & 3-7pm, Sun 10am–6pm; free) and **Bishop's Palace**, between the two squares, were built in the twelfth century, replacing a two-hundred-year-old fortress of which part of a tower remains, incorporated in the palace that now serves as the Hôtel de Ville. The cathedral, despite endless additions and alterations, still has its high gaunt nave in which the starkly unadorned ribbed vaulting is supported from the side walls. Its astonishing, weighty columns and the walls surrounding the altar were fractured in a fierce fire that blazed through the church after the Revolution, giving the masonry an incredible, organic, cave-like feel that is most arresting. In the south aisle hang various paintings, a Fragonard, three early Rubens and, best by far, a well-lit triptych by the sixteenth-century Niçois painter Louis Bréa.

You can see more works by Jean-Honoré Fragonard in the delightful **Villa-Musée Fragonard** at 23 bd Fragonard (June–Sept daily 10am–6.30pm; Oct & Dec–May Wed–Mon 10am–12.30pm & 2–5.30pm; €3). The celebrated Rococo painter was the son of an early and not very successful Grassois perfumed-glove maker and returned to live in this villa after the Revolution, when his work fell out of favour. The staircase features impressive wall paintings by his son Alexandre-Evariste, while the salon is graced by copies of the panels

There are around thirty-odd major **parfumeries** in and around Grasse, most of them producing the different essences-plus-formulas which are then sold to Dior, Lancôme, Estée Lauder and the like, who make up their own brand-name perfumes. To extract 1kg of essence of lavender takes 200kg of lavender; for 1kg of cabbage rose essence, over 3000kg of roses are needed. Perfume contains twenty percent essence (eau de toilette contains ten percent; eau de Cologne five or six percent) and the bottles are extremely small. The major cost to this multi-billion-pound business is marketing, with millions spent on advertising alone. The grand Parisian couturiers, whose clothes, on strictly cost-accounting grounds, serve simply to promote the perfume, go to inordinate lengths to sell their latest fragrance. As you might imagine, however, the rates paid to those who pick the raw materials, mostly in the Third World, are notoriously low.

A good place to get an overview, and a fairly close-up look at the production, is the **Parfumerie Fragonard** (Feb–Oct daily 9am–6pm; Nov–Jan Mon–Sat 9am–12.30pm & 2–6.30pm; free), which is spread over two venues, the **Usine Historique** in the centre of town at 20 bd Fragonard and the **Fabrique des Fleurs** 3km towards Cannes at Les Quatre Chemins. The first shows traditional methods of extracting essence and has a collection of antique cosmetics bottles and bejewelled flagons. The one outside town is more informative and at least admits to modernization of the processes. A map of the world shows the origins of all the various and strange ingredients: resins, roots, moss, beans, bark join civet (extract of a wild cat's genitals), ambergris (whale intestines), bits of beaver, and musk from Tibetan goats all help to produce the array of scents the "nose" – as the creator of the perfume's formula is known – has to play with. A professional "nose" (of whom there are less than fifty in the world) can recognize up to five or six thousand different scents.

Other parfumeries to tour include **Galimard** at 73 rte de Cannes (guided visits daily: summer 9am–6.30pm; winter 9am–noon & 2–6pm; free) and at 5 rte de Pégomas (two-hour workshops by appointment at 10am, 2pm & 4pm, €35; you create your own fragrance under the guidance of a master *parfumeur*; ☏04.93.09.20.00; otherwise winter 9am–12.30pm & 2–6pm, summer same hours daily, free), and **Molinard** at 60 bd Victor-Hugo (March–Sept daily Mon–Fri 9am–6pm, Oct–Feb Mon–Sat 9am–12.30pm & 2–6pm; free). All have shops and give frequent tours in French and English. Others that open to the public include **Salon des Parfums** (Z.I. des Bois de Grasse; summer daily 9am–7pm, rest of year Mon–Sat 9am–1pm & 2–6pm), **Guy Bouchera** (14 rue Marcel-Journet, July–Aug daily 9.30am–8pm, Sept–June daily 10am–7pm) and **Fleuron de Grasse** (190 rte de Pégomas; July–Aug Mon–Sat 8.30am–noon & 1.30–7pm; Sept–June Mon–Fri 8.30am–noon & 1.30–5pm).

depicting *Love's Progress in the Heart of a Young Girl*, which Jean-Honoré painted for Louis XV's mistress, Madame du Barry.

Another museum worth a quick visit is the **Musée d'Art et d'Histoire de Provence**, 2 rue Mirabeau (same hours and entrance fee as the Villa-Musée Fragonard), set in a luxurious town house commissioned by Mirabeau's sister for her social entertainment duties. As well as all the gorgeous fittings and the original eighteenth-century kitchen, the historical collection adds an eclectic touch. It includes wonderful eighteenth- to nineteenth-century faïence from Apt and Le Castellet, Mirabeau's death mask, a tin bidet, six prehistoric bronze leg bracelets; costumes, *santons* and oil presses. There is an opulent eighteenth-century Turkish bed, a collection of brutal, leaden-faced portraits of the seventeenth-century Provençal nobility, and a tremendous sunset painted by René Seyssaud a century ago, whose cracked surface augments the movement of a hazy evening sky near the Étang de Berre.

Just around the corner are another couple of museums: the small **Musée Provençal du Costume et du Bijou**, 2 rue Jean-Ossola (winter Mon–Sat 10am–1pm & 2–6pm; summer also open Sun; free), with displays of the region's traditional dress and jewellery, and the **Musée International de la Parfumerie**, 8 place du Cours (closed for reconstruction until 2008, usually same hours as villa-Musée Fragonard) whose exhibits are fascinating and fun, even if you're not an enthusiast of the perfume industry.

A more relaxed flower-smelling takes place at the **Jardin de la Villa de Noailles**, 59 av Guy-de-Maupassant (tours for groups and individuals can be arranged through Grasse tourist office ☎04.93.40.55.83), to the west of the town centre: take rue Jeanne-Jugan off avenue Général-de-Gaulle, then left down chemin Noailles, and left again. Camelias, magnolias and peonies are the star attractions here.

Eating and drinking

Grasse's best **restaurant** is *La Bastide St-Antoine*, at the hotel of the same name on the south side of the town (☎04.93.70.94.94; menus at €55, €140 & €180): its owner Jacques Chibois is a former Gault Millau chef of the year. Cheaper eating options include the simple *Brasserie de l'Évêché*, on the pretty place de l'Évêché below the cathedral (☎04.93.36.40.12), which serves decent midday menus from about €15 and which faces the square's fountains. Alternatively, *Lou Fassum*, 5 rue de Fabreries (☎04.93.42.99.69, closed Sun & Mon; menu €32) is a traditional Provençal restaurant serving specialities from the pays de Grasse. If you want to make your own picnic, the *Maison Venturini*, 1 rue Marcel-Journet (closed Sun & Mon), sells fabulous sweet *fougassettes*, flavoured with the Grasse speciality of orange blossom. The **bars** on place aux Aires offer the best opportunity for encounters with the locals; the *Bar-Tabac L'Ariel* is a good place to start.

Around Grasse

The countryside around Grasse is pleasant for a day or two's stay, especially if you have a car. To the north is the **Plateau de Calern**, almost deserted save for the British archeologists who arrive every September to map the changing patterns of land use and ownership by the commune of **Cipières**. Running northwest is the **Route Napoléon**, and to the northeast the gorges of the **Loup River** pass the cliff-hanging stronghold of **Gourdon** and **Le-Bar-sur-Loup**'s reminders of mortality. To the west, towards the Upper Var, there are good dinners to be had at **Cabris** and musical caves to witness at **St-Cézaire**.

Cabris

CABRIS, just 6km southwest of Grasse, has all the trappings of a picture-postcard village: a ruined château providing panoramas from the Lac de St-Cassien to the Îles de Lérins, sometimes even Corsica, arty residents who decamped here from Grasse, and no shortage of *immobiliers* trading on fat local property prices. If you want to **stay**, the *Auberge du Vieux Château* on place Mirabeau (☎04.93.60.50.12; ⓦwww.aubergeduvieuxchateau.com; ❹) is the best bet, with wonderful views. The warm and welcoming *Le Petit Prince* **restaurant** at 15 rue Frédéric-Mistral (☎04.93.60.63.14; closed Tues & Wed out of season, Wed only in July-August), overlooking the park lined with chestnut trees, is a treat, with menus at €22, €25 and €31. The delicacies include a *parmentier* of *boudin noir* with apples and a cider sauce.

The Grottes des Audides and Grottes de St-Cézaire

Three kilometres northwest of Cabris, on the road to St-Vallier, are the **Grottes des Audides** (July-Aug daily except Mon am 11am-6pm; rest of year groups on request; ℡04.93.42.64.15; €5), former neolithic dwellings. You descend 60m into the caves, to see scenes of prehistoric life that have been re-created using stone tools and implements found in the caves.

A further set of caves, the **Grottes de St-Cézaire** (Jan & Nov Sun 2.30-5pm, Feb, March & Oct daily 2.30-5pm, April & May 2.30-5.30pm, June & Sept 10.30am-noon & 2-6pm, July-Aug 10.30am-6.30pm; €6) can be found just outside St-Cézaire-sur-Siagne (signed off the road from Cabris). The visit to the caves doesn't involve a deep descent, and visually it is no great treat. What *is* special is the aural experience of the stalagmites and stalactites with the most iron in them; the guide plays them like a xylophone, with an eerie resonance in this most irregular of acoustic chambers.

Heading west from Grasse towards Draguignan along the D562, there's a great **lunch** stop, *Chez Arlette* (℡04.93.66.10.36; closed Tues), about ten kilometres out of town, where the €23 menu is an enormous feast in the best French tradition, served with a minimum of pomp but with considerable respect and designed to be eaten leisurely over a couple of hours.

The Route Napoléon: St-Vallier-de-Thiey

The road north from Grasse is the **Route Napoléon**, the path taken by the emperor in March 1815 after his escape from Elba, in pursuit of the most audacious recapture of power in French history. In typically French fashion the road was built in the 1930s specifically to commemorate their greatest leader's journey.

The route doesn't follow the imperial boot tracks precisely, going miles off course in some places, but it serves a useful purpose. After several kilometres of zigzagging bends you get fantastic views back to Grasse, its basin and the coast. The first village you come to is **ST-VALLIER-DE-THIEY**, 12km from Grasse, with some prehistoric dolmens and tumuli: the **tourist office** on place du Tour (March–Oct Mon–Sat 9am–noon & 3–6pm; Nov–Feb 9am–noon & 3–5pm; ℡04.93.42.78.00, Ⓦsaintvallier.ifrance.com) can provide a walking map of how to get to the prehistoric sites. The place to **stay** is *Le Préjoly* at place Rougière at the entrance to the village (℡04.93.60.03.20, Ⓕ04.93.42.67.80; ❸; closed Jan), which is gradually undergoing refurbishment under new ownership. The restaurant of the same name at the front of the building (℡04.93.42.60.86, menus €16.50 & €21, closed Sun eve, Tues eve & Wed out of season) is under different ownership. There's also a **campsite** in the vicinity, the three-star *Parc des Arboins* on the Route Napoléon, (℡04.93.42.63.89, Ⓕ04.93.09.61.54).

Beyond St-Vallier, the Route Napoléon heads, almost uninterrupted by settlements, towards Castellane (see pp.257–258). Wayside stalls sell honey and perfume; each little hamlet has a petrol station and hotel-restaurant, and every so often you see a commemorative plaque carved with Napoléon's winged eagle.

Along the Gorges de Loup

The main southern approach to the Gorges de Loup is via **LE-BAR-SUR-LOUP**, 10km from Grasse. The little **Église de St-Jacques** contains an altarpiece attributed to the Niçois painter, Louis Bréa, and a fifteenth-century *Danse Macabre* painted on a wooden panel at the west end of the nave. The latter is a tiny but detailed illustration of courtly dancers being picked off by Death's arrows, their souls gathered up by devils, failing Saint Michael's test of blessedness and being thrown into the teethed and tongued mouth of hell. Alongside is a poem, in Provençal, warning of mortality and of the heavy risk involved in committing sins as grievous as dancing.

From here, you can follow the **gorges road**, through dark, narrow twists of rock beneath cliffs that look as if they might tumble at any minute, through the sounds of furiously churning water, to corners that appear to have no way out. Alternatively, you could miss out Le-Bar-sur-Loup and take the D3 from **Châteauneuf-Grasse** up along the northern balcony of the gorges to Gourdon.

Gourdon

Tiny **GOURDON** teeters on the edge of the Gorges de Loup, and the view from place Victoria at the top is as extraordinary as any in the Pays de Grasse. Unfortunately, you have to run the gauntlet of this *village perché*'s many souvenir shops to get there.

The village's **château**, to the right of the main street as you walk up from the car park (June–Sept daily 11am–1pm & 2–7pm; Oct–May Mon & Wed–Sun 2–6pm; €4), is an immaculately restored private residence containing a historical museum and a **museum of decorative arts and modernity** (guided tours only: July-Aug noon-3pm & 5-6pm, Sept-June by appointment; €10). The first houses a self-portrait by Rembrandt (not always on show), a glowing *Descent from the Cross* by Rubens and other religious paintings of the early sixteenth century, as well as Saracen helmets made in Damascus, a writing desk used by Marie-Antoinette and letters signed by Henri IV. Highlights of the latter include a complete Art Deco ensemble by Eileen Gray. It's also possible to visit the gardens (groups only by appointment; ☏04.93.09.68.02; €4). The best **place to eat** in Gourdon is *Le Nid d'Aigle*, place Victoria (☏04.93.77.52.02; closed Sun eve & Mon), at the top of the village and with breathtaking views. It has a reasonable brasserie menu (lunch €19, otherwise around €35).

Antibes, Cap d'Antibes and Juan-les-Pins

Graham Greene, who lived in **Antibes** for more than twenty years, considered it the only place on this stretch of coast to have preserved its soul. And it is true that whilst Antibes and its twin, **Juan-les-Pins**, have not completely escaped the overdevelopment that blights much of this region, they have avoided the worst excesses suffered by some of their immediate neighbours. Antibes itself is a pleasing old town, with animated streets full of bars and restaurants, lots of Anglophones and yachting types and one of the finest **markets** along the coast. Its castle has a superb **Picasso collection**, and the views from the town's ramparts towards the Alps are wonderful. **Cap d'Antibes** is dominated by the world's super-rich, many of whom live, or at least maintain homes, here, though the southern cap still retains its pinewoods to hide the exclusive mansions. There's intermittent access to the wonderful rocky shore here, as well as a couple of beautiful gardens to visit, the **Jardin Thuret** and the **Villa Eilenroc**. Though perhaps not as glamorous as it once was, Juan-les-Pins is one of the region's more appealing beach resorts, with intriguing reminders of its former Art Deco glory, plenty of nightlife and a renowned **jazz festival**.

Antibes

Very little remains of the medieval centre of **ANTIBES**, thanks to border squabbles from the fifteenth century until the Revolution, when Antibes belonged to France and Nice to Savoy. Today, luxury yachts and humble fishing boats shelter in the harbour, beneath the splendidly situated **Fort Carré** (mid-June to mid-Sept Tues–Sun 10am–6pm; mid-Sept to mid-June 10.15am–4.30pm; €3), transformed in the seventeenth century by Vauban into an impregnable fortress. Solid ramparts separate the port from the Vieille Ville, whose twin points of focus are the medieval **Château Grimaldi** and the belfry of the former **cathedral** rising above the sea wall.

Arrival, information and orientation

The Vieille Ville fits into a triangle formed by the coast, the port and the main railway line, with Antibes' **gare SNCF** at the apex. From the station, turn right

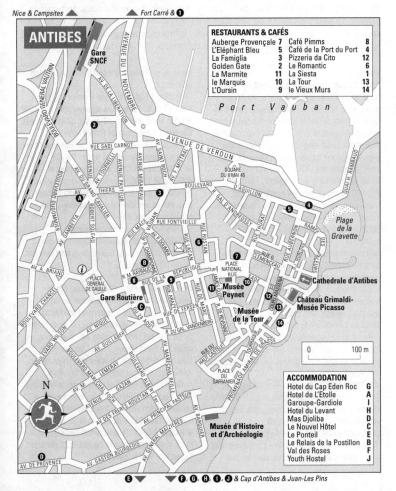

Nice & Campsites ▲   ▲ Fort Carré & ❶

ANTIBES

Gare SNCF

Port   Vauban

RESTAURANTS & CAFÉS

Auberge Provençale	7	Café Pimms	8
L'Éléphant Bleu	5	Café de la Port du Port	4
La Famiglia	3	Pizzeria da Cito	12
Golden Gate	2	Le Romantic	6
La Marmite	11	La Siesta	1
le Marquis	10	La Tour	13
L'Oursin	9	le Vieux Murs	14

AVENUE DE VERDUN

SQUARE DU 8 MAI 45

BOULEVARD   D'AGUILLON

Plage de la Gravette

RUE SADI CARNOT

RUE FONTVIEILLE

PLACE NATIONAL RUE

Cathedrale d'Antibes

Musée Peynet

Château Grimaldi- Musée Picasso

Gare Routière

Musée de la Tour

PLACE GENERAL DE GAULLE

PLACE DU SAFRANIER

0   100 m

N

Musée d'Histoire et d'Archéologie

ACCOMMODATION

Hotel du Cap Eden Roc	G
Hotel de L'Etolle	A
Garoupe-Gardiole	I
Hotel du Levant	H
Mas Djoliba	D
Le Nouvel Hôtel	C
Le Ponteil	E
Le Relais de la Postillon	B
Val des Roses	F
Youth Hostel	J

❺ ▼   ▼ ❻, ❼, ❽, ❾, ❿ & Cap d'Antibes & Juan-Les Pins

and it's a short walk along avenue R–Soleau to place du Général-de-Gaulle and the **tourist office**, at no. 11 (July–Aug daily 9am–7pm; Sept–June Mon–Fri 9am–12.30pm & 1.30–6pm, Sat 9am–noon & 2–6pm; ☏04.97.23.11.11; Ⓦwww.antibesjuanlespins.com). The **gare routière** is east of here on place Guynemer with frequent buses to and from the *gare SNCF*. Bus #2 goes to Cap d'Antibes; bus #3 to Juan-les-Pins, and #10 to Biot. **Bikes** can be hired from Midi Location Service, Galerie du Port, rue Lacan (☏04.93.34.48.00), and Holiday Bikes, 122 bd Wilson in Juan les Pins(☏04.93.61.51.51).

From the *gare routière*, rue de la République leads into the heart of Vieux Antibes around **place Nationale**, which in turn is linked by rue Sade to the **cours Masséna**, the limit of the original Greek settlement and the daily **market place**. The castle and cathedral stand between cours Masséna and the sea.

Accommodation

Though really cheap **hotels** are thin on the ground, there's no shortage of moderately priced two and three star accommodation in Antibes, and there's a **youth hostel** on the Cap. Booking in advance for the summer is recommended. Antibes' **campsites** are a few kilometres north of the city in the quartier de la Brague (bus #10 or one train stop to Gare de Biot).

Hotels

Hôtel du Cap Eden Roc bd Kennedy
☏04.93.61.39.01, Ⓦwww.edenroc-hotel.fr. A celebrity haunt since F. Scott Fitzgerald used it as the setting for *Tender is the Night*, this luxury hotel has a prime position in 25 acres on Cap d'Antibes. With all the usual comforts you'd expect at this price, it even has its own landing stage. Closed mid-Oct to mid-April. ❾

Hôtel de L'Étoile 2 av Gambetta
☏04.93.34.26.30, Ⓦwww.hoteletoile.com. Good-value, comfortable if slightly characterless modern two-star hotel between the *gare SNCF* and town centre, with a/c and WiFi access. ❹

Hôtel Garoupe-Gardiole 60–74 chemin de la Garoupe ☏04.92.93.33.33, Ⓦwww.hotel-lagaroupe-gardiole.com. Lovely location on a lane in Cap d'Antibes; friendly, quiet and with a terrace overlooking the garden on which to dine. Closed mid-Oct to March. ❻

Hôtel du Levant bd de la Garoupe
☏04.92.93.72.99, Ⓕ04.92.93.72.60. On Cap d'Antibes, backed by woods and overlooking the sea, with parking and a garden. Closed mid-Sept to mid-May. ❾

Mas Djoliba 29 av de Provence ☏04.93.34.02.48, Ⓦwww.hotel-djoliba.com. Between the Vieille Ville and the main beach, with a large garden and pool; very pleasant. Closed Nov–Jan. ❼

Le Nouvel Hôtel 1 av du 24 Août
☏04.93.34.44.07, Ⓕ04.93.34.44.08. Right next to the *gare routière* and nothing special, but

about as cheap as you'll find in Antibes in high season. ❹

Le Ponteil 11 impasse Jean-Mensier
☏04.93.34.67.92, Ⓦwww.leponteil.com. In a quiet location at the end of a cul-de-sac close to the sea, this pretty, small Logis de France hotel is surrounded by luxuriant vegetation. Half board only in high season. Closed mid-Nov to Jan. ❼

Le Relais du Postillon 8 rue Championnet
☏04.93.34.20.77, Ⓦwww.relaisdupostillon.com. Centrally located and gay-friendly, with comfortable, individually decorated rooms above a high-quality restaurant. ❹

Val des Roses 6 chemin des Lauriers
☏06.85.06.06.29, Ⓦwww.val-des-roses.com. Stylish chambre d'hôte tucked away on a lane just off the plage de la Salis. ❾

Hostel and campsites

Caravelle 60 Relais International de la Jeunesse 272 bd de la Garoupe, Cap d'Antibes ☏04.93.61.34.40, Ⓦwww.clasjud.fr. Youth hostel by the sea that needs booking well in advance; meals are taken outdoors under the pine trees. Take bus #2 from *gare routière* stop "Auberge de Jeunesse". €15 per night. Closed Oct–April.

Antipolis au du Pylone Ⓦwww.camping-antipolis.com. Four-star campsite, 800m from the sea. €28 per tent in high season. Closed Oct–March.

Les Embruns 63 rte de Biot ☏04.93.33.33.35, Ⓕ04.93.74.46.70. Three-star site just north of Biot's station; and close to the sea. €22 per tent. Closed late Sept to early May.

The Town

The most atmospheric approach to the castle and cathedral is from the south through the **quartier du Safranier**. Place du Safranier and the little residential streets hereabouts, including rue de Lavoir with its old public **wash house**, have an appealing villagey atmosphere. By turning right on rue de l'Orme – rather than continuing straight into cours Masséna, then left into rue du Bateau, you'll find yourself on place Marie-Jol, in front of the **Château Grimaldi**.

Rebuilt in the sixteenth century but still with its twelfth-century Romanesque tower, the château served briefly as Picasso's studio in 1946, and is now home to the **Musée Picasso** (check with tourist office for further information). Picasso spent several extremely prolific months in the château before moving to Vallauris, and leaving all his Antibes output to the museum. Although he donated other works later on, the bulk of the collection belongs to this one period. At this time, he was involved in one of his better relationships; his friend Matisse was just up the road in Vence; the war was over; and the 1950s had not yet arrived to change the Côte d'Azur for ever. There's an uncomplicated exuberance in the numerous still lifes of sea urchins, the goats and fauns in Cubist non-disguise, and the wonderful *Ulysses and the Sirens*, a great round head against a mast around which the ship, sea and sirens swirl. The materials reveal postwar shortages – odd bits of wood and board instead of canvas, and boat paint rather than oils. Picasso is also the subject here of other painters and photographers, including André Villers, Brassai, Man Ray and Bill Brandt. The photo of him holding a sunshade for Françoise Gilot catches the happiness of this period in the artist's life.

By contrast, on the second floor, in Picasso's old studio, are displayed the anguished works of Nicolas de Staël, who eventually killed himself. He stayed in Antibes for a few months from 1954 to 1955, painting the sea, gulls and boats with great washes of grey. A disturbing red dominates *The Grand Concert* and purple the *Still Life with Candlestick*. Works by other great twentieth-century artists are included in the museum's **modern art** collection, including several by German artist Hans Hartung. The wonderful terrace overlooking the sea is adorned by Germaine Richier sculptures along with works by Miró, César and others, and a violin homage to Picasso by Arman.

Alongside the castle is the **cathedral**, built on the site of an ancient temple. The choir and apse survive from the Romanesque building that served the city in the Middle Ages, while the nave and stunning ochre facade are Baroque. Inside, in the south transept, is a sumptuous altarpiece by Louis Bréa surrounded by immaculate panels of tiny detailed scenes.

One block inland, on cours Masséna, the **covered market** (June–Aug daily 6am–1pm; Sept–May Tues–Sun 6am–1pm) overflows with Provençal goodies including delicious olives, and a profusion of cut **flowers**, the traditional and still flourishing Antibes business. In the afternoons, a **craft market** (Easter–Sept Thurs–Sun; Oct–Easter Thurs–Sat) takes over from about 3pm (4.30pm on Sat), and when the stalls pack up, café tables take their place.

As well as the Picasso museum, there's a trio of further museums that may take your fancy. The one on local history, the **Musée de la Tour** (Wed & Fri–Sun 2–6pm; €3) in a medieval tower at the southern end of cours Masséna, is not wildly interesting, but it does house the world's first ever water-skis, invented locally in the 1930s. Further south, on the ramparts along parade Amiral-de-Grasse, the Bastion St-André houses the **Musée d'Histoire et d'Archéologie** (Tues–Sun 10am–noon & 2–6pm; €3), which gathers together the Greek, Roman, medieval and later finds of the region. The **Musée Peynet** on place

Nationale (Tues–Sun: mid-June to mid-Sept 10am–6pm; mid-Sept to mid-June 10am–noon & 2–6pm; €3) pays homage to the Antibes cartoonist whose most famous creation was the 1940s series of *The Lovers*, a truly old-fashioned conception of romance which, if you're not careful, may even induce nostalgia. North of Vieille Antibes at 4 av Tournelli, the **Musée de la Carte Postale** (Tues-Sun 2-6pm, €3.50) has a permanent collection of hundreds of postcards from all eras and countries, charting the history of the postcard with particular reference to the 'golden age' of 1900-1914.

Eating and drinking

You're unlikely to go hungry in Antibes, with places to eat at every turn: Place Nationale and cours Masséna are lined with **cafés**; rue James-Close has nothing but **restaurants**, and rue Thuret and its side streets also offer numerous menus to browse through. Places to **drink** are especially thick on the ground by the port.

Auberge Provencale 61 place Nationale ☎04.93.34.13.24. Carpaccio of *salmon au pistou*, lamb chops with onion-and-pepper compote and the like, served in an attractive covered garden. €19.50 lunch menu, otherwise from €34.50.

Restaurant de Bacon bd de Bacon, Cap d'Antibes ☎04.93.61.50.02. One of the coast's best fish restaurants, overlooking Vieux Antibes and serving fabulous fish soups and stews, including a superb bouillabaisse. Lunch menu €49, dinner €79. Closed Mon, Tues lunch & Nov–Jan.

L'Eléphant Bleu 28 bd de l'Aguillon ☎04.93.34.28.80. Reasonably authentic Chinese, Thai and Vietnamese specialities, plus good vegetarian dishes and sushi, in smart surroundings on the port. Menus at €19 & €21; veggie menu €16.

La Famiglia 34 av Thiers ☎04.93.34.60.82. A cheap, family-run outfit serving good pasta and pizzas from €8 and pasta, with lunchtime *plats* from around €11. Closed all day Wed, Sat & Sun lunch.

La Marmite 20 rue James-Close ☎04.93.34.56.79. One of the best restaurants along this street, with *cassoulet de moules* or *terrine de poisson* on the €25 fish menu, plus cheaper menus at €13.50 and €19.50. Closed Mon.

Le Marquis 4 rue Sade ☎04.93.34.23.00. Inventive Provençal food – such as crayfish salad with foie gras shavings, filet mignon of pork with honey sauce - in a charming setting.

L'Oursin 16 rue de la République ☎04.93.34.13.46. Superb fish and traditional seafood, with menus starting at €24.

Café Pimms corner of rue de la République and place Guynemer. Brasserie with carousel decor and a friendly atmosphere.

Pizzeria da Cito in the covered market, at 23 cours Masséna. Café with a wide selection of beers; *moules* for around €12.50. Open daily.

Café de la Porte du Port rue Aubernon by the archway through the ramparts. One of many lively cafés in the rampart arcades.

Le Romantic 5 rue Rostan ☎04.93.34.59.39. Charming, small restaurant with the likes of langoustine ravioli and *pot au feu* of monkfish or veal in cider on €22 and €28 menus. Closed Mon & Tues lunch.

Les Vieux Murs near the castle at av Amiral-de-Grasse ☎04.93.34.06.73. In a perfect setting on the ramparts, this restaurant serves very classy food, such as king crab with niçois ratatouille or scallops with orange butter. Lunch menu €29, otherwise €42 or €60. Closed Mon lunch in season, all day Mon out of season.

Nightlife

Many **cafés** and **bars** stay open late, with boulevard Aguillon next to the port being the liveliest spot for a drink. Antibes' most popular **nightclub** is the refurbished *La Siesta*, on the route du Bord-de-la-Mer, between Antibes and La Brague, with gaming rooms, a disco, restaurant and bar. Serious dancers, however, will have more choice in neighbouring Juan-les-Pins (see p.390). Antibes has a couple of decent **jazz** clubs – *La Tour International*, 6 cours Massena, Vieille Antibes, and *Bar en Biais*, 600 1iere av, Nova Antipolis – and one **gay club**, the *Golden Gate* at 4 rue Honoré-Ferrare.

Cap d'Antibes

The sandy **Plage de la Salis**, Antibes' longest beach, runs along the eastern neck of **Cap d'Antibes** and is a rarity along the Riviera – access to it is free, with no big hotels blocking the way. The success of Juan-les-Pins spared this side of the Cap from unchecked development in the days before planning laws were tightened. Above the southern end of the beach, at the top of chemin du Calvaire, stands the **Chapelle de la Garoupe** (daily 10am–noon & 2.30–7pm), full of ex-votos for deliverances from accidents, ranging from battles with the Saracens to collisions with speeding Citroëns. It also contains a medieval Russian icon and a painting on silk, both spoils from the Crimean War. Much the best reason to make the trail up here, however, is for the stunning panoramic views across Cap d'Antibes towards both Juan-les-Pins and Antibes; the views

△ Beach on Cap d'Antibes

extend as far as the Esterel and to Nice and beyond. Next to the church is a powerful lighthouse whose beam is visible 70km out to sea.

A second public beach, **Plage de la Garoupe**, stretches along boulevard de la Garoupe before the promontory of Cap Gros. From here a footpath follows the shore to join the chemin des Douaniers. At the southern end of the Cap d'Antibes, on avenue Mrs L.D.-Beaumont, stands the grandiose **Villa Eilenroc** (gardens Tues & Wed 9am–5pm; free; villa out of season Wed 9am–noon & 1.30–5pm, closed in summer; free), designed by Charles Garnier, architect of the casino at Monte Carlo, and surrounded by 28 acres of lush gardens. Its equally magnificent neighbour, the Château de la Croé, was the home, after the 1936 abdication crisis, of the Duke and Duchess of Windsor.

Much of the southern tip of the Cap d'Antibes is a warren of private roads with no entry signs barring all but residents, and if you want to see the fabled "bay of millionaires", east of **Point de l'Ilette**, it's simpler to take a **boat trip** from Juan-les-Pins (departures hourly in summer from Ponton Courbet; Ⓦwww.visiobulle.com; €12). West of the *Hôtel du Cap Eden Roc*, however, the shore is accessible once again at the Batterie du Graillon, where you'll find the **Musée Napoléonien** (Tues–Sat: mid-June to mid–Sept 10am–6pm, mid-Sept to mid-June 10am-4.30pm; €3), which documents the general's return from Elba (see p.468) with the usual paraphernalia of hats, cockades, model ships and signed commands. There are lovely views from the slightly grubby public beach adjacent to the fort. From here walking or cycling up the western side of the Cap is very pleasant; you pass the tiny **Port de l'Olivette** full of small, unflashy boats, as well as rocks, jetties, tiny sandy beaches, and grand villas hiding behind high walls.

Dominating the middle of the Cap, on boulevard du Cap between chemins du Tamisier and G-Raymond, is the **Jardin Thuret** (Mon-Fri: Summer 8am-6pm, winter 8.30am-5.30pm; free; groups by appointment; €1.50 per person; ☏04.97.21.25.00) established in the mid-nineteenth century by a botanist, Gustav Thuret. It now belongs to INRA, a national research institute which tests out and acclimatizes subtropical trees and shrubs in order to diversify the Mediterranean plants of France. You can wander freely around the gardens, and are sure to be surprised by some of the species of trees and shrubs that grow here.

Juan-les-Pins

JUAN-LES-PINS, just 1.5km west of Antibes, is another of those luminous Côte d'Azur names. It had its heyday in the interwar years, when the summer season on the Riviera first took off and the resort was the haunt of film stars like Charlie Chaplin, Maurice Chevalier and Lilian Harvey, the polyglot London-born 1930s musical star who lingered here until 1968, long after her fame had faded. Juan-les-Pins isn't as glamorous as it once was either, though it still has a casino and a certain cachet, the beaches are sand, and there are haunting reminders of its glory days to enjoy. These days it's known above all for its annual jazz festival, **Jazz à Juan**.

Arrival, information and accommodation

Walking from the **gare SNCF** on avenue de l'Esterel down avenue Dr-Fabre and rue des Postes you reach the carrefour de la Nouvelle Orléans, beyond which is La Pinède; by bus from Antibes the most central stops are "Pin Doré" and "Rond Point Joffre". The **tourist office** is at 51 bd Guillaumont on the seafront at the western end of the town (July & Aug daily 9am–7pm; Sept–June Mon–Fri 9am–noon & 2–6pm, Sat 9am–noon; ☏04.97.23.11.10).

Most of the town's **hotels** are clustered around avenue Gallet, between avenue de l'Esterel and the seafront, and avenue Alexandre III which crosses it. *Hôtel de la Pinède*, 7 av Georges-Gallice (☏04.93.61.03.95; ❹), has some cheap rooms and is right in the centre, while the *Parisiana*, 16 av de l'Esterel (☏04.93.61.27.03, ⓔhotelparisiana@orange.fr; ❹), is close to the station. For something more luxurious, try the peaceful *Pré-Catelan* in attractive gardens on the corner of avenue des Palmiers and avenue des Lauriers (☏04.93.61.05.11, ⓦwww.hotel-precatelan-antibes-juan-pins.cote.azur.fr; ❾); or the gorgeous Art Deco *Belles Rives*, 33 bd Edouard-Baudoin (☏04.93.61.02.79, ⓦwww.bellesrives.com; ❾), which preserves an aura of 1930s glamour better than anywhere else in Juan-les-Pins, and where even the cheapest rooms start at €240 in high season.

The Town

Unlike St-Tropez, Juan-les-Pins was never a fishing village, just a pine grove by the sea, and although its casino was built in 1908, it wasn't until the late 1920s that it really took off as the original summer resort of the Côte d'Azur. In the 1930s, revealing swimsuits were reputedly first worn here and water-skiing was invented. Juan-les-Pins' trail-blazing style continued to attract aristocrats, royals, writers, dancers and screen stars throughout the 1950s and 1960s. Today, the eerily beautiful Art Deco bulk of the derelict **Hotel Provençal** looms over Juan from the eastern side of boulevard Baudoin like a standing rebuke. Reputedly one of the largest ruined hotels in the world, it was built by the American railroad magnate, Frank Jay Gould, who was also responsible for the Palais de la Méditerranée in Nice, and it is still the most impressive thing in the town. It's slated for conversion into apartments, though as it closed in 1976 it wouldn't seem anyone is in too much of a hurry. Gould's own home, the 1912 **Villa Vigie**, stands behind high walls across the road from the hotel. Compared with this, the modern *Meridien* hotel and casino is merely a blandly oversized blot on the seafront. Nevertheless, as a **beach** resort Juan has more appeal than many, with 2km of sheltered sand, much of it almost entirely obscured by the many private beach and restaurant concessions, and half a dozen waterskiing outfits if you fancy emulating those 1930s pioneers. The ancient, beautiful pine grove, **Jardin de La Pinède** (known simply as La Pinède), plays host to the region's best **jazz festival** and boasts a Hollywood-style **celebrity walk** with the handprints of Sydney Bechet, B.B. King, Stéphane Grappelli, Dave Sanborn and others. At the western end of the seafront at 1 bd Charles-Guillaumont stands another wonderful, peeling remnant from Juan's heyday, the **Villa El Djezair**, built in exuberant neo-moorish style by the Antibes architect Ernest Truch in 1922 and complete with minaret, cupolas and domes.

Eating and drinking

La Passagère at the *Hôtel Belles Rives* (☏04.93.61.02.79) serves up modern Mediterranean delights in lovely, restored Art Deco surroundings, with menus at €45 for lunch, and €95 at other times. The terrace has wonderful views over the bay. That apart, Juan-les-Pins is not blessed with particularly memorable **restaurants**, so take pot luck from the countless menus on offer on the boulevards around La Pinède. *Le Café de la Plage*, at 1 bd Edouard-Baudouin (☏04.93.61.37.61; lunchtime *plats* €12), is a good bet, serving seafood, cocktails and ice cream in a pleasant seafront spot, while *Helios Plage*, promenade du Soleil (☏04.93.61.85.77, open mid-April to end Sept) is about the smartest of the beach concessions, with *plats* from around €22. Similar, but a little more affordable, is *Le Colombier* (promenade du Soleil, ☏04.93.61.24.66, open March-Oct) with *plats du jour* around €15. Many restaurants in Juan-les-Pins stay open until midnight.

The Côte d'Azur Festival International de Jazz

The best jazz event on the Côte d'Azur, the **Festival International de Jazz** (known simply as Jazz à Juan), takes place during the **last two weeks of July** in the open air. The main venue is La Pinède Gould, just above the beach by the casino.

The festival attracts performers of the calibre of Joe Cocker, Keith Jarrett, Wynton Marsalis, and Didier Lockwood. The music is always chosen with serious concern for every kind of jazz, both contemporary and traditional, rather than commercial popularity. Programme details and **tickets** are available from the tourist offices in Antibes and Juan-les-Pins, and tickets can also be bought from FNAC and Virgin shops.

Nightlife

Juan-les-Pins still cuts a dash in the nightlife stakes. The fads and reputations of the different **discos** may change, but in general opening hours are midnight to dawn, and you can count on searching appraisal of your attire and on paying around €16 for entrance plus your first drink. Some of the current hotspots include *Whisky a Gogo*, on rue Jacques Leonetti, *Le Milk* on avenue G-Gallice and *Minimal* on avenue Guy-de-Maupassant. The perennially popular **live music** venue *Le Pam-Pam*, 137 bd Wilson, often has Brazilian bands, but you'll need to go early to get a seat.

Biot and Sophia-Antipolis

Twenty years ago, the area inland from Antibes above the autoroute was still the more or less untouched Forêt de la Brague, stretching from Mougins in the west to Biot in the east. Now transnational companies have offices and laboratories linked by wide roads cut through the forest, notably at **Sophia-Antipolis**, a futuristic science park. Nearby **Biot**, meanwhile, has become one of the most visited places on the Côte for its glassworks and the Fernand Léger museum.

Biot

Although the *village perché* of **BIOT**, above the coast 8km north of Antibes, is pretty enough, the real draw is its rich arts and crafts tradition. Formerly a centre of pottery production and now home to several glassworks, the village has long been a magnet for artists and craftspeople. Inevitably, Biot is nowadays packed out in high season, and equally inevitably not everything on sale necessarily rises above the level of tourist tat – some of the 'fine' art is anything but. Even so, Biot remains a rewarding place to visit, and it's not to be missed if you can help it.

Arrival, information and accommodation

Biot's **gare SNCF** is actually 4km from the village, by the sea at La Brague. It's not a very pleasant walk along a dangerous road to the village, so you're better off catching one of the Antibes buses (Mon–Sat every 20–30min; Sun around 8 buses). From the bus stop in the village head up chemin Neuf, and rue St-Sébastien, the main street, runs off to your right. The **tourist office** (July–Aug Mon–Fri 10am–7pm, Sat & Sun 2.30–7pm; Sept–June Mon–Fri 9am–noon &

The Route Napoléon

The pines and silver sand between Juan-les-Pins and Cannes, now **Golfe-Juan**, witnessed Napoléon's famous return from exile in 1815. The emperor knew the bay well, having been in command of the Mediterranean defences as a general in 1794 with Antibes' Fort Carré as his base. This time, however, his emissaries to Cannes and Antibes were taken prisoner upon landing, though the local men in charge decided not to capture him. The lack of enthusiasm for his return was enough to persuade the ever-brilliant tactician to head north, bypassing Grasse, and take the most isolated snowbound mule paths up to Sisteron and onwards – the path commemorated by the modern **Route Napoléon**. By March 6 he was in Dauphiné. On March 19 he was back in the Tuileries Palace in the capital. One hundred days later he lost the battle of Waterloo and was finally and absolutely incarcerated on St Helena.

An anecdote relates that on the day of landing at Golfe-Juan, Napoléon's men accidentally held up the prince of Monaco's coach travelling east along the coast. The Revolution incorporated Monaco into France but the restored Louis XVIII had just granted back the principality. When the prince told the former emperor that he was off to reclaim his throne, Napoléon replied that they were in the same business and waved him on his way.

For **other sections of the Route Napoléon**, see 'Grasse' on p.383, 'Sisteron' on p.215, and 'Castellane' on p.258.

2–6pm, Sat & Sun 2–6pm; ⊤04.93.65.78.00; ⑭www.biot.fr) is at no. 46, and can provide copious lists of art galleries, should you need them.

There's not a lot of **accommodation** in Biot. If you book well in advance you could stay at the very reasonable *Hôtel des Arcades*, 16 place des Arcades (⊤04.93.65.01.04, Ⓕ04.93.65.01.05; ❸), in the medieval centre of the village. There are plenty of **campsites** in the vicinity – the best are the one-star *Le Mistral* on route de la Mer (⊤04.93.65.61.48), and the three-star *L'Eden*, chemin du Val-de-Pôme (⊤04.93.65.63.70; closed Nov–March), a couple of hundred metres from the Léger Museum.

The village

The highlight of a visit to Biot is its stunning collection of paintings by Fernand Léger, who lived in the village for a few years at the end of his life. His life-affirming works of art are on display at the **Musée Fernand Léger**, southeast of the village on the chemin du Val-de-Pôme, a thirty-minute walk from the *gare SNCF* (Mon & Wed–Sun: July–Sept 10.30am–6pm; Oct–June 10am–12.30pm & 2–5.30pm; €4.50). Even the museum building itself is a pleasure: with its giant murals, it transcends the mundane suburban setting. The museum closed for substantial rebuilding work in 2004 and was scheduled to reopen as this book went to press at the beginning of 2007.

Léger was turned off from the abstraction of Parisian painters by his experiences of fighting alongside ordinary working people in World War I. Not that he favoured realism, but he wanted his paintings to have popular appeal: he understood that in the modern world art competed with images generated by advertising, cinema and public spectacle. Léger set himself the task of producing paintings that could rival the visual power of such images. He was vocal on the politics of culture, too, arguing for museums to be open after working hours; for making all the arts more accessible to working people; and for public spaces to be adorned with art in the way of "incidental background", on which he often collaborated with Le Corbusier.

Without any realism in the form or facial expressions, the people in such paintings as *Four Bicycle Riders* or the various *Construction Workers* are forcefully present as they engage in their work or leisure, and are visually on an equal footing with the objects. Léger's art has the capacity for instant pleasure – the pattern of the shapes, the vibrant colour, particularly in his ceramic works – though he can also draw it back to stark horror as with *Stalingrad*. It's instructive to compare Léger's life and work with that of Picasso, his fellow **Cubist** pioneer and long-time comrade in the Communist Party. While Léger's commitment to working-class life never wavered, Picasso waved at it only when he needed it.

It was the **potteries** that first attracted Léger to Biot, where one of his old pupils had set up shop to produce ceramics of his master's designs. Today, the former Chapelle des Pénitents Blancs in the village houses a small **Musée d'Histoire et de Céramique Biotoises** (Wed-Sun: July-Sept 10am-6pm; Oct-June 2-6pm; €2) underlines the importance of the potteries to the historical development of the village.

A year after Léger's death, in 1956, the Biot **glassworks** were established, confirming Biot's position as a centre for arts and crafts. Today, there are several glass-makers in the area, all keen for you to visit and buy their products. The **Verrerie de Biot** on chemin des Combes, the third turning off the D4 after the turnoff for the Léger museum (summer Mon-Sat 9.30am-8pm, Sun 10am-1pm & 2.30-7.30pm; winter Mon-Sat 9.30am-6pm, Sun 10.30am-1pm & 2.30-6.30pm; free), is a good choice, where you can watch the glass-blowers at work, visit an **Eco-musée du Verre** (guided tours only Mon-Fri 11.30am & 4.30pm; €6), and admire the famous and beautiful hand-blown bubble glass (*verre bullé*). Opposite the atelier itself is the **Galerie Internationale du Verre** (summer Mon-Sat 10am-8pm, Sun 10.30am-1.30pm & 2.30-7.30pm; winter Mon-Sat 10am-6pm, Sun 10.30am-1.30pm & 2.30-6.30pm; free), which displays stunning contemporary fine-art glass.

There's no shortage of attractions for **children**, all back on the main sea road. They include the performing dolphins of **Marineland** on the N7 (daily 10am-6.30pm; later in high season; adult €34, child €25, closed Jan), which is also home to the water toboggans, chutes and slides of **Aquasplash** (open daily June-Sept 10am-7pm; adult €21, child €17). Opposite Marineland, there's a funfair, **Antibesland** (April to mid-June Sat, Sun & public hols 2-7pm; mid-June to end Aug Mon-Fri 8.30pm-1am, Sat 4pm-1am, Sun 3pm-1am; Sept Sat & Sun 4pm-2am; free entry, rides €1.50-4).

Eating and drinking

Among the **restaurants**, *Le Jarrier*, 30 passage de la Bourgade (☎04.93.65.11.68; menus at €23 & €30; closed Tues & Wed) serves up Biot's best dinners, while the *Hôtel des Arcades* (closed Sun evening & Mon; *plats du jour* around €16) has an appealing combination of café, art gallery and restaurant with traditional Provençal dishes. For lighter meals and snacks there's an appealing *salon de thé*, *Le Mas des Orangers*, at 3 rue des Roses (€10 lunch *formule*; closed Wed) There's also a weekly **market** in the old village on Tuesdays (8am-1pm).

Sophia-Antipolis

If Cap d'Antibes symbolizes old money, **SOPHIA-ANTIPOLIS** represents the power of the multinational. When capital and plant can be shifted anywhere, the hills above Antibes make a tempting location to lure skilled R&D staff. Bayer, France Telecom and Motorola are among the companies to have set up in this vast **science park**, cut out of the forest 6km west of Biot.

You can explore Sophia-Antipolis with your own transport (it's signed off the D4 from Biot, and from the A8 Antibes exit) but despite some daring architecture, the low-density design and extensive shrubbery makes it all rather elusive. **Buses** #1 or #9 will bring you up from Antibes.

Villeneuve-Loubet and Cagnes

Villeneuve-Loubet and **Cagnes** flash past on the speedy train and road connections between Cannes, Antibes and Nice. Glimpses in transit suggest these places are the direst consequence of modern commercial development, but the messy seaside extensions have little to do with Cagnes and Villeneuve-Loubet proper. Both are worth a look: Villeneuve for its castle and place in culinary history; Cagnes for its wonderfully preserved medieval quarter and its artistic connections, with Renoir in particular.

Villeneuve-Loubet

The Riviera shore reaches its trashy nadir at **Villeneuve-Loubet-Plage**, dominated by the giant marina, **Baie des Anges**, built in the 1970s to a design by André Minangoy, its petrified sails visible all the way from Cap d'Antibes to Cap Ferrat. By the time the French government began to be concerned at the despoliation of the Côte d'Azur, apartments in this marina were worth far too much for it to be demolished. So there it stands, a clever, well-maintained but hugely conspicuous piece of modernism. The commercial squalor immediately surrounding it, however, is rather harder to stomach – an unsightly mess of drive-in restaurants, petrol stations and out-of-town retail sheds wedged between the autoroute and the sea.

On the other side of the autoroute, the quiet village of **VILLENEUVE-LOUBET**, on the River Loup, is altogether more attractive. It clusters around an undamaged twelfth-century castle (closed to the public), which was once home to François I. Villeneuve's riverside park and pastures are a stopover point for migrating birds, but its main claim to fame is the **Musée de l'Art Culinaire**, 3 rue Escoffier (July-Aug Sun-Fri 2-7pm, Sept-Oct & Dec-June Tues–Sun 2–6pm; closed Nov; €5), in the house where a king of culinary arts was born in 1846. The son of a blacksmith, **Auguste Escoffier** began his career in restaurants at thirteen, skivvying for his uncle in Nice. By the end of the century he had reached the top in a business the French value as much as design or art – he was known as 'the king of chefs and the chef of kings'. In London he was the *Savoy's* first head chef, then the *Carlton's*, and he fed almost every European head of state. *Pêche melba* was his most famous creation, but its significance for the history of *haute cuisine* was in breaking the tradition of health-hazard richness and quantity. He also showed concern for those who would never be his clients, publishing a pamphlet in 1910 proposing a system of social security to eliminate starvation and poverty.

Items related to Escoffier's life include an antique duck press, copper pans from the Savoy Hotel in London and a 1914 menu from the Carlton Hotel. A technical innovator, Escoffier invented dried potato and a breadcrumb maker as well as his famous recipes. His *Guide Culinaire*, written in 1903, was known as the bible of chefs. The museum includes a recreation of an eighteenth-century Provençal kitchen. It was the invention of the stove or *potager* that revolutionized French cooking, making it possible for the first time to cook dishes simultaneously at a wide variety of different temperatures, and thus paving the way for the development of elaborate menus. Menus were first used at private dinner parties from around the mid-eighteenth-century; in 1765, the first restaurant, *Boulanger*, opened in Paris, with the courses hand-written on a board. The exhibits culminate with a collection of menus, including one printed on a cushion which commemorates the coronation dinner for Queen Elizabeth II held at the *Café de Paris* in London in 1952 and another from a dinner at the *Waldorf-Astoria* in New York in 1945 in honour of Charles de Gaulle. The pervasive influence of culinary French at the dawn of the twentieth century is seen in a menu from the Prussian court in Berlin.

If all this has made you hungry, there are a couple of **restaurants** worth trying in the village. *Le Chat Plume*, just down the hill from the museum at 5 rue des Mesures (☎04.93.73.40,91; closed Mon & Sun) serves hearty *cuisine de terroir* in cheerfully quirky surroundings, with dishes such as *cuisse de lapin* on marinated artichokes at around €14; *L'Auberge Fleurie* close by at no. 11-13 rue des Mesures (☎04.93.73.90.92; menus from €26, closed Wed & Thurs) offers the likes of salmon escalope with saffron or carpaccio of beef with truffle oil, in a more formal setting.

Cagnes

Slashed through by three major roads and with an awe-inspiring traffic problem, the various parts of the **CAGNES** agglomeration are rather confusing. The narrow coastal strip is known as **Cros-de-Cagnes**; **Cagnes-sur-Mer**, which constitutes the town centre, is actually inland above the autoroute; while **Haut-de-Cagnes**, the original medieval village, overlooks the town and coast from the northwest heights. Cros-de-Cagnes has fishing boats pulled up on its broad, pebbly beach, a small, pleasant old quarter and a Hippodrome wedged between the seafront and the A8 autoroute, with horse-racing from December to March and trotting in July and August (ⓦwww.hippodrome-cotedazur.com). Cagnes-sur-Mer is a bustling but rather characterless town, notable only for Renoir's house. Haut-de-Cagnes, however, has a stunning **castle** containing the fabulous **Donation Suzy Solidor** (see p.398) and a changing array of contemporary art.

Arrival and information

The **gare SNCF Cagnes-sur-Mer**, one stop from the *gare SNCF* Cros-de-Cagnes, is southwest of the centre beneath the autoroute. Turn right on the northern side of the autoroute along avenue de la Gare to reach the town centre. The sixth turning on your right, rue des Palmiers, leads to the **tourist office** at 6 bd Maréchal-Juin (July & Aug Mon–Sat 9am–7pm, Sun 9am–noon & 3-7pm; June & Sept Mon–Sat 9am–noon & 2–7pm; Oct–May Mon–Sat 9am–noon & 2–6pm; ☎04.93.20.61.64; ⓦwww.cagnes-tourisme.com).

Boulevard Maréchal-Juin, which becomes avenue de l'Hôtel-des-Postes and then avenue Mistral, is the main street. It runs parallel to avenue de la Gare, which becomes avenue Renoir then veers eastwards into place M.-Bourdet. This is where you'll be dropped if you arrive from Cannes or Nice by **bus**. From here, local bus #42 runs the short distance back to the *gare SNCF*; bus #41 to Cros-de-Cagnes and the seafront; bus #49 to the Renoir museum; and #44 to Haut-de-Cagnes. On foot it's a steep ascent along rue Général-Bérenger, which forks left at the end of avenue de la Gare and turns into montée de la Bourgade.

Accommodation

Cros-de-Cagnes has the largest choice of **hotels** but also plenty of traffic noise: *Beaurivage*, 39 bd de la Plage (☎04.93.20.16.90, ⓦwww.beaurivage.biz; ❹), is a good choice, but ask for one of the quieter rooms at the back; or try *Le Turf*, 13 rue des Capucines (℡04.93.20.64.00; ℱ04.93.73.92.64; ❹), which is set back slightly from the seafront. Top choice in Haut-de-Cagnes, if your budget will stretch, is the luxurious *Le Cagnard*, rue Sous Barri (℡04.93.20.73.21, Ⓦwww .le-cagnard.com; ❾), the ancient guard room for the castle. Small and slightly cheaper but still chic and full of character is *Le Grimaldi*, 6 place du Château (℡04.93.20.60.24, Ⓦwww.hotelgrimaldi.com; ❽). Also in Haut-de-Cagnes, on place Notre Dame de la Protection, *Les Terrasses du Soleil* (℡04.93.73.26.56, Ⓦwww.terrassesdusoleiel.com; ❻) is an attractive chambre d'hôte in the former home of songwriter Georges Ulmer.

Campsites are plentiful, and mostly in wooded locations inland. Try the three-star *Le Todos*, 4km north of Cros-de-Cagnes at 159 chemin Vallon des Vaux (℡04.93.31.20.05, Ⓦwww.letodos.fr; €19.20 per tent; closed Oct–March), with a pool, bar and restaurant, or the well-equipped two-star *le Val de Fleuri*, adjacent to *Le Todos*, at 139 chemin Vallon des Vaux, also with a pool and children's playground (℡04.93.31.21.74, Ⓦwww.campingvalfleuri.fr; €16.50 per tent; closed Nov–Jan). There is also a two-star site, *La Rivière*, at 168 chemin des Salles, 4km north of Cros-de-Cagnes (℡04.93.20.62.27, ℱ04.93.20.72.53, closed Nov–Jan).

Renoir's house

Les Collettes, the house that **Renoir** had built in 1907 and where he spent the last twelve years of his life, is now a museum, the **Musée Renoir**, chemin des Collettes (Mon & Wed–Sun: May–Sept 10am–noon & 2–6pm; Oct & last week in Nov to April 10am–noon & 2–5pm; €3), surrounded by olive and rare orange groves. Renoir was captivated by the olive trees and by the difficulties of rendering "a tree full of colours": remarking on how a gust of wind would change the tree's tonality, he said, "The colour isn't on the leaves, but in the spaces between them." One of the two studios in the house, north-facing to catch the late afternoon light, is arranged as if Renoir had just popped out. Despite the rheumatoid arthritis that had forced him to seek out a warmer climate than Paris, he painted every day at Les Collettes, strapping the brush to his hand when moving his fingers became too painful. There are portraits of him here by his closest friends: a painting by Albert André, *À Renoir Peignant*, showing the ageing artist hunching over his canvas; a bust by Aristide Maillol; and a crayon sketch by Richard Guido. Bonnard and Dufy were also visitors and there are works of theirs here, including Dufy's *Homage to Renoir*, transposing a detail of *Moulin de la Galette*. Renoir himself is represented by several sculptures including two bronzes – *La Maternité* and a medallion of his son Coco – some beautiful, tiny watercolours in the studio, and ten paintings from his Cagnes period (the greatest, the final version of *Les Grandes Baigneuses*, hangs in the Louvre).

To **get to Les Collettes**, take bus #49 from place Bourdet or, on foot, follow avenue Renoir eastwards and turn left up passage Renoir – it's uphill, but not far – around 700m from the *gare routière*.

Haut-de-Cagnes

For many years the haunt of successful artists, **HAUT-DE-CAGNES** is as perfect a hilltop village as you'll find on the Riviera: there are no architectural excrescences to spoil the tiers of tiny streets, and even the flowers spilling over terracotta pots or climbing soft stone walls appear perfect.

The ancient village backs up to the crenellated **château**, which once belonged to the Grimaldis of Monaco and now houses the **Château-Musée**

Grimaldi, comprising the **Musée de l'Olivier,** the **Donation Solidor** and exhibition space for **contemporary art** (May–Sept daily 10am–noon & 2–6pm; Oct–April daily 10am–noon & 2–5pm; €3). The castle's Renaissance interior is itself a masterpiece, with tiers of arcaded galleries, vast frescoed ceilings, stuccoed reliefs of historical scenes and gorgeously ornamented chambers and chapels. The Donation Solidor consists of wonderfully diverse portraits of the cabaret star, Suzy Solidor, whose career spanned the 1920s to the 1970s, and who spent the last 25 years of her life in Cagnes. She was painted by many of the great painters of the period, including Dufy, Cocteau, Laurençin, Lempicka, Van Dongen and Kisling, all of whom have works on display here. Solidor was quite a character: extremely talented, independent and sexy, she declared herself a lesbian years before the word, let alone the preference, was remotely acceptable and was the inspiration for the British music-hall song "*If you knew Suzy, like I know Suzy*". The qualities that most endeared her to each artist, or the fantasies she provoked, are clearly revealed in every one of the canvases, giving a fascinating insight into the art of portraiture as well as a multifaceted image of the woman.

Downstairs is a reconstruction of an olive mill and exhibitions concerning the importance of the olive to the region, whilst upstairs plays hosts to temporary exhibitions of modern art.

On place du Château, the former cabaret where Solidor performed now houses the **Espace Solidor**, a venue for regular displays of contemporary arts and crafts (Wed–Sun: June & Sept 2-6pm, July & Aug 10am–noon & 3–7pm, Oct–May 2–5pm, free). There's also a small **tourist office** here (June & Sept Wed–Sun 11am–1pm & 3–7pm; July & Aug daily 10am–1pm & 3–7pm; Oct–March Wed–Sun 2–5pm), and in July and August jazz concerts are held on the square.

Eating and drinking

Haut-de-Cagnes and Cros-de-Cagnes have the town's best eating places, and for café lounging, place du Château or place Grimaldi, to either side of the castle in Haut-de-Cagnes, are the obvious spots.

In Haut-de-Cagnes, the area around montée de la Bourgade is thick with **restaurants**: a good choice is *Fleur de Sel* at no. 85 (☎04.92.20.33.33; closed Wed & Tues lunch), which serves octopus salad and *pieds et paquets* on a €23 lunch menu. *Le Cagnard* hotel has a predictably smart restaurant (☎04.93.20.73.21; menus from €55; closed mid-Nov to mid-Dec), or there's *Josy-Jo*, 2 rue du Planastel (☎04.93.20.68.76; around €25; closed Sat lunch, Sun & mid-Nov to late Dec), with Provençal delicacies dished up in the space that served as Soutine's workshop in the interwar years.

In Cros-de-Cagnes, *Le Neptune* on route du Bord de Mer (☎04.93.20.10.59; menus from €18) and the smart *La Reserve du Cros* at 91 bd de la Plage (☎04.93.31.00.17; menus from €39) both serve good seafood.

Haut de Cagnes was once quite a lively spot for **nightlife**. It's quieter these days, but there is a jazz club, *Le Black Cat*, at 4 place du Château, with live music Thurs-Sun from 9.30pm.

Vence and around

Set up in the hills 10km from the sea, and with abundant water and the sheltering Pre-Alpes behind, **VENCE** has always been a town of some significance. Its Ligurian inhabitants, the Nerusii, put up stiff opposition to Augustus Caesar, but to no avail; Roman funeral inscriptions and votive offerings from the period remain embedded in the fabric of the old cathedral. In the Dark Ages of Visigoth and Ostrogoth invasions, the bishop of Vence, **Saint Véran** from the St-Honorat seminary, was as effective in organizing the defence of the city as in rebuilding its moral fabric. When he died in 481 he was canonized by popular request – in those days the democratic principle of *vox populi vox Dei* (the voice of the people is the voice of God) operated. But the people of Vence had no spiritual or temporal power to call on to save them from the Saracens who razed both the town and St-Véran's cathedral to the ground.

In the twelfth century the second patron saint of Vence, St-Lambert, took up residence at the same time as the baron **Romée de Villeneuve**, chief minister of Raymond Béranger IV, count of Provence. It was Villeneuve who arranged the powerful marriages of Béranger's four daughters, as part of his strategic scheming (see p.462). From then on, until the Revolution, Vence was plagued by rivalry between its barons and its bishops.

In the 1920s Vence became yet another haven for painters and writers, including André Gide, Paul Valéry, Soutine, Dufy and D.H. Lawrence (who died here, in 1930). Near the end of World War II **Matisse** moved to Vence to escape the Allied bombing of the coast and his legacy is the town's most famous building, the **Chapelle du Rosaire**, built under his design and direction. **Vieux Vence** too has its charms, with its ancient houses, gateways, fountains and chapels as well as the **St-Véran Cathedral**.

From mid-July to mid-August the open-air Latin and World music festival, **Les Nuits du Sud**, takes place. The festival attracts a high calibre of bands and its reputation is growing fast.

Arrival and information

From Cagnes-sur-Mer there are two **roads into Vence**. One enters the town as avenue Général-Leclerc, leading straight up to the eastern end of the old walled city. The other, along with the roads from Grasse, St-Paul and the north, arrives at carrefour Maréchal-Juin and the two main avenues of the modern town, avenue de la Résistance and avenue des Poilus/Henri-Isnard. Coming by bus you'll be dropped at the **gare routière** on place du Grand-Jardin, next door to place du Frêne and the western gateway of Vieux Vence. On place du Grand-Jardin you'll find the **tourist office** (mid-June to mid-Sept Mon–Sat 9am–7pm; Sun 10am–6pm; mid-Sept to mid-June Mon–Sat 9am-6pm; ☎04.93.58.06.38, ⊛www.ville-vence.fr). You can hire **bikes** from Vence Motos on avenue Henri Isnard.

Accommodation

Although Vence has a good choice of **places to stay**, catering for all budgets, it's as well to book ahead in the summer.

Hotels

Hôtel des Alpes 2 av Général-Leclerc ☎04.93.58.13.30, ℮hotel-desalpes@orange.fr. On the eastern edge of Vieux Vence and nothing fancy, but double glazed, friendly and the most economical option. ❷

La Closerie des Genêts 4 impasse Maurel, off av M-Maurel on southern edge of Vieux Vence ☎04.93.58.33.25, ℻04.93.58.97.01. Peaceful, slightly old-fashioned and very welcoming, with an attractive garden and sea views from some rooms. ❸

Diana av des Poilus ☎04.93.58.28.56, ⊛www .hotel-diana-vence.com. Modern building in a quiet and convenient location. ❼

Le Provence 9 av Marcellin-Maurel ☎04.93.58.04.21, ⊛www.hotelleprovence.com. Decent value for the price, with a lovely garden. ❸

Auberge des Seigneurs place du Frêne
☎04.93.58.04.24, 🖷04.93.24.08.01. Just within
Vieux Vence, with rooms named after the painters
who lodged there; the food is excellent. Closed Nov
to mid-March. ❹

La Victoire place du Grand-Jardin
☎ & 🖷04.93.24.21.15. Soundproofed, very central
and reasonable for the money. ❸

Villa Roseraie 14 av H-Giraud ☎04.93.58.02.20,
🖲www.villaroseraie.com. Classic, rich Provençal
homestead with ancient cedars and magnolias

overhanging the terrace on the road to the Col de
Vence northwest of town. Charming reception and
lovely pool in the garden. ❻

Campsite

La Bergerie rte de la Sine ☎04.93.58.09.36,
🖲www.camping-domainedelabergerie.com.
Three-star site 2km west off the road to
Tourrettes-sur-Loup. Closed mid-Oct to late
March. €20 per tent.

The Town

Diminutive **Vieux Vence** has its fair share of chic boutiques and arty restaurants, but it also has an everyday feel about it with ordinary people going about
their business, seeking out the best market deals, stopping for a chat and a *petit
verre* at run-of-the-mill cafés. The **castle** and the **cathedral** are the two
dominant buildings in this part of town; while **Matisse's chapel** (with its
limited opening hours) is the main diversion in the modern town.

Vieux Vence

The 450-year-old ash tree that gives its name to **place du Frêne** stands in front
of Vence's castle, the **Château de Villeneuve Fondation Emile Hugues**
(summer Tues–Sun 10am–6pm; winter Tues–Sun 10am–12.30pm & 2–6pm;
€5), built just outside the city walls in a calm period of fifteenth-century
expansion. It was rebuilt in the seventeenth century and renovated in 1992 to
become a beautiful temporary exhibition space for the works of artists like
Matisse, Dufy, Dubuffet and Chagall – all associated with the town – along with
other modern and contemporary art.

The **Porte du Peyra**, and its sheltering tower that adjoins the castle, have
remained more or less untouched from the twelfth century and provide the best
entry into Vieux Vence. **Place du Peyra**, within the medieval walls, has the
town's oldest fountain. The narrow, cobbled **rue du Marché** off to the right is
a wonderfully busy street of tiny and delectable food shops, all with stalls; it is
said to be one of the most expensive streets in France for food. Behind rue du
Marché you'll find **place Clemenceau**, which centres on the cathedral and
hosts the Tuesday and Friday clothes **market**, spilling into place Surian.

The **St-Véran Cathedral** is a tenth- and eleventh-century replacement for
the church St-Véran presided over in the fifth century, which in turn was built
on the ruins of a Roman temple to Mars and Cybele. Like so many of the
oldest Provençal churches, it is basically square in shape, with an austere
exterior which gives the appearance of monastic exclusion. Over the centuries
bits have been demolished and other bits added, leaving none of the clear lines
of Romanesque architecture. But with each project, including the initial
construction, fragments of the Merovingian and Carolingian predecessor and
Roman Vence were incorporated. In the chapel beneath the belfry two reliefs
from the old church show birds, grapes and an eagle. More stone birds,
flowers, swirls of leaves and interlocking lines are embedded in the walls and
pillars throughout the church. Roman inscriptions from an aqueduct adorn
the porch and more have found their way into the walls of the southwestern
tower. The purported **tomb of St-Véran**, in the southern chapel nearest the
altar, is a pre-Christian sarcophagus. St-Véran and his fellow patron saint of
Vence, St-Lambert, survive in reliquary form in the neighbouring chapel. Of

later adornments there are some superb, irreverent Gothic carved **choir stalls** that are housed alongside some powerfully human, if crude, polychrome wooden statues of the calvary, up above the western end of the nave (irregular hours). In the baptistry, a Chagall **mosaic** depicts the infant Moses being saved from the Nile by the Pharaoh's daughter. Church-as-museum devotees can have a field day examining all the treasures, but those who go for a sense of awesome space will probably be disappointed.

On the east side of the cathedral is **place Godeau**, almost totally medieval save for the column in the fountain that was given to the city, along with its twin on place du Grand-Jardin, by the Republic of Marseille some time in the third century. Rue St-Lambert and rue de l'Hôtel-de-Ville lead from place Godeau down to the original eastern gate, the **Porte du Signadour**, with another fifteenth-century fountain just outside on place Antony-Mars celebrating the town's expansion. In the thirteenth century the only other gate was the Portail Levis on the opposite corner of the city to Porte du Signadour.

The fountain on **place Vieille**, between the Portail Levis and the cathedral, was redesigned in 1572, this time to celebrate the town getting the better of both its feudal and spiritual lords. The town's bishop had been condemned as a heretic for his dabblings with Protestantism. The people of Vence kicked him out not because of the new religion, but because he'd sold his seigneurial rights to Baron Villeneuve, who now had exclusive jurisdiction over them. Using the courts both of Rome and of Provence, the town acquired the illegally transferred rights itself. What is more, when the baron laid siege to Vence with Protestant troops in 1592, the town held out. The townspeople didn't like it when Rome sent a new envoy the same year, accepting him only after he had won the approval of the new king in 1594.

Matisse's Chapelle du Rosaire

Henri Matisse was never a Christian believer, though some have tried to explain the **Chapelle du Rosaire** at 466 av Henri-Matisse, the road to St-Jeannet from the carrefour Jean-Moulin at the top of avenue des Poilus (Mon, Wed & Sat 2–5.30pm, Tues & Thurs 10–11.30am & 2–5.30pm; Sunday Mass 10am; additional openings during school hols, check with the tourist office; closed mid-Nov to mid-Dec; €2.60), as proof of a late-life conversion. "My only religion is the love of the work to be created, the love of creation, and great sincerity," he said in 1952, when the five-year project was completed.

A serious illness in 1941 had left Matisse an invalid. In August 1943, during his convalescence in Vence, where he was nursed by the Dominican sisters who were to involve him in the design of the chapel, he wrote to Louis Aragon: "I am an elephant, feeling, in my present frame of mind, that I am master of my fate, and capable of thinking that nothing matters for me except the conclusion of all these years of work, for which I feel myself so well equipped."

The artist moved back to his huge rooms in Nice in 1949 in order to work on the designs using the same scale as the chapel. There is a photograph of him in bed drawing studies for the figure of St-Dominic on the wall with a paintbrush tied to a long bamboo stick. It's not clear how much this bamboo technique was a practical solution to his frailty, and how much a solution to an artistic problem. According to some critics, Matisse wanted to pare down his art to the basic essentials of human communication, and to do this he needed to remove his own stylistic signature from the lines.

The **drawings** on the chapel walls – black outline figures on white tiles – succeed in this to the extent that many people are disappointed, not finding the

"Matisse" they expect. The east wall is the most shocking; it shows the *Stations of the Cross*, each one numbered and scrawled as if it were an angry doodle on a pad. Matisse described the ceramic murals as "the visual equivalent of an open book where the white pages carry the signs explaining the musical part composed by the stained-glass windows." The full-length windows in the west and south walls are the aspect of the chapel most likely to live up to expectations. They are the only source of colour in the chapel, changing with the day's light through opaque yellow, transparent green and watery blue, and playing across the black and white murals, floor and ceiling.

Every part of the chapel is to Matisse's design (with some architectural input from Auguste Pérret): the high cross with oriental leanings on the roof; the brightly coloured silk vestments (still worn by the priest at Mass), chasubles, crucifix and candelabra; the layout of the chapel; the decoration on the floors, steps and roof. It is a total work and one with which Matisse was content. It was his "ultimate goal, the culmination of an intense, sincere and difficult endeavour".

Eating and drinking

There are plenty of **cafés** in the squares of Vieux Vence: *Le Clemenceau* on place Clemenceau is the best location, though *Henry's* on place de Peyra is more congenial. *La Régence* on place du Grand-Jardin serves excellent coffee to sip beneath its stylish parasols. Rue du Marché is the place for **picnic** food: *Au Poivre d'Âne* at no. 12 specializes in **cheeses** and also sells regional wines.

Restaurants

La Commanderie Château Saint-Martin av des Templiers ☎04.93.58.02.02. Housed in a Templars' castle perched on a rock and complete with stunning views, this is the most beautiful place to eat. Refined Mediterranean food is served with due pomp and ceremony, with menus at €62, €75 and €105.

La Farigoule 15 av Henri-Isnard ☎04.93.58 .01.27. Sea bream fillet or stuffed octopus with saffron *jus* on a €29.50 menu.

Jacques Maximin Table d'Amis 689 chemin de la Gaude ☎04.93.58.90.75. Gourmet cuisine from one of France's fabled chefs, Jacques Maximin, with à la carte dishes such as lobster salad with green asparagus or sauté of prawns with crustacean *jus* weighing in at €70, and menus at €50 and €130. Closed Mon & Tues.

Le Pêcheur du Soleil 1 place Godeau ☎04.93.58.32.56. An astounding choice of pizzas from €7.50, in a pretty location close to the cathedral. Closed Sun eve & Mon.

Le P'tit Provençal 4 place Clemenceau ☎04.93.58.50.64. Provençal dishes like stuffed breast of rabbit with olive gravy & polenta on a €24 menu, close to the cathedral.

St-Paul-de-Vence and the Fondation Maeght

Three kilometres south of Vence, on the road down to Cagnes, is the fortified village of **ST-PAUL-DE-VENCE**, where visitors flock to see the simple grave of **Marc Chagall** on the right-hand side of the little **cemetery** (summer 7.30am-8pm, winter 8am-5pm) at the southern end of the village, or to browse through the seventy or so contemporary art galleries and ateliers. In summer in particular the village is swamped with visitors, but it's undeniably a very beautiful place and the crowds are easily enough left behind – just take any turning off the main street, rue Grande, and enjoy the peace. There's a peculiar little local history **museum** on place de la Castre (Mon & Wed-Sat 10am-noon & 2-5pm; €3) with historical dioramas to tempt visitors weary of shopping. A more expensive but celebrated stop is

△ St-Paul-de-Vence

the hotel-restaurant **La Colombe d'Or** (☎04.93.32.80.02, ⓦwww
.la-colombe-dor.com; ⓞ; *plats du jour* from around €20, closed Nov to late
Dec) which is celebrated not for its food but for the art on its walls, donated
in lieu of payment for meals by the then-impoverished Braque, Picasso,
Matisse and Bonnard in the lean years following World War I.

The chief draw, however, is the remarkable **Fondation Maeght** (daily: July–
Sept 10am–7pm; Oct–June 10am–12.30pm & 2.30–6pm; €11), the artistic
centre that most fully represents the link between the Côte d'Azur and modern
European art. The foundation was established by Aimé and Marguerite Maeght,
art collectors and dealers who knew all the great artists who worked in
Provence. They commissioned the Spanish architect José Luis Sert to design the
building, and a number of the painters, sculptors, potters and designers who
were on their books to decorate it. Both structure and ornamentation were
conceived as a single project, with the aim of creating a museum in which the
concepts of entrance, exit and *sense de la visite* would not apply. It worked. The
Fondation opened in 1964.

Once through the gates, any idea of dutifully checking off a catalogue of
priceless museum pieces crumbles. Giacometti's *Cat* is sometimes stalking along
the edge of the grass; Miró's *Egg* smiles above a pond and his totemed *Fork* is
outlined against the sky. It's hard not be bewitched by the Calder mobile
swinging over watery tiles, by Léger's flowers, birds and a bench on a sunlit
rough stone wall, by Zadkine's and Arp's metallic forms hovering between the
pine trunks, or by the clanking tubular fountain by Pol Bury. And all this is just
a portion of the garden.

The **building** itself is a superb piece of architecture: multilevelled and flooded
with daylight, with galleries opening on to terraces and courtyards, blurring the
boundaries between inside and outside. The collection it houses – sculpture,
ceramics, paintings and graphic art by Braque, Miró, Chagall, Léger, Kandinsky,
Dubuffet, Bonnard, Dérain and Matisse, along with more recent artists and the
young up-and-comings – is impressive. Not all the works are exhibited at any
one time, however, and during the summer, when the main annual exhibition
is mounted, the only ones on show are those that make up the decoration of
the building.

There are several major **exhibitions** every year, from retrospectives to shows
on contemporary themes, along with workshops by musicians or writers with
strong links to the visual arts.

Bus #400 from Nice to Vence serves St-Paul via Cagnes. The Fondation
Maeght is approximately ten minutes' walk from the bus stop in the village. By
car or **bike**, follow the signs just before you reach the village, off the D7 from
La-Colle-sur-Loup or the D2 from Villeneuve.

Tourrettes-sur-Loup

Six kilometres west of Vence, **TOURRETTES-SUR-LOUP** is an artisans'
paradise, preserving just the right balance between crumbly attractiveness and
modern comforts. The three towers from which the village derives its name -
plus the rose-stone houses that cling to the high escarpment – almost all date
from the fifteenth century; the best views can be had from the curious rock
shelf known as Les Loves, just above the town. The Grande-rue is lined with
expensive ateliers selling clothes, sculpture, jewellery, leather, fine art and many
other desirable designer items.

The town is famous for its **violet festival**, held on the first or second Sunday
in March, when floats are decorated with thousands of these blooms. Violets,

which thrive in the mild microclimate, are grown here in vast quantities for the perfume trade as well as for subsidiary cottage industries such as old-fashioned candied violets.

Tourrettes' **tourist office** is at 2 place de la Libération (Mon–Sat 10am–6.30pm; ☎04.93.24.18.93, ⓦ www.tourrettessurloup.com). In terms of **accommodation**, first choice is the classy 🏠 *L'Auberge de Tourrettes*, 11 rte de Grasse (☎04.93.59.30.05, ⓦ www.aubergedetourrettes.fr; ❼), on the edge of the village, with good views. Local **campsites** include the three-star *La Camassade*, 523 rte de Pie-Lombard (☎04.93.59.31.54, ⓦ www.camassade.com), about 3km along the road to Pont du Loup, and, further on, the three-star *Les Rives du Loup*, route de la Colle (☎04.93.24.15.65; ⓦ www.rivesduloup.com; tent €23.50 per night; closed Oct–March). For somewhere to **eat**, try *Le Médiéval* at 6 Grand' Rue (☎04.93.59.31.63; menus at €18 and €38; closed Wed eve & Thurs), or the fancier *Les Bacchanales* at 21 Grand' Rue (☎04.93.24.19.19; menus at €26, €38 or €48; closed Tues & Wed). You may like to try the local violet-flavoured **ice cream** while you're in Tourrettes, too.

Travel details

Trains

Cannes to: Antibes (approx every 20min peak time; 10–15min); Biot (every 40–50min; 18min); Cagnes-sur-Mer (every 25–50min; 20min); Cros-de-Cagnes (every 40–50min; 30min); Golfe Juan-Vallauris (every 40–50min; 7min); Juan-les-Pins (every 25–50min; 11min); Marseille (approx every 30min–1hr; 2hr); Nice (approx every 20min peak time; 40min); St-Raphaël (every 30min–1hr; 35min–1hr 5min); Villeneuve-Loubet-Plage (every 40–50min; 22min).

Buses

Antibes to: Aéroport Nice-Côte-d'Azur (every 20min; 20–45min); Biot (hourly; 35–40min); Cannes (every 20min; 30–35min); Juan-les-Pins (every 20–30min; 8min); Nice (every 20min; 45min–1hr 10min)
Cannes to: Aéroport Nice-Côte-d'Azur (every 20min; 1hr 5min–1hr 15min); Antibes (every 20min; 25–35min); Cagnes *Gare SNCF* (every 20min; 50min–1hr); Le Cannet (every 15–30min; 20–25min); Golfe-Juan (every 20min; 15–20min); Grasse (every 20min; 40–50min); Mouans-Sartoux (every 20min; 22min); Mougins (every 20min; 20min); La Napoule (every 15–45min; 40min); Nice (every 20min; 1hr 20min – 1hr 35min); Vallauris (every 30min; 15min).
Grasse to: Le-Bar-sur-Loup (11 daily; 15min); Cagnes (every 30–50min; 50min); Cannes (every 15–45min; 40min–1hr); Digne (1 daily; 2hr 25min); Grenoble (1 daily; 6hr 15min); Mouans-Sartoux (every 15–45min; 15–25min); Mougins (every 15–45min; 20–30min); Nice (every 30–50min; 1hr 25min); St-Vallier (7 daily; 20–30min); Tourrettes-sur-Loup (3 daily; 30–45min) Vence (3 daily; 50–55min).
Vence to: Cagnes *Gare* (every 20–30min; 15–35min); SNCF Nice (every 15–30min; 50min); St Paul de-Vence (approx every 20min–1hr, 5–10min).

❼

Nice and the eastern Riviera

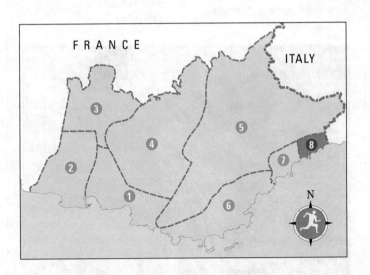

CHAPTER 8

Highlights

* **Vieux Nice** From the flower market at dawn to bar hopping in the early hours, Nice's mellow, Mediterranean heart buzzes with street life. See pp.416-419

* **Niçois villages** Explore craggy Peillon and unspoilt Luceram, the *villages perchés* of Nice's wild and under-populated hinterland, where villagers still live off the land, producing olives, goats' cheese, herbs and vegetables. See p.427 and p.431

* **Villa Ephrussi de Roth-schild** Visit this handsome mansion and its exquisite gardens to find out how the other half used to live. See p.434

* **Plage Mala** Just minutes from Monaco, relax on this secluded, idyllic Riviera beach. See p.437

* **The Casino at Monte Carlo** Break the bank at the world's most famous casino. See p.443

△ Villa Kerylos, Beaulieu

Nice and the eastern Riviera

E ast of the Var, the Riviera is subtly different. For much of its history the coastline between Nice and the Italian border was part of the Kingdom of Savoy, only becoming securely French in 1860. Even today a certain Italianate influence lingers, in the cooking of Nice and in the architecture of Vieux Nice, Villefranche and Menton. The landscape changes too: east of Nice the Alpes-Maritimes come crashing down to the sea and the coastline is often thrillingly scenic.

The Riviera's largest city, **Nice**, became fashionable as a winter resort in the eighteenth century, as aristocratic visitors – many of them invalids – made the journey south to escape the brutal northern winters on the Riviera's sunny shore. Right up to World War I they built their villas here or sojourned in the opulent palace hotels, most of which have long since been converted to apartments, though their architecture remains and often lends the city an appealing, eccentric face. Gradually, other resorts grew to rival Nice, each with its own speciality: **Menton** for tuberculosis sufferers, **Monte Carlo** in the comic-opera principality of Monaco with its casino.

After the Great War many of the old aristocratic visitors never returned: they were dead, impoverished or scattered by revolution and war. In their place came artists and intellectuals - **Matisse** and **Dufy** made Nice their home, **Isadora Duncan** famously met her end there; **Cocteau** favoured Villefranche, and **Somerset Maugham** bought a villa on Cap Ferrat. Later, the introduction of *congés payés* in 1936 brought thousands of ordinary French men and women to a coast that had hitherto been an élite retreat for wealthy foreigners.

The democratization continued after the war, and though the marriage in 1956 of film star Grace Kelly to Prince Rainier of Monaco set the seal on the Riviera's glamour image, the reality was increasingly rather different. The

Museum pass

The **Carte Musées Côte d'Azur** allows unlimited access to 65 of the most important art and history museums, monuments and gardens in the Riviera region. A one-day pass costs €10, a three-day pass costs €17 and a seven-day pass €27. Available at participating museums and principal tourist offices.

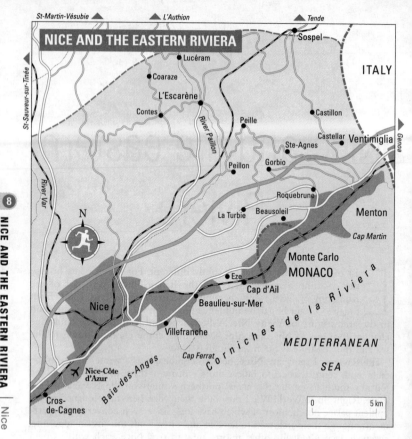

bucolic Mediterranean coast of Smollett's day is nowadays a thing of distant memory.

Nevertheless, there's much to enjoy: the food, vivacious street life and superb culture of the great Mediterranean city of **Nice,** and the unspoilt villages in the Nice hinterland, which guard superb artworks from the medieval School of Nice in their churches and chapels. There are the thrills of the **corniches** running across the mountains between Nice and Menton, and the vicarious pleasures of the independent principality of **Monaco.**

Speedy and inexpensive **train connections** make it easy to visit all the coastal towns and villages without committing yourself to staying overnight.

Nice

The capital of the Riviera and fifth-largest town in France, **NICE** lives off a glittering reputation, its former glamour now gently faded. First popularized by English aristocrats in the eighteenth century, Nice reached its zenith in the Belle Époque of the late nineteenth century, an era that left the city with several extraordinary architectural flights of fancy. Today, more than a quarter of Nice's permanent residents are over 60, their pensions and investments contributing to the high ratio of per capita income to economic activity. Among visitors Italians dominate, especially on summer weekends.

Far too large to be considered simply a beach resort, Nice nevertheless manages to be a delightful, vibrant Mediterranean metropolis with all the advantages and disadvantages its city status brings: superb cultural facilities, wonderful street life and excellent shopping, eating and drinking, but also a high crime rate, graffiti and – in summer – a truly horrendous traffic problem. Yet somehow things never seem as bad as they might be: the sun shines, the sea sparkles and a thousand sprinklers keep the lawns and flowerbeds lush even as temperatures soar into the thirties. Along the famous seafront the frayed but sturdy palms survive, and on summer nights the old town buzzes with contented crowds. It's hard not to be utterly seduced by the place.

Nice's easy-going charm, however, is at odds with its reactionary **politics**. For decades municipal power was the monopoly of a dynasty whose corruption was finally exposed in 1990, when Mayor Jacques Médecin fled to Uruguay, only to be extradited and jailed. From his prison cell, Médecin backed Jacques Peyrat, the former Front National member and close friend of Jean-Marie Le Pen, in the 1995 local elections. Peyrat won with ease and has been mayor ever since, while the Front National retains significant support in the city.

Nice has retained its historical styles almost intact: the medieval rabbit warren of **Vieux Nice**, the Italianate facades of **modern Nice** and the rich exuberance of **fin-de-siècle residences** dating from when the city was Europe's most fashionable winter retreat. It has also retained mementoes from its ancient past, when the Romans ruled the region from here, and earlier still, when the Greeks founded the city. Nice's many museums are a treat for art lovers: within France the city is second only to Paris for the sheer range on offer. The **Musée Matisse**, the **Musée d'Art Moderne**, the **Musée des Beaux-Arts**, **Musée International d'Art Naïf**, Chagall's **Message Biblique** and the **Musée Départmental des Arts Asiatiques** all vie for the visitor's attention. Many of the artists represented by these collections have a direct connection to the city. Of late Nice is smartening up its act with extensive **refurbishment** of its public spaces and the construction of a new **tramway**. Conservative it may be, but this is not a city that rests on its laurels.

Arrival, information and city transport

From terminal 1 at the **airport**, two fast bus services connect with the city: – #99 goes to the *gare SNCF* on avenue Thiers, just west of the top end of avenue Jean-Médecin (14–28min; €4 day pass required) and #98 to the *gare routière* (14-34 min; €4 day pass), which is close to Vieux Nice beneath the promenade du Paillon on boulevard Jean-Jaurès. The regular bus #23 (40min; €1.30) also serves the *gare SNCF* from the airport. It continues up to place Général-de-Gaulle, a couple of blocks from the **Gare de Provence** on rue A-Binet. **Taxis** are plentiful at the airport and will cost about €20-28 into the town centre.

The main **tourist office** is beside the **gare SNCF** on avenue Thiers (June–Sept Mon–Sat 8am–8pm, Sun 9am–7pm; Oct–May Mon–Sat 8am–7pm, Sun 10am–5pm; ☏08.92.70.74.07, ⓦwww.nicetourisme.com). It's one of the most useful, helpful and generous of the Côte tourist offices – though it can be a nightmare trying to get through by phone - and has annexes at 5 promenade des Anglais (June–Sept Mon–Sat 8am–8pm, Sun 9am–6pm; Oct–May Mon–Sat

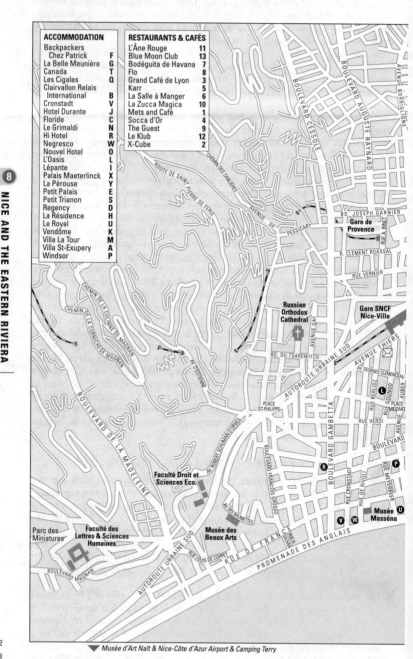

ACCOMMODATION

Backpackers	
Chez Patrick	F
La Belle Meunière	G
Canada	T
Les Cigales	Q
Clairvallon Relais	
International	B
Cronstadt	V
Hotel Durante	J
Floride	C
Le Grimaldi	N
Hi Hotel	R
Negresco	W
Nouvel Hotel	O
L'Oasis	L
Lépante	I
Palais Maeterlinck	X
La Pérouse	Y
Petit Palais	E
Petit Trianon	S
Regency	D
La Résidence	H
Le Royal	U
Vendôme	K
Villa La Tour	M
Villa St-Exupery	A
Windsor	P

RESTAURANTS & CAFÉS

L'Âne Rouge	11
Blue Moon Club	13
Bodéguita de Havana	7
Flo	8
Grand Café de Lyon	3
Karr	5
La Salle à Manger	6
La Zucca Magica	10
Mets and Café	1
Socca d'Or	4
The Guest	9
Le Klub	12
X-Cube	2

Gare de Provence

BD. JOSEPH GARNIER

R. CLEMENT ROASSAL

RUE VERNIER

Russian Orthodox Cathedral

Gare SNCF Nice-Ville

AVENUE THIERS

AV GEORGES CLEMENCEAU

BD. DU TSAREWITCH

PLACE ST-PHILIPPE

PLACE MOZART

RUE VERDI

BOULEVARD GAMBETTA

Faculté Droit et Sciences Eco.

AV. DES BAUMETTES

Musée Masséna

Parc des Miniatures

Faculté des Lettres & Sciences Humaines

Musée des Beaux Arts

PROMENADE DES ANGLAIS

BOULEVARD MAGNAN

▼ *Musée d'Art Naïf & Nice-Côte d'Azur Airport & Camping Terry*

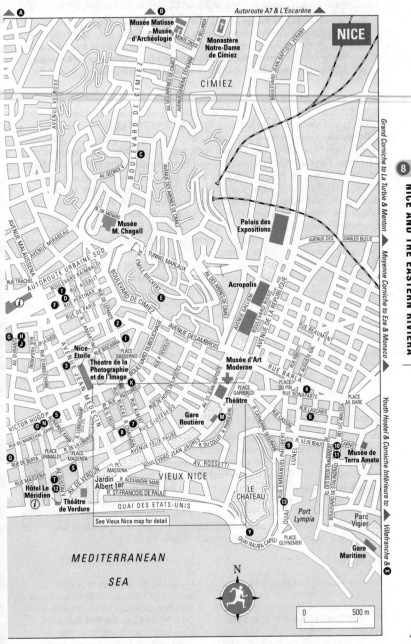

Autoroute A7 & L'Escarène

NICE

Musée Matisse
Musée
d'Archéologie

Monastère
Notre-Dame
de Cimiez

CIMIEZ

BOULEVARD DE CIMIEZ

AVENUE VELROSE

AVENUE MIRABEAU

AVENUE MALAUSSÈNE

RUE TRACHEL

AUTOROUTE URBAINE SUD

BOULEVARD RAIMBALDI

Palais des
Expositions

AVENUE DES DIABLES BLEUS

Musée
M. Chagall

TUNNEL MARLAUX

Acropolis

Nice-
Etoile

Théâtre de la
Photographie
et de l'Image

Musée d'Art
Moderne

Théâtre

Gare
Routière

VICTOR HUGO

Musée de
Terra Amata

Grand Corniche to La Turbie & Menton ▸

Moyenne Corniche to Èze & Monaco ▸

Youth Hostel & Corniche Intérieure to

Villefranche & ⊗ ▸

Hôtel Le
Méridien

Théâtre
de Verdure

Jardin
Albert 1er

VIEUX NICE

QUAI DES ETATS-UNIS

See Vieux Nice map for detail

LE
CHATEAU

Port
Lympia

Parc
Vigier

PLACE
GUYNEMER

Gare
Maritime

MEDITERRANEAN

SEA

N

0   500 m

The **Chemin de Fer de Provence** runs one of France's most scenic and fun railway routes from the Gare de Provence on Nice's rue Alfred-Binet (4 daily; 3hr 12min). The line runs up the Var valley into the hinterland of Nice, and climbs through some spectacular scenery, past places such as the tremendous fortified town of **Entrevaux** (see p.276), before terminating at **Digne-les-Bains** (see pp.266–271).

9am–6pm; ☎08.92.70.74.07), and at terminal 1 of the airport (June–Sept daily 8am–9pm, Oct–May Mon–Sat 8am–9pm; ☎08.92.70.74.07).

Buses are frequent and run until early evening (roughly 7.30–9pm, after which four Noctambus night buses serve most areas from place Masséna until 11.10pm. Fares are flat rate and you can buy a single ticket (€1.30), a Multi+ carnet of seventeen tickets (€20), or a day pass (€4) on the bus; a 10-journey Multi pass (€10) and seven-day passes (€15) are available from *tabacs*, kiosks, newsagents and from Ligne d'Azur, the transport office, at 10 av Félix-Faure, where you can also pick up a free route map. From the *gare SNCF*, bus #4 will take you to place Masséna and along rue Gioffrédo, from where it's a short walk to the Ligne d'Azur office (stop "Alberti-Gioffrédo", ⓦwww.lignedazur.com). For some years the streets of central Nice have been torn apart to construct the first line of a new **tramway** system, which is scheduled to begin operation on a v-shaped course through the city centre during 2007.

Taxis around town are hard to come by, and cost €1.56 per kilometre by day; night rates operate from 7pm to 7am and all day at weekends, and are €2.08 per kilometre. Note that there are additional surcharges for the airport run, for each item of baggage and for being stuck in traffic; the minimum fare is €5.50. Note too that there are scams: if you allow a restaurant or bar to call a çab for you, you may enjoy a luxurious ride home in a top of the range Mercedes – with a hefty bill at journey's end. **Bicycles**, **mopeds** and **motorbikes** can be rented from Holiday Bikes at 34 av Auber, just by the *gare SNCF* (☎04.93.16.01.62).

Accommodation

Before you start doing the rounds, it's well worth taking advantage of the NiceRes **reservation service** offered by the tourist office (ⓦwww.niceres .com). The area around the train station teems with cheap, occasionally seedy hotels, but it's usually possible to find reasonably priced rooms close to the sea or to **Vieux Nice**, even in summer. Options for **camping** are poor: the nearest site is the two star *Camping Terry*, 768 rte de Grenoble St-Isodore (☎04.93.08.11.58), 6.5km north of the airport on the N202 – take bus #59 from the *gare routière* to "La Manda" stop (or ask the driver to drop you at the site), or the Chemin de Fer de Provence railway to Bellet.

Hotels

Canada 8 rue Halévy ☎04.93.87.98.94, ℱ04.93.87.17.12. Plain but clean and reasonable with a good, central location and air conditioning. ❸
Du Centre 2 rue de Suisse ☎04.93.88.83.85; ⓦwww.nice-hotel-centre.com. Gay-friendly hotel, with funky Matisse-style murals and simple but comfortable rooms. ❹

Les Cigales 16 rue Dalpozzo ☎04.97.03.10.70, ⓦwww.hotel-lescigales.com. Stylish tourist hotel with simple decor; quiet and close to the beach. ❽
Cronstadt 3 rue Cronstadt ☎04.93.82.00.30, ⓦwww.hotelcronstadt.com. Hidden inside the garden courtyard of a large residential block, slightly gloomy but extremely tranquil and near the

seafront, with old-fashioned, clean and comfortable rooms. ⑤

Hôtel Durante 16 av Durante ☏04.93.88.84.40, ⓦwww.hotel-durante.com. Great value mid-range hotel, with smart, pretty rooms and an attractive garden. ⑤

Floride 52 bd de Cimiez ☏04.93.53.11.02, ⓦwww.hotel-floride.fr. Charming small hotel in Cimiez, close to the Chagall museum. Free private parking. ④

Le Grimaldi 15 rue Grimaldi ☏04.93.16.00.24, ⓦwww.le-grimaldi.com. Highly-regarded, smart and central, with chic, individually-designed rooms. ⑥

Hi Hotel 3 av des Fleurs ☏04.97.07.26.26, ⓦwww.hi-hotel.net. Swish designer hotel with vibrant colour schemes, individually themed rooms and a lobby that resembles a beauty parlour. ⑨

Lépante 6 rue Lépante ☏04.93.62.20.55, ⓦwww.hotellepante.com. Smart, comfortable and gay-friendly, with a convenient, central location. ⑤

Negresco 37 promenade des Anglais ☏04.93.16.64.00, ⓦwww.hotel-negresco-nice .com. This legendary, somewhat eccentric seafront palace hotel is a genuine one-off, with two top-class restaurants, its own private beach and all the luxury you'd expect. ⑨

Nouvel Hôtel 19 bis, bd Victor-Hugo ☏04.93.87.15.00, ⓦwww.nouvel-hotel.com. Refurbished Belle Époque hotel in a central location, close to av Jean-Médecin. ⑥

L'Oasis, 23 rue Gounod ☏04.93.88.12.29, ⓦwww.hoteloasis-nice.fr. In a quiet and leafy setting, with small, modern rooms. In summer breakfast is served in the garden. ④

Palais Maeterlinck 30 bd Maurice-Maeterlinck ☏04.92.00.72.00, ⓦwww.palais-maeterlinck.com. Stunning resort hotel on a steeply terraced site

between Nice and Villefranche, with great views. It has a wonderful al fresco restaurant and a funicular railway down to the sea. ⑨

La Pérouse 11 quai Rauba-Capeu ☏04.93.62.34.63, ⓦwww.hotel-la-perouse.com. Quite simply the best-situated hotel in central Nice, at the foot of Le Château. Wonderfully peaceful for such a central location. ⑨

Petit Palais 17 av Émile-Bieckert ☏04.93.62.19.11, ⓦwww.petitpalais.fr. Attractive Belle Époque mansion in hilly Cimiez, the former home of writer and actor Sacha Guitry. Quiet and comfortable. ⑥

Petit Trianon 11 rue Paradis ☏04.93.87.50.46, ⓔhotel.nice.lepetittrianon@orange.fr. Cheerful, if basic hotel close to place Masséna and the Vieille Ville, with free internet access and beach towels. ②

La Résidence 18 av Durante ☏04.93.88.89.45, ⓦwww.hotel-laresidence.com. On a side turning near the *gare SNCF*, with decent rooms for the price. ④

Le Royal 23 promenade des Anglais ☏04.93.16.43.00, ⓦwww.vacancesbleues.com. Vast seafront palace hotel, slightly institutional but good value for the location, with spacious, comfortable rooms. ⑦

Vendôme 26 rue Pastorelli ☏04.93.62.00.77, ⓦwww.vendome-hotel-nice.com. Traditional hotel with high ceilings, chandeliers and smart, comfortable rooms and friendly staff. ⑦

Villa la Tour 4 rue de la Tour ☏04.93.80.08.15, ⓦwww.villa-la-tour.com. A good, if potentially noisy, location in Vieux Nice, with a roof terrace and individually-designed rooms. ⑤

Windsor 11 rue Dalpozzo ☏04.93.88.59.35, ⓦwww.hotelwindsornice.com. Fashionable modern boutique-style hotel, with rooms individually designed by artists, a relaxation suite on the top floor and a swimming pool in the verdant courtyard at the back. ⑦

Hostels

Backpackers Chez Patrick first floor, 32 rue Pertinax ☏04.93.80.30.72, ⓦwww .backpackerschezpatrick.com. Cheerful hostel close to the station, with self-catering kitchen and no curfew. €21 per dorm bed.

La Belle Meunière 21 av Durante ☏04.93.88.66.15, ⓦwww.bellemeuniere.com. Efficiently run backpacker hotel in fabulously wasted old bourgeois house. The top-floor rooms get rather hot. €15.

Clairvallon Relais International de la Jeunesse 26 av Scudéri ☏04.93.81.27.63, ⓦwww.clajsud.fr. Slightly cheaper than the youth hostel but 10km north of the centre; take bus #15 (stop "Scudéri"). Location apart, it's pleasantly

informal and has a pool. €15 per dorm bed.

HI Youth Hostel rte Forestière du Mont-Alban ☏04.93.89.23.64, ⓦwww.fuaj.org. Four kilometres out of town and not a lot cheaper than sharing a hotel room. Take bus #14 from place Masséna (direction "place du Mont-Boron", stopover "L'Auberge"); the last bus from the centre leaves at 7.50pm. €15.70 per dorm bed. Reception 7am–noon & 5–11pm. Open Feb–Oct.

Villa Saint-Exupery 22 av Gravier ☏04.93.84.42.83, ⓦwww.vsaint.com. Impressive modern hostel, some way out of central Nice but well-run and well-equipped, with WiFi internet access, kitchens and laundry facilities. Bus #1 or #2 from av Jean-Médecin, stop "Gravier". €22.

The City

It doesn't take long to get a feel for the layout of **Nice**. Shadowed by mountains that curve down to the Mediterranean east of its port, it still breaks up more or less into old and new. Vieux Nice groups beneath the hill of **Le Château**, its limits signalled by boulevard Jean-Jaurès, built along the course of the **River Paillon**. Along the seafront, the celebrated **promenade des Anglais** runs for 5km until forced to curve inland by the runways of the airport. The central square, **place Masséna**, is at the bottom of the modern city's main street, **avenue Jean-Médecin**, while off to the north is the exclusive hillside suburb of **Cimiez**.

Le Château

For initial orientation, with brilliant sea and city views, fresh air, a cooling waterfall and the scent of Mediterranean vegetation, the best place to head for is the park of **Le Château** (daily: April, May & Sept 8am–7pm; June–Aug 8am–8pm; Oct–March 8am–6pm). In fact, there's no château here; the city's fortress was destroyed by the French in the early eighteenth century when Nice belonged to Savoy. This is, however, where Nice began as the ancient Greek city of Nikea: hence the mosaics and stone vases in mock Grecian style. Excavations have revealed Greek and Roman levels beneath the foundations of the city's first, eleventh-century cathedral on the eastern side of the summit. Rather than ruin-spotting, however, the real pleasure here lies in looking down on the scrambled rooftops and gleaming mosaic tiles of Vieux Nice, on the yachts and fishing boats in the port on the eastern side, along the sweep of the promenade des Anglais, and, of course, at the sea itself in the smooth arc of the Baie des Anges between Antibes and the rock on which you stand. At the top of the hill a viewing platform points out the direction of St Petersburg among other places. In the **cemetery** to the north of the park are buried the two great Niçois revolutionaries, Giuseppe Garibaldi and Léon Gambetta, though casual visitors aren't particularly welcome. A moving Jewish war memorial includes an urn of ashes from the crematoria of Auschwitz.

To reach the park, you can either take the lift (€0.80) by the **Tour Bellanda**, at the eastern end of quai des États-Unis, or climb the steps from rue de la Providence or rue du Château in Vieux Nice.

Vieux Nice

Only a few years ago, any expat or police officer would tell you that picturesque **Vieux Nice** was a dangerous place, brimming with drug-pushers, muggers and car thieves. That was always a gross exaggeration, but it still reveals how much the teeming *quartier* has changed. Over the last twenty years or so most of the

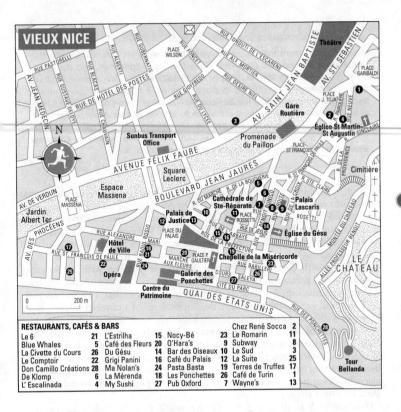

VIEUX NICE

RESTAURANTS, CAFÉS & BARS

				Chez René Socca	2
Le 6	21	L'Estrilha	15	Nocy-Bé	23	Le Romarin	11
Blue Whales	5	Café des Fleurs	20	O'Hara's	9	Subway	8
La Civette du Cours	26	Du Gésu	14	Bar des Oiseaux	10	Le Sud	3
Le Comptoir	22	Grigi Panini	16	Café du Palais	12	La Suite	25
Don Camillo Créations	28	Ma Nolan's	24	Pasta Basta	19	Terres de Truffes	17
De Klomp	6	La Mérenda	18	Les Ponchettes	26	Café de Turin	1
L' Escalinada	4	My Sushi	27	Pub Oxford	7	Wayne's	13

former residents – ethnic minorities and native Niçois alike – have moved out and a host of restaurants, souvenir shops and classy commercial art galleries have moved in. Yet Vieux Nice certainly doesn't feel sanitized: like any tourist honeypot it attracts its share of dodgy characters, its dark and mysterious side alleys are resistant to over-prettification and alongside the galleries and elegant home-furnishing boutiques ordinary life goes on. Clothes lines are strewn high across the streets and in summer there's an almost Neapolitan vibrancy and chaos to the place. What is undeniable, however, is the extent to which Vieux Nice today is dominated by visitors: throbbing with life day and night during August, much of it seems eerie and deserted in winter.

The streets of Vieux Nice are too narrow for buses and much of it is effectively car- (though not necessarily scooter-) free. It's an area made for walking. The central square is **place Rossetti** where the soft-coloured Baroque **Cathédrale de St-Réparate** (Mon-Sat 9am-noon & 2-6pm; Sun 3-6pm) just manages to be visible from the eight narrow streets which meet here. There are cafés to relax in, with the choice of sun or shade, and a magical ice-cream parlour, *Fenocchio*, with an extraordinary choice of flavours.

The real magnet of Vieux Nice, however, is the **cours Saleya**, with its splendidly Baroque **Chapelle de la Miséricorde** (Tues 2.30-5pm) and its adjacent places Pierre-Gautier and Charles-Félix. These wide-open, sunlit spaces, lined with grandiloquent municipal buildings and Italianate chapels, are the site of the city's main **market** (Tues–Sun 6am–1.30pm), where there are gorgeous displays of fruit, vegetables, cheeses and sausages – along with cut flowers and potted roses, mimosa and other scented plants. On Monday the stalls sell bric-a-brac and second-hand clothes (7.30am-6pm). On summer nights café and restaurant tables fill the *cours*. Leading west off the *cours*, rue St-François-de-Paule is home to the suitably grand Belle Époque **Opéra**, opened in 1885, with its plush red and gold interior.

Heading north past the **place du Palais de Justice** with its Saturday market of old paintings, books and postcards, the narrow **rue du Marché** and its continuations – rue de la Boucherie, rue du Collet, rue St-François-de-Paule and rue Pairolière – have the atmosphere of a covered market, lined with food stores and invitingly laid out clothes, with special offers and sales year-round. The diminutive **fish market** is in place St-François (Tues–Sun 6am–1pm), its odours persisting till late at night when all the old streets are hosed down with enough water to go paddling. A short detour north from here will bring you to the Baroque **L'Église St-Martin-St-Augustin** on place St-Augustine (Tues–Sun 9am–noon & 2-5pm), which contains a fine *Pietá* by Louis Bréa.

Heading back south along rue Droite, you'll pass the **Palais Lascaris** at no. 15 (daily except Tues; 10am–6pm; free), an extravagantly decorated, seventeenth-century palace built by a family whose arms, engraved on the ceiling of the entrance hall, bear the motto "Not even lightning strikes us". It's all very noble, with frescoes, tapestries and chandeliers, along with a collection of porcelain vases from an eighteenth-century pharmacy. The Palais Lascaris is also the departure point for Tuesday **walking tours** of Baroque Nice (June-Sept 5pm, Oct-May 3pm; €3). Further down the road, more Baroque splendours can be seen at the seventeenth-century **Église du Gésu** (open Thurs pm, Sat am & Sun eve).

A worthwhile detour onto the quai des États-Unis brings you to the **Centre du Patrimoine/Centre Dóu Patrimoni** (Mon-Fri 8.30am-5pm; free), a mine of information (in French) on Nice's rich artistic, architectural and historic heritage. The Centre also organizes numerous themed **walking tours** of the city.

Place Masséna and the course of the Paillon

The stately, red-ochre **place Masséna** is the hub of the new town, built in 1835 across the path of the River Paillon, with good views north past fountains and palm trees to the mountains. A balustraded terrace and steps on the south of the square lead to Vieux Nice; the new town lies to the north. To the west, the **Jardins Albert-1er** lead down to the promenade des Anglais; to the east, the **Espace Masséna** provides cooling fountains, and a focus for al fresco music concerts and the city's Christmas decorations. Further east, along the covered course of the Paillon, the **Jardins Suspendus** are an unsuccessful attempt to camouflage car parking with a latter-day hanging garden of Babylon.

The course of the Paillon is the site of the city's more recent municipal prestige projects, which create an unfortunate physical barrier between Vieux Nice and the modern city. The giant, unsubtle concrete **Acropolis** conference centre, up beyond traverse Barla, is the most banal of the buildings. Far more impressive is the vast, futuristic **Musée d'Art Moderne et d'Art Contemporain** (MAMAC; Tues–Sun 10am–6pm; €4), composed of four marble-clad towers linked by steel and glass bridges. It's undeniably a bold and confident work of architecture, though the building's fabric is ageing badly, with cladding panels crumbling and the roof terrace – which affords wonderful views over Vieux Nice – decaying. The piazza outside the museum is also a favourite gathering place for Nice's drunks. Nevertheless, MAMAC is one of the cultural highlights of Nice and not to be missed. It has a rotating exhibition of its collection of the avant-garde French and American movements of the 1960s to the present. **Pop Art** highlights include Lichtenstein cartoons and Warhol's Campbell's soup tin, while the **French New Realists** are represented in Arman's *The Birds II* – a flock of flying wrenches – and Nice artist Yves Klein's two massive sculptures, *Wall of Fire* and *Garden of Eden*, along with works by other members of the school, including César, Spoerri, Christo and Jean Tinguely. The **Supports-Surfaces** group, led by Alocco, Bioulès and Viallat, take paintings themselves as objects, concentrating on the frame, the texture of the canvas, and so on, and there are also sections on the **Fluxus International** artists like Ben, who were into 'Happenings', street life and graffiti. The collection also includes American Abstractionists and Minimalists, and the 1980s return to figurative art. A delightful antidote to all this artistic testosterone comes in the form of the vibrant, colourful work of the Franco-American sculptor, painter and *Vogue* fashion model **Niki de Saint Phalle**, who died in 2002 having donated 170 works to the museum.

The modern city centre

Running north from place Masséna, **avenue Jean-Médecin** is the city's rather dull main **shopping** street, named after a former mayor, the father of Jacques Médecin. The late nineteenth-century architecture and trees make it indistinguishable from any other big French city, as do the usual chain stores – including FNAC, Galeries Lafayette and Virgin, though the extensive refurbishment work on the Centre Nice Etoile mall has recently cheered things up a little. More inviting shopping, including Nice's densest knot of **couturier shops**, is concentrated west of place Masséna on rue du Paradis and rue Alphonse-Karr. Both intersect with the pedestrianized **rue Masséna**, a tourist haunt full of bars, *glaciers* and fast food outlets. A side turning off avenue Jean-Médecin brings you to the **Théatre de la Photographie et de l'Image** at 27 bd Dubouchage (Tues–Sun 10am–6pm; free); a photographic museum which displays the fascinating works of Charles Nègre, who shot local views of Nice from 1863–66, just after the city and surrounding area had been ceded to France. In addition, the attractive white painted space has regular temporary exhibitions on photographic themes.

The chief interest of the modern town, however, is its architecture: eighteenth- and nineteenth-century Italian Baroque and Neoclassical, florid Belle Époque, the occasional slice of Art Deco, and unclassifiable exotic aristo-fantasy. The most

△ Russian Orthodox Cathedral, Nice

gilded, elaborate edifice is the early twentieth-century **Russian Orthodox Cathedral**, beyond the train station, at the end of avenue Nicholas II, off boulevard Tsaréwitch (daily except Sun am: May–Sept 9am–noon & 2.30–6pm; Oct & mid-Feb to April 9.15am–noon & 2.30–5.30pm; Nov to mid-Feb 9.30am–noon & 2.30–5pm; €3), reached by bus #14 or #17 (stop "Tzaréwitch").

The promenade des Anglais

The point where the Paillon flows into the sea marks the start of the famous palm-fringed **promenade des Anglais**, which began as a coastal path created by nineteenth-century English residents for their afternoon stroll. It was on the promenade des Anglais that the dancer **Isadora Duncan** met a dramatic death one September evening in 1927, throttled by her own scarf as it caught in the wheel of the open car in which she was travelling. Today it's the promenade itself that is slowly being throttled by the pounding traffic that crawls past some of the most fanciful architecture on the Côte d'Azur.

Past the first building, the glittery Casino Ruhl, is the 1930s Art Deco facade of the **Palais de la Méditerranée**, all that remains of the original municipal casino, closed due to intrigue and corruption, and finally demolished; a new casino and hotel has subsequently been inserted behind the original façade. Nearby, at 2 rue du Congrès, **Galerie Ferrero** is something of an institution in the art world, with a collection including works by Yves Klein. Further along, with its entrance at 65 rue de France, is the **Musée Masséna**, which houses Gothic art, primitive paintings, armour and porcelain, but which has been closed for some years for renovation.

The most celebrated of all the promenade buildings is the opulent **Negresco Hôtel** at no. 37, filling up the block between rues de Rivoli and Cronstadt. Built in 1912, it's one of the great surviving European palace-hotels, still independently owned and run. If you are dressed smartly enough you can wander past the liveried doormen to take a look at some of the public rooms. The Salon Louis XIV, on the left of the foyer, has a seventeenth-century painted oak ceiling and mammoth fireplace plus royal portraits that have all come from various French châteaux. The Salon Royale in the centre of the hotel is a vast oval room with a dome built by Gustav Eiffel's workshops. The stucco and cornices are decorated with 24-carat gold leaf, the carpet is the largest ever made by the Savonnerie factory and the bill for it accounted for a tenth of the cost of the hotel. The chandelier is one of a pair commissioned from Baccarrat by Tsar Nicholas II – the other hangs in the Kremlin. For all its swank though, the Negresco's exterior seems permanently in need of a lick of paint – and the plastic chairs on its terrace simply don't cut it in a hotel of this class.

A kilometre or so west and a couple of blocks inland at 33 av des Baumettes, is the **Musée des Beaux-Arts** (Tues–Sun 10am–6pm; €4), housed in a mansion built by a Ukrainian princess in 1878. The museum's highlights include 28 works by Raoul Dufy, the result of a bequest to the city from Mme Dufy. There are also whimsical canvases by Jules Chéret, who died in Nice in 1932, a great many Belle Époque paintings, a room dedicated to Vanloo, plus a bust of Victor Hugo by Rodin and some very amusing Van Dongens, including the *Archangel's Tango*. In addition, works by Monet, Sisley and Degas grace the walls. The museum is reached by bus #38 (stop "Chéret").

Further west still, the **Musée International d'Art Naïf Anatole Jakovsky** is behind the promenade and the expressway at avenue de Fabron (Mon & Wed–Sun 10am–6pm; €4), and reached by bus #9, #10 or #12 (stop "Fabron"), then bus #34 (stop "Art Naïf"). Housed in the Château Ste-Hélène, former home of the parfumier Coty, the museum displays six hundred examples of art naïf from the eighteenth century to the present day, including works by Vivin, Rimbert, Bauchant and the Yugoslavian masters of the art, Yvan, Generaliă and Laakoviă.

Right out by the airport, the **Phoenix Parc Floral de Nice**, 405 promenade des Anglais (daily: April–Sept 9.30am–7.30pm; Oct–March 9.30am–6pm; €2; exit St-Augustin from the highway or bus #9, #10 or #23 from Nice), is a cross between botanical gardens, bird and insect zoo, and theme park: a curious jumble of automated dinosaurs and mock Mayan temples, alpine streams, ginkgo trees, butterflies and cockatoos. The greenhouse full of fluttering butterflies is the star attraction. The park is also home to the **Musée Départmental des Arts Asiatiques**, beside the lake (Mon & Wed–Sun: May to mid-Oct 10am–6pm; mid-Oct to April 10am–5pm; €4.50). Housed in a beautiful building designed by Japanese architect Kenzo Tange, the museum displays artworks from India, China, Japan and Cambodia, as well as hosting touring exhibitions: there are also regular afternoon tea ceremonies.

The beaches and the port

Although the water is reasonably clean, Nice's beach is painfully pebbly, and the stretch west of Le Château is broken up by twenty private beaches that, from April to October, charge steep fees to enter. East of the port a string of rocky coves includes the **Plage de la Réserve** opposite Parc Vigier (bus #20 or #30), and Coco Beach, popular with the local gay community.

The **port**, flanked by gorgeous red-ochre eighteenth-century buildings and headed by the Neoclassical Notre-Dame du Port, is full of bulbous yachts but has little quayside life despite the restaurants along quai Lunel. There is a **flea market** at place Robilante (Tues–Sat 10am–6pm). Just to the east of the port at 25 bd Carnot is the **Musée de Terra Amata** (Tues-Sun 10am-6pm, €4, bus #81 or #100, stop "Gustavin"), a museum of human palaeontology on the site of an early human settlement dating back 400,000 years – a time when the sea level was much higher than it is today and much of the site of present-day Nice was submerged. The site was the camp of a tribe of hunters, located on a pebbly beach. The exhibits include a reconstruction of a simple shelter.

Cimiez

Nice's northern suburb, **Cimiez**, has always been posh. The approach up boulevard de Cimiez is punctuated by vast Belle Époque piles, many of them former hotels; at the foot of the hill stands the gargantuan *Majestic*, while the summit is dominated by the equally vast *Hôtel Régina*, built for a visit by Queen Victoria. The heights of Cimiez were the social centre of the town's elite some 1700 years ago, when the city was capital of the Roman province of Alpes-Maritimes. Part of a small amphitheatre still stands, and excavations of the Roman baths have revealed enough detail to distinguish the sumptuous facilities for the top tax official and his cronies from the plainer public and women's baths. The **archeological site** is overlooked by the impressive, modern **Musée d'Archéologie**, 160 av des Arènes (Mon & Wed–Sun 10am–6pm; €4), which displays all the finds and illustrates the city's history up to the Middle Ages; take bus #15, #17 or #22 to the "Les Arènes" stop.

Close by is the **Musée Matisse**, 164 av des Arènes (Mon & Wed–Sun 10am–6pm; €4; closed until mid 2007 for renovation), housed in a seventeenth-century villa painted with *trompe l'oeil*. Matisse wintered in Nice from 1916 onwards, staying in hotels on the promenade – from where he painted *Storm over Nice* – and then from 1921 to 1938 renting an apartment overlooking place Charles-Félix. It was in Nice that he painted his most sensual, colour-flooded canvases featuring models as oriental odalisques posed against exotic draperies. In 1942, when he was installed in the *Régina*, he said that if he had gone on painting in the north "there would have been cloudiness, greys, colours shading off into the distance". As well as the Mediterranean light, Matisse loved the cosmopolitan life of Nice and the presence of fellow artists Renoir, Bonnard and Picasso in neighbouring towns. He returned to the *Régina* from Vence in 1949, having developed his solution to the problem of "drawing in colour" by cutting out shapes and putting them together as collages or stencils. Most of his last works in Nice were these cut-out compositions, with an artistry of line showing how he could wield a pair of scissors as deftly as a paintbrush. He died in Cimiez in November 1954, aged 85.

The museum's collection has work from every period, including an almost complete set of his bronze sculptures. There are sketches for one of the *Dance* murals; models for the Vence chapel plus the priests' robes he designed; book illustrations including those for a 1935 edition of Joyce's *Ulysses*; and excellent examples of his cut-out technique, of which the most delightful are *The Bees* and *The Creole Dancer*. Among the paintings are the 1905 portrait of Madame Matisse; *Storm over Nice* (1919–20), which seems to get wetter and darker the further you step back from it; *Odalisque Casquette Rouge* from the place Charles-Félix years; the 1947 *Still Life with Pomegranates*; and one of his two earliest attempts at oil painting, *Still Life with Books*, painted in 1890.

The Roman remains and the Musée Matisse back onto an old **olive grove**, one of the best open spaces in Nice and venue for the July **jazz festival** (see p.392). At its eastern end on place du Monastère is the **Monastère Notre-Dame de Cimiez** (Mon–Sat 10am–noon & 3–6pm; free), with a pink flamboyant Gothic facade of nineteenth-century origin topping a much older and plainer porch. Inside there's more gaudiness, reflecting the rich benefactors the Franciscan order had access to, but also three masterpieces of medieval art: a *Pietá* and *Crucifixion* by Louis Bréa and a *Deposition* by Antoine Bréa. Adjoining the monastery is the **Musée Franciscain** (same hours), which paints a picture of the mendicant friars and relates the gruesome fate that befell some early martyrs. You can also look into the first cloister of the sixteenth-century **monastic buildings**, and visit the peaceful **gardens**. To the north of the monastery is the **cemetery** where Matisse and Raoul Dufy are buried.

At the foot of Cimiez hill, just off boulevard Cimiez on avenue du Docteur-Menard, **Chagall's Biblical Message** is housed in a perfect custom-built museum (Mon & Wed–Sun: July–Sept 10am–6pm; Oct–June 10am–5pm; €6.50, €7.70 during temporary exhibitions), opened by the artist in 1972. The rooms are light, white and cool, with windows allowing you to see the greenery of the garden beyond the pinky red shades of the *Song of Songs* canvases. The seventeen paintings are all based on the Old Testament and are complemented by etchings and engravings. To the building itself, Chagall contributed a mosaic, the painted harpsichord and the *Creation of the World* stained-glass windows in the auditorium. To get there, take bus #15 (stop "Musée Chagall").

The Villa Arson

The **Villa Arson**, 20 av Stephen-Liégeard (July–Sept daily 1–7pm; Oct–June Tues–Sun 1–6pm; free; bus #36 stop "Villa Arson"), lies in the district of St-Barthélemy, also in the north of the city but much further west than Cimiez. It is an unlikely mix of seventeenth-century mansion surrounded by 1960s concrete construction and houses a national school for the plastic arts and an international centre for the teaching of contemporary art. Along with several exhibitions a year and displays of work by pupils, the school has fantastic views over the city to the sea, a café and bookshop and a friendly unelitist atmosphere.

Just to the south, at 59 av St-Barthélemy, the **Prieuré du Vieux Logis** (guided visits organized by Centre du Patrimoine: June-Sept at 5pm, Oct-May at 3pm, €3, assemble at Church of St-Barthélemy, montée Claire-Virenque) contains a collection of fourteenth- to sixteenth-century furniture, household objects and works of art in a sixteenth-century farm, turned into a priory by a Dominican father in the 1930s.

Eating and drinking

Nice is a great place for **food**, whether you're picnicking on market fare, snacking on **Niçois specialities** like *pan bagnat* (a bun stuffed with tuna, salad and olive oil), *salade niçoise*, *pissaladière* (onion tart with anchovies) or *socca* (a chickpea flour pancake), or dining in the palace hotels. The **Italian** influence is strong, with pasta on every menu; **seafood** and **fish** are also staples, with good *bourride* (fish soup), *estocaficada* (stockfish and tomato stew), and all manner of sea fish grilled with fennel or Provençal herbs. The local Bellet wines from the hills behind the city provide the perfect light accompaniment. For **snacks**, many of the cafés sell sandwiches with typically Provençal fillings such as fresh basil, olive oil, goats' cheese and *mesclun*, the unique green-salad mix of the region.

Despite the usual fast-food chains and tourist traps dotted around, most areas of Nice have plenty of reasonable **restaurants**. Vieux Nice has a dozen on every street catering for a wide variety of budgets, while the port quaysides have excellent, though pricey, fish restaurants. From June till September it's wise to **reserve** tables, or turn up before 8pm, especially in Vieux Nice.

Vieux Nice restaurants

The restaurants below are all marked on the Vieux Nice map on p.417

Chez René Socca 2 rue Miralhéti, off rue Pairolière ℡04.93.85.95.67. The cheapest meal in town: you can buy helpings of *socca*, *pissaladière*, stuffed peppers, pasta or calamares at the counter and eat with your fingers on stools ranged haphazardly across the street; the bar opposite serves the drinks. Closed Mon & Jan.

Le Comptoir 20 rue St-François-de-Paule ℡04.93.92.08.80. Very chic 1930s-style brasserie by the Opéra. Serves superb sea bass in salt crust, though the waiting staff can be a little superior and unhelpful. Main courses from €20. Evenings only: Mon-Thurs until 11pm, weekends until midnight.

Don Camillo Créations 5 rue des Ponchettes ℡04.93.85.67.95. Elegantly modern restaurant with contemporary Nicois/Italian cooking on a €36 menu. Closed Mon lunch & Sun.

🏃 **L'Escalinada** 22 rue Pairolière ℡04.93.62.11.71. Good Niçois specialities on a €23 menu – *pissaladière* to start, then you help yourself to chickpea salad from a huge pot. The location is pretty, at the foot of a stepped sidestreet. Open daily.

L'Estrilha 13 rue de l'Abbaye ℡04.93.62.62.00. Reservations essential in summer for this popular restaurant that serves *bourride*, *civet de lapin* and *daube niçoise*. *Plats* around €12.50.

Café des Fleurs 13 cours Saleya ℡04.93.62.31.33. Huge salads and *bruschetta*, plus a grandstand view of the flower market. *Plats du jour* around €12.50. Open 5.30am-midnight daily.

Du Gesú 1 place du Jésus ℡04.93.62.26.46. Extremely popular restaurant with a great atmosphere, serving no-nonsense Niçois/Provençal food,

including good *daube* and pizzas. In an attractive church square in the heart of Vieux Nice. Pizzas from €7, main courses around €11. Closed Sun.

Grigi Panini 5 rue St-Réparate. Hot *panini* from the counter, plus salads and pasta from around €6.50.

La Mérenda 4 rue de la Terrasse. Courgette fritters, *tripe à la* niçois and the like from Dominic le Stanc, former chef at Chantecler. À la carte only, around €25. No phone, no smoking, no credit cards. Closed Sat, Sun & two weeks in Aug.

My Sushi 18 cours Saleya ℡04.93.62.16.32. Chic and reasonably priced sushi bar, with menus from €18. Open daily until 10pm.

🏃 **Pasta Basta** 18 rue de la Préfecture ℡04.93.80.03.57. Excellent fresh pasta from €4.40 plus a bewildering variety of sauces from €2.40 – and they hand you the block of parmesan to grate yourself.

Le Romarin 2/4 place de la Halle aux Herbes ℡04.93.85.65.20. A plum Vieux Nice position on a small square, and generous portions of Niçois specialities. Mixed crowd of tourists and locals. Menus from €15. Closed out of season all day Mon & Tues lunch.

Terres de Truffes 11 rue St-François-de-Paule ℡04.93.62.07.68. Fashionable but intimate and tasteful restaurant with dishes based on a wide variety of fresh truffles. Highly recommended. From around €29.

Café de Turin 5 place Garibaldi ℡04.93.62.29.52. Queues around the block for the spectacular seafood at this restaurant on the edge of Vieux Nice. *Plateaux de fruits de mer* from just under €20. There are seafood stalls in the street outside if you get tired of waiting. Closed Wed.

Greater Nice restaurants

The restaurants below are all marked on the Nice map on pp.412–413.

L'Âne Rouge 7 quai des Deux-Emmanuel ℗04.93.89.49.63. Lobster is the speciality of this port-side gourmet's palace. Monkfish with shellfish, black rice & lemon cream or sea bream with parsnip mashed potatoes and cardamom and viognier sauce are some of the other delights. Classic and very expensive. Menus from €26. Closed all day Wed, Thurs lunch & most of Feb.

Chantecler and La Rotonde Hôtel Negresco, 37 promenade des Anglais ℗04.93.16.64.00. The *Chantecler* is the best restaurant in Nice, seriously expensive à la carte, but chef Bruno Turbot provides a lunchtime menu, including wine and coffee, for €55, which will give you a good idea of how sublime Niçois food is at its best. At *La Rotonde* you can taste less fancy but still mouthwatering dishes on the €25 menu. Closed Mon, Tues & 7 Jan-7 Feb.

Chez Flo 4 rue Sacha-Guitry ℗04.93.13.38.38. Wonderful big brasserie in the grand, Parisian manner, serving *choucroute*, *confit de canard*, seafood and great *crème brûlée* in the Art Deco surroundings of a theatre where Mistinguett and Piaf performed. Lunch menu €22.50, evening €29.50. Last orders midnight. Open daily.

Karr 10 rue Alphonse Karr ℗04.93.82.18.31. Elegantly modern restaurant with an international menu of grilled fish, chicken and steak. Popular pit stop for the designer shopping crowd. Lunchtime *formule* €14.50.

Mets and Café 28 rue Assalit ℗04.93.80.30.85. Good value, busy budget brasserie close to many of the backpacker hostels, with a €9 menu and no shortage of custom. Closed Sun.

La Salle à Manger 7 rue Fodéré ℗04.93.56.00.94 Tiny, brightly modern gay/lesbian friendly restaurant north of the port, with *amuse bouches* and a welcome glass of *kir* on the €23 menu. Eves only, closed Mon.

Socca d'Or 45 rue Bonaparte ℗04.93.56.52.93. Extremely cheap *socca* and pizza a few blocks back from the port. Closed Wed.

La Zucca Magica 4 bis quai Papacino ℗04.93.56.25.27. Long-established, homely Italian vegetarian restaurant on the port, with a sound reputation but a tendency to overdo the cheese. Around €25, no credit cards. Closed Sun & Mon.

Cafés and bars

The bars and cafés below are all marked on the Vieux Nice map on p.417, except Grand Café de Lyon, which is marked on the Nice map on pp.412–413.

Bar des Oiseaux 5 rue St-Vincent. Eccentric cabaret bar named for the birds that fly down from their nests in the loft and the pet parrot and screeching myna bird that perch by the door. Live jazz, bossa nova, *chanson* and flamenco. Open Tues-Sun until 1am.

Grand Café de Lyon 33 av Jean-Médecin. One of the more attractive big *terrasse* cafés on the main street.

Nocy-Bé 6 rue Jule-Gilly. Diminutive Vieux Nice tea bar, with oriental pastries and a huge selection of teas. Mon-Sat until 12.30am.

Le Café du Palais place du Palais. A prime alfresco lounging spot on the handsome square by the Palais de Justice.

Les Ponchettes and La Civette du Cours cours Saleya. At Le Château end of the marketplace, neighbouring cafés with cane seats fanning out a good 50m from the doors. Open late in summer.

Le Sud 10 Félix-Faure. Grungy, laid-back café-bar with good value panini. Open until 9pm. Closed Sun.

Nightlife

British- and Irish-style **pubs** have long been a very popular element of Nice nightlife, particularly with the young. For the older, more affluent generation, the luxury **hotel bars** with their jazzy singers and piano accompaniment have justly held sway for decades, as an essential ingredient of Riviera nightlife. There are plenty of **discos**, too, and, particularly in Vieux Nice, a wide choice of venues for drinking and dancing, though the music tends not to be very original. As for the **clubs**, bouncers judging your wallet or exclusive membership lists are the rule. Nice's **lesbian and gay** scene has broadened in recent years, with a wider selection of venues and a more relaxed attitude: the annual Pink Parade takes place in early June.

Bodéguita del Havana 14 rue Chauvain. Wildly popular Cuban salsa bar with DJs and live music. Open Tues-Sun until 2.30am. Smart dress required.

Blue Moon Club 26 quai Lunel. Bar and mainstream disco. Entrance free until midnight, then €10 and finally €16 with *conso*.

Blue Whales 1 rue Mascoïnat. Intimate venue with a friendly atmosphere and live music on Fridays. Open daily till 2.30am.

The Guest 5 quai des Deux-Emmanuel. Very stylish (and expensive) portside bar with a dance floor, attracting a slightly older crowd. Cocktails from €9.50.

De Klomp 6 rue Mascoïnat. Dutch-style brown café with 12 beers on draught, 60 whiskies and regular live music. Mon-Sat 5.30pm–2.30am.

Ma Nolan's 2 rue St-François-de-Paule. Vast, slick Irish pub with regular live music, televised Irish & British sport plus Murphy's & Guinness on draught. Popular with a younger crowd.

O'Hara's 22 rue Droite. Tiny, long-established Irish folk bar on the corner of rue Rosetti, serving up food and satellite TV sports. Live music Fri and Sat. Open daily until 2am.

Pub Oxford 4 rue Mascoïnat. English-style pub, with an excellent range of beers; live music every evening from 10pm; closes at 5am.

La Suite 2 rue Bréa. A fashionable late-night disco bar in Vieux Nice. You won't get in unless they like the look of you. Open Tues-Sat until 2.30am.

Subway 19 rue Droite. Reasonably priced disco, specializing in reggae, soul and rock. Thurs, Fri & Sat until dawn; €8 with *conso*.

Wayne's 15 rue de la Préfecture. Big, popular rock bar on the edge of Vieux Nice, still the lynchpin of the area's nightlife despite its vaguely Neandertheatre sexual politics. Regular live British bands plus theme nights including quizzes, ladies and student nights. Open daily.

Lesbian and gay bars and clubs

Le 6 6 rue de la Terrasse. Smart lesbian & gay music bar, with regular live entertainment including drag, *rai* (Algerian funk/rap music) and karaoke. Tues–Sun from 10pm.

Le Klub 6 rue Halevy. Nice's largest and best gay club attracts a young, stylish crowd including women and some heteros. Wed–Sun from midnight.

X-Cube 13 av Maréchal-Foch. Slick, stylish minimalist gay men's lounge bar attached to a sex shop and cruising club. Daily until 2.30am.

Entertainment, sport and festivals

Of Nice's many festivals – which begin with the celebrated Mardi Gras **Carnival** and associated flower processions in February – probably the most interesting is the **Festival de Jazz**, staged in late July in the amphitheatre and gardens of Cimiez (for details, check ⓦwww.nicejazzfest.com). The city's biggest sporting event is the **Triathlon de Nice** in June when competitors from all round the world swim 3.8km in the Baie des Anges, cycle 180km in the hills behind the city and run 42km ending up along the promenade des Anglais.

Nice's **opera**, Opéra de Nice, 4–6 rue St-François-de-Paule (ⓣ04.92.17.40.00), and **theatre**, Théâtre National de Nice, promenade des Arts (ⓣ04.93.13.90.90), are the city's twin temples to high culture, with classical music and ballet also finding a home at the opera house. Some of the smaller independent theatres, such as Théâtre de la Cité, 3 rue Paganini (ⓣ04.93.16.82.69), stage the most exciting shows. The best **cinemas** are Cinéma Mercury, 16 place Garibaldi (ⓣ08.36.68.81.06), and the art house Cinémathèque de Nice, 3 esplanade Kennedy (ⓣ04.92.04.06.66), which show subtitled films in the original language, as does the more mainstream UGC Rialto, 4 rue de Rivoli (ⓣ08.92.68.00.41). The major touring **rock concerts** are usually held at the Palais Nikaïa, 163 rte de Grenoble (ⓣ04.92.29.31.29).

The best place for up-to-date **listings** for concerts, plays, films and sporting events is FNAC at 44-46 av Jean-Médecin, where you can also buy **tickets** for most events.

Listings

Airlines Aer Lingus ☎01.70.20.00.72;
Air France ☎36.54; Air Transat
☎08.25.12.02.48; bmi baby ☎08.90.71.00.81;
British Airways ☎08.25.82.54.00; British Midland
☎01.41.91.87.04; Delta ☎08.11.64.00.05;
Easyjet ☎08.99.70.00.41, United
☎08.10.72.72.72.

Airport information ☎08.20.42.33.33.

Boat trips Trans Côte d'Azur, quai Lunel
(☎04.92.00.42.30, ⌨www.trans-cote-azur.com)
runs summer trips to Îles de Lérins, Cannes,
Monaco, St-Tropez and the Esterel.

Bookshop English-language books are available
from The Cat's Whiskers, 30 rue Lamartine
☎04.93.80.02.66.

Car breakdown Nice Dépannage 24hr service
☎04.97.00.03.33.

Car parks Acropolis; promenade du Paillon;
promenade des Arts; *gare SNCF*; place Masséna;
and cours Saleya.

Car rental Major firms have offices at the airport
and/or at the *gare SNCF*, on av Thiers. Try also:
Avis, 2 av Phocéens ☎04.93.80.63.52; Europcar,
3 av Gustave V ☎04.92.14.44.50; or Hertz, 9 av
Gustav V ☎04.93.87.11.87.

Consulate Canada, 10 rue Lamartine
☎04.93.92.93.22; UK, 22 av Notre Dame
☎04.93.62.94.95; USA, 7 av Gustave V, 3rd floor
☎04.93.88.89.55.

Disabled access Transport for people with
reduced mobility ☎04.93.96.09.99.

Emergencies SAMU ☎15; SOS Médecins
☎08.10.85.01.01; Riviera Medical Services
(English-speaking doctors) ☎04.93.26.12.70;
Hôpital St-Roch, 5 rue Pierre-Dévoluy
☎04.92.03.33.75; SOS Dentaire ☎04.93.80.77.77.

Ferries to Corsica SNCM *gare maritime*, quai du
Commerce ☎04.93.13.66.66, ⌨www.sncm.fr;
Corsica Ferries, quai Amiral Infernet
☎08.25.09.50.95.

Internet Internet Café, 30 rue Pertinax; Taxi Phone
Internet, 10 rue de Belgique and at 25 rue Paganini.

Laundry Best One, 16 rue Pertinax; Lavomatique,
11 rue du Pont-Vieux and at corner of rue
Lamartine & Pertinax; du Mono 8 rue de Belgique.

Lost property 1 rue Raoul-Bosio
☎04.97.13.44.10.

Money exchange American Express, 11
promenade des Anglais; Change Or, 7 av Thiers;
Thomas Cook, 12 av Thiers.

Pharmacy 7 rue Masséna ☎04.93.87.78.94, 66
av Jean-Médecin, ☎04.93.62.54.44.

Police Commissariat Central de Police, 1 av
Maréchal-Foch ☎04.92.17.22.22.

Post office 21 av Thiers.

Taxis ☎04.93.13.78.78.

Trains General information and reservations
☎36.35; for information on the Chemin de Fer de
Provence, go to 4 bis rue Alfred-Binet
☎04.97.03.80.80.

Youth information Centre Information Jeunesse,
19 rue Gioffredo ☎04.93.80.93.93.

Niçois villages

The **foothills of the Alps** come down to the northern outskirts of Nice, and right down to the sea on the eastern side of the city: a majestic barrier, snowcapped for much of the year, beyond which crest after crest edges higher while the valleys get steeper and livelihoods more precarious. From the sea, the wide course of the Var to the west appears to be the only passage northwards. But the hidden river of Nice, the **Paillon**, also cuts its way to the sea through the mountains past small, fortified medieval settlements. The **Nice–Turin railway line** follows the Paillon for part of its way – one of the many spectacular train journeys of this region. If you have your own transport you'll find this is serious, hairpin-bend country where the views are a major distraction. **Buses** from Nice to its villages are infrequent.

With their proximity to the metropolis, the *villages perchés* of **Peillon**, **Peille**, **Lucéram**, **L'Escarène**, **Coaraze** and **Contes** are no longer entirely peasant communities, though the social make-up remains a mix. You may well hear Provençal spoken here and the **traditional festivals** are still communal affairs, even when the participants include the well-off Niçois escaping from the coastal heat. The links between the city and its hinterland are strong: the villagers still live off the land and sell their olives and olive oil, goats' cheese or vegetables and herbs in the city's markets; many city dwellers' parents or grand-parents still have homes within the mountains, and for every Niçois this wild and underpopulated countryside is the natural remedy for city stress.

Peillon

For the first 10km or so along the River Paillon, after you leave the last of Nice, the valley is marred by quarries, supplying the city's constant demand for building materials. However, once you reach Peillon's nearest *gare SNCF* at Ste-Thècle, the road begins to climb, looping for 5km through olive groves, pine forest and brilliant pink and yellow broom before you reach the gates of **PEILLON**'s medieval enclave. By bus from Nice, the closest you can get is the "Les Moulins" stop, from where it is a 3.5-kilometre uphill walk.

Peillon is beautifully maintained, right up to the lovely place de l'Église at the top. There is very little commerce and very little life during the week – most of the residents commute to their jobs in Nice. Just outside the village stands the **Chapelle des Pénitents Blancs**, decorated with violent fifteenth-century frescoes similar to those by Jean Canavesio at La Brigue (see p.297). You can peer through the grille across the chapel door; depositing a 20 Euro cent coin illuminates the interior. From the chapel a path heads off across the hills north-wards to Peille. It's a two-hour walk along what was once a Roman road, and a more direct route than going via the valley.

Peillon has an extremely attractive **hotel–restaurant**, *Auberge de la Madone* (℡04.93.79.91.17, ℻04.93.79.99.36; booking essential; closed early Nov to mid-Dec & three weeks in Jan; ❻), with balconies overlooking the valley. If you're on a tighter budget, try *Le Pourtail*, under the same management, across the street (❷). The **restaurant** at the *Auberge de la Madone* (closed Wed) is excellent, offering a €30 lunch menu.

Peille

PEILLE lies at the end of a long climb from the valley below, the journey up from the *gare SNCF* replete with hairpin bends. The atmosphere here is very different to that in Peillon. It was excommunicated several times for refusing to pay its bishop's tithes, and the republicanism of the small town was later manifested by the domed thirteenth-century Chapelle de St-Sébastien being turned into the **Hôtel de Ville**, and the Chapelle des Pénitents Noirs into a communal **oil press**. Peille claims to be the birthplace of the Roman emperor Pertinax who was assassinated within thirteen weeks of his election on account of his egalitarian and democratic tendencies.

The main square, **place de la Colle**, is graced with a Gothic fountain and two half-arches supporting a Romanesque pillar. It's also home to the medieval **court house** bearing a plaque recalling Peille's transfer of its rights over Monaco to Genoa. On nearby rue St-Sébastien the former salt tax office, the **Hôtel de la Gabelle**, still stands. Peille's small **Musée du Terroir** on place de l'Armée (Sun pm only; free) is fascinating, not so much for the exhibits but because the captions are written in the village's own dialect, Peilhasc. The only thing detracting from the beauty of the village is the view to the southwest, marred by the cement-quarrying around La Grave, its suburb down in the valley by the rail line. You can, however, take labyrinthine winding routes to La Turbie, Ste-Agnes or L'Escarène from the village, on which precipitous panoramas – and slow progress – are assured. More adventurous visitors to Peille make the circuit of its **Via Ferrata**, which includes a rope bridge and rockface; there's a

€3 charge to make the circuit and you can hire the necessary equipment locally. Enquire at the *Bar l'Absinthe*.

Three **buses** a day make the connection between Nice and Peille from Monday to Saturday, but there's no Sunday service; the **gare SNCF** is 6.5km from the village. It's worth timing your visit for lunchtime so that you can **eat** at the superb ✦ *Restaurant Cauvin/Chez Nana* on place Carnot (☎04.93.79.90.41; closed Tues & Wed; menu at €25) which does a great blow-out Sunday lunch with real Provençal cooking and a generous choice of hors d'oeuvres; or you can snack at the *Bar la Voute* (sandwiches €3.50) or drink at *L'Absinthe* (closed Tues & Thurs lunch in winter) – both at the end of rue Centrale. If you want to **stay** there are various gîtes, bookable through the Gîtes de France website.

L'Escarène

At **L'ESCARÈNE** the rail line leaves the Paillon and heads northeast to **Sospel**. In the days before rail travel, this was an important staging post on the road from Nice to Turin, when drivers would rig up new horses to take on the thousand-metre Braus pass, which the rail line now tunnels under. The village's single-arched bridge (rebuilt after its destruction in World War II) was the crucial river crossing, yet the people who first lived beside it obviously mistrusted all travellers; their houses had no windows overlooking the river, nor any doors, and access was by retractable ladders.

If you want to stop off for the day – there's nowhere to stay – head for the beautiful **place de l'Église** surrounded by pale yellow, green and ochre houses; opposite the great Baroque church of **St Pierre-es-Liens** is the *Café de l'Union* bar.

Lucéram

Following the Paillon upstream for 6km from L'Escarène, you pass the outwardly unobtrusive fifteenth-century **Chapelle de St-Grat** with gorgeous frescoes by Jean Beleison, a colleague of Louis Bréa. Just 1km further on, clinging to the side of the valley, the village of **LUCÉRAM** has the friendliness of a still-peasant community, full of thin cats and mangy dogs. Its communal oil press remains in service and at the start of the olive season in October the villagers dip their traditional *brissaudo* – toasted garlic bread – in the virgin oil. At Christmas the shepherds bring their flocks into church and after Mass make their offerings of dried figs and bread.

Lucéram is well-known locally for its annual **Circuit des Crèches,** which brings around 50,000 visitors to the village in the weeks before Christmas. During this period more than 400 nativity scenes are displayed in the streets of Lucéram and the neighbouring community of Peïra-Cava; at other times of year there's a smaller selection on display at the **Musée de la Crèche** (enquire at tourist office for admission). The museum is en route to the church of **Ste-Marguerite** (Tues, Wed & Thurs 10am–noon & 2–6pm, Sun 2–6pm, €1.50) whose belfry rises proudly above the village houses, its Baroque cupola glittering with polychrome Niçois tiles. Inside are some of the best late-medieval artworks in the Comté de Nice, though several have been removed and taken to Nice's Musée Masséna (see p.421). All these works belong to the School of Nice, and both the Retable de Ste-Marguerite, framed by a tasteless Baroque baldaquin, and the painting of Saints Peter and Paul, with its cliff-hanging castle in the distance, are attributed to Louis Bréa. There are more local landscapes in the Retable de St-Antoine, painted on flamboyant Gothic panelling, with generous additions of gold, and said to be by Jean Canavesio.

Popular art is present in a thirteenth-century plaster *Pietá*, probably by a local craftsman, to the left of the choir, and the black and red processional lanterns kept in the choir. Another of Lucéram's chapels, the Chapelle St-Jean, has a pretty painted baroque bell tower and houses a collection of old agricultural and hunting tools, the **Musée des Vieux Outils et des Traditions Locales** (enquire at tourist office to gain admission).

You can see more examples of work by Jean Beleison, who painted the walls and ceilings of the **Chapelle de Notre-Dame de Bon Coeur**, 2km northwest of the village off the road to the St-Roch pass. Although you can't go inside the chapel, you can view the paintings from outside.

Lucéram has a small **tourist office** on place Adrien-Barralis (Tues–Sat 9am–noon & 2–6pm, Sun 2–6pm; ☎04.93.79.46.50), which organizes tours of all the village's various museums and monuments (Tues–Sun 11am, 2.30pm & 4pm; €5; tour of the church only €2.50). There's a small cluster of eating places around the *Mairie*, including the rather swish *Retour aux Sources* (☎04.93.13.84.57, closed Sun eve) and the pizzeria *Bocca Fina*, with menus at €24.

Coaraze

COARAZE overlooks the valley of the Paillon de Contes, a tributary running west of the main Paillon. From Lucéram and the pass of St-Roch the road hangs over near-vertical descents, turning corners onto great open views of these beautiful but inhospitable mountains.

The population of Coaraze is less than five hundred, though this is one of the more chic Niçois villages, with many an artist and designer in residence. The facades of the post office and *mairie*, and place Félix-Giordan near the top of the village, are decorated with **sundials** signed by various artists including Cocteau and Ponce de Léon. The latter decorated the **Chapelle Notre-Dame du Gressier** just north of the village in 1962, known now as the Chapelle Bleue from the single colour he used in the frescoes. Place Félix-Giordan also has a **lizard mosaic** and a Provençal poem engraved in stone. The church, destroyed and rebuilt three times, is famous for the number of angels in its interior decoration, 118 in all.

Coaraze has a volunteer-run **tourist office** on place Sainte-Catherine below the village (Mon 10am–noon & 3–6pm, Tues, Thurs & Fri 10am–noon & 3–5pm; ☎04.93.79.37.47), which has the key to the church and chapel. There's also an excellent **hotel-restaurant**, the ⚜ *Auberge du Soleil*, 5 chemin de la Bégude (☎04.93.79.08.11, ✉auberge.du.soleil@orange.fr; ❹), with wonderful views from the rooms and the dining terrace. Access is on foot only, but you won't be expected to drag your cases up yourself.

Contes

The story always told about **CONTES**, 9km downstream from Coaraze, is of its **caterpillar plague** in 1508, which was so bad the bishop of Nice had to be called in to exorcise the leaf-eating army. With the full weight of ecclesiastical law the caterpillars were sentenced to exile on the slopes of Mont Macaron on the other side of the valley. A procession to the mountain was organized with all the villagers plus saintly relics, holy oil and so forth, and lo and behold, every last caterpillar joined the ranks and never bothered Contes again.

Contes has spread down the valley from its old village, and is quite a major town for these parts with a population of over four thousand and a small hotel, *Le Chaudron* (☎04.93.79.11.00, ❸) though there's no real reason to stay. The

Châteauneuf-de-Contes

Across the river from Contes a road winds up the mountainside to **CHÂTEAUNEUF-DE-CONTES**, a hilltop gathering of houses around an eleventh-century Romanesque church. About 2km further on a path to the left leads to a more recent but **ruined village**, the Bourg Mediéval also called Châteauneuf-de-Contes, which was last inhabited before World War I. That this village was abandoned gradually is evident from the varying degrees of building decay and vegetation growth. Ivy-clad towers and crumbling walls rise up among once-cultivated fig trees and rose bushes, and insects buzz in the silence and butterflies flit about the wild flowers that have replaced the gardens. The crescent of walled terraces where the people grew their vegetables is still clearly defined. The passing of time rather than some cataclysm saw its decline – there are no ghosts, nor even a whiff of eerieness; just immense, unthreatening horizons on either side.

There's a boom across the track leading to the site which supposedly closes it to vehicular traffic at 8pm nightly, though this appears not to be too rigorously enforced. Otherwise there are few gates or fences and you can wander around at any time of the day or night. On the Monday of Pentecost the inhabitants of the surviving village make a pilgrimage to the ruins which finishes with a communal meal.

The corniches

Three **corniche roads** run east from Nice to the independent principality of Monaco and on to Menton, the last town of the French Riviera. Napoleon built the **Grande Corniche** on the route of the Romans' Via Julia Augusta. The **Moyenne Corniche** dates from the first quarter of the twentieth century, when aristocratic tourism on the Riviera was already causing congestion on the coastal road, the **Corniche Inférieure**. The upper two are popular for shooting car commercials, and action films. They're dangerous roads: Grace Kelly, princess of Monaco, who was filmed driving the corniches in *To Catch a Thief*, died more than 25 years later when she took a bend too fast as she descended from La Turbie to the Moyenne Corniche.

Buses serve all three routes; the **train** follows the lower corniche; and all three are superb means of seeing the most mountainous stretch of the Côte d'Azur. For long-distance panoramas you follow the Grande Corniche; for precipitous views the Moyenne Corniche; and for close-up encounters with the architectural riot of the continuous coastal resort, take the Corniche Inférieure.

Staying along the corniches, anywhere between Nice and Menton, is expensive and impractical if you haven't booked well in advance. On a limited budget it makes more sense to base yourself in Menton or Nice and treat the corniches as pleasure rides.

The Corniche Inférieure and Cap Ferrat

The characteristic **Côte d'Azur mansions** that represent the unrestrained fantasies of the original owners parade along the **Corniche Inférieure**, a series

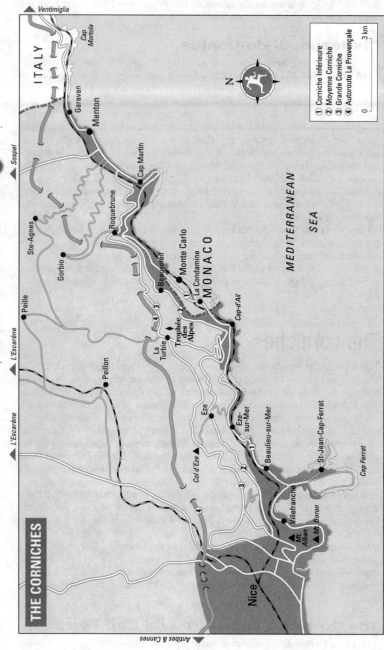

THE CORNICHES

① Corniche Inférieure
② Moyenne Corniche
③ Grande Corniche
④ Autoroute La Provençale

0   3 km

Ventimiglia

ITALY

Cap Mortola

Garavan

Menton

Sospel

Cap Martin

Roquebrune

Ste-Agnes

Gorbio

Beausoleil

Monte Carlo

La Condamine

MONACO

Peille

Cap-d'Ail

L'Escarène

La Turbie

Trophée des Alpes

Peillon

Èze

MEDITERRANEAN SEA

L'Escarène

Col d'Èze

Èze-sur-Mer

Beaulieu-sur-Mer

St-Jean-Cap-Ferrat

Cap Ferrat

Villefranche

Mt. Alban

Mt Boron

Nice

Antibes & Cannes

of pale dots among the lush pines. Others lurk screened from view on the promontory of **Cap Ferrat**, their gardens full of man-eating cacti and piranha ponds if the plethora of *"Défense d'entrer – Danger de Mort"* signs are anything to go by.

Villefranche-sur-Mer

VILLEFRANCHE-SUR-MER, the resort closest to Nice, marks the beginning of one of the most picturesque and unspoilt sections of the Riviera, though the cruise liners attracted by the deep anchorage in Villefranche's beautiful bay ensure a steady stream of tour buses climbing the hill from the port. However, as long as your visit doesn't coincide with the shore excursions, the old town on the waterfront, with its active fishing fleet and its covered, medieval **rue Obscure** running beneath the houses, is a tranquil and charming place to while away an afternoon.

The tiny fishing harbour is overlooked by the medieval **Chapelle de St-Pierre** (Tues–Sun: autumn & winter 10am–noon & 2–6pm, spring 10am–noon & 3–7pm, summer 10am–noon & 4–8pm; €2), decorated by **Jean Cocteau** in 1957 in shades he described as "ghosts of colours". In the guide to the chapel written by Cocteau, the artist invites travellers to enter without any aesthetic preconceptions. The ghostly colours fill drawings in strong and simple lines, portraying scenes from the life of St Peter and homages to the women of Villefranche and to the gypsies. Above the altar Peter walks on water supported by an angel, to the amusement of Christ. The fishermen's eyes are drawn as fishes; the ceramic eyes on either side of the door are the flames of the apocalypse and the altar candelabras of night-time fishing forks rise above single eyes. On June 29, the local fishermen celebrate the feast day of St Peter and St Paul with a Mass, the only time the chapel is used.

To the west of the fishing port, the massive **Citadelle de St-Elme** shelters the Hôtel de Ville, an open-air cinema, a conference centre and a series of **art museums** (June & Sept Mon & Wed–Sat 9am–noon & 2.30–6pm, Sun 2.30–7pm; July & Aug Mon & Wed–Sat 10am–noon & 2.30–7pm, Sun 2.30–7pm; Oct–May Mon & Wed–Sat 9am–noon & 2–5.30pm, Sun 1.30–6pm; free). One is dedicated to the voluptuous works of Villefranche sculptor **Volti**, whose bronze woman lies in the fountain outside the citadel gates; another, dedicated to the couple **Henri Goetz** and **Christine Boumeester**, contains two works by Picasso and one by Miró. A third collection, the **Roux**, is devoted to ceramic figurines.

Practicalities

Villefranche's **tourist office** is in the Jardins François-Binon (June & Sept Mon–Sat 9am–noon & 2–6.30pm; July & Aug Mon–Sat 9am–7pm; Oct–May Mon–Sat 9am–noon & 2–6pm; ℡04.93.01.73.68, Ⓦwww.villefranche-sur-mer.com), just below the corniche as it changes from avenue Foch to avenue Albert-1er. Of the local **hotels**, *Pension Patricia*, 310 av de l'Ange Gardien, Pont St-Jean (℡04.93.01.06.70, Ⓦhotel-patricia.riviera.fr; ❸), is a good-value, low-budget option, while the highly recommended *Hôtel Welcome*, 1 quai Amiral-Courbet (℡04.93.76.27.62, Ⓦwww.welcomehotel.fr; closed mid-Nov to mid-Dec; ❽), is the former convent where Cocteau used to stay, in a prime position overlooking the port. Of the fish **restaurants** on quai Amiral-Courbet, *La Mère Germaine* (℡04.93.01.71.39) is the most famous, founded in 1938 and known for its *bouillabaisse*, but you might also try *L'Oursin Bleu* (℡04.93.01.90.12; menus from €34) and *La Fille du Pecheur* (tapas from around €3.50, *bouillabaisse* for two €45), while inland, the welcoming *La Grignotière*, 3 rue du Poilu (℡04.93.76.79.83; closed

Wed pm in winter), is a delightful small restaurant serving dishes such as stuffed crab or veal escalope with green lemon; plats from around €10.

Cap Ferrat

Closing off Villefranche's bay to the east is **Cap Ferrat**, justifiably among the Côte d'Azur's most desirable addresses, due to the lack of through traffic and its pretty, indented coast; past residents include not only Rothschilds and the King of Belgium, but also the actor David Niven and writer Somerset Maugham. The one town, **ST-JEAN-CAP-FERRAT**, is a typical Riviera hideout for the wealthy: old houses overlooking modern yachts in a fishing port turned millionaires' resort. The #81 **bus** service from Nice and Ville-franche does a circuit of the promontory.

The St-Jean **tourist office** is at 59 av Dénis-Séméria (July & Aug Mon–Sun 8.30am–6pm; June & Sept Mon–Sat 8.30am–6pm, Oct–May Mon–Fri 10am–5pm, ℡04.93.76.08.90, ⓦwww.ville-saint-jean-cap-ferrat.fr). Cheaper **hotel** options are thin on the ground, with *La Frégate*, 11 av Dénis-Séméria (℡04.93.76.04.51, ℻04.93.76.14.93; ❸) being the best bet. For deeper pockets, *Brise Marine*, 58 av J-Mermoz (℡04.93.76.04.36, ⓦwww .hotel-brisemarine.com; ❽; closed Nov–Jan) has spacious rooms 100m from the sea, while the pleasant *Clair Logis*, 12 av Prince-Rainier-de-Monaco (℡04.93.76.51.81, ⓦwww.hotel-clair-logis.fr; ❻), boasts a lovely garden and most rooms have balconies or a terrace. If you really want to blow your savings, the *Grand Hôtel du Cap Ferrat*, 71 bd du Général-de-Gaulle (℡04.93.76.50.50, ⓦwww.grand-hotel-cap-ferrat.com; ❾) is a classic Riviera palace in a stunning site near the southern tip of the cap, with opulent rooms and prices to match: expect to pay upwards of €480 for a double in high season. The *Royal Riviera* (3 av Jean-Monnet, ℡04.93.76.31.00; ⓦwww .royal-riviera.com; ❾) is only a little less opulent, with a hint of Art Deco to its chic decor and doubles from €315 in high season.

Both of these palaces have suitably opulent **restaurants**: otherwise, the best places to eat in the area are on or close to the pleasure port and both have exceptional service: *Le Sloop* (℡04.93.01.48.63; menu at €28; closed Tues eve & Wed out of season) serves prime fish cooked in delicate and original ways; and *La Voile d'Or* (℡04.93.01.13.13; around €90; closed Nov–March) in the boutique hotel of the same name overlooking the port provides very sophisti-cated and imaginative Mediterranean cuisine. There are also cheaper options on the port: *Le Pirate* (℡04.93.76.12.97) serves good-value *plats du jour* from around €12, plus *bouillabaisse* and paella.

East of St-Jean's pleasure port you can follow av Jean-Mermoz then a **coastal path** out along the little peninsula, past the Plage Paloma to **Pointe Hospice**, where a nineteenth-century chapel cowers behind a twelve-metre-high turn-of-the-twentieth-century metal *Virgin and Child*. Back in St-Jean, another coastal path runs from avenue Claude-Vignon right round to chemin du Roy on the opposite side of the peninsula. At the southernmost point of the Cap you can climb a **lighthouse** for an overview of what you cannot reach – most of Cap Ferrat. Two exceptions to the formidable restrictions of passage are the **zoo** at the northern end of boulevard Général-de-Gaulle (daily: July & Aug 9.30am–7pm; Sept–June 9.30am–5.30pm; €14), in the park of King Léopold of Belgium's old residence, and the Villa Ephrussi on the road from the mainland.

The **Villa Ephrussi** (Feb-June & Sept to early Oct daily 10am–6pm; July-Aug daily 10am-7pm; Nov–Jan Mon-Fri 2-6pm, Sat & Sun 10am–6pm; last entry 30min before closing; €9.50, €2 extra to visit first-floor collections) was built in 1912 for Baroness Ephrussi, née Rothschild, a woman of unlimited wealth and highly eclectic tastes. The result is a wonderful profusion of decorative art, paintings, sculpture and artefacts ranging from the fourteenth to the nineteenth century and from European to Far Eastern origin. Among the highlights are a fifteenth-century d'Enghien tapestry of fabled hunting scenes; paintings by Carpaccio and other works of the Venetian Renaissance; Sèvres and Meissen porcelain; Ming vases; Mandarin robes; and canvases by Fragonard, Monet, Sisley and Renoir. The baroness had a particular love of the eighteenth century, and would receive guests dressed as Marie Antoinette. Visits to the ground floor of the villa and its gardens are unguided, allowing you to wander round at your own pace. In order to make the beautiful **gardens**, the baroness had a hill removed to level out the space in front, and then had tons of earth brought back in order that her formal French design could grow above the rock. She named the house after an ocean liner and had her 35 gardeners wear sailors' costumes. They tended Spanish, English, Japanese and Florentine gardens, all on a grand scale with attendant statuary and pools. One part of the park, the eastern slope, remained wild, because funds eventually ran out. Today, the highlights include the **musical fountains**, which perform every 20 minutes, and – when in bloom – the stunning **rose garden**, which offers wonderful views over the bay of Villefranche. In 1916 the baron died; when the baroness herself died in 1934 she bequeathed the house and 5000 works of art to the Académie des Beaux-Arts de l'Institut de France with the aim of creating a museum with an intimate feel, comparable to London's Wallace Collection.

Beaulieu

To the eastern side of the Cap Ferrat peninsula, overlooking the pretty Baie des Fourmis and accessible by foot from St-Jean along the promenade Maurice-Rouvier, is **BEAULIEU**, sheltered by a ring of craggy hills that ensures its temperatures are amongst the highest on the Côte, and that the town itself is one of its less developed spots. It's an appealing place, more tranquil than the bigger resorts and with a working harbour where you can buy freshly caught fish from the quayside, and it retains a couple of fine examples of Belle Époque architecture – most notably La Rotonde on avenue Fernand-Dunan, an opulent former hotel. Undoubtedly its most interesting attraction, however, is the **Villa Kérylos** (Jan to mid-Feb & early Nov to Dec Mon–Fri 2–6pm, Sat & Sun 10am–6pm; mid-Feb to June & Sept to early Nov 10am–6pm; July & Aug 10am–7pm; €8), a near perfect reproduction of an ancient Greek villa, just east of the casino on avenue Gustave-Eiffel. The only concessions made by Théodore Reinach, the archeologist who had it built, were glass in the windows, a concealed piano, and a minimum of early twentieth-century conveniences. He lived here for twenty years, eating, dressing and behaving as an Athenian citizen, taking baths with his male friends and assigning separate suites to women. However perverse the concept, it's visually stunning, with faithfully reproduced frescoes, ivory and bronze copies of mosaics and vases, authentic antiquities and lavish use of marble and alabaster. Not the least of its attractions is the fabulous waterside location with views across to St Jean Cap Ferrat.

Practicalities

The **tourist office** on place Georges-Clémenceau (July & Aug Mon–Sat 9am–12.30pm & 2–7pm, Sun 9am–12.30pm; Sept–June Mon–Sat 9am–12.15pm & 2–6pm; ℡04.93.01.02.21; ⓦwww.ot-beaulieu-sur-mer.fr) is next to the **gare SNCF**, five minutes' walk from Villa Kérylos. A couple of economical **accommodation** options include the family-run *Hôtel Riviera*, at 6 rue Paul-Doumer, right in the centre near the sea (℡04.93.01.04.92, ⓦwww.hotel-riviera.fr; ❹) and *Select*, 1 place Général-de-Gaulle (℡04.93.01.05.42, Ⓔselect.beaulieu@orange.fr; ❹), which is basic but clean and comfortable, and excellent value for this part of the coast. For those on a bigger budget, *Quality Hôtel Carlton*, 7 av Edith Cavell (℡04.93.01.44.70, Ⓦwww.carlton-beaulieu.com; ❼), has pretty rooms with balconies, a short walk from the sea.

The best **restaurant** in town is *La Réserve* at 5 bd du Général-Leclerc (℡04.93.01.00.01; closed mid-Nov to mid-Dec; around €90+), which features refined Mediterranean cuisine in suitably opulent palace hotel surroundings. If you prefer something a little more low-key, *Le Petit Darkoum*, 18 bd Maréchal-Leclerc (℡04.93.01.48.59), is an atmospheric Moroccan restaurant with menus from €30, and *Le Berlugan*, 48 bd Maréchal-Leclerc (℡04.93.01.02.97), is an amiable, relaxed brasserie serving up *faux* filet, escalope milanaise and – on Mondays – fish and chips, from around €16. *Le Beaulieu*, 45 bd Marinoni, is a good bet for **drinks** and coffee in smart surroundings.

Èze-sur-Mer and Cap d'Ail

The next stop on the train is **ÈZE-SUR-MER**, the little seaside extension of **Èze** village on the Moyenne Corniche (see below), with a narrow shingle beach and fewer pretensions than its western neighbours – though that doesn't stop Bono from U2 from owning a villa here. There's a small **tourist office** (May–Oct Mon–Sat 10am–1pm & 3–6.30pm) by the train station and a shuttle bus #83 up to Èze village every hour or so. Reasonable **accommodation** is available at *Auberge Le Soleil*, avenue de la Liberté (℡04.93.01.51.46, Ⓦwww.auberge-lesoleil.com; ❸; closed Nov), right on the seafront.

CAP D'AIL feels equally informal, though it suffers from the noise and congestion of the lower and middle corniches running closely parallel. As you descend to the sea from the main road, however, the noise is quickly left behind. Cap d'Ail's tiny eastern promontory has for years maintained one of the few open public spaces left on the Riviera, around the little **bar-restaurant**

△ The coastal path between Cap d'Ail and Cap Mala

Le Cabanon on Point des Douaniers, which serves its faithful customers who come down here to fish, play boules or just look out to sea. A coastal path leads east from here to **Monaco** and also – rather more temptingly – winds west around the headland to the pretty little **Plage Mala**, one of the most secluded and attractive beaches on the eastern Riviera. The way there is dotted with imposing old villas; in places the path is a bit of a scramble, and it can get slippery if the sea is rough. If you're tempted to **stay**, the *Thalassa Relais International de la Jeunesse* (2 av R-Gramaglia, ℡04.93.78.18.58, Ⓦwww.clajsud.fr; open April-Oct, €15 dorm, reception open 5-11pm) is right on the coastal path near the **gare SNCF**. The *Hôtel de Monaco* (1 av-Pierre Weck, ℡04.92.41.31.00, Ⓦwww.hoteldemonaco.com, Ⓞ) offers rather more luxurious accommodation close to Plage Mala and has a private cinema and secluded garden. You can **eat** seafood in idyllic surroundings at *La Pinède* (10 bd de la Mer, ℡04.93.78.37.10, menus €27 up, open March–Oct, closed Wed) in a pine grove just above the coastal path.

The Moyenne Corniche

The first views from the **Moyenne Corniche** are back over Nice as you grind up Mont Alban, which, with its seaward extension, Mont Boron, separates Nice from Villefranche. Two forts command these heights: **Fort Boron** which is still in naval service, and **Fort Alban**, as endearing a piece of military architecture as is possible to imagine – though now overgrown, it still remains in one piece, with its four tiny turrets glimmering in glazed Niçois tiles. The fort was continually taken by the enemies of Villefranche, who could then make St-Elme surrender in seconds. You can wander freely around the fort and see why Villefranche's citadel, so unassailable from the sea, was so vulnerable from above. To reach it you turn sharp right off the corniche along route Forestière before you reach the Villefranche pass. The #14 bus from Nice stops at Chemin du Fort from which the fort is signed.

Once through the pass, the cliff-hanging car-chase stretch of the Moyenne Corniche begins, with great views, sudden tunnels and little habitation.

Èze

ÈZE is unmistakable long before you arrive, its streets wound around a cone of rock below the corniche, whose summit is 470m above the sea. From a distance the village has the monumental medieval unity of Mont St-Michel and is a dramatic sight to behold, but seen up close, its secular nature exerts itself. Of the *villages perchés* in Provence, only St-Paul-de-Vence can compete with Èze for catering so single-mindedly to tourists. It takes a mental feat to recall that the labyrinth of tiny vaulted passages and stairways was designed not for charm but from fear of attack.

The ultimate defence, the castle, no longer exists, but the cacti **Jardin Exotique** (July & Aug daily 9am–10pm; Sept–June 9am–6/7pm; €5) which replaces it offers fantastic views from the ruins and a respite from the commerce below. Also worth visiting for atmosphere alone is the **Chapelle des Pénitents Blancs** on place du Planet, where the crucifix, of thirteenth-century Catalan origin, has Christ smiling down from the cross.

From place du Centenaire, just outside the old village, you can reach the shore through open countryside, via the **sentier Frédéric-Nietzsche**. The philosopher Nietzsche is said to have conceived part of *Thus Spoke Zarathustra* on this path. You arrive at the Corniche Inférieure at the eastern limit of **Èze-sur-Mer**.

Practicalities

Èze's **tourist office**, on place du Général-de-Gaulle just above the main car park (April–Oct daily 9am–7pm; Nov–March Mon–Sat 9am–6.30pm; ☎04.93.41.26.00, ⓦwww.eze-riviera.com), can supply a map of the many footpaths through the hills linking the three corniches.

If you want to stay, *Hôtel le Belèze*, place de la Colette on the Moyenne Corniche (☎04.93.41.19.09, ⓦwww.eze-riviera.com/eze/beleze; closed Jan, ③), is the most reasonable option, if a bit noisy. Alternatively, if you want to really splash out, there are two four-star luxury **hotels**, both with top-quality **restaurants**: *Château Eza* (☎04.93.41.12.24, ⓦwww.chateza.com; menus €37, €47; ⑨), where you can feast on foie gras with poached strawberries, and rooms in high season start at €320; and the *Château de la Chèvre d'Or*, on rue de Barri (☎04.92.10.66.66, ⓦwww.chevredor.com; ⑨; closed Nov–mid March), where rooms in high season start at €270, and the cheapest menu is a cool €85. Far more affordable meals can be found at the same hotel's *Le Grill du Château*, rue du Barri ☎04.93.41.00.17; menu €24), which serves Mediterranean food; *Le Nid d'Aigle*, at the very top of the village (☎04.93.41.19.08; à la carte from €10; closed Wed and all evenings November–Easter, otherwise closed Tues eve, Wed eve & Thurs eve), which serves simple Provençal fare, salads and the like; and the *Auberge du Cheval Blanc* as you enter the village (☎04.93.41.03.17; around €13) which serves hearty Provençal dishes washed down with pitchers of *vin de pays*.

The Grande Corniche

At every other turn on the **Grande Corniche** you're tempted to park your car and enjoy the distant views, which uniquely extend both seaward and inland, but there are frustratingly few truly safe places to do so. At certain points, such as **Col d'Èze**, you can turn off upwards for even higher views.

Col d'Èze

The upper part of Èze is backed by the **Parc Forestier de la Grande Corniche**, a wonderful oak forest covering the high slopes and plateaux of this coastal range. Paths are well signed, and there are picnic and games areas and orientation tables – in fact it's rather over-managed, but at least it isn't built on. If you take a left (coming from Nice) to cross the col and keep following route de la Revère, you come, after 1.5km or so, to an observatory, **Astrorama** (July & Aug Mon–Sat 6–10.30pm; Sept–June Fri & Sat 6–10.30pm; €10), where you can admire the evening and night sky through telescopes.

If you want **to stay**, the *Hôtel L'Hermitage*, on the corniche (☎04.93.41.00.68, ⓦwww.ezehermitage.com; ⑦), has magnificent views, and a **restaurant** serving passable meals (closed mid-Jan to mid-Feb; menus from €20).

La Turbie

After eighteen stunning kilometres from Nice, you reach **LA TURBIE** and the **Trophée des Alpes**, a sixth-century monument to the power of Rome and the total subjugation of the local peoples. Originally a statue of Augustus Caesar stood on the 45-metre plinth which was inscribed with the names of 45 vanquished tribes and an equally long list of the emperor's virtues. In the fifth century the descendants of the suppressed were worshipping the monument, to the horror of St Honorat who did his best to have the graven image destroyed. However, it took several centuries of barbarian invasions, quarrying, and incorporation into military structures before the trophy was finally reduced to rubble in the early eighteenth century by Louis XIV's engineers, who blew the fortress up to prevent it being used by the king's enemies. Its painstaking reconstruction was undertaken in the 1930s, and it now stands, statueless, at 35m.

Viewed from a distance along the Grande Corniche, however, the *Trophée* can still hold its own as an imperial monument. If you want to take a closer look and see a model of the original, you'll have to buy a ticket for the fenced-off plinth and its little **museum** (Tues–Sun: mid-May to mid-Sept 9.30am–1pm & 2.30–6.30pm; mid-Sept to mid-May 10am–1.30pm & 2.30–5pm; €5). You can climb up to the viewing platform and enjoy the spectacular view, extending to the Esterel in the west and Italy in the east.

In the town, just west of the *Trophée*, the eighteenth-century **Église de St-Michel-Archange** is a Baroque concoction of marble, onyx, agate and oil paint, with pink the overriding colour, and, among the paintings, a superb *St Mark writing the Gospel* attributed to Veronese. The rest of the town is less colourful, with rough-hewn stone houses, most of them medieval, lining rue Comte-de-Cessole, the main street which was part of the Via Julia leading to the *Trophée*.

For those thinking of **staying**, there's plenty of style and atmosphere at the thirteenth-century ⚘*Hostellerie Jérôme*, 20 Comte-de-Cessole (℡04.92.41.51.51, ⓦwww.hostelleriejerome.com; ❼), on the Via Julia in the heart of the old village and with a beautiful *restaurant gastronomique* (menus €60, €110). The same team owns the smart but much more affordable *Café de la Fontaine* on the main road through the village (℡04.93.28.52.79; *plats du jour* around €11).

Roquebrune Cap Martin

As the corniche descends towards Cap Martin, it passes the eleventh-century castle of **ROQUEBRUNE** and its fifteenth-century village nestling round the base of the rock. The **castle** (daily: Jan, Nov & Dec 10am–12.30pm & 2–5pm; Feb, March & Oct 10am–12.30pm & 2–6pm; April–June & Sept 10am–12.30pm & 2–6.30pm; July & Aug 10am–12.30pm & 3–7.30pm; €3.50) might well have become yet another Côte-side architectural aberration, thanks to its English owner in the 1920s. He was prevented from continuing his "restorations" after a press campaign brought public attention to the mock-medieval tower by the gateway, now known as the *tour anglaise*. The local authority has since made great efforts to kit the castle out in an authentic medieval fashion, and one of the best, if perhaps not most authentic, ideas has been to create an **open-air theatre** for the concerts and dance performances held here in July and August, with a spectacular natural backdrop down the precipitous slopes to Monaco and the coast.

The village itself is a real maze of passages and stairways that eventually lead either to one of the six castle gates or to dead ends. If you find yourself on rue de la Fontaine you can leave the village by the Porte de Menton and see, on the hillside about 200m beyond the gate, an incredible spreading **olive tree** that was perhaps one hundred years old when the count of Ventimiglia first built a fortress on Roquebrune's spur in 870 AD.

Southeast of the old village, just below the joined middle and lower corniches and the station, is the peninsula of **Cap Martin**, with a **coastal path** giving you access to a wonderful shoreline of white rocks and wind-bent pines. The path is named after **Le Corbusier**, who spent several summers in Roquebrune and drowned tragically off Cap Martin in 1965. His grave – a work of art designed by himself – is in the cemetery (square J near the flagpole), high above the old village on promenade 1er DFL, and his beach house (guided visits booked in advance through the tourist office; assemble Tues & Wed at tourist office, 10am; €8) is on the shore just east of the pretty **Plage du Buse**, the beach just below the station. It's a restful, low-key spot, with a simple café right on the beach. Further west, the **Plage du Golfe Bleu** is similar. East of Plage du Buse, a coastal path threads its way right round the tip of **Cap Martin**, linking up with avenue Winston Churchill on the eastern side to bring you to Roquebrune Cap Martin's main **beach**, the Plage de Carnolès. It's a spacious enough stretch of shingle, though much less restful than the beaches west of the cap. At the junction of the Via Aurelian and Via Julia is a remnant from the Roman station. Known as the **Tombeau de Lumone**, it comprises three arches of a first-century BC mausoleum, with traces of frescoes still visible under the vaulting.

Practicalities

There's limited **parking** at the entrance to Roquebrune's *Vieux Village*. If you come by train, it's a forty-minute walk uphill from the **gare SNCF**: turn east and then right up avenue de la Côte d'Azur, then first left up escalier Corinthille, across the Grande Corniche and up escalier Chanoine-JB-Grana. Down in the modern town centre and just up from the beach, you'll find the **tourist office** at no. 218 av Aristide-Briand (July & Aug Mon–Sat 9am–1pm, 3–7pm, Sun 10am–1pm & 3–7pm; Sept–June Mon–Sat 9am–12.30pm & 2–6pm; ℡04.93.35.62.87, ⊛www.roquebrune-cap-martin.com).

Hotels to try on the coast in Roquebrune are *Westminster*, 14 av Louis-Laurens (℡04.93.35.00.68, ⊛www.westminster06.com; closed late Nov to late Dec & mid Jan–early Feb; ❺), close to the sea, west of the station, and *Reine d'Azur*, 29 promenade du Cap (℡04.93.35.76.84, ⊛www.hotelreinedazur.com; ❺), overlooking the Plage de Carnolès. In the old village, try ⚑ *Les Deux Frères*, place des Deux-Frères (℡04.93.28.99.00, ⊛www.lesdeuxfreres.com; ❼), where rooms #1 and #2 have awesome views, so it's worth booking these well in advance.

There's no shortage of **restaurants** in Roquebrune village: try the atmospheric *Au Grand Inquisiteur*, 18 rue du Château (℡04.93.35.05.37; menus at €26 & €37; closed all day Mon & Tues lunchtime) or the restaurant at *Les Deux Frères*, place des Deux-Frères (℡04.93.28.99.00; lunch menu €24, otherwise €45; closed Sun eve, all day Mon, Tues lunch). Alternatively, the **bar** *La Grotte*, on place des Deux-Frères (closed Wed & Thurs lunch), serves generous *plats du jour* for around €10.50. For a real gourmet treat, try the panoramic **restaurant** *Le Vistaero* in the *Vista Palace Hotel* on the Grande Corniche (℡04.92.10.40.00), with lunch menus at €40 and €55.

Monaco

Viewed from a distance, there's no mistaking the thick cluster of towers that is **MONACO**. Rampant property development rescued the principality from postwar decline but in the process elbowed aside much of its former Italianate prettiness, leaving it looking like nowhere else on the Riviera. Not for nothing was **Prince Rainier**, who died in 2005, known as the Prince Bâtisseur.

Though it may have lost its looks, this tiny state, no bigger than London's Hyde Park, retains its comic opera independence. It has been in the Grimaldi family's hands since the fourteenth century – save for the two decades following the French Revolution – and, in theory, Monaco would again become part of France were the royal line to die out. For the last hundred years the principality has lived off gambling, tourism and its status as a tax haven.

Prince Albert II is the one constitutionally autocratic ruler left in Europe. There is a parliament, but it is of limited function and elected only by Monégasque nationals, about sixteen percent of the population. A copy of every French law is automatically sent to it, reworded and put to the prince. If he likes the law it is passed; if not, it isn't. The only other power is the Société des Bains de Mer (SBM), which owns the casino, the opera house and some of the grandest hotels.

Along with its reputation for great wealth, Monaco latterly acquired an unwelcome reputation for wheeler-dealer **sleaze**. On his accession in July 2005, the US-educated Albert declared he no longer wished Monaco to be known – in the words of Somerset Maugham - as "a sunny place for shady people". He signaled the principality would be more discriminating in granting residence, then set about complying with EU banking regulations and trying to get Monaco off an OECD list of uncooperative tax havens. As a demonstration of the new approach, in January 2006 the authorities froze $25 million from the local branches of two Swiss banks at the request of Sicilian authorities prosecuting a businessman with alleged links to the Cosa Nostra, while Sir Mark Thatcher, the son of former British Prime Minister Margaret Thatcher, was told he would be expected to leave when his residency expired in 2006. The principality now levies a withholding tax on the interest income of EU citizens resident in Monaco, which it rebates to the resident's country of origin. Even so, it remains home to 6000 mostly well-heeled British expats - including Roger Moore and Shirley Bassey – out of a total population of 32,000. Prince Albert is also reputedly an ardent environmentalist, and future development may be on a more sensitive scale.

One time to avoid Monaco – unless you're a motor-racing fan – is the end of May, when racing cars burn around the port and casino for the **Formula 1 Monaco Grand Prix**. Every space in sight of the circuit is inaccessible without a ticket, making casual sightseeing - or sneaky free views of the race - out of the question.

Arrival and information

The three-kilometre-long state consists of several distinct quarters. The pretty old town of **Monaco-Ville** around the palace stands on the high promontory, with the densely built suburb and marina of **Fontvieille** in its western shadow. **La Condamine** is the old port quarter on the other side of the rock; **Larvotto**, the rather ugly bathing resort with artificial beaches of imported sand, reaches to the eastern border; and **Monte Carlo** is in the middle. French **Beausoleil**, uphill to the north, is merely an extension of the conurbation, and the border is often unmarked and always easily crossed on foot.

The **gare SNCF** is on avenue Prince-Pierre in La Condamine, a short walk from place d'Armes, which is where most **buses** arrive, including those following the middle and lower corniches. Buses from other destinations arrive at a variety of places throughout the principality, but most also stop in Monte Carlo. There's an annexe of the **tourist office** at the gare SNCF (Tues–Sat 9am–5pm), but the

Phone codes in Monaco

When **phoning** Monaco from France you must use the international dialling code ☏00377 (instead of the ☏04 French area prefix); calls to France from Monaco begin ☏0033, dropping the first zero of the local code.

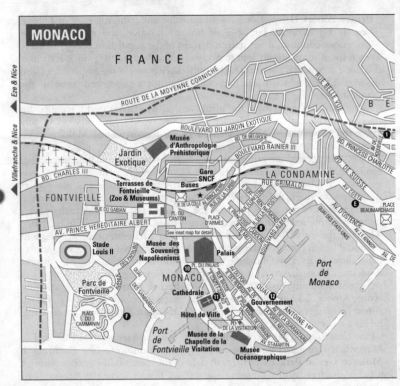

main office is at 2a bd des Moulins near the casino (Mon–Sat 9am–7pm, Sun
10am–noon; ☎92.16.61.16, ⓦwww.monaco-tourisme.com); local bus #4 from
the train station stops here ("Casino-Tourisme" stop).

Buses in Monaco run from 7am to 9pm, with flat-rate tickets (€1.50).
Unusually for the region, **car parking** in Monaco is plentiful and very clean,
if expensive. **Bikes** can be rented from Monte-Carlo-Rent, quai des Etats-Unis
(☎99.99.97.79) on the port. One very useful public service is the incredibly
clean and efficient free **lifts** linking lower and higher streets (marked on the
tourist office's map).

As for the practicalities of statehood, there are no **border formalities** and the
Euro is valid **currency**.

Accommodation

La Condamine is the best area for cheaper **hotels** within the principality,
though don't expect bargains. For something a little more affordable, you can
cross the invisible border and look for a room in Beausoleil. The prestige hotels
cluster around the casino in **Monte Carlo**.

Monaco has no **campsite**, and **caravans** are illegal in the state (as are
bathing costumes, bare feet and chests once you step off the beach). Camping
vehicles must be parked at the Parking des Écoles in Fontvieille, but can't be
parked overnight.

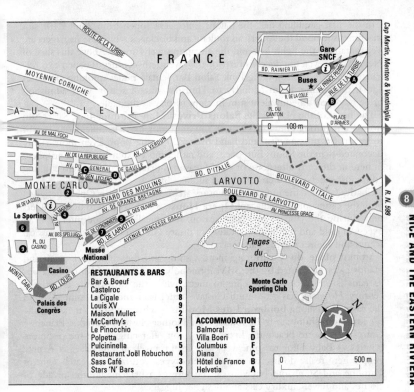

RESTAURANTS & BARS

Bar & Boeuf	6
Castelroc	10
La Cigale	8
Louis XV	9
Maison Mullet	2
McCarthy's	7
Le Pinocchio	11
Polpetta	1
Pulcininella	5
Restaurant Joël Robuchon	4
Sass Café	3
Stars 'N' Bars	12

ACCOMMODATION

Balmoral	E
Villa Boeri	D
Columbus	F
Diana	C
Hôtel de France	B
Helvetia	A

Hotels

Balmoral 12 av Costa ☎93.50.62.37, ⓦwww
.hotel-balmoral.mc. An elegant old building in
Monte Carlo, with good views over the port. ⓻

Villa Boeri 29 bd du Général-Leclerc, Beausoleil,
France ☎04.93.78.38.10, ⓦwww.hotelboeri.com.
A cheapish option with reasonably sized rooms,
some with sea views, and only a couple of minutes'
walk from Monte Carlo centre. Don't be put off by
the scruffy exterior – it's rather better inside. ④

Columbus 23 av des Papalins ☎92.05.90.00,
ⓦwww.columbushotels.com. Luxurious boutique
hotel in Fontvieille, with crisp modern decor, sea
views and prices a little lower than the palace
hotels. ⑨

Diana 17 bd du Général-Leclerc, Beausoleil,
France ☎04.93.78.47.58, ⓕ04.93.41.88.94.
Cheap and fairly comfortable, if somehow
rather glum, but very close to Monte Carlo
centre. ②

Hôtel de France 6 rue de la Turbie ☎93.30.24.64,
ⓦwww.monte-carlo.mc/france. Bright rooms, good
value for the principality and plenty of cheaper
eating options nearby. ⑤

Helvetia entrances at 1bis rue Grimaldi and rue de
la Turbie ☎93.30.21.71, ⓕ92.16.70.51. A fairly
basic option, but clean and comfortable, with
optional a/c. ④

Monte Carlo

The heart of **MONTE CARLO** is its **casino**, the one place not to be missed
on a trip to Monaco. Entrance is restricted to those over 21 and you may have
to show your passport; dress code is strict, with shorts and T-shirts frowned
upon, and skirts, jackets, ties and so forth more or less obligatory. Any coats or
large bags must be left in the cloakroom, which charges a fee.

In the first gambling hall, the Salons Européens (open from 2pm; €10), slot machines surround the American roulette and blackjack tables, the managers are Vegas-trained, the lights low and the air oppressively smoky. Above this slice of Nevada, however, the decor is turn-of-the-twentieth-century Rococo extravagance, while in the adjoining Pink Salon Bar, female nudes smoking cigarettes adorn the ceiling. From Monday to Thursday out of season your admission price buys you an equivalent sum in chips to play at the tables.

The heart of the place is the **Salons Privés** (Mon–Fri from 4pm, Sat & Sun from 3pm), through the Salles Touzet. You must look like a gambler, not a tourist to get in (so no cameras), and hand over €20 at the door. Even more richly decorated than the Salons Européens and rather more extensive, the atmosphere in here in the early afternoon or out of season is that of a cathedral: no clinking coins, just quiet-voiced croupiers and sliding chips.

Charles Garnier, the nineteenth-century architect of the Paris Opera, designed both the casino and the adjacent **Opera House** which is open to ticket holders only during the January to March season. Its typically Baroque interior is an excess of gold and marble with statues of pretty Grecian boys, frescoed classical scenes and figures waving palm leaves.

Around **place du Casino** are more casinos and the city's *hôtels-palais* and grands cafés, all owned by the SBM monopoly. The *American Bar* of the *Hôtel de Paris* is *the* place for the elite to meet, while the turn-of-the-twentieth-century *Hermitage* has a beautiful Gustave Eiffel iron-and-glass dome. Around the casino and along **boulevard des Moulins** is where most of the principality's luxurious shops are to be found, with another cluster on avenue Princesse Grace by Larvotto beach; the luxury goods on offer range from the cashmere booties at Baby Dior to some very grown up jewels at Van Cleef & Arpels. People here really do live up to their stereotypes: you may not catch sight of Caroline and Stéphanie, but you can be sure of a brilliant fashion parade of clothes and jewels, luxury cars and designer luggage.

For an alternative to people-watching, head for the **Musée National** at 17 av Princesse-Grace (Easter–Sept daily 10am–6.30pm; Oct–Easter daily 10am–12.15pm & 2.30–6.30pm; €6). Dedicated to the history of **dolls and automata** from eighteenth-century models to the latest Barbie dolls, it's better than you might think. Some of the doll's-house scenes and the creepy automata are quite surreal and fun.

Monaco-Ville

Though rather over-restored and lifeless, **MONACO-VILLE** is the one part of the principality where the developers have been reined in, and it retains a certain toy-town charm despite the surfeit of shops selling Grimaldi mugs and assorted junk. It is also home to the **Palais Princier**, whose state apartments and throne room can be visited on a self-guided tour (April 10.30am-6pm, May-Sept 9.30am-6.30pm, Oct 10am-5.30pm, closed Nov-March; €7). Despite the palace's modest size and military origins as a thirteenth century Genoese fortress, the part you see certainly feels suitably palatial, thanks in part to major embellishment by the Grimaldis during the latter half of the sixteenth century. The palace courtyard conceals a massive sixteenth-century cistern designed to ensure a water supply in time of siege. These days, the main group besieging it is camera-clicking tourists; if you're outside the palace at 11.55am, you'll catch the daily changing of the immaculate, white-uniformed guard.

There are also a number of small museums and attractions in Monaco-Ville more or less connected to the Grimaldis: you can look at Napoléonic relics and

△ Changing of the guard, Palais Princier

items from the palace's historical archives at the **Musée des Souvenirs Napoléoniens et Collection des Archives Historiques du Palais**, place du Palais (Jan–March Tues–Sun 10.30am–12.30pm & 2–5pm, April daily 10.30am–6pm, May–Sept daily 9.30am–6.30pm, Oct 10am–5.30pm, Dec 10.30am–5pm, closed Nov; €4); see the tombs of Prince Rainier and Princess Grace in the rather dull nineteenth century **cathedral** (daily 9.30am–7pm summer, until 6pm winter) on rue Colonel; and even watch Monaco the movie, at the **Monte Carlo Story**, parking des Pecheurs (July & Aug 2–6pm; Jan–June & Sept–Oct 2–5pm; €7).

If you've had your fill of Grimaldis, check out the **Musée de la Chapelle de la Visitation**, place de la Visitation (Tues–Sun 10am–4pm; €3), which displays part of the religious art collection of Barbara Piasecka Johnson (an heir to the Johnson & Johnson fortune). This small but exquisite collection includes works by Zurbarán, Rivera, Rubens, and a rare, early religious work by Vermeer, *St Praxedis*.

One of Monaco's best, though pricey, sites is the **aquarium** in the basement of the **Musée Océanographique**, avenue St-Martin (April–June & Sept 9.30am–7pm, July & Aug 9.30am–7.30pm; Oct–March 10am–6pm; €11), where delicate leafy sea dragons, living nautiluses and hideous angler fish are just some of the bizarre and colourful creatures you will witness. This is also an institute for serious scientific research, and claims to be the only place in the world that has succeeded in keeping living corals in its aquariums. Films by the famous underwater explorer Jacques Cousteau, who for many years was the director of the institute, are screened in the museum's conference hall.

Bus #1 or #2 will take you from place d'Armes to Monaco-Ville; **by car** head for the Parking du Chemin des Pêcheurs from where there's a lift up to avenue St-Martin by the Musée Océanographique. Only Monégasque- and Alpes Maritimes-registered cars are allowed in Monaco-Ville itself.

Fontvieille, the Jardin Exotique and La Condamine

Below the rock of Monaco-Ville, by the Port de Fontvieille, a modern complex, the **Terrasses de Fontvieille** (bus #5 or #6), houses yet more museums. The **Collection de Voitures Anciennes de SAS le Prince de Monaco** (daily 10am–6pm, €6), is an enjoyable miscellany of old and not so old cars, both prestigious and humble – there's everything from a 1928 Hispano-Suiza worthy of Cruella de Ville to Princess Grace's elegant 1959 Renault Florida Coupé; hardened petrol heads will doubtless gravitate to Nigel Mansell's 1989 Formula 1 Ferrari, but gentler souls might prefer the cute little Autobianchi 110 FB5 convertible or the lovely 1963 Facel Vega. The **Musée Naval** (daily 10am–6pm; €4) contains 250 model ships; the **zoo** (June–Sept 9am–noon & 2–7pm; Oct–Feb 10am–noon & 2–5pm; March–May 10am–noon & 2–6pm; €4) has exotic birds, a black panther and a white tiger, and the museum of stamps and coins, the **Musée des Timbres et des Monnaies** (July–Sept daily 10am–6pm; Oct–June 10am–5pm; €3) has rare stamps, money and commemorative medals dating back as far as 1640.

Monaco's parks and gardens are uniformly immaculate. High above Fontvieille on boulevard du Jardin Exotique is Monaco's prime garden, the **Jardin Exotique** (mid-May to mid-Sept 9am–7pm; mid-Sept to mid-May 9am–6pm or dusk; €6.90; bus #2), full of bizarre cacti emerging from the hillside Admission also includes entry to the **Musée d'Anthropologie Préhistorique**, tracing the history of the human race from Neanderthal man to Grimaldi prince, and the

Grotte de l'Observatoire, prehistoric caves with illuminated stalagmites and stalactites.

The yachts in the **Port de Monaco** in **La Condamine** are, as you might expect, gigantic. Also on the port at quai Albert-1ᵉʳ is a fabulous public Olympic-size, saltwater **swimming pool** with high-dive boards (May to mid-Oct 9am–6pm except during the Grand Prix; €4.50).

Eating and drinking

La Condamine and Monaco-Ville are replete with **restaurants**, **brasseries** and **cafés**, but good food and reasonable prices don't often coincide: the best-value cuisine is usually Italian. It's really not worth going upmarket in Monaco unless you're prepared to contemplate €90 or more a head, in which case there are a few worthy contenders for your money. As for **food shopping**, you can buy caviar, champagne and smoked salmon without any problem on and around avenue St-Charles, but finding *boulangeries* can be difficult. The best daily food **market** is in rue du Marché in Beausoleil.

Cafés and restaurants

Bar & Boeuf Sporting Monte Carlo, 26 av Princesse Grace ☎92.16.60.60, closed Mon out of season, €60–90. The funkier of the two Alain Ducasse operations in Monaco, with a trendy fusion menu based on seabass (*bar*) and beef.
Castelroc place du Palais ☎93.30.36.68. A crowded but smart and convenient place if you've been doing the palace tours. It serves fish dishes and Monégasque specialities, with a lunch menu at €21. Closed Mon & mid-Dec to late Jan.
Restaurant Joël Robuchon Hôtel Métropole, 4 av de la Madone ☎93.15.15.10. Luxurious surroundings and superlative cooking under the aegis of one of France's most respected chefs. €90+.
Louis XV Hôtel de Paris place du Casino ☎92.16.29.76, closed Tues, Wed, Dec & second half of Feb. Alain Ducasse's Monaco flagship, in the *Belle Époque* splendour of one of the grandest

palace hotels and making plentiful use of excellent local produce. €150 upwards.
Maison Mullet 19 bd des Moulins ☎97.98.15.60. Clean, bright patisserie and chocolatier on Monte Carlo's main strip, with a good selection of ice creams.
Le Pinocchio 30 rue Comte F-Gastaldi ☎93.30.96.20. Dependable Italian joint in Monaco-Ville, with a pretty outdoor terrace; *plats* from €11. Closed mid-Dec to early Jan.
Polpetta 2 rue Paradis ☎93.50.67.84. A pleasant restaurant with attractive terrace and vaulted dining hall in Monte Carlo, serving Provençal and Italian food; €30–55. Closed Tues & Sat lunch.
Pulcinella 17 rue du Portier ☎93.30.73.61. Traditional Italian cooking in Monte Carlo; menu at €28, *plats* from €13.

Nightlife, entertainment and festivals

There are better places for **nightlife** than Monaco, and the top discotheques like *Jimmy'z*, by the Monte-Carlo Sporting Club, are not going to let you in unless you're decked out in designer finery. The alternatives include traditional piano bars like Sass Café in avenue Princesse Grace, American- or British-style **bars** and pubs like the large, informal *Stars 'N' Bars* on the quai Antoine-1er, packed out on Fridays and Saturdays and with a lively club upstairs, or the ubiquitous Irish pub, *McCarthy's*, 7 rue du Portier, for Guinness and occasional live music.

By contrast, the **opera season** (Nov–March) is pretty exceptional, the SBM being able to book up star companies and performers before Milan, Paris or New York gets hold of them. The programme of **theatre**, **ballet** and **concerts** throughout the year is also impressive, with the **Printemps des Arts** festival (April) seeing performances by famous classical and contemporary dance troupes from all over the world. The main booking office for ballet, opera and concerts is the casino foyer, place du Casino, Monte Carlo (Tues–Sun 10am–5.30pm; ☎98.06.28.28); for theatre, book at the Théâtre Princesse Grace, 12 av de l'Ostende, Monte Carlo (Tues–Fri 10am-1pm & 2-5pm, ☎93.25.32.27).

Monaco's **festivals** are spectacular, particularly the **International Fireworks Festival** in July and August, which can be seen from as far away as Cap d'Ail or Cap Martin. Mid- to late-January sees vast trailers entering Monaco for the **International Circus Festival** at the Espace Fontvieille, a rare chance to witness the world's best in this underrated performance art (details on ☎92.05.23.45). **Holidays** in Monaco are the same as in France, with the addition of January 27 (Fête de Ste-Dévote) and November 19 (Fête Nationale Monégasque).

The **Monte-Carlo Automobile Rally** takes place at the end of January and the **Formula 1 Grand Prix** at the end of May. Every space in sight of the circuit, which runs round the port and the casino, is inaccessible without a ticket (☎93.15.26.00). Monaco also has a first-division **football team**, AS Monaco, whose home ground is the enormous Stade Louis II in Fontvieille, 3 av des Castelans (☎92.05.40.11).

Listings

Banks Most banks have a branch in Monaco around bd des Moulins, av de Monte-Carlo and av de la Costa; hours are Mon–Fri 9am–noon & 2–4.30pm.

Bookshop Scruples, 9 rue Princesse-Caroline (☎93.50.43.52), sells English-language books.

Consulates Britain, 33 bd Princesse-Charlotte (☎93.50.99.54); Canada 1 av Henry-Dunant (☎97.70.62.42); Ireland, 5 av des Citronniers (☎93.15.70.00); South Africa 30 bd Princesse-Charlotte ☎93.25.24.26.

Emergencies ☎18 or 93.30.19.45; Centre Hospitalier Princesse Grace, av Pasteur (☎97.98.97.69).

Money exchange Cie Monégasque de Change, parking du Chemin des Pêcheurs; Monafinances, 17 av des Spélugues.

Pharmacy Call ☎141 or 93.25.33.25 from public phones.

Police and lost property ☎18 (emergency) or 3 rue Louis-Notari (☎93.15.30.15).

Post office PTT Palais de la Scala, place Beaumarchais (Mon–Fri 8am–7pm & Sat 8am–noon).

Taxis ☎93.15.01.01.

Menton and around

Of all the Riviera resorts, **MENTON**, the warmest and the most Italianate, is the one that most retains an atmosphere of genteel, aristocratic tourism. It got its first boost as a resort in 1861 when a British doctor, James Henry Bennet, published a treatise on the benefits of Menton's mild winter climate to tuberculosis sufferers, and soon thousands of well-heeled invalids were flocking to the town in the vain hope of a cure. Today it is even more of a rich retirement haven than Nice, and it's precisely that genteel, slow promenading pace of the town that makes it easy to imagine the presence of arch duchesses, grand dukes, tsars and other autocrats, as well as sick artists such as Guy de Maupassant and Katherine Mansfield. It's also a classic border town, and in summer the streets and beaches are thronged with relaxed Italian day-trippers munching ice cream. Menton does not go in for the ostentatious wealth of Monaco nor the creative cachet of Cannes or some of the hilltop towns. What it chiefly glories in is its climate and its all-year-round lemon crops. Ringed by protective mountains, hardly a whisper of wind disturbs the suntrap of the city. Winter is when you notice the difference most, with Menton several vital degrees warmer than St-Tropez or St-Raphaël.

Perched in the hills around Menton are some stunning little unspoilt villages, with spectacular views: **Ste-Agnes** and **Castillon** are both known for their arts and crafts studios, while **Castellar** and **Gorbio** are great for walkers.

Arrival and information

Roquebrune and Cap Martin merge into Menton along the three-kilometre shore of the **Baie du Soleil**. The modern town is arranged around three main streets parallel to the promenade du Soleil. The **gare SNCF** is on the top one, rue Albert-1er, from where it's a short walk northeast to the **gare routière** on avenue de Sospel. The **tourist office** is at 8 av Boyer (mid-June to mid-Sept daily 9am–7pm; mid-Sept to mid-June Mon–Sat 8.30am–12.30pm & 2–6pm; ℡04.92.41.76.76, ⓦwww.villedementon.com), inside the Palais de l'Europe, a former casino which now hosts various cultural activities, including regular contemporary art exhibitions. The Vieille Ville lies further east, above the old port and the start of the Baie de Garavan. The district of Garavan, further east again, is the most exclusive residential area and overlooks the modern marina.

Accommodation

Accommodation, though good value, is difficult to find. Menton is as popular as the other major resorts, so in summer you should definitely book ahead. The tourist office won't make reservations for you, though they will tell you where rooms are still available.

Hotels

L'Aiglon 7 av de la Madone ℡04.93.57.55.55, ⓦwww.hotelaiglon.net. Spacious rooms in a nineteenth-century residence surrounded by a large garden, with a heated pool. ⑦

Hôtel des Ambassadeurs 3 rue Partouneaux, ℡04.93.28.75.75, ⓦwww.ambassadeurs-menton .com. A chic, revamped grand hotel that nevertheless retains some of its *Belle Époque* atmosphere. ⑨

Auberge Provençale 11 rue Trenca ℡04.93.35.77.29, ⓕ04.93.28.88.88. Centrally located above a restaurant, with soundproofed rooms and a garden. ③

Beauregard 10 rue Albert-1er ℡04.93.28.63.63, ⓕ04.93.28.63.79. Traditionally furnished rooms and a relaxed atmosphere. ③

Belgique 1 av de la Gare ℡04.93.35.72.66,

ⓕ04.93.41.44.77. A bit mundane but clean, friendly and conveniently close to the station. ③

Chambord 6 av Boyer ℡04.93.35.94.19, ⓦwww .hotel-chambord.com. Large modern rooms, many with balconies. Well located. ⑦

Moderne 1 cours George-V ℡04.93.57.20.02, ⓦwww. hotel-moderne-menton.com. Good-value modern, central hotel: many rooms have balconies. ④

Napoléon, 29 porte de France, Garavan ℡04.93.35.89.50, ⓦwww.napoleon-menton .com. Elegantly modern seafront hotel with pool and garden. Mountain or sea views from the rooms. ⑦

Le Terminus place de la Gare ℡04.92.10.49.80, ⓕ04.92.10.49.81. Basic and inexpensive, right by the station and with a cheap restaurant. ③

Hostel, chambres d'hôtes and campsite

HI youth hostel plateau St-Michel ℡04.93.35.93.14, ⓦwww.fuaj.org. This well-run hostel is up a gruelling flight of steps (signposted Camping St-Michel) from the northern side of the railway to the east of the station, or take bus #6 from the *gare routière* (direction "Ciappes de Castellar"; stop "Camping St-Michel"). Good food and views; 10pm curfew. €15.60 per dorm bed. Reception 7–10am & 5–10pm. Closed Nov-Jan. **Chambre d'hôte** M. Paul Gazzano, 151 rte de Castellar ℡04.93.57.39.73. Two kilometres from

Menton, a delightful house with a terrace and pool looking down over the wooded slopes to the sea. Open all year. ④

Camping St-Michel rte des Ciappes ℡04.93.35.81.23, ⓕ04.93.57.12.35. Reasonably priced campsite in the hills above the town, with plenty of shade and good views out to sea; follow directions for HI youth hostel. €17.75 per tent. Closed Nov–March except for Fête du Citron.

The Town

Menton's history, like that of Monaco, almost took an independent path. In the revolutionary days of 1848, Menton and Roquebrune, both at the time under Monaco's jurisdiction, declared themselves an independent republic under the protection of Sardinia. When the Prince of Monaco came to Menton in the hope that his regal figure would sway the people, he had to be rescued by the police from a furious crowd and locked up overnight for his own protection. Eventually, following an 1860 vote by Roquebrune and Menton to remain in France, Grimaldi agreed to the sale of the towns to the French state for four million francs. Shortly afterwards, sick travellers from the north began to arrive in numbers.

Today, the town's greatest attraction is not the health-giving properties of its winter climate but the fabulous **Vieille Ville** around the parvis St-Michel. Other highlights include the works of **Jean Cocteau** – in particular his

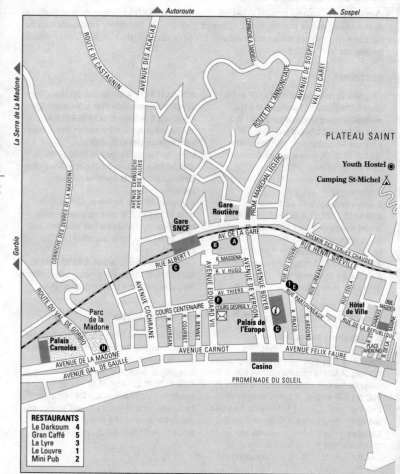

RESTAURANTS
Le Darkoum 4
Gran Caffé 5
La Lyre 3
Le Louvre 1
Mini Pub 2

decoration of the registry office – and the **gardens** in Garavan. Menton's beaches may be stony but they're popular, and in summer the gritty plage des Sablettes on the harbour has a fashionable edge.

The modern town

The **Salle des Mariages**, or registry office, in the Hôtel de Ville on place Ardoino, was decorated in inimitable style by **Jean Cocteau** (1889–1963) and can be visited without matrimonial intentions by asking the receptionist by the main door (Mon–Fri 8.30am–12.30pm & 2–5pm; €1.50). On the wall above the official's desk a couple face each other, with strange topological connections between the sun, her headdress and his fisherman's cap. The *Saracen Wedding Party* on the right-hand wall reveals a disapproving mother of the bride, spurned girlfriend of the groom and her armed vengeful brother amongst the cheerful guests. On the left wall is the story of *Orpheus and Eurydice* at the doomed moment when Orpheus has just looked back. Meanwhile, on the ceiling are

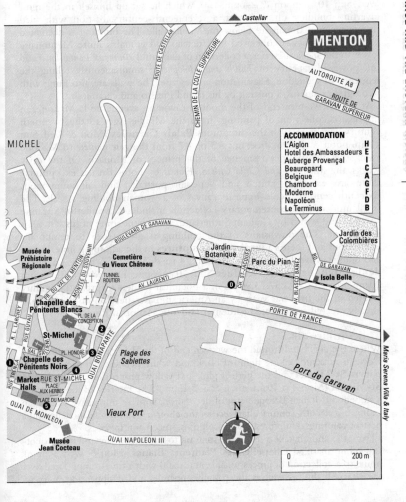

Poetry rides Pegasus, tattered *Science juggles with the Planets* and *Love*, open-eyed, waiting with bow and arrow at the ready. Just to add to the confusion, the carpet is mock panther skin.

The **Musée de Préhistoire Régionale**, at the top of rue Lorédan-Larchey close to the Hôtel de Ville (Mon & Wed–Sun 10am–noon & 2–6pm; free), is one of the best on the subject. There are good videos to watch, life-size recreated scenes of early human life, and the famous 27,000-year-old skull of "Menton Man" found in a cave near the town, encrusted with shells and teeth from his headgear.

Close to the museum are the pretty **market halls** of place du Marché off quai de Monléon, where food and flowers are sold every morning. Behind place du Marché is the attractive place aux Herbes with a bric-a-brac market every Friday morning, and the pedestrianized rue St-Michel, lined with cafés and restaurants and citrus trees, linking the old and modern towns.

There are other works by Cocteau in the **Musée Jean Cocteau** (Mon & Wed–Sun 10am–noon & 2–6pm; €3), which he set up himself in the most diverting building on the front, a seventeenth-century bastion with tiled turrets on quai Bonaparte below the Vieille Ville. The building is decorated with pebble mosaics conceived by Cocteau and contains more Mentonaise lovers in the *Inamorati* series, a collection of delightful *Animaux Fantastiques* and the powerful tapestry of *Judith and Holopherne* simultaneously telling the sequence of seduction, assassination and escape. The walls are also hung with photographs, poems, a portrait by his friend Picasso and ceramics.

At the far western end of the modern town, on avenue de la Madone, an impressive collection of paintings from the Middle Ages to the twentieth century can be seen in the sumptuous **Palais Carnolès** (Mon & Wed–Sun 10am–noon & 2–6pm; free; bus #3 or #7 from the *gare routière* to Madone Parc), the old summer residence of the princes of Monaco. Of the early works, the *Madonna and Child with St Francis* by Louis Bréa is exceptional; there are excellent Dutch and Venetian portraits; and an anonymous sixteenth-century École Français canvas of a woman holding a scale. The small modern and contemporary collection includes a wonderful Suzanne Valadon and works by Graham Sutherland, who spent some of his last years in Menton. The downstairs of the building is given over to temporary exhibitions and there's a **jardin des sculptures** in the adjoining lime, lemon and orange grove. Due north of here, at 74 rte du Val de Gorbio, is **La Serre de la Madone** (April–Oct Tues–Sun 10am–6pm; Dec–March Tues–Sun 10am–5pm; ☎04.93.57.73.90; €8), a botanical garden of great tranquillity created in the interwar years by an American, Lawrence Johnston, who had already created a celebrated garden at Hidcote Manor in England.

The Vieille Ville

Where the *quai* bends round the western end of the Baie de Garavan from the Cocteau museum, a long flight of black-and-white pebbled steps leads to the **parvis St-Michel** and the perfect pink and yellow proportions of the **Église St-Michel** (Mon–Fri 10am–noon & 3–5.15pm). The interior of the church is a stupendous Italian Baroque riot of decoration, with an impressive vast organ casing, a sixteenth-century altarpiece in the choir by Antonio Manchello and a host of paintings, sculptures, gilded columns, stucco and frescoes.

From the church, take a few more steps up to another square and the apricot-and-white marbled **Chapelle des Pénitents Blancs** (Mon & Wed 3–5pm), home to a collection of processional lanterns and with a fine trompe-l'oeil over the altar. All this, as well as the pastel campaniles and disappearing stairways between long-lived-in houses, are a sure sign that you've arrived at the most Italianate and beautiful of the Riviera's *Vieilles Villes*.

From here, head north, or uphill. At the top you'll reach the bewitchingly beautiful and hauntingly sad **Cimetière du Vieux Château**, with cream-coloured mid-nineteenth-century sculpted stone and diverse foreign names ranging from Russian princes to William Webb-Ellis, credited, in public schools throughout England, with the invention of rugby. It was here that many of Menton's young and consumptive visitors were buried, and the grief etched in the gravestones is palpable, from the grave of 24-year-old Englishman James MacEwan – "gentle in spirit, patient in suffering" – to the Liverpool-born Arthur Edward Foster, who died aged 23 in 1887 – "God's finger touched him, and he slept" and the achingly romantic tribute (in German) from a widowed husband to the "unforgettable" Henriette van der Aue of Prague, who died at 33. If all this untimely death is a tad gloomy, there can at least be few lovelier final resting places, with sweeping views along the coast into Italy. The cemetery is in rather crumbly condition, and parts of it are fenced off.

Garavan

If it's cool enough to be walking outside, the public **parks** up in the hills and the **gardens** of **Garavan**'s once-elegant villas make a change from shingle beaches. From the Vieux Cimetière you can walk or take bus #8 along boulevard de Garavan past houses hidden in their large, exuberant gardens.

The first public garden you come to from the cemetery along the boulevard de Garavan is the **Jardin Exotique** (Mon & Wed–Sun: April–Sept 10am–12.30pm & 3.30–6.30pm; Oct–March 10am–12.30pm & 2–5pm; €5), which surrounds the Villa Val Rahmeh. Though there's a good variety of plants, it's not brilliantly maintained and you can get the same views for free from the **Parc du Pian**, an olive grove reached from the boulevard just past the Jardin Botanique. Further on, down avenue Blasco-Ibañez, is the garden of **Fontana Rosa** (guided visits Friday at 10am; €5), surrounding the former home of the Spanish author Vincente Blasco-Ibañez, bright with ceramic decoration and currently undergoing restoration. North up rue Webb-Ellis and chemin Wallaya behind the Garavan *gare SNCF* is the villa **Isola Bella**, the former Menton home of author Katherine Mansfield, with a couple of plaques to identify it, though sadly it is not open to the public. Back on the seafront, the very last house before the Italian border is the **Maria Serena Villa** (guided tours on Tues at 10am; €5), designed by Charles Garnier for the family of Ferdinand de Lesseps.

Eating, drinking and entertainment

Menton has few exceptional **restaurants** so most people usually cross into Italy for a blowout meal. If you're not that bothered what you eat as long as it's cheap, the pedestrianized rue St-Michel is promising ground. There are plenty of snack bars among the burger houses, as well as outlets for omelettes or steak and chips and occasionally interesting *plats du jour*. There's also an excellent Moroccan restaurant, *Le Darkoum*, 23 rue St-Michel (℡04.92.07.34.72) offering *plats* from around €12. Close by, *La Lyre* at 15 quai Bonaparte (℡04.93.35.38.16) offers grilled swordfish, calamares and the like from around €11.50. Fancier modern Mediterranean fare is available in the *Ambassadeurs' restaurant gastronomique*, *Le Louvre* (2 rue du Louvre; ℡04.93.28.75.75) with a €35 lunch menu. Many of Menton's **bars** are on the seafront and port, including *Gran Caffè*, at 25 quai de Monléon, and *Mini Pub*, 51 quai Bonaparte. In summer, the Plage des Sablettes between the Vieux Port and the Port de Garavan is lined with beach bars, some of them quite stylish.

In August the pebbled mosaic of the Grimaldi arms on the parvis St-Michel is covered by chairs, music stands, pianos and harps for the **Festival de Musique de Menton**. The nightly concerts are superb and can be listened to from the quaysides without buying a ticket. If you want a proper seat, make a reservation at the tourist office.

More bizarrely, the town's **lemons** are celebrated in a citrus fruit festival every February and March. Sadly, despite the profusion of local produce, a *citron pressé* served in a Menton bar still costs twice as much as an imported Belgian beer.

Around Menton

In the hills above Menton and Roquebrune are the tiny villages of **Gorbio** and **Ste-Agnes**, and on the road to Sospel, **Castellar** and **Castillon**. All give stupendous views over steep, forested slopes to the sea.

Ste-Agnes

Ten kilometres northwest of Menton and 800m above sea level is **STE-AGNES**, the place which claims to be the highest coastal village in Europe – a claim you'll readily believe after the tortuous journey up to the village. It's milling with crystal engravers, painters, herbalists, jewellers and leather workers, but in spite of that it's still a peaceful spot. Perched at the foot of a cliff, it commands breathtaking views, especially from the ancient Saracen fortress at the top of the crag above. The Saracens had an impeccable eye for choosing defensive positions: such is the site's commanding vantage point that another important **fort** was built into the mountain top a millennium later, this time as part of the Maginot defences of the 1930s (July–Sept daily 3–6pm; Oct–June Sat & Sun 2.30–5.30pm; daily during Fête du Citron; €4).

The village is also an excellent starting point for **walks**, and the *syndicat d'initiative*, in the Espace de Culture et Traditions at the entrance to the village, will provide you with a free list (in French only) of suggested hikes. One

△ Ste-Agnes

popular route, offering the best chance of glimpsing Corsica, is up the **Pic Cime de Baudon** (1hr 45min to the summit at 1264m), with possibilities of continuing on to Gorbio or Peille.

A hospitable place to stay in the village is the **hotel–restaurant** *Saint Yves* (☎04.93.35.91.45, ⓦwww.le-saint-yves.com; ②), some of whose rooms have good views. The best-quality **food** is served in *Le Logis Sarrasin* (☎04.93.35.86.89; closed Mon; menus at €16 & €19), where they prepare a fine *tarte Agnésoise*, made with courgette flowers; while *Le Righi*, around the Maginot fort (☎04.92.10.90.88; menus from €15), has the best views. Three **buses** make the trek up to the village from the *gare routière* in Menton; the trip takes 30 minutes.

Gorbio

GORBIO, to the southwest of Ste-Agnes, is an exquisite hilltop village with very few arts and crafts boutiques or other tourist fodder, lending it a tranquil atmosphere that's rare for so scenic a place. Though the two villages are only 2km apart as the crow flies, the roads between them meet approximately 8km away, below the autoroute. Walkers can take a more direct route (a 45min walk): the road from Ste-Agnes drops downhill, and then crosses the path to Gorbio at L'Auribel bus stop, on a sharp hairpin bend after about 2km. You can also get to the village directly from Menton; bus #901 makes the climb five times daily from the *gare routière* in thirty minutes.

On the Thursday after Corpus Christi in June, the annual rite of the **Procession des Limaces** takes place, when the streets are illuminated by tiny lamps of snail shells filled with olive oil – a custom dating back to medieval times and occurring in villages throughout this area (check with the tourist office in Menton for exact dates).

Castillon and Castellar

A railway used to run along the Carei Valley from Menton up to Sospel. Though the tracks and tunnels are still there, it's been closed for over forty years and there are currently no plans to revive it, which is a great pity as this valley offers one of the best roller-coasting descents to the sea. The villages are few and far between and much of the valley is thickly forested. The Sospel bus (#910) from Menton passes through **Castillon** (5 daily; 25min); for **Castellar** there's a local bus (#903; 5 daily; 25min).

To the east of the Carei Valley, and closer to Menton, **CASTELLAR** marks the point where the pines start to take over from the lemon groves. It is another old *village perché*, but not overrun by tourist commerce. It's also good for **walks**, with several paths radiating out into the hills around it as well as the GR52 from Gorbio and Ste-Agnes, which turns north along the Italian border to Sospel. Details of the paths, plus **rooms** and **food**, can be found at the rather basic *Hôtel des Alpes*, place Georges-Clemenceau (☎04.93.35.82.83, ❸), whose terrace has lovely views.

CASTILLON, a few kilometres south of Sospel, has twice been destroyed and rebuilt, by an earthquake in 1887 and by bombing in 1944. The current village, a short way down from Vieux Castillon, dates from the 1950s, with **Les Arcades des Serres**, a terrace of artists' and crafts workers' studios, added in the 1980s. Its status as an artists' village – the turning from the main road is marked by a dazzling ceramic – is not based on the normal Riviera riches market; the studios and galleries are provided at low rents in a genuine attempt to help local practitioners; and the works you see are very original and of a high standard. The **hotel–restaurant** *La Bergerie* (☎04.93.04.00.39; ❹), on the southern edge of the village, has great views and pleasant rooms.

Travel details

Trains

Nice to: Annot (4 daily; 1hr 55min); Beaulieu (every 15–30min; 12min); Breil-sur-Roya (6 daily; 1hr 5min); Cannes (every 10–35min; 25–40min) Cap d'Ail (every 35min–1hr; 20min); Cap Martin-Roquebrune (every 35min–1hr; 30min); Digne (4 daily; 3hr 16min); Entrevaux (4 daily; 1hr 35min); L'Escarène (6 daily; 40min); Èze-sur-Mer (every 35min–1hr; 15min); Marseille (6 daily; 2hr 24min); Menton (every 15–35min; 25–40min); Monaco (every 15–35min; 20–25min); Peille (6 daily; 30min); Peillon (6 daily; 25min); Puget-Théniers (4 daily; 1hr 26min); St-Raphaël (frequent; 1hr–1hr 20min); Sospel (6 daily; 50min); Tende (3 daily; 1hr 50min); Touët-sur-Var (4 daily; 1hr 14min); Villars-sur-Var (4 daily; 1hr 5min); Villefranche (every 15–55 min; 9min).

Buses

Menton to: Monaco (every 15min; 35min); Nice (every 15min; 1hr 30min); Sospel (3–5 daily; 35–45min).
Monaco to: Èze *gare SNCF* (every 15min; 17min); Menton (every 15min; 45min); Nice (every 15min; 55min); La Turbie (3–6 daily; 30min).
Nice to: Aix (3–5 daily; 2hr 15min–4hr 10min); Beaulieu (every 15min; 10–15min); Cagnes-sur-Mer (every 20 min; 35–40min); Cannes (every 20min; 1hr 25min–1hr 55min); Cap d'Ail (every 15min; 30min); Coaraze (3 daily; 1hr); Contes (hourly; 30min); Digne (2 daily; 2hr 50–3hr 25min); L'Escarène (9 daily; 40–50min); Èze-sur-Mer (every 15min; 27min); Èze-Village (14 daily; 20min); Grasse (every 30–45min; 1hr 10–1hr 35min); Grenoble (1 daily; 7hr 15min); Lucéram (6 daily; 1hr); Marseille (5 daily; 2hr 45min–4hr 30min); Menton (every 15min; 1hr 25min); Monaco (every 15min; 30–40min); Peille (3 daily; 1hr); Roquebrune (every 15min; 1hr); St-Paul (every 35–40min; 55 min); Sisteron (2 daily; 3hr 30min–4hr 10min); Toulon (2 daily; 2hr 30min); La Turbie (5 daily; 40min); Vence (every 20–35min; 1hr–1hr 10min); Villefranche (every 15min; 10min).

Ferries

Nice to: Corsica (summer 2–8 daily; winter 1 weekly; 3hr–5hr 30min).

Flights

Nice to: Amsterdam (4 daily; 2hr 10min); Birmingham (2 weekly; 2hr 15min); Bristol (4 weekly; 2hr 10min); Dublin (4 weekly; 2hr 40min); Liverpool (1 daily, 2hr 20min); London (9 daily; 2hr 10min); New York (5 weekly; 9hr 15min); Paris (28 daily; 1hr 30min); Rome (2–3 daily; 2hr 5min–2hr 15min).

Contexts

Contexts

The historical framework

From the Stone Age to the Celto-Ligurians

lmost all the great discoveries of **Stone Age** life in France have been made in the southwest of the country. In Provence a few Paleolithic traces have been found at Nice and in Menton (the skull of "Grimaldi man", for example), but nothing to compare with the cave drawings of Lascaux. It's assumed, however, that the area, including large tracts now submerged under the sea, was equally populated.

The development of farming, characterizing the **Neolithic Era**, is thought to have been started in Provence around 6500 BC with the domestication of the indigenous wild sheep. Around 3000 BC the **Ligurians** came from the east, settling throughout southern France and cultivating the land for the first time. It is to these people that the carvings in the Vallée des Merveilles, the few megalithic standing stones, and the earliest *bories* belonged. It's also thought that certain Provençal word endings in place names and names of rivers and mountains, such as *-osc*, *-asc*, *-auni* and *-inc*, derive from the Ligurian dialects passed down through Greek and Latin.

At some later point the **Celts** from the north moved into western Provence, bringing with them bronze technology. The first known fortified hilltop retreats, the *oppidi* (of which traces remain in the Maures, the Luberon, the upper Durance and the hills in the Rhône Valley), are attributed to this new ethnic mix, the **Celto-Ligurians**.

The Ancient Greeks discover Provence

As the Celto-Ligurian civilization developed, so did its trading links with the other Mediterranean peoples. The name of the River Rhône may have been given by traders from the Greek island of Rhodes (in French the name can be made into an adjective, *Rhodien*). Etruscans, Phoenicians, Corinthians and Ionians all had links with Provence. The eventual **Greek colonies** set up along the coast, starting with **Massalia** (Marseille) around 600 BC, were not the result of military conquest but of gradual economic integration. And while Massalia was a republic with great influence over its hinterland, it was not a base for wiping out the indigenous peoples. Prestige and wealth came from its port, and the city prided itself on its independence, which was to last well into the Middle Ages.

The Greeks introduced olives, figs, cherries, walnuts, cultivated vines and money. During the two hundred years following the foundation of Massalia, **colonies** were set up in La Ciotat, Almanarre (near Hyères), Bréganson, Cavalaire, St-Tropez (known as Athenopolis), Antibes, Nice and Monaco.

Mastrabala at St-Blaize and Glanum by St-Rémy-de-Provence developed within Massalia's sphere of influence. The **Rhône** was the corridor for commercial expeditions, including journeys as far north as Cornwall to acquire tin. Away from the coast and the Rhône Valley, however, the Celto-Ligurian lifestyle was barely affected by the advantages of Hellenic life, continuing its harsher and more basic battle for survival.

Roman conquest

Unlike the Greeks, the **Romans** were true imperialists, imposing their organization, language and laws by military subjugation on every corner of their empire. During the third century BC Roman expansion was concentrated on Spain, the power base of the Carthaginians – from where Hannibal had set off with his elephants to cross the Rhône somewhere above Orange and the Alps in order to attack the Romans in upper Italy. During this time Massalia nurtured good diplomatic relations with Rome which stood the city in good stead when Spain was conquered and the Romans decided to secure the land routes to Iberia.

This they achieved in a remarkably short time. From 125 to 118 BC, **Provincia** (the origin of the name Provence) became part of the Roman Empire. It encompassed the whole of the south of France from the Alps to the Pyrenees, stretching as far north as Vienna and Geneva, and with Narbonne as its capital.

While Massalia and other areas remained neutral or collaborated with the invaders, many Ligurian tribes fought to the death, most notably the Salyens, whose Oppidum d'Entremont was demolished and a victorious new city, Aquae Sextiae (Aix), built at its foot in 122 BC. Pax Romana was still a long way off, however. **Germanic Celts** moving down from the Baltic came into conflict with the ruling power, managing to decimate several Roman legions at Orange in 105 BC. A major campaign was undertaken to prevent the Barbarians from closing in on Italy. The northern invaders were defeated, as were local uprisings. Massalia exploited every situation to gain more territories and privileges; the rest of Provence knuckled under, suffering the various battles and the requisitions and taxes to pay for them. Finally, from 58 to 51 BC all of Gaul was conquered by **Julius Caesar**.

It was then that Massalia finally blew its hitherto successful diplomatic strategy by supporting Pompey against Caesar, who then laid siege, defeated the city and confiscated all its territories which had stretched from the Rhône to Monaco. Unlike earlier emperors, Julius Caesar started to implant his own people in Provence (St-Raphaël was founded for his veterans). His successor Octavian followed the same policy. While the coastal areas duly Latinized themselves, the **Ligurians** in the mountains, from Sisteron to the Roya Valley, refused to give up their identity without a fight. Fight they did, keeping Roman troops busy for ten years until their eventual defeat in 14 BC, which the Trophie des Alpes at La Turbie gloats over to this day.

This monument to Augustus Caesar was erected on the newly built **Via Aurelia**, which linked Rome with Arles, by way of Cimiez, Antibes, Fréjus and Aix, more or less along the route of the present-day N7. The **Via Agrippa** went north from Arles, through Avignon and Orange. Only the rebellious mountainous area was heavily garrisoned. Western Provence, with Arles as its main town (Narbonne was still the capital of Provincia), dutifully served the imperial interests, providing oil, grain and, most importantly, ships for the superpower that ruled western Europe and the borders of the Mediterranean for five centuries.

Christianity appeared in Provence during the third century and spread fairly rapidly in the fourth when it became the official religion of the Roman Empire. The **Lérins Monastery** was founded around 410 AD and the **Abbey of St-Victor** in Marseille about six years later.

Rome falls: more invasions

For a while in the early fifth century, when the Roman Empire was beginning to split apart, the invasions by the Germanic tribes bypassed Provence. But by the time the Western Roman Empire was finally done for in 476 AD, Provence was under the domination of both the **Visigoths**, who had captured Arles and were terrorizing the lower Rhône valley, and the **Burgundians**, another Germanic tribe, who had moved in from the east. The new rulers confiscated land, took slaves and generally made life for the locals even more miserable than usual.

Over the next two hundred years **Goths** and **Franks** fought over and partitioned Provence; famine, disease and bloodshed diminished the population; lands that had been drained returned to swamp; intellectual life declined. Under the **Merovingian dynasty** in the eighth century Provence was, in theory, part of the **Frankish empire**. But a new world power had emerged – **Islam** – which had spread from the Middle East into North Africa and most of Spain. In 732 a Muslim army had reached as far as Tours before being defeated by the Franks at Poitiers. At this point the local ruler of Provence rebelled against the central authority, and called on the **Saracens** (Muslims) to assist. Armies of Franks, Saracens, Lombards (allies of the Franks) and locals rampaged through Provence, putting the Franks back in control.

Though the ports had trouble carrying on their lucrative trade while the Mediterranean was controlled by Saracens, agriculture developed under the Frankish **Carolingian dynasty**, particularly during the relatively peaceful years of **Charlemagne's rule**. But when, during the ninth century, Charlemagne's sons and then grandsons started squabbling over the inheritance, Provence once again became easy prey.

Normans took over the lower Rhône, and the **Saracens** returned, pillaging Marseille and destroying its abbey in 838, doing over Arles in 842, and attacking Marseille again in 848. For a century they maintained a base at Fraxinetum (La Garde-Freinet), from where they controlled the whole Massif des Maures.

The **hilltop villages** along the coast are commonly explained as the frightened response to the Saracens, though few date back this far. Well inland, people were just as prone to retreat to whatever defensive positions were available. In the cities this would be the strongest building (the Roman theatre at Orange, for example). The Rhône Valley villagers took refuge in the Luberon and the Massif de la Ste-Baume.

For all the terrors and bloodshed, the period was not without its evolution. The Saracens introduced basic medicine, the use of cork bark, resin extraction from pines, flat roof tiles, and the most traditional Provençal musical instrument, the tambourine.

The counts of Provence

The Saracens were expelled for good at the end of the tenth century by **Guillaume Le Libérateur**, count of Arles, who claimed Provence as his own feudal estate. After several centuries of anarchy a period of relative stability ensued. Forestry, fishing, irrigation, land reclamation, vine cultivation, beekeeping, salt-panning, river transport and renewed learning (under the auspices of the Benedictine monasteries) began pulling Provence out of the Dark Ages.

Politically, Guillaume and his successors retained considerable independence from their overlords (first the kingdom of Burgundy then the Holy Roman Empire). In turn they tended to confine their influence to the area around Arles and Avignon, while local lords held sway throughout the rest of the countryside and the cities developed their own autonomy. The Rhône formed the border between France and the Holy Roman Empire but for much of the time this political division failed to cut the old economic, cultural and linguistic links between the two sides of the river.

In the **twelfth century**, Provence passed to the counts of Toulouse and was then divided with the counts of Barcelona, while various fiefdoms – amongst them Forcalquier, Les Baux and Beuil on the eastern side of the Var – refused integration. Power was a bewildering, shifting pattern, but, sporadic armed conflicts apart (confined mainly to the lower Rhône Valley), the titleholder to Provence hardly affected the ordinary people who were bound in serfdom to their immediate seigneur.

As a consequence of the Crusades, **maritime commerce** flourished once again, as did trade along the Rhône, giving prominence to Avignon, Orange, Arles and, most of all, Marseille. In Nice, then under the control of the Genoese Republic, a new commercial town started to develop below the castle rock. The cities took on the organizational form of the Italian consulates, increasingly separating themselves from feudal power.

Troubadour poetry made its appearance in the langue d'oc language that was spoken from the Alps to the Pyrenees (and from which the **Provençal dialect** developed). Church construction looked back to the Romans for inspiration, producing the great Romanesque edifices of Montmajour, Sénanque, Silvacane, Thoronet and St-Trophime in Arles.

Raymond Béranger V, Catalan count of Provence in the early thirteenth century, took the unprecedented step of spending time in his domains. While fighting off the count of Toulouse and the Holy Roman Emperor, he made Aix his capital, founded Barçelonnette and travelled throughout the Alps and the coastal regions. Provence became, for the first time since the Romans, an organized mini-state with a more or less **unified feudal system** of law and administration.

The Angevins

After Béranger's death, Provence turned towards France, with the **house of Anjou** gaining control and holding it until the end of the fifteenth century. The borders changed: Nice, Barçelonnette and Puget-Théniers passed to Savoy in 1388 and remained separate from Provence until 1860. New extraneous powers claimed or bought territories within the country – the **popes at Avignon** (see p.141) and in the **Comtat Venaissin**; the Prince of Nassau in Orange. Though armed conflicts, revolts and even civil war in 1388 chequered its medieval history, Provence was at least spared the devastations of the Hundred Years' War with England, which never touched the region.

By the end of this period the established trading routes from the Orient to Genoa and Marseille, and from Marseille to Flanders and London, were forming the basis of **early capitalism**, and spreading new techniques and learning. Though Marseille was not a great financial centre like Antwerp or Florence, its expanding population became ever more cosmopolitan. Away from the coast and the Rhône, however, feudal villages continued to live in isolation, unable to survive if a harvest failed. For a shepherd or forester in the mountains, life in Marseille or in the extravagant papal city of Avignon would have appeared to belong to another planet.

Provençal Jews exercised equal rights with Christians, owning land and practising a wide variety of professions in addition to finance and commerce. Though concentrated in the western towns, they were not always ghettoized. But the moment any kind of disaster struck, such as the Black Death in the mid-fourteenth century, latent hostility would violently manifest itself. **The Plague**, however, made no distinctions between Jew or Christian, rich or poor: around half the population died from the recurring epidemics.

In **cultural and intellectual life** the dominant centres were the **papal court at Avignon**, and later **King René of Anjou's court at Aix**. However, despite the area's key position between Italy and northern Europe, and the cosmopolitan influence of the popes, Angevin rulers and foreign trade, art and architecture remained surprisingly unmarked by the major movements of the time. The popes tended to employ foreign artists and it was not until the mid-fifteenth century that native art developed around the **Avignon School** – represented by such works as Nicolas Froment's *Le Buisson Ardent* and *La Couronnement de la Vierge* by Enguerrand Quarton. At the same time the **School of Nice** developed, more directly under Italian influence, represented by the frescoes of Canavesio and Baleison and the paintings of Louis and François Bréa. Avignon was the chief city of great **Gothic architecture** – the Palais des Papes and many of the churches – but outside this city the only major examples of the new style were Tarascon's castle and the basilica of St-Maximin-de-la-Ste-Baume.

The **legends of the saints** fleeing Palestine and seeking refuge in Provence began to take root around this time, too, with pilgrimages to the various shrines bringing glimpses of the outside world to small towns and villages. It was at this time that the popes founded a **university in Avignon** (1303) which became famous for jurisprudence; Aix university was established a century later and in the mid-fourteenth century the first paper mills were in use. By King René's time, French was the official language of the court.

Union with France

The short-lived Charles III of Provence, René's heir, bequeathed all his lands to **Louis XI of France**, a transfer of power that the *parlement* of Aix glossed over and approved in 1482. Within twelve months every top Provençal official had been sacked and replaced by a Frenchman; the castles at Toulon and Les Baux were razed to the ground; garrisons were placed in five major towns.

The *parlement* protested in vain, but after Louis XI's death a more careful approach was taken to this crucial border province. The **Act of Union**, ratified by *parlement* in 1486, declared Provence to be a separate entity within the kingdom of France, enshrining the rights to its own law courts, customs and privileges. In reality, the ever-centralizing power of the French state was systematically to erode these rights as it did with Brittany and the other once-autonomous provinces.

The **Jewish population** provided a convenient diversion for Provençal frustrations. Encouraged, if not instigated, by the Crown, there were massacres, expulsions and assaults in Marseille, Arles and Manosque in the last two decades of the fifteenth century. The royal directive was convert or leave – some, such as the parents of **Nostradamus**, converted, many fled to the Comtat. During the sixteenth century more expulsion threats and special taxes were the rule. In 1570 the Jews lost their papal protection in the Comtat.

Meanwhile Charles VIII, Louis XII and François I involved Provence in their **Italian Wars**. **Marseille** became a **military port** in 1488, and in 1496 **Toulon** was fortified and its first **shipyards** opened. While the rest of the province suffered troop movements and requisitions, Marseille and Toulon benefited from extra funds and unchecked piracy against the enemies of France. Genoese, Venetian and Spanish vessels were regularly towed into Marseille's port.

The war took a more serious turn in the 1520s after the French conquest of Milan. **Charles V**, the new Holy Roman Emperor, retaliated by sending a large army across the Var and into Aix. The French concern was to protect Marseille at all costs – the rest of the province was left to fend for itself. After the imperial forces had failed to take Marseille and retreated, the city was rewarded with the pomp and carnival of a royal wedding between François' second son, the future Henri II, and **Catherine de Medici**. The Château d'If was built to protect the roadstead.

Another round in the war soon commenced. Charles V took back Milan, the French invaded Savoy and occupied Nice. In 1536 an even bigger **imperial army invaded**, and again the French abandoned inland Provence to protect Marseille and the Rhône Valley. The people of **Le Muy** stopped the emperor for one day with fifty local heroes, who were subsequently hanged for their pains. Elsewhere people fled to the forests, their towns and villages pillaged by the invaders. **Marseille** and **Arles** held out; French troops finally moved south down the Durance; dysentery and lack of sure supply lines weakened the imperial army. Twenty thousand Savoyards were dead or imprisoned by the time the imperial troops were safely back across the Var.

One effect of the Italian Wars was that Provence finally now identified itself with France, making it easier for the Crown to diminish the power of the *États*, impose greater numbers of French administrators, and, in 1539, decree that all administrative laws were to be translated from Latin into French, not Provençal.

Life in the early sixteenth century

Sixteenth-century Provence was ruled by two royal appointees – a governor and grand *sénéchal* (the chief administrator) – but the **feudal hierarchy** failed to achieve the same command over the structure of society as it did elsewhere in France. Few nobles lived on their estates and those that did were often poorer than the merchants and financiers of the major cities. In remoter areas people cultivated their absent seigneur's land as if it were their own; in other areas towns bought land off the feudal owners. It is estimated that nearly half the population had their own holdings. Advances in irrigation, such as **Craponne's canal through the Crau**, were carried out independently from the aristocracy.

While not self-sufficient in grain, Provence had surpluses of wine, fish and vermilion from the Camargue to export; as well as **growing industries** in textiles, tanneries, soap and paper; and new foods, such as oranges, pepper, palm dates and sugar cane, introduced along the coast from across the Mediterranean. Olives provided the basic oil for food, orchards began to be cultivated on a commercial scale, and most families kept pigs and sheep: only vegetables were rare luxuries. People lived on their land, with the **old fortified villages** populated only in times of insecurity. Most small towns had weekly **markets**, and **festivals** celebrated the advance from survival being a non-stop struggle. Epidemics of the plague continued, however, and sanitation left a lot to be desired – a contemporary noted that even in Aix it "rained shit as often as it did in Arles or Marseille".

Free schools were set up by some of the larger towns, and secondary colleges established in Aix, Marseille, Arles and Avignon. **Nostradamus** (1503–66) achieved renown throughout France – from the royal court down to his Salon and St-Rémy neighbours. His books had to be printed in Lyon, though, as there was as yet no market for printers in Provence.

Châteaux such as La Tour d'Aigue, Gordes and Lourmarin, with comfort playing an equal part to defence, were built at this time, as were the rich Marseille town houses of the Maison Diamentée and the Hôtel Cabre. The facade of St-Pierre in Avignon shows the Renaissance finally triumphing over Provence's artistic backwardness.

The Wars of Religion

Though the Italian Wars temporarily disrupted social and productive advances, they were nothing compared with the **Wars of Religion** that put all France in a state of **civil war** for most of the second half of the sixteenth century. The clash between the new reforming ideas of Luther and Calvin and the old Roman Catholic order was particularly violent in Provence. Avignon, as papal domain, was inevitably a rigid centre of Catholicism. The neighbouring principality of Orange allowed Huguenots to practise freely and form their own organizations. Haute Provence and the Luberon became centres for the new religion due to the influx of Dauphinois and Piedmontais settlers.

Incidents began to build up in the 1540s, culminating in the massacre of Luberon Protestants and the destruction of Mérindol (see p.150). In Avignon heretics were displayed in the iron cages where they'd been slung to die; in Haute Provence churches were smashed by the reformers; while in Orange the Protestants pillaged the cathedral and took control of the city. The regent Catherine de Medici's **Edict of Tolerance** in 1562 only made matters worse. Marseille demanded and received an exemption; Aix promptly dispatched a Catholic contingent to massacre the Protestants of Tourves; Catherine's envoys prompted a massacre of Catholics at Barjols. The notorious Baron des Adrets, who had fought for the Catholics, now switched sides and carried out a series of terrifying attacks on Catholic towns and villages. The *parlement* chose to resign rather than ratify a new edict of tolerance in 1563, even though by this point Orange had been won back to the established Church, the garrison of Sisteron had been massacred for protecting the Protestants and the last armed group of reformers had fled north out of the province.

When Catherine de Medici and her son Charles XIV toured Provence in 1564, all seemed well. But within a few years fighting again broke out, with Sisteron once more under siege. In the mid-1570s trouble took a new turn with the rivalry between Henri III's governor and *sénéchal* adding to the hostile camps. This state of civil war was only terminated by another major outbreak of the **plague** in **1580**.

With the Protestant **Henri de Navarre** (the future Henri IV) becoming heir to the throne in 1584, the *Guerres de Religion* hotted up even more. The pope excommunicated Henri; and the leaders of the French Catholics (the de Guises) formed the **European Catholic League**, seized Paris and drove out the king, Henri III. Provence found itself with two governors – the king's and the League's appointees; two capitals – Aix and Pertuis; and a split *parlement*. After Henri III's assassination, Catholic Aix called in the duke of Savoy whose troops trounced Henri de Navarre's supporters at Riez. At this point the main issue for the Provençaux was loyalty to the French Crown against invaders, rather than religion. Even the Aix *parlement* stopped short of giving Savoy the title to Provence, and after Marseille again withstood a siege, the duke gave up and went back home to Nice in 1592. For another year battles continued between the Leaguers and the Royalists, with Marseille refusing to recognize either authority. Finally Henri IV said his Mass; troops entered Marseille; and the war-damaged and impoverished Provence reverted back to **royal control**.

Louis XIII and Louis XIV

The **consolidation of the French state** initiated by Louis XIII's minister, **Richelieu**, saw the whittling away of Provençal institutions and ideas of independence, coupled with ever-increasing tax demands plus enforced "free gifts" to the king. The power and prestige of the *États* and *parlement* were reduced by force, clever negotiation or playing off the different cities' rival interests.

Political power switched from governors and *sénéchals*, who were part of the feudal structure, to *intendants*, servants of the state with powers over every aspect of provincial life, including the military. The *États*, having refused to provide the royal purse with funds in 1629, were not convoked again. These changes, along with the failure of the aristocratic rebellions during Louis XIV's minority (the Frondes), and the increasing number of titles bought by the bourgeoisie, left the *noblesse d'épée* (the real aristos) disgruntled but impotent. The clergy (the First Estate) also lost a measure of their former power.

It was a time of **plague**, **famine**, further outbreaks of **religious strife and war**. To deal with opposition the Château d'If became a state prison. The **war with Spain**, for which Toulon's fortifications were upgraded and forts added to Giens and the Îles d'Hyères, increased taxation, decimated trade and cost lives. Marseille attempted to hold on to its ancient independence by setting up a rebel council in 1658. The royal response was swift. Troops were sent in, rebels were condemned to the rack or the galleys, a permanent garrison was established and the foundations laid for the Fort St-Nicolas to keep an eye on "*ce peuple violent et libertin*".

While the various upheavals and ever-multiplying tax burden caused untold misery, progress in production (including the faïence industry), education and social provision (mostly the work of the burgeoning Pénitents orders outside the Church establishment) carried on apace. The town houses of Aix, Marseille and Avignon, the Hospice de la Charité in Marseille, the Baroque additions to churches and chapels, all show the wealth accumulating, gained, as ever, by maritime commerce. But the greatest Provençal sculptor of the period, **Pierre Puget**, never received royal patronage and Provençal was still the language of all classes in society, though French for the first time was imposed on certain disciplines at Aix University.

As the reign of **Louis XIV**, the **Sun King**, became more grandiose and more aggressive, Provence, like all of France outside Versailles and Paris, was eclipsed. The **war with Holland** saw Orange and the valley of Barçelonnette annexed; Avignon and the papal Comtat swung steadily into the French orbit; attempts were made again to capture Nice. But for the Provençaux, the people of Orange, Avignon and the Comtat had always been their fellow countrymen and women, while Nice was a foreign city they had never wished to claim. Wars that involved the English navy blockading the ports were as unwelcome to the local bourgeois as they were to those who had to fight.

As the *ancien régime* slowly dug its own grave the rest of the country stagnated. The pattern for Provence of wars, invasions and trade blockades became entrenched. To add to the gloom, another outbreak of the **plague** killed half the population of Marseille in **1720**. The extravagance of Louis XV's court, where the Grassois painter Fragonard found his patrons, had few echoes in Provence. Aix had its grandiose town planning, Avignon its mansions, Grasse its perfume industry, but elsewhere there was complete stagnation.

The Revolution

Conditions were ripe for revolution in Provence. The region had suffered a disastrous silk harvest and a sharp fall in the price of wine in 1787, and the severe winter of 1788–89 killed off most of the olive trees. Unemployment and starvation were rife and the hurtling rise in the price of bread provoked serious rioting in the spring of 1789. There was no lack of followers for bourgeois *députés* exasperated by the incompetent administration and constant drain on national resources that the court represented.

So in **July 1789**, while the Bastille was stormed in Paris, Provençal peasants pillaged their local châteaux and urban workers rioted against the mayors, egged on by the middle classes. There was only one casualty, at Aups. The following year **Marseillaise revolutionaries** seized the forts of St-Jean and St-Nicolas, with again just one lashing of violence when the crowd lynched St-Jean's commander. **Toulon** was equally fervent in its support for the new order, and at **Aix** one counter-revolutionary lawyer and two aristocrats were strung up on lampposts. In the **papal lands**, where the crucial issue was reunion with France, Rome's representative was sent packing from Avignon and a revolutionary municipality installed.

Counter-revolutionaries regrouped in Carpentras and there were several bloody incidents, including the ice-house massacre. However, 1792 saw Marseille's staunchly Jacobin National Guard, the **Féderés**, demolish the counter-revolutionary forces in the Comtat and aristocratic Arles. Marseille's authorities declared that kingship was contrary to the principles of equality and national sovereignty. When the Legislative Assembly summoned all the Féderés to Paris to defend the capital and celebrate the third anniversary of the Bastille, five hundred Marseillais marched north singing Rouget de Lisle's **Hymn to the Army of the Rhine**. It was written for the troops at the front in the war declared that April with Germany and Austria. But for the Parisian *sans-culottes* it was a major hit, becoming the **Marseillaise**, France's national anthem – even more so after the attack on the Tuileries Palace that was swiftly followed by the dethronement of the king. According to the Swedish ambassador of the time, "Marseille's Féderés were the moving force behind everything in August 1792."

Provence had by now incorporated the papal states and was divided into **four départements**. Peasants were once again on the pillage, and still starving, while royalists and republicans fought it out in the towns. In 1793 the Var military commander was ordered to take Nice, a hotbed of émigré intrigue and part of the great European coalition out to exterminate the French Revolution. Twenty thousand people fled the city but no resistance was encountered. The Alpes-Maritimes *département* came into existence.

In the summer of the same year, political divisions between the various factions of the Convention and the growing fear of a dictatorship by the Parisian *sans-culottes* provoked the **provincial Federalist revolt**. The populace was fed up with conscription to the wars on every frontier, and a hankering after their old Provençal autonomy reasserted itself. Revolutionary cities found themselves fighting against government forces – a situation speedily exploited by the real **counter-revolutionaries**. In Toulon the entire fleet and the city's fortifications were handed over to the English. (In the battle to regain the city, the government's victory was secured by the young Napoléon.) Reprisals, in addition to the almost daily executions of the Terror, cost thousands of lives.

Much of Provence, however, had remained Jacobin, and so fell victim to the **White Terror of 1795** that followed the execution of Robespierre. The prisons of Marseille, Aix, Arles and Tarascon overflowed with people picked up on the street with no charge. Cannons were fired into the cells at point-blank range and sulphur or lighted rags thrown through the bars. By the time the Revolution had given up all hopes of being revolutionary in terms of its 1789 manifesto, **anarchy reigned**. Provence was crawling with returned émigrés who had no trouble finding violent followers motivated by frustration, exhaustion and famine.

Napoleon and restoration

Provence's experience of **Napoleon's reign** differed little from that of the rest of France, despite the emperor's close connection with the region (childhood at Nice; military career at Antibes and Toulon; then the escape from Elba). Order was restored and power became even more centralized, with *préfets* enlarging on the role of Louis XIV's *intendants*. The **concordat with the pope** re-establishing Catholicism as the state religion was widely welcomed, particularly since the new ecclesiastical authorities were not all the old First Estate, *ancien régime* representatives. However, secular power reverted to the old seigneurs in many places – the new mayor of Marseille, for example, was a marquise.

It was the **Napoleonic wars** that lost the emperor his Provençal support. Marseille's port was again blockaded; conscription and taxes for military campaigns were as detested as ever; the Alpes-Maritimes *département* became a theatre of war and in 1814 was handed over (with Savoy) to Sardinia. Monaco followed suit the following year, though with the Grimaldi dynasty reinstalled in their palace.

The **restoration of the Bourbons** after Waterloo unleashed another White Terror. Provence was again bitterly divided between royalists and republicans. Despite this split there was no major resistance to the **1830 revolution** which put Louis-Philippe, the "Citizen King", on the throne. The new regime represented liberalism – well tinged with anti-clericalism and a dislike of democracy – and was welcomed by the Provençal bourgeoisie. Despite the ardent Catholicism of the *paysans*, and the large numbers of émigrés that had returned under the Bourbons' amnesties, the attempt by the duchess of Berry to bring back the "legitimate" royalty (which had some initial success in western France) failed totally here.

1848 and 1851

The first half of the nineteenth century saw the first major **industrialization** of France, and, overseas, the conquest of Algeria.

In Provence, Marseille was linked by rail with Paris and expanded its port to take steam ships; iron bridges over the Rhône and new roads were built; many towns demolished their ramparts to extend their main streets into the suburbs. By the 1840s the arsenal at Toulon was employing over three thousand workers.

This emerging proletariat was highly receptive to the visit by the socialist and feminist **Flora Tristan**, who was doing the rounds of France in 1844. A year later all the different trades in the arsenal went on strike. Throughout industrialized Provence – the Rhône Valley and the coast – workers overturned their traditional *compagnons* (guilds) to form more radical trade-union organizations. Things hardly changed, however, in inland Provence, as protectionist policies hampered the exchange of foodstuffs, and the new industries' demand for fuel eroded the forestry rights of the *paysans*. In 1847 the country (and most of Europe) was in severe economic crisis.

News of the **1848 revolution** arrived from Paris before the representatives of the new republic. Town halls, common lands and forests were instantly and peacefully reclaimed by the populace. In the elections that followed, very moderate republicans were returned, though they included three manual workers in Marseille, Toulon and Avignon. Two months later, however, the economic situation was deteriorating again, and newly won improvements in working hours and wages were being clawed back by the employers. A demonstration in Marseille turned nasty and the **barricades** went up.

Elsewhere, the most militant action was in Menton and Roquebrune, both under the rule of **Monaco**, where the people refused to pay the prince's high taxes on oil and fruit. Sardinian military assistance failed to quell the revolt and the two towns declared themselves independent republics. With his main source of income gone, the Grimaldi prince turned the focus of his state shrewdly towards tourism – already well established in Nice and Hyères – and opened the casino at Monte Carlo.

The 1848 revolution turned sour with the election of **Louis-Napoleon** as president in 1850. A law was introduced which in effect annulled the 1830 universal male suffrage by imposing a residency requirement. Laws against "secret societies" and "conspiracies" followed. Ordinary *paysans* discussing prices over a bottle of wine could be arrested; militants from Digne and Avignon were deported to Polynesia for belonging to a democratic party. Newly formed cooperatives were seen by the authorities as hotbeds of sedition. All this inevitably accelerated politicization of the *paysans*.

When Louis-Napoleon made himself emperor in the **coup d'état of 1851**, Provence, as many other regions of France, turned again to revolt. Initially there were insufficient forces in the small towns and villages to prevent the rebels taking control (which they did without any violence). In order to take the *préfectures*, villagers and townspeople, both male and female, organized themselves into disciplined "*colonnes*" which marched beneath the red flag. Digne was the only *préfecture* they held, though, and then for only two days. Reprisals were bloody – another White Terror in effect, with thousands of the rebels caught as they tried to flee into Savoy. Of all the insurgents in France shot, imprisoned or deported after this rebellion, one in five were from Provence.

The Second Empire

The **Second Empire** saw greater changes in everyday life than in any previous period. **Marseille** became the premier port of France, with trade enormously expanded by the colonization of North and West Africa, Vietnam and parts of China. The depopulation of inland Provence, which had been gradually increasing over the last century and a half, suddenly became a deluge of migration to the coast and Rhône Valley. While the railway was extended along the coast – encouraging the nascent Côte d'Azur tourism – communications inland were ignored.

At the end of the **war for Italian unification** in 1860, **Napoléon III** regained the Alpes-Maritimes as payment for his support of Italy against Austria. A plebiscite in Nice gave majority support for **reunion with France**. To the north, Tende and La Brigue voted almost unanimously for France but the result was ignored: the new king of Italy wished to keep his favourite game-hunting grounds. Menton and Roquebrune also voted for France. While making noises about rigged elections, Charles of Monaco agreed to sell the two towns – despite their independence – to France. The sum was considerably more than the fledgling gambling and tourism industry was as yet bringing in and saved the principality from bankruptcy. **Monaco's independence**, free from any foreign protector, was finally established.

One casualty of this dispersal of traditional Provence, combined with the spread of national primary education, was the Provençal language. This prompted the formation of the **Félibrige** in 1854, by a group of poets including Frédéric Mistral – a nostalgic, backward-looking and intellectual movement in defence of literary Provençal. There were other, more popularist, Provençal writers at the time, but they too were conservative, railing against gas lighting and any other modern innovation. The attempt to associate the language with some past golden age of ultra-Catholic primitivism only encouraged the association of progress with the French tongue – particularly for the Left.

By the end of the 1860s the **socialism** of the First International was gaining ground in the industrial cities, and in Marseille most of all. Opponents of the empire had the majority in the town hall, and in the plebiscite of 1870, in which the country as a whole gave Napoleon III their support, the Bouches-du-Rhône *département* was second only to Paris in the number of "nons". It was not surprising therefore that Marseille had its own commune (see p.72) when the Parisians took up arms against the right-wing republic established after the Prussians' defeat of France and the downfall of Napoleon III.

Honoré Daumier, the Marseillais caricaturist and fervent republican, was the great illustrator of both the 1851 and the 1871 events. In the middle of the century the **Marseille school of painting** developed under the influence of foreign travel and orientalism, attracting to the city such artists as Puvis de Chavannes and Félix Ziem. Provence's greatest native artist, **Cézanne**, though living in Paris from the 1860s to the 1880s, spent a few months of every year in his home town of Aix, or in Marseille and L'Estaque. He was sometimes accompanied by his childhood friend **Zola**, and by **Renoir** whom he introduced to this coast.

Third Republic: 1890–1914

Under the **Third Republic**, the division between inland Provence and the coast and Rhône Valley accentuated. Port activity at Marseille quadrupled with the opening of new trade routes along the Suez Canal and further colonial acquisitions in the Far East. Manufacturing began to play an equal role in commerce. The orchards of the Rhône Valley were planted on a massive scale, and light industries producing clothes, foodstuffs and paper developed in Aix and other cities to export to the North African colonies. Chemical works in Avignon produced the synthetics that spelt the rapid decline of the traditional industries of the small towns and villages of the interior – tanning, dyeing, silk and glass. Wine production, meanwhile, was devastated by phylloxera.

The one area of brilliance connected with the climate but not with commerce was art – painting in particular. Following on from Cézanne and Renoir, a younger generation of artists was discovering the Côte d'Azur. The Post-Impressionists and Fauves flocked to St-Tropez in the wake of the ever-hospitable Paul Signac. Matisse, Dufy, Seurat, Dérain, van Dongen, Bonnard, Braque, Friesz, Marquet, Manguin, Camion, Vlaminck and Vuillard were all intoxicated by the Mediterranean light, the climate and the ease of living. The escape from the rigours of Paris released a massive creative energy and resulted in works that, in addition to their radical innovations, have more *joie de vivre* than any other period in French art. Renoir retired to Cagnes for health reasons in 1907; for Matisse, Dufy and Bonnard the Côte d'Azur became their permanent home; and Van Gogh, always a man apart, had a spell in Arles.

Ignoring these bohemian characters, the **winter tourist season** on the coast was taking off. **Hyères** and **Cannes** had been "discovered" in the first half of the nineteenth century (and Nice many years earlier). But increased ease of travel and the temporary restraint of simmering international tensions encouraged aristocratic mobility. The population of **Nice** trebled from 1861 to 1911; luxury trains ran from St Petersburg, Vienna and London; Belle Époque mansions and grand hotels rose along the Riviera seafronts; and gambling, particularly at Monte Carlo, won the patronage of the Prince of Wales, the Emperor Franz Joseph and scores of Russian grand-dukes.

The native working class, meanwhile, were forming the first French Socialist Party, which had its opening congress in Marseille in 1879. Support came not just from the city but from towns and villages that had fought in 1851. In 1881 Marseille elected the first socialist *député*. By 1892 the municipal councils of Marseille, Toulon, La Ciotat and other industrial towns were in the hands of socialists. In Aix, however, the old legitimist royalists (those favouring the return of the Bourbons) still held sway, managing to block the erection of a monument to Zola in 1911.

World War I and the interwar years

The battlefields of **World War I** may have seemed far away in northern France and Belgium, but conscription brought the people of Provence into the war. The socialists divided between pacifists and patriots, but when, in 1919, France took part in the attack on the Soviet Union, soldiers, sailors and workers joined forces in Toulon and Marseille to support the mutinies on French warships in the Black Sea. The struggle to have the mutineers freed continued well into 1920, the year in which the **French Communist Party** (PCF) was born; the party's adherents in Provence were again the heirs to the 1851 rebellion.

The casualties of the war led to severe depopulation in the already dwindling villages of inland Provence, some of which were actually deserted. **Land use** also changed dramatically, from mixed agriculture to a monocrop of vines, in order to provide the army with its ration of one litre of wine per soldier per day. Quantity, thanks to the Provençal climate, rather than quality was the aim, leaving acre upon acre of totally unviable vineyards after demobilization. With the growth in tourism, it was easier to sell the land for construction rather than have it revert to its former use.

The **tourist industry** recovered fairly quickly from the war. The *Front Populaire* of 1936 introduced paid holidays, encouraging native visitors to the still unspoilt coast. International literati – Somerset Maugham, Katherine Mansfield, Scott and Zelda Fitzgerald, Colette, Anaïs Nin, Gertrude Stein – and a new wave of artists, Picasso and Cocteau amongst them, replaced the defunct grand-dukes, even if anachronistic titles still filled the palatial Riviera residences.

Marseille during the interwar years saw the evolution of characteristics that have yet to be obliterated. The activities of the fascist *Action Française* led to deaths during a left-wing counter-demonstration in 1925. Modern-style **corruption** snaked its way through the town hall and the rackets of gangsters on the Chicago model moved in on the vice industries. Elections were rigged and even revolvers used at the ballot boxes.

The increasing popularity of the Communist Party in the city was due to its anti-corruption platform. After the failure of the *Front Populaire* (which the great majority of Provençaux had voted for, electing several Communist *députés*), there were constant pitched battles between the Left and Right in Marseille. In 1939 a state administrator was imposed by Paris, with powers to obstruct the elected council.

World War II

France and Britain declared **war on Germany** together on September 3, 1939. The French Maginot line, however, swiftly collapsed, and by June 1940 the Germans controlled Paris and all of northern France. On June 22, Marshall Pétain signed the **armistice with Hitler**, which divided France between the Occupied Zone – the Atlantic coast and north of the Loire – and "unoccupied" Vichy France in the south. Menton and Sospel were occupied by the Italians, to whom the adjoining Roya Valley still belonged.

With the start of the British counteroffensive in 1942, **Vichy France** joined itself with the Allies and was immediately occupied by the Germans. The port of Toulon was overrun in November, with the French navy scuppering its fleet rather than letting it fall into German hands.

Resistance fighters and passive citizens suffered executions, deportations and the wholesale destruction of Le Panier quarter in Marseille (see p.69). The **Allied bombings** of 1944 caused high civilian casualties and considerable material damage, particularly to Avignon, Marseille and Toulon. The **liberation** of the two great port cities was aided by a general armed revolt by the people, but it was in the Italian sector – in Sospel and its neighbouring villages – that the fighting by the local populace was the most heroic.

Modern Provence

Before the Germans surrendered **Marseille** they made sure that the harbours were blown to bits. In the immediate **postwar years** the task of repairing the damage was compounded by a slump in international trade and passenger traffic. The nationalization of the Suez Canal was the next disaster to hit the city, spelling an end to its prime position on world trading routes. Company after company decamped to Paris, leaving a growing problem of unemployment.

Marseille's solution was to orient its **port** and industry towards the Atlantic and the inland route of the Rhône. The **oil industries** that had developed in the 1920s around the Étang de Berre and Fos were extended. The mouth of the Rhône and the Golfe de Fos became a massive tanker terminal. **Iron and steel works** filled the spaces behind the new Port de Marseille that stretched for 50km beyond the Vieux Port. In the process, the city's population boomed. The urgent demand for housing was met by badly designed, low-cost, high-rise estates proliferating north and east from the congested city centre.

The depopulation of **inland Provence** was never halted, but considerably slowed by the massive **irrigation schemes** and development of hydroelectric power which greatly increased the agricultural and industrial potential of regions impoverished earlier in the century. The isolated *mas* or farmhouses, positioned wherever there happened to be a spring, were left to ruin or linked up to the mains. Orchards, lavender fields and olive groves became larger, the competition for early fruit and vegetables fiercer, and the market for luxury foods greater. The rich **Rhône Valley** continued to export fruit, wine and vegetables, while the river was exploited for irrigation and power, both nuclear and hydroelectric, and made navigable for sizeable ships.

After Algeria won back its independence in 1962, hundreds of thousands of French settlers, the **pieds noirs**, returned to the mainland, bringing with them a virulent hatred of Arabic-speaking people. At the same time, the government encouraged immigration from its former colonies, North Africa in particular, with the promise of well-paid jobs, civil rights and social security, none of which was honoured. The resulting tensions, not just in Marseille but all along the coast, made perfect fodder for the **parties of the Right**. From being a bastion of socialism at the end of World War II, Provence gradually turned towards intolerance and reaction.

Municipal fiefdoms, corruption and vice

The activities of the local mafia, known as the **milieu**, with their invisible and inextricable ties to the town halls, have continued more or less unchecked since the 1920s. Not until the shocking assassination of Hyères' *député*, **Yann**

Piat, in 1994 did the demand for a "clean hands" campaign really begin in earnest.

Drug trafficking became a major problem in Marseille in the early 1970s and is now prevalent all along the coast. Prostitution and protection rackets also flourish from Menton to Marseille, much of it controlled by either Eastern European crime rings, or the Cosonostra Italian mafia, which has been spreading its tentacles westwards, taking advantage of the large numbers of Italians running businesses along the coast, the casinos and cash sales of high-priced properties for money laundering, and the lack of specific anti-mafia laws in France.

As elsewhere in France, but particularly in Provence, **municipal fiefdoms** evolved – particularly with the huge budgets and planning powers that came with increasing decentralization – offering opportunities for patronage, nepotism and corruption, along with the financial muscle that, until very recently, ensured incumbents a more-or-less permanent position.

In **Marseille**, the town hall was controlled by **Gaston Defferre** for 33 years until his death in 1986. As well as being mayor, he was a socialist *député* and minister, and owned the city's two politically opposed regional newspapers. Though people had their suspicions about underworld links with the town hall, no one pointed the finger at Defferre.

In 1995, **Bernard Tapie**, the most popular politician in Marseille and millionaire owner of Olympique Marseille (OM), the town's football team, was unable to run for mayor because he'd just been sentenced to a year in prison for **match-rigging** his football team in the French League. A flamboyant businessman, *député* and European Member of Parliament for the Bouche-du-Rhône *département*, Tapie had already been debarred from all public office for four years due to **bankruptcy**. Despite – or perhaps because of – his many legal entanglements, which include a long-running dispute over a 100-million-euro debt to Crédit Lyonnais, and fresh allegations from a former OM player of corruption and doping, Tapie continues to remain a popular figure in the public eye, though he no longer has any official political office. Rather surprisingly for a figure of the political left, in 2007 Tapie supported UMP Nicolas Sarkozy instead of the socialist candidate Ségolène Royal in the race for the presidency.

Nice's police and judiciary were accused by Graham Greene in 1982 of protecting organized crime. Greene claimed he slept with a gun under his pillow after his *J'Accuse* was published (and banned in France) in which he detailed the corruption. The late **Jacques Médecin**, who succeeded his father as mayor of Nice in 1966, controlled just about every facet of public life until his downfall in 1990 for political fraud and tax evasion – only when Médecin fled to Uruguay were his mafioso connections finally discussed in public. But Médecin had so successfully identified his name with all the city's glamour that after his departure most Niçois gladly supported his sister Génevieve Assemat-Médecin. Those who didn't, backed his daughter, Martine Cantinchi-Médecin, a Le Pen supporter. Finally extradited in 1994, Médecin served a very short prison term and was able to use his popularity to back the successful candidate in the 1995 municipal elections – one Jacques Peyrat, a close friend of Le Pen and former member of the *Front National*. Re-elected in 2001, Peyrat has made no secret of his desire to have the new public prosecutor, Eric de Montgolfier – who made his reputation fighting white-collar crime (notably Bernard Tapie) and political corruption – removed from his post, before his investigations into the Riviera underworld put yet another city magistrate into prison. More constructively, Peyrat was instrumental in creating CANCA, the Communauté d'Agglomération de Nice-Côte d'Azur, a loose grouping of communities in the

Greater Nice area that aims to improve regional coordination on a range of topics, including parking, transport and the environment.

Toulon was another classic fiefdom, run for four decades by **Maurice Arreckx** and his clique of friends with their underworld connections, until he was put away when financial scandals finally came to light. His successor, and former director of finances, tried in vain to win back the voters but merely ran up more debts and lost to the *Front National* in 1995. Arreckx was sentenced to prison on two separate occasions (in 1997 and 2000), before dying of cancer in 2001. Previous to his death, investigators had found several Swiss bank accounts, under the names "Charlot [Charlie Chaplin]" and "Waterloo", where some of the money paid to Arreckx's campaign fund in return for a major construction contract was secreted.

In neighbouring **La-Seyne-sur-Mer** a planning officer, who attempted to stop a corrupt planning deal, was **murdered** in 1986. More recently, a British project for a World Sea Centre, that would have provided much-needed jobs after the closure of the shipyards, was disbanded after the British refused to pay protection money to the tune of £1 million.

François Léotard, the right-wing mayor of Fréjus, who held cabinet office (under Chirac in the late 1980s) and a seat in the *Assemblée Nationale*, was investigated for financial irregularities, but the case eventually ran out of time and the charges were dropped. **Cannes' mayor**, **Michel Mouillot**, was debarred from public office for five years and given a fifteen-month suspended sentence in 1989, then won his appeal and returned to the town hall only to be given an eighteen-month suspended sentence in 1996. **Pierre Rinaldi**, mayor of **Digne**, was investigated for fraud, **Jean-Pierre Lafond**, mayor of **La Ciotat**, for unwarranted interference, two successive mayors of **La Seyne** for corruption and abuse of patronage … and so the list goes on.

Ethnic tensions and the rise of the Front National

The corruption, waste and general financial incompetence of right-wing municipal power was one element in the rise of **Jean-Marie Le Pen's neo-fascist Front National** (FN) party. Another has been the significance of military bases to the region's economy. While the right-wing national government has made cuts in defence spending, Le Pen has trumpeted his ardent support for France retaining its maximum military capability. However, the most important factor has been the combination of rampant racism, high unemployment and the rising crime rates in the region. Whichever way one looks at it, fear is the underlying current of the extreme right's success.

Although coastal Provence, and Marseille in particular, has always boasted a cosmopolitan mix, the experience of centuries has not bred tolerance. **North Africans** now suffer the discrimination meted out in the past to Jews, Armenians, Portuguese, Italians and other ethnic groups. Many locals are quick to complain of the high taxes they pay to support immigrants, while segregated low-income housing has not only helped to enforce the social boundaries, it has also created a severe gap in the level of education available, consequently serving to limit future opportunities and social integration for most foreigners. One of the ugliest ironies is in inland Provence, where many of the North African populations grew in response to the demand for seasonal labourers; thus, the vineyard owner who votes Le Pen is likely to employ Algerian, Moroccan or Tunisian workers when harvest season comes along.

Jean-Marie Le Pen's *Front National* party developed its major power base, after Paris, in **Marseille**, and in 1986 four FN *députés* were elected in the

Bouches-du-Rhône *département*. They lost their seats when proportional representation was abandoned, but in 1989 the "respectable" parties of the right joined forces with the *Front National* in Grasse, Le Muy and elsewhere to oust Socialist and Communist mayors.

That the FN failed to win outright control of any councils then was due not to any great counterbalance to racism but rather to the similarity in policies of Gaullists such as Jacques Médecin of Nice, and because of the unassailable fortresses of municipal power.

In 1995, however, the *Front National* won **Toulon**, the ninth-largest city in France, plus **Orange** and **Marignane**. The main electoral promise was "Priority for the French", by which, of course, they meant the ethnically pure French. Despite the fact that giving priority to white citizens over non-white citizens is illegal, there were instances in Toulon of people of Algerian origin being overtaken in the housing queue. The town hall also used municipal grants to promote their political preferences. So, for example, a book fair lost its subsidy when the organizers refused to include ten far-right authors, including a historian who denies the Holocaust took place.

In December 1998 **internal feuding** split the party into two camps. **Bruno Mégret**, Le Pen's deputy, attempted to seize leadership of the party only to be expelled by Le Pen, along with several of Mégret's supporters including one of Le Pen's daughters. The ousted members immediately formed a new extreme-right breakaway party, the *Mouvement National Républicain* (MNR), headed by Mégret.

With the **municipal elections** of 2001, it looked as if the FN was splintering apart for good. Six years of misrule in Toulon convinced voters to back Hubert Falco of the *Démocratie Libérale* (DL) party, and Jacques Bompard of Orange was the only *Front National* mayor to be re-elected. The MNR made minor headway around Marseille, picking up Marignane and Vitrolles, though the victory in Vitrolles was later overturned in court due to "unfair campaigning techniques". Moreover, neither party managed to pick up any seats in the 2002 legislative elections for *l'Assemblée Nationale*.

It therefore came as a major shock when Le Pen returned in full force for the 2002 **presidential elections**, with first-round victories in five out of six *départements* in the PACA (Provence, Alpes, Côtes d'Azur) region, soundly defeating both Chirac and Jospin. A cursory glance at the results, even if one is familiar with the area's political leanings, is frightening. His highest support was registered in the Alpes-Maritimes (Nice, Cannes), where he took 26 percent of the vote, followed by the Vaucluse (25.8 percent) and the Var (23.5 percent); in the region's urban districts his most notable victories were Orange (33 percent), Carpentras (30 percent) and Marseille (22.4 percent). But Le Pen was unable to build on this success; his candidature for the 2004 PACA presidential elections, the equivalent of a regional governor, was rejected on the grounds of non-residence in the region.

At about the same time as the presidential elections, **ethnic tensions** of other kinds began to manifest themselves, notably among France's Arab and Jewish communities – both the largest of their kind in Europe. In April 2002, pro-Palestinian groups firebombed and burnt to the ground a number of French synagogues, including one in Marseille, and another in Montpellier. The series of attacks led to an outcry about "French anti-semitism" across Europe and the US. The **civic unrest** across France during 2005, which saw youths – many, though not all, from deprived ethnic minority backgrounds - clash with police and hundreds of cars torched, was however focused on Paris, rather than the south, and, perhaps surprisingly, Marseille was relatively little affected. However, an ugly echo of the 2005 events came in the city in October 2006, when teenagers threw a firebomb into a bus, burning several passengers, the most grievously injured of whom was a woman of French-Senegalese origin. Sharpening his tough-guy law-and-order credentials, Interior Minister and presidential candidate Nicolas Sarkozy sent riot police to Marseille in response to the incident.

Mass tourism and the environment

A crucial factor in Provence's postwar history has been the development of **mass tourism**. Beginning with the St-Tropez boom in the 1960s, the number of visitors to the Côte d'Azur has steadily grown beyond manageable – in any sane sense – proportions. By the mid-1970s the coast had become a nearly uninter-rupted wall of concrete, hosting eight million visitors a year. Agricultural land, save for a few profitable vineyards, was transformed into campsites, hotels and holiday housing. **Property speculation** and construction became the dominant economic activities, while the flaunting of planning laws and the ever-increasing threat to the **environment** – the area's prime asset – were ignored.

When **Brigitte Bardot** started to complain that her beloved **St-Tropez** was becoming a mire of human detritus, the media saw it as a sexy summer story. But when **ecologists** began warning that the main oxygenating seaweed in the Mediterranean was disappearing because of yacht anchors damaging the sea bed, new jetties and marinas modifying the currents, and dust from building sites clouding the water, no one was particularly interested. The loss of *Posidonia oceanica* is now affecting fish, and since the 1980s a non-native toxic algae, *Caulerpa taxifolia* has spread from the Côte d'Azur around the Mediterranean, obliterating sea grasses and replacing them with largely sterile algal beds. According to some experts, nearly half of all current developments need to be demolished and a total embargo put on new developments, if the sea is to recover.

Since the late 1990s, Provence has been suffering from a further environ-mental menace – the **sanglochon**, a cross between a wild boar (*sanglier*) and a pig (*cochon*). These animals have been multiplying far beyond the constraints of their ever-shrinking natural habitat, and the boar population in the Var and elsewhere along the Riviera has rocketed from 3000 to over 30,000 in the past decade – not including the 17,000 killed annually. Originally bred on special farms to provide hunters with prey, the hybrid species has two very undesirable characteristics: the first is an ability to reproduce two to three times faster than a regular wild boar; the second is their lack of timidity around people. The boars can wreak a fair amount of havoc, as well as cause considerable damage to property in built-up areas, with dustbins, vegetable gardens, orchards and golf courses being some of the more common casualties of their daily foraging. Locals shoot the animals freely in an attempt to keep numbers at bay, but so far have had little success in curbing the increasing population.

Urban expansion on the coast

If sun-worshipping set the region's tone for the first three postwar decades, the 1980s saw different forces at work. While the encouragement of summer tourism exacted its toll, a new type of visitor and resident was being encour-aged: the expense-account delegate to **business conferences** and the well-paid employee of **multinational firms**. Towns like Nice and Cannes led the way in attracting the former, while the business park of **Sophia–Antipolis** north of Antibes showed how easy it was to persuade firms to relocate their information technology operations to the beautiful Côte d'Azur hinterland. The result is a further erosion of Provençal identity and greater pressure on the environment. The Dutch, American, Parisian and Lyonnais employees of the high-tech industries need more roads, more housing, more facilities, since, whatever its architectural or economic merits, Sophia-Antipolis is a classic ex-urban business park, with rush-hour traffic to match.

The business visitors, rather than countering the seasonal imbalance of tourism, have made consumption and congestion a year-round factor. A black market has even developed in game meat: venison and other game is shot with high-tech weaponry in areas such as the Clues de Haute Provence, and then sold to the promenade restaurants.

The money from business services and industry on the Riviera now outstrips the income from tourism, and whilst in the big cities the distinctive Marseillaise and Niçois identities have recognizably remained, elsewhere along the coast, and inland, continuities with the past have become ever harder to detect.

Inland Provence

Inland Provence has undergone a parallel transformation to the coast, with second homes in the sun becoming a requisite for the high-salaried French from the 1960s onwards.

Though some villages were certainly saved from extinction by the new property buyers, all suffered from the out-of-season closed shutters syndrome. With the growth of ski resorts, however, the population of the Alpine valleys started to increase, reversing a centuries-old trend. The damage to trees, soil and habitats caused by the ski resorts has in part been offset by the creation of the **Parc National du Mercantour**, an enclave that has saved several Alpine animal and plant species.

In central Provence the Durance Valley, alongside the new Marseille–Grenoble autoroute, has become the latest corridor for sunrise industries. Meanwhile, the *paysans* keeping goats and bees, a few vines and a vegetable plot are all of pensionable age. The cheeses and honey, the vegetables, olive oil and wine (unless it's AOC) must compete with Spanish, Italian and Greek produce, from land that doesn't have the ludicrously high values of Provence. In order to exploit the consumption patterns of the twenty-first century the scale has to be larger than the traditional peasant plots, and there must be speedy access to the biggest markets. The emergence in recent years of successful international companies such as l'Occitane en Provence and Oliviers & Co, however, offers one pointer to a viable economic future, trading on the magic of a Provençal image to target upmarket consumers, with prices to match.

Transport mania

Fast access to the Côte d'Azur has become the obsession of planners in Paris, the most recent move being the extension of the **TGV to Marseille**. However, whether or not the region's infrastructure can deal with the corresponding increase in tourist traffic is another matter. The Riviera has long suffered from the lack of a regional mass transportation system and the resulting chronic gridlock: heavy traffic and stop-go jams have long been the norm, not the exception, on the A8 autoroute.

A variety of alternatives has been proposed to ease the transport problems, including the construction of an environmentally dubious autoroute, the **A8 bis**, which would shadow the A8 along the most congested stretch from Fréjus to Monaco. More obviously constructive was the reopening of the Cannes-Grasse railway to passengers in 2005; the first line of Nice's much-delayed tramway was scheduled to begin operation in the summer of 2007.

Books

M ost of the books listed below are in print and in paperback – those that are out of print (o/p) should be easy to track down in second-hand bookshops. Publishers are detailed with the British publisher first, separated by an oblique slash from the US publisher, where both exist. Where books are published in only one country, UK, US or France precedes the publisher's name; where the book is published by the same company in both the UK and US, the name of the company appears just once. Titles marked with the ⚡ symbol are particularly recommended.

History

Robin Briggs *Early Modern France, 1560–1715* (Oxford UP). Readable account of the period in which the French state started to assert control over the whole country. Strong perspectives on the provinces, including coverage of the Marseille rebellion of 1658.

James Bromwich *The Roman Remains of Southern France* (Routledge). The only comprehensive guide to the subject; detailed, well illustrated and approachable. In addition to accounts of well-known sites, it will lead you off the map to all sorts of discoveries.

Alfred Cobban *A History of Modern France* (3 vols: 1715–1799; 1799–1871; 1871–1962. Penguin/Viking Press). Definitive account of three centuries of French political, social and economic life, from Louis XIV to mid-de Gaulle.

Margaret Crosland *Sade's Wife* (Peter Owen/Dufour Editions). Expert on Provence's most notorious resident examines how Renée-Pélagie de Montreuil coped with being married to the Marquis de Sade.

FX Emmanuelli *Histoire de la Provence* (o/p). Huge, well-illustrated tome by a group of French academics, which covers the province in as much detail as anyone could conceivably want.

Colin Jones *The Longman Companion to the French Revolution: A Companion* (Longman). Original quotes and documents, good pictures and an unusually clear explanation of events. Good background on Marseille's Fédérés and Mirabeau.

Emmanuel Le Roy Ladurie *Montaillou* (Penguin/Vintage). Just outside the area but well worth reading, nevertheless, as the classic account of peasant life in a fourteenth-century Pyrenean village, reconstructed using the original court records of an anti-Cathar Inquisition.

⚡ **John Noone** *The Man Behind the Iron Mask* (Sutton/St Martin's Press). Fascinating enquiry into the mythical or otherwise prisoner of Ste-Marguerite fort on the Îles de Lérins, immortalized by Alexander Dumas.

Jim Ring *Riviera: The Rise and Fall of the Côte d'Azur* (John Murray). Highly readable social history of the French Riviera and of the many nationalities who have shaped the region's history, culture and architecture.

Simon Schama *Citizens* (Penguin/Vintage). A fascinating, accessible treatment of the history of the Revolution, with a fast-moving narrative and a reappraisal of the customary view of a stagnant, unchanging nobility in the years preceding the uprising.

Jean Tulard *Napoléon: The Myth of the Saviour* (Todtri Productions). One of the classic French accounts of the rise and fall of the great man. Its interest is with the phenomenon rather than the personal life and characteristics of the man.

🏃 Theodore Zeldin *France, 1848–1945* (2 vols, Oxford Paperbacks). Two thematic and very accessible volumes on all matters French over the last century.

Society and politics

John Ardagh *France in the New Century* (Penguin). Long-time writer on France gets to grips with the country over the last twenty years. It attempts to be a comprehensive survey, but gets rather too drawn into party politics and statistics.

Roland Barthes *Mythologies* (Vintage). Brilliant analyses of how the ideas, prejudices and contradictions of French thought and behaviour manifest themselves, in food, wine, travel guides and other cultural offerings.

Mary Blume *Côte d'Azur: Inventing the French Riviera* (o/p). This attempt to analyse the myth only reconfirms it, mainly because the people Blume has interviewed all have a stake in maintaining the image of the Côte as a cultured millionaires' dreamland. Great black and white photos.

Laurence Wylie *Village in the Vaucluse* (Harvard UP). Sociological study of Roussillon, full of interesting insights into Provençal village life.

Travel

Carol Drinkwater *The Olive Farm* (Abacus). Soft-focus memoir of the joys of expatriate life in rural Provence, written by a well-known British actress.

🏃 MFK Fisher *Two Towns in Provence* (Vintage). Evocative memoirs of life in Aix-en-Provence and Marseille during the 1950s and 1960s.

John Flower and Charles Waite *Provence* (o/p). Waite's gorgeous photographs encompass landscapes, architectural details, markets and images obscure and familiar. Flower's text draws on over thirty years of residence and visits.

William Fotheringham *Put Me Back on My Bike: In Search of Tom*

Simpson (Yellow Jersey Press). An in-depth study of Simpson's life as a cyclist, leading up to his tragic death on Mont Ventoux.

Peter Mayle *A Year in Provence* (Penguin/Vintage). A month-by-month account of the charms and frustrations of moving into an old French farmhouse in Provence; with entertaining accounts of everything from the local cuisine, tips for wooing fickle French contractors, handicapping goat races, and enduring winter's icy mistral.

Julian More *Tour de Provence* (Pavilion). Easy-to-digest travelogue arranged by *département*, starting with More's home in northwestern Provence; good selection of colour photos.

Art and artists

Good introductions to the modern artists associated with Provence are published by Thames and Hudson (UK/US), Clematis and Phaidon (UK) and Abrams (US). Bracken Books (UK) published a series "Artists by Themselves" – small, attractively produced books with extracts of letters and diaries to accompany the pictures – which includes Matisse, Picasso, Cézanne, Van Gogh and Renoir. More substantial editions of artists' own writings include *Matisse on Art* (University of California Press), *My Life: Marc Chagall* (Peter Owen), and *Cézanne by Himself: Drawings, Paintings, Writings* (Little/Brown).

Provence and the Côte d'Azur in literature

The Côte d'Azur has inspired many twentieth-century English, American and French writers, indulging in the high life like Scott Fitzgerald, slumming it with the bohemians like Anaïs Nin, or trying to regain their health like Katherine Mansfield. The two best-known Provençal writers of the twentieth century, Jean Giono and Marcel Pagnol, wrote about peasant life in inland Provence; many of their works have been turned into films. Nineteenth-century Provence features in Alexander Dumas' rip-roaring tale of revenge, *The Count of Monte Cristo*, and in some of Aix-born Émile Zola's novels, while the horrors of eighteenth-century Provence are brought to life in Victor Hugo's *Les Misérables*.

Below is a selective recommendation of literary works in which the region plays a significant role, including poetry – spanning the ages from Petrarch troubadour songs to Bonnefoy and Mistral – and a play by Anouilh set in Marseille.

Jean Anouilh *Point of Departure*

Yves Bonnefoy *In the Shadow's Light*

Anthony Bonner (ed) *Songs of the Troubadours*

Colette *Collected Stories*

Alphonse Daudet *Letters from My Windmill; Tartarin de Tarascon; In the Land of Pain;* and *Tartarin on the Alps*

Alexandre Dumas (Père) *The Count of Monte Cristo*

Lawrence Durrell *The Avignon Quintet*

F. Scott Fitzgerald *Tender is the Night*

Jean Giono *Joy of Man's Desiring; Blue Boy; The Man Who Planted Trees; The Horseman on the Roof; To the Slaughterhouse;* and *Two Riders of the Storm*

Graham Greene *Loser Takes All*

Victor Hugo *Les Misérables*

Sébastien Japrisot *One Deadly Summer*

Katherine Mansfield *Collected Stories*

Frédéric Mistral *Mirèio*

Anaïs Nin *Diaries*

Marcel Pagnol *The Water of the Hills: Jean de Florette and Manon of the Springs; My Father's Glory and My Mother's Castle; Marius;* and *Fanny*

Francesco Petrarch *Canzoniere*

Françoise Sagan *Bonjour Tristesse*

Patrick Süskind *Perfume*

Émile Zola *Abbé Mouret's Transgression; Fortune of the Rougons;* and *The Conquest of Plassans*

Martin Bailey (ed) *Van Gogh: Letters from Provence* (o/p). Attractively produced in full colour. Very dippable and very good value.

Barbara Ehrlich *Renoir: His Life, Art and Letters* (Abrams). A thorough and interesting work.

Françoise Gilot *Matisse & Picasso: A Friendship in Art* (UK Bloomsbury). A fascinating subject – two more different men in life and art would be hard to find.

D and M Johnson *The Age of Illusion* (UK Thames & Hudson). Links

French art and politics in the interwar years, featuring Provençal works by Le Corbusier, Chagall and Picasso.

Jacques Henri Lartigue *Diary of a Century* (o/p). Book of pictures by a great photographer from the day he was given a camera in 1901 through to the 1970s. Contains wonderful scenes of aristocratic leisure and Côte d'Azur beaches.

Sarah Whitfield *Fauvism* (Thames & Hudson). Good introduction to a movement that encompassed Côte d'Azur and Riviera artists Matisse, Dufy and Van Dongen.

Food and drink

Alain Ducasse *Flavours of France* (Artisan). Celebrity cookbook that follows Ducasse from the kitchens of the *Louis XV* restaurant in Monte Carlo to *la Bastide de Moustiers*.

Hubrecht Duijker *Touring in Wine Country: Provence* (Mitchell Beazley). Guide to the top vineyards and wine cellars of Provence.

Kenneth James *Escoffier: the King of Chefs* (Hambledon Continuum). Biography of the famous chef who started his career on the Côte d'Azur.

Richard Olney *Lulu's Provençal Table* (Pavilion/Ten Speed Press). Classic

Provençal recipes and interesting commentary from Lulu Peyraud, proprietor of the Domaine Tempier vineyard in Bandol. Great black and white photos.

Roger Vergé *Cuisine of the Sun* (o/p). The classic cookbook of modern Provençal cuisine, from the legendary chef of the *Moulin de Mougins*.

Patricia Wells *The Provence cookbook* (Harper Collins). More than 200 recipes rooted in the *terroir*, plus vignettes on suppliers, markets and wine-pairing suggestions.

Botany

W. Lippert *Fleurs de Haute Montagne* (France Miniguide Nathan Tout Terrain). Palm-sized

colour guide to flowers, available from French bookshops in the trekking areas.

Language

Language

French

rench can be a deceptively familiar language because of the number of words and structures it shares with English. Despite this, it's far from easy, though the bare essentials are not difficult to master and can make all the difference. Even just saying *"Bonjour, Madame/Monsieur"* and then gesticulating will usually get you a smile and helpful service. People working in tourist offices, campsites, hotels and so on, almost always speak English and tend to use it if you're struggling to speak French – be grateful, not insulted.

On the Côte d'Azur you can get by without knowing a word of French, with menus printed in at least four languages, and half the people you meet fellow foreigners. In Nice, Sisteron and the Roya Valley a knowledge of Italian would provide a common language with many of the natives. But if you can hold your own in French – however imperfectly – speak away and your audience will warm to you.

Provençal and accents

The one language you don't have to learn – unless you want to understand the meaning of the names of streets, restaurants or cafés – is **Provençal**. Itself a dialect of the *langue d'oc* (Occitan), it evolved into different dialects in Provence, so that the languages spoken in Nice, in the Alps, on the coast and in the Rhône Valley, though mutually comprehensible, were not precisely the same. In the mid-nineteenth century the *Félibrige* movement established a standard literary form in an attempt to revive the language. But by the time Frédéric Mistral won the Nobel Prize in 1904 for his poem *Mirèio*, Provençal had already been superseded by French in ordinary life.

Two hundred years ago everybody spoke Provençal whether they were counts, shipyard workers or peasants. Today you might, if you're lucky, hear it spoken by the older generation in some of the remoter villages. It just survives as a literary language: it can be studied at school and university and there are columns in Provençal in some newspapers. But unlike Breton or Occitan proper, it has never been the fuel of a separatist movement.

The French that people speak in Provence has, however, a very marked **accent**. It's much less nasal than northern French, words are not run together to quite the same extent, and there's a distinctive sound for the endings – *in*, *-en*, and for *vin*, and so on, that is more like *ung*.

Pronunciation

One easy rule to remember is that **consonants** at the ends of words are usually silent. *Pas plus tard* (not later) is thus pronounced "pa-plu-tarr". But when the following word begins with a vowel, you run the two together: *pas après* (not after) becomes "pazaprey".

Vowels are the hardest sounds to get right. Roughly:

a	as in h**a**t
e	as in g**e**t
é	between g**e**t and g**a**te
è	between g**e**t and g**u**t
eu	like the **u** in h**u**rt
i	as in mach**i**ne
o	as in h**o**t
o, au	as in **o**ver
ou	as in f**oo**d
u	as in a pursed-lip version of **u**se

More awkward are the **combinations** *in/im, en/em, an/am, on/om, un/um* at the ends of words, or followed by consonants other than n or m. Again, roughly:

in/im	like the **an** in **an**xious
an/am, en/em	like the **don** in **Don**caster when said with a nasal accent
on/om	like the **don** in **Don**caster said by someone with a heavy cold
un/um	like the **u** in **u**nderstand

Consonants are much as in English, except that: "*ch*" is always sh, "*c*" is s, "*h*" is silent, "*th*" is the same as t, "*ll*" is like the y in "yes", "*w*" is v, and "*r*" is growled (or rolled).

Learning materials

French Dictionary Phrasebook (Rough Guides). Mini dictionary-style phrasebook with both English–French and French–English sections, along with cultural tips for tricky situations and a menu reader.

Get By In French (BBC Publications). Phrasebook and cassette. A good stepping-stone before tackling a complete course.

Mini French Dictionary (Harrap/Larousse). French–English and English–French, plus a brief grammar and pronunciation guide.

Breakthrough French (Palgrave/McGraw Hill;

book and two cassettes). An excellent teach-yourself course.

Pardon My French! Pocket French Slang Dictionary (UK Harrap). The key to understanding everyday French.

A Comprehensive French Grammar (Blackwell). Easy-to-follow reference grammar.

À Vous La France; France Extra; France-Parler (BBC Publications; EMC Paradigm). Comprising a book and two cassettes, these BBC radio courses run from beginner's to fairly advanced French.

French words and phrases

Basics

French nouns are divided into masculine and feminine. This causes difficulties with adjectives, whose endings have to change to suit the gender of the nouns they qualify. If you know some grammar, you will know what to do. If not, stick to the masculine form, which is the simplest – it's what we have done in this glossary.

aujourd'hui	today	**demain**	tomorrow
hier	yesterday	**le matin**	in the morning

l'après-midi	in the afternoon	fermé	closed
le soir	in the evening	grand	big
maintenant	now	petit	small
plus tard	later	plus	more
à une heure	at one o'clock	moins	less
à trois heures	at three o'clock	un peu	a little
à dix heures et demie	at ten-thirty	beaucoup	a lot
		bon marché	cheap
à midi	at midday	cher	expensive
un homme	man	bon	good
une femme	woman	mauvais	bad
ici	here	chaud	hot
là	there	froid	cold
ceci	this one	avec	with
cela	that one	sans	without
ouvert	open		

Talking to people

When addressing people you should always use *Monsieur* for a man, *Madame* for a woman, *Mademoiselle* for a girl. Plain *bonjour* by itself is not enough. This isn't as formal as it seems, and it has its uses when you've forgotten someone's name or want to attract someone's attention.

Pardon	Excuse me	d'accord	OK/agreed
Vous parlez anglais?	Do you speak English?	s'il vous plaît	please
		merci	thank you
Comment ça se dit en français?	How do you say it in French?	bonjour	hello
		au revoir	goodbye
Comment vous appelez-vous?	What's your name?	bonjour	good morning/ afternoon
Je m'appelle .-.-.	My name is .-.-.		
Je suis anglais[e]/	I'm English/	bonsoir	good evening
irlandais[e]/	Irish/	bonne nuit	good night
écossais[e]/	Scottish	Comment allez-vous?/ Ça va?	How are you?
gallois[e]/	Welsh/		
américain[e]/	American/	Très bien, merci	Fine, thanks
australien[ne]/	Australian/	Je ne sais pas	I don't know
canadien[ne]/	Canadian/	Allons-y	Let's go
néo-zélandais[e]	a New Zealander	À demain	See you tomorrow
oui	yes	À bientôt	See you soon
non	no	Pardon, Madame/ Excusez-moi	Sorry
Je comprends	I understand		
Je ne comprends pas	I don't understand	Fichez-moi la paix!	Leave me alone! (aggressive)
S'il vous plaît, parlez moins vite	Can you speak slower?	Aidez-moi, s'il vous plaît	Please help me

Finding the way

autobus/bus/car	bus	autostop	hitchhiking
gare routière	bus station	à pied	on foot
arrêt	bus stop	Vous allez où?	Where are you going?
voiture	car	Je vais à ...	I'm going to ...
train/taxi/ferry	train/taxi/ferry	Je voudrais descendre à ...	I want to get off at ...
bateau	boat		
avion	plane	la route pour ...	the road to ...
gare (SNCF)	train station	près/pas loin	near
quai	platform	loin	far
Il part à quelle heure?	What time does it leave?	à gauche	left
		à droite	right
Il arrive à quelle heure?	What time does it arrive?	tout droit	straight on
		à l'autre côté de	on the other side of
un billet pour ...	a ticket to ...	à l'angle de	on the corner of
aller simple	single ticket	à côté de	next to
aller retour	return ticket	derrière	behind
compostez votre billet	validate your ticket	devant	in front of
		avant	before
valable pour	valid for	après	after
vente de billets	ticket office	sous	under
combien de kilomètres?	how many kilometres?	traverser	to cross
		pont	bridge
combien d'heures?	how many hours?		

Questions and requests

The simplest way of asking a question is to start with *s'il vous plaît* (please), then name the thing you want in an interrogative tone of voice. For example:

S'il vous plaît, la boulangerie?	Where is there a bakery?	S'il vous plaît, la route pour la tour Eiffel?	Which way is it to the Eiffel Tower?

Similarly with requests:

S'il vous plaît, une chambre pour deux.	We'd like a room for two.	S'il vous plaît, un kilo d'oranges?	Can I have a kilo of oranges?

Question words

où?	where?	quand?	when?
comment?	how?	pourquoi?	why?
combien?	how many/ how much?	à quelle heure?	at what time?
		quel est?	what is/which is?

Accommodation

une chambre pour un/deux personnes	a room for one/two people	faire la lessive	do laundry
		draps	sheets
		couvertures	blankets
un lit double	a double bed	calme	quiet
une chambre avec douche	a room with a shower	bruyant	noisy
		eau chaude	hot water
une chambre avec salle de bain	a room with a bath	eau froide	cold water
		Est-ce que le petit déjeuner est compris?	Is breakfast included?
pour un/deux/ trois nuits	for one/two/ three nights		
		Je voudrais prendre le petit déjeuner	I would like breakfast
Je peux la voir?	Can I see it?		
une chambre sur la cour	a room on the courtyard	Je ne veux pas de petit déjeuner	I don't want breakfast
une chambre sur la rue	a room over the street	On peut camper ici?	Can we camp here?
premier étage	first floor	un camping/terrain de camping	campsite
deuxième étage	second floor		
avec vue	with a view	une tente	tent
clef	key	un emplacement	tent space
repasser	to iron	auberge de jeunesse	youth hostel

Driving

garage	service station	ligne à air	air line
service	service	gonfler les pneus	put air in the tyres
garer la voiture	to park the car	batterie	battery
un parking	car park	la batterie est morte	the battery is dead
défense de stationner/ stationnement interdit	no parking		
		bougies	plugs
		tomber en panne	to break down
station essence/ station service	gas station	bidon	gas can
		assurance	insurance
essence	fuel	carte verte	green card
faire le plein	(to) fill it up	feux	traffic lights
huile	oil	feu rouge	red light
		feu vert	green light

Health matters

médecin	doctor	mal à l'estomac	stomach ache
Je ne me sens pas bien	I don't feel well	règles	period
		douleur	pain
médicaments	medicines	ça fait mal	it hurts
ordonnance	prescription	pharmacie	chemist
Je suis malade	I feel sick	hôpital	hospital
J'ai mal à la tête	I have a headache		

Other needs

boulangerie	bakery	banque	bank
alimentation	food shop	argent	money
supermarché	supermarket	toilettes	toilets
manger	to eat	police	police
boire	to drink	téléphone	telephone
camping gaz	camping gas	cinéma	cinema
tabac	tobacconist	théâtre	theatre
timbres	stamps	réserver	to reserve/book

Numbers

un	1	vingt-deux	22
deux	2	trente	30
trois	3	quarante	40
quatre	4	cinquante	50
cinq	5	soixante	60
six	6	soixante-dix	70
sept	7	soixante-quinze	75
huit	8	quatre-vingts	80
neuf	9	quatre-vingt-dix	90
dix	10	quatre-vingt -quinze	95
onze	11		
douze	12	cent	100
treize	13	cent-et-un	101
quatorze	14	deux cents	200
quinze	15	trois cents	300
seize	16	cinq cents	500
dix-sept	17	mille	1000
dix-huit	18	deux milles	2000
dix-neuf	19	cinq milles	5000
vingt	20	un million	1,000,000
vingt-et-un	21		

Days and dates

janvier	January	décembre	December
février	February		
mars	March	dimanche	Sunday
avril	April	lundi	Monday
mai	May	mardi	Tuesday
juin	June	mercredi	Wednesday
juillet	July	jeudi	Thursday
août	August	vendredi	Friday
septembre	September	samedi	Saturday
octobre	October		
novembre	November	le premier août	August 1

le deux mars	March 2	dix-neuf-cent-	1999
le quatorze juillet	July 14	quatre-vingt-	
le vingt-trois	November 23	dix-neuf	
novembre			

Food and drink terms

Basic terms

Pain	Bread	Cuillère	Spoon
Beurre	Butter	Cure-dent	Toothpick
Céréales	Cereal	Table	Table
Lait	Milk	L'addition	Bill
Huile	Oil	Offert/Gratuit	Free
Confiture	Jam	(Re)chauffé	(Re)heated
Poivre	Pepper	Cuit	Cooked
Sel	Salt	Cru	Raw
Sucre	Sugar	Emballé	Wrapped
Vinaigre	Vinegar	Sur place ou à	Eat in or take away?
Moutarde	Mustard	emporter?	
Bouteille	Bottle	À emporter	Takeaway
Verre	Glass	Fumé	Smoked
Fourchette	Fork	Salé	Salted/spicy
Couteau	Knife	Sucré	Sweet

Snacks (*Casse-croûte*)

Un sandwich/	A sandwich	Omelette . . .	Omelette . . .
une baguette		nature/aux fines	plain/with herbs
...au jambon/	...with ham/cheese	herbes	
fromage		au fromage	with cheese
...au jambon beurre	...with ham & butter	Croque-monsieur	Grilled cheese and
...fromage beurre	...cheese & butter		ham sandwich
...au pâté	...with pâté	Croque-madame	Grilled cheese,
(de campagne)	(country-style)		ham or bacon and
Oeufs ...	Eggs...		fried egg sandwich
au plat(s)	Fried eggs	Pan bagnat	Bread roll with egg,
à la coque	Boiled eggs		olives, salad, tuna,
durs	Hard-boiled eggs		anchovies and olive oil
brouillés	Scrambled eggs	Tartine	Buttered bread or
poché	Poached eggs		open sandwich

Soups (*soupes*) and starters (*hors d'œuvres*)

Bisque	Shellfish soup	Bouillabaisse	Soup with five fish and
Baudroie	Fish soup with		other bits to dip
	vegetables, garlic and	Bouillon	Broth or stock
	herbs		

Bourride	Thick fish soup with garlic, onions and tomatoes
Consommé	Clear soup
Pistou	Parmesan, basil and garlic paste or cream added to soup
Potage	Thick vegetable soup
Rouille	Red pepper, garlic and saffron mayonnaise served with fish soup
Velouté	Thick soup, usually fish or poultry
Assiette anglaise	Plate of cold meats
Crudités	Raw vegetables with dressings
Hors d'œuvres variés	Combination of the above plus smoked or marinated fish

Pasta (pâtes), pancakes (crêpes) and flans (tartes)

Pâtes fraîches	Fresh pasta
Nouilles	Noodles
Raviolis	Pasta parcels of meat or chard, a Provençal, not Italian invention
Crêpe au sucre /aux œufs	Pancake with sugar /eggs
Socca	Thin chickpea flour pancake
Panisse	Thick chickpea flour pancake
Pissaladière	Tart of fried onions with anchovies and black olives

Fish (*poisson*), seafood (*fruits de mer*) and shellfish (*crustaces* or *coquillages*)

Aiglefin	Small haddock or fresh cod
Anchois	Anchovies
Amande de mer	Small sweet-tasting shellfish
Anguilles	Eels
Araignée de mer	Spider fish
Baudroie	Monkfish or anglerfish
Barbue	Brill
Bigourneau	Periwinkle
Brème	Bream
Bulot	Whelk
Cabillaud	Cod
Calmar	Squid
Carrelet	Plaice
Chapon de mer	Mediterranean fish (related to Scorpion fish)
Claire	Type of oyster
Colin	Hake
Congre	Conger eel
Coques	Cockles
Coquilles St-Jacques	Scallops
Crabe	Crab
Crevettes grises	Shrimp
Crevettes roses	Prawns
Daurade	Sea bream
Écrevisse	Freshwater crayfish
Éperlan	Smelt or whitebait
Escargots	Snails
Favou(ille)	Tiny crab
Flétan	Halibut
Friture	Assorted fried fish
Gambas	King prawns
Girelle	Type of crab
Grenouilles (cuisses de)	Frogs (legs)
Grondin	Red gurnard
Hareng	Herring
Homard	Lobster
Huîtres	Oysters
Langouste	Spiny lobster
Langoustines	Saltwater crayfish (scampi)

Limande	Lemon sole	Poutine	Small river fish
Lotte de mer	Monkfish	Praires	Small clams
Loup de mer	Sea bass	Raie	Skate
Maquereau	Mackerel	Rascasse	Scorpion fish
Merlan	Whiting	Rouget	Red mullet
Morue	Salt cod	Rouquier	Mediterranean eel
Moules (marinière)	Mussels (with shallots in white wine sauce)	St-Pierre	John Dory
		Saumon	Salmon
Oursin	Sea urchin	Sole	Sole
Pageot	Sea bream	Telline	Tiny clam
Palourdes	Clams	Thon	Tuna
Poissons de roche	Fish from shoreline rocks	Truite	Trout
		Turbot	Turbot
Poulpe	Octopus	Violet	Sea squirt

... and fish terms

Aïoli	Garlic mayonnaise/ or the dish when served with salt cod and vegetables	Darne	Fillet or steak
		En papillote	Cooked in foil
		Estocaficada	Stockfish stew with tomatoes, olives, peppers, garlic and onions
Anchoïade	Anchovy paste or sauce		
Arête	Fish bone		
Assiette de pêcheur	Assorted fish	La douzaine	A dozen
		Frit	Fried
Béarnaise	Sauce of egg yolks, white wine, shallots and vinegar	Friture	Deep-fried small fish
		Fumé	Smoked
		Fumet	Fish stock
Beignets	Fritters	Gelée	Aspic
Bonne femme	With mushroom, parsley, potato and shallots	Gigot de mer	Baked fish pieces, usually monkfish
Brandade	Crushed cod with olive oil	Goujon	Several types of small fish, also deep-fried pieces of larger fish coated in breadcrumbs
Colbert	Fried in egg with breadcrumbs		
Croûtons	Toasted bread, often rubbed with garlic, to dip or drop in fish soups		

Meat (*viande*) and poultry (*volaille*)

Agneau (de pré-salé)	Lamb (grazed on salt marshes)	Boudin noir	Black pudding
		Caille	Quail
Andouille, andouillette	Tripe sausage	Canard	Duck
		Caneton	Duckling
Bœuf	Beef	Cervelle	Brains
Bifteck	Steak	Châteaubriand	Porterhouse steak
Boudin blanc	Sausage of white meats	Cheval	Horse meat

493

Contrefilet	Sirloin roast
Coquelet	Cockerel
Dinde, dindon, dindonneau	Turkey of different ages and genders
Entrecôte	Ribsteak
Faux filet	Sirloin steak
Fricadelles	Meatballs
Foie	Liver
Foie gras	Fattened (duck/goose) liver
Gésier	Gizzard
Magret de canard	Duck breast
Gibier	Game
Graisse	Fat
Jambon	Ham
Langue	Tongue
Lapin, lapereau	Rabbit, young rabbit
Lard, lardons	Bacon, diced bacon
Lièvre	Hare
Merguez	Spicy, red sausage
Mouton	Mutton

Museau de veau	Calf's muzzle
Oie	Goose
Os	Bone
Pintade	Guinea fowl
Porc, pieds de porc	Pork, pig's trotters
Poulet	Chicken
Poussin	Baby chicken
Ris	Sweetbreads
Rognons	Kidneys
Rognons blancs	Testicles
Sanglier	Wild boar
Saucisson	Dried sausage
Steack	Steak
Taureau/Toro	Bull meat
Tête de veau	Calf's head (in jelly)
Tournedos	Thick slices of fillet
Travers de porc	Spare ribs
Tripes	Tripe
Veau	Veal
Venaison	Venison

Meat and poultry dishes

Aïado	Roast shoulder of lamb, stuffed with garlic and other ingredients
Bœuf à la gardane	Beef or bull meat stew with carrots, celery, onions, garlic and black olives, served with rice
Canard à l'orange	Roast duck with an orange-and-wine sauce
Canard périgourdin	Roast duck with prunes, pâté de foie gras and truffles
Cassoulet	A casserole of beans and meat
Choucroute	Pickled cabbage with peppercorns, sausages, bacon and salami

Coq au vin	Chicken cooked until it falls off the bone with wine, onions, and mushrooms
Gigot (d'agneau)	Leg (of lamb)
Grillade	Grilled meat
Hâchis	Chopped meat or mince hamburger
Pieds et paquets	Mutton or pork tripe and trotters
Steak au poivre (vert/rouge)	Steak in a black (green/red) pepper corn sauce
Steak tartare	Raw chopped beef, topped with a raw egg yolk

Meat and poultry terms

Blanquette, civet, daube, estouffade, hochepôt, navarin and ragoût	All are types of stew

Aile	Wing
Blanc	Breast or white meat
Broche	Spit-roasted

Brochette	Kebab	Pavé	Thick slice
Carré	Best end of neck, chop or cutlet	En croûte	In pastry
		Farci	Stuffed
Civit	Game stew	Au feu de bois	Cooked over wood fire
Confit	Meat preserve	Au four	Baked
Côte	Chop, cutlet or rib	Garni	With vegetables
Cou	Neck	Grillé	Grilled
Cuisse	Thigh or leg	Marmite	Casserole
Épaule	Shoulder	Mijoté	Stewed
Mariné	Marinated	Rôti	Roast
Médaillon	Round piece	Sauté	Lightly cooked in butter

For steaks:

Bleu	Almost raw	Bien cuit	Well done
Saignant	Rare	Très bien cuit	Very well cooked
À point	Medium		

Garnishes and sauces:

Américaine	White wine, Cognac and tomato	Chasseur	White wine, mushrooms and shallots
Arlésienne	With tomatoes, onions, aubergines, potatoes and rice	Chatêlaine	With artichoke hearts and chestnut purée
Au porto	In port	Diable	Strong mustard seasoning
Auvergnat	With cabbage, sausage and bacon	Forestière	With bacon and mushroom
Beurre blanc	Sauce of white wine and shallots, with butter	Fricassée	Rich, creamy sauce
		Galantine	Cold dish of meat in aspic
Bonne femme	With mushroom, bacon, potato and onions	Mornay	Cheese sauce
		Pays d'Auge	Cream and cider
Bordelaise	In a red wine, shallots and bone-marrow sauce	Piquante	Gherkins or capers, vinegar and shallots
		Provençale	Tomatoes, garlic, olive oil and herbs
Boulangère	Baked with potatoes and onions	Véronique	Grapes, wine and cream
Bourgeoise	With carrots, onions, bacon, celery and braised lettuce		

Vegetables (*légumes*), herbs (*herbes*) and spices (*épices*), etc

Ail	Garlic	Avocat	Avocado
Anis	Aniseed	Basilic	Basil
Artichaut	Artichoke	Betterave	Beetroot
Asperges	Asparagus	Blette/bette	Swiss chard

Cannelle	Cinnamon	Laitue	Lettuce
Câpre	Caper	Laurier	Bay leaf
Cardon	Cardoon, a beet related to artichoke	Lentilles	Lentils
		Maïs	Corn
Carotte	Carrot	Marjoline	Marjoram
Céleri	Celery	Menthe	Mint
Champignons: cèpes, chanterelles, girolles, morilles	Mushrooms of various kinds	Navet	Turnip
		Oignon	Onion
		Panais	Parsnip
		Pélandron	Type of string bean
Chou (rouge)	(Red) cabbage	Persil	Parsley
Chou-fleur	Cauliflower	Petits pois	Peas
Ciboulettes	Chives	Piment	Pimento
Concombre	Cucumber	Pois chiches	Chickpeas
Cornichon	Gherkin	Pois mange-tout	Snow peas
Échalotes	Shallots	Pignons	Pine nuts
Endive	Chicory	Poireau	Leek
Épinard	Spinach	Poivron (vert, rouge)	Sweet pepper (green, red)
Épis de maïs	Corn on the cob		
Estragon	Tarragon	Pommes de terre	Potatoes
Fenouil	Fennel	Radis	Radishes
Férigoule	Thyme (in Provençal)	Raifort	Horseradish
Fèves	Broad beans	Riz	Rice
Flageolets	White beans	Romarin	Rosemary
Fleur de courgette	Courgette flower	Safran	Saffron
Genièvre	Juniper	Sarrasin	Buckwheat
Gingembre	Ginger	Sauge	Sage
Haricots verts	String (French) beans	Serpolet	Wild thyme
...rouges	kidney beans	Thym	Thyme
...beurres	butter beans	Tomate	Tomato
...blancs	white beans	Truffes	Truffles

Dishes and terms

Beignet	Fritter	Râpé(e)s	Grated or shredded
Farci	Stuffed	Pistou	Ground basil, olive oil, garlic and parmesan
Gratiné	Browned with cheese or butter		
		Primeurs	Spring vegetables
Jardinière	With mixed diced vegetables	Salade verte	Lettuce with vinaigrette
À la parisienne	Sautéed in butter (potatoes); with white wine sauce and shallots	Gratin dauphinois	Potatoes baked in cream and garlic
		Mesclum	Salad combining several different leaves
À l'anglaise	Boiled		
À la grecque	Cooked in oil and lemon	Pommes château, fondantes	Quartered potatoes sautéed in butter

Pommes lyonnaise	Fried onions and potatoes	Salad niçoise	Salad of tomatoes, radishes, cucumber, hard-boiled eggs, anchovies, onion, artichokes, green peppers, beans, basil and garlic (rarely as comprehensive, even in Nice)
Ratatouille	Mixture of aubergine, courgette, tomatoes and garlic		
Rémoulade	Mustard mayonnaise, sometimes with anchovies and gherkins, also salad of grated celeriac with mayonnaise	Duxelles	Fried mushrooms and shallots with cream
		Fines herbes	Mixture of tarragon, parsley and chives
Parmentier	With potatoes	Frisé(e)	Curly
Sauté	Lightly fried in butter	Gousse d'ail	Clove of garlic
À la vapeur	Steamed	Herbes de Provence	Mixture of bay leaf, thyme, rosemary and savory
Je suis végétarien(ne).	I'm a vegetarian.		
Il y a des plats sans viande?	Are there any non-meat dishes?	Petits farcis	Stuffed tomatoes, aubergines, courgettes, peppers
Biologique	Organic	Tapenade	Olive and caper paste
Raclette	Toasted cheese served with potatoes, gherkins and onions	Tomates à la provençale	Tomatoes baked with breadcrumbs, garlic and parsley

Fruits (*fruits*), nuts (*noix*) and honey (*miel*)

Abricot	Apricot	Marrons	Chestnuts
Amandes	Almonds	Melon	Melon
Ananas	Pineapple	Miel de lavande	Lavender honey
Banane	Banana	Mirabelles	Small yellow plums
Brugnon, nectarine	Nectarine	Myrtilles	Bilberries
Cacahouète	Peanut	Noisette	Hazelnut
Cassis	Blackcurrants	Noix	Nuts
Cerises	Cherries	Noix	Walnut
Châtaignes	Chestnuts	Noix de cajou	Cashew nut
Citron	Lemon	Orange	Orange
Citron vert	Lime	Pamplemousse	Grapefruit
Dattes	Dates	Pastèque	Watermelon
Figues	Figs	Pêche (blanche)	(White) peach
Fraises (de bois)	Strawberries (wild)	Pistache	Pistachio
Framboises	Raspberries	Poire	Pear
Fruit de la passion	Passion fruit	Pomme	Apple
Grenade	Pomegranate	Prune	Plum
Groseilles	Redcurrants	Pruneau	Prune
Mangue	Mango	Raisins	Grapes
		Reine-Claude	Greengage

Agrumes	Citrus fruits	Flambé	Set aflame in alcohol
Beignet	Fritter	Fougasse	Bread flavoured with
Compôte	Stewed fruit		orange flower water
Coulis	Sauce of puréed fruit		or almonds, can also
Crème de	Chestnut purée		be savoury
marrons		Frappé	Iced

Desserts (desserts or entremets), pastries (patisseries) and confectionery (confiserie)

Bombe	A moulded ice-cream dessert	Macarons	Macaroons
		Madeleine	Small sponge cake
Brioche	Sweet, high-yeast breakfast roll	Marrons	Chestnut purée and cream on a Mont
Calissons	Almond sweets		Blanc rum-soaked
Charlotte	Custard and fruit in lining of almond		sponge cake
	fingers	Mousse au chocolat	chocolate mousse
Chichis	Doughnuts shaped in sticks	Nougat	Nougat
Clafoutis	Heavy custard and	Palmiers	Caramelized puff pastries
	fruit tart	Parfait	Frozen mousse,
Crème Chantilly	Vanilla-flavoured and sweetened whipped		sometimes ice cream
	cream	Petit Suisse	A smooth mixture of cream and curds
Crème fraîche	Sour cream	Petits fours	Bite-sized cakes
Crème pâtissière	Thick eggy pastry-filling		/pastries
Crêpes suzettes	Thin pancakes with	Poires Belle Hélène	Pears and ice cream in chocolate sauce
	orange juice and liqueur	Tarte Tropezienne	Sponge cake filled with custard cream
Fromage blanc	Cream cheese		topped with nuts
Gaufre	Waffle	Tiramisu	Layered pudding of
Glace	Ice cream		mascarpone cheese,
Île flottante	Soft meringues floating		alcohol and coffee
	on œufs à la neige	Truffes	Truffles
	custard	Yaourt, yogourt	Yoghurt

Terms

Barquette	Small, boat-shaped flan	Coupe	A serving of ice cream
Bavarois	Refers to the mould,	Crêpes	Pancakes
	could be a mousse	En feuilletage	In puff pastry
	or custard	Fondant	Melting
Biscuit	A kind of cake	Galettes	Buckwheat pancakes
Chausson	Pastry turnover	Gênoise	Rich sponge cake
Chocolat amer	Unsweetened	Pâte	Pastry or dough
	chocolate	Sablé	Shortbread biscuit

| Savarin | A filled, ring-shaped cake | Tarte | Tart |
| | | Tartelette | Small tart |

Cheese (fromage)

The cheeses produced in Provence are all either *chèvre* (made from goats' milk) or *brebis* (made from sheeps' milk). The most renowned are the *chèvres*, which include Banon, Picodon, Lou Pevre, Pelardon and Poivre d'Ain.

Le plateau de fromages is the cheeseboard, and bread, but not butter, is served with it. Some useful phrases: *une petite tranche de celui-ci* (a small piece of this one); *je peux le gouter?* (may I taste it?).

And one final note: when in a restaurant or café always call the waiter or waitress Monsieur or Madame (Mademoiselle if a young woman). **Never** use garçon, no matter what you've been taught at school.

GLOSSARY

French terms

These are either terms you'll come across in the Guide, or come up against on signs, maps, etc while travelling around.

ABBAYE abbey

ARRONDISSEMENT district of a city

ASSEMBLÉE NATIONALE the French parliament

AJ (*Auberge de Jeunesse*) youth hostel

BASTIDE medieval military settlement, constructed on a grid plan

BEAUX-ARTS fine arts museum (and school)

BORIE dry-stone wall, or building made with same

CALANQUE steep-sided inlet on coast, similar to Norwegian fjord, but not glacially formed

CAR bus

CFDT Socialist trade union

CGT Communist trade union

CHAMBRE D'HÔTE room for rent in private house

CHASSE, CHASSE GARDÉE hunting grounds

CHÂTEAU mansion, country house or castle

CHÂTEAU FORT castle

CHEMIN path

CIJ (*Centre d'Informations Jeunesse*) youth information centre

CODENE French CND

COL mountain pass

CONSIGNE luggage store

CÔTE coast

COURS combination of main square and main street

COUVENT convent, monastery

DEFENSE DE . . . It is forbidden to . . .

DÉGUSTATION tasting (wine or food)

DÉPARTEMENT county – more or less

DL (*Démocratie Libérale*) free-market party

led by Alain Madelin

DONJON castle keep

ÉGLISE church

EN PANNE out of order

ENTRÉE entrance

FAUBOURG suburb, often abbreviated to fbg in street names

FERME farm

FERMETURE closing period

FN (*Front National*) fascist party led by Jean-Marie Le Pen

FO Catholic trade union

FOUILLES archeological excavations

GARE station; **ROUTIÈRE** – bus station; **SNCF** – train station

GÎTE D'ÉTAPE basic hostel accommodation primarily for walkers

GOBELINS famous tapestry manufacturers, based in Paris; its most renowned period was in the reign of Louis XIV (seventeenth century)

GR (*grande randonée*) long-distance footpath

HALLES covered market

HLM public housing development

HÔTEL a hotel, but also an aristocratic town house or mansion

HÔTEL DE VILLE town hall

JOURS FÉRIÉS public holidays

MAIRIE town hall

MARCHÉ market

MNR (*Mouvement National Républicain*) extreme-right party led by Bruno Mégret

PCF Communist Party of France

PLACE square

PORTE gateway

PRESQU'ÎLE peninsula

PS Socialist party

PUY peak or summit

QUARTIER district of a town

RELAIS ROUTIERS truckstop café-restaurants

RC (*Rez-de-Chaussée*) ground floor

RN (*Route Nationale*) main road

RPR Gaullist party led by Jacques Chirac

SANTON ornamental figure used especially in Christmas cribs

SI (*Syndicat d'Initiative*) tourist information office; also known as OT, OTSI and maison du tourisme

SNCF French railways

SORTIE exit

TABAC bar or shop selling stamps, cigarettes, etc

TABLE D'HÔTE meal served in lodging at the family table

TOUR tower

TRANSHUMANCE Routes followed by shepherds for taking livestock to and from suitable grazing grounds

UDF (*Union pour la Démocratie Française*) centre-right party headed by François Bayrou

UMP Right-wing coalition consisting of the RPR, UDF and DL parties; formed in 2002

VAUBAN seventeenth-century military architect – his fortresses still stand all over France

VIEILLE VILLE old quarter of town

VIEUX PORT old port

VILLAGE PERCHÉ hilltop village

VOUSSOIR sculpted rings in arch over church door

ZONE BLEUE restricted parking zone

ZONE PIETONNÉ pedestrian precinct

Architectural terms

AMBULATORY covered passage around the outer edge of a choir of a church

APSE semicircular termination at the east end of a church

BAROQUE High Renaissance period of art and architecture, distinguished by extreme ornateness

CAROLINGIAN dynasty (and art, sculpture, etc) founded by Charlemagne, late eighth to early tenth century

CHEVET east end of church, consisting of apse and ambulatory, with or without radiating chapels

CLASSICAL architectural style incorporating Greek and Roman elements – pillars, domes, colonnades, etc – at its height in France in the seventeenth century and revived in the nineteenth century as NEOCLASSICAL

CLERESTORY upper storey of a church, incorporating the windows

FLAMBOYANT florid form of Gothic

FRESCO wall painting – durable through application to wet plaster

GALLO-ROMAN period of Roman occupation of Gaul (first to fourth century AD)

GOTHIC architectural style prevalent from the twelfth century to the sixteenth century, characterized by pointed arches and ribbed vaulting

MEROVINGIAN dynasty (and art, etc) ruling France and parts of Germany from the sixth to mid-eighth century

NARTHEX entrance hall of church

NAVE main body of a church

RENAISSANCE art-architectural style developed in fifteenth-century Italy and imported to France in the early sixteenth century by François I

RETABLE altarpiece

ROMANESQUE early medieval architecture distinguished by squat, rounded forms and naive sculpture

STUCCO plaster used to embellish ceilings, etc

TRANSEPT cross arms of a church

TYMPANUM sculpted panel above a church door

VOUSSOIR sculpted rings in arch over church door

Travel store

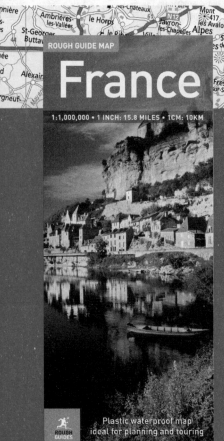

Small print and

Index

A Rough Guide to Rough Guides

Published in 1982, the first Rough Guide – to Greece – was a student scheme that became a publishing phenomenon. Mark Ellingham, a recent graduate in English from Bristol University, had been travelling in Greece the previous summer and couldn't find the right guidebook. With a small group of friends he wrote his own guide, combining a highly contemporary, journalistic style with a thoroughly practical approach to travellers' needs.

The immediate success of the book spawned a series that rapidly covered dozens of destinations. And, in addition to impecunious backpackers, Rough Guides soon acquired a much broader and older readership that relished the guides' wit and inquisitiveness as much as their enthusiastic, critical approach and value-for-money ethos.

These days, Rough Guides include recommendations from shoestring to luxury and cover more than 200 destinations around the globe, including almost every country in the Americas and Europe, more than half of Africa and most of Asia and Australasia. Our ever-growing team of authors and photographers is spread all over the world, particularly in Europe, the USA and Australia.

SMALL PRINT

In the early 1990s, Rough Guides branched out of travel, with the publication of Rough Guides to World Music, Classical Music and the Internet. All three have become benchmark titles in their fields, spearheading the publication of a wide range of books under the Rough Guide name.

Including the travel series, Rough Guides now number more than 350 titles, covering: phrasebooks, waterproof maps, music guides from Opera to Heavy Metal, reference works as diverse as Conspiracy Theories and Shakespeare, and popular culture books from iPods to Poker. Rough Guides also produce a series of more than 120 World Music CDs in partnership with World Music Network.

Visit www.roughguides.com to see our latest publications.

Rough Guide travel images are available for commercial licensing at www.roughguidespictures.com

Rough Guide credits

Text editor: Keith Drew, Geoff Howard, Anne Marie Shaw
Layout: Pradeep Thapliyal
Cartography: Rajesh Chhibber
Picture editor: Jj Luck
Production: Aimee Hampson
Proofreader: Anita Sach
Cover design: Chloë Roberts
Photographer: Michelle Grant
Editorial: London Kate Berens, Claire Saunders, Ruth Blackmore, Polly Thomas, Richard Lim, Alison Murchie, Karoline Densley, Andy Turner, Edward Aves, Nikki Birrell, Alice Park, Sarah Eno, Lucy White, Jo Kirby, Samantha Cook, James Smart, Natasha Foges, Roisin Cameron, Joe Staines, Duncan Clark, Peter Buckley, Matthew Milton, Tracy Hopkins, Ruth Tidball; **New York** Andrew Rosenberg, Steven Horak, AnneLise Sorensen, Amy Hegarty, April Isaacs, Ella Steim, Anna Owens, Joseph Petta, Sean Mahoney
Design & Pictures: London Scott Stickland, Dan May, Diana Jarvis, Mark Thomas, Harriet Mills, Chloë Roberts, Nicole Newman; **Delhi** Umesh Aggarwal, Ajay Verma, Jessica Subramanian, Ankur Guha, Sachin Tanwar, Anita Singh, Madhavi Singh, Karen D'Souza

Production: Katherine Owers
Cartography: London Maxine Repath, Ed Wright, Katie Lloyd-Jones; **Delhi** Jai Prakash Mishra, Ashutosh Bharti, Rajesh Mishra, Animesh Pathak, Jasbir Sandhu, Karobi Gogoi, Amod Singh, Alakananda Bhattacharya, Athokpam Jotinkumar
Online: New York Jennifer Gold, Kristin Mingrone; **Delhi** Manik Chauhan, Narender Kumar, Rakesh Kumar, Amit Kumar, Amit Verma, Rahul Kumar, Ganesh Sharma, Debojit Borah
Marketing & Publicity: London Liz Statham, Niki Hanmer, Louise Maher, Jess Carter, Vanessa Godden, Vivienne Watton, Anna Paynton, Libby Jellie, Rachel Sprackett, Lenalisa Fornberg; **New York** Geoff Colquitt, Megan Kennedy, Katy Ball; **Delhi** Reem Khokhar
Custom Publishing Coordinator: Emma Traynor
Manager India: Punita Singh
Series Editor: Mark Ellingham
Reference Director: Andrew Lockett
Publishing Coordinator: Helen Phillips
Publishing Director: Martin Dunford
Commercial Manager: Gino Magnotta
Managing Director: John Duhigg

Publishing information

This sixth edition published June 2007 by
Rough Guides Ltd,
80 Strand, London WC2R 0RL
345 Hudson St, 4th Floor,
New York, NY 10014, USA
14 Local Shopping Centre, Panchsheel Park,
New Delhi 110017, India
Distributed by the Penguin Group
Penguin Books Ltd,
80 Strand, London WC2R 0RL
Penguin Group (USA)
375 Hudson Street, NY 10014, USA
Penguin Group (Australia)
250 Camberwell Road, Camberwell,
Victoria 3124, Australia
Penguin Books Canada Ltd,
10 Alcorn Avenue, Toronto, Ontario,
Canada M4V 1E4
Penguin Group (NZ)
67 Apollo Drive, Mairangi Bay, Auckland 1310,
New Zealand

Cover concept by Peter Dyer.
Typeset in Bembo and Helvetica to an original design by Henry Iles.
Printed in Italy by LegoPrint S.p.A
© Rough Guides 2007

520pp includes index
A catalogue record for this book is available from the British Library
ISBN: 978-1-84353-784-7

1 3 5 7 9 8 6 4 2

SMALL PRINT

Help us update

We've gone to a lot of effort to ensure that the sixth edition of **The Rough Guide to Provence** is accurate and up to date. However, things change – places get "discovered", opening hours are notoriously fickle, restaurants and rooms raise prices or lower standards. If you feel we've got it wrong or left something out, we'd like to know, and if you can remember the address, the price, the time, the phone number, so much the better. We'll credit all contributions, and send a copy of the next edition (or any other Rough Guide if you prefer) for the best letters. Everyone who writes

to us and isn't already a subscriber will receive a copy of our full-colour thrice-yearly newsletter. Please mark letters: "**Rough Guide Provence Update**" and send to: Rough Guides, 80 Strand, London WC2R 0RL, or Rough Guides, 345 Hudson St, 4th Floor, New York, NY 10014. Or send an email to **mail@roughguides.com** Have your questions answered and tell others about your trip at
www.roughguides.atinfopop.com

Acknowledgements

Neville would like to thank: Geoff Hinchley and Kathryn Walker, Liliane Siréta in La Ciotat and Patricia Chaniel in Biot.

Nick wishes to thank: Louise Armstrong for keeping me company around the Verdon and sorry she was stung on the head by a bee for her troubles.

Readers' letters

Thanks to all the readers who have taken the time to write in with comments and suggestions (and apologies if we've inadvertently omitted or misspelt anyone's name):

Tony Bellworthy, Gerald Chapman, Stuart Connell, Hans Deseure, Noemie and Cedric Dewavrin, Jenny Green, Jen Gold, Sam Hardie, Panu Kalmi, Elizabeth, Malcolm & Rosina Lanyon, John & Carole LeBrun, Marcus Loxton, Jo Nicol, Sally Pabst, Charlie Pearman, Gwerfyl Price, Nancy Trasande, Jim Salmon, Jonathan Snicker, Catherine Van de Wiele

Photo credits

All photos © Rough Guides except the following:

Introduction
Yachts and small boats in the Calanque d'En Vau © Dylan Reisenberger
The cliffs of the Calanque d'En Vau © Dylan Reisenberger
L'Estaque, View of the Gulf of Marseilles by Paul Cezanne © The Art Archive/Corbis
Cannes Film Festival © Agence Images/Alamy
Pont St Benezet, Avignon © Dylan Reisenberge

Things not to miss
01 Calanque d'En Vau © Dylan Reisenberger
02 Les-Baux-de-Provence © Bruno Morandi/ Robert Harding   03 Gypsy pilgrimage © Cristian Baitg reportage/Alamy
05 La Croisette © Ian Dagnall/Alamy
06 Cafe in Nice Old Town © Michael Juno/Alamy
07 Fondation Maeght © Neville Walker
09 Montagne Sainte Victoire au dessus de la route du Tholonet © Visual Arts Library (London)/Alamy
10 Festival d'Avignon © Christophe Raynaud de Lage
11 Peille © Neville Walker
13 Relaxing on the Riveria © G P Bowater/Alamy
14 Avignon's Palais des Papes © Franz-Marc Frei/Corbis
15 Matisse Museum © Neville Walker
18 Marseille © Neville Walker
19 Bouillabaisse © B.Marielle/photocuisine/ Corbis

20 Roman Amphitheatre © Gail Mooney/Corbis
23 Driving Riviera's cornices © images-of-france/ Alamy
24 Camargue © Art Kowalsky/Alamy
25 Cassis © Werner Dieterich/Image Bank/Getty

Colour section: A taste of Provence
Beehives in lavender field © Aguilar Patrice/Alamy
Bouillabaisse © Tor Eigeland/Alamy
Olive oil © Agence Images/Alamy
Daube de boeuf © Cephas Picture Library/Alamy
Calissons from Aix-en-Provence © Agence Images/Alamy
Socca in Nice © Barry Mason/Alamy

Colour section: La Provence sportive
Tree-lined road, Provence © JLImages/Alamy
Tour de France © Reuters/Corbis
Hyeres Sailing week © Eric Estrade/AFP/Getty Images
Boules © images-of-france/Alamy
Monaco Grand Prix © Dominique Faget/AFP/ Getty Images

Black and whites
p.130 Gypsy pilgrimage in Stes-Maries-de-la-Mer © Cristian Baitg reportage/Alamy
p.389 Beach on Cap d'Antibes © Neville Walker
p.454 Saint-Agnes Hill Town © Michael Busselle/ Corbis

Index

Map entries are in colour.

INDEX